Seventh Canadian Edition

Choices

Interviewing and Counselling Skills for Canadians

Bob Shebib
Faculty Emeritus
Douglas College

 **Pearson**

Pearson Canada Inc., 26 Prince Andrew Place, North York, Ontario M3C 2H4.

ISBN 13: 978-0-13-484248-6

6 2021

Library and Archives Canada Cataloguing in Publication

Shebib, Bob, author
    Choices : interviewing and counselling skills for Canadians
/Bob Shebib. -- Seventh edition.

ISBN 978-0-13-484248-6 (softcover)

    1. Counseling--Textbooks. 2. Interviewing--Textbooks.
3. Textbooks. I. Title.

BF636.6.S48 2019   158.3   C2018-903645-1

Dedication

For my children and grandchildren,
Kevin, Jodie, Eli, and Audrey.

Brief Contents

Contents

Preface

"There is a crack in everything, that's how the light gets in"

Leonard Cohen (1968)

Cohen's iconic words are a message of hope reminding us that hardship, setbacks, and obstacles are opportunities for growth, change, and learning. His poetic insight inspires us to believe that we need not fear our imperfections because resilience and empowerment can grow from obstacles and hardships.

"Cracks" in *Choices* have enabled the evolution of seven editions and left me with the inescapable conclusion that it will forever remain a work in progress. In each new edition, user feedback, emergent research, and practice experience have helped me to re-examine my beliefs, discard outmoded ideas, and replace them with fresh perspectives.

The seventh edition of *Choices* maintains its basic format and its objective as an introductory textbook for students in counselling training programs and a practice reference for professionals in social work, criminology, nursing, child and youth care, addictions, psychology as well as professionals and volunteers in other professions whose work involves interviewing and counselling. A continuing best-seller in Canada, *Choices* combines theory, practice examples with sample interviews, and challenging self-awareness exercises in a comprehensive, yet readable format. It is aimed at professionals aspiring to gain a wide range of skills based on supported theory and evidence-based best practices. Although framed in the Canadian ethical and cultural context, the content of the book is designed to appeal to a broad international audience of professionals.

This book aims to contribute to the development of professional competence in five ways:

1. Introducing basic concepts and models to help learners understand the theory and philosophy of effective counselling intervention skills.

2. Providing realistic examples to illustrate concepts in action.

3. Offering challenging exercises that promote skill development, conceptual understanding, and self-awareness.

4. Promoting the importance of a range of skill choices for interviewing, rather than rules and recipes.

5. Presenting connections to relevant neuroscience research.

In the seventh edition of *Choices*, all chapters have been rewritten to improve clarity and include current research, with updated references and weblinks. This edition continues my commitment to producing a readable and practical text. As much as possible, I have avoided the use of unnecessary jargon, and I have tried to be transparent and explicit regarding my assumptions, a practice that parallels my approach to counselling.

Significant changes and enhancements to the seventh edition include:

- A new Chapter 11 exploring neuroscience and counselling
- Significant new content in many chapters related to understanding and working with seniors
- Updated references and content in all chapters
- New and/or updated success tips
- New and/or revised conversations, BRAIN BYTES, and sample interviews including the addition of a "reflections" section
- New material on counsellor burnout, vicarious trauma, and wellness
- Additional content on substance misuse including drug withdrawal, detox, and the opioid crisis
- Content related to understanding and working with paranoia
- Reconfigured Chapter 10: Cultural Intelligence

THEORY AND PHILOSOPHY

Choices promotes an eclectic approach that encourages counsellors to draw techniques and ideas from various theoretical models depending on the specific needs of the client and situation, not the comfort level of the counsellor. Counselling is a complex blend of skill, attitude, and creativity, with the work based on best-practice techniques that are supported by research. Core skills can be learned and practised, but they are not recipes. Based on individual client need and context, high-level professionals create, adapt, and customize skills and strategies, thus avoiding any "one-size-fits-all" approach. Among the models that have heavily influenced this book's content are the following:

- Person-centred counselling, pioneered by Carl Rogers
- Trauma-informed practice
- Cognitive behavioural therapy/counselling (CBT)
- Motivational interviewing
- Short-term and solution-focused counselling
- Emergent insights from neuroscience

The term "cognitive reserve" describes the brain's capacity to creatively find ways to cope with life's challenges. Social workers and other counsellors who have high level of cognitive reserve can "switch gears" when one way of solving a problem does not work. Put simply, they have choices and they are not discouraged or defeated when one approach to working with clients fails. They can vary their approach to meet the unique needs of different clients, cultures, and situations. Over a lifetime of a professional career, through reflection, education and practice experience that builds on success and learns from failure, they can grow their counselling skills and cognitive reserve.

Every interview requires an intelligent choice of skills and strategies. To make wise choices, counsellors need to develop a wide range of practice skills based on supported theory (science) and proven practice (evidence-based best practice). When counsellors have a repertoire of skills, they can make knowledgeable choices based on the unique needs of clients and situations, rather than their own personal comfort levels or established routines. In simplest terms, the more choices counsellors have, the greater their ability to match their work to the needs and wants of their clients, and the less their need to repeatedly use the same skill. Effective counsellors are wise enough to know when to–and when not to–use particular skills. Similarly, the goal of counselling is to help clients achieve versatility in their capacity to solve problems and achieve goals.

Skill and technique can be impressive, but alone they are insufficient. Compassion, caring, empathy, an ability to suspend judgment, objectivity, professionalism, self-awareness, and sufficient psychological health are some of the personal qualities and commitments that must operate in tandem with knowledge and skill. Counsellors need to be genuine, maintain warm and caring regard for their clients, and recognize the inherent worth of people. Kadushin (1990) discusses the important mix of skill and feeling:

> Many might say that if they had to choose between feeling and technique they would choose feeling as the more important prerequisite. Perhaps so, but if one has to make a choice between these qualifications, an injustice has already been done to the client. It should be possible to offer the client an interviewer who is both attitudinally correct and technically proficient. (p. xii)

Respect for Diversity and Culture

Diversity includes differences in such major variables as race, religion, age, sex, sexual orientation, physical and mental ability, economic capacity, language, culture, values, beliefs, preferences, and ways of thinking and behaving. The diversity of today's counselling caseloads requires that counsellors develop a range of interviewing and counselling skills. Competent counsellors are able to vary their style depending on the unique culture and worldviews of their clients.

Choices emphasizes cultural competence. Since everyone is unique, each with his or her own mix of values and beliefs, culture is a variable for work with all clients. When working with clients from visible minorities and those who are marginalized by poverty or discrimination, counsellors must examine the sociopolitical realities that frame the clients' circumstances. They also need to develop sufficient self-awareness to escape or manage any tendency to be culture-bound—the assumption that all clients share their values, perspectives, and ambitions or, worse still, that client differences represent deficiencies. By sustaining a multicultural perspective that recognizes and prizes diversity, counsellors can avoid the pitfalls of ethnocentrism (the belief that one's own views and culture are superior). Culturally competent counsellors view cultural differences as opportunities to widen their horizons and deepen their versatility. They remember to be humble enough to learn from their clients.

Phases of Counselling

This book divides the counselling relationship into four phases: preliminary, beginning, action, and ending. Each phase involves common as well as unique tasks and skills. For example, the beginning phase focuses on relationship development and problem exploration. Predictably, skills for developing relationships, like active listening, are most useful in the beginning phase, whereas skills such as confrontation are not recommended. But the subsequent action phase focuses on helping clients develop new perspectives, set goals, and implement change strategies; thus, skills such as reframing and confronting are used extensively in this phase.

The four phases are developmental, with success at one phase dependent in part on success at previous phases. For example, clients are more willing to accept confrontation in the action phase if a solid relationship or trust has already been established in the beginning phase. In general, reference to the four-phase model allows counsellors to make some predictions about the climate of the interview and to determine which skills and tasks will be needed. However, practitioners must be cautious in applying the model too rigorously to every counselling interview because there are always circumstances for which the sequence of events will differ sharply from the model.

Values and Ethics

Ethics are principles of acceptable conduct. Professional associations such as the Canadian Association of Social Workers and the Canadian Counselling and Psychotherapy Association have formal statements that define ethics and standards of practice for their members. Similarly, *values* are ideas and principles that individuals and groups consider important or worthwhile. In counselling, certain core values are of particular importance:

1. Belief in the dignity and worth of people
2. Respect for the client's right to self-determination (i.e., for freedom of choice and the right to control one's own life)
3. Commitment to work for social justice

The Counselling Relationship

All editions, including this one, have prioritized the importance of the client/counsellor relationship as a major determinant of success. The counselling relationship is something very special. It's negotiated. It's non-reciprocal. It has a purpose. It is designed to recognize and mobilize strengths. It requires counsellors to abandon their biases and suspend any tendency to give advice in order to listen and respond in a manner that creates the conditions for trust, growth, and change.

Counselling should empower clients and strengthen their self-esteem. It has very little to do with giving "good advice," but it might involve providing information and assisting clients to evaluate alternatives in order to support them to make informed and self-determined choices. Best-practice counselling draws on the expertise of clients to participate in decisions related to the goals and process of counselling. For this reason, counsellors should demystify their work through open discussion of their methodologies, assumptions, and intentions. Moreover, commitment to client self-determination restrains counsellors from abuse of power or control. In promoting client self-determination, counsellors use a strengths approach that empowers clients by assuming their capacity to cope and change.

The counselling relationship creates the conditions for change to occur and the motivation for change to proceed. The counselling relationship nurtures the natural need that everyone has to grow and change. **The cornerstone of this is empathy, a unique and powerful way of listening that alone is sufficient to help many people.** It is not a technique that we activate when counselling, but rather an empathic approach to life that Roger's describes as a "way of being."

Counsellor Self-Awareness

Effective counsellors are self-aware, open to feedback, and willing to learn. As counsellors become deeply involved in a relationship with their clients, they need to control their own biases, and constantly monitor their feelings and thoughts so that they are able to separate their experiences and feelings from those of their clients.

Knowledge of self, including consciousness of one's values and beliefs and the impact of one's behaviour on others, is a prerequisite for effective counselling. Counsellors who lack self-awareness may confuse their clients' feelings with their own. When counsellors are unaware of their own needs, including those that are unmet, they risk unconsciously using their counselling relationships to meet personal goals instead of client goals. In addition, without self-awareness, counsellors will be ignorant of those areas of practice in which they are competent and those in which it will be difficult for them to work with objectivity.

Competent professionals know themselves, and they ensure that their values and beliefs do not become a burden to their clients. They accept that exploring and reflecting on one's competence and the limits of one's role and expertise are fundamental to professional practice. For counsellors, this process of self-examination continues throughout their careers.

Neuroscience and Counselling

In recent years, neuroscience has emerged as an important new force in counselling. Since the 1990s new technologies have spawned an explosive interest in the brain. These imaging technologies have resulted in enormous progress in our understanding of the brain. One of the most relevant and exciting findings is the discovery that our brains are "plastic" and in a constant state of change. Life experience, adversity, trauma, risk taking, and learning shape and reshape the brain in ways that help us cope with the challenges in our lives. Or, alternatively, they may drive us to depression, anxiety, and substance abuse.

A growing body of neuroscience research has confirmed the validity of counselling by demonstrating in dramatic ways how counselling changes the brain. Counselling works! Now, we have the science to prove it. We have learned how counselling basics such as listening, empathy, asking questions, and the establishment of relationship counselling harness brain plasticity and promote positive brain growth. It's already exciting, even though we are still at the beginning stages of what is certain to be an avalanche of profound developments in coming years. Neuroscience is providing answers to the question, "How can counselling help create conditions that promote positive, empowering brain growth or repair?" As a result, I think that in the near future college and university counselling programs will require courses on the brain and neuroscience.

Social Justice and Advocacy

Although the topic is beyond the scope of this text, counsellors should also consider their responsibility to extend beyond their role as counsellors to social and political action. As advocates for social justice, they should strive to reduce gender, cultural, and other forms of discrimination. They should also promote changes in social policy as well as modification in the functioning of formal organizations and institutions to meet the needs of clients.

STRUCTURE OF THE BOOK

The book is divided into 11 chapters.

Chapter 1 explores professional identity and introduces readers to the basic concepts of ethics, values, and self-awareness.

Chapter 2 explores the basic nature of counselling skills and strategies. In this chapter, four major skill clusters are introduced: relationship building, exploring/probing, empowering, and challenging. The four-phase model of counselling (preliminary, beginning, action, and ending) is proposed as a model for understanding the evolution of the counselling relationship. As well, the important components of a trauma-informed approach are introduced and discussed.

Chapter 3 examines the helping relationship and considers the core conditions of effective counselling. Sessional and relationship contracting are featured in this chapter.

Chapters 4, 5, and 6 explore the active listening skills of attending, silence, paraphrasing, and summarizing (Chapter 4), questioning (Chapter 5), and empathy (Chapter 6). Specific ideas for interviewing and working with youth are discussed in these chapters.

Chapter 7 is concerned with action-phase skills that motivate clients to think differently and make changes in their lives. Two important theoretical models, cognitive behavioural counselling and motivational interviewing, are featured.

Chapter 8 presents information on working in difficult situations, such as when clients are resistant or potentially violent.

Chapter 9 looks at concepts for working with various populations, including those who are dealing with mental disorders, contemplating suicide, or who have addictions.

Chapter 10 explores important concepts and issues related to counselling clients from different cultures. This chapter includes a discussion of spirituality and counselling, reflecting a growing interest in and acceptance of spiritual issues in counselling. In this chapter, multicultural competencies for Canadian counsellors are introduced.

Chapter 11, new to this edition, explores issues related to neuroscience and counselling including a discussion of brain problems.

Features

People learn in different ways, so this book includes a range of features designed to assist learners in understanding at the cognitive, emotional, and behavioural levels. Each chapter contains the following elements:

- **Learning Objectives:** key concepts that will be addressed in the chapter
- **Summary:** a short review at the end of each chapter that summarizes important ideas
- **Conversations:** a unique feature presenting teacher–student dialogues about frequently asked questions
- **Sample Interviews:** annotated interview excerpts that illustrate and explain chapter concepts
- **Success Tips:** short, practical ideas for counselling success
- **Illustrative Figures:** diagrams that support or embellish chapter concepts
- **Brain Bytes:** short links to interesting and relevant neuroscience
- **Exercises:** end-of-chapter reflective questions to give readers practice developing self-awareness, practice skills, and conceptual knowledge
- **Weblinks:** links to websites related to the chapter's material
- **Glossary:** definitions of key terms

SUGGESTIONS FOR STUDENTS

If you are studying this book as part of a course on counselling skills, you will probably have the opportunity to develop skill competence in a number of different ways:

- Watching instructor demonstrations
- Conducting practice interviews using role-played or (preferably) real-life scenarios
- Completing the chapter exercises

- Receiving feedback and evaluation from instructors and student colleagues who observe your work
- Using audio and video recordings to understand and assess your verbal and non-verbal responses
- Working with clients in practicum field settings

In most counselling skills courses, learning groups are used to practise skills. Usually, these learning groups use classroom simulations and practice interviews in which you assume the roles of client, counsellor, and observer. Each of these roles offers unique challenges and opportunities for learning.

Practice Interviewing: When You Are the Client

The client's role offers a powerful opportunity for you to understand client feelings and expectations. You may find that your reactions are similar to those that clients you will work with in the field experience:

- Ambivalence about sharing feelings or details about personal issues
- Feelings of vulnerability and fear of being judged, embarrassed, or ridiculed

As a client, it will be up to you to control how much you wish to disclose; however, by taking reasonable risks, you can enhance your learning opportunities and insights. However, you should remember that a training environment does not provide the time or setting to address complex problems.

Practice Interviewing: When You Are the Counsellor

When you are asked to practise your newly learned skills as a counsellor, you may feel clumsy and insecure as you take risks to change established communication patterns or experiment with new skills and strategies. As a student with limited training, you may be reluctant to ask questions that seem to invade the privacy of your colleagues. Moreover, when dealing with sensitive issues you may fear that your lack of experience will damage your clients. You may also fear that your colleagues will judge you as inept. As well, when you are being observed by others, the intense focus on your work can be unsettling and anxiety-provoking. But all these reactions are common, and you will probably find that your colleagues feel the same way. Most professional counsellors take many years of practice and study to become competent and comfortable using a full range of skills. What is important is that you persist and avoid the natural temptation to stick with familiar patterns of communicating. Skills that are awkward in the beginning will, with practice, become part of your natural and preferred style.

SUCCESS TIP

If you create the right conditions, others will help you with feedback that will support the development of your skills and self-awareness.

Practice Interviewing: When You Are the Observer

Student observers are responsible for watching the interview and providing feedback to student colleagues who are practising their counselling skills. At first, you may be reluctant to offer feedback, perhaps worrying that your remarks will generate anger or hurt feelings. But keep in mind that the observer's role gives you an excellent opportunity to develop the skill of giving feedback and practise this skill.

Helpful feedback is energizing and does not detract from another person's self-esteem. As people learn and practise interviewing and counselling skills, they may feel vulnerable and awkward. Hence, it is important to remain sensitive to their emotional and psychological needs, while balancing their needs for information and correction.

Observer feedback may be of two types: supportive or corrective.

- **Supportive feedback** recognizes strengths. Consider how you respond differently when your strengths are acknowledged rather than when your weaknesses are targeted. Yet despite how obvious this idea seems, many students and professional counsellors are very problem-oriented and fail to acknowledge client or colleague strengths. Supportive feedback must be genuine (true) and delivered without rescuing or patronizing. If you lie to others to avoid hurting them, your credibility as a source of feedback will diminish.

- **Corrective feedback** challenges others to examine or change behaviour. But before giving corrective feedback, consider your relationship with the other person. If your relationship is based on trust and caring, corrective feedback has the potential to be effective. However, if your relationship has unresolved conflict, corrective feedback is more likely to be perceived as an attack. If people think your feedback is harsh, demanding, or controlling, there is a higher probability that they will resist. Here are some general feedback guidelines:

  - Be specific. Avoid generalities such as, "Your interview was great." Anchor your assessment by identifying the specific behaviours and responses that you observed that contributed to the success of the interview.

  - Don't use corrective feedback as a means to control, impress, or punish. Pay attention to your tone of voice and other nonverbal behaviour. Make sure that you avoid lecturing and pointing fingers.

  - Timing and pacing are important variables. Supportive feedback is more useful when self-esteem is low. In addition, feedback is most effective when given as soon as possible, but ensure that you protect personal privacy.

  - Avoid overwhelming student counsellors by providing too much feedback. Watch for nonverbal cues or ask them to let you know when they would like to stop the process.

  - Ask people to self-evaluate before offering your opinions. You may be surprised to find that they already have insight into the problem areas; thereby reducing the number of areas in which you have to provide direct feedback.

  - Feedback has the most potential for success if it is invited or targeted to perceived areas of need. Contract with others to deliver feedback. Ask questions such as "Would you like me to offer my ideas on what happened?" or "Are there specific issues that you're concerned about?"

  - Everyone is different. Some people prefer feedback to be direct and to the point. Others may prefer it "sandwiched" between positives. Others need time to reflect before responding, or they may profit from visual and written illustrations. Discuss preferences with student counsellors, then respond accordingly.

Some people have an immediate reaction to feedback that will differ from their reaction once they have had time to ponder what you have said. For example, a person who responds defensively or even with anger may, on reflection, come to accept your input and see things differently. The opposite can also be true—people who react favourably may later develop other feelings, such as resentment or confusion. Checking back during future encounters is one strategy for keeping abreast of others' reactions.

Remember that giving helpful and caring feedback is one way of developing and strengthening relationships. If you are honest and supportive with others, you greatly increase the probability they will be honest and supportive with you when you ask for their helpful feedback.

Developing an Effective Learning Group

When you work with student colleagues in each of the three roles, discuss your fears as well as your expectations of one another. You will need to work to develop a contract or agreement on how you will work together. Practice interviews are powerful learning opportunities when they are based on real rather than role-played feelings and issues. Consequently, it will be important to establish a climate of safety, where confidentiality will be respected. Some important principles to remember:

- Colleagues who are in the client's role are disclosing personal issues and feelings, so it is essential to respect their dignity and right to privacy.

- Everyone has different capacities for intimacy. Do not expect that all members of a learning group will disclose at the same level. Accept individual differences.

- Learning the skills of counselling requires a willingness to give up familiar patterns of communication and attempt new approaches. Expand your limits by taking appropriate risks to try new skills and be tolerant of colleagues who are engaged in similar risk-taking.

- Feedback from others is an important part of learning. Therefore, try to make it easy for others to give you feedback by consistently responding nondefensively. Help others give specific feedback by asking targeted questions.

SUCCESS TIP

Expect that the process of learning and experimenting with new skills will result in a period of awkwardness and self-consciousness. For a time, it may seem as though your capacity to counsel others is regressing.

Keeping a Personal Journal

A personal "for your eyes only" journal can be a significant adjunct to your learning. The journal is a tool for introspection that provides a private means for documenting and exploring your thoughts and feelings related to the development of your counselling skills. There are no rules for journal writing other than the need to make entries on a regular basis and to try to avoid self-censorship.

Using This Book

If you are using this book as part of a course on counselling, your instructor will propose a suggested reading schedule that structures your reading over the semester, and he or she will assign or adapt the chapter exercises to fit your learning needs. Another way to use the book is on an "as you need it" basis, using the index or chapter headings to locate specific content. As well, you are encouraged to use other books, journals, and tools, such as Internet research, to supplement your learning. However, you should read this book (or any book) critically and seek to understand and explore the ideas and try them out.

Counselling Skills as a Way of Life

You may be surprised to discover that the skills of counselling are also the skills of effective everyday communication, and that the process of developing your counselling competence may begin to influence your personal relationships. As counselling skills become part of your style, you may find yourself becoming a little more inquisitive and more sensitive to the feelings of others. However, you may find that others in your life do not welcome the changes in your manner and style. When you change, others around you have to accommodate your changes. If you become more probing in your questions, they must be forthcoming with their answers. When you become more empathic, their feelings become more transparent. These changes move the relationship to a deeper level of intimacy, which may be frightening for some, particularly if the pace is too fast for their comfort level.

Acknowledgments

I have appreciated the help offered by the editorial and production staff at Pearson Canada, who have been very helpful in guiding this book through the many steps required to bring the manuscript to publication:

- Portfolio Manager: Keriann McGoogan
- Marketing Manager: Euan White
- Content Developer: Eileen Magill
- Content Manager: Madhu Ranadive
- Project Manager: Susan Johnson
- Copyeditor: Susan Adlam
- Cover Designer: SPI Global

Thank you to Venkat Perla Ramesh and Aishwarya Panday for their terrifc copy edit of this edition. A special thanks to Collen Murphy and John Fox from Douglas College and Joyce Shebib for their comprehensive review of the new Chapter 11. An adapted version of Chapter 11 was published in the online journal, The Neuropsychotherapist (2017), and I am grateful to its' editiors, Matthew Dahlitz and Richard Hill for their assistance in making this happen.

All editions of this book have benefited from the feedback provided by reviewers, readers, colleagues, clients, and students. Over the years, students from Douglas College, have offered candid and helpful feedback, and professional colleagues who have contributed ideas and suggestions that I have assisted me. Thanks to Andrew Buntin, Barbara Picton, Irene Carter, Jason Carter, Michelle Gibbs, Winnie Benton, Irene Carter, Susan Davis, Karen Marr, Sheri McConnell, Sara Menzel, Karen Moreau, Neil Madu, Robert Owens, Alyson Quinn, Melissa Medjuck, John Fox, Doug Estergaard, Bruce Hardy, Lawrence Becker, Elizabeth Jones, Colleen Murphy, and Tabitha Brown.

Each edition of *Choices* has included reviews from professionals in the field. In this seventh edition, 10 reviewers, each of who was intimately familiar with the content of the book, offered their perspectives on how the book could be improved. Their invaluable and intelligent suggestions helped to shape this addition. Thank you to these colleagues who reviewed the seventh edition:

Alana Abramson, *Kwantlen Polytechnic University*

Andrew Buntin, *George Brown College*

Barbara Picton, *Vancouver Community College*

Irene Carter, *University of Windsor*

Jason Carter, *Fleming College*

Michelle Gibbs, *Mohawk College*

Patricia Miller, *Mount Royal University*

Sue Davis-Mendelow, *Humber College*

As always, a special thanks to my wife, Joyce Shebib, who continues to offer support and very helpful critical comments.

Reader comments and critical feedback are always welcomed. Please email me at shebib@telus.ca.

Bob Shebib
Faculty Emeritus
Douglas College
New Westminster, BC

Customized workshops and staff training based on this book are available. Contact the author at shebibb@telus.net for details.

Chapter 1
Professional Identity: Ethics, Values, and Self-Awareness

Stuart Miles/123RF

LEARNING OBJECTIVES

- Identify the Canadian professionals that provide counselling services.

- Identify how counsellors can work within the limits of their competence.

- Define and describe professional ethics, including standards related to dual relationships and confidentiality.

- List and describe the core values of counselling.

- Identify principles for understanding and resolving ethical dilemmas.

- Understand the importance of counsellor objectivity and self-awareness.

- Understand and manage personal needs and values in counselling.

- Recognize and address burnout and vicarious trauma as workplace hazards.

PROFESSIONAL COUNSELLORS IN CANADA

Many professionals, such as social workers, child and youth care workers, psychologists, psychiatrists, nurses, and psychiatric nurses, do counselling work. Most are members of professional associations like the Canadian Association of Social Workers (CASW) and the Canadian Counselling and Psychotherapy Association (CCPA; see Table 1.1).

TABLE 1.1   Professional Associations in Canada

Canadian Addiction Counsellors Certification Federation	www.caccf.ca
Canadian Art Therapy Association	www.catainfo.ca
Canadian Association of Music Therapists	www.musictherapy.ca
Canadian Association of Rehabilitation Professionals	www.carpnational.org
Canadian Association of Social Workers	www.casw-acts.ca
Canadian Counselling and Psychotherapy Association	www.ccpa-accp.ca
Canadian Criminal Justice Association	www.ccja-acjp.ca
Canadian Indigenous Nurses Association	www.anac.on.ca
Canadian Nurses Association	www.cna-aiic.ca
Canadian Psychiatric Association	www.cpa-apc.org
Canadian Psychological Association	www.cpa.ca
Canadian Therapeutic Recreation Association	www.canadian-tr.org
Council of Canadian Child and Youth Care Associations	www.cyccanada.ca
Psychosocial Rehabilitation Canada	www.psrrpscanada.com

As members, they are subject to codes of ethics governing acceptable professional behaviour. Membership in these associations usually requires a university degree and, in some cases, a master's degree or Ph.D.

Social workers generally have university training with a bachelor's degree in social work (BSW) or a master's degree in social work (MSW). In addition, they may have specialized training in areas such as family therapy or group work. Social workers might work in private practice or be employed in hospitals, prisons, schools, or community social service agencies. Many social workers also work for government agencies investigating incidents of child abuse and neglect. Social workers are the largest professional group providing support and counselling to people with psychiatric disorders. Increasingly, with the aging of the Canadian population, social workers are deployed to work with seniors.

Counselling psychologists are usually qualified at the Ph.D. level, but some jurisdictions allow registration for those with a master's degree. They may work as counsellors or may specialize in other areas, such as in administering and interpreting psychological tests. Psychologists are often employed in private practice, but they may also work in settings such as prisons, hospitals, schools, and private industry.

In contrast, psychiatrists are medical doctors with advanced training in psychiatry. They are specialists in the treatment of people with mental disorders. Psychiatrists are the only counselling professionals licensed to prescribe medication. Psychiatric nurses generally have two to four years of training. Historically, they worked in psychiatric hospitals and wards, but today, increasingly, they are working in community based mental health settings.

Community college graduates with one to two years of college training also provide counselling services in settings such as transition homes, addiction centres, employment counselling agencies, and community mental health. The nonprofit social service sector also uses volunteers to deliver services in settings such as crisis phone lines, where people in distress call for assistance or referral. In addition, the professional counselling community is often supported or replaced by an array of self-help support groups, such as Alcoholics Anonymous (AA) or Narcotics Anonymous (NA).

Social Work and Social Justice

Like other professionals in the helping professions, social workers counsel clients to help them develop insight, solve problems, deal with emotional pain, and enhance relationships. They may also support clients by providing information, social skills training, or resources. One special feature that distinguishes social work counselling from that performed by other professionals is its dual focus on working with individuals as well as their social environment (Dale, Smith, Norlin, & Chess, 2009). Social workers assume that an individual can be understood only in the context of his or her environment; thus, they pay particular attention to the interaction of the person and the environment.

Unique to social work is the important professional responsibility to promote social justice or "fairness and moral rightness in how social institutions such as government, corporations, and powerful groups recognize and support the basic human rights of all people" (Sheafor & Horejsi, 2008, p. 6). Social justice commitment involves advocacy to promote human rights and more equitable income redistribution, political action to change oppressive legislation or policy, public education to shape public opinion, and efforts to build community. Social workers recognize that social problems arise, at least in part, from ineffective social systems.

While counselling is important in helping individuals cope, it is insufficient in dealing completely with these great challenges. Thus, because this book explores only the counselling component of social work practice, practitioners are cautioned to approach this task with the broader mission of social work in mind. Value 2 of the *Code of Ethics* of the Canadian Association of Social Workers (2005) outlines the obligations of social workers to advocate for social change:

Pursuit of Social Justice

As a result, social workers believe in the obligation of people, individually and collectively, to provide resources, services and opportunities for the overall benefit of humanity and to afford them protection from harm. Social workers promote social fairness and the equitable distribution of resources, and take action to reduce barriers and expand choice for all persons, with special regard for those who are marginalized, disadvantaged, vulnerable, and/or have exceptional needs. Social workers oppose prejudice and discrimination against any person or group of persons on any grounds, and specifically challenge views and actions that stereotype particular persons or groups.

Principles:

- Social workers uphold the right of people to have access to resources to meet basic human needs.
- Social workers advocate for fair and equitable access to public services and benefits.
- Social workers advocate for equal treatment and protection under the law and challenge injustices, especially injustices that affect the vulnerable and disadvantaged.
- Social workers promote social development and environmental management in the interests of all people. (p. 5)

ETHICS

Ethics are the principles and rules of acceptable or proper conduct. All professions have ethical guidelines, designed to protect both clients and members. Ethical codes define the limits of permissible behaviour and the sanctions or remedies for member violations of ethical standards. Codes of ethics serve the following broad purposes:

ethics: Guidelines that define the limits of permissible behaviour.

- Professionals can use their codes to assist them with decision making and as a reference for their practice.
- Ethical codes help shelter clients from incompetent and unethical practice by members of the profession. Ethical codes recognize that clients may be vulnerable and subject to manipulation and abuse of power by professionals, so they constrain professionals from taking advantage of clients.

- Ethical codes also provide guidance on how counsellors can deal fairly with colleagues and their employers, including the responsibility to address the unethical conduct of colleagues.

- Codes outline the philosophical and value principles of the profession. For example, the code of the Canadian Association of Social Workers has six core social work values:

> Value 1: Respect for the Inherent Dignity and Worth of Persons
>
> Value 2: Pursuit of Social Justice
>
> Value 3: Service to Humanity
>
> Value 4: Integrity of Professional Practice
>
> Value 5: Confidentiality in Professional Practice
>
> Value 6: Competence in Professional Practice (CASW, 2005, p. 4)

These ideals are echoed by the Canadian Counselling and Psychotherapy Association, which articulates the following fundamental principles as the basis for ethical conduct:

a. Beneficence: being proactive in promoting clients' best interests

b. Fidelity: honouring commitments to clients and maintaining integrity in counselling relationships

c. Nonmaleficence: not willfully harming clients and refraining from actions that risk harm

d. Autonomy: respecting the rights of clients to self-determination

e. Justice: respecting the dignity and just treatment of all persons

f. Societal interest: respecting the need to be responsible to society (CCPA, 2007, p. 2)

Unethical behaviour typically arises from issues related to one or more of the following: breaking confidentiality; misrepresenting or working beyond one's level of expertise; conducting improper relationships, including sexual activity with clients; and causing conflicts of interest, such as entering into business or other dual relationships with clients.

Professional associations are responsible for monitoring their own policies and for investigating and resolving violations of ethical conduct. The CASW and CCPA are examples of professional bodies that can formally discipline members who violate their codes of ethics. As well, counsellors who are not members of professional associations may work with agencies that provide guidelines for ethical behaviour and decision making.

In addition, legislation defines and restricts the use of certain titles, such as social worker, psychologist, and psychiatrist, to those who have the appropriate degree or training. The clients of these professionals can report misconduct or concerns to the appropriate professional association; however, there may be no legislation preventing people from offering counselling services under a wide range of other titles, such as counsellor, personal therapist, family and marital counsellor, and personal growth consultant. These practitioners may not have had formal preparation or training, and clients should be cautious when they seek their services.

Although the codes are the primary source for professional decision making, counsellors should also consider relevant theory, research, laws, regulations, and agency policy. When faced with ethical dilemmas, they should consider consultation with colleagues, supervisors, professional associations, and legal counsel. In addition, the CCPA has published an ethics casebook (Shulz, 2000) designed to assist counsellors in clarifying ethics and standards of practice, and the CASW has published *Guidelines for Ethical Practice* (2005) as a reference point for social workers on ethical practice.

Dual Relationships

A **dual relationship** is a relationship in which there is both a counselling relationship and another type of relationship, such as a business relationship, a friendship, or one of sexual intimacy. The essential purpose of counselling is to meet the needs of clients, but dual relationships lead to the risk that counsellors could misuse (or be perceived to be misusing) their professional relationships for personal gain. In dual relationships, the counsellor has a personal interest that may conflict with the client's interests. This may lead to intended or unintended exploitation, harm, manipulation, or coercion of clients. To prevent these problems and any conflict of interest, dual relationships must be avoided because of their potential harm to clients and the risk of damage to the image of the profession.

Not surprisingly, the codes of ethics for the various counselling professions strictly prohibit certain types of dual relationships, especially those of sexual involvement. Generally, they also prohibit sexual intimacies with former clients for a specified period after terminating the counselling relationship, but this injunction may extend indefinitely "if the client is clearly vulnerable, by reason of emotional or cognitive disorder, to exploitative influence by the counsellor. Counsellors, in all such circumstances, clearly bear the burden to ensure that no such exploitative influence has occurred and to seek consultative assistance" (CCPA, 2007, p. B12).

> **dual relationship:** A relationship in which there is both a counselling relationship and another type of relationship, such as friendship or sexual intimacy.

Professional Boundaries

Despite ethical guidelines, boundary violations and abuses do occur. Reviewing the available research, (Thoreson and colleagues 1993) found that the incidence of sexual contact between counsellors and clients ranges from 3.6 to 12.1 percent. Conducting their own study, the researchers found after surveying 1000 randomly selected male members of the American Counseling Association (ACA) that 1.7 percent of the respondents reported engaging in sexual contact with a client during a professional relationship, and 7 percent reported engaging in sexual contact after a professional relationship (Thoreson et al., 1993).

Physical Contact The CASW's *Guidelines for Ethical Practice* (2005) offers this guidance on the issue of physical contact with clients:

> Social workers avoid engaging in physical contact with clients when there is a possibility of harm to the client as a result of the contact. Social workers who engage in appropriate physical contact with clients are responsible for setting clear, appropriate and culturally sensitive boundaries to govern such contact. (p. 12)

While the CASW guidelines do not define appropriate physical contact, common sense needs to prevail. Fear of the implications and repercussions of touching has led some settings to become "no touch" environments; however, this practice may negate the needs of some clients, particularly children who need physical contact. In an editorial on the importance of touching in child and youth care settings, Tom Garfat (2008) emphasized the importance of touch when working with youth, but he also stressed that workers need to learn when not to touch. He distinguishes "between those who would touch youth in the most normal and healthy of ways; a pat on the back, a touch on the shoulder, a comforting hug when the world is a difficult place, a hand held in a moment of crisis, and those who use the opportunity to touch a young person as an opportunity to satisfy their own needs and desires" (p. iii). Garfat strongly endorses the elimination of inappropriate touching, but urges us to remember that "touch is part of human nature, touch is developmentally necessary, touch is part of healing, touch is a form of communication, and touch builds bridges" (p. x).

While sexual intimacy is clearly unethical, the appropriate boundaries of other relationships may be less clear. As Reamer (2002) observes,

> Other dual and multiple relationships are more ambiguous and require careful analysis and consultation. Examples include social workers in rural communities who cannot avoid contact with clients in social settings, social workers who are invited by clients to attend an important life event, social workers' relationships with former clients, and social workers' unanticipated encounters with clients at an Alcoholics Anonymous meeting when both parties are in recovery. (p. 66)

Miller (2007) discusses the challenges that professionals who work in rural or small towns face when applying and interpreting ethical standards such as "the need to maintain professional boundaries and at the same time achieve a sense of personal belonging in the community" (p. 168). She also notes the vulnerability that workers feel, due to their high visibility, when their actions are scrutinized by members of the community.

Pierce and Schmidt (2012) suggest that rural dynamics and culture affect how professional boundaries are defined:

> For example, over time, the professional may be invited to community events, a wedding, or a celebration for which attendance is viewed as significant by the community. Not attending may cause disharmony or barriers between the practitioner and the community. (p. 248)

Confidentiality

The rules regarding confidentiality are integral to every code of ethics. Ethical guidelines stress that the confidentiality of clients must be protected. Indeed, most clients enter counselling with an expectation that what they say will be kept private. For the most part, counsellors can assure clients that they will keep their disclosures confidential; however, often it is not so simple. **Absolute confidentiality** means that client disclosures are not shared with anyone. **Relative confidentiality** means that information is shared within the agency with supervisors or colleagues, outside the agency with the client's permission, or in courts of law owing to legal requirements, such as child abuse legislation. Usually, clients can be assured only of relative confidentiality.

absolute confidentiality: An assurance that client disclosures are not shared with anyone.

relative confidentiality: The assumption that client disclosures may be shared within the agency with supervisors or colleagues, outside the agency with client permission, or with others because of legal requirements, such as those contained within child abuse legislation.

To provide optimum service to clients, counsellors must share information about them within the agency. To monitor the quality of work and help counsellors improve their skills, supervisors need to review client files or consult with counsellors by reviewing audio and video recordings of their interviews. Other counsellors within the agency also have access to files.

Many people believe that counsellors and other professionals enjoy "privileged communication," that is, they are legally protected from having to share information that they have obtained while exercising their professional duties. However, the courts can subpoena counsellors' records because Canada has no legislative protection for licensed or unlicensed psychotherapists.

There are valid reasons, including some legal requirements, for sharing information. For example, all jurisdictions in Canada have legislation that requires counsellors to report suspicions of child abuse and neglect to the appropriate authorities. Similarly, counsellors might have to break confidentiality when they believe that clients might harm themselves or others. Counsellors need to become familiar with the precise wording of relevant statutes in their area since laws may vary significantly among jurisdictions.

One often-quoted legal precedent is the 1976 Tarasoff case, in which the client told his counsellor of his intent to kill his girlfriend, Tatiana Tarasoff. The counsellor told the campus police of the threat, but he did not warn his client's girlfriend or her family.

The client, a student at the school, subsequently carried out his threat and killed the young woman. The young woman's parents brought a successful lawsuit against the counsellor and the university. This litigation established that, when counsellors believe that a client represents "a serious danger of violence to another," they have a **duty to warn** potential victims (cited in Nesbitt, 2017.).

SUCCESS TIP

Become familiar with the legislation in your area that requires you to report suspected cases of child abuse or neglect, but remember it is not your job to conduct an investigation unless you are legally assigned this role.

Since the Tarasoff decision, there have been numerous Canadian applications and legal precedents that address the duty to warn issue. The CASW's *Guidelines for Ethical Practice* (2005) allows for disclosure when "necessary to prevent serious, foreseeable, and imminent harm to a client or others" (p. 6). The guidelines also obligate social workers in such circumstances to notify "both the person who may be at risk (if possible) as well as the police" (p. 8). The CCPA Code of Ethics (2007) has a similar duty to warn obligation that requires counsellors to "use reasonable care to give threatened persons such warnings as are essential to avert foreseeable dangers" (p. 7).

Clients have a right to be fully informed regarding the limits of confidentiality, including any legal or ethical responsibilities that require counsellors to share information. Through discussions regarding confidentiality, counsellors can reassure clients that computer and file records are safe.

Counsellors can take a number of steps to protect client confidentiality. They should discipline themselves not to discuss clients in public places and at parties or other social events. Counselling work is demanding, and an important part of dealing with the stress of the job is to unwind by talking about difficult cases and personal reactions with colleagues and supervisors. This is a healthy and necessary component of professional wellness. Unfortunately, time pressures and large caseloads may leave little or no time for this process during the working day, so it is easy to fall into the trap of discussing clients over lunch or in other settings where confidentiality cannot be ensured. The obvious risk is that the conversation will be overheard. Even when names are not used, accidental listeners may think that they know the person being discussed. In addition, they may decide that they will never go for counselling because what they say would soon be spread all over town.

Although it is tempting for counsellors to discuss clients with family and friends because they are available as supportive listeners, they should avoid doing so. Family and friends are not bound by the same ethics as counselling professionals. They could easily disclose what they have heard, perhaps with a seemingly innocent observation or comment.

Sometimes counsellors breach confidentiality by failing to take simple precautions. For example, taking phone calls during a counselling session can lead to careless breaches of confidentiality and suggest to clients that the counsellor treats their private matters casually. In addition, counsellors should remove all case records, phone messages, and notes from their desk. This prevents clients from seeing the names of other clients and reinforces the fact that the counsellor will not leave private records in public places.

SUCCESS TIP

When leaving phone messages for clients, give just your first name and say nothing about the nature of the call. Clients may not have informed room-mates or family members that they are seeing a counsellor.

TABLE 1.2 Confidentiality Guidelines

- Review professional guidelines such as the CASW's *Guidelines for Ethical Practice* and the CCPA's *Code of Ethics*.
- Involve clients. Keep them informed and seek their permission to release information. Remember that freedom of information statutes may give clients the right to access your files.
- Become familiar with relevant legal statutes (e.g., child abuse or mental health legislation) that define and limit confidentiality. Disclose only the information that is required.
- Protect client records with secure filing systems. Do not leave files, notes, or phone messages about clients out where they may be read by others. Ensure that electronically stored data is protected.
- Ensure that consultations with others concerning clients are legitimate and conducted in a private and professional manner. This precludes conversations about clients at social gatherings or in public places such as restaurants.
- Ensure that interviews are private and free from interruptions.
- Discuss clients only with supervisors and use only support staff for processing necessary paperwork and documentation.
- Never use client names, initials, or identifying data in emails or text messages.
- Exceptions to the rules may, and sometimes must, be made when there are suspicions of child abuse or neglect, when required by law (such as a subpoena), and when there is a risk to self or others (suicide threat or threat of violence).
- Never use social media to discuss clients, even if you change names and identifying information.

The interview itself should be conducted in private, not where other staff or clients may overhear. When greeting a client in the waiting room, counsellors should refrain from using surnames; however, they need to be sensitive to the fact that many seniors and people from some cultures are insulted by the casual use of their first names.

Sometimes counsellors meet clients by chance in public places. When this happens, counsellors should ensure that they maintain confidentiality, even when the client appears unconcerned. They should gently shift the conversation to a neutral topic or suggest a private time and place to continue the discussion. At that time, counsellors can explain why they avoided a public discussion.

Table 1.2 outlines some important confidentiality guidelines.

VALUES FOR PROFESSIONAL PRACTICE

values: What individuals and groups consider important or worthwhile.

Values are principles or qualities that individuals and groups consider important or worthwhile. Ethics are derived from values. Values represent beliefs about what is desirable and good. Personal values describe what individuals consider desirable and what they believe is right and wrong. Professional values describe fundamental beliefs that the profession holds about people and ways the work of the profession ought to be conducted. Clearly, professional values (as reflected in ethical codes of conduct) and personal values have a major impact on shaping the practice of counselling professionals. Two key values of counselling are the belief in the dignity and worth of people and the client's right to self-determination.

Belief in the Dignity and Worth of People

Belief in the dignity and worth of people is the core value of counselling. This value commits counsellors to ensuring that their clients are treated with regard for their rights. It obligates counsellors to demonstrate acceptance of the individual and to uphold confidentiality. Counsellors who value the dignity of their clients appreciate diversity and reject stereotyping, labelling, and other dehumanizing practices.

Counsellors must treat clients fairly, regardless of personal feelings toward them. For example, counsellors must resist the natural temptation to spend more time with clients they favour and less time with those whom they find difficult. Counsellors are expected to apply their skills and knowledge at an optimum level for each client, regardless of their personal reaction toward any client. Clients may have behaved in ways that counsellors perceive to be offensive, but this belief does not give counsellors licence to be disrespectful or to withhold services. Discriminatory practices are strictly prohibited by both major codes:

■ Counsellors actively work to understand the diverse cultural background of the clients with whom they work, and do not condone or engage in discrimination based on age, colour, culture, ethnicity, disability, gender, religion, sexual orientation, marital, or socioeconomic status. (CCPA, 2007, p. 9)

■ Social workers recognize and respect the diversity of Canadian society, taking into account the breadth of differences that exist among individuals, families, groups and communities. (CASW, 2005, p. 4)

These ethical guidelines underscore the need for professionals to learn about other cultures. Such learning increases sensitivity and awareness of how values, beliefs, and worldview define one's behaviour and thinking. This topic will be explored in more depth in Chapter 10.

Counsellors, especially those who work with high-risk clients (such as those with chronic addiction problems) need to be careful that their view of, and attitudes toward, clients do not become jaded. Jaded counsellors often have a cynical and pessimistic perspective on the willingness and capacity of their clients to change and grow. Counsellors who believe that clients are incapable of growth are likely to invest less energy in supporting change. Moreover, they may be more prone to using controlling responses because of their expectation that the "clients cannot do it on their own." What would you predict to be the likely outcome of a counselling session when the counsellor labels the client "a hopeless alcoholic"? Conversely, belief in the dignity and worth of people is expressed through positive practices:

■ involving clients in decision making, goal setting, and problem solving

■ adopting a strengths approach

■ maintaining an optimistic view of human nature, including the belief that people are capable of change and growth

Client Self-Determination

Self-determination is the principle that clients have a right to autonomy and freedom of choice to make their own decisions, insofar as is possible. Counsellors have a duty to respect and promote this right even when they disagree with the decisions of their clients. Moreover, choice is an integral part of client self-determination. When clients have no choices, or believe that they have none, self-determination is not possible; however, adherence to the principle does not prevent counsellors from helping clients understand how their actions might violate the rights of others. Nor does it prevent counsellors from helping clients appreciate the potential consequences of their actions. Some clients, such as people with mental disabilities and young children, may be unable to make competent choices. If so, counsellors may need to prevent them from acting in ways that are potentially harmful to themselves or others.

Sometimes beginning counsellors are misinformed about the nature of counselling. They believe that their role is to listen to their clients' problems and then offer helpful

self-determination: The principle that promotes the rights of clients to have autonomy and freedom of choice.

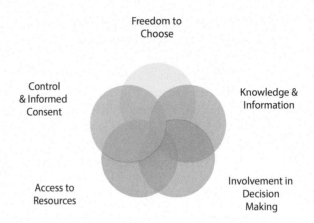

Freedom to
Choose

Control
& Informed
Consent

Knowledge &
Information

Access to
Resources

Involvement in
Decision
Making

Figure 1.1   Essential Elements of Self-Determination

advice or solutions. The principle of self-determination obligates counsellors to avoid behaviours that control and manipulate clients. Instead, they must employ strategies that empower clients to make independent and informed decisions. The counsellor's expertise lies not in knowing what is best for the client, but in being able to manage the process through which problems are solved, feelings are managed, or decisions are made. Empowerment is the process of assisting clients to discover personal strengths and capacities. In other words, through empowerment, counsellors seek to help clients take control of their lives and realize that they can improve their situation through their actions. (See Figure 1.1 and Table 1.3.)

Effective counsellors accept that clients have a right to be involved in counselling decision making. They have the right to be treated as active partners in the counselling process and to participate in decisions affecting their lives. This right is underscored in the CCPA's *Code of Ethics* (2007):

> **Clients' Rights and Informed Consent.** When counselling is initiated, and throughout the counselling process as necessary, counsellors inform clients of the purposes, goals, techniques, procedures, limitations, potential risks and benefits of services to be performed, and other such pertinent information. Counsellors make sure that clients understand the implications of diagnosis, fees and fee collection arrangements, record

TABLE 1.3   Strategy Choices for Promoting Client Self-Determination

- Use advocacy skills to help clients access resources or remove barriers to existing options.
- Avoid prescriptive advice and other controlling responses.
- Help clients identify, access, and explore options.
- Encourage clients to make their own decisions based on informed choices of the costs and benefits of any course of action.
- Assist clients in evaluating the consequences of their actions on others.
- Fully inform clients about counselling strategies and the potential risks. Promote collaborative decision making on goals. Whenever possible, provide access to records.
- Invite clients to evaluate the progress of counselling and the counselling relationship.
- When under court order or similar nonvoluntary conditions, provide information on the client's right to decline service, as well as the possible consequences of such denial. Whenever possible, empower clients with choices.
- Adopt a mindset that recognizes the client as the "expert" on his or her own problems, feelings, and preferred solutions.
- Avoid dependency-promoting behaviours, such as doing for clients what they can do for themselves, excessive involvement, and indiscriminate advice giving.
- Encourage optimism and foster a relationship of safety to help clients take risks.
- Honour client lifestyle choices.

STUDENT: I have just started my field placement, and I am disturbed by what is happening. When the team goes for coffee, everyone jokes and makes fun of the clients. If they knew how their counsellors talked about them, they would never come back. I did not know that professionals could be so cold-hearted. Is their behaviour unethical?

TEACHER: Just before his execution by hanging, a condemned man is offered a cigarette. "No thanks," he says, "I'm trying to quit." Such "gallows humour" is one of the ways many people deal with the enormous stress of their jobs. Jokes about tragic events or client misfortunes help counsellors sustain their emotional well-being. It does not mean that they have become hardened or uncaring toward their clients; rather it is a way of unwinding and relieving constant pressure. As you've discovered, one of the dangers of gallows humour is that others will overhear it and draw conclusions about the person's attitudes. Is it unethical? What do you think?

keeping, and limits of confidentiality. Clients have the right to participate in the ongoing counselling plans, to refuse any recommended services, and to be advised of the consequences of such refusal. (pp. 7–8)

Rights of Children

As a rule, "capable" children are entitled to confidentiality unless there is a reason to suspect that the child might harm himself or herself or others. As well, situations involving child abuse or neglect must be reported. In this respect, a child can receive medical treatment or consultation on issues such as birth control/abortion, mental health problems, and addictions counselling (Justice Education Society, 2015).

In 1991, Canada signed the United Nations Declaration of the Rights of the Child, which obligates it to enforce children's rights as outlined in the Declaration. Nevertheless, United Nations officials have criticized the country for its failure to adequately address the needs of Aboriginal, disabled, and immigrant children as well as those living in poverty (Scoffield, 2008).

ETHICAL DILEMMAS

An **ethical dilemma** exists when a choice must be made between competing values and potential courses of action. A decision to remove a child from a home where there is obvious and significant abuse is not an ethical dilemma since the gravity of the situation gives no room for choice. On the other hand, removing a child when the home situation is marginal requires weighing the risks of potential abuse against the drawbacks of separating a child from his parents.

By virtue of their role, counsellors may have simultaneous obligations to different people and groups, including the agency that employs them, their clients, the community at large, and the legal system. When obligations conflict, an ethical dilemma is created with risks and benefits to each potential solution.

ethical dilemma: A situation involving competing or conflicting values or principles.

Functional magnetic resonance imaging (fMRI) has enabled researchers to identify areas of the brain that are active when people address moral and ethical dilemmas. The results showed that areas of the brain associated with emotions tend to predominate, particularly when there is a more personal involvement in the dilemma (Science Daily, 2001). Another study reported by Riddle (2013) in Scientific American concluded that "our professed moral principles can be shifted by subtle differences in mood and how a question is posed." These findings underscore the value of counsellors consulting with others and avoiding impulsive actions when confronted with difficult ethical decisions.

While ethical codes that are based on the values of the profession attempt to define acceptable behaviour, they usually do not offer answers about specific situations that arise for counselling professionals. Even though they do not provide precise guidelines for resolving all dilemmas, codes are an important reference aid for decision making.

Types of Ethical Dilemmas

1. **Distribution of scarce resources (time, money, and opportunity to participate in a program)**
   - An agency has limited funds available to assist clients with retraining. Who should get the money—the client with the greatest potential for success or the client who needs it most?

2. **Professional competence and ethical behaviour of colleagues**
   - A student on internship (field placement) becomes aware that her supervisor is attending an AA meeting with one of her clients.
   - One of the staff informs you of his intention to phone in sick to extend his vacation a few more days.

3. **Policies and procedures of the agency setting that appear oppressive or insensitive to the cultural/diversity needs of the clients it serves**
   - A worker has information about a client that, if made known to the agency, would make her ineligible for services that she badly needs.
   - You become aware that your client, a single mother on welfare struggling to care for her four children on a meagre budget, received a cheque from her mother to help with expenses. Legally, she is obligated to declare this income, which will be fully deducted from her next welfare payment, thus, depriving her and her children of much-needed assistance.

4. **Behaviour of clients**
   - A 17-year-old girl asks for your help to obtain an abortion without involving her parents.
   - Your client informs you that he has tested positive for HIV, but he hasn't informed his partner.
   - A 16-year-old boy tells you that he is working as a prostitute.
   - Your client casually mentions that he robbed a bank several months ago but was not caught.

5. **Competing values, needs, procedures, or legal requirements**
   - A 15-year-old girl discloses that her father has been abusive, but in recent weeks, he seems to have changed. She asks that you do not make a report to the authorities. She says she knows her father will retaliate if he finds out that she has told anyone.
   - A young 16-year-old Jehovah's Witness asserts her belief that she should not be given a blood transfusion to deal with a terminal illness.
   - An abused child says he will not cooperate with removal from his parents and that he will run away from any foster home.

Resolving Ethical Dilemmas

Erford (2010) describes five ethical rules or principles that can be used to help resolve ethical dilemmas:

1. *Autonomy:* Honour clients' self-determination and their freedom to make their own decisions.
2. *Beneficence:* Pursue the welfare and benefit of others.
3. *Nonmaleficence:* In simple terms, do no harm to others.

4. *Justice:* Strive for an equal distribution of resources and equitable effort among participants.

5. *Fidelity:* Be loyal and honest and keep promises.

Under ideal conditions, counsellors can honour all five principles, but ethical dilemmas by nature represent competing principles, and each choice involves unique consequences. Ethical decision making involves identifying and weighing which of the five principles ought to take priority in any given situation.

The application of any model for ethical decision making does not mean that resolution of ethical dilemmas will be easy. When values and ethics compete, deciding which one should have priority can be painfully difficult. Consider a case where an individual in remission from cancer stipulates that if his cancer returns he does not want further surgery or other invasive treatment. Suppose years later, he develops dementia and his cancer returns. He now asserts that he wants treatment. Which "person's" wishes should a caregiver honour, the one with sound mind from the past or the current one with diminished capacity? (Adapted from Locke, 2014.)

Intimate knowledge of ethical principles and legal guidelines can make the decision-making process clearer, albeit no less difficult. For example, a client's right to confidentiality and self-determination must be given up when that client discloses child abuse, and the duty to warn principle means that professionals must break confidentiality to warn potential victims. However, it is not always clear when a client's behaviour constitutes danger to the safety of others.

The principle of self-determination protects the right of people to make errors and carry out actions that others might consider wrong. Counsellors must consider when the application of this principle must be abandoned because the individual's behaviour might result in death, such as in a case where a client threatens suicide. While counsellors have a clear legal and ethical responsibility to intervene to prevent suicide, their responsibilities are not as clear for other challenges. For example, the lifestyles of homeless persons may reach the point where their hygiene, living, and eating habits become dangerous for them. The point at which their right to self-determination should yield to their right to health and well-being is not easy to establish. An ethical dilemma exists.

There are four steps counsellors can take to resolve ethical dilemmas (see Figure 1.2).

Step 1: Gather Facts During this stage, it is important to control any tendency to act impulsively. Remember that assumptions and hearsay are not the same as facts. Most ethical codes require that professionals seek resolution with colleagues before proceeding. For example, the CCPA code advises a counsellor who has concerns about the ethical behaviour of another counsellor "to seek an informal resolution with the counsellor, when feasible and appropriate" (2007, p. 6). In many cases, frank discussion with colleagues reveals additional information or results in a satisfactory solution.

Step 2: Identify Ethical Issues and Potential Violations At this point, refer to the appropriate code of ethics (CASW, CCPA, etc.) to identify whether the matter under question is addressed in the code. If the person in question is not governed by a professional code, then agency policies and procedures or local legislation may

---

⟫⟫ BRAIN BYTE   Ethics and Neuroscience

Current and emerging neuroimaging techniques raise the possibility that one day these tools could be used to read minds, perhaps to determine if a person is lying or harbouring prejudicial views. In fact, rudimentary tools to do this are already being used. This raises important ethical questions: to what extent might neuroscience be used in legal settings to determine guilt or whether or not a person should be granted parole (Smith, 2013)?

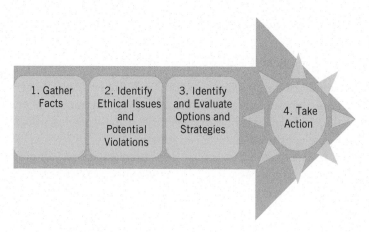

Figure 1.2 Model for Resolving Ethical Dilemmas

provide important reference points. For example, matters of discrimination in Canada are addressed under the *Canadian Human Rights Act* (1985).

Step 3: Identify and Evaluate Options and Strategies   Here the goal is to list the potential action strategies. Where appropriate, consulting with colleagues, professional organizations, and supervisors can assist in generating alternatives.

Reflective questions help you consider the merits and ramifications of any action plan. Here are some sample questions:

- What are the advantages and disadvantages of not taking action?
- What are the advantages and disadvantages of taking action?
- What are the potential consequences (short-term and long-term) of action or inaction?
- Who might gain or lose?
- What other individuals or organizations are likely to be affected?
- To what extent might other factors be influencing my judgment (e.g., unresolved relationship problems, bias, and hidden agendas)?
- What values and principles have priority? Boyle and colleagues (2006) suggest a rank order of ethical principles (see Figure 1.3). They identify seven ethical principles,

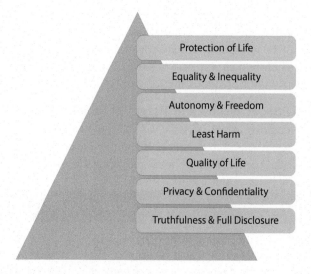

Figure 1.3 Ethical Principles Hierarchy

Adapted from Boyle et al., 2006, p. 97.

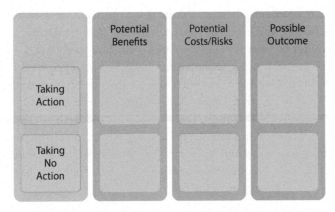

Figure 1.4 Matrix Decision-Making Chart for Ethical Dilemmas

giving the highest priority to protection of life, which supersedes all of the other rights. The equality and inequality principle entitles people to be treated equally, and this right supersedes an individual's right to autonomy and freedom. The least harm principle aims to minimize the adverse consequences of any course of action. The quality of life principle suggests that counsellors should choose alternatives that enhance quality of life over those that diminish it. Privacy and confidentiality, while important, are given lesser priority than those rights higher on the hierarchy. Similarly, truthfulness and full disclosure are important ethical principles, but they may be compromised if overridden by other, higher-rated principles.

A matrix chart, such as that illustrated in Figure 1.4, can be used as a tool to compile and compare the benefits and risks of the alternatives. A separate analysis should be done for each choice. Entries should consider both the short- and long-term costs and benefits of a given course of action. Consult with experts and others when completing this task.

Step 4: Take Action A good action plan should include details of the intended outcome, a list of the people who need to be involved, required resources (e.g., information, meeting space, and external facilitator), and the sequence of events that must be accomplished. A concrete timetable with clearly defined steps ensures that you will not lose time wondering what to do next. The action plan should also anticipate obstacles and identify strategies for addressing them. For example, if you are confronting a colleague on a breach of ethical behaviour, it would be wise to consider what you might do if the colleague

■ launches a counterattack.

■ reacts with feelings such as anger, remorse, or shame.

■ denies that the behaviour occurred.

■ asks that you keep your knowledge of the breach confidential between the two of you.

SUCCESS TIP

Resolution of ethical dilemmas is intellectually challenging and emotionally taxing. Seek appropriate consultation and supervision for planning and debriefing.

Objectivity

Effective counsellors may become intimately familiar with the lives of their clients, yet they are required to remain objective. **Objectivity** is defined as the capacity to understand situations and people without bias or distortion. When counsellors are objective,

objectivity: The ability to understand feelings, thoughts, and behaviour without allowing personal values, beliefs, and biases to interfere.

they understand their clients' feelings, thoughts, and behaviours without allowing their personal values, beliefs, and biases to contaminate that understanding. They also do not directly or subtly try to impose their preferred solutions on clients.

Counsellors can fail to be objective in a number of ways. The first is to make assumptions. **Assumptions** are distortions or false conclusions based on simplistic reasoning, incomplete information, or bias. Counsellors who have had similar experiences to their clients' may assume that their clients' problems and feelings are the same as their own. Consequently, they do not take the time to investigate the distinctive viewpoints of their clients. Counsellors also may make assumptions about the meaning of words, but this danger can be avoided if counsellors remain alert to the need to probe for individual client definition and meaning, as in the following example:

> **Client (speaking to a First Nations counsellor):** I moved here about five years ago. I guess you know how tough it is for an Indian in this city.
>
> **Counsellor (Choice 1):** I sure do. Prejudice is everywhere.
>
> **Counsellor (Choice 2):** As you say, it is not easy. But it's different for everyone. I need your help to understand better what it's been like for you.

assumptions: Distortions or false conclusions based on simplistic reasoning, incomplete information, or bias.

▶▶▶ CONVERSATION 1.2   Personal Feelings Get in the Way

STUDENT: I know what I'm supposed to do, but I'm worried about how I can control my personal feelings when I'm interviewing someone who has done something terrible, such as rape a child or beat up his wife. How do you stay objective in situations like those?

SUPERVISOR: Tell me a bit about what you think you are supposed to do.

STUDENT: I need to make sure that I am objective and that I do not let my personal feelings interfere.

SUPERVISOR: Sure, that is the overall goal. However, all of us will have some personal feelings about what clients have done. Your fears are very normal for someone just starting in the field. Usually, with a bit of experience, most people are able to manage their feelings.

STUDENT: What if the client's behaviour involves things that do not allow me to get past my initial revulsion?

SUPERVISOR: If that happened to me, I would have to ask myself, "Can I be sufficiently in control of my own feelings to work effectively with this person?" In some cases, I can compensate for a bias, and in other cases, I probably should not be involved in the therapeutic relationship. However, I am not sure that anyone is able to stay truly objective in situations where they are involved with someone who has perpetrated a violent crime or harmed a young child. The big questions for me are, "How do I maintain an awareness and openness about my personal feelings?" and "How do I mitigate those feelings when dealing with a person who has done such a

thing?" Sometimes such cases bring up unresolved issues from our own past that need to be re-examined or processed further. Sometimes we simply need to acknowledge that there are certain practice areas that are not the "best fit" for us individually as practitioners. The value of supervision in such circumstances is clear.

STUDENT: Do I have to like my clients in order to work with them?

COUNSELLOR: There will always be clients who rub us the wrong way. Some are demanding, insulting, or threatening, and it's a challenge to feel any real empathy. If that's part of the client's usual style (and it often is), then this provides important information that can be addressed in counselling. If a client "pushes our buttons," sometimes a little introspection is in order. Do our reactions trigger memories of other unresolved issues or experiences in our lives?

STUDENT: Transference?

COUNSELLOR: Yes, it sure could be. We also need to deal with a range of other feelings that can arise such as feelings of overprotectiveness toward a client. Or, when we have strong positive feelings. These responses may need to be managed just as much as when we work with clients who arouse our disgust, anger, or frustration.

STUDENT: From what you've been saying, in all cases, the goal is the same. Be aware of our personal reactions, then manage them. If this isn't possible, refer the client or seek supervision and support for yourself.

In this example, Choice 1 cuts off the discussion, and the counsellor loses a valuable opportunity to appreciate the client's experience. Choice 2, on the other hand, offers gentle empathy and then probes for more detail. This second response reduces the risk that the counsellor will make errors of assumption.

A second way that counsellors can lose objectivity is by over-identifying with clients. When over-identification occurs, counsellors lose their capacity to keep sufficient emotional distance from their clients. Their own feelings and reactions become mixed up with those of their clients, clouding their judgment. Counsellors who find themselves in this position may find that personal counselling or consultation with a supervisor is sufficient to help them regain objectivity, or they may conclude that referral to another counsellor is necessary.

A third way that counsellors can lose objectivity is by becoming overly involved with clients. This over-involvement includes dual relationships prohibited by ethical codes, as well as relationships in which counsellors rely on clients to meet their social and psychological needs. To prevent this from happening, counsellors need to make sure that they are meeting their personal needs in other ways. As well, counsellors should be alert to signs that they may be over-involved with particular clients.

SUCCESS TIP

Warning signs of over-involvement: Interviews that consistently run over time, relief when a client misses an appointment, excessive worry about clients, reluctance to end a counselling relationship that has reached a point of termination, "buttons" being pushed, or strong feelings (negative or positive) toward the client evoked.

Table 1.4 summarizes protective strategies counsellors can use to avoid loss of objectivity.

TABLE 1.4 Maintaining Objectivity

Loss of Objectivity	Protective Strategy Choices
Making assumptions	• Attempt to understand and monitor your prejudices, preferences, and biases (e.g., cultural, gender, and religious). • Develop self-awareness regarding personal needs and values. • Listen to but do not be controlled by the opinions of others. • Be inquisitive. Explore each client's situation to discover his or her unique perspective. • Brainstorm or seek information from all perspectives. • Check your conclusions with clients to see if they match theirs—seek definition, detail, and examples.
Over-identification	• Monitor reactions and discover areas of vulnerability; be alert to strong negative or positive reactions to clients. • Refer clients when you are not impartial or able to control your feelings. • Know why you want to be a counsellor—understand your needs. • Use colleagues to analyze your reactions and give you feedback. • Use tools such as video recordings to review interviews for inappropriate attempts to influence or control.
Over-involvement	• Avoid promoting client dependency. • Develop a wellness program to ensure that you are not relying on your clients to meet your needs for social and psychological involvement and acceptance. • Recognize warning signs of over-involvement.

STUDENT: Is it ever okay to be sexually intimate with clients?

TEACHER: No! Universally, ethical codes of behaviour prohibit sexual intimacies with clients. For example, the CASW's *Guidelines for Ethical Practice* (2005) succinctly states that "social workers do not engage in romantic relationships, sexual activities or sexual contact with clients, even if such contact is sought by clients" (p. 12). A similar injunction explicitly stated in the CCPA's *Code of Ethics* (2007) prohibits any type of sexual relationship with clients and any counselling relationship with clients with whom they have had prior sexual relationships.

STUDENT: That seems straightforward. What about becoming involved with former clients?

TEACHER: That's a more difficult question. My opinion is that you never should, but you should consult individual codes of ethics for specific guidelines. For example, the CCPA code requires a minimum of three years between the end of the counselling relationship and the beginning of a sexual relationship. The period is extended indefinitely if the client is clearly vulnerable. In any case, counsellors "clearly bear the burden to ensure that no such exploitative influence has occurred" (2007, p. 9). A review of the literature concludes that harm to clients does occur when professionals have sexual contact with clients, including "denial, guilt, shame, isolation, anger, depression, impaired ability to trust, loss of self-esteem, difficulty expressing anger, emotional liability, psychosomatic disorders, sexual confusion, and increased risk of suicide" (Beckman et al., 2000, p. 223).

STUDENT: What about other types of involvement? If you are a counsellor in a small town, it's impossible to avoid social contact with clients. Your client might be the owner of the only grocery store in town.

TEACHER: Codes of ethics for the various counselling professions (e.g., psychology or social work) frown upon dual relationships when there is a possibility that counsellors will lose objectivity or where there is potential for client exploitation. In large cities, it's usually easy to refer clients to avoid the conflict of interest of dual relationships. As you point out, it's much more difficult in a small town, and some dual relationship arrangements may be inevitable. However, relationships should never include sexual intimacy with current clients.

THE COMPETENT COUNSELLOR

A high level of self-awareness enables counsellors to make important decisions regarding areas in which they are competent and those in which referral to other professionals is warranted. Counsellors must practise only within the range of their competence, and they should not misrepresent their training or experience. This helps to ensure that they do no harm to clients. The following guidelines provide reference for working with competence:

1. *Work within the limits of competence.* Counsellors should offer counselling services that are within the limits of their professional competence, as measured by education and professional standards. Competent counsellors use only those techniques and strategies that they have been adequately trained to apply. They know that the support and assistance of other professionals is necessary for issues that exceed their expertise. Until counsellors have received the necessary training and supervised practice, they should not work in specialized areas of practice, such as interviewing children in abuse situations or administering or interpreting psychological tests. For example, reading a book or attending a workshop on mental health does not qualify untrained counsellors to make psychiatric diagnoses, nor would attendance at a short seminar on hypnosis qualify them to use hypnosis in their work. Such specialized interventions usually require certification by their professional body.

   Counselling requires skilled interviewing but includes the additional goal of helping clients with such activities as problem solving, dealing with painful feelings, and developing new skills. Psychotherapy involves intensive counselling with emphasis on personality change or the treatment of more severe mental disorders.

2. *Pursue professional training and development.* Counsellors should monitor their work and seek supervision, training, or consultation to evaluate their effectiveness. They should pursue continued professional development to increase their competence and keep their knowledge current. This helps to ensure that their work is based on evidence-based best practice derived from accepted theory supported by empirical research. People would not want to see a doctor whose most recent training was decades ago in medical school. Similarly, clients should not be expected to work with counsellors who are not current in their field.

   Professional counsellors need a core knowledge base, which typically requires two or more years of academic training, including supervised clinical experience in a recognized counselling or social service setting. Moreover, throughout their careers, counsellors should expect to spend time in reading books and journals to increase their knowledge. As well, regular attendance at courses, seminars, and conferences should be a part of everyone's professional career.

   By keeping their knowledge base current, counsellors are better able to be empathic because they are more aware of the issues and feelings that their clients face. Moreover, keeping up to date helps counsellors avoid judgmental responses based on only their own frames of reference. The range of knowledge that counsellors need to pursue includes the following:

   - Specific issues, problems, and challenges that their clients are facing. For example, counsellors working in corrections need to know something about finding a job if one has a criminal record and coping with the stigma of a criminal record. As another example, many clients are dealing with poverty, and counsellors need to be aware of its social and psychological effects.
   - Relevant medical and psychiatric conditions (e.g., attention deficit disorder, multiple sclerosis, schizophrenia, bipolar disorder, and autism). Counsellors credibility and competence is greatly enhanced if their knowledge of these conditions is current.
   - Lifestyle variations (e.g., same-sex relationships, single parents, extended families, and blended families).
   - Cultural awareness about the values, beliefs, and customs of others.
   - Lifespan development (i.e., developmental changes and milestones from birth to death). Life experience can greatly increase a counsellor's capacity for empathy and understanding. Of course, life experience may also cloud judgment and objectivity, so it is important that counsellors seek training and consultation to increase their understanding of others' experiences.
   - Monitoring emerging trends in neuroscience.

3. *Be self-aware of personal reactions and unresolved issues.* Counsellors need to be aware of situations where their clients' problems parallel unresolved issues in their own lives. This awareness is important to help counsellors know when to seek consultation or supervision, when to refer clients to other workers, and when to enter counselling to address their own needs. Clients have a right to expect that their counsellors are objective about the issues being discussed and that their judgment is not impaired by bias, unresolved personal problems, or physical illness. If counsellors have emotional or physical problems that affect their ability to give competent services, they should discontinue service to the client.

In addition, large caseloads and the emotional demands of counselling work may result in emotional and physical fatigue, thereby weakening a counsellor's competence. Competent counsellors monitor their emotional health; by setting limits on their amount of work, they are able to leave time to pursue personal wellness and balance in their lives. Familiar with the dangers of burnout and vicarious trauma, they develop strategies to prevent these career threatening reactions.

STUDENT: I'm just a beginner. So, if I am supposed to work within the limits of my competence, I shouldn't do anything.

TEACHER: Like many counsellors who are just starting, you may feel a bit overwhelmed.

STUDENT: I don't want to say or do the wrong thing. What if I don't know the right answers, or I don't say the right thing to clients?

TEACHER: First, there is rarely a single right way to respond. Most often, there is a range of choices of things to say or do in any situation. Second, no one knows all the right answers. Be honest with clients about the fact that you are still a student, and don't be afraid to admit your limitations, as this provides great

modelling for clients. One goal of training is for you to expand your range of choices so that you can respond based on the needs of your clients and their situations. Remember, learning to be an effective counsellor is a lifelong process. At this stage, your professional responsibility is to make effective use of supervisors to monitor your work. Use them to develop your skills. Make it easy for them to give you feedback. Seek it out, and then try to be nondefensive. Look for opportunities to apply your developing knowledge base by taking some risks to learn new skills.

When I first started in the field, I also feared saying something that would damage my client. When I shared this feeling with one of my professors, he put it in perspective by saying, "What makes you think you're so important to the client?"

In general, interviewing is a process of gathering information without any expectation of influencing or changing clients. Competent interviewing requires an ability to explore and understand clients' attitudes, feelings, and perspectives. The basis for this competence is a nonjudgmental attitude and intelligent application of the active listening skills of attending, using silence, paraphrasing, summarizing, and asking questions (see Chapters 4 to 6). Although the principal goal of interviewing is information gathering, the process of interviewing may lead clients to release painful or forgotten feelings. Thus, adept interviewers are capable of dealing with unpredictable reactions that the interview elicits or of referring clients to appropriate alternative resources. Moreover, they know when and how to probe effectively.

SELF-AWARENESS

Everything that irritates us about others can lead us to an understanding of ourselves.

—Carl Jung (public domain)

The Importance of Self-Awareness

Competent counsellors need to acquire a high level of awareness of who they are. Until counsellors develop self-awareness of their own needs, feelings, thoughts, and behaviours, including their personal problems and their areas of vulnerability, they will be unable to respond to their clients with objectivity. Table 1.5 contrasts the characteristics of counsellors who have high levels of self-awareness with those who have low levels of self-awareness.

Counsellors who lack self-awareness and are not motivated to pursue it are destined to remain unaware of the ways they influence clients. For example, they may be unaware of how their nonverbal reactions to controversial topics betray their biases and discomfort. Capuzzi and Gross (2009) highlight the importance of counsellors developing awareness of their own spiritual and religious beliefs to appropriately engage with their clients' spiritual issues: "Counsellors may not pick up on their clients' concerns because of their own bias or may pick up on these themes too readily to the exclusion of other issues" (p. 304). They may avoid particular topics, or they may behave in certain ways to mask their insecurities. As another example, counsellors with personal needs for control may meet this need through excessive and inappropriate advice giving.

TABLE 1.5 Self-Awareness

Counsellors with Self-Awareness	Counsellors without Self-Awareness
• Recognize and understand their emotional reactions.	• Avoid or are unaware of their feelings.
• Accept that everyone's experience is different	• Assume clients will respond or feel the same as them
• Know where their feelings end and those of their clients begin.	• Project personal feelings onto clients.
• Recognize and accept areas of vulnerability and unresolved issues.	• Respond inappropriately because unresolved problems interfere with their capacity to be objective.
• Understand personal values and their influence on the counselling relationship.	• React emotionally to their clients but don't understand why or how.
• Recognize and manage internal dialogue.	• Unconsciously use clients to work out their own personal difficulties.
• Understand and control personal defence mechanisms.	• Remain blind to defensive reactions.
• Know how they influence clients and counselling outcomes.	• Remain unaware of how their behaviour influences others.
• Modify behaviour based on reactions of clients.	• Behave based on personal needs and style rather than in response to the needs and reactions of clients.
• Set professional goals based on knowledge of personal and skill strengths and limitations.	• Avoid or limit goal setting because they are unaware of personal and professional needs.
• Accurately identify and appraise counselling skill competence.	• Overestimate or underestimate counselling skill competence.
• Know those areas that are likely to trigger unhelpful feelings or responses.	• Are reactive without insight.

Increasing Self-Awareness

Counsellors who are serious about developing their self-awareness are secure enough to risk exploring their strengths and limitations. Self-awareness means becoming alert and knowledgeable about personal ways of thinking, acting, and feeling. Self-aware counsellors are strong enough to be open to discovering aspects of themselves that they might prefer to keep hidden. This is a continuing, career-long process that requires courage as counsellors look at themselves and their ability to relate to others.

Colleagues, supervisors, and clients can be extremely helpful sources of information, but their feedback needs to be cultivated. Generally, people are reluctant to deliver critical feedback, however helpful it may be. Therefore, it is important that counsellors create the conditions that encourage feedback. They can invite input from others through a number of strategies.

The first strategy is to create a safe climate. People balk at giving feedback to others, because they fear how it will be received. One concern is the risk of retaliation: "If I say something, will I be attacked or made to feel guilty?" Another common worry is that feedback will damage the relationship. The major concern also might be that feedback will cripple the other person's self-esteem.

Therefore, counsellors must demonstrate that they are ready, willing, and able to respond nondefensively to feedback. They have a responsibility to consider feedback and, when appropriate, to act on it. They don't have to agree unconditionally with what has been said to them, but they must listen and give nonaggressive responses—in other words, without blame or excuses. Sometimes such control can be difficult to sustain, particularly if feedback is delivered in an uncaring and hostile manner. A general rule when dealing with clients is that, no matter what clients say or do, counsellors must maintain a professional role. Of course, this does not preclude setting appropriate limits, nor does it mean that counsellors have to tolerate personal or physical abuse. It means staying calm, being nondefensive, and refraining from retaliatory responses, such as name calling or making punishing statements.

The second strategy is to use active listening skills to ensure that feedback is concrete or specific. Counsellors can ask questions to get details, definitions, examples, and clarification. Summarizing and paraphrasing can also be used to confirm understanding.

Who Am I? How Do Others See Me?

Self-awareness for counsellors involves answering two basic questions: Who am I? and How do others see me? These questions require counsellors to explore and understand their personal feelings, thoughts, and behaviour.

Feelings Effective counsellors are comfortable discussing a wide range of emotions. They do not avoid feelings; in fact, they recognize that, for many clients, understanding and managing painful emotions is the greatest outcome of counselling. To understand client emotions, counsellors must be in tune with their own emotional reactions. Empathy, the basic tool for understanding the feelings of others, will be contaminated unless counsellors are fully in touch with their own feelings. This includes knowing where their feelings end and those of their clients begin.

Work and personal stress may also negatively affect a counsellor's capacity to relate effectively to clients. Counsellors must be aware of stressful situations and understand how they react to them. Self-aware counsellors avoid or reduce stressors by developing personal wellness plans for coping with the inevitable demands of the job.

Thoughts Counsellors need to be aware of their own internal dialogue—the inner voices that evaluate their actions. Counsellors with low self-worth typically find that the inner voice is critical, issuing messages such as "I'm no good." Negative self-talk can lead to emotional distress and interfere with counselling performance in several ways:

■ Counsellors may be reluctant to be assertive with clients and may be excessively gentle or nonconfrontational.

■ Counsellors may be unable to assess counselling relationship outcomes objectively if they tend to interpret problems as personal failures and to discount positive feedback or outcomes.

Counsellors need to become watchful of negative self-talk as a crucial first step in developing a program to combat its effects. Subsequently, systematic techniques such as thought-stopping can be used to replace depreciating self-talk with affirmations or positive statements.

Behaviour Counsellors need to take time to discover how clients are reacting to them. Personal needs and defence mechanisms may lead counsellors to assume blindly that problems in the counselling relationship arise from their clients' inadequacies or failings. Although effective counsellors have confidence in their own abilities, they have to accept that occasionally they may say or do the wrong thing. Counsellors need to be mature and open enough to evaluate their work and to take responsibility for their errors and insensitivities. For example, open minded counsellors consider the possibility that clients may be angry for good reason, perhaps because of oppressive agency routines.

Counsellors who lack self awareness may fail to understand or accept the needs of their clients and are more likely to take their clients' behaviour too personally. Ultimately, counsellors need to be self aware enough to know which client reactions are reactions to their behaviour or personalities and which are the result of other variables beyond their control.

Sigmund Freud first described defence mechanisms in 1894. A **defence mechanism** is a mental process or reaction that shields a person from undesirable or unacceptable

defence mechanisms: Mental process or reaction that shields a person from undesirable or unacceptable thoughts, feelings, or conclusions that, if accepted, would create anxiety or challenges to one's sense of self. Common defence mechanisms include denial, displacement, rationalization, suppression, and regression.

thoughts, feelings, or conclusions that, if accepted, would create anxiety or damage one's self-esteem. Defence mechanisms, which are unconscious, distort reality and serve to protect people from perceived threats. Simple defences include blaming others or making excuses for their own failures. For example, counsellors might take credit for counselling successes but blame failure on their clients. Common defence mechanisms used by counsellors include the following:

- *Denial*: Refusing to acknowledge the existence of feelings or problems. When counsellors use denial, they fail to consider that their actions might be the reason for their clients' inappropriate behaviour.
- *Displacement*: Shift of emotions or desires from one person or object to another person or object. For example, counsellors deal with their own work stress by behaving aggressively with clients.
- *Rationalization*: Developing excuses or explanations to protect their self image. For example, counsellors justify their inability to confront clients by concluding that it is best to offer only positive feedback.
- *Suppression*: Averting stressful thoughts by not thinking about them. For example, counsellors refuse to consider that personal biases might be affecting their decisions.
- *Regression*: Dealing with conflict or stress by returning to behaviour from an earlier stage of life. For example, counsellors deal with aggressive clients by becoming overly compliant or overly pleasing.

Counsellors should be alert to circumstances where they use defence mechanisms instead of confronting reality. Facing reality requires courage and taking risks because giving up one's defences means sacrificing safety. Moreover, feedback from others can be threatening because it challenges counsellors to let down their defences by addressing aspects of their situations that they might prefer to avoid.

When counsellors understand themselves, they recognize when their defences are up and can take steps to change their reactions and behaviour. They know when and where they are vulnerable; then, they use this knowledge to cue or trigger nondefensive alternatives. For example, when clients are angry or hostile, rather than yielding to the natural impulse to fight back, counsellors can discipline themselves to take time to empathize and encourage clients to ventilate.

Self aware counsellors know their skill strengths and limitations. This self awareness enables them to avoid overusing particular skills simply because they are strengths, and it helps them to know when it is appropriate to refer clients to other counsellors. It also helps them to set goals for professional skill development. Knowing the limits of one's ability is a measure of competence.

Personal Needs

Counsellors have the same basic needs as everyone else, including the need to be loved, respected, and valued by others. This is natural; however, counsellors must understand how their personal needs can adversely affect counselling outcomes. Lack of self-awareness regarding personal needs can lead to unconscious structuring of the session to meet the counsellor's needs instead of the client's. One student was told by her supervisor that her clients really liked her as a person, but when they had a problem, they would go to someone else because they did not believe she was capable of dealing with tough issues or giving critical feedback. Through supervision and reflection this student learned how her need to be liked left her vulnerable and overly sensitive to client reactions. As a defence, she avoided doing anything that might arouse anxiety.

A range of counsellor needs may interfere with counselling, including the need to be liked; the need to achieve status or prestige, control, and perfection; and the need to cultivate social relationships. Table 1.6 summarizes the major warning signs and risks of these needs.

Need to Be Liked   In Chapter 3, we will explore the importance of a warm and trusting counselling relationship. Largely, counselling depends on establishing and maintaining a safe environment, one in which clients feel safe enough to take risks. Obviously, this is easier if clients like their counsellors; however, counsellors need to remember that having clients like them is not the primary goal of counselling. The aim of counselling is to support client change or problem management. This means that counsellors have to be assertive enough to risk making reasonable demands on their clients, which, in turn, may generate tension and anxiety. Otherwise, clients can easily stay locked into established but unhealthy patterns. The need to be liked becomes problematic when it becomes more important than achieving the goals of counselling. One beginning counsellor, a young male, wrote in his journal: "When a client says something negative or behaves in a self-destructive way, I realize I hold back. I don't say anything because I want to be liked. I want the client to like me, not see me as an authority figure. I'd rather be seen as a pal or a friend." This journal entry highlights the dangers of this counsellor's need to be liked and signals an important insight that will help him question some of his assumptions about counselling. He will need to re-evaluate how his behaviour may be sabotaging client progress.

TABLE 1.6   Managing Personal Needs in Counselling

Personal Need	Warning Signs and Risks
To be liked and to be helpful	• Withholding potentially helpful but critical feedback • Inappropriately avoiding controversy or conflict • Trying to ingratiate (e.g., excessively praising, telling clients what they want to hear) • Acting with rescuing behaviour • Expecting or reaching for compliments from clients
Status or prestige	• Trying to impress with "exotic" techniques or brilliant interpretations • Taking credit for client success • Name-dropping • Bragging about successes
Control	• Advice giving • Interfering with client self-determination (e.g., unnecessarily using authority, manipulating, and dominating) • Imposing personal values • Stereotyping clients as needy and inadequate (which creates a role for someone to be "helpful")
Perfectionism	• Focusing on mistakes • Pushing clients toward unrealistic goals • Responding with self-deprecation to mistakes (e.g., "I'm a failure")
Social relationships	• Becoming over-involved with clients (e.g., meeting clients socially, continuing counselling relationships beyond the normal point of closure) • Indiscriminate self-disclosure

Need for Status or Prestige   Counsellors who have an excessive need to impress others, perhaps because of insecurity, may become technique-centred instead of client-centred. With this switch in priorities, the needs of the client may be overlooked as counsellors act to impress clients or others. The priority of counselling should be to bolster the self-esteem of clients.

Need for Control   Codes of ethics recognize that clients are vulnerable to exploitation. Consequently, counsellors need to pay substantial attention to refraining from behaviours that result in undue control of clients. The principle of self-determination (introduced earlier in this chapter) is a basic value that upholds the right of clients to make independent decisions. Counsellors interfere with this right when they attempt to take over clients' problems and orchestrate their solutions.

In some settings, such as government agencies, counsellors may have the legal mandate to impose their services. This situation requires counsellors to be especially vigilant. As Brammer and MacDonald (1999) observe, helpers in these settings "must be wary of identifying too closely with the power of the agency under the guise of carrying out the agency's mission. Often the helpee becomes lost in such settings, and the helping services tend to support the power of the organization. The result may be an exaggerated emphasis on adjustment or pacification rather than on actualization and liberation" (p. 40).

Perfectionism   Perfectionism, an unrealistic pursuit of excellence, can negatively affect counselling. Counsellors who are perfectionists may be unable to appraise their work accurately, and they may have an unjustified tendency to blame themselves for client failures. Sometimes counsellors who are perfectionists push clients toward unrealistic goals or challenge them to move at too fast a pace.

Need for Social Relationships   Counsellors with unmet social needs risk over-involvement with clients. If counsellors do not have outlets in their own lives for social interaction, they may misuse the counselling relationship for that purpose.

Personal and Cultural Values

Counsellor self-knowledge of personal values and preferences is indispensable for effective counselling. Values constitute a frame of reference for understanding and assessing clients and for making decisions and choices.

Self-awareness of personal values is an important element of competence. All counsellors have personal values, and it is crucial that they understand what these values are to avoid imposing them on clients. Self-awareness of personal values is a first step for counsellors to take to manage the bias that comes from interpreting clients' behaviour from their own perspectives or cultures rather than from the clients'.

Cultural self-awareness refers to knowledge of the customs, traditions, role expectations, and values of one's culture of origin. Language is a particularly important variable. The word *authority* will have a very different meaning for individuals who come from totalitarian countries and for those who come from egalitarian societies. Cultural self-awareness prepares counsellors to recognize and value the diversity of other cultures. Such awareness needs to be accompanied by a belief that one's own ethnic group is only one of many and that there are other appropriate beliefs and behaviours.

Inevitably, the personal values of counsellors influence the way they assess clients, the techniques and procedures they use, and the goals that they deem reasonable, including which topics will get more or less attention. Moreover, certain topics are more value-charged (e.g., abortion, assisted suicide, sexual orientation, religion, and abuse), and the beliefs of counsellors may bias their work in these areas. For example, counsellors who find that they never discuss sexuality in their counselling work need to determine why.

TABLE 1.7 Values, Beliefs, and Attitudes That Help and Hinder Counsellors' Effectiveness

Unhelpful Values & Beliefs	Helpful Values & Beliefs
To accept help from others is a sign of weakness.	To accept help is a sign of strength.
Some people are just not deserving of our respect or caring.	Everyone has intrinsic worth and the capacity to be productive.
People are inherently evil. Unless you are careful, they will take advantage of you.	People are essentially good.
I know what is best for my clients.	People are capable of finding their own answers and making decisions.
It is essential that my clients like me.	The purpose of counselling is to help clients exercise choice, not to make clients like me.
I've been there myself, so I know what my clients are feeling.	I can't know what my clients are feeling until I take the time to let them teach me.
People are incapable of changing.	People can and do change.
My religion/culture/viewpoint is the best.	I can accept a wide variety of cultures, religions, and viewpoints.
In this world, it is survival of the fittest.	We depend on one another, and we have a responsibility to help others.
Counsellors have a right to impose service when it is in their clients' best interest.	With some exceptions, clients can choose to refuse service.

Are they avoiding this topic because of personal inhibitions? Are they unconsciously judging the sexual behaviour of their clients?

One way for counsellors to address this problem is to disclose their values to their clients; however, they should do this in such a way that clients do not feel pressured to adopt similar values. Clients should feel free to maintain their own values without fear that they are in some way disappointing their counsellors.

A counsellor's value system is an important variable that influences the methods and outcomes of counselling. In general, counsellors are most effective when their values reflect an optimistic and nonjudgmental view of people. Intellectually and emotionally, they accept and treasure the widest possible variations in lifestyle. They believe in the inherent strength and capacity of people and in their intrinsic right to freedom of choice. Table 1.7 examines some of the values that might impede or enhance counsellors' effectiveness. When counsellors have values that hinder effectiveness, they are more likely to find themselves behaving contrary to the ethics of the field, such as acting in ways that inhibit self-determination or failing to respect the dignity of their clients. Conversely, counsellors who have values that enhance their ability are more naturally inclined to support the ethics of the profession and are more likely to behave in ways that empower their clients.

PROFESSIONAL SURVIVAL

Working as a counsellor can be immensely stressful and, for some, emotionally dangerous, particularly for those who are working with clients who have experienced trauma and abuse. People who work in hospitals and mental health settings, as well as those who work with children are particularly vulnerable. Continued exposure to client troubles can leave counsellors with little patience and resilience for dealing with their own issues. Some experience burnout or vicarious trauma.

Burnout is a state of emotional, mental, and physical exhaustion that hinders or prevents people from performing their jobs. Burnout may affect people in different

Burnout: A state of emotional, mental, and physical exhaustion that reduces or prevents people from performing their job.

ways, but certain symptoms are typical. The stress of burnout may show itself as a general state of physical exhaustion, including signs of diminished health, such as headaches, sleep disruptions, and digestive upset. Emotional and mental burnout may reveal itself as increased anxiety, inability to cope with the normal demands of work, depression, excessive worry, discouragement, pessimism toward clients, loss of a sense of purpose, general irritability, and an inability to find joy in one's career or life.

Vicarious trauma is a risk for anyone in the helping professions who works with people who have been traumatized. Sheafor and Horejsi (2008) offer this caution:

> After repeated exposures to clients who have been traumatized and are in great distress, social workers and other helpers may develop symptoms of trauma themselves, such as intrusive thoughts and images, sleeplessness, bystander guilt, feelings of vulnerability, helplessness, self-doubt, and rage. Workers who feel especially overwhelmed by disaster, those who have had a prior experience of severe emotional trauma, and those who are inexperienced in disaster-related work are especially vulnerable to developing these symptoms. (p. 571)

Counsellors who suspect that they suffer from burnout or vicarious trauma should first consult a physician to rule out any medical condition that might be a factor. Obviously, the best way to deal with burnout is to prevent it from happening. For counsellors, this means balancing the demands of their work life by taking care of themselves. Counsellors need to develop personal wellness plans that address their own emotional, physical, and spiritual needs. An essential part of this plan is time away from the job. Counsellors need to avoid becoming over-involved by working unreasonably long hours and weekends or by skipping vacations. They need to make intelligent decisions about the limits of what they can do.

Counsellors can also prevent burnout by setting up and using a support system of family, friends, supervisors, and colleagues. By doing so, they ensure that they have people to whom they can turn for assistance and emotional support. Work colleagues and supervisors are essential for helping counsellors manage their emotional reactions to clients, such as fear and anger. Counsellors need to recognize that being able to accept help from others is a sign of strength and that they should model this belief in their own behaviour. Talking to others reduces isolation and allows for team participation and support with difficult decisions or situations. It is particularly important for counsellors to have someone to debrief with after stressful interviews, such as those with angry or abusive clients.

Continued professional development is another important strategy for preventing burnout. Seminars, courses, and conferences expose counsellors to new ideas and the latest research and can help them renew their enthusiasm and creativity.

vicarious trauma: An occupational hazard for people in the helping professions, in which they develop the same symptoms as their clients who have been traumatized.

SUCCESS TIP

Preventing Workplace Burnout

Among the many proven strategies for preventing burnout are: awareness and early intervention to deal with symptoms, exercise, nutrition, healthy personal relationships, lifestyle balance, laughter/having fun, mindful breathing, mindfulness, debriefing with trusted colleagues and supervisors, use of a mentor or role model, distancing oneself from negative coworkers, sleep, recreation, spirituality, taking a vacation, ensuring workplace breaks, maintaining reasonable office hours, scheduling client interviews to minimize sustained periods of stress, working within the limits of one's competence, and accepting that you can't help everyone.

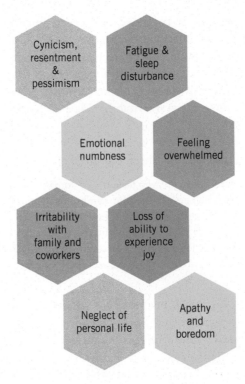

Figure 1.5 Common Symptoms of Workplace Burnout

SUMMARY

- Counselling services are provided by a wide range of different professionals, including social workers, nurses, psychologists, and others.

- Professional codes of ethics define the acceptable limits of behaviour for professionals who provide counselling services. They aim to protect clients from misuse of position and power by professionals, and they strictly prohibit dual relationships that are sexual or exploitive.

- Ethics, derived from values, are the principles and rules of acceptable conduct. The values of the counselling profession are rooted in a few basic principles: belief in the dignity and worth of people, respect for diversity, and respect for the client's right to self-determination.

- An ethical dilemma exists when a choice must be made between competing values. Five principles can help resolve ethical dilemmas: autonomy, beneficence, non-maleficence, justice, and fidelity. Ethical decision making involves weighing the five principles and deciding which ought to have priority in a given situation.

- Objectivity is the capacity to understand situations and people without bias or distortion. Counsellors can lose their objectivity by making assumptions, over-identifying with clients, or becoming overly involved with their clients.

- Self-awareness is essential for counsellors to work with objectivity. Self-aware counsellors know themselves—their feelings, thoughts, behaviour, personal needs, and areas of vulnerability. They understand how they affect clients, and they know the limits of their competence. They can answer the question, "Who am I?"

- Burnout and vicarious trauma are workplace hazards that can be addressed using a variety of strategies such as lifestyle balance, nutrition, exercise, and effective use of trusted colleagues and supervisors.

EXERCISES

Self-Awareness

1. What strong beliefs do members of your cultural/ethnic group hold?

2. Use the questions and situations below to examine your values in relation to sexual orientation issues.

   a. If a client of yours is gay or lesbian, how might it influence the way you work with him or her?

   b. What would you do if a friend told you an anti-homosexual joke or story? What if the person telling the joke was a client or a colleague?

   c. Do you have gay or lesbian friends?

   d. Do you think homosexuality is an illness? How do the teachings of your religion mesh with your personal values and beliefs?

   e. Your daughter discloses that she is lesbian. Predict how you might feel, think, and behave.

   f. Your best friend confides that he feels he is the wrong gender and that he is in the early stages of transitioning. How do you respond?

   g. What are your views on same-sex marriage?

3. Write an essay that explores your values and beliefs. Explore issues and questions such as:

   - Why do you want to become a counsellor?

   - What needs do you expect to meet through your work? In what ways might your personal needs be an impediment?

   - Are people inherently good or bad?

   - What is your understanding of the meaning of life?

   - Should people have the right to take their own lives?

   - Should immigrants be required to speak one of Canada's two official languages?

   - What are the characteristics of the client you would most and least want to work with? (Be specific regarding as many variables as possible, such as age, gender, personality, culture, and religion.) Why would you choose these characteristics?

   - What topics or issues are likely to evoke strong personal reactions from you?

   - What does authority mean to you? How do you behave and feel when you are relating to people in authority?

   - Where do you draw your strength?

   - When you die, what do you most want to be remembered for?

4. Explore your personal strengths and limitations. Use the following topics to structure your assessment:

   - capacity to be assertive (as opposed to shy or aggressive)

   - degree of self-confidence

   - comfort dealing with a wide range of emotions

   - need to control or be in charge

   - capacity to relate to diverse populations (age, gender, culture, religion, etc.)

   - ability to give and receive feedback (positive and critical)

   - need to be helpful

   - anxieties and fears

   - competence in initiating relationships (beginnings)

   - ability to deal with conflict

   - self-awareness regarding how others see you

   - overall awareness of personal strengths and limitations

   - values and attitudes that will help or hinder your work as a counsellor

   - capacity and willingness to change

   Based on your answers, identify what you consider your five major strengths and your five major limitations to be.

5. Evaluate your capacity for handling feedback from others. Are you generally open and nondefensive when others critically evaluate your behaviour or performance? Do you tend to avoid asking for feedback? Do you actively solicit feedback? Interview friends and colleagues for their opinions.

6. Are you excessively dependent on your clients? Rate yourself for each statement below using the following scale:

   4 = always

   3 = frequently

   2 = sometimes

   1 = rarely

   0 = never

   _____ I feel responsible for the feelings, thoughts, and behaviour of my clients.

   _____ I get angry when my help is rejected.

   _____ I feel worthless or depressed when clients don't change.

   _____ I feel compelled to help people solve problems by offering unwanted advice.

   _____ I want to take care of my clients and protect them from painful feelings.

_____ When clients don't like me, I feel rejected or inadequate.

_____ I do things to make my clients like me, even if what I do is not helpful.

_____ I avoid confronting or challenging clients.

_____ I tell clients what they want to hear.

_____ I feel most safe when I'm giving to others.

_____ When clients fail, I take it personally.

_____ I spend too much time proving to myself and my clients that I'm good enough.

_____ I tend to be very controlling with clients.

_____ I tolerate abuse from clients to ensure they like me.

_____ I feel responsible for solving my clients' problems.

Carefully review any statements where you scored 4 or 3. Use your awareness of problem areas to develop a program of self-change.

7. Imagine that you are a client. What might your counsellor need to know about you (e.g., values, needs, and preferences) to work effectively with you?

8. Take an inventory of your friendship circle. To what extent do your friends come from the same cultural group and have the same values base as your own? Predict what might happen if you broadened your circle to include more diversity. Develop a plan to learn about the cultures and world religions in your community.

9. What personal and religious values do you have that would generate ethical dilemmas?

Skill Practice

1. Interview one or more colleagues who deliberately introduce issues, feelings, or behaviours that represent "triggers" for you. What did you learn from this interview?

2. Imagine that you are addressing a situation where you believe a colleague has acted unethically, for example, by breaching confidentiality or speaking rudely to a client. Assume that you have decided to approach the colleague informally to share your observation. Role-play what you might say.

Concepts

1. Can we promise our clients absolute confidentiality? Why or why not?

2. What are some advantages and disadvantages to allowing clients access to files?

3. Under what conditions would you make exceptions to the principle of self-determination?

4. Use the concepts in this chapter to explore ethical issues and strategies for each of the following situations:

   a. An elderly, frail woman suffering from inoperable cancer decides to kill herself.

   b. A client decides to give his or her life's savings to his or her church.

   c. A 16-year-old male client boasts that if his girlfriend tries to leave him, he will kill her.

   d. A client from a counselling relationship that terminated six months ago phones to ask you for a date.

   e. Your client leaves your office in anger, determined to "teach my wife a lesson for the way she treated me."

   f. Knowing that you are in the market for a new car, your client, a used-car salesperson, offers to help you buy a car at the wholesale price.

   g. Your client is a young woman (age 17) who is questioning her sexual identity. She inquires about your sexual orientation.

   h. Your client asks for your email address so that he can keep in touch

   i. Your client, a bisexual male, has tested HIV-positive, but he informs you that he does not wish to tell his wife. He says that he will practise safe sex.

   j. You receive a call from a client's wife. She says she is concerned about her husband and asks whether you think her husband might be gay.

   k. Your colleagues begin to talk about a client. You are with them at a local restaurant.

   l. One of your colleagues tells you that she has just returned from a one-day workshop on hypnosis. She says that she can hardly wait to try it on some clients.

   m. You encounter one of your colleagues having lunch with a client. You notice that they are drinking a bottle of wine.

   n. You have an erotic dream about one of your clients.

   o. While you are counselling a student (in your role as school counsellor), he discloses that he is selling marijuana to classmates. (Would your response be different if you were a counsellor in a community agency unconnected to the school?)

   p. You are a counsellor working with a young gay client in downtown Toronto. He has been socially isolated and is slow to trust anyone, but over time, you have managed to form a strong working relationship. Imagine that he approaches you with a request that you walk with him in Toronto's annual gay pride parade. What variables would you consider in making your decision? What are the implications of going with him? What are the implications of not going?

   q. Your client is down to her last two dollars. She offers to buy you a coffee.

   r. Your car is broken and requires an expensive repair. Your client has been struggling to set up a mobile repair service, but business has been slow. He offers to fix your car for a discounted price.

5. A good friend invites you to a small dinner party. When you arrive, you are introduced to the other guests, including a marital-counselling client whom you have been working with for the past year. You note that her companion

for the evening is not her husband. From observing their behaviour, there is no doubt that this is a romantic relationship. She has never mentioned this relationship in the past. What would you do for the rest of the evening? Should you disclose this relationship to the woman's husband? If she asks you to keep your knowledge of this relationship from her husband, could you continue to see them for marital counselling?

6. Assess the extent to which you believe that each of the following counsellor behaviours might be acceptable using the following rating scale:

5 = always

4 = often

3 = sometimes

2 = seldom

1 = never

Be prepared to defend your answer. How might your answer vary depending on the circumstances?

_____ seeing a client after having had one alcoholic drink

_____ accepting an invitation for dinner at a client's home

_____ hugging a client

_____ inviting a former client to a party at your home

_____ dating a former client

_____ having sex with a client

_____ driving your client home

_____ discussing your client with a supervisor

_____ assisting a client to end his or her life

_____ accepting a client's decision to commit suicide

_____ allowing your teenager to babysit for your client

_____ buying a car from your client

_____ lending money to a client

_____ reporting your client to the police (after the client tells you that he or she committed a crime)

_____ reporting suspected child abuse by your client

_____ sharing personal experiences, feelings, problems, and so on with your client

_____ getting angry with your client

_____ discussing a client with your family or friends (without mentioning names)

_____ giving a present to a client or receiving a present from a client

_____ sharing information about clients with other counsellors

_____ warning a person that your client has threatened to harm himself or herself

_____ telling a client's partner that he or she is HIV-positive

_____ advising a client to leave an abusive marriage

_____ crying in the presence of a client

_____ counselling a friend or neighbour at your agency (adapted from Shebib, 1997)

7. Give examples of appropriate physical contact between counsellors and clients. How might cultural, age, or gender variables affect your answer?

8. The case below is based on a case record completed by a social work student. Use the CCPA and CASW codes to evaluate the appropriateness of the language used.

I visited the Smith home to investigate allegations of child neglect. I was met at the door by Mrs. Smith, a single parent. I was surprised by her size; she was morbidly obese and smelled as if she had not showered in weeks. Rolls of fat hung out of Mrs. Smith's shirt, and portions of her legs were covered with dirt. Mrs. Smith's slovenly appearance suggests she is unable to care for herself, much less her children (Reamer, 1998, p. 93).

9. Explore the issues involved in discussing clients with friends and relatives. Is it acceptable to discuss clients if you change their names and other identifying data? Defend your answer.

10. Should some clients be forced to attend counselling?

11. Do you think gallows humour is ethical? Defend your answer.

12. Review the codes of ethics for three or four different Canadian professional organizations. What common and unique features can you identify?

13. Work in a small group to develop confidentiality guidelines for electronic storage and sharing of data. What are the risks of sharing information with other professionals using email?

14. Social Media

   a. Discuss the ethics of using Google or other search engines to find posted information about a client without their consent. Suppose a search reveals information that is contradictory to discussions held during a counselling session. Or, what if a search finds posted information critical of the counsellor?

   b. What personal information about themselves is appropriate and inappropriate for counsellors to post online?

   c. Explore the appropriateness of counsellors connecting with clients on Facebook. What about former clients?

15. Imagine that you are director of a social service agency. With limited funding, you have to make a difficult decision to fund one program and terminate another. Both programs have been successful. Discuss how you might approach the resolution of this ethical challenge.

WEBLINKS

The Canadian Counselling and Psychotherapy Association website has links to notes on ethics, legal issues, and standards for counsellors

www.ccpa-accp.ca/ethics/

The Canadian Association of Social Workers website has links and information for social workers

www.casw-acts.ca

The Markkula Center for Applied Ethics at Santa Clara University website provides articles and links on the topic of ethics

www.scu.edu/ethics

This website has links to resources, articles, and discussions on the topic of dual relationships and boundary issues

http://kspope.com/dual/index.php

Chapter 2
The Skills, Process, and Pitfalls of Counselling

Is approachable

Chooses the right setting

Does not overreact

Seeks to understand the problem

Effective counselor

Maintains confidentiality

Helps with painful emotions

Gives specific counsel

Knows his limitations

Dizain/Shutterstock

LEARNING OBJECTIVES

- Define what is meant by counselling.
- Describe the necessary range of skill versatility for counsellors.
- Describe the essential elements of a trauma-informed approach to counselling.
- Identify and classify the skills and strategies of counselling
- Summarize the developmental objectives of the four phases of counselling.
- Describe counselling pitfalls.

WHAT IS COUNSELLING?

Counselling is a time-limited relationship in which counsellors help clients increase their ability to deal with the demands of life. Typically, people are referred to or seek counselling because of an unmanageable crisis, such as the loss of a job, relationship problems, or feelings of distress. The immediate goal of counselling is to provide assistance so that people seeking help (clients) can gain some control over their problems. The long-term goal of counselling is to restore or develop a client's ability to cope with the changing demands of their lives (empowerment).

counselling: An empowerment process of helping clients to learn skills, deal with feelings, and manage problems.

Recent research and developments in neuroscience confirm that counselling has the potential to change client brains in very positive ways. This research supports the value of core counselling skills such as listening and empathy. Research also endorses placing an emphasis on client strengths and the centrality of the client/counsellor relationship as a basis for change. Counselling enhances neurogenesis (the production of new neurons in the brain) and it takes advantage of the brain's neuroplasticity (the capacity of the brain to change) (Ivey, Ivey, & Zalaquett, 2010).

The Canadian Counselling and Psychotherapy Association (CCPA, 2012) offers this perspective:

> Counselling is the skilled and principled use of relationship to facilitate self-knowledge, emotional acceptance and growth and the optimal development of personal resources. The overall aim of counsellors is to provide an opportunity for people to work toward living more satisfyingly and resourcefully. Counselling relationships will vary according to need but may be concerned with developmental issues, addressing and resolving specific problems, making decisions, coping with crisis, developing personal insights and knowledge, working through feelings of inner conflict or improving relationships with others.

Counselling is defined by three variables: the needs and wants of the client, the mandate of the counselling setting, and the expertise or competence of the counsellor. As discussed in Chapter 1, professional counsellors are aware of the limits of their competence and know when to refer their clients to other appropriate services. They are also aware of their own needs and unresolved issues and they refer clients to other professionals when they cannot work with reasonable objectivity. In addition, they accept that no one counsellor is qualified to work with all clients. Table 2.1 summarizes how counselling knowledge and skills evolve from beginning to advanced levels.

The work of counselling may entail a broad range of activities, including the following:

- helping clients cope with painful feelings
- teaching clients new problem-solving skills

TABLE 2.1 Counselling Skill Levels

Beginning Level Counsellors	Advanced Level Counsellors
Basic use of core listening and responding skills	Exemplary use of a broad range of listening and counselling skills and strategies; capacity to be creative to meet the unique needs of individual clients
Sensitivity to overt nonverbal cues	Responsiveness to subtle nonverbal cues and themes
Basic content knowledge of field of practice	In-depth knowledge of evidence-based best practices; ability to analyze and adapt published material
Rudimentary understanding of self	Sophisticated knowledge of self and cultural worldview, one's impact on others, and one's ability to selectively use aspects of self to influence others
Tendency to "mimic" mentors and textbook responses	Capacity to customize their approach; development of individual styles
Struggle to manage biases, personal reactions	"Second nature" capacity to stay appropriately detached and in control of self even when "tested" by clients
Self-conscious	Focus on clients
Tendency to want to fix, rescue, or solve client problems	Acceptance of the client as "expert;" focus on client empowerment

- mediating relationship communication difficulties
- aiding clients in identifying and accessing resources
- helping clients make decisions and implement action plans
- supporting or motivating clients

Interviewing skills are indispensable to effective counselling. The goal of **interviewing** is to acquire and organize relevant information through timely listening and responding skills. The primary goal is information gathering; however, clients may feel relief from sharing and organizing their thoughts in response to systematic interviewing.

Good interviewers are comfortable with silence and know when to listen without interrupting. Counsellors who listen to their clients give them a chance to air their feelings, and this step can be therapeutic in itself. Patient listening shows clients that counsellors are willing to accept them without judgment and without burdening them with quick-fix solutions to complex problems and feelings.

At the beginning of counselling sessions or interviews, silent listening may also give counsellors valuable clues about the potential focus of the interview. Listening also helps counsellors learn about their clients' priorities; it reveals which methods clients may have used and not used to try to solve their problems.

> **interviewing:** Acquiring and organizing relevant information using active listening skills, including attending, silence, paraphrasing, summarizing, questioning, and empathy.

SUCCESS TIP

However self-defeating it may appear, all human social behaviour has a purpose.

Good listeners also know when and how to respond. Paraphrasing, summarizing, questioning, and showing empathy constitute the foundation of effective listening. These skills enable counsellors to focus and deepen the interview. Good listeners use questions to clarify meaning and seek details and examples; whereas they paraphrase and summarize responses to confirm understanding and highlight important information. A good interview involves methodical questioning and exploration of issues, a process that can help clients clarify and organize their thoughts. Finally, counsellors use empathy skills to confirm their understanding of the client's feelings.

> **psychotherapy:** Advanced counselling targeting severe emotional or behavioural difficulties or disorders.

⟩⟩⟩ CONVERSATION 2.1   Counselling and Psychotherapy

STUDENT: What is the difference between counselling and psychotherapy?

TEACHER: The terms **psychotherapy** and *counselling* are often used interchangeably, and there is no accepted distinction between them. Both counselling and psychotherapy are used to help clients learn skills, deal with feelings, and manage problems. In counselling and psychotherapy, appropriate relationships with clients are the crucial success medium that establishes a foundation of safety and security for clients to undertake the change process.

Although there is no clear dividing line between the two terms, the major difference between counselling and psychotherapy is that psychotherapy tends to be more long-term than counselling, with an emphasis on severe emotional and behavioural difficulties or disorders. On the other hand, counselling is targeted at assisting clients in managing situational problems. While psychotherapy can greatly assist people, it can be harmful if undertaken without appropriate training, experience, or supervision. Attending a short workshop or reading a book is insufficient preparation.

Currently, there are hundreds of different therapeutic approaches, such as Gestalt, transactional analysis, psychodrama, rational emotive, Rogerian or person-centred, motivational interviewing, cognitive behavioural, music therapy, art therapy, and Adlerian.

CHOICES: THE NEED FOR VERSATILITY

diversity: Variations in terms of lifestyle, culture, behaviour, sexual orientation, age, ability, religion, and other factors.

versatility: The need for counsellors to develop a broad range of skills so they can adapt their approach to fit the distinctive complexities of each individual and context.

The typical counselling caseload is characterized by its **diversity**. Culture, gender, age, religion, sexual orientation, language, education, economic ability, and intellectual capacity, as well as beliefs, values, preferences, and personal style, make every client different. Skill versatility means that counsellors have choices that give them the freedom to adapt to individual differences—**versatility** enables counsellors to customize their approach. For example, although most clients respond favourably to empathy, some clients see empathy as intrusive and respond with defensiveness, preferring to keep their feelings private. Effective counsellors are alert to such reactions and have the ability to use skills other than empathy with these clients.

Brill and Levine (2005) stress the importance of the counsellor's personal influence in the counselling process. Counsellors "must consider their weaknesses as well as their capacities and strengths in selecting methods, techniques, and procedures. Because each individual is different, all workers must develop their own styles and their own ways of handling the tools of the trade. This is the element of artistry that is a vital part of such work" (p. 175). Successful counsellors model high congruence between who they are and how they act. They are sincere and real in the way they relate to clients.

In order to work effectively with diversity, the following key principles are essential:

1. *There is no "one-size-fits-all" model of counselling.* Respect for client diversity requires counsellors to be versatile in adapting their methods to fit the needs of each client or context. They may work from a model or process for exploring problems and helping clients build solutions, but they adapt that model to each client situation. Most counsellors now accept that no single counselling approach is best, and they are willing to draw ideas from different theoretical schools. In the process, they learn to use an assortment of counselling tools, including drama, role play, toys, music, art, films, visual charts such as genealogical diagrams, personality tests, and audio or visual recordings.

2. *Expert counsellors draw on evidence-based best practices and experience as guides in determining which skills and procedures will best meet their clients' needs.* Evidence-based empirical data can help counsellors predict which skills and approaches have the highest likelihood of success with particular problems.

3. *Adaptation of skills for individual clients and circumstances is required.* Counsellors who persist in using the same strategy for all clients, without regard to individual differences, will never become effective. Skill versatility gives counsellors choices and the freedom to adapt to individual differences. When one strategy fails or is inappropriate, another can be utilized. Culture, spiritual values, gender, developmental level, the presence of mental disorders or addiction, the nature of the problem, and the capacity of the client are some of the variables to be considered when adapting skills.

⟫⟫ BRAIN BYTE Music

By using a range of counselling strategies, counsellors can activate different areas of their clients' brains and stimulate the development of new neural pathways or even the growth of new neurons. For example, research has demonstrated that using music, dance, and exercise with Alzheimer's patients helps them to recall memories and emotions. Drawing on a different part of the brain (music is one of the last parts of the brain to go with Alzheimer's), physical and emotional connections with the person are made possible that would not be available through talk alone. Music can also be used to "shift mood, manage stress-induced agitation, stimulate positive interactions, facilitate cognitive function and coordinate motor movements" (Alzheimer's Foundation of America, 2015).

Versatility means being flexible regarding variables such as the location of the interview, the duration, the pace, the fees, and the people involved. Although some counsellors work in office settings with scheduled 45-minute or hour-long interviews, many work in settings where counselling interviews are less structured. Process versatility gives counsellors choices regarding the sequence and pace of counselling activities. With most clients, the beginning phase is concerned with exploring problems and feelings, but with other clients, counsellors may move immediately to action and problem solving. With some clients, counsellors spend a great deal of time helping them explore their feelings, but with others, counsellors spend little or no time in this activity.

Versatility also extends to other factors, such as the amount of expected or desired eye contact, the seating arrangements, and the physical distance. Some clients are comfortable in an office setting, but others prefer to work in their own home or to meet in a neutral setting. Adolescent boys, for example, might prove more approachable if counselling interventions are combined with some activity. Some clients favour an open seating arrangement with no desk or obstacle between them and their counsellors. Others prefer to work over the corner of a desk.

4. *Adaptive counsellors know how and when to use skills, and they know when to refrain from using them.* This requires intelligent consideration of a wide range of variables, including setting, problem, client capacity and receptivity, time available, and so on. For example, at the beginning of a counselling relationship, counsellors usually want to use skills that promote the development of the working alliance, so they avoid more demanding strategies such as confrontation. Once they have established a firm working relationship, counsellors will want to use skills that help clients gain new perspectives, so confrontation may be warranted. As another example, empathy often encourages clients to share deeper feelings. Therefore, counsellors who use empathy should be willing to invest the time that this sharing requires; however, if the interview is near an end, the counsellor might decide to avoid empathic responses that stimulate emotions that cannot be dealt with in the time available.

5. *Clients are at different stages of motivation and each stage suggests unique counsellor skills and strategies.* For example, clients who are precontemplative (not thinking about change in their behaviour) will not respond to approaches that might work very well with clients who are in the midst of change.

6. *Effective counsellors are "multilingual."* They adapt their use of language and idiom to match the language of their clients. Careful listening helps counsellors learn their clients' communicative language and metaphors, which helps counsellors modify their language to fit that of their clients. Counsellors will find it easier to establish rapport and build trust when they match their clients' words with similar language. The following examples illustrate:

Client 1: My view of the problem is . . .

Counsellor 1: If I get the picture correctly, the way you see it is . . .

Client 2: When I listen to myself, I know what I have to do.

Counsellor 2: Tell me more about what you are saying to yourself.

Counsellors need to pay attention to variables such as voice tone, volume, and tempo and then respond appropriately. To a depressed client, a high-energy, fast-talking counsellor might be annoying. Similarly, the counsellor who responds in a monotone to a client who is ecstatic about finding a job might come across as cold and indifferent. There are constraints on this principle, though: Counsellors should not yell at clients who yell at them, nor is it necessary for counsellors to use vulgar language to match their clients.

The challenges of today's diverse caseload may require a counsellor to interact in one interview with a client who has a sophisticated and articulate command of English, then meet with a client whose language skills are rudimentary. For each, a different vocabulary is appropriate and necessary.

Brief Encounters

Some counsellors work in settings where they are able to schedule clients with protected time over a period of many months; however, in many social service and community centres, interactions are brief, limited to a single encounter or even a few minutes. Nevertheless, the potential impact of this work, however brief, should not be discounted (Presbury, Echterling, & McKee, 2008; Carpetto, 2008). Among the possible positive outcomes are the following:

■ When clients are ambivalent about change, support from the relationship can tip the scales in favour of change by creating an atmosphere of trust and safety.

■ Counsellors can motivate by conveying optimism that change can occur, particularly when they focus on client strengths, not weaknesses.

■ Short sessions can provide an outlet for clients to ventilate feelings.

■ Counsellor empathy and nonjudgmental responses help clients accept their feelings as normal.

■ Questions and reflective responses can help clients organize ideas and plan for systematic change.

■ A client's way of thinking about a problem and its resolution can shift when counsellors offer fresh ideas or reframed reflections (i.e., looking at a problem from a new perspective).

■ Counsellors can help remove barriers to change through information or the provision of resources.

TRAUMA-INFORMED PRACTICE

Traumatic experiences can include single events such as violence/rape or natural disasters, as well as those that arise from ongoing abuse or neglect. A person can also experience trauma from witnessing, reading, or hearing about the experiences of others. In fact, counsellors may experience vicarious trauma from exposure to the stories of trauma from their clients.

People respond in unique ways to trauma. Some continue their lives with little or no emotional disruptions while others experience "anxiety, terror, shock, shame, emotional numbness, disconnection, intrusive thoughts, helplessness and powerlessness" (BC Provincial Mental Health and Substance Use Planning Council, 2013, p. 11). Counsellors can expect that a significant proportion of their client caseload has experienced trauma, as 76 percent of Canadians have experienced trauma at some point in their lives. Moreover, up to 90 percent of women in treatment for substance abuse have been subject to abuse-related trauma (BC Provincial Mental Health and Substance Use Planning Council, 2013), for which their use of substances is a way of coping.

After trauma or ongoing stress, the hippocampus, a part of the brain associated with memory, may be damaged and become smaller, which leads to more difficulty in problem solving. At the same time, the amygdala, a part of the limbic system responsible for emotions such as danger and fear, becomes larger and more sensitive, which helps explain the hypersensitivity and paranoia that develops after trauma. Damage to the prefrontex cortex after trauma may impair the individual's ability to plan and make appropriate decisions (Bremner, 2006).

The BC Provincial Mental Health and Substance Use Planning Council (2013) has identified four essential elements of a trauma-informed approach: trauma awareness, emphasis on safety and trustworthiness, opportunity for choice, collaboration and connection, and strengths-based skill building.

1. **Trauma Awareness**
   Here, the focus is on building both client and counsellor knowledge about trauma and how it can affect one's life (mental, emotional, and behavioural), including chronic pain, sleep difficulties, depression, anxiety, emotional numbness, memory problems, loss of life meaning, feelings of shame/self-hate, inability to trust in relationships, difficulty setting boundaries, substance misuse, self-harm, high-risk sexual behaviour, suicide, isolation, and criminal behaviour (see BC Provincial Mental Health and Substance Use Planning Council (2013, p. 22) for a complete list). The National Child Traumatic Stress Network (2015) notes that children may respond to trauma with a wide range of reactions, including difficulty attaching, increased vulnerability to stress, relationship problems (e.g., friends and teachers), trouble with authority figures (police), and problems expressing or managing emotions. Post-traumatic stress disorder (PTSD) is one common result of the trauma of experiencing or witnessing a traumatic event. Its symptoms may include a wide range of symptoms, including uncontrollable flashbacks, distressing thoughts and nightmares about the event, a need to avoid people and places associated with the trauma, severe anxiety, emotional numbness, inability to form trusting relationships, sleep problems, substance misuse, guilt, shame, and anger (Mayo Clinic, 2017b; American Psychiatric Association, 2013).

2. **Emphasis on Safety and Trustworthiness**
   The immediate focus following any traumatic experience is to make sure that the person is safe, that basic needs are met, and that he or she is able to connect with supportive people and resources. Trauma upsets one's sense of physical and emotional security so it is essential that the counselling environment be structured in a way that contributes to the restoration of safety. Establishing a welcoming environment from reception to physical space to service delivery that involves and keeps clients informed is important. Counsellors need to be predictable and reliable with consistent follow through. The Substance Abuse and Mental Health Services Administration (2014) emphasizes the importance of offering cultural and gender responsive service, including utilizing cultural connections and recognizing and addressing historical trauma. An important part of this practice is to use, or support clients to use, culturally appropriate healing practices.

3. **Opportunity for Choice, Collaboration, and Connection**
   Trauma disempowers people. Trauma-informed practice aims to restore client power and control in their lives and as participants in the counselling relationship. Open communication, freedom for clients to express opinions and feelings, nonjudgmental counsellor attitudes, support of client choices, and collaborative work with clients all contribute to this element.

Focusing on strengths helps to change the focus of the prefrontal cortex (the part of the brain responsible for judgment, planning, and decision making) from negative to positive thinking (Ivey, Ivey, & Zalaquett, 2010). This finding has huge implications for counselling clients with low self-image and pessimistic thought patterns. Counselling from a strengths perspective takes advantage of the brain's neuroplasticity to enhance important determinants of change, such as capacity to take appropriate risks, optimism about one's ability, and resilience to handle obstacles without damage to self-esteem.

4. **Strengths-Based Counselling and Skill Building**

Strengths-based practice shifts the focus from problems to opportunities and solutions. Counsellors "hold the belief that children, youth, and their families have strengths, resources and the ability to recover from adversity (as opposed to emphasizing problems, vulnerabilities, and deficits)" (Hammond, 2010, p. 4). Clients and counsellors work as partners, and the "expertise" of clients to make their own decisions is respected.

Relationship Issues

People who have been traumatized often have difficulties in their personal and family relationships. Sensitive counsellors who utilize a trauma-informed approach recognize that some of these same difficulties may emerge in the client/counsellor relationship. Some of these problems include the following:

- difficulties trusting others and a reluctance to share feelings
- general loss of interest in establishing intimate relationships
- hypersensitivity and a tendency to be suspicious about the motives of others
- tendency to become easily frustrated and trouble managing anger

It is critical that counsellors manage their own feelings when working with people who have been traumatized to ensure that they do not respond defensively to client behaviours that are provocative. They need to communicate to their clients that the counselling relationship is safe and that counselling will not exacerbate their trauma. Consequently, patience, empathy, honesty, and proceeding at an appropriate pace for each client are particularly important when working with clients who have been traumatized. Fully involving clients and respecting their rights to self-determination and decision making will help to restore a sense of control, so crucial to recovery from trauma. As a result, clients who achieve intimacy and find support in a counselling relationship find that they are also more able to communicate in their personal relationships.

Counsellors who have their own history of trauma need to ensure that this does not negatively impact their ability to counsel clients who have been traumatized. Utilizing supervision as a tool to increase self-awareness of their behaviour, emotions, and impact on clients is recommended.

SUCCESS TIP

With a trauma-informed approach, counsellors understand that their clients' behaviour, thoughts and emotions, however troubling, misguided, or confusing, are coping strategies that enable them to deal with and survive the impact of their trauma. Counselling can help clients develop more effective choices—for example, healthy communication skills, anxiety or anger management, assertiveness, and interpersonal relationship/intimacy skills.

Treating Post-Traumatic Stress Disorder   The goal of post-traumatic stress disorder treatment is to help clients regain control by dealing with those emotions, behaviour, and thoughts that are interfering with their quality of life. Counselling (psychotherapy) is the primary treatment, but this may be supplemented with antidepressant or anti-anxiety medication. Medication, by itself, is insufficient. Combining medication with meditation and wellness initiatives such as exercise and nutrition will help with recovery. The principles of trauma-informed counselling discussed in this section are the foundation for any intervention. A number of different counselling strategies have proven effective, including the following:

- **Cognitive behavioural therapy** (CBT) to help clients deal with unhelpful thinking patterns. (See Chapter 7.)

- **Exposure therapy,** which involves revisiting traumatic events until they are no longer troublesome.

- **Eye movement desensitization and reprocessing (EMDR)** a very specialized approach designed to help clients process traumatic memories. (Shapiro, 2001).

- **Use of groups** for support and sharing of coping skills.

COUNSELLING SKILLS AND STRATEGIES

There is no standardized method for classifying counselling skills and strategies. Nevertheless, it is useful to think about skills and strategies in terms of their function or intended purpose. In this book, four major **skill and strategy clusters** are discussed (see Tables 2.2, 2.3, 2.4, and 2.5):

1. Relationship building

2. Exploring & probing

3. Empowering & strength building

4. Promoting change

skill and strategy clusters: Categories of skills and strategies based on their intended purpose or helping activity.

   Some skills achieve multiple purposes. Sensitive active listening, for example, contributes to the development of the relationship because it communicates acceptance and the sincere desire to understand. At the same time, active listening is essential for getting information, so this skill can also be classified as an exploring and probing skill. Reframing is both an empowering and a challenging skill. It serves to empower when it shifts a client's attention to something positive (emotion, perception, or experience) that has been overlooked or never interpreted as such, but it challenges by influencing the client to entertain new interpretations that generate new behaviours or changes in

TABLE 2.2 Relationship Building	
Goal: Establish a productive and professionally intimate relationship, sustain trust	
Skills	**Strategies**
• Active Listening: Attending, silence, paraphrasing, summarizing, empathy, and asking questions • Core Conditions: Congruence, positive regard, and warmth • Define and Sustain Relationship: Contracting, Immediacy, and Relationship Problem Solving • Appropriate counsellor self-disclosure • Humour	• Maintain a safe, confidential, and professional environment • Focus on collaboration • Be trustworthy, reliable, and consistent • Help clients "tell their stories" without judgment • Remember important details

TABLE 2.3 Exploring & Probing

Goal: Acquire and deepen understanding and motivate clients to "tell their stories."

Skills	Strategies
• Active Listening: Attending, silence, paraphrasing, summarizing, empathy, and asking questions • Seek examples • Directives • Simple encouragers • Open-ended sentence completion statements • Pay attention to nonverbal channel of communication	• Maintain focus on key issues • Manage interview transitions (change of topic) • Monitor pacing to fit individual client needs

TABLE 2.4 Empowering & Strength Building

Goal: Increase client choice, control, and opportunity.

Skills	Strategies
• Recognize and search for client strengths • Reframing for new perspective such as viewing problems as opportunities for change • Identify resources to assist client (referral) • Provide information • Teaching: *role playing, modelling* • Positive reinforcement: praise, reassurance, and reward	• Prioritize collaboration • Foster optimism • Focus on growth and potential for change • Advocate on behalf of client • Utilize skills training programs • Use of mentors

TABLE 2.5 Promoting Change

Goal: Focus on solution and the possibilities for feeling and problem management

Skills	Strategies
• Challenging: confronting and correcting distortions • Providing feedback • Using reframing to add new perspectives on problems and solutions • Action Planning: defining clear goals, exploring alternative change options, and making changes • Helping clients identify and modify unhelpful thinking patterns (see Chapter 7) • Helping clients manage problematic feelings: relaxation and mindfulness • Using power and authority	• Focusing on helping clients change: goal setting, exploring/evaluating alternatives, and implementing action plans for change • Utilizing client strengths

emotional perspective (see Chapter 7 for an in-depth discussion of this skill). Counsellors do not use skills compulsively. They have the knowledge, ability, and assertiveness to use a skill when necessary, but they also use self-restraint to avoid using a skill when it is not in the client's best interest. Counsellor self-disclosure, for example, is an option, not a requirement.

SUCCESS TIP

A trauma-informed approach features core conditions, relationship-building skills, and empowerment skills as this combination of skills and attitudes works best to provide safety and ensure collaboration with clients.

Practitioners need to be versatile, building skill competence based on knowledge of the following:

1. Skills and strategies and their intended purpose
2. Best methods and situations for using each skill
3. Self-awareness of personal strengths and limitations with each skill
4. Acquired understanding of each client's capacity, need, and willingness

Relationship-Building Skills

Relationship-building skills and strategies are the basic tools for engaging clients, developing trust, and defining the purpose of the counselling. A strong counselling relationship is universally accepted as essential for counselling success. The relationship establishes and sustains the necessary safety, trust, and intimacy for clients to explore their issues and feelings, then deal with the challenges and emotions associated with change. The strength and support of the relationship provides a base for clients to risk engagement in the change process.

Relationship-building work is of central importance during the beginning phase of helping, but effective counselling requires that the relationship be sustained and deepened through all phases of helping.

Core Conditions Rogers (1951, 1961, 1980) and others have written extensively about the **core conditions** necessary for forming a helping relationship—namely, congruence or genuineness, empathy, and positive regard. Rogers believed that people are essentially good, self-deterministic (able to make their own decisions), and goal-directed. Thus, he believed that these core conditions are necessary for establishing the rapport and therapeutic alliance needed in a purposeful counselling relationship. Central to his theory was the notion that the core conditions create the environment within which change and growth will occur with the client seen as "the expert on his or her own life . . . responsible for the direction of change and growth within counselling" (Erford, 2010, p. 16).

Congruence, or **genuineness**, is the capacity to be real and consistent with clients. Congruent counsellors are open with their reactions and feelings and demonstrate consistency in what they believe, say, and do. Congruency also requires counsellors to be "transparent"— without hidden agendas or false demeanours. Rogers believed that the more counsellors are aware of their feelings and the more they genuinely express these feelings in the counselling relationship, the more effective their counselling will become. An important part of congruence is counsellor self-disclosure, particularly with their "here and now" feelings.

Empathy is the most important core condition. In simple terms, it means being able to see the world through the eyes of the client. Essential to empathic understanding is the ability to understand feelings without imposing one's own feelings or reactions. Counsellor experiences have the potential to increase empathic understanding, providing counsellors are on guard to ensure that they do not become prescriptive of how the client must feel. **Positive regard**, or respect for clients, is the ability to recognize the inherent worth of people, regardless of their behaviour.

Active Listening **Active listening** is crucial for building relationships and for understanding. If counsellors are preoccupied with what to say in reply, they cannot truly listen. Until they listen there is no way for them to understand the complexities and uniqueness of their clients' situations. Active listening is an interactive process involving six skills: attending, using silence, paraphrasing, summarizing, questioning, and showing empathy:

■ **Attending** is the manner in which counsellors communicate that they are physically and psychologically interested in what their clients are saying or doing.

■ Appropriate **silence** gives clients time to think and respond. Effective counsellors understand the multiple meanings of silence. Is the client confused? Have

relationship-building skills and strategies: Tools for engaging clients and developing trust.

core conditions: Warmth, empathy, positive regard, and genuineness.

congruence: The capacity to be real and consistent with clients; matching behaviour, feelings, and actions.

genuineness: A measure of how authentic or real one is in a relationship.

empathy: The process of accurately understanding the emotional perspective of another person and the communication of this understanding without imposing one's own feelings or reactions.

positive regard: The ability of counsellors to recognize the inherent worth of people.

active listening: A term describing a cluster of skills that are used to increase the accuracy of understanding. Attending, using silence, paraphrasing, summarizing, questioning, and showing empathy are the basic skills of active listening.

attending: A term used to describe the way that counsellors communicate to their clients that they are ready, willing, and able to listen. Verbal, nonverbal, and attitudinal cues are the essence of effective attending.

silence: A tool used in counselling when the client is thinking, the client is confused and unsure of what to say or do, or the client has encountered painful feelings. Because it is culturally defined, silence can also signal trust issues or closure.

we reached the end of the topic? Is the client thinking? Skilled counsellors know when to interrupt a silence and when to allow it to continue.

- **Paraphrasing** involves restating (usually in shortened form) the client's thoughts to clarify the essence of what he or she has said.

- **Summarizing** means condensing the essential content and identifying important themes and ideas.

- **Questioning** involves probing for information to confirm understanding and seek clarification, such as by saying, "Do you mean that . . . ?" When combined with nonjudgmental counsellor responses that confirm understanding, questioning provides an opportunity for clients to "tell their stories," a process which is often cathartic and therapeutic.

- Empathy is "the process of accurately understanding the emotional perspective of another person and the communication of this understanding" (Shebib, 1997, p. 177).

Active listening is the psychological incentive for clients to open up with further disclosure. When clients sense deeply that they have been heard, that their ideas are not judged or rejected, that their feelings are accepted and validated, trust develops. Active listening makes it safe for clients to explore ideas and feelings. Together with the core conditions, active listening says to the client, "I have heard you," "I am willing to understand your feelings and problems without judgment," and "I accept you." Active listening is a powerful tool for establishing rapport and understanding, the basis for strong working relationships.

Defining and Sustaining the Relationship
Rogers (1961) emphasizes the importance of avoiding moral judgment of the client. He vividly captures the significance of nonjudgmental exploration to the development of the relationship:

> It is only as I understand the feelings and thoughts which seem so horrible to you, or so weak, or so sentimental, or so bizarre—it is only as I see them as you see them, and accept them and you, that you feel really free to explore all the hidden nooks and frightening crannies of your inner and often buried experience. (p. 34)

Two major skills are associated with defining and sustaining the relationship: contracting and immediacy. Counselling contracts may change, sometimes frequently, as the work proceeds.

- **Relationship contracting** involves negotiating the intended purpose of the counselling relationship, including agreeing on the expected roles of both counsellor and client.

- **Sessional contracting** is concerned with setting the purpose of an individual session. Sessional contracting defines a work plan that is individualized to meet the needs of the client. Consider, for example, three women who seek counselling for the same problem—a relationship breakdown. Because of contracting, the first client may conclude that she needs help in managing her stress and pain. The second client may want to focus on developing her assertive communication skills for dealing with an abusive spouse. The third client might want help with decision making in choosing between leaving the relationship and remaining in hopes of solving the relationship problems. (See Chapter 3 for a detailed discussion of relationship and sessional contracts.)

- **Anticipatory contracting** focuses on planning strategies and responses for events that may occur during counselling, such as how to give feedback or how to respond to a drug use relapse. Clients are often able to give counsellors valuable input and advice on how they (counsellors) can best deal with these events.

paraphrasing: A nonjudgmental restatement of the client's words and ideas in the counsellor's own words.

summarizing: A way of condensing content. (See also *Content Summary* and *Theme Summary*.)

questioning: An active listening skill that involves probing for information to confirm understanding and seek clarification.

relationship contracting: Negotiating the intended purpose of the counselling relationship, including agreeing on the expected roles of both counsellor and client.

sessional contracting: An agreement between counsellor and client regarding the topic and expected outcome of an interview or session. (See also *Contracting*.)

anticipatory contracting: An agreement between counsellors and clients that plans for predictable events. Anticipatory contracts provide guidance for counsellors and answer the question, "What should I do if . . . ?"

Immediacy (Egan & Schroeder, 2009) is a tool for examining and deepening the counselling relationship. It involves a process of evaluation that addresses the quality of the relationship in terms of its contracted objectives. The skill of immediacy can be used to troubleshoot relationship problems. It promotes candid discussion regarding ways the relationship might be changed to fulfill its objectives. With immediacy, relationship problems and feelings are addressed before they have a chance to have a lasting destructive impact. (See Chapter 3 for an extensive discussion of this skill.)

> **immediacy:** A tool for exploring, evaluating, and deepening counselling relationships.

Exploring and Probing Skills

Exploring and probing skills are basic tools of interviewing that counsellors use to gather information, clarify definitions, seek examples, and obtain necessary detail. These skills enable counsellors to avoid making assumptions. Active listening skills are the primary tools of exploration and probing. Because they communicate counsellor willingness to listen nonjudgmentally, they motivate and encourage clients to tell their stories. When clients are helped to explore their problems, they often gain insight from questions that provoke thinking in areas that may have been overlooked. As well, reflective responses such as empathy help them gain perspective on emotions.

> **Exploring and probing skills:** Skills counsellors use to gather information, clarify definition, seek examples, and obtain necessary detail.

Directives, such as "Tell me more" or "Please expand on your feelings," control the direction and pace of the interview. Directives can also be used to focus the client on relevant priorities. Directives are the "road signs" of the interview.

> **directives:** Short statements that provide direction to clients on topics, information, and pace (e.g., "Tell me more").

Simple encouragers are short verbal and nonverbal cues that motivate clients to continue. Verbal statements such as "Uh-huh" or "Yes" and short directives such as "Please continue," along with nonverbal signals such as head nods and an attentive posture, make up this skill set.

> **simple encouragers:** Short phrases and gestures such as "Tell me more," "Go on," "Uh-huh," and head nods that encourage clients to continue with their stories.

Counsellor self-disclosure, used sparingly, can be a useful tool that models appropriate sharing of feelings. Counsellor self-disclosure may reduce the clients' sense that their experiences or feelings are strange or abnormal. Subsequently, when experiences are "normalized," clients are more apt to open up and share. In this way, counsellor self-disclosure acts as an exploring/probing skill.

> **counsellor self-disclosure:** When counsellors disclose personal opinions, feelings, or anecdotes, it can be a useful tool that models appropriate sharing, and it might normalize the clients' feelings or experiences. Counsellor self-disclosure should be used sparingly solely to meet the needs of clients in a way that does not shift the focus to the counsellor.

Humour, if timely, can be used to reduce tension or encourage clients to take a lighter view of their situation, but humour must be used cautiously so that it does not offend clients or trivialize their problems.

> **humour:** a counselling tool that when appropriate and well timed, may support the development of the relationship, reduce tension, encourage the client to take a lighter view of their problems, or provide an alternate perspective on their situation.

Open-ended sentence completion statements give clients an opportunity to "fill in the blanks." The counsellor presents an incomplete statement, then pauses to allow the client to complete the thought. Almost always, clients will finish the statement with their own content. This is a powerful strategy that gives clients full control of the answer while the counsellor controls the focus area. Here are some examples:

How might you finish this statement?

- The one thing I need most from my husband is . . .
- You're feeling . . . .
- So, the options you've considered are . . . .
- Finish this statement. The one thing I need most is . . . .
- The next step is . . . .

By responding to nonverbal cues, counsellors pay attention to such things as voice tone, posture, eye contact, and facial expressions. Sometimes the content expressed by a client's words is sufficient for understanding. But not infrequently, the major meaning or intent of a client's message comes through the nonverbal channel. Counsellors should never ignore the nonverbal channel, which enhances, contradicts, or embellishes verbal messages.

Managing transitions involves paying attention to or suggesting shifts between phases or topics. This skill can be used to organize the flow of the interview or to link themes and ideas (see Chapter 5 for an extensive discussion.)

Empowering Skills

empowering skills: Skills used to help clients mobilize confidence, self-esteem, and control over their lives.

Empowering skills help clients mobilize confidence, self-esteem, and control over their lives. Counsellors who are committed to empowering their clients must start with a basic belief that their clients are capable of managing their own lives. They must relinquish the mistaken notion that clients depend on them for advice, decision making, and problem solving. Clients are empowered when they participate in decisions about counselling goals and procedures.

The principle of self-determination introduced in Chapter 1 promotes empowerment by helping clients recognize choices and encouraging them to make independent decisions. To avoid promoting unhealthy client dependency, counsellors should not do for clients what clients can, and should, do for themselves. Counsellors should acknowledge and give clients credit for their success. When clients are successful and they "own" their success, their confidence and self-esteem increase.

Four skill sub clusters are the essence of empowering: teaching, giving information, supporting, and above all searching for strengths.

Teaching   Teaching may be used in counselling as a way to assist clients in developing strengths. Skills training, role-playing, and other tools can be used to help clients develop their capacities.

Giving Information   Information giving empowers clients with knowledge of alternative courses of action, including resources that might assist them in dealing with their problems. Counsellors may also offer suggestions and advice regarding problem management.

Supporting   Supporting is used to bolster clients' energy and optimism. To some extent, all counselling skills are supportive. Supporting reduces clients' feelings of isolation and provides them with incentives to address their problems, express their feelings, and begin a process of change. Supporting can also be used to tell clients that they are on the right track and that their feelings and reactions are normal. As well, supporting helps clients manage anxiety and stress, thus, increasing their energy, self-confidence, and capacity for problem solving.

Searching for Strengths   Clients are often besieged by debilitating problems and chaos. Counsellors cannot ignore real problems, but in the process, they should not focus all their attention on problem situations and what is dysfunctional in their clients' lives. The **strengths approach** assumes the inherent capacity of people. Individuals and communities are seen to have assets and resources that can be mobilized for problem solving (Sheafor & Horejsi, 2008; Saleeby, 2009; Glicken, 2004). Empowering skills and principles will be explored in more detail in Chapter 7.

strengths approach: A counselling perspective that assumes the inherent capacity of people. Individuals and communities are seen to have assets and resources that can be mobilized for problem solving.

Promoting Change Skills and Strategies

challenging skills: Skills used to encourage clients to critically evaluate their behaviour and ideas.

Challenging skills are used to encourage clients to evaluate their behaviour and ideas. They push clients toward change and growth to fulfill the fundamental reason for the counselling relationship; however, excessive or premature reliance on challenging skills may strain the counselling relationship.

Confrontation prods clients to critically examine their actions or consider other viewpoints. Counsellors may need to provide critical or corrective feedback, identify overlooked strengths, correct distortions, suggest other viewpoints (reframing), or

confrontation: Counselling initiatives that challenge clients to critically examine their actions and/or consider other viewpoints.

request that clients assume responsibility. Confrontation skills are most effective when there is a strong relationship of trust and when clients understand and accept the value of their use. Brill and Levine (2005) offer this perspective on the challenging skill of confrontation:

> Misuse of confrontation can be devastating, destroying all previous efforts. Workers must assess the amount and quality of confrontation the client is willing or able to use, and they must be able to give support if the reality is overwhelming. Workers must not use confrontation to express their own anger and frustration, although these are certainly a part of the reality with which both workers and clients must deal. (p. 186)

Ideally, confrontation skills increase clients' motivation for change. The counselling relationship provides the necessary base for confrontation. Clients are more likely to accept confrontation as credible when counsellors have first listened and fully understood them. Clients *may* be appropriately confronted when they:

- are working from false assumptions or incomplete information.
- misread the actions of others.
- lack **self-awareness** regarding the impact of their actions (e.g., when they blame others for their problems rather than examining their own responsibility).
- demonstrate contradictions in their behaviour, thoughts, and feelings.
- deny or do not recognize their personal strengths, capacities, or resources.

self-awareness: The process of becoming alert and knowledgeable about one's own way of thinking, acting, and feeling.

Action planning is a way of helping clients bring about changes in their lives. These changes may include finding new ways of managing feelings, forming strategies for modifying ways of thinking, or developing new skills or behaviours. Action planning helps clients define clear and measurable targets for change (goals), identify and evaluate alternative strategies, and select and develop plans for reaching these goals.

action planning: Helping clients make changes in their lives; involves setting goals, identifying strategies for change, and developing plans for reaching goals.

Use of Power and Authority Counsellors derive or are given power by virtue of their position. Such power comes from many sources: competence, knowledge, education, control of resources, position in the agency or status in the community, or simply the fact that the client is the one who is in the position of needing or seeking help. Counsellors are also representatives of agencies that wield power. For example, child protection social workers frequently make decisions and judgments that have a large impact on clients' lives. However gentle and caring counsellors are, clients may perceive them as persons with power and influence, and often as people to be feared. Compton and Galaway (2004) note that families may have "negative expectations, lack of trust, and fear of commitment" (p. 152) because of experiences where they perceived professional authority to have been misused. Miller (2007) advocates the importance of an anti-oppressive model of practice that recognizes the inherent imbalance of power between clients and professionals. She promotes the use of methods such as the strengths approach, transferring power to clients, and involving them in decisions (i.e., an anti-oppressive approach). As well, she invites dialogue on the important issue of what professionals "can or should do in the presence of organizational and societal policies that do not support practising according to the framework" (p. 132).

THE PHASES OF COUNSELLING

Counselling relationships can vary greatly in terms of time. Some evolve over a long period, but others may be limited to a few or even a single session while some may last for only a few minutes. Counselling interventions usually move through a planned change process involving sequential steps or phases, each characterized by unique as well

phases of counselling: Sequential
steps through which counselling tends to
evolve. The four phases are preliminary,
beginning, action, ending.

as common objectives and skills. For our purposes, four **phases of counselling** will be discussed: (1) preliminary, (2) beginning, (3) action, and (4) ending. This model builds on similar models presented by others such as Egan and Shroeder (2009), Shulman (2009), and Young (1998).

Each phase is distinguished by its focus on different activities. The preliminary phase is essentially for planning. Proper planning increases the likelihood that clients will perceive that their needs can be met through counselling. The beginning phase is a time of engagement, when both the client and the counsellor make decisions about whether they will work together and, if so, under what structure. The beginning phase is also a time for exploring problems and feelings. Although clients may begin to change their behaviour or manage their feelings more effectively during the beginning phase, the action phase is more concerned with initiating change. During the ending phase, the working relationship is brought to a close, perhaps with a referral to another resource or counsellor.

SUCCESS TIP

Every counselling relationship will have many beginnings and endings and the presence and dynamics of each should be considered. The most significant beginning is the start of the relationship, but each session or encounter also has a beginning. When the focus of discussion shifts to a different topic, this is also a beginning. Similarly, each encounter also has an ending and as each topic draws to a close, this is also an ending. The end of the relationship is a important ending that deserves the full attention of the counsellor.

One common objective of each phase is forming and sustaining a working relationship. This counselling relationship is the vehicle for change and provides a base of safety and security for clients to explore and understand their emotions and difficulties. The counselling contract, an agreement on the goals and roles of the participants, is the reference point for the relationship. It is continually reviewed and revised as the work progresses.

A second common objective of all phases is to establish open, honest, and productive communication. Effective communication enables counsellors to learn about their clients' needs and feelings. As well, it empowers clients to learn new ways of handling old problems.

The third common objective of all phases is evaluation. Ongoing evaluation can review the essential elements of the counselling plan (goals and methods), the working relationship, or the overall satisfaction of all participants with the pace of the work and its results. By using a problem-solving approach, counsellors and clients can explore ways to ensure that the work is relevant and efficient.

Skill clusters help organize skills based on function. Since each phase of counselling supports different activities, each phase also favours different skills. For example, during the beginning phase of counselling, relationship-building skills are the priority, and challenging skills are usually avoided, at least until a foundation of trust and safety has been established. Exploration/probing skills are also vital during the beginning phase. They enable counsellors to acquire information for understanding, thus, helping them avoid assumptions. Challenging and directing/teaching skills tend to be more effective in the action phase, when a strong relationship and a solid base of understanding have been established. Table 2.6 summarizes the principal activities and priority skills of each phase.

Counselling tends to move through the phases sequentially, with success at each phase depending, in part, on the success of preceding phases. For example, the

TABLE 2.6 Counselling Activities and Skills

Phase	Principal Activities	Priority Skills
Preliminary	• Interview preplanning • Reviewing files and other information sources • Preparing the interview setting	• Planning • Establishing self-awareness
Beginning	• Establishing a collaborative, professional working relationship • Interviewing for understanding • Evaluating	• Active listening • Promoting core conditions • Defining the relationship (contracting) • Searching for strengths
Action	• Goal setting • Action planning • Helping clients change behaviour, manage feelings, and change unhelpful thinking patterns • Revising the contract, deepening the relationship, and managing communication difficulties • Evaluating goal progress and the ongoing relationship	• Teaching • Information giving • Supporting • Confronting • Action planning
Ending	• Ending the helping relationship • Referring client to other resources • Evaluating goal achievement	• Giving information • Supporting

preliminary phase is designed to support the work of the beginning phase. It allows the counsellor to complete the preparations that will help welcome the client to the agency. As well, it works as a kind of warm-up, so counsellors can be ready and sensitive to the needs of their clients. Weak planning results in weak beginnings. Similarly, effective work in the action phase is easier when the beginning phase has been successful. A solid base of understanding permits counsellors and clients to set more goals, and a foundation of trust allows counsellors to be more challenging in their approach. In contrast, counsellors who attempt to challenge clients from a thin base of trust are likely to meet with resistance or rejection. Even in the action phase, it is important to try to sequence the steps. If clients try to develop action plans before they have set clear goals, their action plans are more likely to be vague and directionless.

Although counselling work tends to evolve sequentially through the four phases, usually it does not move forward in a neat and orderly manner:

> The logical progression of these phases makes the process appear to be a linear, step-by-step set of activities. In reality, change rarely proceeds in an orderly fashion; rather, it is more of a spiral, with frequent returns to prior phases for clarification or a reworking of various tasks and activities. (Sheafor & Horejsi, 2008, p. 126)

The phases of counselling also provide a systematic and useful checklist of the key activities and logical steps that are part of the change or problem-solving process. By referring to the phases of counselling, counsellors and clients can remain clear on where they are in the counselling process, what has been done, what remains to be accomplished, and what options remain open. However, as any experienced counsellor will attest, "each counselling encounter is different, each relationship is uniquely complex, and the work may evolve in unpredictable ways" (Shebib, 1997, p. 71).

Sometimes clear divisions between the phases of counselling are apparent. But more frequently, there are overlaps between the phases and shifts forward and backward between one phase and another, and, in some cases, phases may be skipped altogether. Some typical counselling scenarios are provided here:

- Jessica, a very private person, was distraught over the breakup of her marriage. Aware of her inability to cope and not knowing what to do, she attended several sessions with a counsellor. Her counsellor proceeded slowly, gently encouraging Jessica to talk about her feelings. Jessica was surprised that during the second counselling session, she began to weep. Afterward, she remarked that she felt as if a great weight had been lifted from her shoulders. She never felt the need to return for a third session.

- Bert was not interested in exploring his problem beyond a superficial level. Anxious to effect change in his life, he wanted to brainstorm ideas for dealing with his problems. Counselling work focused on helping him set goals. As this work progressed, client became more trusting, and the sessions began to focus on exploring his feelings.

- When Joyce was challenged by her counsellor to examine how she might be contributing to the problems she blamed on her boss, she became angry and stormed out the office, never returning. A year later, a series of events caused her to recall her short-lived counselling experience, and she decided to take some responsibility for her difficulties. The counsellor never knew about the ultimate positive outcome of the relationship that appeared to end so badly.

- As Fernando talked about his problem, he suddenly realized that his situation was not as hopeless as he thought. Discovering another way to look at his problem allowed him to identify several new ways to solve it.

- After a single session, Bob remarked to his counsellor, "My problem is the same as when I came in here, but somehow it doesn't seem to bother me as much."

The Preliminary Phase

The preliminary phase of counselling is essentially a time of planning with a focus on two central tasks. First, the agency setting is made attractive for clients so they are motivated to engage and remain with the agency. Second, counsellors prepare themselves for the interview.

⫸ CONVERSATION 2.2 | Helpful Friends and Counsellors

STUDENT: What is the difference between a conversation with a helpful friend and a counselling interview?

TEACHER: The goal of a friendship is to meet the needs of both people. Friends (and family) are important. If they are understanding, caring, and supportive, they can be an effective source of help. As with a counselling relationship, just talking to a friend can be cathartic to the individual. The reality is that there are limits to what friends can offer. Sometimes friends and family don't have specialized knowledge, or they may not know what resources or services are available to deal with specific problems. Friends and family may also be so emotionally involved with you that it is hard for them to be objective.

STUDENT: You're right. I find my family can't separate their feelings from mine, and they always end up giving me well-intentioned but not very helpful advice.

TEACHER: Effective counsellors are comfortable discussing feelings, and they don't tell clients how they should feel. Good counsellors are excellent listeners, and they invest time to make sure they accurately understand clients' feelings and concerns. Counsellors know how to systematically explore problems, set goals, and develop plans for action. They assist clients in identifying and evaluating alternatives, while recognizing that the clients must choose for themselves. Therefore, counsellors do not impose advice or try to rescue clients by taking on their problems. Unlike friendships, counselling relationships are directed to meet the needs of one person only—the client.

The Agency Setting   Ideally, the agency is set up to appeal to the client groups that it serves. A drop-in counselling centre for teens should look different from a day program centre for seniors. Dim lighting and beanbag chairs meet the needs of teens but present a safety hazard for seniors. Tea is appropriate for seniors, but a soft drink makes more sense when the clients are teens. Ideally, the agency should:

- have uncrowded waiting rooms.
- allow for reception and interview space that is private and confidential.
- greet clients in a warm and friendly manner.
- provide for the needs of children (e.g., by supplying a play area with age-appropriate toys).
- allow for wheelchair access.
- have posters and other art that do not violate the values, religion, or culture of the agency's clients (generally, they should also be politically neutral).
- have up-to-date reading material in the waiting room.

But often counsellors fail to ensure that their interviews are protected from phone calls and other interruptions that impede the flow of conversation. When interruptions are allowed, the message to clients is, "I have other concerns that are more important than you. Hurry up and finish."

Moreover, flexible office arrangements are best. Some clients and many counsellors prefer an unobstructed arrangement without a desk between the participants, but others favour working over the desk. The office needs to be arranged with careful consideration to the messages that the design communicates. Chairs and desks should be arranged so that no psychological advantage or power is given to the counsellor. Seating arrangements should allow for adequate personal space between counsellors and clients. A comfort zone of about 1 to 2 metres (4 to 7 feet) is adequate for most clients, but other factors might result in a need for more or less distance.

Counsellors also need to be careful in choosing personal items to display. Pictures and memorabilia that punctuate differences between counsellors and their clients should be avoided. Of course, clients may have different reactions. For example, some clients expect and appreciate seeing their counsellor's degrees or diplomas hung on the wall. For these clients, knowing something about the training and credentials of their counsellors helps to establish confidence and credibility. Other clients, however, may react negatively to such a display. For them, the display sets up social and intellectual barriers. Generally, counsellors should structure their offices with the needs and background of their clients in mind. In this respect, clients can be an invaluable source of consultation. Their opinions on office decor and layout should be solicited.

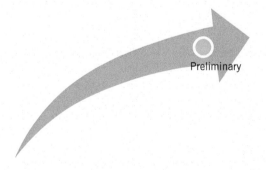

Preliminary

Figure 2.1

Interview Preparation   Counsellors can use the preliminary phase to predict how the interview time will be used and to make decisions related to the time, place, and structure of the interview. As well, counsellors can think about specific questions and responses for working with particular clients, without setting up a script or rigid agenda.

Shulman (2009) suggests that for a variety of reasons, clients often do not share feelings and concerns directly. They may be ambivalent about sharing, or they may hold back because of societal and cultural taboos about talking about sex, authority, or money. As a result, clients may raise these concerns indirectly, and counsellors must be alert to recognize clues about their clients' concerns. For example, a single parent who asks her welfare worker if he has ever been on welfare may be indirectly expressing her fear that the worker will be insensitive to the stress she faces in trying to cope with a limited budget. Sometimes questions regarding personal background or circumstances may be indirect ways for clients to explore concerns about trust.

Shulman (2009) recommends the preliminary phase skill of *tuning in* as a tool for anticipating the feelings and concerns that clients might bring to the interview. By tuning in, counsellors can think about what clients might express and how they will do so. The preliminary phase is also a time when counsellors examine their own readiness. For example, counsellors should take a few moments prior to each interview to self-examine through questions such as the following:

- Am I dealing with personal stress or problems that might make me less effective or more vulnerable?
- Am I sufficiently disengaged from my last client to be open and objective?
- What personal biases do I need to manage to work effectively with this client?
- What reservations do I have about meeting this client?
- Do I have unfinished business with this client that I have not addressed?
- What feelings do I have toward the client that might impede my objectivity?

Client Files   The preliminary phase is also a time for fact-finding to help understand a client's situation. For example, a counsellor could research Tourette's syndrome in preparation for meeting a client with a child who has been diagnosed with this condition.

Typically, most agencies have files on each client that may contain considerable information regarding the client's age, place of birth, address, marital status, work history, educational background, prior experiences with counselling, and assessments of personality, values, past problems, ability to handle stress, communication patterns, and so on. Client files can also alert counsellors to any past incidents of violence and point out any need to take special precautions.

A review of client files can greatly speed the intake process, but it is important to maintain an open mind and avoid prejudgment, particularly with respect to the assessments other counsellors have made regarding the client's manner and personality. Client reactions are influenced in part (and occasionally) by the personality and behaviour of their counsellors, as shown in the following example:

> Russ waited for his counsellor, who was half an hour late for the scheduled interview. Russ was stressed because of personal problems and was anxious to get home to care for his sick children. Estelle, his counsellor, was also stressed because of a difficult week of work. During her interview with Russ she was also aware that her next appointment was already waiting for her to finish with Russ. Determined to catch up, she moved quickly with questions to complete her assessment of Russ's situation. Russ, taken aback by Estelle's abrupt style, proceeded cautiously, hesitating to share personal information quickly. Later, when completing her file notes on the interview, Estelle wrote: "Client was defensive and guarded. He appeared unusually resistant to exploring his feelings."

STUDENT: If there's already a file on the client, should I read it before seeing the client for the first time?

TEACHER: There are pros and cons to reading client files in advance. It's important to be aware of the risks of either route. Some counsellors prefer to conduct their first interviews without reading their clients' files. They argue that by not reading the files, they are prevented from being unduly influenced (biased) by prior information. After a first interview, they feel more able to evaluate the validity of previous records. In addition, they argue that clients can change, and approaching the interview with a fresh perspective makes it easier to relate to the client's present condition.

STUDENT: But suppose the client has a history of violence that is reported in the file. How would I be able to get that information to protect myself while still keeping an open mind? Is there a way of getting only the pertinent information from the file that would allow me to identify those problems?

TEACHER: That's one of the drawbacks of not reading the file. I like your idea of setting up some kind of process for identifying clients who might be dangerous. Clients who present safety concerns could be "red-flagged" in some way.

STUDENT: I think another drawback is that if you do not look at the file, you will miss out on knowing what's been done, what worked, what issues are key, and so forth. Is there a way of reading a file without being influenced by other writers?

TEACHER: Being aware of the potential for influence is crucial. It is important to remind ourselves that opinions in files are not the clients' opinions but those of the person writing the record. Ideally, records should be shared with clients and the conclusions jointly supported. Of course, this is not always possible.

STUDENT: Could I share the file with the client to get his or her reactions?

TEACHER: Probably not, at least not without the permission of the person who wrote the record. Depending on where you live, freedom of access to information legislation may give clients the right to petition for access to the file. Usually, the onus is on the agency or government department to provide a reason for withholding information. Counsellors need to be familiar with the regulations in their area.

The Beginning Phase

Successful preliminary phase work establishes a base for the first major task of the beginning phase—namely, developing a safe and trusting helping relationship through which clients can work toward their goals. This relationship between counsellors and their clients influences whether clients will be willing to risk disclosure and is a significant variable that determines whether clients will continue with counselling. The counselling relationship is time-limited and based on a contract that outlines the objectives and terms of the relationship.

Some clients come willingly to counselling, perhaps because of an unresolved crisis or because they have been persuaded by others to seek help. Other clients are involuntary and, in some cases, overtly antagonistic to the counsellor. They may also be coming because of a current crisis or pressure from others. An employer, for example, may insist that a staff member seek counselling to address attitudinal or addiction problems.

Many clients are also under considerable stress, and this stress is intensified if the clients perceive counsellors negatively. Predictably, clients' experiences with other agencies and counsellors shape their perceptions and expectations. Clients who have had bad experiences with counsellors will understandably be guarded against further disappointment. In addition, because counsellors are often in a position of authority, or clients see them in such a position, clients' experiences with others in authority will come into play. Most clients, however strongly they may be motivated, will have some degree of resistance or ambivalence to change. Involuntary clients may be especially resistant and, in some cases, hostile. They may perceive any initiative by their counsellors as a hostile act, however, well meaning it was.

The counselling relationship is fundamental to counselling success. Even in short, one-session encounters, when a high level of intimacy is not crucial, clients will be more apt to engage and share when the counsellor gives some attention to developing the relationship. Chapter 3 more fully explores the importance of the helping relationship and specific skills for developing and maintaining it.

A second major task of the beginning phase is to acquire and deepen an understanding of the client's situation or problem. In the beginning phase, clients are asked to tell their stories, describe their feelings, and explore their problems and dilemmas. For their part, counsellors must be prepared to listen, and this means being prepared to learn. Preliminary phase work may help counsellors predict possible themes, and experience may teach counsellors a great deal about common needs and issues; however, in the beginning phase, counsellors need to put aside all assumptions as they attempt to appreciate the unique nature of each client. The active listening skills of attending, using silence, summarizing, paraphrasing, questioning, and showing empathy are the basic tools for this exploration. These skills tend to motivate clients to gradually open up, organize their thoughts, and identify their feelings. They move the relationship beyond superficiality and help both the counsellor and the client achieve shared understanding. Active listening also enables counsellors to probe for details, definitions, and examples—information that is essential for preventing assumptions.

The Therapeutic Value of the Beginning Phase The therapeutic value of counsellors listening without judgment can be enormous. Active listening enables what is often the most important part of any counselling encounter—the opportunity to tell one's story and express feelings without interference. Since intense listening is rare in everyday encounters, clients may be visibly moved when they feel heard. Moreover, when counsellors accept clients without judgment, clients become better able to accept themselves. Effective counsellors also encourage clients to explore the emotional components of their lives. When clients share emotions, counsellors need to be careful not to sabotage this sharing by rescuing, telling clients not to feel as they do, changing the subject, or conveying discomfort or judgment. In addition, as clients talk, they may release a flood of emotions. A client might remark, "I've told you things that no one

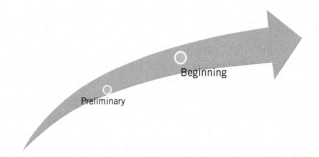

Figure 2.2

else knows." As clients open up, they may begin to feel unburdened, a process that is known as **catharsis** or ventilation.

catharsis: An emotional release of feelings about past or current experiences that results in a powerful release of pent-up feelings such as anxiety or anger.

Effective counsellors probe for detail by asking questions systematically. They identify feelings and mirror them with empathic statements. This work enables clients to organize their thinking and to explore and accept their feelings. When clients are confused or indecisive, orderly questioning helps them categorize information and pinpoint details or issues that they may have overlooked.

Cautions For some clients, a single session may be sufficient to meet their needs, and they may not return for the next scheduled interview. Sometimes they decide not to return because they feel they do not need to. The cathartic release of emotions in a single session empowers them enough to deal with their problems.

Other clients may quickly respond to the power of the counselling relationship and disclose at a level they would not have predicted. Later, they may feel embarrassed, fearing that they have gone too far, or they may resent their counsellors for probing into areas they would have preferred to keep private. In response, clients may cut off the counselling relationship prematurely, or they may come to the next session but remain distant and guarded to protect themselves from over-disclosing.

One way to prevent problems is to be sensitive to individual pacing needs. Clients may give clues that the session is moving too quickly. The counsellor should watch for indicators such as hesitation, questioning why the counsellor wants to know something, or statements that the client would rather not discuss particular issues.

Another strategy is to discuss with clients how they feel about the session. The following excerpt illustrates this technique:

Counsellor: Later tonight, when you think about our time together, how do you think you'll feel?

Client: I think I will have mixed feelings. It was really good to talk, but I wonder if I told you too much. I hope you will not think less of me.

Counsellor: You took a real risk with me in sharing your private thoughts and feelings. I think it's reasonable to worry about how I reacted. Would you like to know?

Client: Yes, very much.

Counsellor: Do you trust me enough to believe that I will not lie to you or tell you something just to make you feel better?

If the client says yes, the counsellor might candidly share his or her reaction to the client disclosure:

Counsellor: I admire your courage to face such painful issues. As a result, I feel closer to you and better able to understand your struggle. No, I don't think less of you.

If the client says no, the counsellor initiates discussion of what work needs to be done to establish trust:

Counsellor: Perhaps we could talk a bit about what needs to happen between you and me in order for you to trust me.

In the previous example, the counsellor helps the client anticipate feelings that might arise after the session. By doing so, the counsellor can help prevent the client from reaching false conclusions or making erroneous assumptions about what happened. For counsellors to have such discussions with clients, a high level of counsellor self-awareness is crucial. Counsellors need to be willing to examine how they are relating to their clients. They should be adept at identifying any personal biases (positive or negative) that they need to manage to work effectively with their clients.

The Action Phase

In the beginning phase, counsellors work to understand their clients' perspectives, and clients organize their thinking and express their feelings. The action phase focuses on solving problems, managing feelings, setting goals, and exploring alternative strategies.

In practice, action-phase work may happen simultaneously with beginning-phase work, as clients may make discoveries or achieve insight from exploring issues, feelings, and problems. Skilled interviewers ask questions systematically, probing for detail as appropriate. This process alone helps clients organize their thoughts on complex issues. As well, summarizing, paraphrasing, and responding with empathy provide an important mirror for reflecting clients' feelings and ideas. As a result, clients may see their problems in a different light, or they may discover choices for action that they had overlooked.

In the action phase, counsellors play a key role by providing new information, ideas, or perspectives. This involves challenging distortions of problems and encouraging clients to consider issues they may have overlooked. As well, counsellors need to encourage the work of change by ensuring that clients set clear and specific goals, which form the basis for the development of realistic action plans. Subsequently, counsellors may assist clients in implementing their plans. This assistance includes helping them anticipate and address potential problems, as well as supporting them through the struggles of the change process. Counsellors also help clients develop new strategies for coping through skill acquisition strategies such as role-playing or techniques for managing self-defeating thought patterns.

When clients experience the core conditions of congruence, empathy, and positive regard, they become better able to accept themselves, less defensive, and more open to experiencing and accepting their feelings. Client attitudes and feelings change as counselling progresses successfully. Some of the important signals that clients are changing and growing include the following:

- cues that they feel less apprehensive about counselling and the counselling relationship
- increased acceptance of feelings and more honest expression of previously denied feelings
- diminished negativism, self-doubt, and blaming of others, and increased optimism and self-acceptance
- increased acceptance of responsibility for behaviours or choices
- reduced sense of responsibility for the actions and choices of others
- increased empathy for others (Gilliland & James, 1998, p. 115)

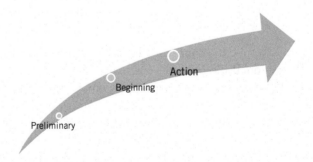

Figure 2.3

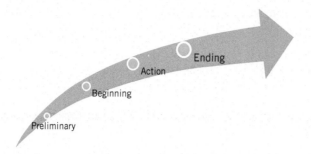

Figure 2.4

As noted earlier, beginning-phase and action-phase activities can happen simultaneously. Shifts between beginning-phase and action-phase work are also common. For example, clients may explore a problem in depth, begin a change program, and then revert to beginning-phase work to tackle another problem area. Some common scenarios include the following:

> Angelo's counsellor encouraged him to describe his situation. As he talked, he discovered aspects of his problem that he had overlooked and that suggested new possibilities for immediate action.

> Parivash tended to keep her feelings so well hidden that she was unaware of their effect or intensity. With gentle encouragement from her counsellor, she began to open up. Talking about her feelings represented a dramatic shift in her behaviour. The therapeutic value of this change was enormous, as she unburdened herself from a lifetime of pent-up emotions.

> Chapter 7 will explore how to assist clients through the work of the action phase.

The Ending Phase

Successful termination starts in the beginning phase, when the nature and limits of the counselling contract are defined. When counsellors and clients agree on the activities and goals of counselling, they have defined a point of termination. This point becomes the target of all counselling work. Although the target may change as client needs and progress are re-evaluated, counsellors should reinforce that termination is a reality of the counselling relationship.

Although evaluation is a component of all phases of counselling, the ending phase is a major opportunity to assess what has been accomplished and what remains to be done. It is a time to help clients make the step to independence and to consider new directions and goals. It may also occasionally be a point of transition, such as when a counsellor refers a client to another service. The ending phase is also a time to evaluate the counselling relationship. This evaluation may involve addressing any unresolved concerns and expressing feelings about the ending of the relationship. See Chapter 3 for a more complete discussion of endings.

COUNSELLING PITFALLS: BARRIERS TO SUCCESS

Counselling relationships are formed to assist people to reach goals such as making a decision, dealing with painful feelings, improving interpersonal skills, or managing an addiction. Outcome success is easy to define: It is measured by the extent that goals are reached. Measuring the success of an interview or communication moment in the interview is more difficult since much of the change work happens outside the interview. An example illustrates:

> Jerome stormed out of the interview when his counsellor asked him to consider how his drinking might be affecting his family. His angry words as he slammed the door left the counsellor feeling rattled: "You're just like all the rest. I thought you were on my side, but it's clear my wife has got to you." Six months later, Jerome's situation deteriorated to the point where he was ready to reflect on his addiction. The counsellor's challenge became an important part of his recovery.

Nevertheless, counselling can and does fail, so counsellors need to develop their capacity to systematically investigate and review failure. They need to be able to distinguish between failures that are beyond their control and those caused by their own mistakes. Failure may originate with the client; it may arise from personal issues associated with the counsellor, such as faulty technique or lack of skill; or it may stem from factors that are outside both the client's and the counsellor's control. Egan and Schroeder (2009) put it bluntly when they described what they call the shadow side of helping:

> Helping models are flawed; helpers are sometimes selfish and even predatory and they are prone to burnout. Clients are sometimes selfish, lazy, and predatory, even in the helping relationship. (p. 31)

Client Variables

Substance abuse or mental disorders may make it difficult or impossible for clients to engage with the work of counselling. Clients may resist or undermine counselling because of secondary gain, where the payoffs from maintaining the problem outweigh the benefits of change. Or clients may resist change because of an unconscious fear of success, because they expect to fail, or because the risks of change are too frightening to face.

Counsellor Variables

Intellectually and emotionally secure counsellors are willing to examine their methods and attitudes, and they are willing to take their share of responsibility for poor counselling outcomes. Counsellor variables include mental attitudes, moods, and behaviours, all of which can dramatically affect how counsellors relate to and assess their clients. Some counsellor variables that affect counselling outcomes are burnout and vicarious trauma, personal problems, and loss of objectivity.

Burnout and Vicarious Trauma   A career working with people in crisis may be intensely satisfying, but it can also be emotionally stressful and draining. Counsellors may experience unrelenting pressure in workplace demands, including high caseloads, limited resources, and crushing paperwork. Counsellors can become depleted from trying to respond to the needs of their clients and the organization. In addition, counsellors are subject to their own family and economic stress and trauma. Counsellors may be resilient, but even the sturdiest person can become debilitated by stress.

Personal Problems   Counsellors are subject to the same stresses in life as other people. They can become depressed, their children can become ill, their marriages can fail, or they can become responsible for caring for ailing or elderly parents. Responsible counsellors accept that there may be times when they need help too. They recognize the importance of having people in their lives to whom they can ask for assistance. When counsellors have healthy reciprocal relationships with others, they are less likely to use (subconsciously) their clients to meet these needs.

During acute periods of stress, counsellors need to recognize their vulnerability and take steps to protect their clients. These steps might include taking a temporary reduction in workload, shifting to a less demanding caseload, taking a "mental health" break, or seeking increased supervision or consultation to monitor their work. In extreme circumstances, they may choose to take an extended leave or switch careers.

Loss of Objectivity   Objectivity is a measure of counsellors' capacity to relate to clients without allowing their own feelings and biases to distort their judgment (see Chapter 1 for a detailed discussion). A number of factors can lead to a loss of objectivity, including unresolved personal problems, difficulty dealing with particular emotions or topics, attraction or revulsion to clients, over-identification with clients, and excessive or unrealistic fear of particular clients.

Counsellors who are not aware of their values and beliefs and the impact of their behaviour on others are limited in their ability to monitor their level of objectivity. Counsellors who are committed to increasing their objectivity make themselves available for feedback or supervision. Moreover, they recognize their personal limitations and their inability to work objectively with every client. They know when to refer clients to other professionals.

Common Mistakes

Counsellors are constantly making choices. They must decide which of the three domains to explore (feeling, thinking, or behaviour). They must choose which skills to use, how much to probe and challenge, how fast to move the process forward, and which material is relevant to pursue. All of this happens in an environment (relationship) that is often ambiguous, occasionally hostile, frequently complex, and constantly changing. Table 2.7 outlines the top 10 most common counselling errors.

Pseudo-Counselling: The Illusion of Work   The goal of every counselling relationship is to improve the quality of life for the client. Achieving this goal may involve problem resolution, assistance with decision making, or management of painful feelings. Counsellors need to screen their responses and activities to ensure that their work supports the objectives of counselling.

Pseudo-counselling involves what Shulman (2009) describes as the **illusion of work**—counselling sessions are animated and active, but they are essentially empty and

pseudo-counselling (illusion of work): A process in which the worker and the client engage in a conversation that is empty and that has no real meaning. Counselling involves irrelevant exploration of issues, use of clichés and patronizing platitudes, intellectual exploration of issues, and avoidance of subjects or feelings that involve pain in favour of "safe" topics.

TABLE 2.7 Top 10 Counselling Errors

1. Rigidity and use of a "one-size-fits-all" approach
2. Insufficient attention to the counsellor–client relationship
3. Advice giving
4. Absence of core conditions—empathy, unconditional positive regard, and genuineness
5. Missing the opportunities offered by paying attention to the nonverbal channel
6. Loss of objectivity and judgmental responses
7. Pacing problems (too fast, too slow, and inappropriate timing of responses)
8. Inappropriate use of self-disclosure (too much, too little, and poorly timed)
9. Rescuing, false reassurance, and minimizing problems
10. Cultural insensitivity

without real meaning. Shulman makes this important observation: "For the illusion to take place, however, two must engage in the ritual. The worker must be willing to allow the illusion to be created, thus, participating in its maintenance" (p. 154). The illusion of work can be created through the following:

- interesting but irrelevant exploration of issues that do not contribute to problem solving, including an excessive focus on finding the root causes of problems
- use of clichés and patronizing platitudes
- overly intellectual exploration of issues
- avoidance of subjects or feelings that involve pain in favour of safe topics. Of course, it is sometimes appropriate to shift the focus to safe areas of discussion (e.g., if the interview is almost over, or if clients are clearly unable to handle additional stress).

Inappropriate Advice Giving   Society conditions us to seek advice from experts, so it's not surprising that many clients come to counsellors expecting "expert advice" on how to manage their lives and solve their problems. Students and beginning counsellors often believe that counselling requires them to listen patiently to their clients' problems and then offer advice on what they should do. However, they need to learn that this approach is rarely helpful and is sometimes harmful to clients, particularly when such advice is based on values that are inconsistent with the client's lifestyle or culture.

Clients often seek advice even when they know what to do to manage their problems. Seeking advice can be a way of expressing dependency or transferring responsibility for decisions and outcomes to someone else. This dependency inhibits the right of clients to make choices, and it may leave clients feeling resentful or frustrated, particularly if the advice was unsolicited.

Advice giving may increase counsellors' self-esteem by underscoring their ability to be resourceful and helpful, but it may also undermine clients' self-esteem, leaving them feeling inadequate because they have been unable to figure out their problems for themselves or because they lack the will or resources to act on the "good advice." Counsellors who tend to give advice can become overly concerned about whether clients follow their advice, and if so, whether the advice is successful. They can also become disappointed when clients do not follow advice.

As Compton and Galaway (2004) conclude: "it is not your job to 'fix' clients. Rather, you help them set and work toward goals. You assist them to recognize and use person-in-situation strengths and resources for problem solving and goal attainment" (p. 82). We are in a better position to empower and promote client self-determination if we refrain from giving advice and if we honour what clients bring to the relationship:

- knowledge regarding themselves and the situation
- knowledge about the origin and development of the problem
- expectations about how you can help
- a network of social relationships
- views about what they would like to accomplish
- strengths for use in pursuing goals (Compton & Galaway, 2004, p. 82)

This injunction against advice giving does not mean that counsellors should withhold information or ideas that might benefit their clients. Here are some examples of information or advice that counsellors might provide:

- tentative suggestions regarding alternative courses of action that the client has overlooked; however, "when counsellors are unwilling or unable to present and explore all viable alternatives neutrally, they have an ethical responsibility to refer the client to another counsellor, or at the very least, to make their biases or limitations explicit" (Shebib, 1997, p. 33)

- expert information based on research or knowledge (e.g., job-search techniques and child-rearing principles)
- ideas for improving communication or problem solving
- suggestions regarding the process of problem resolution
- opinions and information that will help clients avoid unforeseen consequences (dangers) to themselves or impulsive or poorly considered action

Where there is a range of individual choices, such as decisions related to marriage or career, advice giving is inappropriate. In such circumstances, the role of counsellors is to assist clients in identifying alternative courses of action, then to help them weigh the advantages and disadvantages of each alternative. Counsellors may suggest alternatives, but they should do this in such a way that clients feel free to reject their suggestions. As a rule, counsellors should probe for client ideas first with questions such as "What are your thoughts on what to do?" "What are your choices?" "What advice could you give yourself?" "What ideas have you considered but rejected?"

Rescuing Rescuing, or "band-aiding," involves actions that prevent or protect clients from dealing with issues or feelings. Rescuing arises from the counsellor's need to avoid tension and keep the session cheerful, but it is misguided because rescuing diverts clients from addressing important though difficult issues in their lives. Rescuing is therefore a misuse of the support function of helping. Counsellors may become so preoccupied with avoiding or reducing tension that they interfere with their clients' ability to cope or to solve problems. If problem situations are to be worked through successfully, clients must be allowed to experience and express painful emotions. For their part, counsellors must develop their ability to be present for such work without their own needs and anxiety interfering or becoming a burden to their clients.

rescuing: Also called band-aiding, this involves a counsellor's actions that prevent or protect clients from dealing with issues or feelings. Rescuing arises from the counsellor's need to avoid tension and keep the session cheerful.

SUCCESS TIP

Advice giving and rescuing arise more from the counsellor's need to be helpful, intelligent, or powerful than the client's need to receive advice or be rescued.

There are three major types of rescue behaviour:

1. *Tension reducers:* Avoiding tough but otherwise timely and important topics and feelings by changing the subject, using humour to cut off discussion, or suggesting a coffee break.

> Rodney was finally willing to address his sadness over the death of his father. As he began to talk, he cried softly. As he did so, his counsellor reached out and put her hands on his shoulders, reassuring him that his grief would pass.

> Par hesitated for a moment as he struggled to collect his thoughts. Sensing that this might be a painful moment for him, his counsellor suggested that he might prefer to talk about something else.

Counsellor responses such as these impede the work of counselling by preventing or discouraging clients from dealing with their feelings. For clients to learn to manage their emotions, they must be allowed to experience their pain. If counsellors communicate discomfort or disapproval with expressed emotions, important opportunities for work may be lost.

2. *Placating*: Withholding potentially helpful but critical confrontation or offering false feedback and empty reassurance.

> Tara expressed fear about contacting her father, with whom she had not had contact for five years. Her counsellor offered support: "Everything is going to work out well. I'm sure your father will be ecstatic to see you."

> Shirley decided not to confront her client over an obvious hygiene problem. She concluded that it would be best not to upset her client and jeopardize a strong relationship.

3. *Behaviours that impede independence*: Speaking for clients and doing for clients what they are able to do for themselves.

> Jessie's counsellor wanted to be seen as helpful and resourceful. She offered to rewrite her client's résumé and pick up application forms from local employers.

> José was having trouble understanding a school assignment. His child care counsellor phoned his teacher to ask for clarification, even though José was capable of talking to the teacher himself.

For clients to become independent, they need to develop the skills and strength to deal with their lives on their own. This may be a difficult process for clients, requiring counsellors to be supportive without stifling their clients' growth. Counsellors must avoid unduly protecting their clients by interfering with their opportunities and capacity to face their difficulties. This requires counsellors to be fully aware of their own need for power and control and to accept that successful counselling requires clients to be their own problem solvers. Furthermore, counsellors must rid themselves of any fantasy that only they can save their clients.

Communication Stoppers   Some responses tend to bring communication to a halt. Rescuing and advice giving are two prime examples, but others that have the same effect include name calling, "playing psychologist" by offering clever but unsolicited assessments, commanding, moralizing, minimizing the feelings or concerns of others, using platitudes or clichés, and excessive use of interrogating questions, especially *why* questions that tend to ask for justification or communicate subtle judgment. Abrupt subject changes are also communication stoppers. They may communicate that the counsellor is uncomfortable with the topic or feelings expressed.

Faulty Technique   Some of the problems that arise in counselling can be attributed to counsellors' inept use of skills. Poor technique can lead to missed opportunities

---

>>> **CONVERSATION 2.4**   Rescuing and Supporting

STUDENT: What is the difference between supporting clients and rescuing them?

TEACHER: Rescuing robs clients of legitimate opportunities for growth. Supporting promotes self-determination by providing encouragement or resources to motivate clients toward growth and change. Timing is also a factor. Rescuing occurs when clients have the strength to deal with difficult areas or feelings, but their counsellors avoid the work or pain that this would entail. On the other hand, if clients are overwhelmed, some direct assistance by counsellors to lessen their burden is supportive. It may be wise to avoid excessive intimacy in the beginning of a relationship, and it may be hazardous to explore highly emotional topics near the end of an interview. An important question for counsellors to consider is "Whose needs are being met, mine or the client's?" Rescuing behaviour meets counsellors' needs under the guise of helping clients, but supportive behaviour helps clients realize their objectives. In the long run, there are times when it is more supportive to allow clients to face their struggles and experience their pain. Effective counsellors are courageous enough to allow clients to express their pain and accept the reality that they cannot provide solutions to all problems.

and, in extreme cases, can be harmful to clients. For example, counsellors might fail to respond to individual differences (e.g., gender and culture), or they may cling to a rigid "one style fits all" approach to counselling. They may also be poor listeners, or they may lack empathy. They might push clients too quickly, or they might allow them to stagnate by neglecting to motivate them to make changes.

Uncontrollable Variables   Large caseloads may preclude counsellors from spending sufficient time with their clients. Resources may not be available to support clients in their change process, such as at a detox facility. In addition, unexpected events and crises such as illness, death, or job loss may frustrate progress. In some cases, client changes may be subverted by family and friends who are unprepared to support change.

Defence Mechanisms   Sigmund Freud (1856–1939) first used the term **defence mechanism** to describe how people protect themselves from anxiety, unpleasant thoughts, and personal threat. To some extent, the use of defence mechanisms is normal and healthy; it allows us to cope with the demands of life. But defence mechanisms are problematic when they are overused or when they prevent us from dealing with problems that should be addressed. Here are some common defence mechanisms that counsellors are likely to see in their clients.

defence mechanisms: Mental process or reaction that shields a person from undesirable or unacceptable thoughts, feelings, or conclusions that, if accepted, would create anxiety or challenges to one's sense of self. Common defence mechanisms include denial, displacement, rationalization, suppression, and regression.

- *Acting Out.* Expressing emotional distress behaviourally. Example: A young child deals with her frustration by breaking her doll.

- *Denial.* Refusing to accept or acknowledge what may be clearly evident to others. Example: A man with a drug addiction will not admit he has a problem despite considerable evidence and feedback from others.

- *Displacement.* Transferring feelings to a less threatening person or object. Example: A man who is angry at himself for losing his money at the casino takes his anger out on his wife.

- *Dissociation.* Separating or disconnecting from reality. Example: Amnesia as a reaction to a trauma; daydreaming.

- *Humour.* Avoiding emotional conflict by looking at the humorous aspects of the situation.

- *Intellectualization.* Avoiding feelings through excessive abstract thinking, such as focusing on the details of an event, while losing touch with the associated feelings.

- *Passive Aggression.* Indirectly expressing aggression. Example: Withholding helpful ideas or information from someone you dislike.

- *Projection.* Falsely assigning our own unacceptable feelings to others. Example: An aggressive person sees others as hostile and angry.

- *Rationalization.* Using self-serving but incorrect explanations to avoid emotional turmoil. Example: A woman who did not get a job promotion rationalizes that she did not want the job anyway.

- *Reaction Formation.* Substituting behaviour, thoughts, or feelings that are the opposite of those that are unacceptable. Example: Being overly friendly or helpful to someone you dislike.

- *Regression.* Reverting to an earlier form of coping. Example: An adult sulks rather than using problem solving to deal with a difficult situation.

- *Repression.* Keeping feelings and memories out of conscious awareness (but they still continue to influence behaviour). Example: A woman who was sexually abused as a child may have no memory of the event, but she remains uncomfortable with physical touch as an adult.

- *Splitting.* Seeing or experiencing things only as polar opposites. Example: Seeing others as either perfect or totally inadequate. This defence prevents people from considering more balanced views and expectations of self and others.

- *Sublimation.* Involves converting unacceptable feelings or impulses into more acceptable behaviour. Example: Dealing with anger through involvement in martial arts.

- *Suppression.* Deliberately avoiding thinking about feelings or thoughts that provoke anxiety.

(*Source:* American Psychiatric Association, 2000, Grohol, 2015, McLeod, 2008)

SUMMARY

- Counselling involves a time-limited relationship designed to help clients increase their capacity to deal with the demands of life such as dealing with feelings, learning new skills, making decisions, and accessing resources.

- Counselling caseloads are characterized by diversity in culture, gender, age, religion, sexual orientation, language, education, economic ability, and so on. Working with diversity requires counsellors to be adaptive and to be able to use research theory and experience as guides to determine which skills and procedures best meet the needs of their clients.

- There are four essential elements of a trauma-informed approach: trauma awareness, emphasis on safety and trustworthiness, opportunity for choice, collaboration and connection, and strengths-based counselling and skill building.

- Four major skill and strategy clusters define the range of necessary skills for counsellors are (1) relationship-building, (2) exploring/probing, (3) empowering and strength building, (4) promoting change.

- The four counselling phases are (1) preliminary, (2) beginning, (3) action, and (4) ending. Each phase is characterized by unique tasks and skills. During different phases of the relationship, different skill clusters assume priority.

- Many variables can lead to poor outcomes in counselling. Client variables include unrealistic expectations and poor motivation. Counsellor factors such as burnout, personal problems, and loss of objectivity can also lead to failure. Process or faulty techniques, including pseudo-counselling, advice giving, and rescuing, can contribute to failure. Finally, failure may arise from factors outside the control of counsellors and clients.

EXERCISES

Self-Awareness

1. Think of a recent or current problem that you are facing. Describe the ways that counselling might be used to assist you in addressing this problem. Using concepts from this chapter, identify what might be the major activities for each phase of counselling.

2. Review the tasks of each of the phases of helping. With which phase do you feel most comfortable? Least comfortable?

3. Describe a situation in which you gave advice to or rescued someone. Do you have a tendency to give advice or rescue others? Seek feedback from others who know you to see if their perceptions agree with your self-evaluation.

Skill Practice

1. Imagine that you are responding to the following client questions: What is counselling? How does it work?

2. Interview colleagues or counsellors form the field. Explore their answers to the following question: What are some of your biggest counselling mistakes? What did you learn from them?

Concepts

1. Rate the extent that you think each of the following statements is true using the following scale (be prepared to defend your answers):

4 = always

3 = frequently

2 = sometimes

1 = rarely

0 = never

_____ It is important for counsellors to develop a personal style so that they treat all clients the same way.

_____ The counselling process has a lot in common with the processes used by other professionals, such as doctors and lawyers; thus, competent counsellors gather information, diagnose the problem, and offer solutions or advice to their clients on the best resolution.

_____ Usually, clients who seek help are in crisis, and their ability to make decisions is significantly impaired. Therefore, it is important that counsellors are comfortable with making important decisions on behalf of their clients.

_____ The application of skills or techniques detracts from spontaneity.

_____ Professional counsellors strive to be free of biases.

_____ Counsellors who have personal experience with the problem or issues that their clients are experiencing will be more effective.

_____ The counselling process evolves sequentially through a number of phases, with each phase having specific tasks and requiring specific skills.

_____ Effective counsellors are consistent. They use the same skills in the same way throughout the counselling process.

_____ If the principles of counselling are applied effectively, all clients will be helped.

_____ Everything that happens in the counselling interview must be treated as confidential and shared with no one. This is the law in Canada.

_____ Effective counselling involves blending the client's needs with those of the counsellor so that everyone involved is satisfied.

_____ The skills of counselling are also the skills of effective everyday communication.

2. Write a short essay supporting the following argument: The capacity to accept help from another person is a sign of strength.

3. In what ways might advice giving disempower clients?

4. What do you think are the advantages and disadvantages of working from a four-phase model of counselling?

5. Identify and explore clients' legal rights to access file information in your jurisdiction.

6. List the pros and cons of displaying each of the following in your office:

   a. family photos

   b. motivational posters

WEBLINKS

Chapter 3

Relationship: The Foundation for Change

LEARNING OBJECTIVES

- Explore the features of a counselling relationship.
- Explain the importance of the core conditions of warmth, empathy, and genuineness.
- Demonstrate ability to negotiate relationship, anticipatory, and work contracts.
- Demonstrate skills for maintaining the counselling relationship.
- Examine relationship endings.

THE COUNSELLING RELATIONSHIP

One of the most well-documented finding in counselling is the fact that developing and sustaining an effective counselling relationship is widely accepted as critical to success (Cochran & Cochran, 2015; Cozolino & Santos, 2014; Heinonen & Spearman, 2010; Nystul, 2011; Rogers, 1980; and Shulman, 2009). In fact, the relationship itself is often the central reason for client change, and it can be "more important than any information given, referrals made, or practice approaches used . . ." (Heinonen & Spearman, 2010, p. 101). Research by Kivlighan, Gelso, Ain, Hummel, and Markin, (2015) demonstrated that counsellors with better relationships have clients who make better progress.

Having a strong relationship can activate the brain's reward system in the same way as a drug by releasing the neurotransmitter dopamine, which is associated with pleasure and feeling good. Conversely, the loss of the relationship can lead to depression and anxiety (Jantz, 2015).

Capuzzi and Gross (2009) conclude, "specific procedures and techniques are much less important than the alliance between counsellor and client" (p. 65). Significantly, "even clients whose lives have predisposed them to distrust and suspicion often remain alert to clues that this professional relationship may hold promise" (Miley, O'Melia, & Dubois, 2004, p. 130).

Rather than focus on technique, wise counsellors make the helping relationship the centre of their work. Over 50 years ago, Rogers (1961) emphasized that a counsellor's attitudes and feelings are more important than technique and noted that the client's perception of the counsellor's attitudes is what is most crucial. Reflecting on this he wrote, "In my early professional years I was asking the question: How can I treat, or cure, or change this person? Now I would phrase the question in this way: How can I provide a relationship which this person may use for his own personal growth?" (p. 32). The expertise that counsellors bring to the relationship lies less in their ability to solve problems than in their capacity to recognize and mobilize client strengths and resources. When strengths are revealed and resources identified, clients become empowered with new choices and revitalized optimism.

Definition

A **counselling relationship** is a time-limited period of consultation between a counsellor and one or more clients for assisting the client in achieving a defined goal.

Counselling relationships have some of the same components of intimacy, caring, and support that characterize deep personal relationships. High-level communication skills are as important to friendships as they are to counselling. Moreover, many of the skills of counselling are also the skills of effective everyday communication. Friendships grow out of mutual attraction and common interests, whereas counselling relationships focus on helping clients achieve goals such as resolving crises, making decisions, and learning new skills. Counselling relationships are structured for the primary purpose of reaching these goals, and once the clients have achieved them, the counselling relationship is terminated. There is no expectation of reciprocity.

Personal relationships can be terminated for personal reasons. Counsellors, however, are expected to persist in their efforts on behalf of clients even when they are frustrated by lack of progress or client resistance. Counselling may be ended when there is little likelihood of reaching its goals, but not simply because the counsellor prefers other clients. One measure of professionalism is the capacity of the practitioner to sustain commitment, patience, and caring despite frustrating obstacles. Many clients come to counselling with impaired ability to form or sustain healthy relationships, so counsellors must remain sensitive to this fact and not allow their own emotions or "buttons to be pushed."

Rogers's counselling classic, *Client-Centered Therapy* (1951), describes the experience of a client who successfully completed counselling following an unsuccessful experience with another counsellor. The second counsellor asked the client why he had been able to work through his problems on his second attempt. The client responded, "You did about the same things he did, but you seemed really interested in me" (p. 69).

counselling relationship: A time-limited period of consultation between a counsellor and a client dedicated to achieving a defined goal.

Oxytocin is a hormone and a neurotransmitter that plays a significant role in relationship bonding. Both sex and birth increase levels of oxytocin, and it appears that strong relationships also increase oxytocin levels. There is evidence that increased oxytocin levels reduce stress, anxiety, depression, and also increase empathy and one's general ability to communicate emotions (Gravotta, 2013; Simon-Dack & Marmarosh, 2014). "Our brain/body releases oxytocin to strengthen relationships. Oxytocin gets released during light caresses, sex, when someone shows they trust you, and sometimes even simply with talking. When released, oxytocin increases feelings of attachment for another person, as well as feelings of trust. It also decreases feelings of stress, fear and pain" (Korb, 2014: online). These findings underscore the importance of paying attention to the counselling relationship and avoiding a strict task or problem-solving orientation.

The helping relationship provides the necessary security for clients to disclose their feelings and ideas. As trust develops in relationships, so does the capacity of clients to become increasingly open to revealing themselves. Drawing from the strength of their relationships with counsellors, clients may risk new ways of thinking and behaving, and in this way, the relationship becomes the medium for change. In positive counselling relationships, clients perceive their counsellors as allies. They become increasingly willing to disclose because they do not fear that they will be rejected, judged, or coerced to change in ways that they find unacceptable. In its purest form, the counselling relationship becomes a collaborative endeavour.

Counselling sessions are not always comfortable or pleasant. The process may involve exploration of painful feelings or experiences. Personal change involves risk and modification of one's usual way of thinking or behaving, and this can be stressful. Counsellors who are intent on keeping the counselling relationship pleasant may communicate reluctance to deal with sensitive issues, or they may withdraw at the first sign of difficulty by changing the topic or rescuing.

SUCCESS TIP

If you want to influence someone, first pay attention to the relationship.

Relationship and the Phases of Counselling

Each of the four phases of counselling—preliminary, beginning, action, and ending—has associated relationship tasks and challenges (Shebib, 1997). In all phases, counsellors need to develop effective skills and attitudes for engaging and retaining clients, including sincerity, perceptiveness, honesty, respect for diversity, capacity to initiate conversations, ability to be a good listener, comfort with discussing feelings, empathy, ability to communicate confidence without conceit, and warmth. The essential elements of the counselling relationship include core conditions, contracts, goals, and immediacy, with the work conducted within professional boundaries and time limits (Figure 3.1).

Preliminary Phase The goal of the preliminary phase is to create the necessary physical and psychological conditions for the relationship to begin. The counselling environment (e.g., agency setting, office layout, and reception procedures) can have a dramatic impact on the client's mood and expectations even before the interview begins (Knapp & Hall, 2006; Shebib, 1997). Preliminary phase work attempts to create first impressions that say to clients, "You will be respected here. You are important. This is a place where you will be supported."

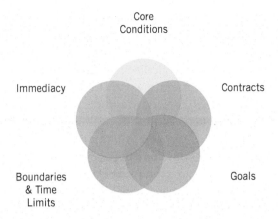

Core
Conditions

Immediacy

Contracts

Boundaries
& Time
Limits

Goals

Figure 3.1   The Essential Elements of a Counselling Relationship

SUCCESS TIP

The stage for the relationship is set long before you meet your client. Experiences with past counsellors, expectations about the process, factors such as the waiting room, how the client is greeted, and waiting time mean the relationship has already started before your first encounter. The relationship is further predefined by issues such as culture, gender, sexual orientation, reactions to authority, and the presence of mental disorders.

Beginning Phase   The relationship goal in the beginning phase is to develop rapport, trust, and a working contract or agreement regarding the purpose of the work and the roles of the participants. The relationship at this phase must provide enough safety for clients that they will engage and continue with counselling. Counsellors create this environment of safety by communicating that they do not judge the client and that change can occur. The relationship enables clients to feel sufficiently free to take on the first risks of counselling—sharing their feelings and concerns. Nevertheless, some clients are poorly equipped to do this, and they may remain guarded or suspicious throughout the whole process.

Action Phase   Ideally, in the action phase, the relationship continues to develop and strengthen. Clients take new risks as they find the courage and strength to examine and change their ways of thinking, feeling, and behaving. During this phase, relationship work may need to focus on addressing communication problems including, at times, tension or conflict.

Ending Phase   Termination of the counselling relationship comes when counselling has served its purpose and clients have reached their goals. Termination focuses on reviewing the work accomplished, helping clients consolidate learning, and saying goodbye. Ending phase work will be discussed in more depth later in this chapter.

CARL ROGERS AND THE CORE CONDITIONS

Carl Rogers (1902–1987), the founder of client-centred therapy (later known as person-centred therapy), has exerted an enormous influence on the counselling profession for the last 65 years.

Rogers (1951, 1961, and 1980) asserted the importance of seeing others as "becoming." This notion underscores a fundamental belief in the capacity of people to change. Clients are not bound by their past, and counsellors should not use diagnosis and classification as tools for depersonalizing clients and treating them as objects. In counselling, clients need to be seen for their potential, strength, inner power, and capacity to change. Rogers's nondirective methods are based on the premise that if core conditions are present, then change is possible. The core conditions act to speed the natural process of healing or recovery from psychological pain or problems.

The essential core conditions are unconditional positive regard, empathy, and genuineness. Core conditions are aspects of attitude that are prerequisites to forming and maintaining effective helping relationships. Although counsellors can use certain behaviours and skills to demonstrate core conditions, the conditions must represent the authentic values and attitudes of counsellors. When counsellors exhibit these core conditions, the potential for change and positive relationships with clients is increased.

However, there is no guarantee that clients will interpret warmth, genuineness, and empathy (or any communication) in the way that they were intended. Prior experiences and expectations, as well as cultural and individual differences, can easily lead to discrepancies in the way communication is perceived. Counsellors can expect to be rejected at least some of the time, despite their best efforts. Moreover, a client may perceive empathy as an intrusive attempt to "get into my head" and may interpret caring attitudes as manipulation. Secure professionals accept this reality, knowing that considerable resistance may be encountered as they work to develop the helping relationship.

Unconditional Positive Regard   Unconditional positive regard accepts the client as a person of worth and dignity. This acceptance is felt and communicated by counsellors without condition, judgment, or expectation. Rogers believed that such unconditional regard creates the very best conditions for client growth to occur. Essential components of unconditional positive regard include caring, respect, warmth, and compassion.

Rogers (1961) urged counsellors to shun any tendency to keep clients at a distance by treating them as objects with detailed diagnostic labels. Instead, he argued that counsellors need to learn that it is safe to express their **warmth** and to let clients know that they care.

warmth: An expression of nonpossessive caring that requires genuineness and involvement, the acceptance of the equal worth of others, a nonjudgmental attitude, and avoidance of blaming.

Warmth is difficult to define; yet its presence or absence can be felt immediately. Warmth communicates comfort and trust, and it is a precursor to trust. It attracts clients to take risks because it indicates the goodwill and motivation of their counsellors. In the beginning, clients often come to counselling reluctantly, perhaps driven by external pressure or by the weight of their problems. Counsellors need to engage or connect with clients to help them find enough acceptance so that they return and sufficient safety so that they can take appropriate risks. Warmth says, "I'm approachable. You do not need to be afraid of me. I won't take advantage of your vulnerability. I'm a kind person." As a result, warmth is particularly important during the formative or beginning stage of the relationship. Warmth is also crucial for supporting clients during a crisis, and it is a necessary partner to caring confrontation. Clients will be more receptive to feedback if it originates from a warm and caring attitude.

Although warmth can to some extent be defined behaviourally, it must arise from genuine feelings of caring for the client. Otherwise, the counsellor's actions will appear lacking in genuineness. Warmth is demonstrated by smiling appropriately and by showing sincere interest in the comfort of the client. Counsellors show warmth when they communicate nonverbally that they are totally focused on their clients. Simple courtesies, such as eliminating distractions from the interview, asking clients if they are physically comfortable, offering them a beverage, and making eye contact all convey warmth. Well-timed humour can also add a warm touch to the interview.

Counsellors need to be flexible with their level of expressed warmth and caring. Highly suspicious clients may interpret warmth as manipulative, and some clients are not comfortable with a high level of expressed emotion. As well, gender may be a variable.

Being warm does not preclude dealing with difficult topics; in fact, warmth provides the necessary foundation for such talk. Nor does it imply that a great deal of the interview needs to be spent making small talk, as one might do during a social visit.

Sometimes in busy social service agencies, caseloads become unmanageable and the pace of the work frantic. Constant crises and unrelenting paperwork exhaust even the most energetic and caring workers, who may begin to lose the "spark" they had when they first entered the field. Unless controlled, the office routine can begin to feel more like an assembly line than a counselling service, as clients become numbers and the work becomes increasingly task-oriented. How does one continue to feel and express warmth under such conditions? The answer must be discovered individually, but we can learn something from the observations of one worker, a senior caseworker with over 25 years' experience:

> What works for me is to remind myself that no matter how overwhelmed I feel, it's worse for my clients. Often, they're broke, in crisis and not sure whether they want to live or die. They don't need me to be part of the problem. What doesn't work for me is to get caught up in coffee room negativism. You know what it's like—the ones who never have anything good to say and always expect things to get worse. It also helps if I take a few moments, sometimes precious seconds, between interviews to meditate. When I meet my client, I try to spend some time just being friendly.

Empathy Empathy describes the capacity to understand the feelings and views of another person. Empathic attitudes and skills can generate powerful bonds of trust and rapport. Empathy communicates understanding and acceptance. An empathic attitude is characterized by one's willingness to learn about the world of another and begins with suspending judgment. To be nonjudgmental requires considerable discipline in controlling personal biases, assumptions, and reactions that might contaminate understanding.

⟫⟫ CONVERSATION 3.1 Unconditional Positive Regard

COUNSELLOR 1: Maybe Carl Rogers could do it, but I find it difficult, sometimes impossible, to have respect and caring for someone who has done something horrendous, such as raping a child.

PROBATION OFFICER: Even Rogers admitted to being challenged. Sometimes he'd share his negative reactions or feelings with his clients—maybe that's why he identified genuineness as a core condition.

COUNSELLOR 2: Even if I have strong negative feelings toward my client, I can still control my behaviour. I can listen; I can use my active listening skills to try to understand. I can empathize, which doesn't mean I agree with the client or sanction the behaviour.

PROBATION OFFICER: One of the first people I worked with was a man who was so abusive and he put his wife in the hospital. I disliked him before I even met him. But as I got to know him, I found myself softening a bit. I still was repulsed by what he did, but I also came to understand his depression, his inability to get a job, and his own abuse as a child. He was much more complicated than I imagined. Now, I've worked in the Alberta correctional system for 15 years, and I've never met anyone who is pure evil, although some psychopaths can come close.

COUNSELLOR 3: We have a professional role to play, and it's not our job to condemn or punish, but the reality is that we won't like or respect every client we meet; however, we have a much better chance of helping the client change if we have a working relationship. This increases the possibility that clients will trust us so that they can express and discuss important feelings and ideas. The bottom line for me is this: respect the client, but reject the behaviour. When you do that the client has a safe relationship, and often that alone can generate movement to constructive change. If the client expresses remorse or self-doubt about his behaviour or if he hints at some desire to change, we can build momentum for change with encouraging questions and reflections such as "Sounds like there's a part of you that would like to be different," or "Suppose you were to make a change in the direction you describe. How would you do it?"

COUNSELLOR 2: Here's another thought. I think it is just as important to understand and control our strong positive feelings because these have the same potential to cloud our objectivity.

In addition, counsellors need to be able to enter the emotional world of their clients without fear of becoming trapped in their pain. Counsellors who are secure with themselves and their feelings have the capacity to enter their clients' worlds without fear of losing their own identity. Brill and Levine (2005) note that when a counsellor communicates acceptance, there is the "freedom to be oneself—to express one's fears, angers, joy, rage, to grow, develop, and change—without concern that doing so will jeopardize the relationship" (p. 118).

Empathy has two components. First, counsellors must be able to perceive their clients' feelings and perspectives. This requires counsellors to have abundant self-awareness and emotional maturity so that they do not contaminate their clients' experience with their own. The second component of empathy is to make an empathic response. This involves putting in words the feelings that the client has expressed. This task can be particularly difficult, since clients often communicate their feelings in abstract, ambiguous, or nonverbal ways. Empathic responses require a vocabulary of words and phrases that can be used to define feelings. At a basic level, empathic responses acknowledge obvious and clearly expressed feelings. At a more advanced or inferred level, empathic responses are framed from hints and nonverbal cues. An empathic response proves to clients that they have been heard, understood, and accepted. Chapter 6 focuses on this critical skill.

Genuineness Being genuine means being authentic and real in a relationship. Counsellors who are genuine show high consistency between what they think and do, and between what they feel and express. Rogers (1961) used the term *congruent* to describe this quality and emphasized the importance of self-awareness to unambiguous communication. To avoid giving contradictory messages, counsellors need to be aware of how they are feeling and how they are transmitting their feelings.

Genuine counsellors are also highly trustworthy. They do not lie to clients, and they are willing to provide feedback that is timely and helpful. They show respect for clients by being open and honest while maintaining warmth and empathy in the relationship. They do not work from hidden agendas, nor do they put on "masks" or play roles to hide their true feelings. As well, genuine counsellors are reliable. They do what they say they are going to do.

Core Conditions: Implications for Counsellors

Rogers's philosophy suggests a number of introspective questions for counsellors to consider regarding their attitudes and behaviour in helping relationships:

- *How can I act so that clients will perceive me as trustworthy?* This means counsellors do what they say they will do and act in a way that is consistent with how they feel. It requires counsellors to communicate without ambiguity and contradiction.

- *Can I permit myself to experience positive attitudes of warmth, caring, liking, interest, and respect toward clients?*

- *Can I be strong enough as a person to be separate from my clients?* This requires a high level of maturity, self-awareness, and courage. Rogers summarizes this challenge: "Am I strong enough in my own separateness that I will not be downcast by his depression, frightened by his fear, nor engulfed by his dependency? Is my inner self hardy enough to realize that I am not destroyed by his anger, taken over by his need for dependence, nor enslaved by his love, but that I exist separate from him with feelings and rights of my own?" (1961, p. 52)

- *Am I secure enough to permit clients their separateness?* Clients are not under their counsellor's control, nor are they to be molded as models of what counsellors feel they should be.

- *Can I let myself fully empathize with my clients' feelings and world perspectives without evaluating or judging?*

STUDENT: How far should I go with genuineness? What if I'm angry with my client? Should I say so? Or suppose I find my client disgusting. Should I express that too?

TEACHER: You've identified an important dilemma. On the one hand, the need for genuineness suggests that we should be open and honest with our clients. We shouldn't put on false fronts, lie to clients, or fake our feelings. At the same time, ethical principles clearly prohibit us from doing harm. Being genuine doesn't entitle counsellors to "dump" on their clients. Genuine counsellors are truthful, but they are also timely. They share personal perceptions and feelings in an assertive way to meet their clients' needs. They might express their anger, but they do so without intending to punish, ridicule, or trap their clients. As for feeling disgust toward a client,

I can't see how sharing that information would serve any purpose. On the other hand, it may be useful to the client if you explored the specific behaviours or attitudes that gave rise to those feelings. With sensitive feedback, your client can have the benefit of learning about his or her impact on others. Once you put it on the table for discussion, you no longer have to hide your reactions. One final point: Strong reactions toward our clients may hint at our own vulnerabilities. If you find a client disgusting, I'd want to ask you, "Where does that feeling come from? Are you sure it is related only to the client?"

STUDENT: Maybe the client "pushes my buttons" the same way my parents did.

TEACHER: Exactly.

COUNSELLING CONTRACTS

A **contract** is a negotiated agreement between the counsellor and the client regarding important variables that define the work. Counsellors typically begin contracting early in the first interview; however, contracting is continuous throughout the life of the helping relationship. Rigid adherence to negotiated contracts is hazardous. Counselling contracts need to be periodically revisited and updated, sometimes even several times during a single session. The reasons for amending contracts include the following:

contract: A negotiated agreement between counsellors and clients regarding the purpose of the work, their respective roles, and the methods and routines that will be used to reach their agreed-on objectives. (See also *sessional contract* and *work contract*.)

- Exploration of problems and feelings may promote insight, and this may lead to changed expectations and revised goals.

- Increased trust may enable clients to address more difficult topics and feelings that they were unwilling to consider at the beginning of the relationship.

- New problems and issues may emerge because of changing circumstances.

SUCCESS TIP

Variables such as culture, level of trust, timing, mood, and stress can affect a client's willingness and capacity to address topics. Similarly, unresolved conflict in the client–counsellor relationship can dramatically affect the contract. Unless these variables are considered and until conflict is resolved, the client may not cooperate or fully participate.

Purpose of Contracting

Contracting ensures that clients and counsellors are on the same page with respect to the goals of the work and the counselling methods that will be used. Contracting also involves discussion that defines the counsellor–client relationship, including roles, rights, and responsibilities. Good counsellors adjust their style to meet the needs, culture, and personality of their clients. They consult and negotiate with their clients to identify and understand these variables. Effective contracting respects clients' freedom to choose, and it gives them knowledge and control of the helping process. When counsellors and their clients are working toward agreed-upon objectives, it is much more likely that clients will "own" the work rather than see it as something that has been imposed on them. Contracting reduces suspicions that counsellors may have hidden agendas.

Contracting directly addresses the reality that there may be (and often are) sharp differences among the following:

- the problem as perceived by any referring source (e.g., another agency, family, employer, etc.)
- the problem as perceived by the client
- your perception (as counsellor) of the problem

The contract is like a road map that provides general directions on how to get from A to B. It confirms that all parties are working toward the same end. A counselling contract also predicts an end to the relationship. Defining tasks and goals makes it clear when the relationship should be ended. In this way, the counselling relationship is clearly distinguished from a friendship, which may last for a lifetime.

SUCCESS TIP

Contracting may change over the life of the relationship or even during a single session. Client insight, changed priorities, mood, trust level, capacity, and emergent issues are variables that drive changes in the contract.

Contracts may be formal and signed by both the counsellor and the client, but more frequently they are informal and ratified with verbal agreement or a handshake. There are three types of contracts: relationship, anticipatory, and work.

Relationship Contracts

relationship contract: A Negotiation of the intended purpose of the counselling relationship, including an agreement on the expected roles of both counsellor and client.

The **relationship contract** outlines how the counsellor and the client will work together. It results in a customized relationship that is uniquely respectful and responsive to the client's expectations, wants, and needs. The process involves candid discussion and exploration of client issues, such as the following:

- communication style (e.g., preferred ways to communicate, problem solve, resolve conflict, and give and receive feedback)
- personal values, worldview, and culture
- exploration of how differences (e.g., gender, age, race, and sexual orientation) might help or hinder the counselling work
- past experiences with counselling

The relationship contract, by its nature, honours diversity and individual differences in communication styles and patterns. The process signals to clients that their needs and wants will be respected and that counsellors are willing to adjust their style to accommodate clients.

Part of the relationship contracting process is discussing the methods and process of counselling. Counsellors should be open about what they are doing and not work from a secret script with mysterious techniques that they hide from clients. They should be willing and able to describe their work in simple, non-jargonistic language. In this way, clients can know something about what is happening, the direction of the work, and what remains to be done.

Shulman (2009) emphasizes the need for workers to provide clear, non-jargonistic statements that describe the range of services available. This is particularly important in settings where the counsellor may be the one who initiates first contact. When the purpose of the meeting is explicit, clients do not have to worry about workers' hidden agendas, and they are in a more informed position to take advantage of assistance. In the example below, a school counsellor is making an excellent attempt to engage with an 11-year-old boy who has transferred to the school in the middle of the academic year and seems depressed and alone:

> **Counsellor:** My name is Mr. Smith. I'm here because your teacher thought I might be able to help you with some of the problems you're having at school. I know that it can be tough to be the new kid. Sometimes it's just not much fun. Maybe we could meet and see if we can figure out a way to make things better. What do you think?

Past Experiences with Counselling Many clients have considerable experience working with counsellors, and they have learned what works and what does not work. Counsellors can learn from this and adapt their approach accordingly. A sample probe illustrates as follows:

> **Counsellor:** I'd like your help. I know you've been coming to this agency for a while, and you have a lot of experience as a user. It would help me if you could tell me a bit about your experiences—like, what did you find helpful and not helpful? Then we can talk about how you and I can best work together.

While clients may have had satisfying and empowering experiences, the reality is that many have felt disempowered by counsellors and other social service providers. Open discussion about this can provide valuable cues for structuring the current relationship. Moreover, the process can help clients who have had a bad experience reach some closure on unresolved feelings. At the same time, the process clearly communicates that this relationship has the potential to be different.

Discussion of the Roles and Expectations of the Participants Counsellors should know something about what clients want from them. Do clients expect them to provide advice on how to manage their problems? Do they want to be challenged with new information and new perspectives? Are they looking for someone who is warm, gentle, and supportive, or someone who will just listen? Similarly, counsellors need to tell clients about any expectations they have. Role discussion may also address issues such as how the participants might address conflict, and how they can provide feedback to each other.

Clients may be aware of their pain and may recognize and accept the need for change and help, but they may have no idea what form this help might take. In such situations, counsellors need to be able to help them understand the potential assistance that counselling can provide.

Some clients also have unrealistic expectations of their counsellors and the process. They may believe that counsellors will tell them what to do and solve all their problems. Or they may have no faith in the process whatsoever. According to Wicks and Parsons (1984), when people enter counselling they often anticipate "either a miracle or complete failure" (p. 175). Contracting is a significant opportunity for demystifying the process and for challenging unreasonable positive or negative expectations.

The following example is taken from the midpoint of a second interview. It illustrates how the counsellor gently encourages the client to re-examine some self-imposed restrictions on the relationship:

> **Client:** Let's keep my feelings out of this. I simply want to look at ways to improve my relationship with my son. If you could teach me some techniques, I'd be most grateful.

> **Counsellor:** Of course you're entitled to privacy on issues or feelings that you don't want to share with me. At the same time, I wonder if you might be too hasty in restricting what we can discuss.

Client: I don't get it. What do you mean?

Counsellor: Well, you've been through a lot. With your son's arrest and his disappearance for over a month, I'd be surprised if you weren't feeling stress.

Client: Who wouldn't?

Counsellor: That's exactly my point. When I don't talk about feelings that are bothering me, I have to keep them inside or pretend they're not there. I've found that doesn't work. Sooner or later, I have to face my feelings.

Client: I'm just afraid that if I start crying, I won't be able to stop.

Counsellor: That tells me that the pain must be very deep. *(Silence as the client tears up.)*

Counsellor: I won't push you, but I hope our relationship can become a safe place for you. It's okay with me if you cry.

Many clients are slow to develop trust, perhaps for good reason. They may have lifelong experiences of betrayal or abuse by people they trusted. Why should it be any different with a counsellor? As a result, it is understandable that they approach counselling with a degree of mistrust. Wicks and Parsons (1984) provide a compelling observation: "Though there may seem to be a great distance between counsellors and their clients during the beginning phase of counselling, they should not be discouraged because at that point their clients may be closer to them than anyone else" (p. 168).

Client: I really don't see the point in being here. My situation is hopeless. I've been to other counsellors and nothing worked. I'm only here because my wife insisted. She thought you might be able to help.

Counsellor (Choice 1): You certainly do sound discouraged, but I think you should give counselling another chance. Maybe by talking about your problems, we can discover some solutions you've overlooked.

Counsellor (Choice 2): Given your past experiences, I can see why you're pessimistic. You're wise to be skeptical until you find out if you can trust me. In the end, the results will be the most important thing.

In this example, Choice 1 is well-meaning but ill-timed and may lead to a power struggle if the client feels compelled to defend his position. Choice 2 is not condescending, it avoids the power struggle trap, and it does not promise success.

Anticipatory Contracts

anticipatory contract: An agreement between counsellors and clients that plans for predictable events. Anticipatory contracts provide guidance for counsellors and answer the question, "What should I do if . . . ?"

Anticipatory contracts enable counsellors and their clients to plan for predictable events. If you know something has been problematic in the past, ask your client for help on how you might respond if the same situation arises in the future. Some examples of what counsellors might say are as follows:

Counsellor (to a client with a history of violence): "I need your help. If I see that you are angry, what would be a good thing for me to do that you would find useful?"

Counsellor (to a client starting a job search): "Suppose three or four weeks into your job search you are getting discouraged. Give me some advice on what I might do to help you recapture some of the positive energy you feel today."

Homebuilders usually prewire new homes so that future installation of services like cable television will be easy. In the same way, relationships can be "prewired" to make resolution of communication difficulties easier. Contracting strategies, such as discussing in advance how conflict will be addressed and working to develop and refine open communication, are the tools for prewiring relationships. If conflicts occur, a mechanism is already in place for resolving them. Here are some examples that illustrate the options:

> **Counsellor:** Suppose that I have some feedback for you. How would you like me to approach you?

> **Counsellor:** Let's talk about what each of us can do if there's a problem between us. Imagine that I say or do something that offends you or you don't like.

All of us have preferences about how we like to give and receive feedback. Some of us want it straight and to the point; some respond better to a "sandwich style," combining critical feedback with support and positive affirmation. Others need visual or behavioural illustrations. Anticipatory contracting identifies these preferences.

SUCCESS TIP

The onus is on the counsellor to adjust his or her style of giving feedback to meet the style of the client. Clearly, this requires counsellor flexibility. Anticipatory contracts tell the counsellor how to be flexible.

Work Contracts

Whereas the relationship contract focuses on the respective roles and expectations of the participants and how they will communicate, the **work contract** defines the focus for the current session and the overall objective of the participants' work together. Sheafor and Horejsi (2008) identify the following basic components of the work contract:

> **work contract:** An agreement that specifies the intended goals or outcome of counselling.

- problems or concerns to be addressed
- goals and objectives of the intervention
- activities [actions] the client will undertake
- tasks to be performed by the worker
- expected duration
- schedule of time and place for interviews
- identification of other persons, agencies, or organizations expected to participate (p. 322)

As well, ethical issues, including the limitations of confidentiality, are also part of the work contract.

Sessional Focus   The sessional contract answers the question, "What are we hoping to talk about and accomplish today?" Although the importance of defining sessional focus seems self-evident, it is surprising how often counsellors proceed without a clear sense of direction or purpose. Or they assume that their clients understand and are working with the same purpose in mind. When clients are involved in negotiating the contract, they are respected and empowered as active partners, not passive recipients of service. With clarity and agreement regarding purpose, clients are more likely to support and participate in the work. Sometimes what counsellors see as client resistance is better understood as legitimate client defence against something (i.e., goals or processes) they experience as imposed.

Sessional contracts can direct attention to one or more of the three major domains: behaviour, thinking, and feeling. Sessional contracts based on behaviour target objectives such as skill development, problem solution (what to do or say), decision making,

TABLE 3.1 Contracting Leads

- What are you hoping to accomplish as a result of our work today?
- Where do you feel most comfortable starting?
- What brings you here?
- What do you need to get out of today?
- What do you need from me?
- Let's talk about how we can use our time here.
- Finish this sentence: When I leave here today, I hope that . . .
- Several times you've hinted at . . . Perhaps it might be important to focus on this a bit.
- (*To an involuntary client*) You feel forced to come. Nevertheless, you could have chosen not to. So I wonder if we could talk about how you could make the best use of the time we have together.
- The examples below are choice options when you wish to introduce clients to the services available at the agency, when clients are stuck, and when clients have limited understanding of the possibilities of counselling.
- If you wish, we could explore . . .
- Here's an idea of where we might go from here.
- In my experience, I have found that it is very helpful, sometimes crucial, to talk about feelings before working on problem solutions. Does this make sense to you or not?
- Let me tell you a bit about the programs here. Then we can discuss which ones, if any, you wish to use.
- Here are two choices: Either we could work now on finding a solution, or perhaps it might be better to just spend time talking about how you feel.
- I wonder if it makes sense to talk a bit about . . .

exploring options, and goal setting. Sessional contracts based on thinking are concerned with helping clients explore values, assumptions, beliefs (including spiritual beliefs), and self-esteem issues. When feeling is the focus of the contract, the work concentrates on clients' emotions.

Counsellors are sometimes too quick to assume that clients need to work on solutions when their primary need may be to "unwind" with a sympathetic listener. Through sessional contracting, counsellors ensure that what is done in the interview is explicit and relevant.

Work Focus If there is no agreement on the purpose of counselling, the work is apt to be directionless. Without an agreed-upon purpose, counsellors tend to make assumptions about the needs and wants of their clients—which are frequently wrong. See Table 3.1 for examples of leads that can be used to initiate contracting.

Every counselling agency has a purpose that defines and limits its service. Specialty agencies, such as employment counselling centres, may focus on career testing and job search skills, while a transition home may provide crisis counselling and shelter. A community centre might provide a broad range of counselling, education, and group support services. The multiple purposes of counselling can include helping clients with problem solving, decision making, and managing feelings. It can also provide support, give information, and foster skill acquisition.

Counsellors define and limit their role based on their position in the agency and their training. An intake worker, for example, may be restricted to initial screening and assessments, while a community outreach worker may specialize in reaching clients who do not voluntarily seek service.

But clients may have specific wants and needs that do not mesh with the mandate of the agency or its workers. Abraham Maslow's (1954) famous hierarchy of needs (Figure 3.2) can be a useful way of understanding client priorities. Maslow suggested that people normally seek to fulfill their basic survival needs before pursuing higher order needs. As one counsellor put it, "You can't counsel a client who hasn't eaten."

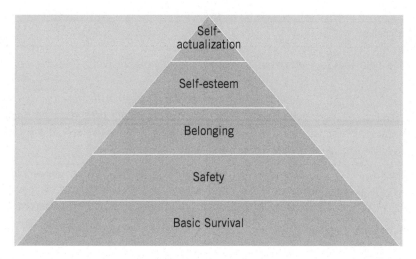

Figure 3.2 Maslow's Hierarchy of Needs

Contracting needs to consider three variables: client need, agency mandate, and counsellor expertise. Contracting works well when the client's needs match the agency's mandate and the counsellor's competence, but when the service the client needs is beyond the mandate of the agency or the competence of the counsellor, referral to another counsellor or agency is appropriate. Interview 3.1 illustrates how contracting is used to engage and map out a plan with the parent of a teen who is abusing drugs.

⟫⟫ INTERVIEW 3.1 | Contracting

This interview is excerpted from the 15-minute mark of the first session with a parent of a teen who is abusing drugs.

Counsellor: Let's take a few minutes to talk about how we might work together. Then we'll both have a shared sense of direction.	**Analysis:** A simple, non-jargonistic statement initiates the contracting process. Contracting is presented as a collaborative process.
Client: Great idea. I was wondering where we go from here.	
Counsellor: Perhaps you have some ideas on what you'd like to achieve. I'd like to hear them. Then, if you wish, I can add some of my own.	**Analysis:** By seeking input, the counsellor communicates respect for the client's needs and signals that the counsellor is not going to take control and make all the decisions. This helps to empower the client and minimize any tendency for the client to become overly dependent.
Client: As I told you, my big goal is to keep my son alive. I don't want to receive a call from the hospital saying he has overdosed.	
Counsellor: Whether your son uses drugs is not under your control. If you wish, we could talk about some of the ways you could deal with his behaviour, such as how to handle it when he breaks curfew or what to do when you think he's high.	**Analysis:** The counsellor gently attempts to contain the work within areas that the client can control, namely her behaviour. The client's reaction confirms understanding and provides agreement on one target for work.
Client: That would be great! Those are two of my biggest problems.	
Counsellor: Obviously, this is a time of stress for you. One of the ways I may be able to work with you is to help you deal with your feelings. Sometimes you might feel overwhelmed by everything that's happening, and I'd be happy just to listen or to help you sort out your feelings.	**Analysis:** Counsellors can suggest additional ideas to help clients make the best use of the services available. In this statement, the counsellor attempts to introduce feelings as one of the areas on which counselling might focus.
Client: You have no idea how tough this has been for me as a single parent. My father was addicted to alcohol, and my son brings back all those memories.	**Analysis:** The client's willingness to begin to share some of her feelings signals to the counsellor that she has accepted the offer to explore feelings.

Counsellor: So, you're no stranger to the pain that is caused by addiction.	***Analysis:*** *Empathy is the preferred response to strong feelings.*
(*Five minutes later.*)	***Analysis:*** *This work sets the stage for feedback. It gives the counsellor a clear picture of the client's preferred style. Knowing this, the counsellor can tailor any feedback to fit the client's expectations.*
Counsellor: What do you need and want from our relationship?	
Client: I want you to be honest with me.	
Counsellor: What do you mean by "be honest?"	***Analysis:*** *The counsellor avoids assumptions of meaning and asks the client to define the word "honest." Words can have very different meanings to individuals. Later, if the counsellor wishes to challenge the client, he or she can use an introductory statement such as the following to remind the client of the contract: "Remember when we agreed that if I had some ideas that were different from yours I should be honest?" Because there has been prior agreement, the client is more likely to support the process and to be open to feedback or challenges.*
Client: Don't try to spare my feelings. If you think I'm wrong, say so. Don't sugarcoat the truth.	
Counsellor: So, if I have some ideas about how you might do things differently or another way of looking at things, I'll just tell you.	
Client: Exactly.	
Counsellor: Can I expect the same from you?	
Client: (*Hesitates.*) I guess so.	
Counsellor: You seem unsure. Would it be tough to confront me if you thought I was wrong?	***Analysis:*** *Some clients have trouble dealing with persons in authority. Even though the client agrees, it is important to pick up on the hesitation. Others are simply shy and have habitual patterns of taking a passive approach to relationship problems. The counselling relationship can be an opportunity to experiment with new ways of relating. When counsellors create conditions of safety for risk-taking, clients can learn skills that they can transfer to other relationships. In this excerpt, the counsellor also finds a way to honour strengths.*
Client: I'm the kind of person who likes to keep those kinds of things inside.	
Counsellor: Sometimes it makes sense to hold back, and that's a strength. Like with your son, you need to pick your battles. Overall, it's better to have choices. In our relationship, I'd like to invite you to risk telling the truth to me.	
(*A few minutes later.*)	
Client: About a year ago, I went to a family counsellor for help. That was a disaster.	
Counsellor: You might be worried that this will turn out the same way.	***Analysis:*** *The purpose of asking clients about experiences is not to engage the client in a gossip session about the mistakes of colleagues. Candid discussions about what was effective and ineffective provide important information on the client's expectations and fears for the current relationship. This gives the counsellor a chance to customize counselling to meet the needs and wants of the client.* *A little shared humour adds warmth to the relationship.*
Client: Yes.	
Counsellor: Now I'm worried too.	
(*Counsellor and client laugh.*) Tell me what went wrong; then, we can talk about how we can avoid the same problems here. Just tell me what happened, but don't tell me who your counsellor was.	
Client: Well, for one thing, he never gave me any information. If I asked for a brochure or something on heroin, he'd always say sure, and then he'd forget.	*Reviewing the client's counselling history helps avoid the mistakes of the past. Of course, this discussion must be conducted in a professional manner that does not involve maligning colleagues.*
Counsellor: I wonder if it might be useful if we kept a few notes.	
Client: Okay.	
(*A few minutes later.*)	***Analysis:*** *Discussion regarding the limits of confidentiality and any other ethical concerns that the client has can now be addressed.*
Counsellor: Do you have any questions?	
Client: Who gets to see my file?	

Reflections:

■ How does the counsellor in this interview promote collaboration?

■ How would you have answered the counsellor's question, "What do you need and want from our relationship"?

Relationships with Youth Establishing a relationship with youth involves all of the same elements of success that are involved in relationship building with adults. With youth, it is important to establish relationships with clear boundaries. It is desirable to have warm and friendly encounters where the conversation feels natural and spontaneous; however, conditions different from friendship are present. For one, there are limits to confidentiality and these should be discussed. Insofar as possible, the youth's right to privacy can be respected, but legal and agency responsibilities need also be considered. In this sense, it is important not to compromise the role of other professionals by withholding information to which they are entitled, or by undermining their authority or competence through collusion with youth. It is also essential for counsellors to avoid assuming a parental role. Unsolicited advice or attempts to control will likely meet resistance.

Many youths who come to counselling have histories of abuse and neglect. Some may still be living in abusive or dangerous situations where fear and caution are constants. Counsellors can expect that these youths will bring these same feelings to the counselling relationship, and initial attempts to connect with youths may be difficult. If they expect that the counsellor cannot be trusted, then whatever defences they use to cope with rejection will come into play. Thus, initiatives to establish counsellor trust, reliability, and predictability are crucial. A trauma-informed approach should be used, which features the core conditions, recognition of the client's strengths, and collaboration as the foundation for relationship engagement and development.

Adolescence is a time when there are enormous physical, emotional, and social developmental challenges. During this period, anxiety, depression, moodiness, and indecision are common experiences. When there are also issues involving substance abuse, poverty, the criminal justice system, mental health, marginalization, abuse, and neglect, the challenges are multiplied and new barriers emerge which may bring youths to counselling. If a warm and trusting counselling relationship can be negotiated, much-needed stability and structure is introduced into their otherwise chaotic lives. Chapter 5 will explore in more detail the skills and attitudes necessary for establishing this relationship.

Engaging with Seniors

Life Stories Counsellors who work with older adults should become familiar with the values and issues that have defined their lives. Just as the rise of terrorism and the events of 9/11 have left an indelible imprint on current generations, seniors were impacted by world events such as the Vietnam War and the cultural changes of the 1960s. As part of relationship building with seniors, counsellors should ask them to share details of significant life events and influences. Some of these will be highly personal such as the birth of their children, death of their spouse, or significant travels. Others will be intimately connected to significant experiences like war (e.g., World War II, the Korean War), the Cuban Missile Crisis, the Beatles, or the fall of the Berlin Wall. One senior related how air raid sirens used in Canada in the 1950s as a drill for nuclear war, left her so terrified that even today, sounds such as the siren from an ambulance rekindle her fear. Hearing such stories will provide counsellors with context for a greater understanding and empathy for lives that have evolved very differently than their own. Here are some sample questions that might be used:

- What were the most significant memories or moments from your life?

- Where have you lived (or travelled) during your life? How did this change or affect you?

- What were your happiest moments (or saddest)? What lasting effect did they have?

- What changes in the world have affected you the most?

- What are the things about your life that are important for me to understand?

Age Differences Significant differences in age between counsellors and their clients is a factor that can be discussed openly. Some seniors may be reluctant to share, fearing that a younger counsellor will not be able to understand their problems. Others may welcome the idea of working with someone younger as a chance to get fresh ideas and a "youth" perspective. A simple lead can be used to initiate the conversation. For example, "How do you think the fact that I am much younger than you might help or hinder our work together"? Counsellor leads can also honour the experience and wisdom of their senior clients. Using a strengths approach, a counsellor might say, "I'm betting that you've learned a lot in your life that you can use to deal with your current problems."

Relationship Dynamics Transference and countertransference are often at play. Some seniors may adopt a parental and protective role toward the counsellor. For their part, counsellors need to be aware of their own feelings (positive or negative) when working with seniors. For example, interaction with an aging client facing declining health might trigger the counsellor's own fears about death and dying. In response, the counsellor might withdraw or become overly protective.

Counsellors need to be ready to examine their own assumptions regarding aging. Seniors are a very diverse group, and there are vast differences among them with respect to health, cognitive ability, capacity for autonomy, lifestyles, and income. Counsellors must be willing to revisit any negative assumptions they might harbour such as the notion that seniors are rigid or not capable of making their own decisions due to cognitive decline. While many seniors have hearing loss, this should not be confused with loss of mental ability.

SUSTAINING THE COUNSELLING RELATIONSHIP

Immediacy

immediacy: A tool for exploring, evaluating, and deepening counselling relationships.

Immediacy is a tool for exploring, evaluating, and deepening counselling relationships (Egan & Schroeder, 2009). All relationships, including counselling relationships, are subject to periodic conflict. This may arise from communication problems, strong emotions, misconceptions, failed expectations, power struggles, value conflict, and many other reasons. Such conflict has the potential to be destructive, but it also presents a great opportunity for further development of the relationship.

The goal of immediacy is to strengthen the counselling relationship by evaluating the general working climate of the counsellor–client relationship. "The relationship is evaluated or reviewed, and relationship strengths and weaknesses are examined by exploring the respective feelings, hopes, and frustrations of the parties involved" (Shebib, 1997, p. 114). All relationships, including the counselling relationship, are occasionally tested with minor or serious personality conflicts and communication breakdowns. Counselling involves risk-taking, which can lead to stress and anxiety. This process of change means that the relationship is not always pleasant. Handled wisely, these conflicts have the potential to deepen rather than impair relationships.

When problems are identified, they can be resolved through discussion, compromise, conflict resolution, or renegotiation of the relationship. Immediacy can address feelings such as anger, resentment, or resistance that are adversely affecting the relationship. Similarly, positive feelings of liking or attraction might also need to be addressed if these feelings are clouding objectivity or progress. The example below illustrates how a counsellor might initiate relationship immediacy:

> **Counsellor:** I want to put aside what we've been talking about and take a look at what's happening between us. I think we have a great rapport, and we both seem relaxed when

we're together, but I believe I've become reluctant to be totally honest. Maybe it's because I don't want the relationship to become unpleasant. If I'm not mistaken, you seem to hold back too.

Immediacy is a powerful tool for preventing communication breakdowns and building trust. By addressing relationship difficulties as they arise, problems that are more serious are prevented from developing because of the buildup of unresolved feelings. This does not imply that every relationship issue must be explored. With immediacy, counsellors can address significant feelings and issues that affect the relationship as they occur, but it is important for counsellors to be sensitive to timing and pacing. Generally, immediacy should *not* be introduced when a session is ending if there is insufficient time to resolve issues. It may also be wise to delay immediacy discussions if clients are unduly stressed with other issues. As well, avoid initiating immediacy discussion too early in the relationship before a base of trust is developed. Counsellors can ensure the appropriateness of using immediacy by asking: Would immediacy be useful for the client? Does the client have the capacity (personal strength and resources) to profit from immediacy at this time? Immediacy is a way to get closer to clients.

A **dependent relationship** arises when clients become overly reliant on their counsellors for decision making. Common indicators that a dependent relationship exists include excessive permission seeking, frequent phone calls or office visits for information, and an inability to make simple decisions or take action without consulting the counsellor. A dependent relationship undermines the principle of self-determination by shifting power away from clients and preventing them from developing independence. A well-timed immediacy discussion can address dependency issues and lead to a new contract that favours client autonomy.

dependent relationship: A counselling relationship in which clients become overly reliant on their counsellors for decision making. Indicators include excessive permission seeking, frequent phone calls or office visits for information, and an inability to make simple decisions or take action without consulting with the counsellor first.

In the following example, the counsellor uses immediacy to identify a sharp change in the mood of the interview:

Counsellor: You seem to have become somewhat quiet. When I ask a question, you give me one- or two-word answers. Usually you're quite expressive. Is something wrong?

Client: Now that you mention it, yes. I'm just not sure how much I'm willing to trust you. At first it was okay, but now you seem intent on pushing me to deal with things I'd rather keep private.

Counsellor: Perhaps I'm moving too fast or bringing up issues we haven't agreed to talk about.

Client: Mostly you don't take no for an answer. When I say I don't want to talk about something, I mean it.

Counsellor: Like earlier today, when I kept coming back to how you felt when you broke up with your wife.

Client: That's a perfect example.

Counsellor: I guess I was pushy. I knew you would rather avoid the topic. At the same time, I could see that there was so much pain involved that I thought it might be useful to talk about your feelings.

Client: You're probably right. I should face it, but I'm afraid.

When responding with immediacy, it is important to use **I-statements** to underscore responsibility and ownership of feelings. In general, the emphasis should be on statements such as "I'm uncomfortable," not "You make me feel uncomfortable."

I-statements: Clear assertions about personal feelings or reactions that do not blame or judge others.

Counsellor: Let's stop for a moment. I'm feeling confused, and I'm not sure where we're headed. What's happening for you?

Client: We do seem to be going in circles. I'm lost too.

Counsellor: All right, let's talk about how we can get back on track.

In Interview 3.2, the counsellor uses immediacy to address concerns that his client has become dependent. Initially, the client is reluctant to discuss this issue, but the counsellor's persistence sets the stage for the client to emerge with some important feedback. Changes in the relationship can then be negotiated. Moreover, the process models communication and relationship problem-solving skills that are transferable to other situations.

Transference and Countertransference

transference: The tendency of clients to communicate with their counsellors in the same way that they communicated to significant people in the past.

Transference is a concept that was first introduced by Freud to describe the tendency of clients to communicate with their counsellors in the same way that they communicated with significant people in the past. Transference can include reactions of both attraction and aversion. When transference is strong, clients have intense feelings and reactions that are unconnected to experiences with their counsellors. Transference is

---

⟫ INTERVIEW 3.2 Immediacy

Counsellor: Do you remember that when we first met, we agreed that from time to time we'd stop to evaluate how things are going? If it's okay with you, I'd like to talk about our relationship—how we're communicating, as well as what's working and what's not working.	**Analysis:** The counsellor signals an interest in looking at the relationship and provides a link to earlier relationship contracting, so the process should not come as a surprise to the client.
Client: I think it's been great. You always seem to know what to say. I don't know if I could cope if it weren't for you.	**Analysis:** Many clients are uncomfortable with immediacy discussions, perhaps because of past failures. The client's praise of the counsellor may be justified, or it may be an attempt to avoid any controversial topics.
Counsellor: Thanks. To be honest, I have mixed reactions to what you're saying. It's nice to be appreciated, but I'm also concerned. I wonder if by relying on me so much, it's becoming harder for you to do it on your own.	**Analysis:** The counsellor self-discloses feelings and concerns. This also models for the client.
Client: I can't do it on my own.	
Counsellor: Okay, so you need help. Being able to seek and accept help is a sign of strength. My concern is that I may be doing things for you that you need to do yourself.	**Analysis:** Without attempting to argue with the client, the counsellor gently persists in encouraging the client to look at the issue.
Client: Now you sound like my father. He's always saying that I should stand on my own two feet more and not rely on him so much, but every time I try to be independent, he interferes.	**Analysis:** The client is able to identify an important parallel to her relationship with her father (transference).
Counsellor: Does that happen between you and me?	
Client: (Hesitates.) A little.	
Counsellor: Can you elaborate?	**Analysis:** The counsellor uses a simple probe to make sure that he understands.
Client: Don't get me wrong, I really want your help, but sometimes it seems like you've already decided what I should do. I figure that you probably know what's best, so I just go along with your plan.	
Counsellor: It sounds as though you have mixed feelings. On the one hand, you value my help, but on the other I also sense some reluctance, maybe a bit of anger at me. I wonder if part of you knows it isn't good for you if you don't have the freedom to make your own decisions.	**Analysis:** An empathic response recognizes the client's ambivalence or mixed feelings.
Client: That's right.	

Counsellor: Can you think of a recent example? I want to make sure I understand.

Client: Earlier today when I mentioned that I wanted to go back to school, you were really supportive, and I appreciated that, but it seemed like you were bulldozing me to take art. I like to paint, but it's a hobby, not something I want to pursue as a career.

Analysis: Asking for an example ensures that both the counsellor and client have the same understanding. As well, the example adds necessary detail and clarity to the issue.

Counsellor: That's a good point. Thanks for the feedback. Let's talk about how we can change our relationship to avoid similar problems in the future. For my part, I'll try to be more sensitive to interfering. What about you?

Analysis: The immediacy discussion deepens the relationship and enables the counsellor and the client to negotiate necessary changes.

Client: I guess I should be more assertive.

Counsellor: Meaning?

Client: If I think you're pushing, I will you tell you.

Counsellor: And, when I sound like your father . . .

Client: Watch out! (*Both laugh.*)

Reflections:

- What might be the outcome if this conversation never happens?
- Suppose the client insists that "all is well." Suggest options for the counsellor.
- The success tip below suggests that relationship patters and problems for both clients and counsellors tend to be duplicated in their relationship with each other. Explore how this might be true in this relationship.

likely present when there are strong feelings of liking or disliking another person based on first impressions (Young, 1998). For example, a client might relate to the authority of a counsellor with the same withdrawal and inner anger that characterized an earlier relationship with parents. In addition, as Egan and Schroeder (2009) note, "Some of the difficulties clients have in their day-to-day relationships are reflected in their relationships to helpers. For instance, when they are compliant with authority figures in their everyday lives, they may be compliant with their helpers. Or they may move to the opposite pole and become aggressive and angry" (pp. 205–206).

SUCCESS TIP

Relationship patterns and problems that clients have in their everyday lives tend to be duplicated in their relationships with counsellors. Similarly, counsellors may bring relationship patterns and problems from their everyday lives to the counselling relationship.

Examples of transference:

- Kevin desperately wants to be liked. He gives his counsellor unsolicited praise and gifts. Increasingly, he begins to act and talk in the same way as his counsellor.
- Claire suffered abuse from her father and both of her brothers. In the first session with a male counsellor, she immediately begins to cry, despite the fact that she felt optimistic and self-confident before she entered his office.
- Amar has a strong need for approval. He withholds information that he thinks might provoke the counsellor's disagreement.

- Jamie, a six-year-old who has been abused, behaves in a sexually provocative way.
- Toby, age 18, has had a very strained relationship with his father. His counsellor notes how easily he becomes angry during the interview at the slightest provocation.

With transference, unresolved issues result in distortions in the way that others are perceived. Consequently, the successful examination and resolution of counsellor–client relationship difficulties helps clients develop communication and problem resolution skills that will be useful to them in their daily lives. It is important that counsellors distinguish client reactions and feelings that arise in the current relationship from those that arise from transference. Counsellors should not be too quick to rationalize clients' feelings and behaviours as transference. Their clients' responses may be valid reactions to what has transpired in the counselling session.

Transference happens to some degree in all relationships, but it is much more likely to occur in relationships in which authority is present. Of significance is the fact that to some extent all counselling relationships involve power and authority. Counsellors such as probation and parole officers may have formal roles of authority. Counsellors may also have power because clients perceive them as having superior or expert knowledge. Some counsellors, such as those in welfare settings, have control over services and benefits that clients are seeking. Clients also may react to other variables, such as age, socioeconomic status, position, gender, marital status, appearance, size, intelligence, and social demeanour.

countertransference: "The positive or negative wishes, fantasies, and feelings that a counsellor unconsciously directs or transfers to a client, stemming from his or her own unresolved conflicts" (Gladding, 2011, p. 42).

Countertransference is defined by Gladding (2011) as "the positive or negative wishes, fantasies, and feelings that a counsellor unconsciously directs or transfers to a client, stemming from his or her own unresolved conflicts" (p. 42). The risks of countertransference underscore the importance of counsellor self-awareness and the responsibility of supervisors to provide opportunities for them to "monitor the tendency to be too helpful, and to deal with feelings of sexual attraction as well as anger, fear, and insecurity" (Young, 1998, p. 169).

Countertransference issues are emotional reactions to clients whereby counsellors come to see clients as projects, sexual objects, friends, or even extensions of themselves (Young, 1998). Below are some signs for counsellors that countertransference is happening or that a risk for countertransference is present:

- having intense feelings (e.g., irritation, anger, boredom, and sexual attraction) for clients you hardly know
- feeling attraction or repulsion
- being reluctant to confront or tending to avoid sensitive issues or feelings

>>> BRAIN BYTE   Transference

Neural networks, formed by learning and experience, are activated by explicit or implicit memory. Explicit memory activates the frontal cortex and the hippocampus to recall experiences, information, or ideas. Implicit memory involves different parts of the brain, the basal ganglia, and the cerebellum. It encompasses motor memory skills such as how to drive a car, as well as associative memory, which includes defences, emotions, and behaviours that emerge from triggers or associations. For example, hearing a particular song may evoke sadness that is connected to a past unpleasant experience. This connection or association is not available to conscious awareness. (Gabbard, 2006). Transference occurs in counselling when implicit memories stimulate emotional and behavioural responses associated with other relationships such as with one's father. A client who feared the harsh discipline of his father and kept his feelings to himself may do the same thing with his counsellor, unaware that there are aspects of his counsellor's appearance or behaviour that remind him of his father and have set off the same guarded response.

Adults who were abused or neglected as children may develop brains that are poorly equipped to form healthy relationships. The amygdala, a part of the brain that is responsible for processing fear, can be damaged by abuse. A person may enter adulthood with excessive fear of taking risks, a necessary part of learning and intimacy. In less than one-half a second and outside of conscious awareness, a damaged amygdala may trigger fear and the "flight or fight" response before the more rational pre-frontal cortex can ascertain that a relationship is potentially safe. In this way, the amygdala erects barriers and generates negative emotions that prevent the formation of meaningful and intimate relationships. (Cozolino, 2010; Cozolino & Santos, 2014). Abused children may feel unworthy of love and "remain in dysfunctional patterns of behavior, hold on to failed strategies, and remain in destructive relationships" (Cozolino & Santos, 2014, p.163). A unique opportunity to alter these patterns is possible if a strong and trusting counselling relationship can be negotiated using a trauma-based approach. Cozolino and Santos (2014) discuss the neuroscience: "A positive emotional connection stimulates rewarding metabolic processes that activate neuroplasticity, and secure relationships protect against stress, which inhibits protein synthesis and other biological processes necessary for brain growth." This is further evidence of the centrality of the counselling relationship as a prerequisite for client growth and change.

- continually running overtime with certain clients and wishing that others would not show up for scheduled appointments
- adopting rescuing behaviour, such as wanting to lend money, adopt abused children, or protect clients
- thinking about client similarities to other people

STUDENT: I think that many counsellors misunderstand self-disclosure. Some of my colleagues make a point of telling their clients about their past, whereas others share little or nothing about their private lives.

TEACHER: Counsellor self-disclosure can be an important part of effective counselling. The problem is knowing what to share, how much to share, and when to share it.

STUDENT: I agree. I think some disclosure conveys that the counsellor is warm and human, and it helps clients overcome the common mistaken belief that they are the only ones with problems.

TEACHER: Self-disclosure models appropriate sharing of feelings and gives clients the courage to open up. Some clients may feel reassured knowing that their counsellors have faced similar problems, but unless it's handled carefully, clients may see their counsellors as needy.

STUDENT: Back to your earlier statement. What do you share? How much? When?

TEACHER: The answers vary depending on the client and the situation. In general, a moderate level of self-disclosure is appropriate (Sheafor & Horejsi, 2008). However, some situations may warrant a great deal of self-disclosure and some none at all. Depending on the situation, too much self-disclosure may be as bad as too little.

STUDENT: As I see it, the most important principle is that self-disclosure should be an option, not a compulsion. Counsellors need to be able to self-disclose, but they also should be able to constrain themselves from always disclosing. If the session is moving smoothly without self-disclosure, then it's probably unnecessary. Self-disclosure must strengthen the relationship or otherwise contribute to the work. The primary goal is to meet the client's needs.

TEACHER: That's right. For me, the most important principle is to avoid letting counsellor self-disclosure shift the focus of the interview from clients to counsellors. That leads to role reversal, with clients counselling counsellors. As I said earlier, too much self-disclosure leads clients to see counsellors as incapable and lose confidence in the process and the capacity of their counsellors to help. The counselling relationship is not mutual, with each person taking turns sharing a problem. What's often forgotten is the fact that self-disclosure involves more than sharing details of your past or your personal problems. Sharing your feelings with clients about the relationship or the work is also self-disclosure and a key element of the skill of immediacy. Rogers (1961 and 1980), a central figure in counselling and the founder of client-centred (person-centred) therapy, emphasized the importance of being transparent and real in the relationship by sharing moment-to-moment feelings that are relevant to the relationship. After all, if we can't be open about our feelings, how can we expect clients to be?

TABLE 3.2 Guidelines for Counsellor Self-Disclosure

- Self-disclosure should not shift the focus from client to counsellor.
- Self-disclosure should be used only to meet the needs of the clients.
- Counsellors need to be able to self-disclose as well as able to not self-disclose.
- Too much can be as inappropriate as too little.
- Revealing current feelings, concerns, and ideas is usually more useful than revealing past history.
- If the work is proceeding smoothly without it, then it probably is not necessary.

- dealing with clients who have problems or personal histories similar to your own
- employing unnecessary or excessive self-disclosure (see Table 3.2)
- feeling reluctant to end the counselling relationship

ENDING THE COUNSELLING RELATIONSHIP

Counselling relationships vary in length from a single interview or a short encounter to many years. Some are superficial, with minimal emotional investment by the participants, while others result in considerable intimacy and emotional involvement. Counsellors need to make intelligent decisions about when to terminate the relationship. Termination of counselling relationships may happen for a number of reasons:

1. The relationship may be ended when the goals of counselling have been reached. Counselling relationships are time-limited, so when clients have developed a sufficient capacity to work on their own, it is time to end the relationship.

2. Counsellors may end the relationship if they do not have the time or competence to fulfill their clients' needs. In such cases, the ending will include referral to other counsellors or agencies.

3. Counsellors may determine that they are unable to work with sufficient objectivity. Here again, referral is the preferred alternative.

4. Situational factors such as illness, moving, or the end of a practicum may necessitate termination or referral.

5. If evidence shows that counselling has not worked and that there is little potential for success, it is time to terminate or refer.

SUCCESS TIP

Clients may decide to opt out of future service and fail to show up for scheduled appointments. However, this does not necessarily mean that the work has been unsuccessful because "as many as two-thirds of dropouts report considerable progress" (Fortune, 2002, p. 459).

The Canadian Counselling and Psychotherapy Association's *Code of Ethics* (2007) offers this guidance on termination:

> Counsellors terminate counselling relationships, with client agreement whenever possible, when it is reasonably clear that: the goals of counselling have been met, the client is no longer benefitting from counselling, when clients do not pay fees charged, when previously disclosed agency or institutional limits do not allow for the provision of further counselling services. However, counsellors make reasonable efforts to facilitate the continuation of counselling services when services are interrupted by such factors as counsellor illness, client or counsellor relocation, client financial difficulties, and so forth. (p. B18)

The end of a counselling relationship may trigger some of the same feelings as those experienced in any relationship breakup. The psychological distress that people feel can now be (partially) explained by functional magnetic resonance imaging (fMRI) of the brain. Imaging shows that parts of the brain that typically fire when people experience physical pain also fire when triggered by cues associated with the ended relationship. In addition, research also found that the reward system of the brain engages in a way similar to the way persons with addictions crave drugs (Greenberg, 2011). This research supports the importance of spending time addressing the loss associated with the end of the counselling relationship.

Endings can evoke painful feelings. All relationships, regardless of their length, have the potential to be intimate. The counselling relationship is not designed to be permanent, but owing to its intimacy the ending of the relationship may trigger powerful feelings and behaviours in both clients and counsellors. For some clients, intense satisfaction and feelings of accomplishment punctuate their success, but others may feel abandoned and deserted. The ending may remind them of the pain and sadness of other endings, so they may need help dealing with their loss and grief (Brill & Levine, 2005; Shebib, 1997; and Shulman, 2009).

The ending of a strong counselling relationship brings attention to the fact that all relationships are temporary. Pending termination may generate a variety of emotions and reactions including anxiety, anger, and denial of the ending. Counsellors need to be sensitive to signals that clients are having trouble with endings. Some clients who have shown progress might regress to previous ways of coping, or they may present new and complex concerns that seem to say, "I'm not ready for this to end." Gladding (2011) emphasizes the importance of mutual agreement to end the relationship, although for a variety of reasons this may not always be possible.

Other clients might express their pain about the ending by expressing unfounded anger and resentment (in effect, avoiding the pain of the ending or denying the importance of the relationship). Still others fail to show up for the final meeting as another way to avoid dealing with the pain of the ending.

Young (1998) suggests that "a helper's feelings of loss at termination may also be due to a reliance on helping relationships to meet needs for intimacy (friendship) as well as a conscious or unconscious sexual attraction" (p. 286). The termination may also remind counsellors of other losses in their lives. When these losses remain unresolved, there is a risk that counsellors may be unable to handle termination with the client. They may feel guilty for leaving the client, and they might delay or avoid termination to elude their own feelings of pain. Counsellors who have invested heavily in the relationship have to deal with their own feelings about the ending. This may result in a variety of denial reactions:

- Denial of the ending by allowing or encouraging clients to remain in counselling longer than necessary. The counselling relationship is not designed to be lifelong, and the counselling contract should set an end point to the relationship. As well, individual interviews should be structured within a time frame. A defined time frame helps to focus and contain the work. Excessively long interviews without time controls can lead to fatigue, unnecessary repetition, and inattention.

- Denial of the ending by making false or unrealistic concessions or promises (e.g., by promising to visit or correspond with clients)

- Denial of feelings by behaving apathetically or avoiding discussion of feelings about the ending

- Denial of feelings by abruptly ending without warning

Dealing with Endings

The ending phase can also be a time of continuing growth for clients, so it is important to involve clients in the process. As Brill and Levine (2005) suggest:

> In termination, as in the other steps of the problem-solving process, the client's participation is of maximum importance. If the helping relationship is at all significant, the way it ends will be important for the client's self-image and capacity for future relationships. The reason for termination should be clear in the minds of both client and worker and, whenever possible, feelings about it expressed and understood. (pp. 140–141)

The ending phase, when handled effectively, offers rich potential for work. Surprisingly, many books on counselling do not examine the therapeutic possibilities of the ending phase. With trust firmly established in the relationship and the urgency of the end approaching, clients may broach significant themes and topics in the ending phase (Shulman, 2009). Shulman (2009) describes the phenomenon of **doorknob communication**, whereby clients bring up important issues at the end of the interview/ relationship when there is little or no time to address them. Clients are typically ambivalent about dealing with the issues, but their need to address them finally overcomes their need to avoid them.

Termination or transfer should not be abrupt but anticipated as an outcome during all phases of counselling. It should be "discussed during the planning and contracting phase of the helping process and the client should be reminded from the beginning that intervention is goal oriented and time limited" (Sheafor & Horejsi, 2008, p. 479).

Generally, termination of the counselling relationship should focus on the following:

- review of the extent to which work contract goals have been realized
- procedures for further contact or services from the agency, if needed
- referral to other services, if necessary
- relationship closure, including discussion of feelings regarding the ending—for example, unresolved feelings and regrets—along with unfinished business
- next steps

The ending might also include some culturally appropriate ritual such as the offering of a small gift, but generally, there is no expectation of counsellor reciprocity. One exception might be the end of a long relationship with a youth, in which case the worker might present a token of remembrance.

It is appropriate for counsellors to express their feelings about the termination of the relationship. This models appropriate sharing for clients, and it stimulates them to risk sharing their reactions and feelings. Of course, this discussion requires counsellors to be open to strong feelings that clients may express, such as sadness and anger. Shulman (2009) underscores the importance of counsellors sharing their own feelings, but he acknowledges that this is a difficult skill to develop. In part, this difficulty arises from the fact that counsellors may be struggling with their own sense of loss as they prepare to end the relationship with a valued client. Continued self-examination can help counsellors develop self-awareness about their own behaviours and feelings regarding endings and separations.

doorknob communication: A phenomenon described wherein clients bring up important issues at the end of the interview/relationship when there is little or no time to address them.

Interview 3.3 illustrates how the ending process can be used to address feelings. The client is a young adolescent about to be discharged from a residential treatment centre. For the last six weeks, he and his counsellor have been actively planning for his return home. The client has been looking forward to more freedom and release from the rules and restrictions of the centre. As part of his pre-release planning, he has spent two weekends with his family.

⟫⟫ INTERVIEW 3.3 | Endings

In this interview, the client, a 16-year-old youth, is about to be released from a treatment centre ending a six-month relationship with the counsellor. During his time at the centre, the youth has grown very close to his counsellor.

Client: How long are we going to be here? I have things I need to do.

Counsellor: If I'm not mistaken, you look a little glum today.

Analysis: The counsellor risks empathy by picking up on nonverbal cues from the client. The counsellor suspects that the client's overt anger may be connected to the ending of the relationship and the more important feeling is sadness, not anger.

Client: Can't you ever let anything pass? Why don't you just get off my back?

Counsellor: Tomorrow you'll be leaving the centre to return home. Maybe we could talk about that. I'm wondering how you feel about it. I wouldn't be surprised if you had mixed feelings of being happy to be leaving but also sad to be leaving your friends here.

Client: It's no big deal, but why should you care?

Analysis: The client's first reaction is to deny his painful feelings about the ending by expressing more anger. The counsellor is careful not to get hooked. The counsellor opts to keep the conversation active in the feeling domain.

Counsellor: I feel sad knowing you're leaving. We've become very close, and I'll miss our time together.

Client: It's been all right. I guess you're okay.

Analysis: By sharing her own feelings, the counsellor communicates her willingness to deal with emotions. Her disclosure underscores that the relationship had meaning. This acts as a model for the client. Of course, any feelings the counsellor shares must be genuine.

Counsellor: Thanks, and you're okay with me too. (*Ten seconds of silence.*) How do you feel about us not seeing each other anymore?

Client: I can handle it.

Counsellor: I know you can. You've really shown a lot of courage dealing your problems.

Analysis: Although his anger softens, he is still reluctant to acknowledge his feelings. The counsellor persists.

Client: I wish it wasn't happening. I don't know if I'm ready to go.

Counsellor: It's very scary thinking about leaving.

Analysis: Although the client has trouble labelling his feelings, he begins to open up. The counsellor uses empathy to acknowledge the feelings suggested by the client's remark.

Client: I want to go home, but my mother and I always seem to end up fighting. You and I can talk and not fight. Why can't it be that way with my mother?

Counsellor: Maybe you have more control than you think. What do you do differently with me than with your mother?

Analysis: The client risks talking about his feelings about going home. The counsellor tries to get the client to accept credit for success in the counselling relationship. She challenges him to consider how he can transfer some of his behaviour from the client–counsellor relationship to his relationship with his mother.

Reflections:

- What might happen if this client is not able to resolve his feelings regarding leaving the centre and the end of his close relationship with the counsellor?
- Explore the importance of counsellor self-disclosure in this encounter.
- What important principles regarding endings are evident in this excerpt?

SUMMARY

- Developing and sustaining an effective counselling relationship is widely accepted as critical to success in counselling.

- Throughout all phases, the core conditions of counsellor warmth, empathy, and genuineness are essential.

- Counselling contracts are important tools for defining roles, purpose, and for anticipating issues that might arise during the life of the counselling relationship.

- Over the four phases of counselling—preliminary, beginning, action, and ending— the counselling relationship needs to be developed, sustained, and then ended. Understanding the concepts of transference and countertransference, the intelligent use of counsellor self-disclosure, and immediacy for dealing with relationship issues is crucial for maintaining the working climate of the relationship.

- The inevitable ending of the counselling relationship may trigger powerful feelings in both clients and counsellors. The ending phase, when handled effectively, offers rich potential for work.

EXERCISES

Self-Awareness

1. What were (or are) the attributes of your most positive relationship with another person? The most negative? How can you use this information to be a more effective counsellor?

2. Pay attention to the people you see and meet over the next week. Who evokes strong emotional reactions? Who seems most similar to your parents or other authority figures? Now examine your feelings and try to identify transference reactions—feelings that you carry over from prior relationships and that are not based on objective reactions to the current relationship.

3. Most of us tend to repeat established patterns when we begin new relationships. Seek feedback from others who know you and explore questions such as the following:
   - What first impressions are you likely to leave with others?
   - How do their perceptions compare with your intentions or inner feelings?

   Now consider the following questions:
   - What are your typical feelings, thoughts, and behaviours as you begin new relationships?
   - How are beginnings the same or different for you when you are relating to different individuals or groups (e.g., clients, colleagues, or supervisors)?
   - What works for you?
   - What doesn't?

4. Examine your own needs with respect to keeping the counselling relationship warm and pleasant. How far would you go to ensure this as an outcome? Under what conditions might you need to sacrifice pleasantness?

5. This exercise is designed to expand your self-awareness regarding issues that might affect your counselling relationships. Complete each sentence quickly, without attempting to edit your thoughts.
   - The one thing I have to have from other people is . . .
   - What's missing in my personal life is . . .
   - Something that people do that bothers me is . . .
   - The one type of person I'd hate to work with is . . .
   - Relationships would be better if . . .
   - What I like most about people is . . .
   - What I dislike most about people is . . .

6. Think about significant relationships in your life that have ended because of separation, death, or other reasons. How did you respond emotionally and behaviourally to these endings? In retrospect, are there things you wish you had said or not said? What remains unresolved in these relationships? (Suggestion: If this exercise evokes strong emotions, you may find it useful to debrief with a friend or colleague.)

7. In your answer to the previous question, what behavioural patterns are evident? What are the implications of your insights for your work as a counsellor?

8. Rate the extent to which you think it would be appropriate for you to disclose the information listed below. Use the following scale:

   5 = always appropriate

   4 = usually appropriate

   3 = sometimes appropriate

   2 = usually not appropriate

   1 = never appropriate

Be prepared to defend your answers with examples.

_____ Details of your education and training

_____ Your philosophy of counselling

_____ Information about your age, marital status, and number of children

_____ Your sexual orientation

_____ Particulars about your life, such as personal problems that you have faced

_____ Details about your everyday life, such as your hobbies, reading preferences, and vacation plans

_____ Intimate details about your personal life, such as marital problems and recovery from addictions

_____ Feelings such as anger, boredom, confusion, or sexual attraction that are influencing the interview

To what extent were your answers influenced by your comfort level with each of the categories?

9. Evaluate your general comfort with self-disclosure and intimacy. What areas of your life are you reluctant or unwilling to talk about? To what extent would your friends and colleagues describe you as open or closed? Do you tend to be guarded about sharing information, or do you generally disclose a great deal to others? How does your comfort with disclosure vary depending on whom you are talking with (e.g., family, friends, authority figures, clients, colleagues, and strangers)? What are the implications of your answers for your work as a counsellor?

10. Imagine you are a client with little knowledge of counselling going for your first interview. Assume you are seeking help managing depression. What are some of the things you would want to know about the counselling process and your pending relationship with the counsellor?

Skill Practice

1. Interview friends and colleagues on the topics of warmth, empathy, and genuineness. Ask them to describe how they know when someone exhibits these inner qualities.

2. Talk to people who are happy in their work. Ask them to describe how they sustain their energy and enthusiasm.

3. Orchestrate an immediacy encounter. Contract with a colleague to spend one hour evaluating and strengthening your relationship. Use the following open-ended statements to develop themes for your discussion, but be sure to explore your ideas and responses:

   • The thing I value most in this relationship is . . .

   • The one thing that is missing in our relationship is . . .

   • When I first met you, my reaction was . . .

   • You are most like . . .

   • When I think about sharing feelings with you . . .

   • For us to become closer, I would have to . . .

   • What I want most from you is . . .

   • When I think of the future of our relationship, I . . .

Periodically, share how you are feeling using a statement such as "Right now I'm feeling . . ." You are free to add other significant themes in your relationship that are not suggested in the above list. When you are finished, discuss what changes you would like to make in your relationship.

4. On the basis of your observations and insights from the previous question, begin the process of developing a range of different skills and strategies for beginning relationships. This will help you avoid becoming locked into established patterns. Define personal goals for development in relation to how you handle beginnings. As part of this, detail three different beginning styles you wish to add to your skill repertoire. Describe when and how you will experiment with these three approaches. What problems do you anticipate might interfere with achievement of these goals?

5. Simulate a relationship contracting session with a colleague in the role of client. Choose your own issue and setting.

6. Imagine you are interviewing a client who believes "counselling is a waste of time." Suggest several approaches.

Concepts

1. Under what conditions do you think it would be wise for a counsellor to avoid self-disclosure?

2. Evaluate the potential appropriateness of each of the following counsellor self-disclosures (the counsellor is speaking to a client):

   a. Your situation reminds me of my own problems. Maybe we can pool our energies and find a solution that works for both of us.

   b. I'm sorry to say that it's none of your business whether I have children.

   c. When my husband abused me for the first time, I knew the marriage was over and I left.

   d. (*In an addictions treatment centre, meeting a client for the first time*) Hi, I'm John, and I'm a recovering alcoholic, so I know what you're going through.

   e. I'm feeling confused. I think we need to stop for a minute and decide where we're going.

   f. Your problems are really getting to me. They remind me so much of my own struggles. They bring back all my pain.

   g. You have the most beautiful eyes.

   h. I like what you're wearing today. It's really sexy.

   i. Generally, I like to try to establish open communication in my relationships, so I push myself to be open with my feelings even when it's difficult.

   j. Your attitude really makes me want to just give up on you.

   k. This has been a bad day for me. There have been some cutbacks at the agency, and I'm worried about losing my job, so if I seem a little preoccupied today I hope you'll understand.

   l. What a weekend! We partied all night. I could hardly make it to work today.

3. Describe how counsellor self-disclosure might be appropriate in response to each of the following client statements or questions. Suggest a response.

   a. Have you ever felt so angry that you wanted to kill someone?

   b. My mother never gives me the support I need.

   c. I began using drugs when I was 11.

   d. Are you gay?

   e. I'm terrified about going back to school. I don't think I can handle it. It's been so many years since I wrote an essay or read a book.

   f. My teenage son is driving me crazy.

   g. I think this counselling session is a waste of time.

   h. I really like you.

   i. I don't think anyone has ever been as depressed as I am.

4. What are the issues (pros and cons) involved in counselling friends?

5. What themes might emerge as important and unique when developing counselling relationships in different fields of practice or settings, such as working with seniors, group homes for youth, foster homes, addictions settings, immigrant clients, correctional facilities, rural settings, hospitals and hospice settings, work in the LGBTQ (lesbian, gay, bisexual, transgender, questioning) community?

6. Explore how a counsellor's age might be a factor when working with youth, such as counsellors who are very young and those who are much older.

WEBLINKS

An overview of the basics of Person-Centered Therapy "The Foundation of Person-Centered Therapy" by Jerold D. Bozarth

www.personcentered.com/therapist.html

This site contains links to major personality theorists, including Carl Rogers

www.ship.edu/~cgboeree/perscontents.html

This *Counselling Today* article examines technology and the counselling relationship

http://ct.counseling.org/2011/10/finding-technologys-role-in-the-counseling-relationship

This site contains an article exploring juvenile offenders' perception of the counselling relationship

www.jtpcrim.org/August_2011/Juvenile-Offenders-Perceptions-John-Ryals.pdf

This site contains YouTube video links where clients discuss their experiences with counselling

www.youtube.com/ – search for Experiences of Counselling Part 2: Developing the Counselling Relationship

Chapter 4

Listening & Responding: The Basis for Understanding

LEARNING OBJECTIVES

- Define the components of listening for understanding.

- Identify and describe strategies for overcoming listening barriers.

- Explain the importance of active listening.

- Describe nonverbal communication.

- List and explain the multiple meanings of silence in counselling.

- Define and demonstrate paraphrasing skills.

- Define and demonstrate summarizing skills.

LISTENING FOR UNDERSTANDING

> *When you talk, you are only repeating what you already*
> *know, but if you listen you may learn something new*
>
> (Dalai Lama)

Proficient counsellors are dynamic and responsive listeners. They are persistent and curious learners committed to understanding. They strive to hear, not just the words of their clients, but also the nonverbal channel of information where variables such as voice tone, posture, and gestures act to support, repeat, enhance, or contradict verbal messages.

Effective listening, not only includes silence, but also involves the components of hearing, observing, interpreting, and responding through a complex process that requires sensory, mental, and behavioural competence. As a mental process, listening involves separating relevant information from irrelevant information, assigning meaning to words and experiences, and remembering and linking related data. High-level listening regards emotional understanding as a prerequisite for fully comprehending the words and content of what the speaker has said. Put simply, listening is making sense of what has been heard from the perspective of the other person.

Counsellors may use questions to obtain clarification, definitions, and examples. They use silence to reflect and communicate respect for the risks that clients have taken to share their stories. Summarizing, paraphrasing, and empathy are, in part, listening checks to ensure the accuracy of their observations and conclusions.

Effective listening as a counsellor requires management of or disengagement from barriers such as personal problems, boredom, lack of interest, or competing demands to fully focus—both psychologically and physically—on the message. Counsellors need to be self-aware and constantly on the alert to ensure that their own perspective does not detract from or contaminate their capacity to understand the words and feelings of their clients. The listening process is outlined in Figure 4.1. Since the challenge to effectively listen is demanding and potentially exhausting, it is not surprising that failure to listen effectively is a primary reason for relationship breakdown.

The Power of Listening

Listening is a cornerstone of counselling and is essential to understanding and relationship development. Often clients come to counselling with considerable experience of not being heard. They may have turned to family and friends for help but found that their concerns were discounted or were met with simplistic advice by people who were so anxious to help that they failed to listen with attention. In contrast, effective counsellors and interviewers have a cultivated ability to listen.

As a fundamental building block for the counselling relationship, listening communicates to clients that their ideas and feelings are important. Our natural inclination is to interpret meaning to words and behaviour based on our own experiences. This can easily lead to assumptions that are very different from those intended or experienced by others. Listening educates counsellors about the uniqueness of their clients, thus, minimizing any tendency to make erroneous assumptions. Moreover, listening encourages clients to tell their stories and disclose their feelings. In the process, they may gain enormous therapeutic value from releasing pent-up emotions. Also, when counsellors listen to clients, clients become better able to listen to themselves. In general, systematic

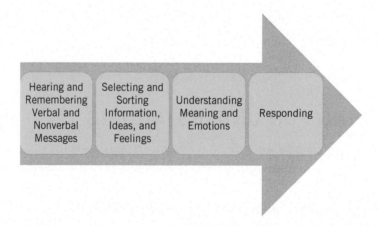

Figure 4.1 The Listening Process

listening, punctuated with appropriate probes, clarification responses, and summaries, helps clients organize confusing and contradictory thoughts.

Listening is an act of acceptance and caring that says, "Your feelings are precious and unique. I won't insult you by assuming that I know what you're going to say before you say it. I won't judge or ridicule what you say. I won't try to change you to fit my idea of what you should be." Listening is an active attempt to understand our clients' perceptions and feelings, which may be different from our own.

Ironically, while listening requires counsellors to be silent, remaining silent does not necessarily mean that one is listening. A silent person may hear the words and even be able to repeat verbatim what has been said, but a tape recorder or a clever parrot can do the same thing. Good listening is an active process that requires hearing the content, emotional tone, and context of what is being said while controlling listening obstacles and using skills such as summarizing, paraphrasing, and empathy to confirm understanding. Without attention and self-control, learning obstacles can contaminate messages with unintended distortion, selective attention, and interpretation. Thus, good listening requires that we open ourselves up to learning.

Listening is not a passive act—effective listeners are busy with the task of trying to comprehend what is happening for their clients. Sometimes counsellors are patiently quiet as they respectfully yield the right to speak to their clients. At other times, they are vocal, with questions and directives for more detail, examples, or clarification. At all times, they should carefully observe and try to understand nonverbal behaviour. Active listening, a collection of skills discussed in this and subsequent chapters, is the way that counsellors show their clients that they are listening. This is possible because they are, in fact, mentally and physically committed to the task of listening. With so much at stake and so much to do, listening is hard work. It requires counsellors to focus all their intellectual and physical attention on clients so that clients have the counsellors' unwavering commitment. Listening is the client's reward for talking.

SUCCESS TIP

To be heard and deeply understood by another person is a rare and profoundly empowering experience. Consequently, all the help that some clients need is the opportunity to share their problems with a patient, nonjudgmental listener who doesn't burden them with advice.

LISTENING BARRIERS

Communication is a process involving a sender and a receiver (for two-person communication). In its purest form, the communication loop begins when one-person frames and sends a message using verbal or nonverbal channels (frequently both); the receiver must hear and interpret the message, then provide feedback that confirms understanding.

▶▶▶ BRAIN BYTE   Listening

Barth (2011) reported on a study by Princeton neuroscientist Lauren Silbert who demonstrated that fMRI scans of good listeners showed their brain activity paralleled that of those to whom they were listening. In addition, the scans showed that key brain areas lit up before words were spoken, suggesting anticipation of what was about to be said. On the one hand, this might support the listening process and add to a person's capacity to be empathic. On the other hand, inaccurate anticipation has pitfalls and can clearly lead to misunderstanding and communication breakdown. To prevent this miscommunication, counsellors must remain very attentive to ensure that their clients' messages are in sync with any messages or feelings they anticipated.

TABLE 4.1 Common Listening Barriers

Sending Messages	Receiving Messages
• Not having the words to express feelings and ideas.	• Assumptions, bias, and judgment
• Lack of insight or awareness	• Errors interpreting messages
• Contradictory verbal and nonverbal messages	• Selective attention
• Bias	• Hearing words, but not emotions
• Unresolved trust issues	• Emotional reaction
• Perspective (cultural/worldview)	• Failure to attend to nonverbal channels
• Unwillingness to communicate (self-censorship)	• Unwilling to hear content or feelings
• Information gaps/incomplete communication	• Distractions such as fatigue, boredom, and preoccupation with personal issues
• Resistance	• Planning what to say instead of listening
	• Interrupting, rushing, or finishing the speaker's sentences
	• Resistance

In counselling, this feedback, usually in the form of summaries, paraphrases, or empathic responses, acts as a powerful incentive for the client to continue. Questions (as discussed in Chapter 5) are also an important tool in communication. They provide a way to get missing information, examples, and definition.

Typically, there are a huge number of barriers to listening (see Table 4.1). Some originate with the sender, others with the receiver. These can interfere with effective communication such that high-level communication is often the exception, not the rule.

Closed-minded listeners respect only those who agree with them. Since they already have the "right" answers, there is neither need to consider new thoughts and ideas, nor is there any reason to seek additional information. In contrast, open-minded listeners are willing to explore new ideas and are secure enough to hear different opinions without distortion.

Overcoming Listening Barriers

Be Patient   To make themselves understood, people need to be able to frame their ideas. Clients who lack the ability to express themselves, perhaps because they have a limited vocabulary or capacity to articulate in precise terms, use words that are vague, ambiguous, or contradictory. Others may not have sufficient awareness or insight to describe their feelings. In such circumstances, counsellors can become impatient, and this becomes an obstacle to listening. They may try to hurry the process by finishing sentences for clients who are struggling to express themselves. Or they can become lazy and assign their own meanings to words and phrases.

Active listening helps to minimize the risks of misinterpretation. Summaries and paraphrases help confirm understanding, and they provide a reflective mirror for clients to hear their own ideas from a different but undistorted perspective. Targeted and systematic questioning encourages exploration and specificity, and it helps clients organize their thinking and engage in problem solving.

》》BRAIN BYTE   The Auditory Alarm System

Ten times faster than a visual image or a thought can be processed, the auditory circuits of the brain respond to sound. (Horowitz, 2012). Neuroscientist Seth Horowitz (2012) depicts this auditory circuit as an alarm system in a constant state of readiness to respond to sounds that signal danger or attraction. Most sounds are ignored as irrelevant, while others, like a ringing phone, demand our immediate attention. But Horowitz warns of the dangers in a new digital world, where effective listening becomes difficult as our brains are being seduced by constant noise. As a safeguard, counsellors need to soundproof their sessions.

Focus on Trust   Client messages can be incomplete or missing information because of trust issues, particularly in the beginning phase of the counselling relationship when the client may be reluctant to share. This is understandable since the counselling relationship has yet to be tested. Consequently, the client may hold back information or feelings that are ultimately vital for understanding and instead present "safe" issues to test the relationship or only hint at concerns that are more important. Ideally, as counselling progresses, clients learn that they can depend on their counsellors to respond with respect and understanding. Unfortunately, in some cases, they may learn that their counsellor cannot be trusted with feelings.

Control Distractions and Stay Focused   Once messages are sent, they must be received and interpreted accurately—hence the importance of a counselling environment that is free from distraction and interruption. Counsellors should never discontinue an interview to answer the phone since that may breach confidentiality, impede relationship rapport, and stop the flow of information. Similarly, pagers, fax machines, cell phones, and even an unanswered ringing phone can destroy the ambience of a meeting. Ideally, all such equipment should be turned off.

Good listening is difficult work that requires effort to stay focused. Since we can think many times faster than others can talk, it's easy to allow our thoughts to wander. The trick is to keep our minds busy with listening. Active involvement in listening, through summarizing, paraphrasing, and asking questions, helps counsellors stay alert and focused. Mental involvement helps counsellors concentrate on and understand what's being said. For example, as they listen, they can ask themselves, "What does the client mean by that? What are the key points in that explanation?" However, counsellors should avoid trying to figure out what clients are going to say next since this will only divert their attention from listening.

Internal noise can also interfere with listening. Counsellors might be preoccupied with their own needs or ideas. They could be looking forward to their vacation and imagining their break. They may be under personal stress, suffering from fatigue or thinking about other clients. A tired counsellor might deliberately neglect to explore or define important ideas.

Stop Assuming   If counsellors believe that they already know what others are going to say and are not open to new information, then listening is not possible. Apparent patient attention and silence could give the illusion of listening, but assumptions and preconceptions quickly become obvious to astute clients. Typically, clients are guarded and defensive with people who have opinions different from their own. In the following example, a high school student has just told her counsellor that she has been offered a scholarship at a prestigious university.

> **Student:** It's one of the finest universities in the area. It is an honour to have been chosen from all the applicants. My father, who never had a chance to go to university, is ecstatic.
>
> **Counsellor (Choice 1):** Wow! That is terrific. You must be so proud of yourself. This is really an outstanding opportunity.
>
> **Counsellor (Choice 2):** How do you feel about it?

The counsellor in Choice 1 in this example assumes feelings and meaning. As a result, further exploration is discouraged or cut off. Choice 2 is a listening response that encourages more information. It allows for the possibility that the client might say, "I'm depressed about it. I've been going to school for 12 years, and I really wanted to take a year off." Choice 2 illustrates a basic principle of effective listening: Good listeners are open to learning.

Personal Reactions   What clients say and how they say it may arouse a counsellor's tension and anxiety. Emotions in the client can trigger emotions in the counsellor, which, if unchecked, can lessen the counsellor's capacity to listen. For example, an angry client might stimulate fear in a counsellor, who, preoccupied with fear or insecurity, then might act defensively. A depressed client might have a contagious effect and cause a counsellor to become similarly despondent. Certain words or messages might act as emotional triggers for counsellors and lead to faulty listening and understanding.

Many beginning counsellors react strongly to clients who have been abusive, and they erect listening barriers. They get so trapped in their own need to condemn the abhorrent behaviour that they have no room left to become aware of their clients' frames of reference. Consequently, they fail to establish any base for understanding and any credibility to promote change. Entering into the private world of clients whose behaviour and attitudes differ sharply from one's own requires emotional maturity, skill, and, often, abundant courage. Such capacities distinguish and define competent counsellors.

Sometimes counsellors become bored (e.g., when dealing with clients who speak in a monotone or clients who are repetitious and long-winded), even to the point of falling asleep during the interview. To stay alert during an interview, counsellors must arrive alert. They should get enough sleep and exercise and avoid heavy lunches that might lead to drowsiness. Short breaks to take a walk, stretch, or clear the mind are important ways of sustaining energy.

When clients share difficult feelings and topics, some counsellors handle their own discomfort by becoming inappropriately quiet or silent, becoming excessively talkative, changing the subject, or offering premature advice or reassurance. Such responses may communicate that the counsellor does not understand or is not listening or, in the case of inappropriate silence, that the counsellor does not care. Counsellors need to become confident in their skills and abilities so that they can tolerate clients' feelings, reactions, and even verbal assaults with a minimum of defensive reactions, which obscure listening and understanding.

Listening Does Not Mean Agreeing   A common misconception occurs when people confuse listening with agreeing. One new counsellor remarked, "If I listen to someone who abuses children, am I not condoning it?" Another person remarks, "I told him what I want. Why doesn't he listen to me?" In fact, the other person may have listened and heard, but has chosen not to comply. In this example, failure to comply is interpreted as evidence that the other person isn't listening. This is a common error in thinking.

Exemplary counsellors are vigilant when they are dealing with clients who test their values and beliefs. They discipline themselves by taking extra precautions to ensure they are listening accurately. They also try to become alert to any internal noise that might impair their capacity to hear. They know they are vulnerable, and they take preventive measures.

Self-Awareness   Since everyone's frame of reference is different, we can never perfectly understand how other people are experiencing their world. Our understanding is always clouded to some extent by the meanings we assign to events and by our own thoughts and feelings. Counsellors may have unrecognized or unresolved problems

---

⟫⟫ BRAIN BYTE   The Right Ear Advantage

Research has shown that when people feel overloaded, they hear better with their right ear. This is because the right ear connects to the left-brain hemisphere which plays a dominant role in processing language. Tilting your head to allow more sound to the right ear may improve listening and memory from 8 percent to as much as 40 percent in some individuals. (Starr, 2017)

parallel to those of their clients. For example, one counsellor experienced unusual discomfort when trying to work with a client who was dealing with an unwanted pregnancy. Ten years before, the counsellor had placed her own child up for adoption, but she had never addressed the emotions she felt over the decision. Whenever her client focused on her options, the counsellor's own feelings made it tough for her to separate her feelings from those of the client.

Table 4.2 summarizes strategies for overcoming common listening problems. These strategies are presented as ideas rather than as recipes for responding. Each interview situation requires individualized and creative responses.

TABLE 4.2 Overcoming Listening Barriers

Problem	Counsellor Choices
The client has problems with language (e.g., misleading word choice and difficulty verbalizing ideas).	Ask questions to clarify meaning. Pay careful attention to nonverbal communication for clues to meaning.
Messages are incomplete, ambiguous, or unclear.	Probe for detail and examples. Paraphrase to confirm understanding. Ask for definition.
Relationship problems/trust issues are resulting in client censorship of feelings and ideas.	Show empathy. Have a candid discussion about the trust or relationship issues. Go at a slower pace and reduce questions. Communicate openness through nondefensive responses.
There is outside interference (e.g., noise and lack of privacy).	Hold phone calls and move interviews to a private setting.
There is internal interference (e.g., counsellor fatigue, difficulty concentrating, boredom, and hearing impairment).	Start a personal wellness plan. Improve time management skills. Defer the interview. Use self-discipline to increase concentration (e.g., mentally summarize key details). Summarize, paraphrase, and empathize.
The counsellor has a loss of objectivity when dealing with ideas that are contrary to his or her values.	Use supervision or consultation to address personal issues that cloud objectivity. Discipline yourself to explore different ideas.
There are cultural barriers between counsellor and client.	Enlist the client's help to understand cultural values and issues; then adapt the interview style to fit. Use translators or refer the client to a counsellor of the same culture. Develop culture-specific knowledge.
Content is overwhelming for the counsellor (e.g., when the client rambles or is long-winded).	Summarize to identify themes and priorities. Selectively interrupt to control the flow of the interview.
The client is inappropriately silent.	Attempt to understand the meaning of the silence; then respond appropriately.
The client has speech problems (e.g., mumbling, stuttering, and whispering).	Remember that problems may decrease as the counsellor becomes more familiar with the client's style. Ask the client to speak up.

ACTIVE LISTENING

Understanding is always tentative—hence the importance of allowing clients to confirm or correct our understanding. Active listening describes a cluster of skills used to increase the accuracy of meaning. Attending, being silent, summarizing, paraphrasing, questioning, and empathizing are the essential skills of active listening (see Figure 4.2). They breathe life into listening so that it becomes a continuous process of paying attention, hearing, exploring, and deepening. Active listening involves hearing what is said as well as what is left unsaid. Counsellors need to use both their eyes and ears to ascertain meaning. Careful attention to such cues as word choice, voice tone, posture, and verbal hesitations is necessary to discover confirming or conflicting messages in the verbal and nonverbal messages. Subtle changes in voice tone or sudden shifts in the topic may signal important areas for the counsellor to explore. In one case, a 28-year-old woman who was describing her career goals happened to mention her sister. As she did so, the counsellor noticed that she avoided eye contact and her voice dipped slightly. He asked how she felt about her sister. The woman began crying as she related how her sister had always been the favoured one in the family and how she had felt rejected by her mother. Subsequently, this relationship became a central issue during counselling, and the client developed insight into how she was using her career as a desperate attempt to gain her mother's acceptance.

Active listening skills defuse critical incidents. The FBI, for example, has recognized active listening skills as essential competencies for resolving crises, including hostage-taking incidents, and it has replaced using force with active listening as the preferred strategy (Van Hasselt et al., 2006; Royce, 2005). Research has shown that active listening, particularly the skills of paraphrasing, empathizing, and open-ended questioning, helps subjects (i.e., hostage takers) release frustration, despair, anger, and other powerful feelings, with the result that they return to a more normal level of arousal and rational thinking. One reason active listening is so effective is because it does not threaten people with an overt attempt to change them. Active listening builds rapport because it shows that the listener is nonjudgmental and is interested in understanding. Individuals in

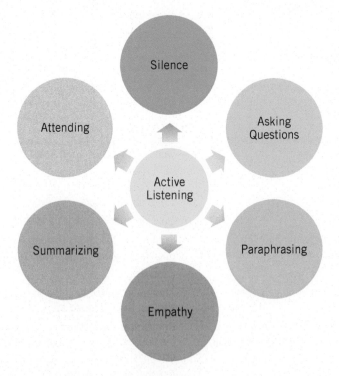

Figure 4.2 The Skills of Active Listening

crisis may erect heavy psychological defences, but "because active listening poses no threat to an individual's self-image, it can help a subject become less defensive" (Noesner & Webster, 1997, p. 16). Active listening is a powerful tool for developing a relationship, which becomes a basis for negotiation.

Attending, nonverbal communication, using silence, paraphrasing, and summarizing will be explored in the following sections. Subsequent chapters will address the skills of questioning and empathy.

ATTENDING

Attending is a term used to describe the way that counsellors communicate to their clients that they are ready, willing, and able to listen. When coupled with understanding and appropriate verbal responses, attending promotes exploration. As a basic active listening skill, attending conveys physical and psychological commitment and openness to the helping interview. Attending says to clients, "I'm here for you. You have my undivided attention. I'm not afraid of your feelings and what you have to say."

Certain core attending skills are universally applicable, and counsellors can use them with confidence. First, counsellors need to ensure that their feelings, attitudes, and commitment to clients are genuine. If a counsellor has negative feelings about a particular client, then referral to another counsellor may be warranted. On the other hand, if such negative feelings permeate a counsellor's attitude toward many clients, then additional remedies may be necessary, such as personal counselling, assistance to deal with burnout, consultation and supervision to manage feelings, or a career change. Sometimes a counsellor's personal reactions can be a valuable clue regarding how a particular client impacts other people. The key consideration here is whether the counsellor's feelings are unique to him or her, or whether they are indicative of a client's general demeanor.

Second, providing a safe and private space is an incentive for clients to open up. This includes efforts by counsellors to control distracting noise and curb their own internal distractions. Self-discipline to suspend hasty assumptions and judgments is also essential. Counsellors need to avoid reacting with verbal or nonverbal messages that express impatience, disagreement, or judgment. As noted earlier in this chapter, this may be difficult when clients present ideas that are offensive or conflict with the counsellor's values and beliefs.

Third, counsellors can show that they are attending by being on time for the interview, remembering important details, and following through with agreed-on plans. A certain physical and verbal presence conveys commitment. Verbal and nonverbal behaviours such as head nods and encouraging probes convey interest. Counsellors need to bring warmth to the interview, which is communicated through appropriate smiling, changes in voice tone, and expressions of caring and support. An unemployed client who reports with glee to his counsellor that he has found work has a right to expect more than a monotone, "That's great."

There may be cultural and individual differences that require adapting how you attend to clients. For example, some clients are not comfortable with sustained eye contact, and others may be suspicious of warmth and humour. This reality underscores the importance of continual work to develop cultural understanding and competence. As always, it is important to remember that individuals vary in the extent they subscribe to the values of their culture of origin.

There is general agreement that the following behaviours convey appropriate attending:

- keeping an open posture (i.e., turning towards the client, arms and legs uncrossed)
- maintaining eye contact

attending: A term used to describe the way that counsellors communicate to their clients that they are ready, willing, and able to listen. Verbal, nonverbal, and attitudinal cues are the essence of effective attending.

- leaning forward
- using responsive facial expressions like appropriate smiling
- encouraging comments and head nods
- speaking in a warm and pleasant voice

As with any counselling skill or procedure, attending must be applied intelligently relative to diversity and cultural variables. For example, among many Middle Easterners, six to twelve inches is a comfortable conversational distance; but an "arm's length" is more comfortable for most Westerners (Hackney & Cormier, 2005). Counsellors should also avoid rigid adherence to one style of attending. For example, the needs of a client who is embarrassed may be best served by averted or less-intense eye contact until more trust and comfort develops.

Careful attention to words, phrases, and nonverbal communication opens counsellors up to learning. Counsellors need to hear what is said, as well as what is not said. They need to reflect on how ideas are communicated through tone of voice, posture, and other clues, and listen carefully for confirming or conflicting messages. As well, they need to sift through what may be complex and sometimes confusing information to identify patterns, priorities, and areas of relevance. This work may involve the major senses of hearing, sight, smell, and touch. Although counselling work generally centres on hearing and sight, significant information can be gleaned from our other senses. For example, alcohol and some other drug use may be detected by smell.

When counsellors are patient, they give clients space to confront painful emotions and to gather their thoughts. When counsellors sit still, maintain culturally appropriate eye contact, and avoid needless questions they do much to convey to their clients their unwavering attention. These actions focus the attention of the interview completely on clients. To accomplish this, counsellors must develop their ability to be comfortable with silence.

SUCCESS TIP

The pitfalls of listening include saying too much as well as too little. Silence is important, but ultimately insufficient for effective listening.

Selective Attention

selective perception (selective attention): A term used to describe the natural tendency to avoid being overwhelmed by information by screening out material that is irrelevant.

Selective perception or **selective attention** is a term used to describe the natural tendency to screen out irrelevant information to avoid being overwhelmed. Of necessity, counsellors must ignore some parts of a client's communication and selectively attend to others. It is not possible (nor desirable) to attend to everything a client says; however, communication breakdown can easily occur if a counsellor ignores issues or feelings that are important to a client. This underscores the importance of the contracting process (see Chapter 3) as a tool for ensuring that counsellors and clients are on the same page.

What a person pays attention to is likely to be influenced by one's frame of reference, which is uniquely defined through influences such as past experiences, personal values, current mood, interests, concerns, fears, prejudices, health, culture, and context. A tow truck driver looks very different depending on whether you have a flat tire on

SUCCESS TIP

Clients also selectively attend. For example, those who are overly anxious are more likely to pay attention to anxiety-provoking stimuli, and those who are suspicious will be more sensitive to cues that the counsellor cannot be trusted.

The brain is unable to pay attention to two things at the same time. In order to divert our attention to a different task, the brain must shut down and shift its focus from the first task (Medina, 2008). Research also shows that shifts in attention result in a greater risk of missing important cues and not remembering what clients have said (Taylor, 2011). This reality underscores the importance of counsellors attending to their clients' communication without becoming preoccupied with what to say next.

a dark and stormy night, or you are being towed for illegal parking. The word *mother* may call up images of love and support or memories of abuse and pain.

Recognizing and Managing the Pitfalls of Selective Attention   Managing the pitfalls begins with self-awareness about how our point of view and life experiences influence our perceptions and interpretations. Counsellors need to reflect on their own listening habits to identify areas of vulnerability. Counsellors need to be alert to the dangers of selective perception in their own thinking and responses. They must be vigilant to make sure they understand how and when prior learning, values, and current expectations influence where they focus. They need to be careful that they don't impose their own sense of what's important, which can easily lead to loss of objectivity as well as missed information and opportunities. Viewing sessional recordings and seeking feedback from informed observers is an important part of this process. Here are some typical counsellor selective perception errors to consider:

1. *Egocentricity*. Hearing only messages that support established opinions and beliefs. We need to remember that what we know is subject to change.

2. *Role bias*. Counsellors will pay more attention to cues that are consistent with their professional focus, training, and responsibility. An employment counsellor will be interested in career and vocational data, whereas a marriage counsellor will be more alert to information on familial communication. This is necessary and appropriate; however, attending to one issue runs the risk that other important areas for inquiry are overlooked. For example, an employment counsellor who does not recognize the symptoms of a mental disorder or substance abuse will have limited effectiveness when dealing with clients who have these issues.

3. *Disengaging*. When this happens, counsellors have simply stopped listening and their attention is focused elsewhere. This may occur for a variety of reasons, including boredom, disinterest, fatigue, or preoccupation with their own issues. As well, counsellors might deliberately disengage when they are uncomfortable with the topic.

4. *Preoccupation with problems*. When counsellors are too fixated on problems, they miss the opportunity that comes from a strengths approach. Recognizing client strengths helps to build confidence and self-esteem, and it mobilizes resources for problem solving.

    It is also important to pay attention to the counselling relationship. Over the life of the counsellor–client relationship, various priorities will emerge related to beginnings, contracting, problem solving, and endings. The vitality of the relationship is a strong predictor of a successful outcome in counselling, so this important variable should never be ignored.

5. *Not attending to the emotional domain*. By focusing on behaviour, counsellors ignore the emotions of their clients, which are often more important to problem resolution than finding behavioural solutions. Emotions can sustain problems, interfere with decision making, and create stress that prevents problem solving. When clients express emotions, active listening, particularly empathy, is crucial. For example,

Miller, Forcehimes, and Zweben (2011) reported that "one of the strongest predictors of a counsellor's effectiveness in treating substance use disorders is empathy" (p. 49). Counsellors should also monitor and deal with the emotions that they bring to an interview or that arise during an interview.

6. *Not considering the nonverbal channel.* Listening to words without considering nonverbal communication may result in counsellors hearing only a small part of what their clients are communicating.

7. *Snap judgments.* Good listeners are curious, patient, and cautious in the pursuit of understanding. Medina (2008), a molecular biologist, notes, "What we pay attention to is often profoundly influenced by memory. In everyday life, we use previous experience to predict whether we should pay attention" (p. 75). This suggests a major pitfall that has profound implications for counsellors. When our clients share stories, their stories may stir our own memories, and we may begin to "fill in the blanks" based on our experience. This shortcut to understanding can result in erroneous assumptions and missed information. While past experience with the same issues as our clients may give us an empathic advantage, this is only true if we remain vigilant to ensure that we do not contaminate our clients stories with those of our own. Perhaps we are safer when clients present unfamiliar issues and problems because our lack of knowledge makes it easier to explore for understanding.

8. *Multitasking.* Neuroscience has demonstrated that the human mind is incapable of multitasking with respect to paying attention (Medina, 2008). Here's the most common problem in counselling: While clients are talking, counsellors are thinking ahead, planning what to say. In order to think ahead, their minds must disengage from listening. Active listening skills can help counsellors maintain focus on what their clients are communicating.

SUCCESS TIP

Too much time exploring content comes at the expense of problem solving and feeling management. While some detail is necessary for understanding, excessive attention to all the details is neither necessary nor productive. Nor is it generally useful to direct the work of counselling to find the "root" causes of problems.

Remember that listening is hard work, and you need to be physically and psychologically ready for the interview. One essential component of this readiness is to address your psychological needs by dealing with your own issues that might make it difficult to hear clients. If you have unresolved difficulties, especially if they mirror those of your client, it will be particularly difficult to listen effectively. A second component is to make sure you fully disengage from your last client before engaging with the next. Finally, make sure you understand before you move on. Summarize, paraphrase, and ask defining questions to enhance and confirm your understanding. As a rule, the more you occupy yourself with the active demands of listening, the less you will be tempted to let your thoughts wander.

NONVERBAL COMMUNICATION

Most people are familiar with the physiological reactions that occur in moments of great fear. Powered by increased adrenal secretions, our bodies respond automatically with elevated heart rate, rapid breathing, dry mouth, and other symptoms. Many of these reactions are clearly visible to any observer, even before any verbal declaration of fear. Nonverbal behaviour is usually outside our conscious control and is less likely

TABLE 4.3 Nonverbal Behaviour: What to Observe

Eyes	Eye contact, movement, tears, dilated pupils
Facial cues and expressions	Frowning, shaking the head, smiling, clenched mouth, blushing
Vocal	Tone, volume, use of silence, hesitation, pace, mood
Use of space	Seating distance, movement, body position
Appearance/Dress	Grooming, hygiene, dress, tattoos, branding, scars
Body language	Posture, gestures, pacing behaviour, arm and hand movements
Touch	Handshake (e.g., limp, aggressive), hugging, hand on shoulder
Distractions	Playing with a ring or pen, touching hair
Affect	Blunted, flat, inappropriate, labile, restricted (see glossary)

to be censored. Consequently, counsellors can often trust nonverbal communication as a more reliable indicator of feelings than verbal communication. Sue and Sue (2008) found that "studies support the conclusion that nonverbal cues operate primarily on an unawareness level, that they tend to be more spontaneous and more difficult to censor or falsify, and that they are more trusted than words" (p. 171). Table 4.3 includes some of the key things to look for in your clients' nonverbal behaviour.

In general, research has shown that often 55 to 65 percent or more of the meaning of a message is conveyed nonverbally (Sheafor & Horejsi, 2008). Sometimes all significant communication comes from the nonverbal channel; for example, people's emotions may be conveyed much more accurately by their body posture and eye contact than by their words. Counsellors who rely only on words will be limited and ineffective by not integrating that part of the interaction that contains the meaning.

Knapp and Hall (2006) offer these conclusions:

Nonverbal communication should not be studied as an isolated phenomenon but as an inseparable part of the total communication process . . . Nonverbal communication is important because of its role in the total communication system, the tremendous quantity of informational cues it gives in any particular situation, and its use in fundamental areas of our daily life. (p. 24)

Meaning of Nonverbal Communication

Counsellors can learn a great deal more about their clients' ideas and feelings if they carefully observe and try to understand the nonverbal channel. Generally, nonverbal communication serves one or more of four purposes:

- *Confirming or repeating:* Nonverbal messages are consistent with messages that are spoken. Alternatively, nonverbal cues embellish the intensity of the client's ideas or feelings. Example: thumbs up with a smile while saying yes.

>>> **CONVERSATION 4.1** Problems with Listening and Responding

STUDENT: I find that I'm so busy trying to think of what to say next that I miss what the client is saying.

TEACHER: Yes, it is tough. That is a common problem, even for experienced counsellors. The brain cannot multitask listening and planning. One task must stop for the other to occur. Of course, it is hard to stay focused on what is being said without some thought of what to do next, but with practice it can be done. One trick is to think about what is being said before thinking about what to say. As you reflect on what is being said, try to identify major themes and feelings. Often, your response will emerge naturally out of this effort. Develop your comfort with silence. If you need a moment to think, ask for it.

- *Contradicting:* Disparities between the verbal and nonverbal messages are apparent. Example: Client might say, "I'm ecstatic," but in a sarcastic manner that conveys the opposite. Another common example occurs when people say, "I'm interested in what you have to say," but at the same time, they continue with another activity, betraying their lack of interest.

- *Substituting:* Ideas and feelings are communicated only in the nonverbal channel. Examples: shaking or nodding the head to say no or yes; shrugging the shoulders, expressing confusion or indecision. Nonverbal communication such as vocal intonations, pauses, and hand gestures can also be used to regulate the flow of conversation (e.g., turn-taking). Yawning might unconsciously signal to your guests that it is time to go home.

- *Expressing emotion:* The client's emotions are suggested through nonverbal means. For example, crying might signify sadness, fear, or joy; a raised voice might suggest anger or frustration.

Counsellors need to interpret nonverbal behaviour cautiously. Nonverbal behaviour can have many meanings, each of which can vary according to culture, context, and individual comfort level. For example, people from some cultures interact at very close personal distances, but others experience the same personal distance as intrusive or even aggressive. Some people consider direct eye contact rude, while others view avoidance of eye contact as cold or as evidence that people are lying. In fact, in some cultural groups averting one's eyes is a sign of respect and courtesy. Hays and Erford (2010) offer this perspective on Native Americans:

> To subtly match this level of eye contact is respectful and shows an understanding of the client's way of being. The eyes are considered to be the pathway to the spirit; therefore, to consistently look someone in the eye is to show a level of entitlement or aggression. It is good to glance at someone every once in a while, but listening in the traditional way is something that happens with the ears and the heart. (p. 320)

kinesics: The study of body language, such as posture, facial expressions, gestures, and eye motion.

Body Language **Kinesics** is the study of body language, including such variables as posture, facial expressions, gestures, and eye motion. Sometimes body language is easily interpreted, such as when people use gestures that have direct verbal equivalents. For example, people might point to indicate direction or use their fingers and hands to signify size or numbers. At other times, body language is ambiguous and more difficult to interpret, particularly when people communicate contradictory messages. For example, a person might appear to be listening intently and making appropriate eye contact, but if these actions are accompanied by fidgeting and rapid finger tapping, then the real message is "I'm bored."

Even a simple smile may have multiple meanings, including warmth, amusement, or nervousness. Tears may convey sadness, amusement, embarrassment, or fear. Consequently, counsellors should look for multiple indicators of meaning rather than a single explanation. Factors such as context, culture, relationship, power dynamics, and gender may be loosely or intimately connected to the meaning of any nonverbal message.

In some situations where verbal and nonverbal messages appear contradictory, the client may be ambivalent and both messages may be correct. For example, a mother might say how proud and happy she is that her son is leaving home to attend college, but at the same time be crying. In this example, it is clear she has mixed feelings, and an appropriate empathic counsellor response might be, "Even though you're proud to see your son taking this important step, it still hurts because he will no longer be at home."

Voice Vocal nonverbal cues include tone, volume, pitch, and rate of speech. These variables can reveal if clients are depressed, euphoric, angry, or sad. For example, Kadushin (1990) concluded that anger tends to be expressed with speech that is more

Email and text messaging communication is often misinterpreted because there is no access to the nonverbal channel which signals the subtle meanings, emotions and intentions of the sender. To fully process meaning, our brains need to access and interpret both the verbal and the nonverbal channel. Note that the nonverbal channel is often more important and reliable, particularly when emotions are involved. Generally, nonverbal communication is processed in the right hemisphere of the brain. Damage to the right side of the brain can lead to a variety of social communication difficulties, including understanding nonverbal cues and other subtleties of communication such as humour or metaphors (American Speech Language Hearing Association, 2015).

rapid and loud, whereas sadness is characterized by more pauses and slowness of speech. Silence is also an important component of nonverbal communication. Counsellors need to be able to read nonverbal cues to decide how, when, and if they should interrupt a silent moment.

Spatial Distance/Proxemics   **Proxemics** describes how people use space and distance. Hall's model (1959) is still widely used to describe the four main distances (for Western-born Canadians):

proxemics: A term used to describe how people use space and distance in social behaviour.

1. Intimate distance is a zone of up to 0.5 metres (2 feet), reserved for private exchanges of intimate thoughts and feelings.

2. Personal distance is a zone of about 0.5 to 1 metre (2 to 4 feet), used for less intense exchanges with friends and family.

3. Social distance is a zone of approximately 1 to 3.5 metres (4 to 12 feet), used for more impersonal meetings and social contact.

4. Public distance beyond 3.5 metres (12 feet) is used for casual exchanges, such as giving a speech or lecture.

How an individual uses space is influenced by many variables, including gender, age, culture, physical characteristics, status, various personality traits, and the nature of the relationship. Thus, counsellors should adapt their seating to meet the needs of individual clients and situations and remember that angry clients usually need more space. Moreover, in such situations, counsellors need more space for safety reasons. Counsellors should also be mindful of spatial shifts during the interview. Often these changes are subtle, such as when a client shifts his or her chair back, as if to say, "I'm not comfortable with what we're talking about." Similarly, as clients lean in and move toward them, counsellors can conclude that intimacy and trust are increasing. When clients physically withdraw, counsellors might want to avoid confrontation or sensitive topics.

Counsellor Self-Awareness of Nonverbal Behaviour   Counsellors need to be aware of their own nonverbal behaviour and the subtle ways it might influence their clients. Counsellors may inadvertently communicate displeasure by frowning, turning away from clients, or increasing the physical distance from clients. Alternatively, they communicate interest by smiling, using a pleasant tone of voice, increasing eye contact, and leaning toward clients.

SUCCESS TIP

Clients can be very adept at noticing nonverbal cues that might betray their counsellors' judgment, bias, deception, disinterest, anxiety, or lack of genuineness.

Some counsellors might laugh nervously when they are anxious or scared, thereby confusing their clients. Counsellors can review videotapes of real or mock counselling sessions to increase their sensitivity to appropriate and inappropriate nonverbal communication habits.

Culture and Nonverbal Communication   All cultures have unique nonverbal languages. In the deaf culture, for example, nonverbal communication is an extremely important adjunct to ASL (American Sign Language). Gestures and facial expressions may be emphasized to define meaning. One Canadian study supported the conclusion that the French speak more often with their hands and typically use more gestures in their interactions (Adler, Towne, & Rolls, 2001). Spatial distance also differs among cultures. Middle Easterners stand and communicate much closer than most Westerners would be comfortable doing. With respect to eye contact, Adler et al. (2001) make this observation:

> Like distance, patterns of eye contact vary around the world. A direct gaze is considered appropriate for speakers in Latin America, the Arab world, and southern Europe. On the other hand, Asians, Indians, Pakistanis, and northern Europeans gaze at a listener peripherally or not at all. In either case, deviations from the norm are likely to make a listener uncomfortable. (p. 231)

Some nonverbal communications such as smiling, laughing, and frowning have the same meaning everywhere; however, some cultures put more emphasis on controlling the expression of personal feelings, which sometimes makes it difficult to gauge the intensity of the client's feelings. An example illustrates how a counsellor might use cultural knowledge:

Counsellor: *(Speaking to a middle-aged Asian woman.)* How are you feeling?

Client: *(With a slight smile.)* I'm fine. I'm doing okay.

Counsellor: On a scale from 1 to 10, with 10 being the best you have ever felt, where would you put yourself?

Client: *(Hesitates.)* Maybe 3 or a 4.

In the preceding example, the counsellor knew that the Asian woman might (as part of her cultural learning) hide and suppress her feelings, perhaps not wanting to burden her counsellor with her pain. The scaling question provides a face-saving way for her to reveal her emotions.

SUCCESS TIP

Client nonverbal cues will tell you when you have spoken too much, when the client wants to talk, and when the mood of the interview has shifted. Trust these cues more than the words you hear.

Working with Nonverbal Communication

Nonverbal communication needs to be considered as part of the total communication process that includes verbal behaviour and context. Here are four ways to respond to client nonverbal communication:

1. *Use it as a basis for understanding.* By paying attention to the nonverbal channel, counsellors can greatly increase their knowledge of those areas that are important or sensitive for the client.

2. *Ignore.* Inconsequential nonverbal behaviour (e.g., a small shift in body position or scratching one's nose) does not need to be addressed.

3. *Defer.* Sometimes nonverbal behaviour is potentially significant, but a sufficient level of trust has not yet been established. Potentially significant nonverbal messages may come at the end of the interview when there is no time to address their meaning. In such circumstances, it may be wise to defer, but a mental note can remind the counsellor to deal with it later when there is more time.

4. *Acknowledge in the verbal channel.* Use responses such as, "Your tears really say how much this means to you." Responding to nonverbal cues communicates a deep sensitivity to the client's experience and (in this example) a willingness to work in the emotional domain.

Metacommunication

Metacommunication is the message that is heard (interpreted), which may differ sharply from the words spoken or the intended message of the speaker. Factors such as nonverbal cues (especially voice tone, volume, and inflection), context, history, relationship trust level (especially regarding unresolved conflict), mood, and many others all influence how someone interprets a message. So, it is important that we stay alert for signs that a different meaning has been ascribed. For example, the seemingly simple offer, "Can I help?" might be understood (heard) by different people as:

<aside>metacommunication: The message that is heard (interpreted), which may differ from the words spoken or the intended message of the speaker.</aside>

- You don't trust me.
- You don't think I'm capable of doing it on my own.
- You need help, and I'm the one who can solve your problem.
- You want the credit for what I'm doing.
- You think I am doing a lousy job.
- You are willing to do it for me.
- You are angry because I didn't ask you to help.

The following example illustrates what some clients might "hear:"

Counsellor 1: Why don't you tell him how you feel?

Meaning of the message for the client: You were not smart enough to think of that on your own.

Counsellor 2: Do you agree with what I said?

Meaning of the message for the client: Do not disagree.

SILENCE

The Personal Meaning of Silence

Another major active listening skill is silence. One distinguishing quality of effective counsellors is their mastery of language to communicate ideas and promote change; however, language fluency alone is insufficient. Counsellors also need to understand the importance of silence in communication. They need to balance their verbal agility with an equally strong capacity for silence. Sometimes the most effective and appropriate counselling response is to say nothing.

Individuals and cultural groups show considerable differences in their comfort with silence. In some cultures, silence is a sign of respect. For many counsellors, silence is unnatural and if pauses occur in the conversation they become anxious and fear that their clients will see them as incompetent. They also often burden themselves with pressure to fill the silent void with words. A silent pause, even as short as a few seconds, may lead to inner panic. Almost on reflex, they act to fill silent moments with questions and interpretations.

Some people judge silence harshly. They see quieter people as unmotivated, uninterested, aloof, rejecting, and ignorant. In a discussion with a group of students in a counselling class, I asked members who rated themselves as "more verbal" to talk to "less verbal" members about their typical reactions to silence. The verbal members made statements such as "I feel judged," "I don't think you're very interested," "I'm boring you," and "I wonder if you care about what we're doing?" Their comments clearly indicated that they felt threatened by silence or viewed it as evidence of judgment or lack of interest.

In contrast, the members who rated themselves as quieter noted that they often did not have enough time to respond and revealed that they were fearful or felt inadequate. Sample comments from this group were: "You don't give me enough time to speak," "I'm scared to talk," "I worry about making a fool of myself," and "By the time, I think of what to say, someone else has already said it."

Silence in Counselling

As noted above, counsellors can have the same anxieties about silence as other people have. Silence may heighten their sense of inadequacy as counsellors and lead to uncertainty in the interview. As a result, counsellors may become impulsive and try to fill silences too quickly.

However, disciplined counsellors who allow silence in their interviews may find that their relationships take on an entirely different tone, with their clients answering their own questions and discovering their own solutions. A repertoire of skills position counsellors for dealing with silence in an interview. Counsellors should become comfortable permitting silence as well as knowing when to interrupt silences appropriately. Knowing when to speak and when not to requires some understanding of the various meanings of silence. A survey of the use of silence in counselling suggested that counsellors use silence "primarily to facilitate reflection, encourage responsibility, facilitate expression of feelings, not interrupt session flow, and convey empathy" (Hill, Thompson, & Ladany, 2003, p. 513). Silence may be ill-advised, however, with clients who are psychotic or with those who are likely to view the silence as punishment.

During silence, counsellors need to do more than just keep quiet; they also need to attend to the silence. **Attended silence** is characterized by eye contact, physical and psychological focus on the client, and self-discipline to minimize internal and external distraction. Silence is not golden if it communicates lack of interest or preoccupation, or if it says, "I'm not listening." This means refraining from fidgeting and other digressions, such as taking notes or answering the phone. At the same time, counsellors should not stare or turn the silence into a contest to see who breaks it first. Counsellors should not automatically assume that silence means failure, nor should they think that a few moments of silence means that the work of counselling has stopped. Passive clients may be busy with thought, or they may be seeking to gain control or understanding of painful and forgotten feelings.

attended silence: Attended silence is characterized by making eye contact, physical and psychological focus on the client, and self-discipline to minimize internal and external distraction.

> ## ⟫⟫ BRAIN BYTE   Silence
>
> Cozolino (2010) suggests that some clients find silence in counselling difficult and they imagine that the counsellor "thinks they are boring, stupid, a waste of time, or a bad client" (p. 88). He suggests that their reactions are activated by implicit memories (unconscious) that mirror difficult relationships with their parents. It seems that for some, "defences to escape negative feelings come to require constant action and distraction to keep us from becoming frightened or overwhelmed" (p. 88). In contrast, Cozolino identifies another group of clients who find silence supportive and a break from the pressures of communication.

Every silent interlude has a different meaning, and counsellors need to be astute to discover the significance of each quiet moment and the most appropriate response. Understanding different types of silence helps counsellors look for cues and consider appropriate responses. Here are the six common meanings of silence in counselling:

1. The client is thinking.

Although all clients need time to process information and frame their responses, some need more time than others do. Some clients talk with only a momentary pause to catch their breath, but others punctuate their speech with periods of reflection. If counsellors do not allow this time for contemplation, their clients may feel disempowered or inadequate. Clients may be formulating their thoughts or feelings, only to be prematurely cut off by counsellors whose own anxiety with silence does not permit them to wait.

When clients need time to reflect, counsellors can simply remain attentive and nonverbally show their interest and involvement through eye contact, open posture, and so on. They can also verbally indicate their willingness to listen by using simple phrases, such as "I sense you need some time to think. That is okay. I'll wait" and "It's okay with me if you just need to think without speaking."

2. The client is confused and unsure of what to say or do.

Sometimes questions are unclear, the focus of the interview is ambiguous, or clients do not know what is expected of them. Clients may sit in silence, shifting uncomfortably and attempting to sort out what to do next.

When clients become quiet because they are confused, allowing the silence to continue sustains or increases the clients' anxiety. These circumstances warrant interrupting the silence to clarify meaning, direction, or expectations. Rephrasing, summarizing, paraphrasing, and even repetition can help in such situations.

Counsellor: Perhaps you're confused.

Client: (Nods.)

Counsellor (Choice 1): I think I might have confused you with my last question. It didn't make sense to me either. Let me reword it.

Counsellor (Choice 2): Let's slow down a bit. Help me to understand what is unclear or confusing.

In addition, clients may have difficulty expressing their ideas, or language problems may be a barrier. Sometimes clients just need a little more time to find the right word or phrase. At other times, counsellors need to tentatively suggest ideas or help clients label feelings.

Clients are more likely to be silent during the beginning phase of counselling and during first interviews. This is normal and usually indicates that clients are unsure of what to say or do. Consequently, they depend on the counsellor to take the lead to clarify role and direction.

3. The client is encountering painful feelings.

Interviewing and counselling can stimulate powerful feelings and memories. Counsellors who can tolerate silence give space to their clients so that they can experience and deal with pain or anxiety. In some cases, clients may be ambivalent about facing their feelings. They may be afraid of their intensity, or they may be unwilling to face their feelings, at least at this time. Silence is a chance for clients to examine the merits of continuing further or retreating to safety. Usually, such moments are obvious because the discussion is intense immediately before the silence.

When clients are struggling with powerful feelings, counsellors may need to use multiple responses. First, you can allow this type of silence to continue. Responding with attentive silence can be very therapeutic and supportive. It says, "I am here. I understand. I have the courage to be with you as you deal with your pain."

Second, you can support silence with empathy when dealing with powerful client feelings. Otherwise, clients might feel ignored or misunderstood. Empathy confirms that feelings have been heard, and subsequent silence gives the client time to process. Empathy might be used to let clients know that they have been understood. As well, empathy tells clients that they have not been abandoned and that their counsellors are ready, willing, and able to be with them while they consider their feelings. Once the counsellor has expressed empathy, silence may be appropriate. In the following example, empathy frames two long, silent moments:

Counsellor: As I listen to you, I am beginning to sense your feeling of resentment that your mother continually tries to run your life.

(15 seconds of silence.)

Client: *(Tears in her eyes.)* Resentment! That's only part of it. I don't think I could ever live up to her expectations.

(Counsellor maintains eye contact, faces client.)

(10 seconds of silence.)

Client: But it's going to be okay. I realize that I have my own expectations to meet. It's me I have to face in the mirror.

Counsellor: Sounds like you are beginning to accept that your mother is not going to change and that only you have control over who you are and how you act.

4. **The client is dealing with issues of trust.**
   Before trust develops in the counselling relationship, clients may be hesitant to share personal information, and they may communicate this reluctance through silence. This is a normal and self-protective way for people to avoid rejection and maintain a sense of control over private matters. A different trust issue may arise with involuntary clients who use silence as a way to control or sabotage the interview or demonstrate hostility. Their silence says what the client may want to express: "I'm here, but you can't make me talk." Silence becomes a way of retaining dignity and control in a situation in which they feel disempowered.

   Generally, counsellors will want to move the interview gently toward more openness and intimacy. One way to proceed is to acknowledge the risk in sharing and to discuss issues of trust. You can open the door with a comment like this: "I know it's not easy to share your feelings with a stranger. You don't know me yet, and you can't be sure how I might respond." Another strategy is to move at the client's pace and discuss less threatening content until trust in the relationship develops.

   Sometimes it is preferable to put trust issues on the table rather than try to proceed when there is obvious resistance. Consider using a lead such as the following:

Counsellor: I'd like to share a perception with you. I've noticed that whenever I ask a question, you answer me quickly, and then you become rather silent. I'm worried that there might be some problems between you and me that we should discuss. Or perhaps you see it differently. In any case, I think it would help if we could discuss it. I'm certainly willing to listen to any of your concerns or feelings.

(Client is silent.)

Counsellor: I'm not you, and without your help I can't understand how you feel, but I suspect you'd rather not be here. That's how I'd feel in the same circumstance.

In the preceding example, the counsellor's invitations do not guarantee that the client will open up to discuss feelings about being forced to attend the interview;

however, such openness to discuss the issue frequently works. In any case, clients will have heard the invitation, and it may help to build trust.

5. Silence is the client's usual way.

Some clients are quiet by nature. They are unused to giving long or spontaneous responses, and they may be more comfortable keeping their ideas to themselves. Silence is not a sign of counselling failure, so counsellors should avoid the temptation to end it prematurely. Sometimes counsellors need to modify their own expectations and ways of relating to allow for the extended silences of some individuals.

As we will see in the next chapter, there are interview techniques that are effective in drawing out quieter clients. For example, open-ended questions that cannot easily be answered with a simple yes or no may help overcome patterns of continued silence. Another technique is to discuss with clients how silence is affecting the counselling work and then to explore ways for them to become more expressive. Sometimes clients don't understand the expectations of their counsellors, but once they do they are willing to cooperate. Professionals should reflect on the fact that whereas they have had training in the skills and process of counselling, their clients have not. Clients may be inaccurately seen as resistant when they are just unsure of what to say. This underscores the importance of counsellors keeping clients fully informed by taking advantage of opportunities to explain their intent and procedures. Simple statements such as the following help demystify the counselling process:

Counsellor: I'm sure there's more that you can tell me. It will help me to understand better if you tell me more details and perhaps give me a few examples.

Counsellors can also adapt their methods by using strategies that require less verbal interaction. Children, for example, may respond better to play, art, music, and drama. Adolescent males may be more motivated to talk if the interview is conducted in conjunction with an activity, such as a walk in the park or a game of pool. Counsellors are wise to remember that while they tend to be most comfortable with verbal interaction, their clients might favour other methods. For example, some clients like to write in a journal, which gives them a chance to think introspectively without time pressures. With these clients, counsellors might seek agreement to use relevant journal entries as reference for discussion. In the following case, a counsellor relates how poetry was used:

> The client was a 20-year-old woman who seemed, at first, reluctant to talk about her depression. Her usual responses were one-word or short answers. I remembered that she had mentioned that she liked poetry, so I asked her if she would be willing to bring some of it to our meeting. She was willing and in fact eager to share her work. She brought a short poem to the next session, which she read to me. The poem revealed her deep depression and her preoccupation with death. Afterward, we talked about her torment at a level that would not have been otherwise possible. Each week, she brought a new poem, and these poems became our starting point. As she began to feel better about herself, her poems became more buoyant and optimistic, and they became one measure of her progress.

6. The client has reached closure.

Silence happens when there is nothing more to say about a particular topic or idea. Silence is a way of saying, "I'm finished. Let's talk about something else."

When counselling topics reach natural and appropriate closure, counsellors need to move on to a new subject. They may break such silence by seeking confirmation that an end point has indeed been reached. One strategy for preventing premature closure is to acknowledge the possibility of closure, as well as the possibility that the client may need time to formulate more ideas. A comment such as the following acknowledges both alternatives:

Counsellor: I'm thinking that we might have gone as far as we can with that idea. Or perhaps there is more you would like to say.

Subsequently, a transition to a new topic is appropriate. It may also be valuable to take a few moments to summarize before moving to a new area of discussion.

Nonverbal Cues and Silence

Sometimes nonverbal cues can reveal the meaning of silence. Presenting the open palms of one's hands may say, "Wait. I need time." Looking away and clenching a fist may signal an angry silence. At other times, the meaning of silence is unclear. In such situations, counsellors may choose to let the silence continue for a while to see if its meaning becomes apparent, or they may wish to seek help from their clients to understand it. Following are some sample responses that counsellors can use:

- You've (We've) become very quiet. I'm wondering what that means.
- Help me understand the meaning of your silence.
- Perhaps you are hesitant to tell me, or maybe you just need some time to think.

Although silence is often ambiguous, and understanding its meaning is difficult, some clues can help counsellors interpret silence. Table 4.4 presents some of the messages of client silence. The table includes a range of nonverbal cues and ideas about how to respond to each; however, all nonverbal behaviour needs to be interpreted with extreme caution. The same behaviour may have multiple meanings. Crossed arms may suggest defensiveness but may also signal that the client is physically cold, or the client may be both defensive and cold. You need to interpret all nonverbal behaviour by considering the individual client and the overall context in which the behaviour occurs, and then check with the client to confirm accuracy.

Encouraging Silence

Silence can serve a number of useful purposes in counselling. It provides time to experience feelings and contemplate. Insight may emerge from moments of uninterrupted thought. Therefore, it makes sense for counsellors to promote periodic silence in their interviews with clients. This may be particularly useful when working with clients who

---

⟫⟫ CONVERSATION 4.2 | Learning to Deal with Silence

STUDENT: How long is a reasonable amount of time to allow a silence to continue?

TEACHER: Without knowing the context, I can't answer your question. Sometimes after a few seconds of silence, it's appropriate to break in and say something. In other circumstances, an extended silence of several minutes is okay. Each situation must be looked at individually.

STUDENT: I agree, but my problem is that I get uncomfortable after a few seconds. I get so anxious that I usually rush to say something, even when I know I should keep quiet.

TEACHER: Try paying attention to what you're saying to yourself during silent moments. Watch for depreciating self-talk, such as "If I don't say something, the client will think I'm incompetent." Counter this by reminding yourself that silence has its place in counselling. If you interrupt too soon, you rob clients of important opportunities to reflect. Remember that comfort with silence can be learned, but as with all skills, learning requires practice. It may help to have a glass of water so that you can take a long, slow sip to prevent speaking prematurely. Deep breathing may also help. Finally, do not overcompensate. Some silences should be interrupted.

TABLE 4.4 Responding to Silence: Nonverbal Cues

Client Actions	Intended Message	Counsellor Response Choices
Palm of one hand raised 90 degrees, squinting, furrowed brow, eye movement, and smiling (positive or pleasing thought).	"Please be patient. I need time to think."	Verbalize willingness to wait. Indicate attended silence with eye contact and other nonverbal expressions of support.
Shoulder shrugging, raised palms, and rapid eye movement.	"Help—I'm confused and don't know what to do next."	Set the direction; clarify instructions. Rephrase the last response.
Ignoring or providing inappropriately short answers, moving the chair back.	"You can't make me talk." "I don't want to be here."	Communicate that it's okay not to talk. Empathize with resistance. Describe your feelings when forced to talk.
Starting to talk, abruptly stopping, shaking head, and stuttering.	"I don't know whether to talk or not."	Empathize with ambivalence. Discuss the risks of sharing and not sharing.
Physical withdrawal, averted eye contact, carefully measured words, and whispering.	"I'm scared of what you might think of me."	Reassure and convey a nonjudgmental attitude.
Tears, covering eyes, quivering lips, flushed face, looking at the floor, and trembling.	"I'm overwhelmed with these feelings."	Show empathy, use attended silence, and then reveal further empathy.
Low voice tone, a pattern of short answers.	"This is the way I am. I don't say much."	Accept it as a cultural or individual norm. Gently encourage with open-ended questions. Explain the importance of sharing.
Leaning back, smiling, saying, "That's it."	"I'm finished."	Summarize. Change the topic and move on.

are impulsive and clients who seem afraid of silence. The following are examples of counsellor leads:

- I think it might be useful if we each took a quiet minute or two to think about this idea.
- Let's pause for a moment.
- It's okay with me if you want to think about it for a while.
- When you're ready, we can talk about it. In the meantime, I'm comfortable if we don't say anything.
- Occasional silence is something that may occur during our time together. Sometimes one or both of us will need time to think.

SUCCESS TIP

Avoid the impulse to respond immediately to a client's question. Sometimes clients ask a question but after a pause go on to answer it themselves, expressing their thoughts and feelings in more depth. This is another example of how silence can be a high-level counselling response.

PARAPHRASING

Paraphrasing means restating the client's words and ideas in your own words, but paraphrasing is not the same as repeating what the client says. Repetition confirms memorization, but it does not mean that the words and ideas have been understood. Paraphrasing is a way of stating thoughts from a different angle. The defining feature of an accurate paraphrase is its interchangeability with the client's ideas.

paraphrasing A nonjudgmental restatement of the client's words and ideas in the counsellor's own words.

Paraphrasing is an important active listening skill that serves two purposes. First, paraphrasing confirms that counsellors have been listening and have understood clients. Second, paraphrasing gives clients an opportunity to correct inaccuracies. In the beginning phase of counselling, paraphrasing is particularly important because the counsellor is just starting to understand how the client thinks and feels. Paraphrasing helps the counsellor "get on board." Paraphrasing, summarizing, and empathy are reflective skills that are crucial to developing the counselling relationship. As well, it helps clients explore their problems in a way that is less forceful and directive than direct questioning techniques.

Paraphrasing concentrates on immediate client statements. It is presented without judgment and without an attempt to solve problems. The important point to remember is that paraphrasing does not add to or alter the meaning of a client's statement. Instead, it promotes more discussion and elaboration. In the following example, notice how the counsellor's paraphrased responses capture the essence of what the client has said:

> **Client:** Losing my job was just the start of a bad year. I have had big marriage problems too, and now my daughter is on the street.
>
> **Counsellor:** You have had a number of serious things go wrong this year.
>
> **Client:** Right now, the most urgent thing is to find some way to get my daughter back home. I need to know she's safe.
>
> **Counsellor:** So the focus of your attention is seeing that your daughter is out of danger.
>
> **Client:** I'd love to be able to leave my husband and move to a new city, but what would happen to my daughter? I can't be selfish.
>
> **Counsellor:** If it were just you, you'd know what to do, but your daughter really is your priority.
>
> **Client:** You're absolutely right. Once she's okay, then I'll take care of myself.

It is always preferable for counsellors to present paraphrases tentatively. This provides the opportunity for clients to correct errors, confirm accuracy, or provide more detail. A tentative paraphrase opens discussion for deeper exploration. Statements such as "Correct me if I'm wrong" and "Would it be fair to say . . . ?" suggest tentativeness. Table 4.5 provides some other examples of paraphrasing statements.

Sometimes counsellors move too quickly by doing two things at once. In the following example, the counsellor offers a potentially useful paraphrase and then abruptly switches to a question that will move the interview in a different direction:

> **Counsellor:** As I see it, you've reached a point in your life where you're not going to take any more abuse. What do you see as your options?

In this example, a vocal pause or short silence should have been given to allow the client the chance to confirm that the paraphrase was correct. Client confirmation may come from both verbal and nonverbal channels.

TABLE 4.5 The Language of Paraphrasing

- Put a different way, you seem to be saying . . .
- As I understand it . . .
- Is this right? You're saying . . .
- In other words, . . .
- It seems as if . . .
- It sounds a bit like . . .
- As I hear it . . .
- The picture I get is . . .

Paraphrasing and Empathy

Paraphrasing differs from empathy because it concentrates on the content of messages—information, facts, details, and descriptions—whereas empathy focuses on feelings. Paraphrasing may be less threatening to clients who have trouble discussing feelings. Paraphrasing can be used as a prelude to empathy, with empathy being introduced as clients become more trusting and willing to address their feelings.

In general, paraphrasing arises from words that the client has actually said, whereas empathy builds on verbal and nonverbal cues, responding to feelings that the client may never have identified. Paraphrasing is more closely related to summarizing. Both paraphrasing and summarizing condense content, and both highlight key ideas in the client's communication.

The following example shows the difference between paraphrasing and empathy:

Client: Not having a job is getting me down. I know it doesn't help to sit in front of the TV all day hoping someone will call with my dream job.

Counsellor paraphrase: You're aware that you have to become more active in searching for a job to stop the downward slide.

Counsellor empathy: You're aware that wishing for a job offer is making you depressed.

In the paraphrase response, the counsellor paid attention to the key message (content) in the client's statement and then restated it in different words. In the empathy response, the counsellor picked up on the emotional component. Counsellors often find that simple paraphrases such as the preceding one have a powerful, positive effect. Paraphrasing helps clients realize that counsellors are listening and that they are interested. Subsequently, clients who feel heard and understood often release their defensiveness and fears about sharing. In turn, the process of sharing and exploring may generate new understanding or insight for clients regarding their feelings and problem situations.

SUMMARIZING

Summarizing is an active interviewing skill that can serve a number of purposes. First, summarizing confirms understanding and checks assumptions. Since client messages may be complex and ambiguous, it is crucial that counsellors validate their interpretations. When they summarize content, counsellors present a snapshot of their clients' main ideas in condensed format for verification.

Counsellor: So far, you seem to be saying that you don't see any point in trying the same old strategies. Talking to her didn't seem to work. Ignoring her was even worse. Now you're not sure what else you can do. Does that seem like an accurate summary?

⟫ CONVERSATION 4.3 | Effective Paraphrasing

STUDENT: If the client has just said something, what's the point in restating it? I think that a client might find paraphrasing very irritating.

TEACHER: You're saying why anger your client by repeating what's obvious?

STUDENT: That's right.

TEACHER: Notice that I just paraphrased what you said, and you seemed okay with it.

STUDENT: (Nods in agreement.)

TEACHER: An effective paraphrase is more than just mechanical restatement or parroting of the client's words. Verbatim restatements may irritate clients because they don't add anything to the interview. A useful paraphrase considers client ideas from a different perspective. Paraphrases are most potent when they invite or stimulate further elaboration and discussion. Nevertheless, I think it's best to avoid excessive use of paraphrasing or any other skill. Use paraphrasing when you need to check your perceptions and when it seems important to let a client know that you understand.

Second, summarizing is a way of organizing complex data and content by tying disjointed but related ideas together. This may help clients look at existing problems differently, thus, permitting new insights. Such summaries can also significantly reduce a client's confusion by ordering ideas in a more coherent sequence. The following example is excerpted from the midpoint of an hour-long counselling session. Prior to this point, the client had been talking about a variety of ways to manage his depression.

Counsellor: Let me see if I can sum up what we've been talking about. Essentially, as you see it, you need to work on long-term solutions, some related to improving your fitness, others targeting your social life. As well, you want to look at things you can do immediately to reduce your depression, including getting a medical and looking for some fun things to do. Is that a fair way to outline our discussion?

The counsellor's summary helps the client systematize his or her action plan. Summaries such as this help clients and counsellors identify priorities. By summarizing, counsellors configure their clients' problems and issues in a way that gives precedence to certain ideas.

Third, summarizing can be helpful in working with clients who are verbose—who introduce irrelevant material and wander from topic to topic. Summarizing separates what is important from what is irrelevant by focusing the interview on particular themes and content.

Counsellor: From what you've been saying, it seems that your problems at work with your supervisor are your top priority. Do you agree?

Summarizing may focus on a short time within an interview or it may encompass a broader period, including the whole interview or the entire helping relationship. Two types of summaries are content (or simple) summaries and theme summaries. A **content summary** focuses on content and is an unedited condensing of the client's words—all ideas are included. A **theme summary** edits unnecessary detail and attempts to identify key patterns and areas of urgency. The following example illustrates the two types of summaries. The client, a 45-year-old male, has been describing how unhappy he has been as a welder.

Client: From the first day on the job, I knew that welding wasn't for me. Even as a child, I always wanted to work with people. As a welder, I spend most of my time on my own. Last week was a good example. From Monday to Thursday, I was in the shop basement, and the only time I had any human interaction was when I went to lunch. It's not much better at home. My wife has gone back to school, so she's busy with homework every night. The kids are grown, and we don't see them that often. All I seem to do is work and watch TV. With the junk on TV, that's not much of a life. The only thing worth watching is CNN.

Content (or simple) summary: From the beginning, you were aware that your welding career didn't meet your long-standing need to work with people. It seems that your work, with last week as a typical example, leaves you on your own. With your wife studying and your children gone, TV offers little comfort.

Theme summary: You're feeling isolated. Neither your job nor your home life gives you much opportunity to satisfy your long-standing need to work with people.

Content summaries make little or no judgment about relevance. The major goal of the content summary is to organize ideas and sum up data. Theme summaries are risky. They require interviewers to determine which information is relevant and which is irrelevant. In the preceding example, different interviewers might focus on different themes, depending on their mandate. A researcher investigating television programming would hear this client's statement differently from a career counsellor or a marriage counsellor.

Good summarizing involves four essential steps that you can remember with the acronym **LIVE**: listen, identify, verbalize, evaluate.

content summary: A summary that focuses on content and is an unedited condensing of the client's words.

theme summary: A summary that edits unnecessary detail and attempts to identify key patterns and areas of urgency.

LIVE: An acronym that describes the four essential steps in summarizing: listen, identify, verbalize, evaluate.

Step 1: Listen   In this step, the task is to listen carefully to verbal and nonverbal messages that provide clues to content and meaning. Counsellors must exercise a great deal of self-discipline to avoid contaminating clients' ideas with personal bias and definition. Counsellors can ask questions, request examples, and probe for definition as ways to reduce any risk of imposing their own biases and assumptions. At the same time, they need to control distractions, including outside noise, daydreaming, attending to other activities, or becoming preoccupied with what to say next. In general, active involvement in what is being said diverts counsellors from any temptation to become distracted. Another technique to avoid distraction is to silently repeat or review client messages.

Listening means paying attention to the five W's—Who? What? Where? When? Why?—plus How? Sample questions to consider are: Whom are clients talking about? What are they saying? What are they feeling? What are they thinking? When does this happen? Where does it occur? Why does it happen? How are clients saying it?

Step 2: Identify and Interpret   The primary goal of this step is to make sense of all that has been said and heard. This involves distinguishing important information from irrelevant information, identifying underlying themes and patterns, and setting priorities. It also means hearing what has been said in context and avoiding a common pitfall in listening: not seeing the forest for the trees. The counsellor's goal is to arrive at as similar a meaning as possible to the meaning the client intended. At this step, counsellors need to remember that their perspectives are biased. What they deem significant and what their clients view as important may differ sharply. This reality underscores the importance of discussing these differences openly within the interview.

One technique that counsellors can use is to listen for keywords in each of the three domains: behaviour, thinking, and feeling. Some sample reflective questions for counsellors include the following:

- What is my client doing?
- How does he make sense of what is happening? What beliefs does she have about her problem situation?
- How is he feeling?

Step 3: Verbalize Your Understanding   The goal of this step is to verbalize your understanding of what the client has said in a summarization response, using words and phrases that the client can understand. Understanding is always tentative, at least until clients have an opportunity to confirm or challenge counsellors' perceptions. So, this step is crucial to test the accuracy of comprehension.

The move to a summarizing statement can be flagged by leads such as the following:

- To summarize what you've been saying . . .
- If I may offer a summary . . .
- To be sure I understand . . .
- Let's summarize . . .
- Summing up . . .
- Let's pause for a moment to recap.

Step 4: Evaluate   After summarizing for clients, the next step is to watch and listen carefully for signs that the summary is correct. Accurate summaries may be signaled nonverbally by the client's head nods, smiles, and relaxed posture, and verbally with short statements, such as "That's right" or "Exactly."

Disagreement may be direct, with expressions like "No, that's not right," or it may be nonverbal, with clients moving back, hesitating, or looking away. Lukewarm responses, such as "Kind of," are subtle clues that your summary is incomplete or inaccurate. In addition, paralinguistic cues, such as speech that is drawn out, may indicate a lukewarm response, even though the words may appear to confirm understanding. When dealing with lukewarm responses, counsellors need to use questions and statements to invite confirmation. This reinforces the notion that the client's right to be heard accurately will be respected, and it empowers clients to take an active role in evaluation. Leads such as the following can be used:

- Does my summary capture the important points?
- I'm wondering if you agree with my summary.
- Is that accurate?
- How does that sound to you?
- What have I missed?

▶▶▶ INTERVIEW 4.1 | Listening, Silence, and Summarizing Skills

The following interview excerpt illustrates some important concepts from this chapter. This is the second interview with a client who is seeking help with anger management. The excerpt begins about five minutes into the interview.

Counsellor: Let's review what we talked about last week. *(Three seconds of silence. Client smiles and nods her head.)*	***Analysis:*** *This opening comment sets the stage for a summary review of the last interview. This is important for re-establishing the contract. It confirms that issues important in the last session still remain priorities.*
Counsellor: I remember two points. First, you indicated that you wanted to find out what your triggers are—the things that lead you to lose control. Second, you wanted to explore some ideas for staying in control. What have I missed?	***Analysis:*** *After offering a summary, it is important to confirm its accuracy. In this case, the counsellor uses the brief silence to allow for the client to respond. This theme summary focuses on what the counsellor considers to have been the priority of the last session. Checking for client agreement is an important component of making sure the process is collaborative.*
Client: Yes, that about sums it up. But I don't want to become a pushover.	***Analysis:*** *The client confirms partial accuracy and then adds a point that the interviewer's summary has missed. This should alert the interviewer to the client's priorities.*
Counsellor: So, anger management, but not at the expense of giving up your rights. *(Ten seconds of silence.)*	***Analysis:*** *A succinct paraphrase offers another perspective. Perhaps the counsellor missed an opportunity to get more clarity on the word "pushover."*
Counsellor: You've become very quiet. I'm struggling to understand what that means. *(Ten seconds of silence. Client looks at the floor, tears in her eyes.)* **Counsellor:** Perhaps this is painful for you to think about.	***Analysis:*** *There is not enough information for the counsellor to understand the meaning of the client's silence. It might be tempting to move on with further questions, but the counsellor suspects that the silence is significant. A gentle statement invites the client to give meaning to her silence. Nonverbal cues (looking away and tears) suggest that the client is encountering strong feelings. The counsellor then focuses on feelings.*
Client: In every relationship I've ever had, I end up being the underdog. I do everything to please my partner, but nothing for me. I always give in. Inside, it's a different story. I'm full of rage and resentment.	***Analysis:*** *The client's comments suggest that she is willing to take a trust risk. This is a critical moment in the interview. The client will be watching carefully for signs of rejection.*

Counsellor: Tell me more. *(Leans toward client, maintaining eye contact.)*	***Analysis:*** *This directive encourages the client to go on with her story. It confirms direction and is short enough not to interfere with the momentum that the client has established. Attending behaviour shows that the counsellor is interested and open to hearing the client's ideas and feelings.*
Client: That's the essence of the problem. I let things build up inside and then I explode. Once, I was even fired when I blew up at my boss.	***Analysis:*** *The client continues to risk. This signals that trust is growing, but the connection may still be very fragile. As we will see in Chapter 6, it is now important for the counsellor to make an empathic connection with the client's feelings.*
Counsellor: So, your anger is a bit like a time bomb, ticking away until you explode.	***Analysis:*** *Here the counsellor paraphrases, using a simile that is consistent with the client's phrasing.*
Client: Exactly. *(Short silence.)*	***Analysis:*** *This silence may be a simple pause that allows the client to decide what to talk about next.*
Client: But, as I think about it, it's not just my anger. I guess what I'm really afraid of is never having things go my way. **Counsellor:** As I hear it, you seem to need to have more control over your life. **Client:** No, that's not it. It's not control so much as validation.	***Analysis:*** *The client does not accept the counsellor's paraphrase as accurate. Secure counsellors need not fear such mistakes or corrections. The client's willingness to correct the counsellor indicates that she has enough trust in the relationship to feel safe in challenging the counsellor. Of course, some clients may challenge because they have no trust.*

Reflections:

- If you were the counsellor in this interview, what feelings might you have experienced during the extended silent moments?

- Early in the interview, the counsellor asks, "What have I missed?" Consider the advantages of this question compared to an alternative, "Have I missed anything?"

- Suggest leads that would enable the counsellor to follow up on the client's statement, "I don't want to be a pushover."

SUMMARY

- Listening is the basis for understanding and a prerequisite for relationship development.

- A wide range of problems, such as cultural and language barriers, difficulty in framing ideas, outside noise, ambiguity, loss of objectivity, and speech problems, can interfere with this listening process. Competent counsellors remain sensitive to these problems and take steps to overcome them.

- Active listening (silence, attending, summarizing, paraphrasing, questioning, and empathizing) is an essential tool for increasing understanding, communicating interest, and letting clients know that they have been heard. Active listening involves counsellors in an ongoing process of paying attention, listening, exploring, and deepening.

- Significant information is communicated through the nonverbal channel.

- Silence may have multiple meanings. Effective counsellors are comfortable with silence, but they also have the wisdom to know how and when to interrupt it.

- Attending is the way that counsellors communicate that they are physically and psychologically committed to the helping relationship.

- Paraphrasing is a way of restating someone's words and ideas in your own words. Paraphrasing is important in counselling because it confirms to clients that counsellors have heard and understood them.

- Summarizing helps clients organize complex thoughts and is used to focus on relevant themes and content.

EXERCISES

Self-Awareness

1. Describe an encounter you have had where nonverbal communication was more important than the content of the verbal messages.

2. List words, phrases, and situations that you think are your emotional triggers that might make it difficult for you to listen.

3. Over the next week or so, pay attention to the vocal pauses and silences that you and others use in everyday and professional communication. What indicators suggest comfort with silence? Discomfort?

4. Deliberately alter your response time in a conversation to experiment with silence.

5. Ask a colleague to observe your use of silence during an interview (e.g., attended silence, appropriate interruptions, and length).

6. Videotape an interview or ask a colleague to observe your attending behaviour.

7. Metacommunication. Describe the possible meaning (for you) of each of the following:

   a. Your teacher asks you to see her right after class.

   b. Your partner forgets your birthday.

   c. A friend asks if you are free next Saturday morning.

   d. A client does not show up for an appointment

   e. Your client asks, "How old are you?"

Skill Practice

1. During interviews with some colleagues or clients, find opportune moments for brief periods of reflective silence; then continue the interview. Discuss with your colleague/client what the impact of the silence was on the interview.

2. Work with a colleague to explore the effects of poor listening. As an exercise, deliberately (but subtly) violate the principles of effective listening and attending. For example, interrupt inappropriately, ask unrelated questions, switch topics prematurely, and avoid eye contact and other indicators of interest. When you are finished, discuss how it feels to not have others listen to you.

3. Conduct an interview with a colleague on any topic of interest. Practise paraphrasing. Watch for verbal and nonverbal indicators that your paraphrase was correct.

4. Conduct a five- or ten-minute interview with a colleague on any topic of interest. As interviewer, you should practise summarizing skills. Try to offer both content and theme summaries. At the conclusion of the interview, offer a complete summary of the session. Ask your partner for feedback.

5. Conduct practice interviews with a colleague to experiment with spatial distance. Deliberately increase or decrease the distance between the two of you to learn about the effect of space. At what point did your space become violated? How did physical distance affect the quality of your verbal exchange?

6. Attempt to communicate with a colleague using only nonverbal cues and gestures.

7. Observe the nonverbal communication patterns of different age groups. What similarities and differences are apparent?

8. Form a small group of four to five colleagues. Identify one of you who is willing to discuss a current problematic situation. Two or three people will observe the interview, and two will act it out.

   Counsellor 1: Conduct a 10-minute interview while paying careful attention to the detail of the problem. Deliberately avoid addressing feelings.

   Counsellor 2: Conduct the interview while paying careful attention to emotions. Deliberately avoid exploring the details of the problem.

   Counsellor 3: Deliberately increase the length of counsellor pauses (silence).

   Debrief and compare the outcomes of the interviews.

Concepts

1. Explain how silence can be used effectively in counselling.

2. Paraphrase each of the following client statements:

   - At a party the other night, I finally met someone with whom I can carry on an intelligent conversation. He seemed interested too, but he didn't ask for my phone number.

- It's a dilemma. I don't know whether to finish the school year or drop out and get a handle on some of my debts.

- My supervisor wants to see me today. I know she wants to talk to me because I've been late for work over the last few weeks.

- If she wanted me to call her, why didn't she say something?

- First my car broke down, then the fridge. Now it's the plumbing. I should marry someone who is good at fixing things.

- I think that with AIDS and all the other diseases you can catch, we should all take precautions. You never know who might be infected.

- Well, to put it bluntly, I think my partner has a lover. But I could forgive that. I just want our relationship to be the way it was when we first met.

- I've tried everything. I have a great résumé. I've called everyone I know. I look for work five to six hours a day. Still, I can't find a job.

- Lately, I've been thinking that there has to be more to life than work and play. I'm not even sure if I believe in God, but I need to find some meaning for my life.

- I just lost it. My anger built up and I hit her. She got so upset that she packed up and left with the kids. I've never done anything like that in my whole life. I realize that I didn't solve anything by losing my temper. Now I may have ruined my marriage and turned my kids against me.

- I guess I'm going to have to find some way of dealing with my drinking problem. The other day, I was so sick from drinking that I couldn't even get out of bed. I just can't let booze continue to jeopardize my work and my family.

3. Interview people from different cultures regarding their use of nonverbal behaviour (e.g., greetings, saying goodbye, summoning a waiter, eye contact, physical contact, and use of space).

4. Explain why counsellors might avoid paying attention to certain topics because of their own needs. Alternatively, explain why counsellors might pay excessive attention to certain topics because of their own needs.

WEBLINKS

Links on listening from the International Listening Association:

www.listen.org

"Tips on Effective Listening," by Larry Alan Nadig:

www.drnadig.com/listening.htm

The International Child and Youth Care Network (click on the "Reading" tab for access to practice hints, a reference library, and other useful connections):

http://cyc-net.org

Chapter 5
Asking Questions: The Search for Meaning

iqoncept /123RF

LEARNING OBJECTIVES

- Describe the importance of asking questions.

- Explore essential questions (closed, open, and indirect) and how they might be used effectively.

- Identify and describe common questioning pitfalls.

- Explore strategies for interviewing youth and seniors.

- Explain how to promote concreteness in counselling.

- Recognize the five different types of interview transitions.

THE ART OF ASKING QUESTIONS
Questions Support Counselling Goals

No single approach to questioning works with every client. Counsellors must consider numerous factors, such as the goals for the session, the context in which questions are asked, and the individual needs of clients, and then adapt their questioning techniques accordingly. With a repertoire of techniques, skillful interviewers use questions to engage clients in higher-order thinking, kindle their curiosity, and prompt them to consider new possibilities.

Asking questions is a cornerstone of active listening and counselling. Purposeful and well-timed questioning considers variables such as the current interview phase, sessional contract, level of trust, and the capacity of the client to handle that level of questioning. Used appropriately, questions support the goals of counselling in a number of ways:

- *Gathering information.* Answered questions provide counsellors with details, definitions, and examples. As an adjunct to empathy, questions help clients explore, clarify, and define emotions. Counsellors who use questions to learn will be less likely to make erroneous assumptions.

- *Providing focus.* Sessional contracting is used to define the purpose of the interview. Subsequently, questions control the topic and direction of the interview consistent with this contract. Focused questions ensure that the interview remains on track.

- *Promoting insight.* Thought-provoking questions stimulate clients to begin a reflective process that can promote insight. Asking the right questions can promote awareness by leading clients to examine issues, ideas, and feelings that they might have otherwise overlooked. Effective questioning can also help clients make connections and uncover patterns in their thinking and problem solving. A series of questions can systematically lead clients through problem exploration, goal setting, and problem solving.

- *Catharsis.* Stimulating questions in combination with nonjudgmental responses fuel the cathartic process by encouraging clients to tell their stories and explore their feelings. Often the therapeutic value of this is sufficient to provide the necessary strength and motivation for clients to address their problems on their own.

Types of Questions

When counsellors vary the way they ask questions, the interview takes on more vitality and the use of time becomes more effective. Effective questioning technique depends on a number of factors, including timing, the nature of the relationship, the purpose of the interview, and the mood of the participants. Moreover, questions that are surprisingly useful with one client may generate hostility in another. There is an art to asking questions that precludes any attempt to structure questioning in the same way for each client.

Closed Questions   **Closed questions** can easily be answered with a yes or a no, and they are useful for confirming facts and obtaining specific information. Since closed questions do not invite detailed responses, they can effectively bring closure to an interview or slow the pace of clients who are overly verbose. On the other hand, closed questions should be avoided with clients who tend to be succinct. For example, clients

closed questions: Questions that can easily be answered with a simple yes or no (e.g., "Did you go by yourself?").

⏵⏵ BRAIN BYTE   Memory

Questions can trigger recall of memories long forgotten. Questions evoke answers or emotional reactions based on stored information and experiences from the past. A simple question such as "where did you attend school?" may trigger a strong emotional response from an Indigenous person who endured the abuses of the Canadian Residential School system. Memory involves all five senses. The smell of cookies in a bakery may produce a pleasant recall of one's grandmother. A loud noise may instantly take a Canadian veteran back to his experiences in Afghanistan. Consequently, when asking questions, counsellors need to consider that their clients may interpret the question from an entirely different frame of reference. Unexpected responses and nonverbal communication are clues that this may be happening.

can easily dismiss the question "Do you have anything you want to talk about today?" with the answer "No." Typically, closed questions begin with words such as *can*, *did*, *are*, *have*, *is*, *will*, *would*, and *do*, as in the following examples:

- Can you tell me what you've done about it?
- Did you have an opportunity to call the school?
- Are you feeling depressed?
- Is my understanding correct?
- Do you agree that the most important problem right now is . . . ?

In general, when counsellors want a definite yes or no answer to an important question, a closed question is preferable. In the following example, the client hints that suicide might be an issue. This possibility is too significant to be ignored, so the counsellor uses a closed question to see if this is a risk.

> **Client:** Lately, I have been so down I wonder, what's the point of going on?
>
> **Counsellor:** Have you been thinking about killing yourself?

Sometimes organizations require an intake interview that requires a great deal of information. A series of closed questions is an efficient way to gather data quickly. Unfortunately, too many closed questions may irritate clients and leave them feeling interrogated and restricted. To minimize these effects, counsellors should blend closed questions with various interview strategies—in particular, other active listening skills.

SUCCESS TIP

At the beginning of an interview, it is usually better to minimize questions and simply encourage clients to "tell their story." By doing so, counsellors may find that they obtain much of the information that they need without having to question clients.

---

open questions: Questions that promote expansive answers. These types of questions cannot be answered with a simple yes or no (e.g., "How do you feel about her?").

Open Questions **Open questions** are distinct from closed questions because they are difficult to answer with a simple yes or no. For this reason, open questions are usually preferable to closed questions. They provide a great deal of freedom for clients to answer the questions in the way they choose, with as much or as little depth as they wish. Open questions may be used to begin an interview, for example, "What brings you here today?" They may also be used to explore thoughts, feelings, or behaviour: "What were you thinking?" "How did you feel?" "How did you respond?"

Open questions begin with *who*, *what*, *where*, *when*, or *why* (the "five W questions") or *how*.

- Who knows about your situation besides your wife?
- What have you been able to do to cope with this problem?
- Where do you see this relationship going?
- When did this begin?
- Why do you think it has been difficult for you to cope? (As will be discussed later in this chapter, *why* questions should be used cautiously.)
- How do you see it?
- At what point do you think you might be ready to make a decision?

Keep in mind that with some clients both open and closed questions yield the same result. With these clients, the closed question "Did you have any feelings about what happened?" and the open alternative "How did you feel?" will generate the same response. However, counsellors should avoid using the closed alternative with less verbal clients. If counsellors want an expansive answer, they should avoid using closed questions, particularly when dealing with clients who tend to provide single-word or short answers to questions. For example, instead of asking, "Did you come here for help with your résumé?" a counsellor might ask a question that conveys a greater expectation for detail, such as "What were your reasons for coming in today?"

Closed questions become leading questions when they suggest the "right" or expected answer to the client. In the following example, a single mother describes her situation:

Client: I often think that my kids do not give me enough respect. Just once, I'd like them to ask me how my day went. When I'm tired, they could help out more.

Counsellor: Do you feel angry?

Client: Sure I do. Who wouldn't?

In this example, the client hints at strong but undefined feelings. Even though the client affirms anger, this may not be her main feeling. The client may indeed be angry, but other feelings may be dominant. Yet many clients find it easier to go in the direction suggested by the counsellor's question than to shift the answer. A less biased question might be "How do you feel about this?"

Kadushin (1997) suggests that open questions can be intimidating for inexperienced clients who are unsure of their expected role: "For such interviewees, open-ended questions provide little structure, little guidance for what they are supposed to talk about and how they are supposed to talk about it" (p. 241). As a rule, clients may remain confused, resistant, or threatened by questions until clarity is established regarding the goals and process of counselling. This underscores the importance of relationship contracting that establishes counselling routines and expectations, which typically leads to more client control and collaboration and a reduction in client resistance.

SUCCESS TIP

Questions can lead to surprising and unexpected client responses (for both clients and counsellors). These responses create options for transitions to new areas of inquiry and for renegotiated agreement on the direction of work (contract). When clients respond to questions with strong emotions, empathy is a preferred response.

Indirect Questions   **Indirect questions**, or embedded questions, are statements that act as questions. Indirect questions are a softer way of seeking information. They are less intimidating than open and closed questions. Indirect questions are effective for breaking up the monotony and threat of constant questioning, particularly when they are combined with other skills, especially empathy. The following are some examples of indirect questions:

indirect questions: Statements that imply questions (e.g., "I'm curious about how you responded").

- I wonder whether you believe that it's possible.
- Perhaps you're feeling confused over her response.
- I'm curious about your opinion.
- Given what you've said, I wouldn't be surprised if you decided to accept the offer.
- I have no idea what you might be thinking.
- I would not be surprised to find that you have strong feelings on the matter.
- You may have already reached a conclusion.
- Your views on this are very important to me.

Table 5.1 summarizes the various types of questions, including their advantages and disadvantages.

TABLE 5.1 Types of Questions

Type	Description	Advantages	Disadvantages	Examples
Closed questions (*do, will can, are, if*)	Questions that can be answered yes or no	• Confirm facts, conclusions, or agreements • Slow the pace of a rambling interview by limiting focus • Are easy for clients to answer	• Restrict answers • When asked repeatedly, can leave clients feeling interrogated	• Will you be going to the parents' group tonight? • Did you say everything that you wanted to say?
Open questions (*who, what, where, when, why, how*)	Questions that promote a more expansive answer	• Allow for an unrestricted range of responses • Empower clients by giving them increased control of answers	• May be more time-consuming process • Are more challenging for clients to answer	• What are your plans for this evening? • How are you feeling?
Indirect questions	Statements that act as questions	• Are less threatening than traditional questions	• May not elicit a response from the client	• I am interested in knowing if you have thought about what to do.

ESSENTIAL QUESTIONS: SOME OPTIONS

Some interviews are highly structured with a series of questions to answer, such as a survey or a standardized assessment tool or protocol. For example, a suicide risk assessment interview will include targeted questions designed to get information about known risk factors. A psychiatric interview gathers data to see whether a client's symptoms match the criteria for particular mental disorders. Although it is possible (and sometimes desirable) to conduct an interview without questions, the ability to formulate targeted questions is an indispensable skill for every counsellor.

structured interview: An interview that follows a predetermined sequence of questions.

A **structured interview** follows a defined sequence of predetermined standard questions. Examples include interviews that require counsellors to complete forms to establish clients' eligibility or to make assessments. In structured interviews, there is little or no freedom of choice regarding the focus and pace of the interview.

unstructured interview: An interview that does not have a preset plan that restricts direction, pace, or content.

An **unstructured interview** gives interviewers and clients freedom to go in any direction without a predetermined set of questions. In this type of interview, the tone is more conversational, and the pace and style of questioning is less rigid. The contract remains flexible.

Typically, most interviews will have the following process goals:

1. Establishing purpose (sessional contract)
2. Defining, strengthening, or trouble shooting the counselling relationship (relationship contract)
3. Exploring and understanding the client's situation and problems
4. Problem solving
5. Evaluating the work

The following sections propose sample questions for each of the preceding areas. It is always preferable to have a variety of ideas (choices) for accomplishing the same task. A repertoire permits flexibility and contributes to keeping the interview interesting and individualized. To increase the chances for rapport, counsellors need to modify questions and word choice to meet the particular needs, educational level, and culture of each client. Other active listening skills such as summarizing and, in particular, empathy are essential to ensure that the interview does not become an interrogation.

Questions for Establishing Purpose

Contracting was introduced in Chapter 3 as a tool for ensuring that clients and counsellors clearly understand the intended purpose of the relationship. When clients come for service, the basic question counsellors need answered is "What brings you here today?" Of course, this does not prevent counsellors from introducing their own ideas, but this question and its variations ensure that clients are consulted regarding their needs and expectations. This is particularly important when working with involuntary or reluctant clients. Here are some sample questions:

- How would you like to spend our time together?
- Do you have feelings and concerns from our last session that you want to address?
- What would you like to talk about?
- What do you think would be a good starting point?
- What would you like to accomplish today?
- What is your goal?

Questions to Define the Counselling Relationship

Clients may come to counselling with clear ideas of what they want from their counsellors, or they may be aware only of their pain and be hopeful that some help will be forthcoming. In any case, it is important that both clients and counsellors understand their respective roles in the process. Relationship contracting (see Chapter 3) gives clients and counsellors an opportunity to define their relationship and how they will work together. Typical questions include the following:

- What experiences have you had with counselling? What did you find helpful/not helpful?
- What are your expectations of me?
- How do you prefer feedback (e.g., soft, direct, and "sandwiched")?
- When you imagined coming here today, what were you hoping would happen?
- How will you know if our time together has been useful?
- Anticipatory feedback helps to plan for things that might arise in the counselling relationship. For example:
  - If I notice that you are getting discouraged, what should I do?
  - What would be a good way for me to approach you if I think there were problems between us?

Questions for Exploring and Understanding

At the beginning of an interview, or when a new topic is introduced, an open-ended question such as "What do I need to know about your situation?" empowers clients to identify areas of immediate concern or willingness to explore. This question communicates to clients that counsellors will respect their needs and wants without making assumptions. It seems to say, "I am willing to listen and learn. I will treat you as a person, not as a number or a category." At least initially, clients may not put forward their most urgent need. They may start with a safe topic to test the waters for understanding and acceptance. Once they feel more trust, they may present matters that are more serious.

Sample variations of this question are "What are the important things I need to understand about you and your problem?" and "Can you tell me the key points we need to explore?" Concreteness probes are used during all phases of the interview to ensure clarity and secure examples. They move the interview from superficial understanding to shared understanding.

Questions designed to learn about a client's situation generally target three important areas or domains:

1. How the client *feels* about the problem—**affective domain**
2. How the client *thinks* about the problem—**cognitive domain**
3. What the client *is doing* about the problem—**behavioural domain**

affective domain: How clients feel.

cognitive domain: How clients think about their situations.

behavioural domain: What clients are doing.

Affective Domain (Feeling)

Sometimes solutions to problems are obvious to clients, and they do not need help with decision making or problem solving but still lack the capacity to cope with their dilemmas. Often this is because their struggles to deal with painful feelings detract from their power to solve the problem. So, in many circumstances, management of emotions is a prerequisite to problem solving.

Questions that explore the feeling or affective domain include the following:

- How do you feel?
- What emotions does this trigger?
- I'm interested in hearing more about your emotions.
- What feelings best describe your reaction?
- Are you feeling . . . ?

The question "How do you feel?" is one way to introduce feelings and to encourage clients to explore the emotional components of their problems.

Cognitive Domain (Thinking)

How people think about their difficulties is often more important than the problem itself. An event that may be no big deal to one client may represent a life-threatening crisis to another. **Self-talk**, or inner dialogue, refers to the mental messages we give ourselves. Negative self-talk is associated with inaction and poor self-image.

self-talk: Mental messages people give to themselves (e.g., "I'm no good").

In contrast, positive self-talk builds confidence and is self-empowering. It moves people away from a victim mentality of feeling powerless. It also enables individuals to deal with crises realistically, without self-imposed rigid and punishing demands.

By seeking to understand how clients think about problems, counsellors can get valuable clues regarding important issues, such as self-esteem, motivation, and irrational thinking. Subsequently, counsellors can directly challenge clients' negative self-talk.

Sometimes counsellors can achieve quick and dramatic counselling interventions by challenging the rationality of the worrier. By offering facts, challenging assumptions, and inviting clients to consider the real probabilities of dreaded events, counsellors introduce much-needed critical thinking that may interrupt the worry cycle (Shebib, 1997, p. 81). This strategy is an essential element of cognitive behavioural counselling, which will be explored in Chapter 7.

Here are sample questions that can prompt exploration of the cognitive area:

- What are you thinking?
- What is the evidence for your belief?
- How do you know this to be true?
- What do you say to yourself about this problem?
- What does your "inner voice" say?

- What messages do you give yourself that are self-defeating?
- What are you telling yourself?

Behavioural Domain   Although it is important not to move too quickly to work on problem solving, an important part of work in the beginning phase involves interviewing clients to learn what they are doing and not doing about their problems. Such information is important for assessment. It tells counsellors whether their clients are active in seeking and working on solutions or whether they have become withdrawn and have given up. Some questions for exploring the behavioural area include the following:

- What have you done?
- Who else is affected by this problem?
- Can you identify what triggered your relapse?
- How did you respond?
- What did you do or say?
- When is the problem worse or better?
- Has the way you have been handling your problem changed?

SUCCESS TIP

Changes in any of the three domains—feeling, thinking, or behaviour—will stimulate changes in the other two areas. For example, when a client is able to alter negative thinking patterns, positive changes are more likely with respect to their feelings and their behaviour. (See Figure 5.1).

Questions for Problem Solving

Questions can assist clients to think systematically about the sequential steps involved in finding remedies to their problems. Questions of this type are more appropriate when the problem has been fully explored. Some key template questions include the following:

- What do you see as possible strategies for overcoming this problem?
- What are the costs and benefits of this alternative?
- How would you feel if you took this step? How would you feel if you did not act?

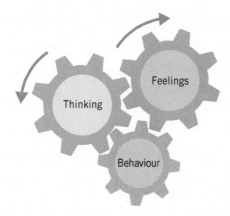

Figure 5.1   The Three Domains

- What prevents you from taking action?
- How can you overcome this barrier?
- What else do you need to make it happen?
- What do you see as your first step toward change?
- How can you make it (your goal) happen?
- What strengths or resources will help you achieve your goal?
- When will you start?

> ### SUCCESS TIP
>
> Avoid the common tendency to move too quickly to problem solving. Make sure that the problem has been fully explored first and that clients have been given an opportunity to express and process their feelings.

Questions for Evaluating

Ongoing evaluation of counselling outcomes and the counselling relationship ensures that the work remains on track. Evaluation enables counsellors and clients to trouble-shoot relationship problems before they become catastrophic. Evaluation also informs contract negotiation and revision. Some examples of questions that might initiate evaluation are as follows:

- How has our work met your expectations?
- Looking back on our session, what were the things that you found helpful? Unhelpful?
- How would you like things to be the same or different next time we meet?
- What remains to be done?
- What changes would you like to make with respect to the way we communicate?
- On a scale of 1–10 how would you rate our time together?
- How would you evaluate our work?

At the end of an interview (or as a significant topic ends), the question "What have we missed?" often yields surprisingly rich information. This question provides a last-chance opportunity for clients to talk about unexpressed issues and feelings. In addition, when clients have been ambivalent about sharing some details, this question may tip the scales in favour of sharing. It also empowers clients by giving them control over content, and a final chance to make sure their needs are on the table for discussion. Some variations of this question include the following:

- What else do we need to discuss?
- What's left to explore?
- Have we covered all that is important?
- What questions haven't I asked?

In the following example, the counsellor prompts the client to examine the session:

Counsellor: Our time is almost up, and I want to make sure I haven't overlooked anything that is important to you. What have we missed?

Client: Well, we haven't even begun to talk about how my divorce has changed my kids. In many ways, they have been the real victims.

Neuroplasticity means that our brains are constantly involved in forming new neural pathways as well as pruning ones that are no longer used. Effective interviewing can help to form a "new brain." For example, questions that focus on setting goals create neural pathways that strengthen the focus on moving forward and change. Questions targeting client strengths activate areas of the brain that stimulate positive emotions, and increase the neurotransmitter serotonin, which is essential to a sense of well-being (Ivey, Ivey & Quirk, 2009).

Counsellor: I agree with you. It's very important that we don't overlook them. Does it make sense to you to make that discussion part of our next meeting? I want to make sure there is enough time.

Client: Yes, that makes sense.

Counsellor: Then let's make that number one on our list for next time.

Remember that there are some risks to opening up new areas of discussion at the end of an interview, particularly if the topic involves strong emotions for the client. In the preceding example, the counsellor suspected that this was a complex topic, so she suggested deferral to the next session. In such circumstances, the counsellor might have been tempted to ask further questions or to empathize, but these responses might have prolonged the interview beyond the time available. It is important to end the interview without leaving the client in a state of distress.

SUCCESS TIP

Six Key Questions

1. What brings you here today?
2. What are your expectations of me?
3. What do I need to know about your situation?
4. What do you mean by . . . ?
5. What did we accomplish?
6. What did we miss?

QUESTIONING PITFALLS

Asking questions is a skill. Faulty questioning may bias answers, antagonize clients, or keep the interview at a superficial level. In addition, insensitive questions that disregard clients' feelings or culture can leave them feeling judged or abandoned. Poorly timed questions may rush the interview or frighten clients with demands for disclosure before trust has been established.

Leading (Biased) Questions

A **leading question** suggest the "correct" answer by conveying a strong clue about the answer the interviewer would prefer to hear. The following examples illustrate this pitfall:

> "Don't you believe it's time you took care of yourself instead of putting your husband first?"

> "You like school, don't you?"

leading questions: A question that suggests a preferred answer (e.g., "Don't you think our session went really well today?").

"Do you really want to keep working for a man who treats you that way?"

"You're not thinking of killing yourself, are you?"

Clients who have a high need to be liked, those who tend to be compliant, and those with dependency needs are especially vulnerable to leading questions. These clients are less likely to be assertive by disagreeing with their counsellors.

How a question is worded can also dramatically change the answer. Asking your spiritual leader, "Is it all right to smoke while praying?" may get a very different answer from asking, "Is it all right to pray while smoking?" (Sudman & Bradburn, 1983, p. 1).

Counsellors may use leading questions to camouflage their own ideas. For example, the counsellor who asks, "Do you think you should be doing that?" is probably saying, "I don't think you should be doing that." Leading questions tend to corner clients, as in the following interview excerpt, in which a counsellor talks to a man about his mother:

Counsellor: Given what you've been saying, it's time for action. Wouldn't you agree that allowing your mother to live alone at home is not in anyone's best interest?

Client: I suppose you're right.

Counsellor: Would you prefer to put her in a seniors' home?

Client: I really don't want to put her in a home. That wouldn't be right.

Counsellor: Don't you think this might be easier on your family than taking on the enormous problems involved in moving her in with you?

Client: *(Hesitates.)* I suppose you're right. But . . .

Counsellor: *(Interrupting.)* I have a list of possible placements. Do you want to make some calls now?

It's easy to see how the counsellor's agenda in the preceding encounter discounted the views and needs of the client. By selectively emphasizing one alternative, the counsellor allowed the client little freedom of choice. Consider how the outcome might have been different had the counsellor used the following lead:

Counsellor: Given what you have been saying, it seems you've reached a point where it's time for action. What do you see as your options?

Such a lead would have allowed the client to identify alternatives, such as arranging for in-home care for his mother or inviting her to live with him. The counsellor's favoured alternative does not contaminate the discussion. Counsellors need to remind themselves that the solution belongs to the client and there may be considerable ambivalence regarding the alternatives. The counsellor's role is to support the management of this ambivalence by paying attention to feelings, exploring the problem, and weighing alternatives.

Excessive Questioning

Although questions can be an important part of most interviews, excessive questioning can quickly leave clients feeling interrogated and bombarded and, as a result, some clients fail to return for a second interview. Others become increasingly defensive and terse with their responses, particularly if they are unsure of the purpose of the questions. Excessive questioning can overwhelm clients, leaving them frustrated, confused, and exhausted. Questions put counsellors in control, and they remind the client who has power in the relationship.

Some clients simply do not respond well to questions. Counsellors may find that rather than getting more information, they are obtaining less. For example, involuntary clients may experience questions as an invasion of their privacy. As well, clients from some cultures may react unfavourably to questions. In such circumstances, reliance on

STUDENT: Sometimes it feels as if all I do is ask questions. I can't help thinking that if I were the client, I'd be really irritated. I don't want to leave clients feeling interrogated, but questions seem to be the only way to get the information I need. Do you agree?

TEACHER: You're right to be concerned. There is a real danger that clients will become defensive if they feel cross-examined. By paying attention to the needs, feelings, and responses of individual clients, you will be able to see if you are alienating them. Sometimes counselling works best if you avoid or minimize questions. For example, clients who have not yet developed trust in their counsellors may respond better in interviews when questions are minimized.

Another drawback to asking too many questions is that too much responsibility for the direction and content of the interview can be left on your shoulders. This can be disempowering for clients and can lead them to become overly dependent.

STUDENT: But are there ways to explore and get information without asking questions?

TEACHER: Yes, there are a number of skill alternatives to questions for gathering information and making assessments. In some cases, pre-interview questionnaires can be used to gather important information. Switching to a nonverbal mode by using tools such as flip charts, pictures, play (with children), or music can also be effective ways to connect with clients. Techniques such as showing empathy, summarizing, using silence, and self-disclosing may be more effective ways of getting details, facts, and examples.

Empathy, for example, is a powerful counselling tool that tells clients that we understand or are trying to appreciate their feelings and perspectives. Empathic responses and summaries create an essential base of trust by showing that counsellors are nonjudgmental and capable of listening and understanding. In response, clients often become more courageous and motivated to share and explore. Appropriate use of silence creates space for clients to speak. Questions are important for effective interviewing, but you should try to add variety to your interviews by using a range of skills.

---

questions will frustrate the goals of the interview. Counsellors should be alert to signs that their clients are reacting poorly to questions. For example, their clients' answers may become briefer, a clear sign of their intention to be less cooperative. Clients also may communicate their displeasure nonverbally by shifting uncomfortably, grimacing, or averting eye contact. Some clients may refuse to answer by becoming silent, but others may be more outspoken with their disapproval, saying, for instance, "I don't see the point of all these questions." If counsellors continue with questions when it is clear that their clients are rejecting this approach, serious damage to the counselling relationship may result.

Consequently, it is important that counsellors are able to modify their approaches to reduce or eliminate questions. Sometimes, for example, an empathic response can achieve the same purpose as a question:

Client: I just don't know what I'm going to do. Since she left, I've felt lost and unsure of what I should do with my life.

Counsellor (Choice 1): What are some possibilities?

Counsellor (Choice 2): Sounds as if you feel all alone and uncertain of what to do next.

Choice 1 seeks more information from the client about what alternatives he sees for himself. This question moves the interview away from feelings to problem solving and decision making. In Choice 2, the counsellor acknowledges the client's feelings as well as his indecision, and the response is much more likely to be perceived as supportive and sensitive.

Sometimes counsellors have to ask many questions, such as in determining eligibility for service or completing an intake (first) interview. One way to lessen the impact of excessive questions is to have periodic pauses to check how their clients are doing. For example, they might say, "I'm asking a lot of questions. How are you doing? I know it can be a bit overwhelming." Respectful comments such as these empower and involve clients in the process.

It is important for counsellors to remember to balance questions with responses that confirm understanding (summaries) and empathic responses that affirm sensitivity to feelings. When questions are clearly linked to the agreed-upon purpose of the interview (contract), clients are much more likely to be cooperative, but if the questions appear meaningless or intrusive to the client, resistance is likely. Asking questions is an appropriate way to get information. However, skilled counsellors have the ability to switch to a non-questioning mode when the situation warrants. The following example shows some of the different options for exploring a client's anger:

Open Question: What happens when you get angry?

Closed Question: When you are angry, do you become violent?

Indirect Question: I'm curious about how you handle your anger.

Self-disclosure: When I'm angry, I always wonder what to do with it.

Empathy: Sounds as though, in addition to your anger, you also have a lot of pain.

Silence: (Appropriate silence avoids arousing the client's defences. It gives the client time to express his or her feelings.)

Contract: Perhaps we can pause for a moment and decide whether this is a good time to explore your feelings of anger.

Directive: Tell me more.

Sentence completion: Use an incomplete sentence (sentence stem) that pauses with an expectation that the client will finish the sentence. Usually the client will fill the pause with his or her thoughts or feelings.

Here are some examples:

- *It seems that when you become angry, you tend to . . .*
- *And you are feeling . . .*
- *The most important thing for you is to . . .*
- *If you were to tell him what you think, you would . . .*

This tool enables counsellors to control the process by providing clients with stimulating prompts while ensuring that the content comes from clients.

Summary: The theme in what you are saying seems to be a strong feeling of anger.

Paraphrase: In other words, you're a person who will deal with your anger in some way.

All of the preceding examples are potential counsellor responses, and each has the potential to achieve the process goal of anger exploration. They illustrate the range of choices that are always available to skilled, versatile counsellors.

SUCCESS TIP

Consider switching to a non-questioning mode (1) to reduce the tone of interrogation and avoid the power struggle trap, (2) when client responses are guarded and defensive, (3) when clients are not responding to questions, (4) for cultural adaptation, and (5) to add variety to your interviews.

Multiple Questions

Multiple questions are two or more questions asked at the same time. If the questions are complementary, they are not problematic. A second question may be asked simultaneously that embellishes or clarifies the first:

Counsellor (Example 1): How did you feel about it? How did you feel when he rejected you?

In Example 1, the second question does not detract from or contradict the first. Of course, the second question alone would have sufficed. In contrast, the following example illustrates how multiple questions can be confusing:

Counsellor (Example 2): How did you feel about it? Did you see any other way of handling the situation?

With Example 2, both questions are potentially useful, but not when they are asked at the same time. The client has to decide which question to answer. Each will take the interview in a different direction: the first focuses on feelings while the second moves the discussion to the behavioural domain. At their worst, multiple questions can inundate and assault clients with complex and conflicting demands. Imagine if you were the client in the following interview:

Counsellor: So, is there anything you can do? Do you think you might have told her how you felt? Or maybe you see it differently. How long do you think you can continue to hang on?

The counsellor may be well-meaning, but responses such as these complicate matters and may add to the client's confusion. As a rule, counsellors need to curb any impulse to ask more than one question at a time. When they ask a question, they should wait for the answer before proceeding to another question or topic.

Irrelevant and Poorly Timed Questions

One way that counselling interviews are distinguished from everyday conversations is that interviews have a definite purpose or intent. When counsellors know the purpose of the interview, they are able to frame questions that support that purpose. Conversely, counsellors who are unsure of the purpose are more likely to ask random questions.

Counsellors should have a purpose for questioning, and they should be prepared to share this purpose with their clients. They might offer a brief explanation, for example, "It would help me to understand your situation better if I asked you some questions. This will give me an idea of how you see things." Preambles such as this inform the client of the counsellor's motives and procedures. When clients know what is happening, they are less likely to be defensive and more likely to support the process.

Sometimes counsellors ask excellent questions but ask them at the wrong time, which leads to inappropriate topic changes. A common error of this type occurs when counsellors ask content questions after clients have expressed their feelings:

Client: I was furious with her. I never imagined that my best friend would be having an affair with my husband. We've been married for 10 years, and I thought I could trust him. I feel like a complete fool.

Counsellor: How did you find out they were seeing each other?

In the preceding example, the counsellor's question may be valid, but it is timed insensitively. Since the client has just risked expressing strong feelings, the counsellor should consider empathy as the preferred response. The next chapter addresses the critical skill of empathy.

A second common error occurs when counsellors shift the topic without exploring beyond a superficial level. This can happen for several reasons. First, counsellors may be unskilled at probing a topic. Second, they may be overly cautious about probing, perhaps fearing that they will be invading their clients' privacy. Third, they may be fixated on problem solving, as in the following example:

Client: We fight all the time.

Counsellor: How do you think you might cut down on the fighting?

In this example, the counsellor jumps to problem solving far too quickly. A better choice would have been questions to find meaning and empathy to connect with feelings. For example, the counsellor needs to learn what the client meant by "fight." Do they yell and scream? Do they refuse to talk to each other? Or is there physical conflict? Perhaps the best response choice would be a probe targeting feelings, such as "How do you feel about the constant fighting?"

Why Questions

Why questions should be used cautiously since they tend to be more threatening for clients if they are perceived as asking for justification, or if the tone of the *why* question communicates judgment, disapproval, or embedded advice. The question "Why don't you leave him?" may put a client on the defensive with the implied message "You should leave." *Why* questions ask people to explain and justify their behaviour. Frequently, this requires a degree of insight that they simply do not have. In response, clients may make up answers or feel exposed and stupid for being unable to answer the question.

Even when judgment is not intended, "when someone asks why you did something, you might feel she or he is judging you for not being able to handle the situation more effectively" (Hill, 2004, p. 121). *Why* questions may provoke defensive reactions, including avoidance and attack because "many clients associate *why* with a past experience of being grilled" (Ivey, Ivey, & Zalaquett, 2010, p. 103). The following excerpt illustrates:

> **Client:** I can't relate to my father anymore. He cannot see that I need my independence.
>
> **Counsellor:** Why don't you just move out and live on your own?
>
> **Client:** Impossible. I have two more years of college, and I can't afford it.
>
> **Counsellor:** Why not just tell him how you feel?
>
> **Client:** It's easy for you to say, but you just don't understand.

Kadushin (1997) suggests asking *what* instead of *why* questions. For example, "What prevents you from sharing your feelings?" is more helpful than "Why don't you share your feelings?" The first question (what) seems to accept that there are explanations and reasons for the client's behaviour, whereas the second question (why) seems to demand justification.

TAILORING THE INTERVIEW TO THE CLIENT
When Clients Do Not Answer Questions

Sometimes clients do not answer questions, or their answers are superficial. To decide how to proceed in such cases, counsellors need to consider some of the reasons why clients might be reluctant to respond.

Questions Are Not Understood Clients may not understand questions because they have not heard them. For example, clients may be hard of hearing or deaf, or counsellors may be speaking too softly, or background noise interferes. As well, clients may not have been listening. In addition, counsellors may be using words, phrases, metaphors, and expressions that are not part of the client's repertoire. Effective counsellors are able to adapt their idiomatic language and voice volume to meet their clients' needs and expectations. They avoid technical terms and jargon, particularly when communicating with clients from different cultures. Furthermore, counsellors are role models for their clients, and one of the interesting and positive outcomes of counselling is that clients may learn how to listen. When counsellors demonstrate effective listening and responding skills, clients tend to imitate them. Alternatively, counsellors can teach clients to use listening tools. For example, to encourage clients to summarize, leads such as this can be used: "Please tell me in your own words what your understanding of our agreement is. I want to make sure we both have the same understanding."

The Purpose of Questioning Is Unclear   Clients have a right to know why questions are being asked, and they are more apt to respond when the purpose is clear. Counsellors may simply state the purpose in an explanatory sentence: "The reason I am asking this question is . . . ?" However, if counsellors do not have a valid reason for asking particular questions, they should not ask them. Questions are crucial for accomplishing the goals of counselling, but they must be used cautiously, either to obtain important information or to direct the interview to relevant channels.

The Answers to Questions Are Unknown   Some questions are difficult for clients to answer. For example, the questions may call for insight and explanations that are beyond the clients' current level of understanding. Sometimes clients are unable to articulate their ideas and inner feelings. Learning disabilities are also a factor for some clients. When clients don't have answers, "why" questions are particularly frustrating.

Client Privacy Is an Issue   If clients are concerned about their privacy, they may say (verbally or nonverbally), "That's not an issue I care to explore." They may change the topic abruptly, or they may respond with silence. Some clients resist questions because of prior experiences of being embarrassed, interrogated, or put on the spot. Moreover, their cultural norms may discourage questions of any type, or they may restrict the areas in which questioning is appropriate. In some situations, clients withhold answers because they fear that their answers will not be understood or that they will be judged. At other times, they are simply not ready or able to address the issues the questions raise.

Unresolved Relationship Issues   It will be difficult to proceed with counselling if there is outstanding tension or conflict in the relationship. Good questions, insightful empathy, accurate summaries, even warmth and caring may be rejected because they are filtered through the relationship discord. In such situations, it may be a better choice to shift the discussion to address the conflict.

Response Choices When Clients Don't Respond to Questions   First, counsellors should honour the rights of clients to control areas of discussion and levels of intimacy during any phase of the relationship. Using the contracting process, counsellors can respect clients' wishes not to explore the particular area and shift the discussion to less threatening content. Nevertheless, some anxiety is normal and potentially productive when difficult topics are being addressed, so counsellors should not automatically shift the topic when anxiety arises.

Second, counsellors can evaluate whether they have given their clients enough time to answer. Some clients are slower to respond, and counsellors may misinterpret their silence as reluctance to speak.

Third, counsellors might tactfully ask clients what is preventing them from answering. Sometimes trust issues impede candor. Candid discussion of barriers usually increases trust, if counsellors are nondefensive. Moreover, by remaining nondefensive, counsellors demonstrate their capacity to be open and nonjudgmental. They show their ability to handle tough issues without retaliating. As well, when questions target sensitive or private information, counsellors can express empathy regarding how hard it might be to share such personal material.

Fourth, counsellors can simply stop asking questions. If they continue to ask questions even though clients refuse or dismiss them, unfortunate consequences will likely result. Moreover, under persistent questioning clients may become increasingly frustrated, angry, and resistant, or they may feel inadequate because they have been unable to meet their counsellors' expectations.

Table 5.2 summarizes conditions for using questions appropriately.

TABLE 5.2 Guidelines for Questioning

Don't:	Do:
Bombard clients with questions.	Balance and add variety to the interview with a range of other skills.
Ask more than one question at a time.	Pause after each question to give clients time to answer.
Use leading questions to control clients and their answers.	Remember that summary and empathy responses are important to confirm understanding.
Use *why* questions, as they usually imply blame or convey judgment.	Ask questions one at a time.
Ask questions unless you have a reason to need, or a right to have, the answer.	Respect cultural norms and individual styles that may make certain questions inappropriate.
Ask a long series of closed questions.	Ask questions for a specific purpose.
Ask closed questions when you need to confirm specific facts or ideas.	Ask open questions to give clients maximum control.

Managing the Rambling Interview

A challenge that all counsellors face is how to focus and control overly verbose clients, who ramble from topic to topic with unnecessary or overwhelming detail. Significantly, the thinking patterns that lead clients to verbose wandering in the interview may be the same patterns that prevent them from handling their problem situations appropriately. Consequently, it is important that counsellors take some responsibility for managing the interview process. In this way, clients learn about sequencing and managing problem exploration and resolution. Here are some strategy choices:

■ Since open questions tend to elicit detailed responses, counsellors can use more closed questions.

■ Identify the problem. For example, the counsellor might make a comment such as, "You're giving me a lot of information, and I want to make sure I don't miss anything. So, can I have your permission to focus on one point at a time?"

■ Ask questions that challenge clients to be brief and focused, such as, "If I asked you to summarize your situation in a sentence or two, what would you say?"

■ Monitor the use of nonverbal cues that might encourage wandering, such as an attentive posture, head nods, and paralinguistic cues (e.g., "Go on," "Yes").

■ Be candid with the client by using a statement such as "It seems to me that whenever we start to talk about a topic, we end up wandering off the subject. What do you think might be happening?"

■ When clients make inappropriate or premature shifts, immediately refocus on the topic being addressed. It may be helpful to let the client know why you are doing this with a comment such as "I'm going to slow you down a bit. I want to make sure we fully explore the issue of . . . before we move on. If we stay with one issue at a time, we are less likely to miss important work."

■ Identify time constraints. Set time limits on the interview and remind clients of the interview time remaining.

Although it may be necessary to cut some clients off, it is important that this be done in a way that the client does not feel devalued or overpowered. Counsellors need to monitor and control their own negative feelings, such as irritation and frustration that may be evoked by their verbose clients. If this is not done, it will be difficult for them to communicate a genuinely caring tone and empathic attitude.

SUCCESS TIP

In the beginning phase, clients often need an uninterrupted opportunity to tell their story and share their feelings. Controlling and focusing the interview too quickly may impede and negate the cathartic benefit for a client that is made possible by attentive listening.

Interviewing Youth

The period from puberty to young adulthood spans 8–12 years and is characterized by enormous biological, psychological, and social development, as well as significant changes in cognitive development and the brain. Even under the best of circumstances, it is often a trying time with rapidly fluctuating emotions, insecurities, and angst as people confront the challenges of developing an adult identity. These challenges are compounded for youth in the social service system who could be dealing with additional issues such as family breakdown, homelessness, poverty, drug abuse, physical and sexual abuse, mental disorders, and conflict with the legal system.

Like all groups, there is no one-size-fits-all script for working with youth. Although they may be dealing with common problems and challenges, each young person is unique and the counselling relationship must honour these individual differences. Paying attention to the counselling relationship makes this possible.

The core conditions (unconditional positive regard, empathy, and genuineness) discussed in Chapter 3 of this text are the foundation for this relationship. Youth may come to counselling with considerable suspicion so counsellors need to be patient, calm, and consistent during what might be a lengthy beginning phase of trust building. Past relationships where trust has been violated may leave youth justifiably suspicious and cautious of the motives of others, including well-meaning counsellors. Counsellor consistency and predictability provides structure that increases a sense of safety for the youth.

The contracting process can be used to explore and understand the youths' needs, what they want from you, as well as individual preferences. Open discussion to achieve clarity on the role of the counsellor and the goals of counselling, as well as the limits of confidentiality, helps to reassure youth that there are no hidden agendas.

Youth may present with behaviours that don't make sense. Intense reactions to seemingly innocuous triggers, resistance to simple rules, anger, acting-out behaviours, and an inability to make simple decisions in their own best interests may signal a history of trauma. Youth who distrust the sincerity or commitment of their counsellors

---

⟫⟫ BRAIN BYTE | The Adolescent Brain

The prefrontal cortex (behind the forehead) is a major area of the brain responsible for regulating behaviour, making good judgment choices, and predicting the outcome of behaviour. It also plays a part in regulating emotions and sexual urges. It is the last area of the brain to fully develop, with full maturation delayed until early adulthood. As a result, adolescents are more likely to act impulsively and to experiment with drugs and high risk or sensation seeking behaviour (Ashwell, 2012). Compounding the problem is the fact that drugs such as alcohol compromise the prefrontal cortex, further limiting its ability to support effective decision making.

may test their relationships repetitively by questioning motives, engaging in provocative behaviour, and exhibiting outright expressions of hostility toward their workers. This requires that workers be exceptionally patient and resilient and not take their clients' actions personally. A trauma-informed approach to youth recognizes that these behaviours and reactions serve a self-protective purpose, and counsellors need to take time to try to understand these clients in the context of their trauma. This underscores the importance of giving youth time to "tell their stories" and the critical importance of counsellors letting them know that their stories have been heard. Active listening skills, in particular empathy, are crucial in this process. On the other hand, excessive questioning can feel intrusive, and it may undermine the intended collaborative goal of the relationship. Table 5.3 offers additional tips for interviewing youth.

Indigenous youth may be dealing with significant issues of marginalization, including a system involving workers who are typically Caucasian. An anti-racist approach such as the one described by Hick (2010) demands that workers "change their own awareness and procedures, and social relations and systems that operate, both overtly and covertly, to perpetuate racism" (p. 267). As part of this, counsellors should actively explore how they can support the use of Indigenous spiritual and healing practices.

Youth can be an incredibly satisfying population to work with, as there is great potential for shifts and changes in their lifestyle that could result in major positive movement. A strengths-based approach shifts the focus from deficits, problems, and identifying what is wrong to collaborative relationship where the emphasis is on helping clients take control by utilizing personal, community, and family strengths. Wayne Hammond (2015), President of Resiliency Initiatives Canada, emphasizes that children can be resilient and grow, even thrive, when faced with adversity and that our approach should emphasize hope, solutions, and possibilities. He says that "those who embrace a strength-based perspective hold the belief that children, youth, and their families have strengths, resources, and the ability to recover from adversity (as opposed to emphasizing problems, vulnerabilities, and deficits)."

TABLE 5.3 Success Tips for Interviewing Youth

- Don't get drawn into power struggles.
- Maintain self-awareness and a nonjudgmental attitude regarding issues such as dress, hair, and body piercings.
- Avoid pressuring youth to make changes they are not ready for, as this is likely to evoke resistance.
- Pay close attention to changes in baseline (established patterns of behaviour) as they may signal increased stress or suicide risk.
- Seek youth input in goal setting and decision making to increase the likelihood that they will engage in and sustain change.
- Be friendly and warm, but remember you are not their personal friend.
- Avoid trying to be "with it" by adopting the language, mannerisms, and dress of this group. It's not expected; it may not be respected.
- Remember that what may seem to be "no big deal" to you may be a major crisis to the youth. What is important is how they see and define the problem.
- Don't assume heterosexuality.
- Support and collaborate with other professionals who may be involved with your client.
- Social media is a big part of most teens' lives. Look for opportunities to discuss safety issues (e.g., the dangers of "sexting"). Encourage clients to utilize appropriate online resources to assist them to understand issues in their lives.

Interviewing and Counselling Seniors

Canada's 6 million seniors are a very diverse population. Interviewing and counselling with this group requires consideration of a large number of variables. In addition to the usual cultural and personality differences that define any group, counsellors will want to consider factors that are significant for seniors, including physical health, cognitive ability, economic status, family, and community supports.

> Mason and Paul are lifelong friends in their early seventies. Mason is physically active and enjoys spending time with his wife and six grandchildren. Paul uses a walker, lives in a long-term care facility, and is dependent on medication for a variety of health issues including diabetes, Parkinson's disease, and depression. Paul invested wisely and is financially independent while Mason continues to work part-time in order to meet his basic needs.

Challenges and problems faced by seniors can be disempowering. As with any group, the goal of counselling is to assist them to restore or sustain elements essential to an empowered life including independence, freedom of choice, and an opportunity to pursue goals and dreams.

All of the principles, values, and counselling strategies discussed in this book are still appropriate when working with seniors. As always, flexibility in the choice of skills is essential in order to accommodate individual difference.

Counsellors who work with seniors need to be exceptionally empathic. They need to invest considerable effort to understand life issues that they have not yet faced. For example, the need for a senior to move to assisted living may, in the face of diminished capacity and failing health, seem self-evident and necessary, yet it is met with considerable resistance. This resistance must be understood from the perspective of the client's emotions which have been aroused by the implications of the multiple losses associate with the prospect of moving. Empathy and patience provide an opportunity for the client to express and process these emotions. Table 5.4 provides further success tips for interviewing and counselling seniors.

Senior Abuse

When interviewing seniors, counsellors should be alert to the possibility of abuse. Senior (elder) abuse includes a wide range of problematic issues including: physical assault, sexual abuse, over/under medication, neglect, denial of personal rights such as the right to practice one's religion, threats, emotional abuse, and harassment. It may come from strangers who target seniors, caregivers, or in any setting providing service, but it is most likely to come from someone known to the senior, usually a family member. Neglect in care facilities may occur as a result of inadequate staffing or training. In recent years, online predators have targeted seniors and have successfully duped many of them out of their life savings.

Counsellors need to be fully familiar with their legal and professional responsibilities with respect to elder abuse. Sometimes the abuse is a criminal offence (e.g., assault, theft, and uttering threats) and protection and investigation are subject to the jurisdiction of the criminal code. The Canadian *Charter of Rights and Freedoms* offers protection against discrimination. There is no specific legislation in Canada that deals with the rights of seniors but each province has enacted its own laws regarding issues such as guardianship (see Canadian Centre for Elder Law, 2017) for details on provincial legislation.

Counsellors should look for clues that suggest abuse such as:

■ Signs of neglect: shaggy appearance, malnourishment, lack of personal hygiene, and being left unbathed

■ Injury: unexplained or untreated wounds, black eyes, or bruises

TABLE 5.4 Success Tips for Interviewing and Counselling Seniors

- Adapt for hearing problems. Minimize noise, and if you need to talk louder, take extra precautions to insure confidentiality.
- Modify the interview as necessary to accommodate vision and mobility problems. For example, provide any written material in a larger font. Ensure that office furniture is not a barrier or an obstacle to the client.
- Be careful with physical contact. For example, a firm handshake may injure someone with fragile bones.
- If your client has cognitive impairment, keep it simple, speak slowly, summarize, use repetition, and simple and focused questions.
- Allow time for the client to reflect and process. Pictures can be used as memory cues.
- Focus on empowerment. Adopt counselling strategies that give clients control and collaborative involvement in decision making.
- Adopt a strengths-based approach that assumes capacity, not incapacity. A client may have vision impairment, but this does not mean that he or she is unable to make independent decisions.
- Explore and understand the events and life experiences that have shaped the values and world view of clients.
- Adapt counselling strategies to the cultural norms, values, and beliefs of the client.
- Facilitate life reviews that help seniors make sense of their lives.
- Be open to discussions that involve spirituality.
- Use "Mr.," "Miss," or "Mrs." unless you are invited to use first names.
- Be sensitive to gender-related issues.
- Eliminate age inappropriate jargon or unfamiliar acronyms.
- When working with families, talk directly to the older person, not through other family members. Similarly, when using a translator, maintain eye contact with the client and speak to them, not about them.
- Remember, some seniors may be meeting social/emotional needs through their relationship with a counsellor. This factor may add more time to the interview. However, older clients may have less energy, so avoid lengthy sessions that cause fatigue.
- Use empathy to convey understanding, but be careful that empathy does not invade the clients' need for privacy as they may not be comfortable with excessive intimacy with a stranger.
- Be sensitive to clues (e.g., bruising or unexplained injury, changes in baseline behaviour in mood or social involvement, lack of hygiene) that the client may be a victim of neglect, or physical, emotional, sexual, and financial abuse.
- Be alert to the fact that depression, social anxiety, and multiple losses may trigger thoughts of suicide. Don't be afraid to ask the "intent question" (see Chapter 9).
- Listen. There is much to learn from the acquired wisdom of seniors.

See Chapter 11 for strategies for working with seniors who have dementia.

- Behavioural changes: withdrawal, depression, defensiveness, and personality changes
- Financial changes: altering a will or power of attorney, large cash withdrawals, and exploitation by unscrupulous business
- Unsafe living conditions

Seniors, even when asked, may be very reluctant or unable to disclose that they are victims of abuse. This may occur because of shame, or fear of the consequences, or a desire to protect family members from legal consequences. In the following example, a social worker notices that her client, age 81, has a black eye.

Social Worker: I can see that your eye is swollen.

Client: It's nothing.

Social Worker: How did it happen?

Client: I must have bumped into a door or something. I really don't remember.

Social Worker: Was your husband with you when it happened?

Client: Like I said, it's nothing to worry about.

Social Worker: I'm wondering if you feel safe when you are alone with him.

Client: The last few years have not been easy for him. He really is a good man. But, since his stroke, there are times when . . . . (*Long pause.*)

Social Worker: You care for your husband, and it sounds like you don't want to cause him any trouble.

Client: I don't know what I'd do without him.

Social Worker: Sure, but it's also important that your needs are met. You need to be able to feel safe in our own home. Maybe, we're at a point where both of you could use some extra support.

In the example, the social worker proceeds with considerable patience and tact while gently maintaining the trust that will set the stage for a referral to appropriate follow-up and support services. Each province and city will have its own resources that can be accessed by seniors for support and protection including police, social service agencies, health authorities, shelters, community care facilities, and other organizations that offer specialized services for seniors.

Cross-Cultural Interviewing

Counsellors need to be careful that their counselling and questioning methods are not culturally biased. For example, cultural groups differ profoundly in the way they react to questions. When attempting to relate effectively to members of other cultures, counsellors need to avoid stereotyping and overgeneralizing. Within a culture, an individual may subscribe to all, some, or none of the cultural norms. Following are some points to consider:

- Clients with histories of oppression may tend to be overly compliant during the interview. Consequently, closed questions such as "Do you understand?" may be answered "yes," when in fact the client does not understand. Open questions are preferable.

- Use staff or interpreters who speak the immigrant client's language. When using an interpreter, look at the client when the interpreter is translating.

- When language skills are limited, pay careful attention to nonverbal cues.

- Some cultures may react negatively to questions, or they might find some questions on particular topics intrusive.

- Speak slowly, repeat or summarize often, and allow frequent pauses. Sometimes visual or written cues will assist communication. Use simple language and minimize jargon and idioms. Speaking louder will not help.

BEYOND THE SURFACE: INTERVIEWING FOR CONCRETENESS

The Need for Concreteness

Concreteness is a term used to measure the clarity and specificity of communication. It is "a way to ensure that general and common experiences and feelings such as depression, anxiety, anger, and so on are defined idiosyncratically for each client" (Cormier & Cormier, 1985, p. 48). When communication is concrete, all participants share an

concreteness: A term used to measure the clarity and specificity of communication.

>>> **BRAIN BYTE** Neural Development and Marginalization

Ivey, Ivey, Zalaquett, and Quirk (2009) reported that neuroscientists have found that the stress of poverty, oppression, sexism, and racism can create unhealthy and damaging levels of cortisol in the brain, which negatively impact neural development in areas of the brain associated with language and memory. This underscores the importance of counsellors supporting social action initiatives to combat oppression. Counselling can also assist clients to explore ways that they can mitigate the toxic damage from marginalization, including ways to deal with oppressive systems.

understanding of words, phrases, ideas, feelings, and behaviours. With selected probing skills, counsellors assist clients to provide necessary definition and detail. Counsellors also need to model concreteness by ensuring that their expressed ideas and feelings are clear and specific. In addition, they need to remain alert to signs (verbal and nonverbal) that their clients may be assigning different meanings from those intended. When client communication lacks concreteness, counsellors can use interviewing skills to raise it to the desired level. Figure 5.2 outlines various strategies counsellors can use to achieve concreteness.

Probing for concreteness is necessary for the following reasons:

■ *People see and experience events differently.* When someone describes a problem or shares a feeling, there is a natural tendency to make assumptions based on our own prior learning and experience. When a client asks a counsellor if he knows how she feels, the counsellor may automatically answer "*yes*" without further inquiry or clarification. Even though personal experience can help them appreciate the problems and feelings of clients, counsellors risk communication breakdowns if they neglect to explore their assumptions for accuracy. Active listening enables them to understand the experiences of others with less risk of contamination.

■ *The meaning of words and ideas is very much influenced by factors such as culture or history.* Although people may have links and similarities in their experiences and common human needs, everyone is unique. All people have different frames of reference based on their learning and experience. Consider the images that a word such as *anger* might evoke for various people. One person might vividly recall an abusive childhood, in which anger always led to someone getting hurt. Another might visualize screaming and hurtful words, while someone else thinks of withdrawing and saying nothing. To a 12-year-old, 30 might seem like old age, but to a man in his late 80s, 70 is young. Similarly, a joke may be perceived as humorous by some people but provocative, insulting, or sexist by others.

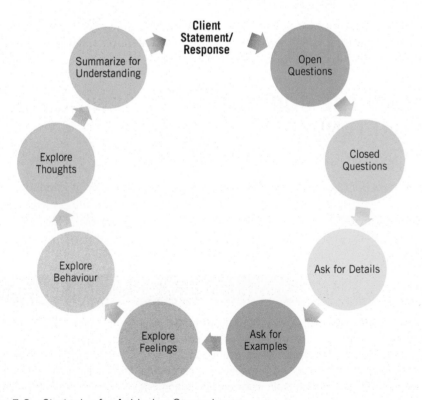

Figure 5.2 Strategies for Achieving Concreteness

- *Jargon and idiom may confuse clients.* Questions must be clear and understandable to the client. Like many other professionals, counsellors and their work settings have their jargon, consisting of abbreviations, distinctive words, and phrases that are commonly understood by the people who work in the field. This jargon allows for a quick shorthand flow of communication and helps to define activities and routines precisely. Unfortunately, jargon is often used inappropriately with clients who do not understand it, as in the following example:

Counsellor: I'm assuming that this is the first time that you've gone through the intake process. After we complete your app, I can refer you to an appropriate community resource.

A new client may have no idea what is meant by the terms *intake process* and *community resource* or the abbreviation *app*. Too embarrassed to ask, such a client may be left feeling demoralized, stupid, and incapable. Nonassertive clients frequently respond to jargon by acquiescing or pretending that they understand when they have no idea what has been said.

- *Messages are often unclear, incomplete, or ambiguous.* Important information may be missing. Shared understanding between two people is possible only when each participant understands a message in the way that the sender intended.

- *People may lack the vocabulary to express their ideas precisely.* When language abilities are limited, it is difficult to communicate ideas and feelings.

- *People may be unaware of their feelings.* Questions can stimulate thinking and bring clients' attention to areas and feelings that they may not have considered.

- *Communication may be superficial.* When counsellors move too quickly without exploration of key ideas and feelings, the interview is likely to remain on a surface level, and it may quickly run out of steam. Here's an example:

Client: I feel strongly about it.

Counsellor: I'm not surprised. From what you have been saying, who wouldn't feel that way?

The counsellor is supportive but does not explore further to find out how the client is feeling. This client hints at feelings but gives no information about their precise nature. Unless the counsellor probes further, assumptions and misunderstanding are the likely outcomes.

Probes for concreteness propel the interview from a superficial level of discussion to an intimate level that requires a deeper investment from everyone involved in the interview. Chapter 2 defined the illusion of work concept as a kind of implicit partnership between counsellors and clients. In this arrangement, counsellors permit clients to avoid the pain and struggle that are often associated with growth, while counsellors avoid the risk that purposeful challenge entails:

We have all developed the capacity to engage in conversations which are empty and which have no meaning . . . Workers have reported helping relationships with clients that have spanned months, even years, in which the worker always knew, deep inside, that it was all illusion. (Shulman 2009, p. 154)

- *Content alone does not fully communicate meaning.* A counsellor can easily miss important information by failing to notice the underlying emotional or personal content in the words.

Counsellor Reluctance to Probe One distinguishing characteristic of exemplary professional interviewers and counsellors is their capacity to be comfortable with any topic. Effective interviewers and counsellors are learners, and they recognize that the best teachers are their clients. This means having the courage and assertiveness to ask difficult questions about private matters. If counsellors have personal needs to avoid certain topics or if they are fearful that the discussion might unleash strong client emotions, they might hold back to meet their own needs to keep the interview pleasant. At the same time, counsellors need to know when to back off and respect their clients' right to declare some topics off limits. Probing too deeply or moving too fast may result in clients revealing a great deal, but having done so, they may react adversely. They might feel violated and not return to future sessions, or they might put up barriers to protect against further unwanted inquiries. To be ethical, counsellors must question wisely, exploring only those matters that are relevant to the work and fit their competence and training. Thus, asking clients for more concreteness requires that counsellors are willing to invest time and energy to listen.

Client Reluctance   Some thoughts may be private, and lack of relationship trust may preclude full disclosure. For example, people fearing judgment or ridicule may tell others what they think they want to hear, or what they believe will result in acceptance. Individuals may also distort or exaggerate messages because of experiences. Embarrassment, fear, uncertainty, taboos about taking help, and simple mistrust of the interview process, including suspicion about the motives of the interviewer, present natural barriers to sharing information. For some people, taking help from someone else suggests dependency and weakness, which may result in feelings of inadequacy. None of this means that the interview relationship is dysfunctional. In relationships, everyone must decide how much, when, and with whom they are willing to reveal personal thoughts and feelings. Everyone differs in the degree to which they are comfortable with disclosing intimate thoughts and feelings. Restraint and self-censorship of some ideas and feelings are normal and necessary. Some people prefer to remain private, sharing little or nothing. Others open up very slowly and only with people whom they deeply trust. Cultural norms may also influence what individuals are willing to share. Clients often view counsellors and interviewers as authority figures, and they tend to relate to them based on their prior experiences and images of people in power. Even though the counsellor may have very little real authority, what is important is the perception of the client that the counsellor has power. Probes for concreteness are invitations to clients to trust their counsellors by revealing thoughts that they might prefer to keep hidden.

Shulman (2009) suggests that the same societal taboos that inhibit open discussion of sensitive topics also affect helping relationships. Among the taboos that Shulman identifies is reluctance to talk about sex, money, dependency, loss, and authority. To Shulman's list of common taboos could be added discussions about spiritual issues and health, as well as others that vary between people and between cultures.

SUCCESS TIP

Competent interviewing requires curiosity and a willingness to learn. This becomes even more important when counsellors have personal and professional experience with the issue on the table. Unless counsellors monitor and control their assumptions, they are vulnerable to assuming they know their client's situation without needing to be told.

Strategies for Achieving Concreteness

Let Clients Know the Purpose   Counsellors should probe for understanding only in those areas that support the purpose of the counselling relationship (contract). Without a clear contract, the counselling interview is more likely to be haphazard and random. However, in the beginning, it may be necessary to give clients some time to tell their story. When counsellors have a need for information or if they wish to explore a particular area, they should consider sharing their objective, as in the following example:

> **Counsellor:** You have not talked much about your feelings. I'm wondering if it might be useful for us to spend a little bit of time exploring this important area. That might help us understand some of the pressure you've been under and how tough it is to move forward. What do you think?

When clients understand and support the purpose, they are much more likely to respond positively to probes for concreteness.

Respect Timing   Here are some broad general guidelines:

- During the beginning phase of a relationship, probe more cautiously until trust is developed, or you get a sense of the client's capacity for more in-depth exploration.
- When there are relationship conflict issues, consider the wisdom of dealing with this reality first.
- Probes for concreteness may stir up feelings that clients need time to process; therefore, during the ending phase of an interview probe more selectively.

Use Simple Encouragers and Directives   The simplest way to probe for more information is to use short phrases and gestures that encourage clients to continue with their stories. Nonverbal gestures, such as head nods, sustained eye contact, and attended silence, convey such support and interest.

Directives are short statements that provide direction to clients. Using directives is another way of gathering information. They can also be used to control the pace and flow of an interview, and in cognitive behavioural counselling (discussed in Chapter 7), they are used to assign homework to clients. Directives such as "Describe your feelings," "List your main reasons," "Give me an example," "Tell me what you did," "Share your thoughts," "Tell me more," "Expand on that," "Don't move too quickly," "Describe your feelings," and "Put it in your own words" all help achieve concreteness.

Since overuse of directives may leave clients feeling controlled, they should be used sparingly. A softer tone and open body language can lessen the command aspect of the directive. Short statements and directives, such as "Tell me more," "Yes, go on," "What else?" "Please expand on that," and simple encouragers such as "Uh-huh, hmm," can be used to sustain client sharing without interrupting the flow of the interview. A short example will illustrate:

> **directives:** Short statements that provide direction to clients on topics, information, and pace (e.g., "Tell me more").

> **Client:** I guess I'm pretty angry.
>
> **Counsellor:** Meaning?
>
> **Client:** Our relationship is on the rocks.
>
> **Counsellor:** Tell me more.
>
> **Client:** My brother always puts me down. It's got to the point where I don't want to be around him.
>
> **Counsellor:** (Nods; attentive silence.)
>
> **Client:** We used to be so close. We were inseparable, but in the last year, it's become so competitive.

Questions   Questions are the primary tool for seeking information. Intelligent questioning can be used to get examples, define terms, or probe for detail. The following interview excerpt demonstrates this process:

> **Counsellor:** I want to make sure I understand. What do you mean when you say *competitive?*
>
> **Client:** It's something ugly. Not just wanting to win but also needing to win. It's as if everything rides on winning.

Counsellor: Is that true for both of you?

Client: At first, it was just him. Now I'm just as bad.

Counsellor: What's a typical example?

Counsellors can use series of questions to explore vague statements beyond a superficial level. The following excerpt illustrates:

Client: I know there are many times when I let my feelings get the better of me.

Counsellor: What kinds of feelings?

Client: Sometimes I let my anger build to the point where I'm ready to explode.

Counsellor: "Ready to explode"—what does that mean?

Client: I would never become physical and hurt someone. I'm just afraid of getting really mean and saying hurtful things.

Counsellor: Has that happened?

Client: Yes. *(Hesitates.)* A lot.

Counsellor: Can you think of a good example?

Client: My mother. She's always trying to control my life. Most of the time, I just try to ignore her constant nagging, but lately it seems that every second day she phones with advice. I don't want it, and I don't need it. Yesterday I blew up at her.

Counsellor: What did you do or say?

Client: I told her in no uncertain terms to butt out of my life. She started to cry. Then I felt guilty.

Empathy Although it is not usually thought of as a probing tool, empathy in fact creates a powerful incentive for clients to open up. Although there are exceptions, successful empathy builds trust and safety for clients to reveal and explore their feelings. Without empathy, clients are more likely to keep their feelings private.

Follow Clues Often clients hint at a concern, which provides counsellors with a natural opportunity to probe for more detail and to open the discussion to a greater level of intimacy.

Client: *(Avoiding eye contact.)* It's not easy to open up to a stranger.

Counsellor: It is tough. You might wonder how I am going to react or whether I will hold what you say against you.

Client: It's just so embarrassing.

Counsellor: One way to overcome that is to take a chance on me. I'm open to anything you have to say. I find that when I avoid talking about a tough area, it becomes even more difficult to deal with later.

Client: Lately, I cannot sleep at night because I'm wondering if I might be gay.

SUCCESS TIP

"To help a client, discuss taboo feelings and concerns, the worker has to create a unique 'culture' in the helping interview. In this culture, it is acceptable to discuss feelings and concerns that the client may experience as taboo elsewhere" (Shulman, 2009, p. 156). To create this culture, look for clues that taboo-related blocks are present, bring discussion of the block to the open, and then renegotiate a new agreement that allows for open discussion of the taboo area (Shulman, 2009).

Making Choices

A theme throughout this book is that effective counsellors have a broad range of alternatives for responding. When they have choices, counsellors are not locked into repetitive patterns, and interviews are more interesting and vibrant for both clients and counsellors. The following example demonstrates some of the many ways that a counsellor might respond to a client:

Client: I suppose I should have expected it. My girlfriend said she needed time to think to "re-evaluate our relationship," as she put it. It was tough, but I gave her some time alone.

Counsellor (Choice 1): How did you feel about what was happening? [an open question that focuses the discussion on the client's feelings]

Counsellor (Choice 2): What was your plan? [an open question concentrating on the client's behaviour and thoughts]

Counsellor (Choice 3): Tell me what you planned to do. [directive]

Counsellor (Choice 4): Sounds like this was a painful time for you. [empathic response directed to the client's feelings]

Counsellor (Choice 5): I'd be interested in knowing how you handled it. [indirect question]

Counsellor (Choice 6): (Silence.) [silence used to give the client an opportunity to continue sharing]

Counsellor (Choice 7): It was hard, but you were able to give her time to reassess your relationship. [paraphrase]

SUCCESS TIP

Choices for promoting elaboration (concreteness) include combining each of the six basic open question stems (who, what, when, where, why, and how) with each of the three basic domains (behaviour, feeling, and thinking). Simple encouragers such as "Tell me more" and "For example . . ." promote further depth and clarity.

INTERVIEW TRANSITIONS

An **interview transition** occurs when the topic of conversation shifts from one subject to another. Such shifts may occur spontaneously in the course of the interview, or they may be orchestrated to further the objectives of the interview. The need for a transition arises in the following situations:

interview transition: A shift in the topic of the interview.

1. Discussion of a particular issue is finished, and it is time to move on.
2. Discussion triggers ideas in another area or links to earlier areas of discussion.
3. The topic is too threatening or painful, and a topic change is needed to reduce tension.
4. The subject has limited relevance or has lost its relevance to the goals of the interview.
5. A change from one phase of the interview to another is necessary (Shebib, 1997, p. 156).

There are five types of transitions: natural, strategic, control, phase, and connect or linking (Shebib, 1997, p. 156).

Natural Transitions

Natural transitions arise as the discussion flows seamlessly from one topic to another, with clear links between the two topics. The most common natural transition occurs when clients mention new themes as part of the interview, and counsellors use this information to jump to the new topic.

> **Client:** As I talk about my dissatisfaction with my job, I realize that the same could also be said about my marriage.
>
> **Counsellor:** Perhaps we could address that now. Tell me what's happening in your marriage.

Clients are unlikely to resist natural transitions since the interview moves clearly in the direction they have suggested. The topic change is not abrupt, and transition responses indicate that counsellors have heard what their clients have just stated.

Strategic Transitions

Strategic transitions arise when counsellors make choices among topic alternatives. Imagine that a client makes a statement such as the following:

> **Client:** This has been the worst year on record for me. My finances were a disaster anyway, and now that I've lost my job I think I'll go under. Needless to say, this hasn't been good for my marriage. I can see how hard it is on my kids. My eldest daughter seems to avoid me entirely, and I'm sure my son is on drugs. It all becomes too much.

How should a counsellor respond to this revelation? Should he or she select finances as a priority for follow-up? Or go with one of the other problems: marriage, relationships with children, drug abuse, or unemployment? Should the counsellor focus on problems or feelings or both? How a counsellor responds is a strategic decision that affects the direction of the interview, at least for the moment. As much as possible, clients should be involved in decisions to make a strategic transition.

Control Transitions

Because counsellors have to orchestrate the flow of the interview, they sometimes use control transitions to manage the interview's direction. Redirecting the flow of an interview is warranted when the discussion topic is irrelevant or when it prevents dialogue on more important issues. Preventing premature subject changes is crucial for ensuring concreteness or full exploration of content and feelings. Moving too quickly from topic to topic results in a rambling and superficial interview where many things are discussed, but few are understood.

Control transitions are used not to dominate clients, but rather to exercise professional duty to ensure that the interview time is productive. In practice, counsellors and their clients should share control, with counsellors giving clients as much power as possible to set the course of counselling based on their needs. For their part, counsellors help by monitoring the process and pace of the interview to ensure that discussions have sufficient intimacy and stimulation. Skilled counsellors are sensitive to the following elements of the interview that are open to control:

1. Specific topics that are the subject of focus
2. The extent that the interview focuses on each of the three domains: feelings (including control on level of emotionality), behaviour, and thinking
3. Sequences in which topics are discussed, including decisions to move the interview from one phase to another
4. Use of time, including depth of discussion as well as interview start and end times
5. The following example illustrates a control transition:

> **Counsellor:** I think we might be moving too quickly here. We haven't had a chance to talk about your feelings. I wonder if you'd agree that we should do that before we move on to a different topic. It might help us both to understand why it's been so difficult for you to make a decision.

In this example, the counsellor gives a brief reason for slowing down the interview and focusing on feelings. Clients who understand what is happening are much more likely to support the process.

But clients themselves may suddenly change the subject of the interview for a variety of reasons. For example, perhaps they were revealing too much, or the material was too painful or personal to discuss. Because of issues of client trust and readiness, counsellors need to use control transitions wisely and be mindful of the underlying feelings that client-initiated shifts signal. One way for counsellors to deal with a topic shift is to openly acknowledge the shift, then gently explore its meaning.

> **Counsellor:** Am I right in thinking that you seemed uncomfortable talking about your relationship with your father?
>
> **Client:** It's not something I want to get into right now.
>
> **Counsellor:** That's okay. I will not force you. On the other hand, you might decide later that you are ready.

Counsellors can use summaries as a way to introduce control transitions. As the following example illustrates, summarizing makes the topic switch seem less abrupt. This is important because abrupt transitions may appear harsh to clients and accentuate their feelings of being cross-examined.

> **Counsellor:** So, as I understand it, drug abuse has had a significant impact on your work. Your boss has reached a point where he will support you, but only if you enter rehab. Let's shift our focus for a minute and talk about problems with your family.

Phase Transitions

Counsellors also use topic changes to help move the counselling process into the next phase. For example, in the beginning phase relationship building and problem exploration are paramount. However, at some point, it becomes clear that sufficient time has been spent on problem exploration, and it is time to move on to the challenges of the action phase, where the activity shifts to problem solving and sessional contract work on feelings, thinking, or behaviour. Thus, phase transitions are needed to bridge the work of one phase to another, as illustrated by the following example:

> **Counsellor:** I wonder if we have reached a point where it makes sense to begin talking about the changes you want to make. We could begin to discuss some of your goals and then think about how to achieve them.

In the following example, the counsellor uses a phase transition to end the interview and to establish a link to the next session:

> **Counsellor:** I'm impressed with your insights about how you tend to put yourself down. It seems to me that the next logical step might be to explore how to combat this tendency. If you agree, we can start with that next time.

Pacing   Generally, interviewers should proceed at a pace that their clients can manage. This does not mean that clients must always be 100 percent comfortable with the intensity of the interview. Indeed, the work of interviewing and counselling can be demanding, and exploring difficult topics can be exhausting. Here are some general guidelines for pacing:

- Move more slowly in new relationships and first encounters.
- Expect differences among clients.
- Don't expect to maintain the same intensity or an ever-increasing intensity throughout the interview. Periodic "rest" periods with nonthreatening or less demanding topics can energize clients.
- End interviews with less demanding questions and responses.

STUDENT: What are your thoughts on taking notes during an interview?

TEACHER: You first.

STUDENT: I have mixed feelings. On the one hand, I don't want to forget anything. On the other hand, it seems so cold and clinical to be writing when clients are talking. It seems to take away from the intimacy of the relationship.

TEACHER: Suppose you were the client, and I were taking notes.

STUDENT: I'd wonder about what you were writing about me. I'd be really scared that someone else might see the notes. I'd probably be really careful about what I said.

TEACHER: What if I told you that you could see the notes?

STUDENT: That would help. Then I'd be able to correct any mistakes. I'd really want to know who would have access to the file.

TEACHER: All clients have a right to that information. They may not ask but, as a rule, you should tell them. You raised a good point earlier about how note-taking can detract from rapport in the interview. I agree. I think it's particularly important to put the pen down when clients are talking about feelings or other private matters. On the other hand, most clients expect that you'll write down information such as phone numbers and addresses.

STUDENT: I'd prefer not to take notes at all during the interview and just write up a summary after the client leaves.

TEACHER: That would be ideal. Of course, that's not always possible. There may be forms or computerized questionnaires to complete that can't be delayed until after the interview. Or you may have other clients waiting, so there may be no time after the interview.

Moreover, counsellors need to manage interview transitions between one topic and another. As well, they should avoid rigid agendas such as might be followed in a formal meeting and instead allow some freedom of movement between topics. Counsellors also need to be careful not to sprint from one topic to another without adequate exploration or completion.

Connect (Linking) Transitions

Connect or linking transitions are used to join or blend ideas from recurrent themes. For example, a client may make continual subtle references to a need to have everything just right. The counsellor might use a connect transition to bring this theme to the foreground:

> **Counsellor:** In all your examples, you talk about how you make sure that you pay attention to every little detail. Then you seem to berate yourself if everything isn't perfect.

The following excerpt illustrates selected interview skills. This is the first interview with the client, a single mother on welfare. The counsellor works in a community service centre that offers a variety of programs.

(During the first five minutes of the interview, the counsellor and the client engage in small talk.)	***Analysis:*** *Interview openings establish first impressions. A few minutes spent on small talk helps clients relax, and it should not be considered time wasted.*
Counsellor: Perhaps you can tell me what brings you here today. You did not tell me much on the phone, but I had the impression that you felt some urgency. **Client:** I've been on welfare for years, and I just can't make ends meet.	***Analysis:*** *A simple phase transition begins the process of establishing the purpose of the interview. By making a link to the intake phone call, the counsellor demonstrates that the client's sense of emergency was heard. This lets the client know that the counsellor is a good listener and sensitive to feelings.*

Counsellor: Sounds rough. Tell me more.

Client: It's not just the money—it's what it's doing to my kids.

Analysis: A supportive and sympathetic reaction communicates warmth and concern. The counsellor uses a directive to seek more detail and concreteness. As well, it creates an opportunity for the client to tell her story.

Counsellor: What do you mean?

Client: My oldest is 18. He doesn't seem to have any motivation. He says he can hardly wait until he is 19 so he can go on welfare too.

Analysis: It would be easy to assume what the client is talking about. Instead, the counsellor probes for definition. An open question gives the client full freedom to speak freely.

Counsellor: I wonder if it seems to you that being on welfare somehow connects with your son's attitude.

Client: Good point. I hadn't thought of that, but it makes sense. It's all we've known for the last five years.

Analysis: This indirect question offers an interesting reframe for the client to consider.

(A few minutes later.)

Counsellor: I need your help to understand what you were hoping would happen when you came here today.

Client: I need to get into some sort of retraining. My skills are way out of date.

Analysis: Here the counsellor might have asked an open question to initiate the working contract. However, an indirect question is substituted. This adds some variety to the interviewer's style and helps to avoid leaving the client feeling interrogated.

Client: I'm willing to work anywhere, but eventually, I want to find something that fits.

Counsellor: Fits?

Client: I'd really like to work with people. I'd like your job. *(Both laugh.)*

Analysis: The counsellor's response accents a key word using a questioning tone. This is yet another way to seek information that is more concrete. The counsellor's interest stimulates the client to say more. Humour lightens the tone, but provides an opportunity to probe further.

Counsellor: I noticed earlier that as you described your volunteer work with kids, you seemed happy.

Client: I'd love to do it full time, but there's no way.

Analysis: A linking transition connects two parts of the interview. Good counsellors try to remember a bit of information that might be relevant or useful later—a kind of "memory Post-It note."

Counsellor: What prevents you?

Client: I need to earn a living. Volunteers aren't paid. To get hired full time, I'd need to get a diploma.

Analysis: An open question to identify barriers.

Counsellor: But . . . ?

Client: But . . . That takes money, and I have no idea how I'd pay for it. Plus, I've never been a good student so going back at my age may be a recipe for disaster.

Analysis: Here, a simple unfinished response is a useful prompt for the client to identify barriers.

Counsellor: Sounds as if you've already looked into it. Although you sound like you'd love to do it, you're worried about all the obstacles.

Client: Yes. As I said earlier, I'm determined to get out of this rut. I suppose I should do something about it.

Reflections:

■ What is the importance of the client telling her story?

■ How does the counsellor in this interview communicate empathy?

■ Suggest what the counsellor might say or do next.

SUMMARY

- Questions are an important interviewing tool for gathering information, providing focus to the interview, promoting client insight, and supporting catharsis. Good questioning can systematically lead clients through problem solving and can help clients examine areas that they might otherwise overlook. It is important to balance questions with responses that confirm understanding (summaries and paraphrases) and empathic responses that confirm sensitivity to feelings. So experienced counsellors use a broad repertoire of skills all the time.

- Questions can be either closed or open. Closed questions can be easily answered yes or no. Open questions are difficult to answer with a simple yes or no. The vast majority of open questions will be "five W" questions (who, what, where, when, why, and how). Another effective questioning tool is the use of indirect questions, which are statements that function as questions.

- Faulty, insensitive, and poorly timed questioning may bias clients' answers, antagonize them, or keep the interview at a superficial level. Common errors include leading questions, excessive questioning, multiple questions, irrelevant or poorly timed questions, and *why* questions. Alternative options to questions are always available for use by skilled counsellors.

- Interviewing youth and seniors involves paying attention to individual differences as well as cognitive ability.

- Concreteness concerns the extent to which the discussion conveys clear and specific meaning. When communication is concrete, all participants share understanding of language, ideas, and feelings. Strategies for promoting concreteness include using simple encouragers, probing for detail with questions and directives.

- Interview transitions occur when the topic of the interview shifts from one subject to another. Such shifts may occur spontaneously in the course of the interview, or counsellors may orchestrate them to further the objectives of the interview. There are five different types of transitions: natural, strategic, control, phase, and connect (or linking).

EXERCISES

Self-Awareness

1. Pick an issue that you have very strong feelings about (e.g., abortion, capital punishment, or Canadian politics). Conduct a 5- to 10-minute interview with a colleague to explore his or her views on the same topic. However, do not reveal any of your feelings or thoughts on the topic. After the interview is over, discuss the experience. To what extent were you able to keep your own views separate?

2. Think about an experience where you had a strong reaction to being questioned. What were your thoughts and feelings during the encounter? How did you react?

3. Ask a friend or colleague to monitor your interactions over the next week or so regarding your use of questions. Seek feedback.

4. Conduct an interview with a colleague. Use questions inappropriately (e.g., ask irrelevant questions, change the topic frequently, bombard with questions, and ask leading questions). After the interview is completed, discuss how it felt to be in both the interviewer and the client role. What did you learn about yourself from this experience?

5. Reflect on the variables that might make it difficult for you to self-disclose to a counsellor. What issues in your life would you be reluctant or unwilling to discuss? How do you think you might react if a counsellor pursued these topics?

6. Think about some of your personal and work relationships. Are you more likely to be the one asking questions or the one answering questions? In what ways does this impact the power dynamics of the relationship?

7. On a scale of 1–10 (1 = easy; 10 = tough), rate how difficult it might be for you to conduct a client interview with the following themes or topics:

- Death
- Spiritual issues
- Sex and intimacy
- Mental health issues
- Hygiene
- Aging
- Your relationship with him/her

What can you learn about yourself from your answers?

Skill Practice

1. Conduct a 10-minute focused interview with a colleague. Your task is to explore one topic in as much depth as possible. However, in this interview, you are not allowed to ask questions. Use a range of skills other than questioning. (Note to the client: Keep your answers very brief. Try not to be overly cooperative.) After the interview is over, discuss the experience. See how many different strategies you can identify for getting information (in addition to open and closed questions).

2. As a conditioning exercise for interviewing quiet clients, conduct an interview with a colleague. Set up the interview so that your colleague does not respond verbally. Use a variety of techniques other than questions.

3. Videotape an extended interview with a colleague. Classify each response that the counsellor makes in terms of type— open question, closed question, summary, and so on. Identify patterns. Are there skills that are overused or underused?

Concepts

1. Classify each of the following questions as open, closed, or indirect.

a. How do you feel about your brother?

b. I'm puzzled about your reaction.

c. Do you have time to see me next week?

d. I'd like to know something about your strategy.

2. Reword the following closed questions as (a) open questions and (b) indirect questions.

a. Are you enrolled in the secretarial program?

b. Did the principal refer you?

c. Are you feeling sad?

d. Do you want to talk about your feelings?

e. Did you tell her how you felt?

3. Imagine that you are responding to the following client statements. Suggest follow-up responses that are open questions, closed questions, indirect questions, and directives.

a. I have mixed feelings.

b. The next step is to solve the bloody problem.

c. It's been a long time.

d. I know exactly what she means.

e. You have no idea how I feel.

f. I'm really angry with you.

g. There are some significant things happening in my life right now.

h. I'm not sure I can handle this problem. I need help.

4. Each of the following client statements has one or more problems with concreteness. First, identify the concreteness problem. Second, suggest a possible counsellor response to promote concreteness.

a. I still have feelings for her.

b. I've given it a lot of thought.

c. I hardly sleep at night.

d. I've tried to control my kids, but nothing seems to work.

e. She's an elderly person.

f. I feel bad.

5. Each of the following counsellor statements contains phrases or jargon that may be unfamiliar to clients. Reword each using everyday language.

a. It seems as though your son has a lot of interpersonal difficulty, and it is generating acting-out behaviour.

b. Cognitively, he seems well within the mean.

c. It appears to me that you are feeling ambivalent.

d. After intake it seems appropriate to make a referral to one of our community resources.

e. Your affect is euthymic.

6. Work in a small group to brainstorm jargon that is used in a setting that you know. Next, reword these terms and phrases so that they are easily understandable.

7. Watch a talk show. See if you can identify the interviewing skills that are used. Look for evidence of improper interviewing technique.

8. Identify six or more different choices for obtaining the following:

- The price of a bottle of soda
- Information about your client's feelings
- Your client's reason for seeking help

9. Imagine that you are a counsellor preplanning an interview with each of the following clients. What information do you think you might need? Identify questions and directives that you might use.

- A patient who has been physically restrained in a hospital emergency ward after a drug overdose.
- An elderly woman who is going blind.
- A man who seeks help for anger management.
- A parent of a child who has been taken into custody.

10. Interview Aerobics

11. Prepare flash cards with the names of various skills on each card (e.g., open question, closed question, paraphrase, summary, empathy, indirect question, directive, silence, wild card [any skill], self-disclosure, and contracting). Then use them in an interview with a colleague.

Note: The following exercises are designed to help you develop a range of skills. The more comfortable you are with a wide array of responses, the more you will be able to respond based on the needs of the client and the situation.

Exercise 1: Shuffle the cards. The counsellor listens carefully to what the client says and then selects the first card in the stack and follows the directions on that card. For example, if the next card reads "closed question," the counsellor must ask a closed question, even if that might not be the best response. (Note: Do not look at the card until the client has finished speaking.)

Exercise 2: Work in a group of three (counsellor, client, and coach). During the interview, the coach chooses an appropriate skill card for the counsellor to use.

Exercise 3: Conduct an interview using the cards in any order that you choose. Continue interviewing until all of the cards are used. Cards may be used more than one time.

Exercise 4: Conduct an interview using the cards in any order that you wish. However, you can use each card only once.

Exercise 5: Develop your own strategy for using the cards.

(Adapted from Shebib, 1997, p. 161)

WEBLINKS

Article on investigative interviewing of children.

"Guidelines on Investigatory Interviewing of Children: What Is the Consensus in the Scientific Community?" by Hollida Wakefield (2006). *American Journal of Forensic Psychology, 24* (3), 57–74.

www.ipt-forensics.com/library/ajfp1.htm

Basic counseling skills for working with teens (Center for Adolescent Studies)

https://centerforadolescentstudies.com/3-basic-counseling-skills-working-teens/

Chapter 6
Empathic Connections

Simikov/Shutterstock

- Explain the importance of emotions in counselling.
- Define what is meant by empathy.
- Identify the types of empathic responses, including when and how to use them.
- Explore key principles (generalizations) for using empathy.

THE EMOTIONAL DOMAIN

At any moment in a counselling interview, counsellors can choose to focus on one of three broad areas: behaviour, thought, or feelings (emotions). All three are potentially important and necessary for problem management and change. Of significance is that change in any one domain will have impact upon and trigger change in the others.

When the emphasis is on behaviour, counsellor questions and responses target what the client is doing or saying. Responses such as, "What did you say?" "How did you handle the situation?" and "What do you see as the next logical step?" are dominant. If the focus shifts to the thinking (cognitive domain), responses such as, "How did you make sense of what happened?" and "What were you thinking?" are evident. Work in the feeling or affective domain will involve counsellors in responses and questions that explore emotions. Questions such as, "How do you feel?" as well as empathy will

161

dominate the work. The balance of this chapter will explore concepts and strategies for working in the important emotional domain. Chapter 7 will explore how counsellors can work in the behavioural and cognitive domains.

Emotions define and shape the course of our lives. They remind us that we are alive, but sometimes they make us long for death. Some emotions—such as joy at the birth of a child—demand to be expressed. Some that are too frightening to acknowledge are destined to remain forever hidden, perhaps even from ourselves. Carl W. Buechner underscored the importance of emotional connections: "they may forget what you said, but they will never forget how you made them feel" (public domain). Shared emotions are the cornerstone of intimacy. One's emotional reaction, while not always rational, clear, or understandable, often controls the final judgment on communicative meaning.

Emotional responses trigger unique physiological responses in our bodies such as nausea or headaches, and they can have a profound impact on our health and well-being (Seligman & Reichenberg, 2010). In fact, "Emotions experienced as positive can activate the inner pharmacopeia, those chemicals that relax, help fight infection, and restore" (Saleeby, 2009, p. 17).

Historically, emotional responses have helped humans respond to important situations:

- *Anger:* The hands swell with blood, making it easier to use weapons or strike back; increased heart rate and adrenalin serve to increase energy and power.

- *Fear:* Blood flow to the legs increases, making it easier to escape; the body may freeze for a moment, giving time to gauge whether hiding is a better response.

- *Happiness:* Brain activity inhibits negative thoughts and fosters increased energy.

- *Love:* General bodily responses promote well-being and a general state of calm and contentment.

- *Surprise:* Raising the eyebrows expands the field of vision, thus, making it easier to figure out what is going on and to plan the best course of action.

- *Sadness:* A general drop in energy and enthusiasm creates an opportunity to mourn. (Goleman, 2005)

Jones (2006) makes this interesting observation: "Emotions are clever design solutions to the problem of making fast decisions in response to significant practical problems posed by the natural and social worlds: we perceive a danger and fear immediately primes us to take protective action" (p. 3). But she also comments on the way that emotions can cause us to act inappropriately: "They prepare us to embrace motivationally actions we should shun and leave us in physical turmoil when we would be better served by calm" (p. 8). Murdock (2009) identifies how problems might arise from emotional reasoning: "Because of the emotional investment in an idea, it is seen as true, regardless of discrepant information" (p. 329).

>>> **BRAIN BYTE** Emotional Memories

Emotional reactions are also linked to our emotional memories. The human brain compares current experience with past events for similarities, and it may command us to "react to the present in ways that were imprinted long ago, with thoughts, emotions, reactions learned in response to events perhaps only dimly similar" (Goleman, 2005, p. 21). This may result in what Goleman (2005) describes as "out-of-date neural alarms" that cause us to react with outdated or ineffective responses. Moreover, emotions can be particularly baffling because "they often date from a time early in our lives when things were bewildering and we did not have words for comprehending events. We may have the chaotic feelings, but not the words for the memories that formed them" (p. 22).

Because the human experience is so closely connected with emotions (feelings), we can expect counselling work to frequently focus on helping clients identify, explore, manage, or accept their emotions. Counsellors engage with clients' emotions in a number of ways. The counselling relationship provides safety for clients to explore and understand their feelings. Friends and family may be well-meaning but poorly equipped to deal with complex emotions. They may be prone to simplistic advice giving, or they may try to change the subject when painful feelings are revealed. Counsellors, on the other hand, are able to deal with feelings. They do not tell clients how they should feel, nor do they insult or frustrate clients with quick-fix solutions. Instead, they allow clients to express emotions without needing to censor what they reveal. Nonjudgmental responses and permissive encouragement from counsellors can be enormously therapeutic for those clients who have struggled on their own to cope with their emotions. The pursuit of empathic understanding opens up an avenue for communication and insight that is seldom accessible in everyday communication.

Goleman (2005) suggests that the ability to recognize feelings as they happen is the cornerstone of emotional intelligence, and that people who are more in touch with their feelings are better able to navigate their lives and are more competent decision makers. Gladding and Newsome (2010) suggest that "people who are unaware of their emotions often experience problems in relationships" (p. 154). Presbury, Echterling, and McKee (2008) conceptualized emotional intelligence in two categories: skills related to understanding the self and skills related to understanding others. Self-skills include abilities such as recognizing, monitoring, managing, and remaining open to our own emotions; being congruent in what we feel and how we behave; and using emotions as part of problem management and creativity. Emotional intelligence when relating to others requires empathic ability, including the capacity to understand, manage, and navigate emotions in others that may be complex and ambivalent. As well, we need to be able to recognize incongruence; that is, inconsistencies between what people feel and what they say or do. Seligman and Reichenberg (2010) give an example:

> A person expressing words of love will speak softly, maintain good eye contact, and have an open and welcoming posture. However, if that person verbalizes love but has poor eye contact, an angry tone of voice, or a tense and closed posture, conflicting and confusing emotions are communicated. The receiver may not know what to believe, only pay attention to part of the message, misinterpret the message, or discredit the message because of its delivery. (p. 132)

However, communication difficulties and problems often occur, since there are wide variations in the extent to which individuals value and express emotions. Many factors impact this, including age, cultural norms, gender, setting, mental disorders, and socialization. For example, people from Asian cultures value emotional restraint, whereas Westerners tend to be more boisterous in expressing feelings. Individuals may openly express emotions when they are with peers or friends, but be guarded or mute with persons in positions of authority (including counsellors).

Counsellors need to be alert to the impact of these variables, and they must also monitor their own emotional reactions and mood to make sure that their feelings do not

>>> BRAIN BYTE   Mirror Neurons

Recent neurological discoveries may help explain the roots of empathy as well as the risks of vicarious trauma for those in the helping professions. When we listen to or observe others, "mirror neurons" in our brains tend to fire in the same way as those of our clients. Put simply, when we hear about or witness an event, our brains respond in the same way as if we experienced the event directly. As a result, our feelings tend to mimic our clients' feelings.

negatively impact the work. Granello and Young (2012) emphasize that "clients in counseling must be allowed to work through their own issues without regard to the changing emotional state of the counselor" (p. 119).

Counsellors can help clients consider how their emotions might be interfering with decision making or everyday life. Decision making, for example, may be difficult when clients' emotions pull them in different directions; however, many unhappy feelings, such as sadness, anger, grief, and disappointment, are part of everyone's life. In fact, feelings like grief are healing responses, and they are not usually pathological or in need of treatment.

The Language of Emotions

> *Our language has wisely sensed the two sides of being alone. It has created the word "loneliness" to express the pain of being alone. And it has created the word "solitude" to express the glory of being alone.*
>
> —*Paul Tillich (The Eternal Now, 1952)*

Much of counselling involves getting in touch with the subjective experience of clients, particularly in the emotional domain. Counsellors are constantly challenged to understand and respond to the range of subtle feelings that clients express in language that they can understand and accept. Despite the fact that there are hundreds of words for emotions in the English language, words alone often fail to communicate precise information about client feelings. A client who says, "I'd kill for a chocolate ice cream," is clearly exaggerating. Another might minimize a problem, saying, "It doesn't bother me," but context and other cues might reveal evidence of profound pain.

Table 6.1 presents a feeling inventory of the most common families of emotions. It is self-evident that emotional intensity varies among people depending on the circumstances. Sometimes, word modifiers (e.g., *very, extremely, somewhat, mostly,* and *little*) serve to limit, quantify, and add further precision to the level and type of emotion expressed. For example, we can expect some difference in emotional level between people who describe themselves as somewhat happy and others who say they are incredibly happy.

Metaphors Metaphors describe a state by using a symbol in a direct comparison. For example, a client who says he is "going around in circles" is using a metaphor to describe his feelings of confusion.

Here are some metaphors with the possible feeling that each one suggests:

- tied up in knots, in a pressure cooker (stressed)
- about to blow up, bent out of shape (furious and angry)
- on a sinking ship, down in the dumps (hopeless)
- tearing my hair out (swamped)
- in a sticky situation (vulnerable)
- between a rock and a hard place (helpless, confused, and ambivalent)
- butterflies in my stomach (fear and excitement)
- on top of the world, on cloud nine (happy and ecstatic)
- taken for granted (devalued and put down)
- going around in circles, feeling pulled apart (confused and ambivalent)
- egg on face, like two cents (embarrassed and shamed)

In addition, sometimes people use metaphoric phrases to describe ways of dealing with emotions, such as "rising above it."

TABLE 6.1 Feeling Inventory

Category of Emotion	Intensity		
	Low Level	**Medium Level**	**High Level**
Anger	annoyed, irritated, miffed, offended, resentful, provoked, displeased, aggravated, put off, ticked, upset, and disturbed	angry, mad, hostile, hateful, disgusted, inflamed, in a tiff, fed up, sore, agitated, and seething	outraged, furious, vengeful, repulsed, boiling, in a rage, irate, and infuriated
Fear	alarmed, nervous, anxious, teased, uneasy, timid, bothered, apprehensive, intimidated, and butterflies	frightened, scared, worried, distressed, fearful, jumpy, and uptight	shocked, horrified, panicked, terrified, mortified, terrorized, and cold sweat
Empowerment	adequate, up to the challenge, able to cope, and stable	confident, capable, adept, healthy, qualified, whole, energized, dynamic, tough, strong, brave, determined, and secure	invulnerable, in control, bold, potent, courageous, and unbeatable
Vulnerability	delicate, insecure, timid, shy, small, fragile, tired, weary, embarrassed, spooked, apprehensive, and concerned	weak, vulnerable, falling apart, burnt out, cowardly, helpless, useless, sick, incompetent, inadequate, and unprotected, frail	defenseless, impotent, worthless, no good, powerless, exhausted, lifeless, useless, and petrified
Joy/pleasure	satisfied, glad, good, pleased, and comfortable	happy, contented, joyful, loved, excited, optimistic, and cheerful	euphoric, jubilant, ecstatic, thrilled, delighted, passionate, elated, marvelous, full of life, terrific, and overjoyed
Sadness	disappointed, hurt, troubled, downcast, upset, and bothered	unhappy, glum, sad, depressed, melancholy, blue, lonely, dismal, and pessimistic	agonized, dejected, despairing, despondent, hopeless, and miserable
Focus	distracted, muddled, uncertain, doubtful, hesitant, mixed up, unsure, and indecisive	confused, baffled, perplexed, puzzled, ambivalent, stumped, jumbled, disjointed, and frustrated	(in a state of) pandemonium or chaos, mystified, and swamped
Shame	embarrassed, humbled, and regretful	belittled, discredited, guilty, shamed, remorseful, and ashamed	disgraced, scandalized, humiliated, and mortified
Surprise	startled, and puzzled	surprised, stunned, and shocked	astonished, astounded, flabbergasted, amazed, overwhelmed, and in awe
Love	attracted, and friendly	close, intimate, warm, tender, cherished, smitten with, and doting on	loved, adored, enraptured, crazy about, wild about, flip over, idolize, and worship

Nonverbal Communication of Emotions   One key to successful communication is monitoring and understanding the nonverbal channel of communication. Body language (especially facial expression); vocal cues such as tone, intensity, rate of speech; and affect are essential components of emotions that confirm, embellish, or contradict verbal statements. All cues should be interpreted cautiously, including these common ones: tears, forced smiles, grimaces, covering clenched fist, shaking, becoming silent, smiling, shaking head, pacing, looking at the floor, turning away, and yelling. For example, lack of eye contact may be culturally appropriate in some Indigenous groups in Canada, and so non-Indigenous helpers should not interpret it as a sign of disrespect. Counsellors need to remember that their own nonverbal communication is not always under their control, and it may be outside their level of awareness. As Sue and Sue (2008) note, a counsellor "who has not adequately dealt with his or her own biases and racist attitudes may unwittingly communicate them to a culturally different client" (p. 171). Despite their words and stated intentions, their nonverbal communications express an uncensored meaning.

Individual Differences and Cultural Context

All feelings can be experienced as positive or negative at varying levels of intensity, but this subjective determination is individually defined. For some people, anxiety can be debilitating, seriously affecting the quality of their lives; however, for an athlete the same emotion may arouse a competitive spirit and the individual might thrive on its physiological consequences. Counsellors need to remember that their clients may respond with emotional reactions very different from their own—with similar feelings, sharply different feelings, without significant emotional reactions, or with markedly increased or decreased intensity; therefore, counsellors should avoid using their own measuring criteria to interpret the emotions of others. For example, if they expect that people in crisis will be verbal and declare their pain, then they might miss the fact that the quiet child is much needier than the one who is acting out.

But circumstances and context are not always good predictors of feelings. One person might be anxious about public speaking but find the experience exhilarating, while another person is terrified by the prospect. One individual might enjoy parties and be stimulated by the chance to meet new people, but a second person looks for any excuse to avoid the panic brought on by crowded social events. Consequently, when the meaning is not obvious, counsellors should ask clients to explain their emotional experiences.

In the following example, the counsellor makes erroneous assumptions and then, sensitive to the client's nonverbal message, works to correct the error. This models openness to the client and serves to reinforce the reality that counsellors are not perfect.

> **Client:** My mother is coming to visit me next week.
>
> **Counsellor:** Oh, that's nice. It's always great when you have a chance to see your folks.
>
> **Client:** *(Hesitating.)* I guess so.
>
> **Counsellor:** *(Picking up on the client's hesitation.)* Perhaps I was too hasty in assuming you would be happy that she was coming. I should have waited until you told me how you felt. How do you feel about her visit?
>
> **Client:** I dread it. My mother always wants to tell me how to run my life.

Individuals are also often governed by cultural norms, and there are wide variances in the extent and manner to which they express emotions. Some cultures value emotional expression, whereas others favour emotional restraint. Cultural empathy (Cormier & Hackney, 2008) requires counsellors to pay attention to both cultural as well as contextual considerations. Note that empathic responses should be culturally appropriate with consideration of issues of pride and shame. For some clients, empathic responses may lead to embarrassment and "loss of face." Thus, client receptivity to empathic responses should be considered.

Ambivalence

Clients interpret their own problems and experiences and find them frequently complicated by multiple and seemingly contradictory feelings from two or more emotional families (see Table 6.2). A great deal of stress and confusion can arise from the pushes and pulls of competing feelings that, if unmanaged, can disrupt a client's life. The terms *ambivalence* and *of two minds* are often used. Ambivalence is normal, and although it can keep people stuck, identification, exploration, and resolution of ambivalence can be a valuable part of decision making. Four key questions can be used to systematically evaluate options:

1. What are the advantages of maintaining the status quo?
2. What are the advantages of changing?
3. What are the disadvantages of the status quo?
4. What are the disadvantages of changing?

TABLE 6.2 Common Mixed Feelings

Happy and scared	This often arises in conjunction with a lifestyle change (e.g., getting married, returning to school, starting a new job, sending children to daycare, and experiencing the "empty nest" when children leave home).
Happy and sad	Some transitional life events, such as leaving one job for another or seeing a child off to college (or kindergarten, etc.), elicit these feelings. A sense of loss as well as gain is often present.
Depressed and fed up	These feelings suggest that the person has "bottomed out." Significantly, the feeling of being fed up may be used as a strong motivator for change (e.g., deciding to change a self-destructive drug habit).
Angry and afraid	Fear is often the more significant emotion, but anger is more commonly expressed (e.g., a parent facing a teenager who is two hours late for curfew).
Hopeful and despairing	Many clients fluctuate between believing that change is possible with the potential for life to get better and that nothing will improve and further effort is futile. Developing and sustaining motivation is crucial in such situations (e.g., a person coping with a life-threatening illness).
Attracted and repelled (approach/ avoid)	Many people who are considering changes in their lives experience these feelings. Part of them wants things to be different, and part wants the security of their present situation, however, distressful (e.g., a person contemplating leaving an abusive relationship).
Love and hate	This usually arises in the face of contradictory evidence (e.g., a friend whose behaviour is erratic—sometimes loving, sometimes abusive).

This method acknowledges that there are costs and benefits to each course of action. It also presents a nonjudgmental way to honour the fact that clients may resist change for good reason, even when they pay a heavy price for doing so. For example, a client may continue to abuse substances despite enormous personal and financial costs because it provides relief from his severe depression.

SUCCESS TIP

Counsellors need to remember that clients are the experts on their own lives and that they have made the best choice from what they consider to be their available options. Counselling empowers clients by helping them identify additional choices and by helping them to address or remove barriers to options that were not seen as viable.

Motivational Interviewing (Miller & Rollnick, 2013) was developed as a collaborative communication style specifically for assisting clients to resolve ambivalence. Empathy, a central feature of Motivational Interviewing "normalizes ambivalence and demonstrates that the counsellor unconditionally accepts the client" (Capuzzi & Stauffer, 2016, p. 153). This popular, evidence-based approach will be explored in detail in Chapter 7. Example:

A woman describes the joy she felt when her son left home to begin training as a counsellor, but as she talks, her eyes well up with tears. Clearly, she is experiencing a strong sense of loss, despite the fact that words speak to her pride and happiness. More accurately, both feelings exist simultaneously.

SUCCESS TIP

When responding to clients who express mixed feelings, say *and* instead of *but*. This is less confrontational and fully honours the presence of both feelings.

People also have feelings about the emotions they experience. Sometimes they are very aware of these mixed feelings, sometimes not. Try this simple experiment. Close your eyes and recall a recent strong emotion, such as anger or joy. Take a moment to get in touch with your feelings. Now try to complete this sentence, "I feel about feeling (your recent strong emotion)." Many readers will find that this simple exercise leads to a deeper understanding of their emotions. Some may find guilt behind their joy; others fear.

Mixed feelings are often associated with anxiety and stress, especially when the feelings require opposing responses. If a person is both attracted to and repelled by a particular choice, anxiety is likely to continue until he or she resolves the dilemma.

Affect

affect: A term that counsellors use to describe how people express emotions.

Affect is a term counsellors use to describe how people express emotions like sadness, excitement, and anger. Culture and context help to define what is considered within the "normal range" of affect. Moreover, affect is communicated through voice tone and quality, posture, facial expressions, and other nonverbal cues. These terms are often used to describe affect:

blunted: Emotional expression is less than one might expect.

flat: There is an absence or near absence of any signs of emotional expression.

inappropriate: The person's manner and mood contradict what one might expect. For example, a client might laugh while describing the death of his mother.

labile: There is abnormal variability in affect, with repeated, rapid, and abrupt shifts in affective expression.

restricted or constricted: There is a mild reduction in the range and intensity of emotional expression.

affective disorders: Disturbances in mood, including depression and mania.

mood disorders: See also *affective disorders*.

dysthymia: A chronic condition with symptoms similar to depression but that are less severe.

- **Blunted**: Emotional expression is less than one might expect.
- **Flat**: There is an absence or near absence of any signs of emotional expression.
- **Inappropriate**: The person's manner and mood contradict what one might expect. For example, a client might laugh while describing the death of his mother.
- **Labile**: There is abnormal variability in affect, with repeated, rapid, and abrupt shifts in affective expression.
- **Restricted or constricted**: There is a mild reduction in the range and intensity of emotional expression. (For more information, see American Psychiatric Association, *Diagnostic and Statistical Manual of Mental Disorders*, 4th ed., 2000.)

Psychologists and other mental health professionals use the terms **affective disorders** or **mood disorders** to describe a variety of disturbances in mood. The most common mood disorders are major depression, dysthymia, and bipolar disorder. Clients with major depression are likely to experience many of the following symptoms: depressed mood; inability to experience pleasure; loss of energy and interest in life and work; changes in appetite; sleep disturbances (especially insomnia); decrease in sexual energy; feelings of worthlessness, helplessness, guilt, anxiety, or pessimism; and thoughts of death or suicide. **Dysthymia** is a chronic condition with symptoms similar to depression but that are less intense. With bipolar disorder, clients have alternating depressive and manic episodes. Manic episodes include these symptoms: abnormally elevated mood, irritability, hostility, grandiosity, overactivity, flight of ideas, decreased need for sleep, and buying sprees or other indicators of poor judgment (Davis, 2006; American Psychiatric Association, 2000). In these situations, referral to a physician should be considered as an adjunct to counselling (see Chapter 9 for a more in-depth discussion).

EMPATHY

It is the mind which creates the world about us, and even though we stand side by side in the same meadow, my eyes will never see what is beheld by yours, my heart will never stir to the emotions with which yours is touched.

—George Gissing (1857–1903)

Empathy Defined

In everyday terms, *empathy* means seeing the world through someone else's eyes. For the purposes of counselling, though, empathy is defined as "the process of accurately understanding the emotional perspective of another person and the communication of this understanding" (Shebib, 1997, p. 177). The primary objective of empathy is to understand and respond to feelings, but there is also a cognitive component. Reiter (2008) defines cognitive empathy as "an understanding of the values, worldview, and intentions of the client" (p. 109). Cognitive empathy is an essential component of appreciating how emotions are experienced and understood from the client's perspective.

But as Baron-Cohen (2003) notes, "empathizing does not entail just the cold calculation of what someone else thinks and feels. . . . Empathizing occurs when we feel an appropriate emotional reaction, an emotion triggered by the other person's emotion, and it is done in order to understand another person, to predict their behavior, and to connect or resonate with them emotionally" (p. 2). To be effective, empathizing needs to come from a position of compassion and caring. Rogers (1980) outlined what he considered to be the essential elements of empathy:

- Entering the private perceptual world of the other and becoming thoroughly at home in it.

- Being sensitive, moment to moment, to the changing felt meanings that flow in this other person.

- Temporarily living in his or her life, moving about in it delicately without making judgments.

- Sensing meanings of which he or she is scarcely aware.

- Not trying to uncover feelings of which the person is totally unaware, since this would be too threatening. (p. 142)

SUCCESS TIP

Empathy needs to be expressed to be effective. The empathic process is not complete until clients have an opportunity to confirm, correct, or embellish their feelings, and they know that their feelings are understood and appreciated.

The Importance of Empathy

Carl Rogers (1902–1987), one of the most influential psychologists of the twentieth century, wrote and lectured extensively on the importance of empathy in counselling. He conceptualized empathy as one of the core conditions of helping (along with unconditional positive regard and congruence) that determine the outcome of counselling. In fact, Rogers argued that the core conditions were not only necessary but also sufficient to effect change. Near the end of his life, he offered this comment on the importance of empathy: "To my mind, empathy is in itself a healing agent. It is one of the most potent aspects of therapy, because it releases, it confirms, it brings even the most frightened client into the human race. If a person can be understood, he or she belongs" (1987, p. 181).

Empathy is a fundamental building block for the helping relationship and is clearly connected to positive outcomes in counselling (Table 6.3 outlines some of the ways that empathy helps clients). It is widely ranked as among the highest qualities that a counsellor can possess (Clark, 2007, 2010; Egan & Shroeder, 2009; Reiter, 2008; Rogers, 1980;

TABLE 6.3   How Empathy Helps

- Encourages expression of emotions, which is cathartic
- Normalizes and validates feelings, reduces isolation, and contributes to the development of the counselling relationship
- Increases awareness of emotions, including ambivalent feelings
- Stimulates further exploration of clients' subjective experiences
- Helps clients recognize the impact of emotions on themselves and others
- Assists clients to understand how emotions influence decision making or how they can impede action
- Provides a starting point for managing and expressing emotions in constructive ways (e.g., recognizing triggers)

and Shulman, 2009). Empathy is a powerful helping tool and a core condition for all helping relationships, regardless of the counselling or therapeutic model adopted. Among clients who abuse substances, research shows that empathy is one of the strongest predictors of success in reducing relapse (Miller, Forecehimes, & Zweben, 2011). Appropriate empathy communicates understanding, builds trust, and assists in establishing the counsellor's credibility. Miller and Rollnick (2002) conclude that the degree of empathy expressed by counsellors is a significant determinant of the success of clients in addictions treatment, whereas confrontational counselling leads to high dropout rates and poor outcomes. People tend to protect themselves from judgment and rejection through defensive reactions or by evading disclosure; however, as Clark (2007) observes, empathic responses reduce psychological threat. Effective empathy is nonjudgmental and it is nonprescriptive (i.e., it does not suggest that the client's feelings need to be changed or "treated"). The counsellor's manner and tone convey acceptance, comfort, and capacity to listen.

When counsellors are empathic, they are less likely to oversimplify complex problems. Because they understand more, they are also less prone to insult their clients with well-meaning but unusable and premature advice. A common counselling error is to move too quickly to problem solving when, for many clients, their difficulty is primarily emotional. They may already have ready solutions to their problems, but emotional turmoil or ambivalence is a barrier preventing action. As a result, they are unable to engage in taking action until their emotional needs are understood and managed. By assisting clients to understand and manage feelings, energy is freed up for problem solving and clients may be able to move ahead without further counsellor involvement.

Counsellors who accept the feelings of their clients help them accept themselves and their feelings. Effective empathy honours the fact that clients have real and rational reasons for feeling as they do. Rogers (1980) notes, "True empathy is always free of any evaluative or diagnostic quality. The recipient perceives this with some surprise: 'If I am not being judged, perhaps I am not so evil or abnormal as I have thought. Perhaps I don't have to judge myself so harshly.' Thus, the possibility of self-acceptance is gradually increased" (p. 154).

Rogers further suggests that empathy is more than just a skill—it is a way of being with another person. As he succinctly put it, "The ideal therapist is, first of all, empathic" (1980, p. 146). As important as empathy is, it should not preclude efforts to understand other parts of clients' experiences, such as their thoughts, experiences, behaviour, and the context in which they live their lives.

Empathy also assists clients in identifying and labelling feelings, which allows them to deal with those feelings. Moreover, with strong and supportive counsellors, clients can find the courage to deal with feelings that may have been too painful or overwhelming to address on their own. In this sense, empathy contributes to therapeutic change.

Recent research at the Mount Sinai Medical Center (2012) has found that an area of the brain known as the anterior insular cortex is where empathy is processed. This finding has huge future implications for conditions such as autism, dementia, and some personality disorders where a lack of empathy is a central feature.

Furthermore, clients often adopt the communication patterns of their counsellors. Thus, counsellors who use empathic communication and other active listening skills are modelling skills that clients can use to improve their relationships with others. Counsellor empathy models a healthy and effective way of communicating.

To empathize effectively, counsellors need to be able to demonstrate comfort with a wide range of feelings. For instance, they need to be able to talk openly about painful feelings such as grief. Just as doctors and nurses need to be able to deal with catastrophic injury without losing control or running away, counsellors must develop their capacity to work with intense feelings without needing to change the subject, intellectualize, or offer quick fixes. Sometimes counsellors misinterpret this capacity as meaning that they need to be emotionally detached and coldly indifferent. In fact, empathic counsellors are deeply involved with their clients. They put aside or suspend their own reactions to their clients' feelings and adopt an accepting and nonjudgmental attitude.

Rogers (1961) emphasizes the need to "sense the client's private world as if it were your own, but without ever losing the 'as if' quality . . . To sense the client's anger, fear, or confusion as if it were your own, yet without your own anger, fear, or confusion getting bound up in it" (p. 284). Rogers also provides this important observation about empathy:

> You lay aside your own views and values in order to enter another's world without prejudice. In some sense, it means that you lay aside your self; this can only be done by persons who are secure enough in themselves that they know they will not get lost in what may turn out to be the strange or bizarre world of the other, and that they can comfortably return to their own world when they wish. (1980, p. 143)

An empathic connection does not mean that we endorse our clients' views or behaviour. As Miller and Rollnick (2002) note, "It is possible to accept and understand a person's perspective while not agreeing with or endorsing it. Neither does an attitude of acceptance prohibit the counselor from differing with the client's views and expressing that divergence" (p. 37). In extreme cases, clients may present with attitudes and behaviour that we find abhorrent—a man who has abused his partner, for example. Understanding this client's inner world in such a case may even be vital, as it establishes the counsellor's credibility for understanding and, subsequently, as a potential influence to help the client move toward non-violent responses. In such situations, empathic efforts often help counsellors to become less reactive with their own feelings after they learn about the complexities of their clients' lives.

 **BRAIN BYTE** Selective Empathy

Gwen Dewar (2015) reviewed recent research on empathy and the brain and reported a number of significant findings. She found that exposure to media violence can blunt our ability to be empathic to others. She also reported that the research suggests that we are less sensitive to the pain and emotions of others when they are strangers, members of a different race or subgroup, or individuals who are subject to social stigma.

Client Reactions to Empathy

Clients may respond to empathy differently. Positive reactions include:

- Reduction of pain through the release of feelings (catharsis);
- Increased insight as feelings are recognized, labelled, and managed; and Increased trust and rapport with the counsellor.

Negative reactions include:

- Anger at the counsellor for creating the conditions that led to their feelings being exposed;
- Embarrassment arising from fear of being judged as weak;
- A sense of intrusion if empathy violates personal, familial, or cultural values that preclude sharing feelings with others; and
- Fear of continuing the counselling work if empathy pushes the client to deal with feelings before they are ready.

Consequently, in sessions where powerful feelings are revealed, counsellors should leave time to process the clients' reactions. This might uncover any feelings or concerns that should be addressed before moving on, or it may prevent clients from dropping out of counselling. Example:

Counsellor: When you go home tonight and reflect about what you shared today, what do you think you might say to yourself?

Client: I think I'll be embarrassed that I cried. You must think I'm really weak and fragile.

Counsellor: Would you like to know how I feel?

Client: Sure!

Counsellor: I'll tell you, but first I want to know if you will believe me.

Client: You've always been up front with me. I'll believe you.

Counsellor: I think it took a lot of courage for you to be open with your feelings, and I respect you for taking that step. For me, it was a sign of strength.

In some cases, the dialogue might take a different route such as the following:

Counsellor: I'll tell you, but first I want to know if you will believe me.

Client: You'll probably just say something to make me feel better.

Counsellor: So, let's talk about what needs to happen before you can trust me.

Sometimes clients who have shared deeply come to the next session determined to exercise more control over their emotions. They may appear defensive or withdrawn. A lead such as, "What are your thoughts and feelings about the last time we met?" can be used to debrief the last meeting. On the other hand, it may be healthy to avoid confronting this apparent resistance; instead, see it as a healthy way for the client to feel safe and gain composure.

Angus and Greenberg (2011) suggest that some clients have developed problematic emotional responses that often originate from trauma. For example, if a client learned as a child that closeness and kindness was followed by sexual abuse, then, as an adult, she may respond to empathy and requests for intimacy as an impending violation. As a result, counsellor empathy may be met with anger and rejection, particularly in the early developmental stages of the relationship. On the other hand, sensitive and well-timed (measured) empathy can provide an opportunity for her to begin to address how prior learning, while protective at one time, now prevents her from developing deep and meaningful relationships. Exploring emotions associated with the trauma can help her become unstuck from automatic emotional reactions and actions that are no longer useful or appropriate.

STUDENT: I would really like to increase my empathy skills, but my vocabulary is so limited. I seem to know only a few feeling words, such as happy, sad, scared, and angry. How can I increase my feeling word choice?

TEACHER: It's not necessary to have an encyclopedic vocabulary, but you should have enough word choice to capture a broad range of feelings. Study Table 6.1 (which appeared earlier in this chapter) for new feeling words; then take advantage of every opportunity to practice empathy and use these words. The Internet has many sites that feature feeling word inventories and these can be useful, but remember that feelings are often mixed. Try reading books and watching TV with a special ear for discerning how people are feeling. One of the best ways is to use invitational empathy to ask others how they feel, then to listen carefully to their words. This will help sensitize you to their unique vocabulary. By adopting an attitude of interest and curiosity and focusing on feelings, you can dramatically increase your vocabulary. Another strategy when listening to clients is to try to recall feelings that you might have had in similar circumstances. This might give you some tentative ideas about what your client could be feeling.

STUDENT: What about the danger of imposing my feelings on them?

TEACHER: Yes, that is always a risk. Hence the need to be tentative, remembering that people may respond to the same situation in widely different ways. Nevertheless, there are often some common and predictable emotions for most people in a given situation. It's also important to work on becoming aware of your own feelings.

TYPES OF EMPATHY

The three types of empathy are invitational empathy, basic empathy, and inferred empathy. With invitational empathy, a counsellor uses strategies to encourage clients to talk about their feelings. With basic empathy, a counsellor mirrors what the client has explicitly said. And with inferred empathy, a counsellor reaches empathic understanding by interpreting subtle clues. At any point in an interview, counsellors can use empathy to explore a client's behaviour, thinking, or feelings. When counsellors focus on behaviour, they explore what clients are doing or saying or they shift attention to problem solving. When they pursue thinking, they are interested in their clients' beliefs and assumptions, including their inner dialogue and self-esteem. Empathy enables counsellors to pay primary attention to the third area—feelings (Figure 6.1). Frequently, counsellors are too anxious to solve problems, and they move the interview focus prematurely to problem

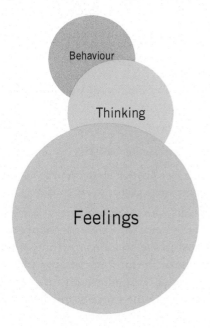

Figure 6.1   Empathy Focuses the Work of Counselling on the Feeling Domain

solving, ignoring, or discounting what may be more important than solutions—their clients' feelings.

Invitational Empathy

Invitational empathy encourages clients to explore emotions. It signals intent (or an invitation) to move the interview away from one of the other domains (behaviour/problem solving or thinking) to a focus on emotions. Invitational empathy is initiated with a simple question such as, "How do you feel?" Another choice is to say something like, "It might be helpful if we put solving this problem aside for a moment to explore how you feel." If appropriate, counsellors can make further process comments about the importance of addressing feelings as an integral part of problem management. Invitational empathy says to the client that the counsellor is ready and able to talk about difficult feelings.

To do this, counsellors can draw on their knowledge of human growth and development, such as ways that people tend to deal with particular life events and crises. Some clients are reluctant to share their feelings for fear of judgment, or they may believe that they shouldn't feel a particular way. Others may think they are the "only one" or that they are "crazy," "evil," or "abnormal." For example, it is common to feel some relief, even happiness (as well as grief) when a loved one who has been struggling with a painful illness dies, but a client may feel guilty for feeling this way. Invitational empathy normalizes the experience, making it easier for the client to talk about it and accept it: "It's normal at a time like this to struggle with mixed feelings—grief, pain, comfort, and perhaps joy that her suffering is at an end."

By encouraging clients to talk about feelings and then responding nonjudgmentally, the counsellor is saying, "It's okay to feel this way." In the following example, the counsellor uses invitational empathy to "give permission" to a client who might otherwise suppress or ignore his pain to experience and verbalize his emotions:

> **Client:** I guess it's no big deal. So, what if they know the scoop on my marital problems?
>
> **Counsellor:** A lot of people in the same situation might feel embarrassed and perhaps disappointed or angry that a friend could be so indiscreet about something said in confidence.

In the following example, the counsellor uses nonverbal cues as a basis for invitational empathy to encourage the client to explore a difficult topic:

> **Counsellor:** Would you mind if I shared an observation with you? I may be wrong, so I'd like your opinion.
>
> **Client:** Sure, go ahead. Say it.
>
> **Counsellor:** I notice that whenever mention of your father comes up, you seem keen to change the topic.
>
> *(Long silence; client stares at the floor.)*
>
> **Counsellor:** Some memories are painful—maybe even too painful to talk about.
>
> **Client:** *(Softly, tears in his eyes.)* It's just that his death was so unexpected. We had a fight that morning, and I didn't even get a chance to say goodbye.

Invitational empathy begins with questions and responses targeted at encouraging clients to express feelings. The choice of strategy is influenced by the usual variables, including the amount of trust in the relationship, time constraints, culture, and the counsellor's role. Timing is one of the most important variables. Since the exploration of feelings can be time-consuming, it is important for counsellors to make sure that they have enough time to complete the process. Intelligent use of silence is another important variable. Clients may need their counsellors to patiently listen and restrain themselves from filling every silent moment with words.

One way to bridge the interview into a discussion of feelings is to use invitational statements, such as "I don't know how you feel, but if you're feeling pain or loneliness, I'm ready to listen." Comments such as "I need your help in understanding your feelings" can also move the interview into the affective—or feeling—area.

Frequently, clients provide natural opportunities when they give hints about how they are feeling. Then the counsellor can use questions to encourage further sharing. Open questions promote clients to share feelings: "How are you feeling?" "What feelings best describe how you reacted?" Closed questions target specific information about feelings: "Did you feel angry?" "Is this something you feel strongly about?"

Helping clients understand the importance of addressing feelings is an important step that keeps clients involved in decision making (contracting). When counsellors inform clients and solicit their support for the process, clients' motivation is higher. Here are some sample leads:

- I think it might help if we shift our focus and talk a bit about how you feel. This might help us both to understand why your decision is so difficult.

- We haven't yet talked about your feelings. In my experience, feelings often present one of the biggest barriers.

- Until feelings are understood and accepted, they can distort our thinking and even reduce the amount of control we have over our behaviour. So you might find it useful if we spend some time exploring how you feel.

In addition, directives can be used to move the interview into the feeling area: "Tell me how you feel." "Let's switch our focus and talk about your feelings." Directives are one way to manage the flow and focus of the interview.

Moreover, with some clients, counsellor self-disclosure is a powerful tool if used sparingly: "I don't know how it is for you, but I know that for many months after my marriage ended, I was in a state of shock."

Another tool for exploring feelings is the sentence completion statement. Sentence completion statements give counsellors a way to focus feelings on a particular area, and they give freedom to clients to control the answer.

- When I think about all my problems, I feel . . .
- If I could use one feeling to describe my situation, it would be . . .
- When I first came for counselling, I felt . . .
- The feelings that I most need to deal with are . . .

But invitational empathy should always respect the clients' rights to privacy. Many variables, especially trust, impact the extent that any client is willing to open up and discuss feelings. In addition, variables such as gender, past experience, socialization, mood, and power issues can also influence how much individuals are willing to share.

Basic Empathy

With **basic empathy**, counsellors perceive and respond to feelings that are explicitly communicated. Basic empathy may involve labelling feelings or summarizing expressed feelings. Frequently, clients want to talk about feelings, particularly those closely related to their problem situations. When they take the initiative to introduce feelings, it is relatively easy and nonthreatening for counsellors to respond with basic empathy. Basic empathy simply says, "I have heard how you feel, and I accept your feelings without judgment." With basic empathy, no attempt is made to interpret, judge, or promote greater awareness or insight beyond that which the client has already articulated.

Despite its apparent simplicity, basic empathy can be a powerful helping tool. When people express feelings in everyday communication, they may be blocked or discouraged

basic empathy: A counsellor's acknowledgment of a client's clearly communicated feelings.

when others react by judging, ignoring, or giving advice. For example, one common but extremely unhelpful response is "You shouldn't feel that way." In contrast, basic empathy creates a climate in which clients do not have to defend or hide their feelings. For many people, basic empathy responses are an unusual and satisfying experience. As one client described it, "For the first time, I felt safe. Someone had finally listened and heard me."

Furthermore, counsellors who punctuate their work with frequent empathy are more likely to build rapport and evoke further information from clients. Simple logic suggests that when people believe that they are accepted and understood, they are more likely to feel secure and less likely to raise defences. As a result, clients are more inclined to share and explore at a deeper level of intimacy than they would under more threatening conditions. The following example illustrates basic empathy:

Client: I was ready to kill her. How could she embarrass me in front of all those people?

Counsellor: So you're angry that she didn't have enough sense to keep quiet.

Client: Angry, but also hurt. After all, she was supposed to be my best friend. How could she double-cross me?

Counsellor: Sounds as if you feel betrayed.

But empathic responses also need to be presented with an air of tentativeness to give clients an opportunity to offer corrections. A simple pause or a question such as "Have I got it right?" can be used to this end.

SUCCESS TIP

To make simple, yet effective, empathic responses, use this format:
"You feel . . . *(add feeling word)* because . . . *(add content)*"

Inferred Empathy

Inferred empathy, sometimes called *advanced empathy* (Egan & Schroeder, 2009), involves identifying clients' feelings based on nonverbal cues, themes, and hints. Counsellors should also pay careful attention to what their clients do not say, including topics they avoid and sudden shifts in focus. Inferred empathy is a powerful counselling tool that enables clients to deal with feelings at a level deeper than expressed emotions.

Some clients find that their trust level increases when counsellors identify their hidden feelings: "My counsellor seemed to know how I felt without my saying so. Finally, I felt understood. In fact, I began to understand myself better." Moreover, inferred empathy may be particularly useful with clients who lack feeling vocabulary or are unaccustomed to expressing feelings. Inferred empathy seems to say, "I have the courage and the ability to hear your feelings."

Client: It was a tough situation. Here I was in front of all those people with my private life laid bare.

Counsellor: From the tears in your eyes, I suspect this was a painful and embarrassing moment for you.

In the preceding example, the client seems willing to explore her experience, yet she stops short of verbally identifying her feelings. The counsellor takes a mild empathic risk and considers context and nonverbal cues to infer empathy. Inferred empathy should always be presented tentatively to allow room for correction and further exploration.

With inferred empathy, some speculation based on the evidence of feelings is necessary. Consequently, there is more risk involved than with basic empathy. There are two significant risks. First, because the information base for inferred empathy is more ambiguous, more errors are likely. Hence, counsellors should be especially tentative with inferred empathy. As well, counsellors should avoid becoming overly speculative to the point where they are simply guessing at their clients' feelings. Second, inferred empathy may be met with resistance from clients who are unwilling or unable to acknowledge their feelings. Inferred empathy notices subtle cues, and clients may be surprised to hear that their feelings have been communicated. They may react with anger and resentment that their feelings have been uncovered. In addition, some clients are afraid of the intensity of their feelings, whereas others have strong needs for privacy. Thus, inferred empathy must be timed appropriately. The counselling relationship should have a reasonable level of trust, and the counselling session should have sufficient time left to process any reactions. Otherwise, it is best to defer inferred empathic responses till later.

Since inferred empathy involves "reading" the client, counsellors need to develop skills in this area. First, clients provide clues to their feelings in a number of ways. They might be embarrassed about sharing their feelings or reluctant to ask for help, so they talk about a "friend who has a problem." Second, as stressed earlier, understanding nonverbal behaviour is crucial. Astute counsellors learn a great deal about their clients' feelings by carefully observing changes in voice tone, sudden shifts in posture, nervous behaviour, tears, grimaces, clenched fists, finger tapping, and smiling. As well, certain behaviours can suggest feelings. For example, a boy who runs away from a group home just before a visit from his mother may be saying something about his fear or anger. A client who arrives late, refuses to take his coat off, and sits with arms folded across his chest might be saying, "I don't want to be here."

SUCCESS TIP

When there are time pressures, counsellors tend to focus more on task at the expense of relationship. Appropriate and proportional empathy, even when time is limited, helps clients to manage better than if the interview or encounter addressed only task.

People often express emotions using analogies. For example, a client who compares his life to a speeding train may be expressing his fears of being out of control. Some clients hint at their feelings by asking questions, such as "Do you worry about your kids when they are out late at night?" In addition, clients who minimize problems, as in "I have a bit of a problem. Do you have a minute?" or "This is probably not important," may be signaling that they have significant issues and feelings that they need to discuss.

Preparatory Empathy

Tuning in, or **preparatory empathy** (Shulman, 2009), is another useful way to prepare for inferred empathy. Preparatory empathy is a preliminary phase skill that involves trying to anticipate the feelings and concerns that clients might bring up in the interview. Since clients often do not directly reveal their feelings, tuning in helps counsellors anticipate how clients might communicate feelings indirectly. Shulman (2009) illustrates tuning in with a common example involving an encounter between a 22-year-old counselling novice and a 38-year-old mother of seven children. The mother asked the worker, "Do you have any children?" The worker responded defensively by talking about her training in child psychology. Shulman suggests that the worker missed the implicit feelings expressed by the mother—the fear that the worker will not understand her. Had she used the tuning-in skill, the worker might have been able to consider in advance the range of feelings that a mother of seven kids might have when meeting with a young counsellor who has no children. With such advance preparation, the worker might have been more sensitive to the mother's real question, perhaps responding, "No, I don't have any children. Why do you ask? Are you wondering if I'm going to be able to understand what it's like for you having to raise so many? I'm concerned about that as well. If I'm

preparatory empathy: A counsellor's attempt to consider (in advance of the interview) the feelings and concerns that the client may communicate indirectly.

to help you, I'm going to have to understand, and you are going to have to help me to understand" (Shulman, 2009, p. 57). This response is an excellent illustration of genuineness, which in this case provides an opportunity for a discussion of the mother's feelings about workers and gives the worker a chance to share her own feelings. Similar counsellor strategies might be appropriate for client questions, such as, "Have you ever been to jail?" "Do you know what it's like to live on the street?" and "How old are you?"

Table 6.4 summarizes the three types of empathy.

TABLE 6.4 Types of Empathy

Type	Description	Major Use	Comments
Invitational	Encouraging clients to talk about feelings	To stimulate discussion of emotions To normalize feelings	Invitational empathy underscores the importance of emotions. It counters any tendency to move too quickly to problem solving without fully considering the role that emotions play.
Basic	Responding to clearly articulated feelings	To encourage continued expression of feelings To confirm capacity to hear feelings	Basic empathy contributes to the development of trust. It signals to clients that counsellors are willing and able to deal with feelings.
Inferred	Responding to nonverbal cues and other indicators of feelings	To move feelings into the verbal channel of communication	Inferred empathy may generate more anxiety in some clients if feelings that they avoided, suppressed, or wanted to keep hidden are made visible. Inferred empathy may promote client insight.

⟫⟫ CONVERSATION 6.2 — When Not to Use Empathy

STUDENT: I don't think empathy is always such a good thing. I watched one taped interview of Carl Rogers and two other therapists interviewing the same client, Gloria. If I had been Rogers's client, I would have been irritated. He seemed to continually regurgitate what the client had just said.

TEACHER: You've raised a good point. Too much empathy, particularly when you get stuck at a basic level, might leave you and your client going in circles. It's also true that if you move too fast with empathy, your clients can feel threatened and put up their defences. This is particularly true with clients who have strong needs for privacy. They may view your empathic statements as an unwanted intrusion into their feelings. Empathy invites greater relationship intimacy, and some clients are not ready for the risks that this entails. As Clark (2007) noted, "some find the emotional closeness of the therapeutic relationship threatening and invasive" (p. 37). Some clients open up to empathic responses only to later regret having revealed too much. They may "clam up" in future sessions, never return to counselling, or they may resent their counsellors for allowing that to happen.

But even though you might have been irritated, it's interesting to note that, years later, Rogers's client Gloria described how her short time with Rogers was life-changing for her. This reminds us that clients respond differently to the same technique. Be careful that your perception of the Rogers tape doesn't deter you from using empathy. It may be exactly what your client needs.

Other clients who may not be ready for empathy are those who are so caught up in their own talking that they do not even hear empathic statements. As Shea (1998) suggests, attempts to empathize with this group may actually be counterproductive because empathy interferes with what they want most—an audience to listen.

STUDENT: I think one way to handle that is to test your client's capacity for empathy with a few basic empathic statements. If they are not well received, you can back off by switching to less demanding content or more basic empathy.

TEACHER: I agree, back off, but not forever! As trust develops, the client may welcome that same empathic response that he or she at first rejected. To continue the list of times when empathy may not be a good idea, I'd add the following:

- Your clients reject empathy.
- It's clearly time to move on to problem solving or another activity.
- Empathy is continuously misinterpreted by the client (e.g., as controlling or intrusive).

We should always remember that counselling techniques will not work the same way with all clients. Cultural norms, trust level, mood, and personal resiliency are all variables that influence how empathy is received.

FOUR GENERALIZATIONS ABOUT EMPATHY

Generalization One   *When clients share feelings, empathy is (more often than not) the preferred response.* A positive reinforcer "presented immediately following a behaviour causes the behaviour to increase in frequency" (Martin & Pear, 2011). Clients take an interpersonal risk when they share their feelings. Empathy acknowledges this risk by conveying recognition and acceptance of the client's feelings. Empathic responses are a reward for sharing that conveys the meta-message: "This is a safe place to bring your feelings." In this way, it reinforces the wisdom of the risk and motivates clients to continue sharing feelings. On the other hand, when clients share feelings and they are not rewarded (or reinforced) with empathy, then they tend to keep their feelings more private. Non-empathic responses to expressed feelings carry the meta-message, "Your feelings are not important," or "I'm not comfortable talking about what you're feeling." This underscores the importance of expressing empathy early in the relationship. When dealing with reluctant or mandated clients, empathy provides a way to acknowledge and validate their strong emotions. Subsequently, as these clients feel understood and listened to, their reluctance will often lessen.

Generalization Two   *Risk expressing empathy early in the relationship.* Norms, once established, are difficult to alter. Early empathy helps form the norm that the counselling relationship is a safe place to express feelings. To become comfortable with empathy, counsellors need to overcome their own fears about bringing emotions into the foreground. Many counsellors fear that by encouraging clients to express emotions, they might trigger extreme reactions, particularly suicide, but this fear is not substantiated by research. In fact, it takes energy to suppress emotions; therefore, by helping clients express and get in touch with their feelings, counsellors can help them decrease the negative effects of these feelings.

Invitational empathy is useful for working with clients who are reluctant or unable to articulate feelings. Counsellor timing is critical, and counsellors should present invitational empathy in a gentle and tentative manner.

Early in the counselling relationship, counsellors should give priority to acquiring, maintaining, and deepening empathic understanding by remaining alert to empathic opportunities. One obvious opportunity arises whenever clients verbalize feelings. In such moments, counsellors can use basic empathy to confirm understanding. Sometimes clients reveal feelings nonverbally, and counsellors can use inferred empathy. When clients have not shared their feelings, counsellors can adopt invitational empathy to encourage them to share their emotions.

Generalization Three   *Never assume that we can know another person's emotions in the way that they know them.* People often try to be understanding and compassionate by saying, "I know just how you feel." While this response has the potential to be supportive, it is more likely that it will sabotage further opportunity for exploration and learning. It does not honour the fact that each of us emotionally processes experiences in our own way. The fact that we have had a similar experience does not give us easy access to instant understanding. Our own experience, with all of its associated memories, emotions, and outcomes, may actually be a barrier to empathizing. Empathy requires that we work to see the world from the client's perspective. This means that we must carefully guard against bias—the natural tendency to assume that how we feel or have felt under like circumstances is how the client is feeling. High-level self-awareness, healthy curiosity, and humility about our limited capacity to appreciate the client's emotions are prerequisites. Active listening, particularly empathy, will help us to get closer to this goal.

"I know just how you feel" also discourages people from the cathartic benefit of telling their story—one of the most therapeutic outcomes of active listening. It hijacks any opportunity for the counsellor to learn. Since we already "know" what the person feels, what point is there in discussing it?

Counsellors should express empathy tentatively. Thus, it is important to check with clients to confirm empathic understanding. Counsellors need to refrain from using empathy as a weapon by insisting that their clients must feel a particular way. Counsellors should also look for indicators that clients have accepted their empathy and that it is accurate. Clients provide confirmation through head nods, smiles, manifesting reduced anxiety, and verbal confirmation (e.g., "That's right" or "You seem to know exactly how I'm feeling even before I tell you"). Clients also implicitly confirm willingness to accept empathy when they continue to share feelings at a deeper level. Conversely, clients may verbally signal that empathy has missed the mark (e.g., by saying "No" or "That's not right") or with subtler nonverbal and paraverbal messages. Some clients who are reluctant to challenge may agree with empathy that is off the mark, so it is important to remain alert for contradictory nonverbal messages such as tentative voice tone (e.g., "I guess so") or hesitation in their responses.

Sometimes, empathy misses the target and clients offer corrections. This is good news and should be viewed as an important and positive outcome of empathic risk. Empathy is a developmental process requiring counsellors to remain open to adjusting and refining their understanding until they reach a point of shared meaning with their clients. Moreover, when clients correct their counsellors, counsellors know that they can trust them not to capitulate.

Generalization Four *Empathy requires flexibility in its use, including the ability to refrain from using it.* Empathy is an important and powerful skill, but counsellors need to use it intelligently. When clients are willing to address feelings, empathic responses are effective (see Table 6.5 for suggestions). With some clients, empathic statements result in the opposite of what was intended. Instead of deepening trust and encouraging clients to open up, empathy arouses defences. This may happen when empathy targets feelings that clients would prefer to hide, or when clients experience empathy as invading their personal space. When clients resist empathy by withdrawing or becoming defensive, counsellors should discontinue using it for a while.

SUCCESS TIP

If clients express feeling, respond with empathy. Risk expressing empathy early in the relationship. Be tentative—we can never fully know how others feel. Develop flexibility (how, when, and when not to use empathy).

Moreover, situational differences influence how the work of empathy unfolds. Some clients are verbal and open with their feelings. They are likely to respond positively to empathy. Others need gentle encouragement to talk about feelings, and they open up discussion of feelings gradually and in a very controlled manner. Counsellors will generally find that they encounter less resistance when they match their clients' pace.

TABLE 6.5 The Empathic Communication Process

- Decide if it is an appropriate time to explore emotions (consider context, timing, and level of trust).
- Use invitational empathy to initiate discussion of feelings.
- Pay attention to verbal and nonverbal indicators of emotion.
- Explore feelings for detail, definition, and example.
- Formulate a tentative empathic response.
- Wait for or encourage the client to confirm or correct your empathic perception.
- Correct or offer a deeper empathic response based on the client's response.

Empathic Response Leads

Using a range of different responses adds interest and variety to the interview. Using the same words and phrases too often can irritate clients and reduce the interview's energy and vitality. Having a range of leads for empathic response prevents the interview from sounding artificial or robotic. The following list suggests some variations.

Invitational Empathy

- How/What do you feel? (open question)
- Do you want to talk about your feelings? (closed question)
- I'm wondering how you are feeling. (indirect question)
- Tell me how you feel. (directive)
- Any thoughts on how that made you feel? (closed question)

Basic Empathy

- You feel . . .
- My sense is that you might be feeling . . .
- From your point of view . . .
- As you see it . . .
- I wonder if what you're saying/feeling is . . .
- You appear to be feeling . . .

Inferred Empathy

- Your tears suggest that you might be feeling . . .
- You've become very quiet. Perhaps you are feeling . . .
- One theme that keeps coming up in what you are saying is . . .
- When you talk about . . . I sense you feel . . .
- What I understand from what you have said is . . .

SUCCESS TIP

A tentative tone and a pause for further client input or correction is an important part of any empathic response.

Why Achieving Empathic Understanding Is So Difficult

Empathic errors are generally unlikely when counsellors are similar to their clients (in age, gender, race, etc.) and when they have had similar problems and experiences; however, even in these situations, empathic errors can happen if counsellors do not separate their own experiences from those of their clients. Counsellors need to remember to allow for individual differences by remembering that, however, similar their own experiences might be, they can never fully understand how their clients feel. Through empathy, they can get a sense of their clients' feelings and rise above imposing their own interpretations, feelings, and judgments, but this understanding will never be perfect.

Empathy is perhaps the most difficult counselling skill to master. Empathy demands a lot of mental energy from counsellors. First, they must manage their own emotional and judgmental reactions. Then they have to find meaning and discover feelings from their clients' verbal and nonverbal communication. This can be exceptionally demanding since clients may keep feelings hidden or suppressed, or lack understanding and awareness of their emotions. Relationship issues, including lack of trust, embarrassment, and fear of being judged, can inhibit clients from disclosing. For example, there may be societal, cultural, or personal norms that prohibit sharing of feelings. Or clients may not have the ability (language) to communicate their emotions.

Further complicating the empathic process is the fact that counsellors must respond right away. In an interview, there is no time to use a thesaurus or a dictionary and no opportunity to consult others, rehearse their empathy, or ponder the feeling state of their clients. Empathic risk means daring to share perceived understanding with clients using concrete words and phrases that are accessible in the situation.

Poor Substitutes for Empathy

When counsellors express empathy, they acknowledge the feelings that clients have expressed (verbally and/or nonverbally). They might include a brief "because" clause that summarizes content. In most situations, they will stop there. This gives clients a chance to process what they have heard, to offer corrections, or possibly to share at a deeper level. At this point, counsellors should avoid cutoff responses, subject changes, empty responses, sympathy, or any other response that diverts attention away from empathy.

Cutoffs Cutoffs are phrases that inhibit the further expression of feeling. Counsellors who make statements such as, "Don't feel . . ." and "You should feel . . ." are demonstrating a low level of understanding and acceptance of how their clients feel. Such statements are not supportive. They force clients to defend their feelings. Similarly, when counsellors ask clients questions such as "Why do you feel like that?" a judgmental tone is present that can leave clients feeling defensive (see Chapter 5).

Another response that may inhibit clients is silence. When clients risk sharing feelings, empathy is better than silence. When counsellors fail to acknowledge feelings, they may be saying, "This is not important" or "I'm not capable of dealing with your emotions." In response, clients might feel abandoned, embarrassed, or judged.

Counsellors can also make the mistake of cutting clients off by changing the subject or offering advice. A subject change gives the meta-message "Let's not talk about that."

> **Client:** Sometimes when he speaks to me that way, I just want to go hide in a corner.
>
> **Counsellor 1 (appropriate empathy):** It sounds like maybe you're feeling embarrassed.
>
> **Counsellor 2 (inappropriate empathy—subject shift):** It sounds like maybe you're feeling embarrassed. Would you like to talk about ways of overcoming it?

Empty Responses Empty responses are devoid of content. Phrases such as "I hear what you're saying" and "I understand what you mean" convey no confirmation that the counsellor has understood. Another empty response is parroting, or repeating what the client has said. Egan and Schroeder (2009) describe parroting as "a parody of empathy" (p. 145). In contrast, empathy communicates the counsellor's effort to go beyond merely hearing the words to understanding the client's feelings and perspectives. Using empathy, the counsellor rephrases the client's statements and assigns labels to feelings that the client has expressed but not named.

Be aware that clichés and platitudes, such as "Everybody has to have a little pain in their life," patronize and reject clients' feelings. As Egan and Schroeder (2009) put it, clichéd responses say, "You don't really have a problem at all, at least not a serious one" (p. 145).

Sympathy Sympathy and empathy are frequently confused, and many people view them as identical; however, there are important and significant differences between the two concepts. Sympathy refers to concern for other people's problems and emotions

The following excerpt illustrates some of the *inappropriate* responses that counsellors sometimes use instead of empathy. Ignoring feelings and offering empty responses, simplistic advice, and sympathy are inadequate substitutes for empathy.

Client: *(Softly, with tears in her eyes.)* I just haven't been the same since he left. I still look out the door and expect him to come home.

Counsellor: How old was he when he ran away?

Analysis: *Inappropriate topic shift: The client is clearly experiencing pain, perhaps grief, and she trusts the counsellor enough to share these feelings. Generally, when clients share feelings, particularly feelings that are strong, empathy is the preferred response. The counsellor's response shifts the focus away from feelings to content. This may subtly signal to the client that the counsellor is uncomfortable with feelings. Continual shifts such as this will "train" the client not to share feelings.*

Client: He was just 16. I still thought of him as my baby. Now I go to sleep at night wondering whether he's dead or alive.

Counsellor: You thought of him as your baby. Now you go to sleep at night wondering whether he's dead or alive.

Silence.

Analysis: *Parroting. Repetition at this point serves no purpose. Sometimes key words or phrases can be emphasized as a way to focus attention, but this type of parroting is inappropriate here.*

Counsellor: I understand how you feel.

Client: *(Buries her face in her hands.)* Sometimes I just don't know whether I can go on living. If something doesn't happen soon, then . . . *(Counsellor interrupts.)*

Analysis: *Superficial response. The counsellor tries to be supportive, but the response is empty. Until the counsellor risks empathy with specific feeling words and phrases, the client cannot know whether she has, in fact, been heard.*

Counsellor: You have to think of your husband and your other children.

Client: Yes, I know, but do you have any idea what I'm going through? How tough it is just to get out of bed in the morning?

Analysis: *Misguided rescue attempt, ignoring feelings. It seems obvious that this counsellor is unable to deal with the powerful feelings that the client presents. After an ill-timed interruption, the counsellor offers a misguided and simplistic solution, while ignoring the emotions the client expressed.*

Counsellor: My guess is that you feel very angry at the world, maybe even some guilt that you are somehow responsible for your son's running away.

Client: No! I don't feel guilty. I was always a good mother. I think if my son were here, he'd say that too. When he became addicted to drugs, it was more than either of us knew how to handle.

Analysis: *Inaccurate empathy. The counsellor attempts inferred empathy. Unfortunately, there is insufficient evidence to support the counsellor's conclusion that the client feels angry or guilty. The counsellor may be right, but as suggested it is merely a guess, a poor substitute for empathy. Moreover, the counsellor is not attending to the feelings that the client has already expressed.*

Counsellor: I hear what you're saying.

Client: So, what am I supposed to do? I feel so empty and useless.

Analysis: *Superficial response. This response has the same problems as her earlier one, "I understand how you feel."*

Counsellor: It's a very bad feeling

(Brief silence.)

Analysis: *Inaccurate empathy, lack of specificity. The counsellor attempts empathy but misses the intensity of the client's feelings. Then, the counsellor quickly shifts the focus without giving the client time to respond.*

Counsellor: You shouldn't feel that way. One day your son might walk in the door. You have to go on living.

Analysis: *The counsellor's response violates the important requirement to accept clients' feelings without judgment and without trying to tell them how they should feel.*

Client: I suppose you're right. Thanks for listening. It felt good to get it off my chest.

Counsellor: I'm glad I was able to help.

Analysis: *Sometimes clients benefit from the interview, even when the counsellor's responses are as poor as those depicted in this encounter. Simply telling one's story and verbalizing feelings can help people deal with pain or problems; however, it is much more likely that this client is ready to dismiss the counsellor. The counsellor may be just as relieved that the interview is over.*

Reflections:

■ Suggest alternate appropriate responses that the counsellor might have used.

■ What might counsellors do when they recognize that their response was inaccurate or inappropriate.

and is related to our own emotional and behavioural reactions. Sympathy is the counsellor's personal reaction, and though it is intimately connected to the client's feelings, it is not the same as empathy. Sympathetic responses are self-disclosures, whereas empathy is a process of seeking to understand another's feelings; however, counsellors are human, and it is normal for them to have emotional responses when listening to their clients. In fact, their reactions are the basis for compassion, an indispensable component of a caring counselling relationship. There are moments when it is appropriate for counsellors to express sympathy by letting clients know that they support them and that they are moved by their pain. At the same time, it is essential for counsellors to develop the ability to separate their emotional reactions (sympathy and compassion) from those of their clients. Counsellors also need to ensure that their sympathy does not detract from the client's feelings by interfering with their need to express feelings, tell their stories, and face the reality of their problems.

> **Client:** I'm really worried about telling my dad that I've dropped out of college. Even when I was a little girl, my father kept saying, "You've got to get an education or you'll never get anywhere in life."
>
> **Counsellor (Choice 1—sympathetic reaction):** I don't think it was very fair for him to have laid such a heavy burden on you. It always makes me somewhat angry when I hear about parents pushing their kids.
>
> **Counsellor (Choice 2—empathic reaction):** So you fear that you've let your father down!.

In the preceding example, Choice 1 is a misguided attempt to offer support. Judgmental in tone, it shifts the focus from the client's feelings to those of the counsellor. Choice 2 expresses basic empathy, setting the stage for further exploration.

Clark (2007) cautions that "A counsellor is subject to being psychologically drawn into the experiences of a client, and the interaction can lead to a distortion of perspectives" (p. 14). For example, an overly sympathetic counsellor might curb discussion of painful emotions or might change the topic or avoid further discussion of the area to "protect" the client from the distress of facing the issue. Too much sympathy might also cut off an opportunity for the client to explore feelings and options for action. The following example illustrates this:

> **Client:** After 15 years of working for the company, they tell me that even though I've done a great job, I have to take a pay cut and a new job because they can't afford to have two supervisors.
>
> **Counsellor:** That's so unfair. What do they expect? You deserve better.

It's easy to speculate how in the preceding example the counsellor's response might curtail a more balanced airing of feelings and later exploration of the merits of a pay cut as one of the options. Here is a more appropriate empathic response:

> **Counsellor:** Perhaps you feel used, believing that their praise was just empty words.

SUCCESS TIP

Clients are often successful in making us feel as they do. Use this as a basis for empathy and as a way to monitor, understand, and control your own emotions.

Tough Empathy

It is easy to feel caring and compassion for most people in pain, such as the aging client who loses his job, the young mother who has had a second miscarriage, and the single parent who is trying to raise children on a limited income; however, some clients may challenge a counsellor's tolerance. Even the most accepting counsellors occasionally find

CONVERSATION 6.3 — How Can I Be Empathic If I Have Not Had the Same Experience?

STUDENT: I haven't had a lot of life experience, and I'm worried that I won't be able to understand what the client is feeling.

TEACHER: Sometimes counsellors do their best work when they admit they don't understand, then take the time to listen. We are constantly challenged to work with clients who are very different from us, so we need to be willing to learn and willing to let clients "teach" us about their experiences and feelings. While we may not have had the same experience, we can draw on events in our own lives that have evoked similar feelings such as pain or loss. If we have been there ourselves, we have some advantages, but only if we are cautious to avoid assuming that our feelings, perspective, and solutions will be the same for our clients. The best way to do this is listening to our clients' stories, even if we think we know what they are going to say.

STUDENT: Maybe there's an advantage to not having had the same experience in that I'll be more ready to listen, learn, and be curious.

it difficult to lay aside personal reaction, suspend judgment, and respond with empathy to clients such as the following:

- Bob, an angry 20-year-old who savagely attacked an elderly woman
- Pernell, a father who argues for the morality of sex with girls over 15
- Eileen, an HIV-positive prostitute who ignores the dangers of having unprotected sex with her customers
- Ruby, a woman who rejects and attacks efforts to help

Counsellors working with clients such as these often experience strong emotional reactions, and they may find it difficult to put aside their personal feelings to feel and express empathy.

Some criminal psychopaths live with cruel disregard for the rights and feelings of others, displaying a complete absence of ability to feel empathy or caring. In fact, "the blotting out of empathy as these people inflict damage on victims is almost always part of an emotional cycle that precipitates their cruel acts" (Goleman, 2005p. 106). Commenting on the research, Goleman offers evidence that suggests a biological basis for a lack of empathy in psychopaths.

Why then should counsellors respond with empathy to such people? First, empathy is a way for counsellors to understand how their clients think and feel. Second, as noted earlier, empathy is instrumental in forming the helping relationship, the prerequisite condition for the contract between client and counsellor. One outcome of empathy is that clients come to feel valued and understood. Because of the empathic relationship, clients begin to reveal more, make discoveries about themselves, and alter their perspectives about themselves and others. With clients who lack empathy for others, counsellor use of empathy obliges them to face their feelings and those of their victims.

In situations in which it is difficult to respond with empathy, counsellors may need to work on their own issues. For example, they can ask themselves, "What is it about this particular client that makes it difficult for me to be empathic?" "Does this client remind me of someone else (e.g., parent and former partner)?" "To what extent do I have unresolved feelings and issues that this client triggers?"

Another strategy for counsellors is to spend time getting to know the client. Usually, familiarity increases empathy, as in the following example:

Carl, an employment counsellor, carefully read Antonio's file. Antonio was a 19-year-old unemployed male. From all indications, Antonio was not very interested in finding a job. His mother complained that he usually slept until noon and that he rarely even read the newspaper want ads. Antonio arrived for his appointment 20 minutes late and gave out a clear message that he didn't want to be there. "How long will this take?" he asked bluntly.

Carl's natural reaction was anger and disgust at Antonio's attitude. He wondered to himself why he should spend time with this client, who was clearly unmotivated. Putting his personal feelings aside, Carl decided to respond with empathy, and he gently replied, "My hunch is that you don't see much point in being here. Maybe you're even a little angry at being forced to come." Antonio, a bit surprised at Carl's perceptiveness, told him how much he resented everyone trying to run his life.

Gradually, Antonio began to let down his defences and a very different picture emerged. Antonio talked about the rejection he felt from countless employers who turned him away. Soon it was clear to Carl that Antonio was deeply depressed. He slept late because he could not sleep at night. He had stopped looking for work because it was his best choice for dealing with the pain of rejection.

Sometimes counsellors fear expressing empathy because they mistakenly believe that empathy endorses their clients' beliefs or lifestyles, but keep in mind that being empathic does not mean agreeing with the client's feelings or perspectives. Empathy simply attempts to say, "I understand how you feel and how you see things." In fact, clients must feel understood before they will respond to any efforts to promote change. Empathy is one of the ways that counsellors establish credibility and win the trust of their clients. When a trusting relationship exists, clients may be willing to consider other perspectives and look at the consequences of their choices.

⟫⟫⟫ INTERVIEW 6.2 | Effective Use of Empathy

Client: For as long as I can remember, I've been drinking on a daily basis. It's no big deal.	
Counsellor: *(Softly, while maintaining eye contact.)* Drinking has been part of your life, and you don't see a problem with it. *(Client nods.)*	***Analysis:*** *The counsellor tries to proceed cautiously with basic paraphrasing. Mirroring the client's thoughts conveys that he has been heard. Suspending verbal and nonverbal judgment helps to develop trust.*
Counsellor: You mentioned that your family gives you a hard time about drinking. How do you feel about that?	***Analysis:*** *An open question encourages the client to talk about his feelings. Such statements also say to the client that the counsellor is willing to listen.*
Client: Yeah. I work hard all day. If I want to have a drink, no one has a right to tell me to stop. Drinking helps me relax.	
Counsellor: Sounds as though you resent it when others interfere with something that gives you pleasure.	***Analysis:*** *Inferred empathy. Although the client does not directly label his feelings, based on the words, context, and nonverbal messages, the counsellor speculates that resentment might be the predominant feeling.*
Client: *(Loudly.)* They should back off and mind their own business. I don't tell them how to live.	***Analysis:*** *The client's response suggests that he is responsive to the counsellor's empathy. He signals this by continuing to share at a deeper level. This is a significant event in the interview, which should give the counsellor confidence to continue to risk empathy.*
Counsellor: It's more than just resentment. Perhaps you're angry that they don't respect your right to live your life as you see fit.	***Analysis:*** *Anger is inferred from the client's nonverbal expression (volume). By labelling the anger, the counsellor gives the client "permission" to discuss his anger.*

Client: I guess I shouldn't be so ticked off. After all, my father was an alcoholic, and I know first-hand what it's like to live with a drunk.	*Analysis: Since the counsellor accepts his anger, the client may feel less that he has to defend it.*
Counsellor: To some extent, your feelings are mixed. You feel anger because you think they should mind their own business, and you also see where they're coming from. You are sympathetic to their fears. **Client:** Well, to be perfectly honest, it's not just their fear. I don't want to drink myself to death like my father did.	*Analysis: The counsellor picks up on and identifies the client's mixed feelings. Mixed feelings can often be a source of anxiety for clients, particularly if they pull their emotions in different directions.*
Counsellor: You've done some thinking about how you'd like your life to be different. When your wife confronts you, it really touches a nerve, and you're reminded of fears you'd rather not have. **Client:** No way I'm going to let that happen to me.	*Analysis: Inferred empathy. This client was initially guarded and defensive, quick to defend his right to drink. As he finds acceptance from the counsellor, he begins to let his guard down. In some interviews, such as this one, trust can develop quickly, but more often, the counsellor requires extended patience.*
Counsellor: You're determined to control your drinking. **Client:** I'm not going to be like my father.	*Analysis: This basic empathic response gives the client some breathing room. Counsellors should avoid constant pressure on clients to move to a higher level of intimacy. The counsellor needs to move deeper, but caution is critical to avoid moving too quickly.*
Counsellor: Correct me if I'm off base, but as you talk, I wonder if a part of you is afraid that your drinking could get out of hand.	*Analysis: The counsellor uses both confrontation and inferred empathy in this statement. Presenting the ideas in a tentative manner softens the confrontation.*

Reflections:

- What might have happened if this counsellor had used a more confrontational approach?
- If you were the counsellor, what would you want to do in the next half-hour with this client?

SUMMARY

- Because of the central role that emotions play in our lives, counsellors must give priority to exploring and understanding clients' feelings. Emotions are characterized by physiological as well as psychological and behavioural reactions. Mixed feelings, including contradictory emotions, are common. A great deal of client stress and confusion can arise from the pushes and pulls of competing feelings, which, if unmanaged, can control a client's life.

- Empathy is a core skill for all helping relationships. Empathy helps build the helping relationship, assists clients in identifying and labelling feelings, models a healthy way of relating to others, and helps clients accept their own feelings. Although counsellors can never know exactly how their clients feel, empathy enables them to move closer to understanding.

- The three types of empathy are invitational, basic, and inferred. Invitational empathy involves strategies to encourage clients to talk about their feelings. Basic empathy mirrors what the client has explicitly said, while inferred empathy attempts to reach empathic understanding from less obvious clues. A variety of strategies can be used to encourage clients to express feelings, including invitational statements, questions targeted at feelings, explanations of the importance of addressing feelings, directives, self-disclosures, and sentence completion statements.

■   There are four key generalizations about empathy: (1) When clients share feelings, empathy is often the preferred response. (2) Counsellors should risk expressing empathy early in the relationship. (3) Counsellors should express empathy tentatively. (4) Empathy requires flexibility in its use, including the ability to refrain from using it.

EXERCISES

Self-Awareness

1. Begin a log to track your feelings. At periodic intervals (e.g., every hour), record words and phrases that best describe how you are feeling at that moment. Try to be as precise as possible, using terms that capture the essence and intensity of how you feel. Maintain your log for at least one week.

   a. What patterns or cycles are apparent? Are there times of the day or week when you are more likely to feel particular emotions?

   b. How could you have altered your emotions (e.g., to increase pleasurable feelings and decrease negative feelings)?

   c. What have you learned about yourself from this exercise that will assist you in your work as a counsellor?

2. Recall the 10 families of emotions: anger, fear, strength, weakness, joy, sadness, confusion, shame, surprise, and love. Rate your ability to show or express each one on a scale of 1 to 5 (5 = strong, 1 = unable to express).

   a. What are the emotions that you have more difficulty expressing? Are there feelings you would never express?

   b. How do your ability and willingness to share emotions vary depending on the person you are with?

3. Would you find it easier to tell your friends (your parents, family, etc.) that you love them or that you are angry with them?

4. What did you learn about expressing emotions when you were growing up? Explore how this might help or hinder your work in your field of practice. For example, if you grew up in a family or culture where emotions were seldom expressed, consider how this has impacted your current willingness to show your feelings or to encourage others to share their emotions.

5. Describe in detail how you feel, think, and act when you experience specific emotions. For example, you might write, "When I feel scared, I want to escape. My breathing is shallow. I tend to look away. I become quiet. I think I might vomit." (Hint: Use your imagination to visualize situations where you might experience the specific emotion.)

Learning Group

1. Work in a small group of four or five students. Take turns making a brief statement about something current in your life that involves emotions. In response, other members attempt to identify the predominant feelings expressed.

2. Practice Interview: Work in pairs with one person acting as a client sharing the details of something current that involves emotions, and the other person acting in the counsellor role. Allow about 15 minutes for the interview. As counsellor, use the three types of empathic responses to keep the interview focused on feelings. When the interview is over, review the experience with each other using the following questions as a guide:

   • Client: What was easy and difficult about sharing your feelings? What responses from your partner were helpful? Unhelpful?

   • Counsellor: What aspects of responding with empathy did you find most challenging?

3. The purpose of this exercise is to develop your ability to "track" the flow of an interview, including identifying the use of particular interviewing and counselling skills. Work with student colleagues. One student will be the counsellor, another the client, with the others as observers. Videotape a 15-minute segment of a counselling interview. Classify each counsellor response (e.g., open question, closed question, silence, empathy, self-disclosure, or mixed response). Use the following table to compile interview statistics. Place a check each time a particular skill is used. Notice that the table is organized to divide the interview into time segments.

	0–5 minutes	6–10 minutes	11–15 minutes
Open question			
Closed question			
Indirect question			
Silence			
Empathy			
Self-disclosure			
Directive			
Summary			
Paraphrase			
Other (specify)			

After the interview, discuss these questions:

a. Did the counsellor use a variety of different responses?

b. To what extent did the counsellor vary his or her approach as the session progressed?

c. What interview transitions were apparent? Were they appropriate? Consider, for example, whether the transition occurred prematurely, before concrete understanding or exploration was completed.

d. What skills were overused or underused?

e. Which responses were productive? Which responses were counterproductive?

4. Interview colleagues or friends from diverse ethnic groups to explore how different individuals express emotions.

5. In a small group, predict and describe the possible emotions that different individuals in the following scenarios might experience. What nonverbal cues might you observe in each case?

a. Man whose wife of 60 years has just died

b. Young teenager on a first date

c. Middle-aged man fired from his job

d. 20-year-old man told by his doctor that he has schizophrenia

e. Mother discovering her teenage daughter is using drugs

f. A young woman subjected to online harassment

g. Person who lost his life savings in the stock market

h. Prisoner about to be sentenced

i. Angry client

j. Client seeing a counsellor for the first (or last) time

k. Patient in hospital waiting for major surgery

l. Child entering a foster home

m. Man who has just abused his wife

n. Couple on the day of their marriage

o. Immigrant who has left his wife and children at home while he settles in Canada

p. Serial killer

q. Compulsive gambler after a big win and after losing his paycheque

r. 11-year-old girl who has been sexually abused by her father

s. 75-year-old woman remarrying three years after the death of her husband. (She was happily married for 45 years.)

6. Identify feeling words and phrases that best describe how each of the following clients may be feeling:

a. "Everyone in my life keeps putting me down. Even my own children constantly criticize me."

b. (Shaking.) "Fifteen hard years with the same company and what do they do? They dump me with three weeks' notice."

c. (A six-year-old boy, crying while speaking to recreation staff.) "No one wants to play with me. No one likes me."

d. "If I started crying, I don't think I could ever stop."

e. (An ex-offender to his or her parole officer.) "Have you ever been to jail?"

f. (A 16-year-old boy.) "I'd rather live on the street than go to another foster home. Five foster homes in five years. I've had enough!"

g. (A gay man.) "I didn't expect to live to see 40."

h. "Why do you want me to go to see a psychiatrist? Do you think I'm crazy? You're the one who's crazy."

i. (Patient speaking to a paramedic.) "Leave me alone. I just want to die."

7. Interview people from different cultures. If possible, interview first-generation immigrants who have been in this country for only a short time. Explore their views on emotional expression, for example, the extent that their personal, familial, and cultural roots value sharing emotions. Remember that peoples' viewpoints do not necessarily represent that of their culture of origin.

Concepts

1. Assume that the following clients are speaking to you and that an empathic response is appropriate. Suggest a response to each statement.

a. (Youth speaking to a youth justice worker.) "You don't care about me. All you guys are the same. You tell me that you want what's best for me. You're just in this job for the money."

b. (Client, smiling.) "For the first time, things are really starting to come together for me. My kids are all doing well in school, my marital problems are on the upswing, and I finally put some money aside for a rainy day."

c. (Parent to a teacher.) "I don't know what to do. I know you said I should try to help my son with his homework and show some interest in his work, but he comes home from school and goes straight to his room. When I ask about his homework, he always says that there wasn't any. When I offer to help, he makes it clear he'd rather do it on his own."

d. (Teenager, crying.) "I'm pregnant. This will kill my dad, but first he'll kill me."

e. "Everyone always says how together I am, but I don't feel together. Sometimes I get so wound up that I think I'm going to burst."

f. (Man, age 57, talking about his family problems.) "I have to make every decision. I can never count on my wife or kids for help."

g. (Parent to a teacher.) "My son does not have ADHD. I don't care what you say. I'm not going to put him on drugs."

h. (Client shouting.) "I am calm!"

i. (Woman, age 50-plus, talking to a 23-year-old worker.) "You're pretty young to be working here."

j. (Patient in an ambulance.) "Don't let me die."

2. Each of the following client statements expresses more than one feeling. Identify feeling words and phrases that best describe the mixed feelings. Next, formulate an empathic response.

   a. "Thanks for seeing me today. It really felt good to get things off my chest. No one has ever listened to me the way you did. I hope you don't think I'm crazy or stupid."

   b. *(Eyes welling up with tears.)* "It's over. I don't care to be with him anymore."

   c. "I was brought up to believe you should handle your problems on your own. Look at me now—sitting here pouring my guts out to a counsellor."

   d. "To tell you the truth, I'd like to just march right in, look him in the eye, and tell him exactly where to go. I don't know what to do."

   e. "Finding out that my former girlfriend had my baby was totally shocking. After we broke up, she didn't even tell me she was pregnant. I'd love to be a father, but I don't want a relationship with her. Maybe it would be best if I just forget the whole thing, but I want to do what's right."

   f. "Living on your own is the pits. Now I don't even know where my next meal is coming from. I used to love being married. I felt as if life really had meaning. At least, I don't have to worry about being beat up by my husband every time he gets drunk. It's just so difficult. Maybe I should give him another chance."

   g. *(Woman, 79 years old, crying.)* "My daughter keeps saying that she is coming for a visit, but it has been weeks since I have seen her. *(Wipes away the tears.)* It's not that important. I really do not want to be a bother. I'm just feeling sorry for myself this morning."

   h. *(A civil engineer from Syria who immigrated to Canada.)* "I was so excited to begin my new life in Canada when I came three years ago. But all my dreams have disappeared. The only work I've been able to find is driving a cab."

   i. *(12-year-old girl.)* "I flashed my breasts on the Internet while I was in an online chat room. Now my life is ruined. Everyone at school calls me a slut. I have no one."

   j. "The 2015 terrorist killings in Paris really messed me up. I haven't been able to sleep, and I constantly think about my kids. I don't travel or even go to movies anymore. It could happen here."

3. This exercise allows you to apply tough empathy. The following statements may evoke strong personal reactions. Assume that the person is speaking to you and that you are responding with empathy, even though empathy may not be the preferred response.

   a. "Canada was much better when it was white and Christian. With such high unemployment, don't you think it's time to stop letting every damn immigrant into the country? No wonder I can't get a job."

   b. "I'm not ashamed to admit it. Once in a while, I hit my wife. It's no big deal."

   c. "I don't care what you say. I won't give up on you until you convert and save your soul."

   d. "I want to die. I've thought about it for months, and I just don't want to live anymore."

   e. "What's the big deal if I have to steal a bit from Safeway to make sure my kids are fed? It's not like it hurts anyone."

   f. *(Student to teacher.)* "I suppose this course is going to be like all the others. Lots of reading, a bunch of papers. I only hope there's some relevance to it all."

   g. *(Client, 35 years old.)* "I had no idea she was only 15. She was the one who wanted to have sex. From the look in her eyes, I could tell she was begging for it. It's really unfair that I'm now charged with rape. Besides, 15 is old enough for someone to make up their own mind."

   h. "This counselling isn't very helpful."

   i. "I really don't worry too much about AIDS. What can I do about it? If I'm meant to get it, then I'll get it. So what? We all have to die sometime."

   j. "I'm not stupid. I know that he shouldn't hit me. But I guess I deserved it, the way I put him down. I should learn to keep my mouth shut. When I see him, I'll apologize."

   k. *(Client, with angry tone.)* "No one is willing to talk to me about the fact that I might be dying. I can accept it, but every time I ask the big question, people change the topic."

   l. "There's no way I'm going to pay for her stupidity. If she didn't want to get pregnant, she should have taken the pill. Now she expects me to support the baby until he's 18. I don't care if I am the father. Not a chance!"

   What do you think are the advantages of responding with empathy to the preceding clients?

4. Each of the following client statements might be a routine inquiry for information or could be an indirect way of expressing feelings. Assume that the client is expressing feelings and formulate an empathic response.

   a. How old are you?

   b. Have you ever been unemployed?

   c. Have you ever lived in a foster home?

   d. Did you use drugs when you were my age?

   e. Have you ever taken psychiatric medications?

5. Record a television program. Watch it with the sound turned off. Pay attention to the nonverbal communication of the actors. Now watch it with the sound turned on. How successful were you in correctly reading the nonverbal cues?

6. The following is the transcript of a portion of a counsellor's interview. The worker is an employment counsellor at

a Vancouver social service agency. Critically evaluate the counsellor's responses (e.g., appropriateness of questions, use of empathy, etc.). What attitude do you think the counsellor conveys to his client? Suggest alternative responses based on empathy.

Counsellor: Hey! Are you Leah? I'm Mr. Short. Won't you come in to my office? *(Brief small talk in office.)*

Counsellor: So what is your problem? How can I help you?

Client: Well, I don't really know where to begin. Right now, my life is a mess. I've gotten along well so far, but lately . . . well, I'm just not coping very well. *(Client pauses, wipes tears with a tissue.)*

Counsellor: Okay, calm down. Try not to cry. Have you been to this agency before? By the way, how old are you?

Client: No, this is the first time. I wonder if anyone will ever give me a chance. Sometimes I think, why not give up? I feel so scared all the time. Don't get me wrong—I really want to work, to be independent, to buy my kids all the things I haven't been able to afford. I just don't know if I can do it. I haven't worked in 10 years. Plus, there's the problem of daycare . . . the things you read . . . it's hard to know who to trust. Things just seemed so much easier when my husband was alive.

Counsellor: You say you haven't worked in 10 years. What was the last job you held? What did you do? What are your job skills?

Client: Mostly, I've worked as a secretary in Toronto. It was okay, but I don't want to do that anymore. I really don't have a clue what I'd like.

Counsellor: So you know you want to get out of clerical work, but you're unsure what else you might do or like.

Client: Yes, exactly.

Counsellor: Have you considered social services? There are lots of good programs that you could complete in a short time.

Client: No, I don't think I'd like that.

Counsellor: How can you be sure until you give it a try? Sometimes volunteer work is a really good way to find out if you like it.

Client: Well . . . I guess so.

Counsellor: Actually, I was in the same boat as you. Then I volunteered. Next thing I knew I was back in school. Now I'm working full time and loving it. I have a friend who works at the volunteer bureau. Why don't I give her a call and set up an appointment for you?

Client: Okay . . . thanks.

Counsellor: No problem. I was glad to be of help. I'll phone her, and then I'll give you a call. It'll probably be next week or so.

WEBLINKS

Roots of Empathy, a program with Canadian origins, to teach empathy skills to children

www.rootsofempathy.org

The Compass DeRose Guide to Emotion Words: A comprehensive list of emotions and feeling words as well as some links to other resources and articles on the topic

www.derose.net/steve/resources/emotionwords/ewords.html

The Association for the Development of the Person Centered Approach (includes links and articles based on the teachings of Carl Rogers)

www.adpca.org

Website offering comprehensive tools and worksheets on emotions and a variety of other relevant topics

http://www.therapistaid.com/

Emotional Intelligence Network

http://www.6seconds.org/

Chapter 7
Supporting Empowerment and Change

LEARNING OBJECTIVES

- Identify the elements of empowering clients.

- Explore the strengths approach.

- Appreciate the complex and diverse challenges of working with seniors.

- Understand the goals and skills of crisis intervention.

- Describe the principles and strategies of motivational interviewing.

- Identify and describe the stages of change model.

- Explore the principles and strategies of cognitive behavioural counselling.

- Understand the process of problem solving.

- Understand the principles and techniques of brief counselling.

EMPOWERMENT: MOBILIZING STRENGTHS FOR CHANGE

Empowerment: The process of helping clients discover personal strengths and capacities so that they are able to take control over their lives; the expected outcome of successful counselling.

Empowerment that results in clients discovering strengths and taking control of their lives is the expected outcome of successful counselling. There are many elements of empowerment that impact all three domains: feelings, thinking, and behaviour

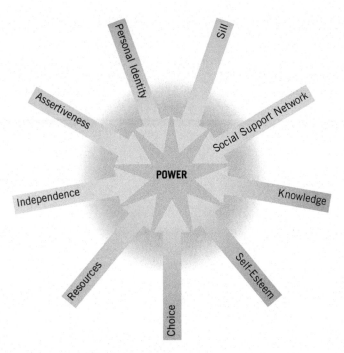

Figure 7.1   The Elements of Empowerment

(see Figure 7.1). Empowered clients have high self-esteem and confidence, enabling them to take appropriate risks without undue anxiety. Able to enjoy success without guilt, they are fully aware of their needs and values. They behave assertively, aware of their rights, yet respectful of the rights of others. With access to knowledge and resources, they make their own decisions by using a range of skills and strategies. Although empowered clients have the ability to act independently, they are also able to draw on social and community supports. Empowerment is the antidote to oppressive systems that deny people access and opportunity to participate in decisions that affect their lives.

Empowerment requires self-determination as well as the means, opportunity, resources, and freedom to exercise choice. Fully exercised, empowerment ensures full participation in decisions affecting clients' lives. Responsible empowerment is founded on the principle of reciprocity and respect for relationships and the rights of others. It is assertive for personal rights and freedoms, but not at the expense of the rights and freedoms of others. In relationships, responsible empowerment commits people, insofar as possible, to negotiating, collaborating, consensus seeking, and remaining accountable. Responsible empowerment is assertive, neither passive nor aggressive.

How Counselling Promotes Empowerment

Counsellors do not empower clients; rather they promote the conditions where empowerment can flourish. Counsellors support client empowerment with the foundational belief that clients are capable of change and have a right to manage their own lives. An empowerment attitude focuses on the capacities and strengths of clients while forgoing any need to control clients by taking on an "expert" role that makes them dependent. When empowerment is the priority, clients become the experts, and there is "collaboration and shared decision making within the professional relationship" (Sheafor & Horejsi, 2008, p. 79). Counsellors demystify the counselling process through open and non-jargonistic discussion with clients of their methods and assumptions.

Self-determination, an important component of client empowerment, is promoted by helping clients recognize choices and by encouraging them to make independent decisions. Counsellors should not do for clients what clients can and should do for themselves.

Anti-Oppressive Practice

Often clients come from disadvantaged and marginalized groups where they "have been 'beaten down' by oppression, poverty, abuse, and other harmful life experiences. They want better lives for themselves and their families, but they feel powerless to make the necessary changes. Some clients have a pervasive sense of failure and feel different from and rejected by other people" (Sheafor & Horejsi, 2008, p. 422).

Sometimes powerlessness arises from negative self-evaluation and low self-esteem or from lack of confidence in one's ability to alter one's life, but sometimes the systems that are set up to assist clients are themselves oppressive and contribute to powerlessness. **Anti-oppressive practice** involves counsellors working for structural changes in organizations or policy, and in promoting equity in the distribution of resources, opportunities, and power (Drolet, Clark, & Allen, 2012). Paul Moore (2001) suggests that an anti-oppressive framework challenges workers to examine and challenge the lenses that may colour our viewpoints on what is "right and acceptable:" racism, sexism, heterosexism, ableism, ageism, and class oppression. Feminist theory addresses the power differential that allows men to enjoy privilege at the expense of women.

Ben Carniol (2010), a Canadian social work educator and advocate, reminds helpers that since racism and other prejudices may deny clients access to jobs and resources such as adequate housing, helpers have a responsibility to advocate for a progressive system and social policy changes.

Since client self-determination is enhanced when clients have more choices, counsellors should also be involved in broader activities such as working to identify and remove gaps and barriers to service and encouraging more humane and accessible policies and services. The counselling process itself offers empowerment to clients. The beginning phase offers many clients a unique opportunity to explore their situation and their feelings. Active listening skills help clients bring long-forgotten or misunderstood feelings to the surface. Ventilation of feelings can energize clients, and it can lead to spontaneous insight into new ways of handling problems that seemed insurmountable. For some clients, the work of counselling is finished at this phase.

anti-oppressive practice: When counsellors work for structural changes in organizations, policy, and in promoting equity in the distribution of resources, opportunities, and power.

THE STRENGTHS APPROACH

The **strengths approach** is a perspective that shifts the focus from client problems and deficits to possibilities, capacities, and resources that can be mobilized in the pursuit of goals and change. Many clients come to counselling with low self-esteem and confidence. Seligman's (1975) concept of **learned helplessness** suggests that individuals can become demoralized through failure to the point that they give up trying to alter their circumstances, even in situations in which change is possible. Persons with learned helplessness can be difficult and frustrating to work with because these clients do not believe their efforts will make a difference. When they are successful, they are likely to attribute it to luck, rather than their efforts or capacity. As long as they hold these beliefs, they are unlikely to engage in risk-taking to solve problems and achieve

strengths approach: A counselling perspective that assumes the inherent capacity of people. Individuals and communities are seen to have assets and resources that can be mobilized for problem solving.

learned helplessness: A state of mind that occurs when individuals have learned through failure that their efforts will not result in change.

empowerment. Significantly, individuals may in fact be quite capable, but believe they are not. For others, anxiety about risk-taking or failure deters them from action. In addition, if clients are locked into a view of themselves as victims, they are likely to resist change, or they may enter into dependency relationships in which they relinquish power and control to others, including their counsellors. The key is to help them set small goals and implement a successful action plan, then accept the connection between their actions and success. Cognitive behavioural techniques are also valuable in helping clients change the way they think about themselves.

SUCCESS TIP

Counsellors need to manage their own unmet needs that might impede their capacity to be helpful. For example, if they have a high need for control, they can potentially take power from clients, who for their part may freely give it away.

Here are some basic strategies for maintaining a strengths approach:

1. Negotiate collaborative relationships with clients where they share responsibility for identifying priorities, goals, and preferred ways of proceeding. Accept that they are the "experts" on their own lives and that with encouragement they can make decisions on what will and will not work. Counsellors need to be flexible and accept that every intervention plan will be individualized to the unique needs and attributes of each client. What works with one client may be counterproductive with another.

2. Trust that clients have the capacity to change, and that they can learn to cope with their problems and challenges. Every experienced counsellor can relate amazing stories of people who have recovered from adversity and overwhelming odds.

3. Stay interested in strengths. Acknowledge clients' skills, resourcefulness, motivation, and virtues. When workers value their clients' strengths, clients learn to value themselves. Discovering overlooked abilities, knowledge, and experience can also energize counsellors and clients.

4. Ask questions or make statements that uncover strengths, such as "Think of a time when you were able to handle problems such as this. What skills and resources enabled you to cope?" Other approaches include these: "When you were able to manage, what were you doing that helped you succeed?" "What are the things in your life that you feel good about?" "What's working well for you?" "What would your friends say are your best qualities?"

5. Help the client identify strengths that come from adversity with questions such as "In what ways have the problems you've faced in your life made you stronger?" To a client who has struggled for six months to find work and get off welfare, you might say, "I'm impressed with your ability to hang in there. Many people would have given up." Look for strengths in the way clients have handled adversity with comments and questions such as "You've been through a lot in your life, but somehow you've managed to survive. How have you been able to do this?" Or you might say, "In what ways have your problems made you stronger?"

6. Use cognitive behavioural techniques to help clients challenge and manage self-deprecating remarks that reinforce low self-esteem.

7. Avoid diagnostic labels as a way of describing clients. Labels tend to ignore strengths by focusing on pathology and deficits.

8. Focus on problem solving and goal setting rather than on discussions of blame or on finding the root causes of current behaviour or problems. There may be

cathartic benefit to discussing history, but once this purpose is achieved, the focus of the work should shift to present and future events. Goal setting energizes clients to action and mobilizes their resources and motivation for change.

9. Use the informal resources of families, neighbourhoods, and communities that are potential sources of help and strength for clients. Use community directories to pinpoint agencies, services, and self-help groups that could be supportive. Challenge clients to identify and discover these resources: "Who do you trust?" "Who supports you when you need help?"

Strengths-based counselling shifts the focus from deficits and problems to a process in which clients' strengths, capacities, and resources are recognized. Strengths are the resources that enable clients to overcome problems. In this sense, client assessment moves beyond identifying obstacles and problems to discussion of personal and environmental resources.

Helping clients realize their strengths empowers them with the belief that they are capable of change. For example, helping clients reframe how they think about problems can enable them to see their problems as opportunities. Saleeby (2009), a major proponent of the strengths approach, offers these perspectives:

> It is a collaborative process . . . . It is an approach honoring the innate wisdom of the human spirit, the inherent capacity for transformation of even the most humbled and abused . . . . Rally clients' interests, capacities, motivations, resources, and emotions in the work of reaching their hopes and dreams, help them find pathways to those goals, and the payoff may be an enhanced quality of daily life for them. (p. 1)

SUCCESS TIP

"Practicing from a strengths perspective requires that we shift the way we think about, approach, and relate to our clients. Rather than focusing exclusively or dominantly on problems, your eye turns towards possibility. In the thicket of trauma, pain, and trouble, you see blooms of hope and transformation." (Saleeby, 2009, p. 1)

The strengths approach reduces some of the power differential that occurs when client vulnerabilities and deficits are given priority over their strengths. Glicken (2004) offers this reminder: "There is usually more about clients that is positive and functional than is negative or dysfunctional" (p. 4). With the strengths perspective, the client is the expert and the primary author of the change process. "Thus, the worker's role is to listen, help the client process, and facilitate by focusing on positive behaviors that might be useful to clients for coping with their current life situations" (Glicken, 2004, p. 6).

►►► BRAIN BYTE   Stress and Crisis

Our minds and bodies react with remarkable speed to deal with crisis and stress. To divert its resources to fighting the crisis, the brain shuts down nonessential activity such as digestion. Our hearts pump faster and our breathing increases to maximize oxygen to the body. Adrenaline, the stress hormone cortisol, and dozens of other hormones are released. The brain signals the liver to release more sugar creating a burst of energy. While cortisol, adrenaline, and other hormones help us cope in the short run, with chronic (prolonged) stress, depression may increase, the production of new brain neurons is reduced, and there is damage to the Hippocampus, a part of the brain associated with memory and learning. Maladaptive attempts to deal with stress using drugs, overeating, and smoking compound the problem by increasing the risk of stroke, heart attack, liver disease, and a myriad of other health problems (Ashwell, 2012; The Franklin Institute, 2015; and University of Maryland, 2015).

EMPOWERMENT AND SENIORS

On July 1, 2017, there were almost 5.8 million people in Canada over 65 years of age representing about 16 percent of the population, and for the first time, the number of seniors over 65 years of age in Canada is greater than the number of children under 15 (Statistics Canada, 2017).

The first of the baby boomers are now in their 70s. Their lives have evolved very differently than past generations, and they are rewriting the book on aging. With improved life expectancy, they can expect to live 15 to 20 years or more and their expectations for an active and productive retirement are high. As a group, they are healthier, more educated, and more financially secure than previous generations.

Today's seniors are very adept at self-advocating for their rights and needs. Generally, they have led lives where they were active participants in decision making, so there is little doubt that they will have an enormous impact on services for this age group. They will want to be very involved in defining and developing programs and services that will meet their needs. Since the foundation for empowerment is choice and control, counsellors will welcome this proactive stance as one that is very consistent with strengths and empowerment counselling philosophy and routines.

Aging offers many opportunities. It is a time when people can have more time to pursue hobbies, spend time with family, assist with raising grandchildren, travel and realize dreams that were not possible in their younger years. Increased attention to fitness and nutrition along with better healthcare results in more seniors living longer, healthier, and independent lives. Financial need, better health, and a general desire to remain active in the labour force has resulted in many seniors working well past the traditional retirement age of 65.

Aging can also present with many unanticipated challenges that lead seniors to seek counselling (see Table 7.1) For example, health issues may have impacted the ability of many seniors to work or participate in activities that have defined their lives. Some, because of mobility or health issues, including loss of eyesight, have become dependent on others for the first time in their lives. Women live longer than men, so they are more likely to face the prospect of living alone without their spouse, sometimes with very limited income or support.

Retirement or unanticipated job loss can result in dramatic changes in role and status that have defined a person's life. Without the demands and time commitments of employment, retirement requires people to find new ways to structure their time and find meaning in their lives. Otherwise, depression, loneliness, and despair may take over. Consequently, helping seniors achieve or maintain a sense of purpose is an essential empowerment goal.

CRISIS INTERVENTION AND EMPOWERMENT

A crisis can take many forms. Natural disasters, terrorist attacks, and war create crises that impact all members of a country or community. Personal experiences such as rape, death, divorce, loss of income, or incarceration clearly affect individuals and their families.

Many factors influence how an individual copes with a crisis, including past experiences, overall physical and psychological health, the presence or absence of social and community supports, substance use, personality factors such as impulse control, and genetics. Catastrophic disasters, assaults, war, and other traumas can disempower even the strongest individuals, and people may experience devastating and debilitating life changes, such as post-traumatic stress disorder. For some, a crisis may stir up past memories of other traumas and the impact may be cumulative, leaving them more vulnerable. As a result, there is further psychological injury leading to depression, physical illness, anxiety, hopelessness, suicide, or withdrawal.

TABLE 7.1 Empowering Seniors

Component	Potential Issues	Support Choices
Medical/Psychiatric	• Complex health, for example, loss of eyesight, hearing, and physical mobility • Depression • Dementia including Alzheimer's Disease	• Family support and education • Lifestyle counselling—nutrition and exercise • Appropriate use of medication and the health system • Respite care
Financial	• Poverty (especially women) • Unexpected job loss • Costs of housing in long-term care • Financial abuse	• Career and job counselling for those remaining in the workforce • Community resources for financial and housing support • Legal remedies
Social	• Discrimination (ageism) • Managing time, use of leisure, and coping with retirement • Emotional and physical neglect and abuse • Isolation and fear of abandonment • Housing • Couples who become separated in different care facilities because one of them needs more complex care	• Wellness counselling • Exploration of meaningful social and recreational opportunities • Use of advocate groups and organizations • Employment of volunteers • Police intervention • Lobbying for systemic change • Pets • Arrangement of transportation (family, volunteers, and seniors' services)
Psychological	• Loss of control, independence, and identity and the need to find purpose in life • Dealing with death and dying • Loss of control, identity, and independence • Isolation and fear of abandonment • Grief exacerbated by multiple losses (friends, family, and spouse) • Sexuality	• Strengths-based counselling • Grief counselling • Maximizing involvement in decision making • Utilization of adult day care and drop-in programs for seniors

Nevertheless, many people adapt and may even thrive during a crisis. They discover their resilience and untapped strengths, including previously unknown resources. Optimistically, the resolution of a crisis is an opportunity for growth. Presbury, Echterling, and McKee (2008) suggest that post-traumatic growth (PTG) happens when people "come away from traumatic events having gained a new perspective on life and having achieved important understandings" (p. 212). Supportive crisis intervention by counsellors and others can increase the probability of post-traumatic growth (James & Gilliland, 2013).

A crisis can overwhelm individuals and disrupt their ability to cope and function normally. Personal crises that may arise from depression, loss of job, or rape may evoke emotions so intense that action or rational thinking is impossible. Sometimes, as in the case of a disaster like a flood or tsunami, people are cut off from their basic physical needs. Whatever the nature of the crisis, the priority goal for counselling is to help clients obtain power and control by re-establishing safety and stability. One central step is to help and encourage connections with supportive family, friends, and community resources to restore equilibrium and to reduce psychological trauma.

SUCCESS TIP

In the immediate aftermath of a crisis, counsellors may wish to minimize (but not prevent) expression of feelings in favour of initiatives that focus on safety and connection with supportive family and community resources.

The ultimate goal of crisis intervention is client empowerment, so that wherever possible counsellors should collaborate with clients; however, because of physical incapacitation or emotional inability, there may be times when counsellors need to assume power and be more directive. For example, if a client is suicidal and not responding to counselling initiatives, the counsellor may need to call for emergency services and hospitalization. If a client is emotionally unable to make rational decisions, the counsellor may be required to take charge. Table 7.2 summarizes counsellor skills and strategies for selected crisis intervention goals.

In the remainder of this chapter, strategies for motivating clients and helping them develop and sustain change will be explored. Motivational Interviewing (Miller & Rollnick, 2002, 2013) is a tool to help clients deal with the ambivalence that inhibits them from making necessary changes. The **stages of change model** (Prochaska & Norcross, 2001) is based on the notion that people go through different motivational stages, each of which requires different counsellor skill choices for success. Frequently, the stages of change model is reflected in Motivational Interviewing. Cognitive behavioural counselling is a collaborative (counsellor and client) approach to helping clients make changes in the three major psychological domains: thinking, behaviour, and emotions.

> **stages of change model:** A theory of motivation that recognizes five changes of stage: precontemplation, contemplation, preparation, action, and maintenance.

MOTIVATIONAL INTERVIEWING (MI)

Motivational Interviewing (MI) (Miller & Rollnick, 2002, 2013) is an empirically validated strategy for helping people overcome ambivalence to change. Motivational interviewing requires a collaborative, nonconfrontational relationship. It assumes that motivation and capacity for change are within the client. Consequently, it honours the client's right to self-determination regarding whether change is to take place, as well as the ultimate goals of any change process. "MI allows clients, both mandated and voluntary, to discover their own reasons for making change. MI allows the impetus to change to emerge from within a client, thus honoring the client's unique circumstances and worldview" (Capuzzi & Stauffer, 2008, p. 145).

> **motivational interviewing (MI):** A nonconfrontational counselling approach that promotes behavioural change by assisting clients to recognize and resolve ambivalence.

TABLE 7.2 Crisis Intervention

Intervention Goal	Counsellor Skill and Strategy Choices
Physical safety	• Link to resources for food, shelter, and medical assistance. • Help client move to a physical or psychologically safe setting. • Access emergency services (e.g., police and ambulance).
Psychological safety	• Encourage client to link with personal supports (family, friends, and religious leader). • Show empathy (allow clients to express feelings). • Normalize feelings. • Carry out trauma counselling.
Empowerment	• Provide information. • Encourage decision making. • Promote and reinforce small goals with realistic time frames. • Mobilize or help client connect with support groups.
Restore balance	• Offer reassurance. • Provide services (information, support, and referral) to significant family. • Communicate hope and optimism. • Encourage resumption of normal routines. • Plan for follow-up.

Miller and Rollnick's (2013) conception of MI highlights the following features:

- The "spirit of motivational interviewing" is more important than technique. "The spirit of motivational interviewing" as conceptualized by Miller and Rollnick (2013) is primarily concerned with the attitude of the counsellor and the counselling relationship. It derives from Roger's person-centered approach with a high emphasis on client self-determination and faith in the ability and capacity of people to change. They identify "four key interrelated elements of the spirit of MI: partnership, acceptance, compassion, and evocation" (p. 15). Partnership emphasizes collaborative conversations to assist people to strengthen their motivation for change. Acceptance involves the essential core conditions described by Rogers (1961) of unconditional positive regard, empathy, and genuineness (See Chapter 3 of this book). Compassion, as defined by Miller and Rollnick, involves a conscious focus on promoting the best interests of clients by giving their needs priority (p. 20). Evocation focuses on the inherent strengths of clients as opposed to detecting problems and deficits. As discussed earlier in this chapter, the strengths approach assumes that clients are experts on their own lives, and they have within them the experience, wisdom, and resources that need to be the focal point for decision making and change.

- Avoidance of the "righting reflex-the desire to fix what seems wrong with people" (p. 6). This desire to fix might involve confrontation (which tends to promote resistance), and advice giving on the best course of action. It often involves trying to persuade clients to change. The righting reflex tends to put clients on the defensive where they take positions that have historically been defined as resistant. In MI, counsellors are encouraged to consider how their behaviours and responses might be evoking resistance. (See Chapter 8 for a further discussion of this important perspective.)

- A belief that the resolution of ambivalence is a critical step in supporting change.

Ambivalence   Miller & Rollnick note that most people who need to change are ambivalent: they have reasons to change as well as reasons to maintain the status quo, however, dsyfuntional that might be (2013). Anxiety and indecision can leave people stuck. Ambivalence is a normal part of the change process. For clients who are not interested in changing, the emergence of ambivalence would signal movement toward change.

When people are ambivalent, they are drawn in opposite directions at the same time. People may be ambivalent for a number of reasons, including the following:

1. The alternatives are equally appealing (Approach/Approach).
2. Neither course of action is appealing (between a "rock and a hard place").
3. Both alternatives have features that are both appealing and unappealing.
4. Conflicted feelings—knowing what is right, but finding one's emotions taking one in the opposite direction (Heart/intellect).
5. Desire to move in one direction, but fear of loss if that direction is chosen.
6. Simply not knowing what is right.

"Change Talk" and "Sustain Talk"   One way counsellors can address ambivalence is by listening for "**change talk**"—client statements favouring change and "**sustain talk**"—client statements favouring the status quo (Miller and Rollnick, 2013, p. 7). Here are some examples of client statements that signal change talk:

- I wish my life was different.
- I want to quit drinking.
- I could ask my family for help.
- I might be able to work part-time.

change talk Client statements favouring change.

sustain talk: Client statements favouring the status quo.

- I probably should go back to school.
- I need to find a way out of this mess.
- I will look into it.
- My intention is to fight this problem.
- I tried to stop using heroin.

When counsellors hear change talk, carefully targeted responses can increase the level of change talk and motivation for change.

Client: "I know that smoking is bad and I need to quit *(change talk)*, but I'm afraid that if I quit I'll gain weight *(sustain talk)*."

Counsellor (MI choices):

- If you made a decision to quit, how would you do it?
- What are your reasons for wanting to quit?
- How important is it for you to give up smoking?

A decisional balance sheet lists the benefits and costs of different choices. By addressing barriers to change, counsellors may help client to "tip the balance" in favour of change. In the above example, exploration of the ways one can control weight gain may help this client overcome resistance to change.

Empathy

Empathy and other active listening skills are now universally recognized as important to any counselling relationship, regardless of the theoretical approach of the counsellor. MI is no exception and empathy is a central feature of this approach. "Within the Spirit of MI," it creates an interview climate where clients are free to explore their values, perceptions, goals, and the implications of their current situation without judgment. Conversely, "confrontational counselling has been associated with a high dropout rate and relatively poor outcomes" (Miller & Rollnick, 2002, p. 7). Active listening, especially with the use of empathy, increases intrinsic motivation for change.

Developing Discrepancy

The overall goal of motivational interviewing is to help people get unstuck. The method is to initiate "change talk" by taking advantage of naturally occurring opportunities in the interview to embellish client statements that suggest differences between the way their life is and the way they would like their lives to be. Simply focusing on a client's goals and aspirations can often help people appreciate how their current lifestyle is inhibiting their ideals. Motivational interviewing uses a number of strategies to evoke change talk, such as the following:

- Asking evocative questions about disadvantages of the status quo, advantages of change, optimism about change, and intention to change.
- Using scaling questions—for example, "On a scale of 1 to 10, where are you in terms of satisfaction with your life?"

- Exploring the positive and negative consequences of the status quo.
- Using elaboration skills (e.g., asking for clarification, examples, description, and further information) to elicit further change talk.
- Querying extremes, such as "Suppose you don't make any changes. What do you think might be the consequences of this in the worst-case scenario?"
- Looking back to help clients remember how things were before compared with the current situation.
- Looking forward by asking clients to describe their hopes and goals for the future.
- Exploring goals and values to target discrepancies between important goals and current behaviour (Miller & Rollnick, 2002).
- Helping clients understand their ambivalence to change using the metaphor of a seesaw—when the costs of continuing present behaviour and the benefits of change outweigh the costs of change and benefits of continuing present behaviour, change will occur.

"Rolling with Resistance"

When counsellors confront clients with arguments for change, they can easily find themselves in power struggles where they are pressing for change and clients are resisting. In MI, client resistance is seen as a message that the counsellor needs to do something different. Power struggles are likely when counsellors do the following:

- Offer unsolicited advice from the expert role.
- Tell clients how they should feel.
- Ask excessive questions.
- Order, direct, warn, or threaten.
- Preach, moralize, or shame.
- Argue for change.
- Blame, judge, or criticize.

SUCCESS TIP

"As long as your clients are going to resist you, you might as well encourage it" (Milton Erickson, source unknown).

radical acceptance: A strategy that involves encouraging expression of statements that you tend to disagree with or philosophically oppose.

Radical acceptance is a strategy that involves encouraging expression of statements that you tend to disagree with or philosophically oppose, for example:

Client: I don't see the point. The only reason I came today is the fact that if I didn't show up, I'd be cut off welfare.

Counsellor: I'm very glad you brought this up. Many people share views such as yours but won't speak up, so I appreciate your willingness to be honest.

amplified reflection: A technique that exaggerates what a client has said with the hope that the client will present the other side of ambivalence.

Amplified reflection is a technique that exaggerates what a client has said with the hope that the client will present the other side of ambivalence. However, as Miller and Rollnick (2002) stress, "[t]his must be done empathically, because any sarcastic tone or too extreme an overstatement may itself elicit a hostile or otherwise resistant reaction" (p. 101).

Client: I don't see what the problem is. What's the harm in having a few drinks after a hard day's work?

Counsellor: So, you're saying that drinking hasn't caused any problems or given you any reason for concern.

Client: Well, I wouldn't go that far.

Support Self-Efficacy

To begin and sustain change, clients must believe in their capacity for change. For their part, counsellors can have an enormous impact on outcome if they believe in their client's ability to change and when they take steps to enhance client confidence. One choice is to help clients identify past success. Another is encouraging clients to make an inventory of their strengths and resources. Working on small achievable goals often starts a change process that gathers momentum. Counsellors can also look for opportunities to affirm their clients' efforts, strengths, and successes.

STAGES OF CHANGE

Risk Taking

Change involves risk, and risk creates anxiety. Even when motivation to change is high, emotions such as fear make it difficult to replace established behaviour with new ways of behaving. As a result, there is often tremendous (self-imposed) pressure on clients to maintain the status quo, however, ineffective it might be. Sometimes change involves a "selling" job, but the results are better when clients, not counsellors, do the selling. Clients need to convince themselves that the benefits of change outweigh the risks, and they need to develop positive attitudes and beliefs about their capacity for change. Counsellors with a strengths perspective believe in the capacity of their clients to change, and this belief in them can be a powerful motivating factor.

Johnson, McClelland, and Austin (2000) identify three factors important for motivation: "the push of discomfort, the pull of hope that something can be done to relieve the problem or accomplish a task, and internal pressures and drives toward reaching a goal" (p. 133). Thus, not only must clients want to change, but they must also believe in their capacity for change.

The concept of **secondary gain** is a useful way of understanding why some people resist change despite the obvious pain or losses involved in maintaining their current situation. Secondary gain refers to the benefits that people derive from their problems, such as increased attention from others, having an available rationale for not changing or participating, financial advantage, or escape from work or other tasks.

Secondary gain: A useful way of understanding why some people resist change despite the obvious pain or losses involved in maintaining their current situation.

▶▶▶ CONVERSATION 7.1 | Working with "Lazy" Clients

STUDENT: The clients I have the most trouble with are the lazy ones—the ones who won't even get out of bed in the morning to go look for a job or the clients who never follow through on commitments.

TEACHER: Sure, these clients can be exceptionally difficult and frustrating to work with. Sometimes it's hard to do, but we should discipline ourselves to be nonjudgmental regarding motivation. Although it might be tempting to label some clients as lazy, we should remember that they may have given up for good reason. They may not have the resources or support they need for change or they may have given up in order to protect themselves from the further damage to their self-esteem that would come from repeated failure. In this way, their behaviour may be seen as adaptive. It's normal for counsellors to lose patience with them and give up, but it's important to remember that precisely what they did to themselves—give up. That's one of the reasons they need counselling.

The stages of change model, also known as the **transtheoretical model of change** (Prochaska & Norcross, 2001), has received a great deal of attention in the literature since its inception in the 1980s. In this model, five stages of change are recognized: precontemplation, contemplation, preparation, action, and maintenance. As well, change is viewed as progressive development in this model, with success at any phase dependent on the success of previous phases. Figure 7.2 illustrates the five stages of change. Although this figure implies an orderly progression from one phase to another, in reality, clients may progress through stages and then drop back to an earlier stage (relapse) before starting again.

An essential assumption is that counselling interventions need to be selected to meet the needs and motivation of the particular stage clients are in. Thus, for example, it makes no sense to talk to a client who is not ready to change (precontemplative) about change strategies, but this talk would be wholly appropriate for a client who is preparing for change.

A client may be at different stages of change for different problems. For example, a client may be precontemplative (not interested in changing) regarding his drinking, but ready to take action with respect to his failing marriage. Accordingly, discussing strategies for cutting down his drinking is likely to meet with failure; however, exploring strategies to improve his marriage is likely to elicit a positive response.

Precontemplative Stage: "I Don't Have a Problem."   Clients at this stage have no intention of changing. These clients do not perceive themselves as having a problem, despite the fact that their behaviour is problematic for themselves or others in their lives. These clients are not thinking about change, and they may rationalize their problems, minimize the consequences of their actions, or blame others.

For these clients, empathic and sensitive listening that encourages them to examine their situation and its consequences can be very helpful. Counsellors can provide information, offer feedback, or encourage reflection with questions such as "Is what you're doing now working to meet your needs?" Obviously, for clients to change, they

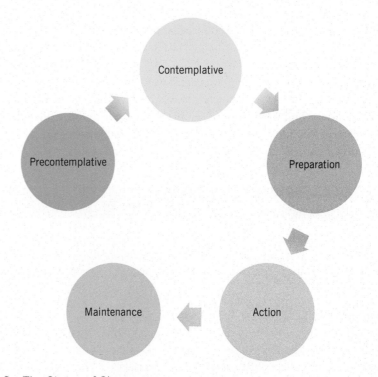

Figure 7.2 The Stages of Change

must move beyond the precontemplative stage. Unfortunately, many people, including some counsellors, believe that confrontation is the remedy for denial. Denial is a defence mechanism that enables people to cope, perhaps by protecting themselves from the risks of change. As a result, confrontation threatens this protection and it often triggers further and deeper resistance. DiClemente and Velasquez (2002) observe that "Sometimes the reluctant client will progress rapidly once he or she verbalizes the reluctance, feels listened to, and begins to feel the tension between the reluctance to change and the possibility of a different future" (p. 205). DiClemente and Valasquez (2002) offer this perspective:

> Clinicians often believe that more education, more intense treatment, or more confrontation will necessarily produce more change. Nowhere is this less true than with precontemplators. More intensity will often produce fewer results with this group. (p. 208)

Contemplative Stage: "Maybe I Should Do Something About It." At the contemplative stage, clients know they have a problem and are thinking about change, but they have not developed a plan or made a commitment to take action. Contemplative clients may be ambivalent and may vacillate between wanting to alter their lives and resisting any shifts in their behaviour or lifestyle. At this stage, clients may be open to new information as they self-assess their problems and the advantages and disadvantages of change.

> Example: Agnes has been in an abusive relationship for years. She wishes that she could leave and start over. In fact, she has left her husband twice in the past, but each time she has returned within a few weeks.

Contemplative stage clients like Agnes are "burnt out" from previous unsuccessful attempts at change. They are often in a state of crisis with considerable associated stress. Although they desire change, they doubt it will happen, and they believe that if change is to occur, it will be beyond their control. They also lack self-esteem and believe that they do not have the skill, capacity, or energy to change.

> Example: Peter (55) has been unemployed for almost two years, but he has not looked for a job in months. He says, "There's no work out there. Besides, who is going to hire a man of my age?"

Seligman's (1975) concept of learned helplessness is a useful perspective for understanding these clients. People with learned helplessness come to believe that their actions do not matter; as a result, they are unlikely to extend any effort to change since they believe that they have no control over their lives and that what happens to them is a result of chance. They believe in a "luck ethic" rather than a "work ethic." Their beliefs are reflected in statements such as the following:

- "You have to be in the right place at the right time to succeed."
- "If I'm successful, it's because the task was easy."
- "It doesn't matter if I work hard."
- "There's nothing I can do about it."

The key to working with people with learned helplessness—indeed, with most clients at the contemplation stage—is to assist them "in thinking through the risks of the behaviour and potential benefits of change and to instill hope that change is possible" (DiClemente & Velasquez, 2002, p. 209). Many people with low self-esteem and learned helplessness are in fact quite capable; it is the way they think and feel about themselves that is problematic. Consequently, it is important that counsellors look for ways to counter the client's self-deprecating remarks (e.g., encourage clients to see their past failures as deficits in the plan, not deficits in them). As well, counsellors can encourage clients to see elements of success in previous efforts (e.g., partial goal achievement, lessening of problem severity, and short-term achievement). Cognitive behavioural techniques, discussed later in this chapter, have also proven to be effective.

Confrontation should be used cautiously. As a rule, confrontation is most effective when it is invited in the context of a collaborative relationship—in other words, when it is invited. Then, it may be useful as a way to help clients understand incongruities between what they believe and the way they act, and recognize self-defeating ways of thinking and behaving, behaviour that is harmful to self or others, blind spots, blaming behaviours, and communication problems. As well, confrontation can also target unrecognized or discounted strengths.

Preparation Stage: "I'm Going to Do It Next Week."   When clients reach this third phase, they have made a decision to change and motivating them is no longer the principal task; however, counsellors need to sustain the energy for change through support, encouragement, and empathic caring. The principal task for the counsellor is to assist the client to develop concrete goals and action plan strategies. Without concrete, systematic plans, change efforts can be quickly frustrated and abandoned like soon-forgotten New Year's resolutions. The essence of good planning consists of setting concrete goals, identifying and evaluating alternative ways of reaching goals, selecting an action plan, and anticipating potential obstacles. For clients with learned helplessness, setting small, achievable goals is crucial for establishing and maintaining a climate of success and hope.

> Example: Iris, a young single parent, is excited about the possibility of returning to school. She sees a school counsellor for assistance with enrollment in the high school's special program for teen moms, but she has not yet considered issues like daycare.

Using a strengths approach, counsellors can assist preparation stage clients to draw from their past experiences (proven success strategies and lessons learned). As well, clients can learn about strategies that have worked for others. Finally, it is very important to coach these clients to anticipate potential obstacles and to plan strategies for addressing them, including the emotional stress of the change process.

Action Stage: "I'm Changing."   At this stage, clients are actively involved in the change process. They are working on the goals and implementing the plans developed in the preparation stage. DiClemente and Velasquez (2002) offer this perspective on counsellor strategies for this stage:

> Clients in action may still have some conflicting feelings about the change. They may miss their old lifestyle in some ways and be struggling to fit into this new behaviour. Careful listening and affirming clients that they are doing the right thing are important in this stage. It is also important to check with the client to see if he or she has discovered parts of the change plan that need revision. (p. 212)

When clients encounter anticipated obstacles, counsellors can remind them of previously developed contingency plans. If there are unanticipated obstacles, counsellors can assist with interventions to support clients as they deal with these potential setbacks.

Maintenance Stage: "I've Done It. I Need to Keep Doing It."   In the final stage, the challenge for the client is to maintain the changes that have been made and to deal with relapses, which may occur for a number of reasons (e.g., unexpected temptation, personal stress, triggers, letting down one's guard, and sabotage by others who are threatened by the change).

Counsellors can help clients accept that relapses, while undesired, are part of the change process, and they can help them to reframe the relapse as an opportunity for better success next time. For example, they can help them develop new or revised strategies for dealing with stress points or triggers.

Table 7.3 outlines the stages of change.

TABLE 7.3 The Stages of Change

Stage/Goal	Strategy Choices
Precontemplative Stage Clients with no desire or intention of changing • *Counselling goal: Increase awareness of need for change.*	• Employ empathy and other active listening skills. • Provide information and feedback (if invited). • Encourage clients to seek information and feedback from others. • Help clients become aware of attractive alternatives. • Use thought-provoking questions. • Avoid directive and confrontational techniques. • Use films, brochures, books, and self-assessment questionnaires as tools to increase client insight. • With involuntary clients, explore feelings and concerns openly, self-disclose your own feelings about being forced, give clients choices, involve them in decision making, and encourage client-initiated goals.
Contemplative Stage Clients who are thinking about change • *Counselling goal: Resolve ambivalence to engage in the change process.*	• Support "change talk." • Discuss risks and benefits of change, but avoid arguing in favour of change. • Help clients understand and manage self-deprecating remarks (e.g., reframe past failures as learning experiences). • Identify elements of success in previous change efforts. • Explore previous relapses emphasizing failure of plans, not failure of clients. • Use support groups. • Convey hope and belief in the client's capacity for success.
Preparation Stage Clients who are committed to change • *Counselling goal: Develop concrete strategies for action.*	• Set goals. • Plan systematic action. • Assemble/mobilize resources to support change. • Make contingency plans (anticipate obstacles).
Action Stage Active change effort • *Counselling goals: Implement change and sustain momentum.*	• Reward (praise, support, and acknowledge) change efforts. • Assist client to anticipate and manage potential obstacles.
Maintenance Stage Sustain change • *Counselling goal: Sustain change.*	• Assist client to deal with periodic obstacles or relapses.

COGNITIVE BEHAVIOURAL COUNSELLING

"I know that you believe you understand what you think I said, but I'm not sure you realize that what you heard is not what I meant."

—Robert McCloskey

Thoughts are the birthplace of emotions, self-esteem, and behaviour. Positive (helpful) thinking creates an "I can do it" attitude, which leads to a greater willingness to embrace new challenges and to take appropriate risks. Negative or unhelpful thinking patterns, on the other hand, create distress and interfere with one's overall sense of well-being. Cognitive behavioural techniques focus on increasing helpful thinking and on changing problematic behavioural patterns.

Cognitive behavioural counselling (therapy), or CBT, has been empirically tested in hundreds of studies. The results have demonstrated its usefulness for a wide range of social, emotional, and mental health problems such as mood disorders (depression and bipolar disorder), anxiety disorders (obsessive-compulsive disorder and post-traumatic stress disorder), substance use problems, eating disorders, gambling problems, anger, personality disorders, stress, unresolved grief, as well as medical problems such as hypertension and low back pain (Butler, Chapman, Fauman, & Beck, 2006; Chambless & Ollendick, 2001; and Beck & Beck, 2011).

cognitive behavioural counselling (therapy): A counselling approach that assists clients to identify and modify unhelpful thinking and problematic behaviour.

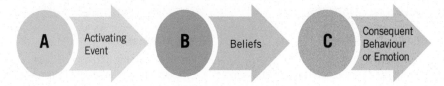

Figure 7.3 ABC Model

American psychiatrist Aaron T. Beck (1921–) is considered the founder of CBT. Wills (2008) identifies the central assumptions behind Beck's approach: "At the heart of the CBT paradigm there is a very simple yet effective working model: the way people think about their situations influences the way they feel and behave" (p. 5). CBT does not focus on finding the root causes of problems; rather, it emphasizes problem solving to help clients find new ways of thinking and responding.

Counsellors can quickly teach clients the basic ideas behind CBT and, in the process, help them learn about how unhelpful thinking impacts behaviour and emotions, and how behaviour and thinking that is learned can be unlearned.

The key to changing problematic behaviour or emotions is to explore and modify distorted thinking, and then to learn and practise new responses. CBT focuses on understanding current thinking (the present) and problem solving to develop new behaviours.

> Marie and Aiesha are passengers on the same airline flight. Marie is consumed by her fear that the plane will crash, thinking, "This is a dangerous situation. What if the engines fail? And air turbulence will surely tear the plane apart." Aiesha boards the plane and quickly immerses herself in a book with no intrusive thoughts of dying.

Ellis (2004) developed the famous ABC model (Figure 7.3) as a tool for understanding why Marie and Aiesha experience the flight so differently. In the model:

- A represents an activating event (in this case, the airplane flight).
- B refers to the beliefs that are triggered by the activating event, A.
- C is the consequent emotion or behavioural reaction.

Clearly, Marie's beliefs about flying are markedly different from Aiesha's. Cognitive behavioural counselling would concentrate on how Marie can modify her thinking about flying, which is based on erroneous and distorted beliefs about its dangers. Moreover, the skills Marie learns will help her adapt to future problems she may encounter in other areas of her life.

SUCCESS TIP

If one's thinking changes, behaviour and emotions also change. If one's behaviour changes, thinking and emotions also change. If one's emotions change, thinking and behaviour also change. See Figure 7.4.

Cognitive behavioural counselling uses a combination of methods to help clients learn more effective coping strategies, including

- helping clients recognize thinking patterns, in particular those that are unhelpful;
- helping clients modify thinking patterns; and
- assisting clients to develop action plans and strategies (modifying behaviour).

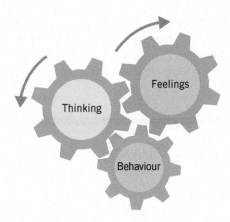

Figure 7.4   Interdependence of Feelings, Behaviour, and Thinking

Helping Clients Recognize Thinking Patterns

> *"Whether you think you can or think you can't—you're right."*
>
> —Henry Ford (public domain)

Frequently, behaviour persists because clients are locked into unhelpful ways of thinking about their problems or solutions. Thinking patterns that drive feelings and behaviours are frequently outside a client's awareness, and they emerge from schema or core beliefs. Schema are the "basic beliefs individuals use to organize their view of the self, the world, and the future" (Sperry, 2006, p. 22). Significantly, a person's thinking may be driven by schema, assumptions and errors in thinking that are not fact based. Individuals who are potentially very capable may act as if they were incapable because of faulty beliefs.

Automatic thoughts occur spontaneously and are often outside of one's awareness. Usually, they repeat well-established themes such as, "I won't succeed," and this repetition strengthens power of the belief. Such unhelpful or maladaptive thoughts can lead to distress, inaction, low self-esteem, depression, and reluctance to engage in healthy risk-taking, such as initiating social relationships. Cognitive behavioural counselling helps clients recognize automatic thoughts, identify "errors in thinking," and explore how thoughts hinder them from reaching goals. Table 7.4 outlines some common helpful and unhelpful core beliefs clients might have. Once clients become aware that an automatic thought is about to happen, they can practise replacing that thought with an alternative. This interrupts the repetitive cycle of problematic behaviour. On a broader level, clients learn to understand and modify schemas that drive dysfunctional behaviour and painful emotions.

automatic thoughts: Thoughts that occur spontaneously and are often outside of one's awareness

TABLE 7.4 Helpful and Unhelpful Core Beliefs	
Unhelpful	**Helpful**
• I am unlovable.	• I am a person worthy of love and respect.
• To seek help is a sign of weakness.	• I can ask for and offer assistance.
• Without a relationship partner, I am nothing.	• I am responsible for my own happiness.
• I will fail. I am helpless.	• I will do my best, savour my success, and learn from my mistakes.
• I have to be loved by everyone.	• I accept that not everyone will love me.
• I must be perfect in everything that I do. I must be seen by others as the best.	• I accept my limitations; they do not diminish me.
• I am special; I can take advantage of people.	• My rights as well as the rights of others need to be respected.

> Example: A new social setting triggers Troy's automatic thoughts: "I don't belong. I won't fit in." These thoughts originate from his core belief, "I am unlovable." His automatic thoughts and his core beliefs create anxiety and fear. His strategy is to use drugs to curb his anxiety, which in turn lead to the new belief that he won't be able to cope unless he uses drugs.

Unhelpful Thinking Patterns

It is the mark of an educated mind to be able to entertain a thought without accepting it.

—Aristotle (public domain)

Most of the time, our thoughts are outside of our awareness. Cognitive behavioural counselling is designed to help clients develop conscious awareness of their thinking patterns, then critically examine their validity and usefulness. Subsequently, clients learn strategies for interrupting unhelpful thinking, while increasing helpful thinking and behaviour.

Thinking errors can easily lead to faulty interpretations and maladaptive behaviour. Other thinking patterns, while they may be accurate, are simply not helpful. In a classic early work, Beck (1976) proposed the notion of "Cognitive Triad" (aka Beck's Triad) consisting of views about self, the world, and the future to explain depression:

Self: "I am worthless." (or unworthy, useless, and deficient)

World: "The world is unsafe." (failure is imminent)

Future: "The future is grim." (problems will persist indefinitely)

The assumption is that the negative triad sustains the client's depression; therefore, CBT focuses on helping clients to change their maladaptive and unhelpful interpretations of self, the world, and the future.

unhelpful thinking patterns: Faulty reasoning caused by distortion, incomplete analysis, egocentricity, rigidity, and self-defeating thought.

It is important to understand the major **unhelpful thinking patterns**, such as emotional decision making, distortion, selective attention, worry, magnification/minimization, mind reading, perfectionism, and self-defeating thought.

Emotional Decision Making   In a Mr. Spock (*Star Trek*) world, all decisions would be based on totally objective, rational analysis of the facts, and emotions would play no part. In everyday life, it's not so simple. Emotions can and often should play a part in most decisions. Emotional decision making is problematic when it results in negative outcomes. Or, emotions might strongly support one conclusion despite evidence to the contrary. For example, people might feel inadequate and unlovable while ignoring the fact that they have achieved success, and they have many friends.

Distortion   Distortion results from misinterpretations, faulty assumptions, or cultural biases. An extreme form of this is delusional thinking, which involves holding beliefs that have no basis in reality. Here are some common examples:

- Misreading another person's silence as lack of interest (mind reading).
- Assuming that others should know what we want, need, or feel without being told.

⟩⟩ BRAIN BYTE   The Emotional Brain

Recent brain research (Naqvi, Shiv, & Bechara, 2006) is mapping how different parts of the brain (some rational and some emotional) are activated during decision making. In some circumstances, the "emotional brain" hijacks rationality and people make (and sometimes repeat) decisions and actions that are not in their best interest. Moreover, this can continue despite full awareness of the continuing error.

- Interpreting lack of eye contact as a sign of disrespect or lying when, in fact, the other person is from a culture where direct eye contact is discouraged.
- Arriving at false conclusions such as believing (after hurting a friend's feelings) that "I am a horrible person', and she'll never speak to me again."

Selective Attention   Selective attention errors arise from a failure to look at all aspects of a problem or situation. For example, people with low self-esteem may overlook evidence of their successes and strengths by looking only at their failures or limitations. Or, people may be egocentric and not consider other people's feelings or ideas. As a result, they may be seen by others as insensitive. Selective attention may involve any of the following:

- Listening only to information and facts that support your point of view.
- Having a selective memory that overlooks or distorts important information.
- Losing focus on what a person is saying (because of factors such as boredom, preoccupation with personal issues, or setting distractions).
- Focusing only on the present without considering the long-term implications.
- Displaying egocentric thinking that does not consider other points of view or the impact of one's behaviour on others.

Worry or Rumination   Excessive worry interferes with problem solving, and it may lead to feelings of anxiety, depression, helplessness, and pessimism. Unhelpful worrying might involve dwelling on past events or failures, or it may focus on events that clients fear might happen in the future.

Magnification/Minimization   These types of thinking patterns distort facts by extreme and exaggerated thinking. Here are some examples:

- Splitting (all or nothing)—the tendency to interpret people, things, and experiences as either totally good or totally bad, with no shades of grey.
- Overgeneralization—drawing conclusions from a single fact or event. For example, after being turned down for a job, a man concludes that he is worthless and no one will ever hire him.
- Discounting—rejecting compliments by refusing to believe that the other person is telling the truth.
- "Catastrophizing"—magnifying small mistakes into disasters or total failures.

Mind Reading   This common error arises when people assume they know how others are thinking or feeling. Mind reading frequently arises from personal insecurities. For example, low self-esteem may result in interpreting the actions of others as rejection.

Perfectionism

Healthy individuals set realistic, challenging, and achievable goals. They are motivated to do their best, and they maintain high standards for themselves. Conversely, people who are perfectionists set unrealistic standards of achievement with an expectation of constant success. Perfectionist individuals are under constant stress caused by the anxiety to perform, or the realization that they have failed to reach or sustain their unrealistic expectations of self. Irrational beliefs that arise from perfectionism include the following:

- I can't make a mistake.
- I am a failure if I am less than perfect.
- I have no value unless I achieve the very best.

- If I can't be perfect, then I might as well give up.
- I have to be the best. To win is the only option.
- I'm probably going to fail anyway, so why try?

The personal cost of perfectionism can include chronic pessimism, low self-esteem, lack of confidence, depression, anxiety, and obsessive concern with order and routine. Perfectionists frequently use the words must, only, always, never, and should (the MOANS acronym introduced in Chapter 5).

self-defeating thoughts: Inner dialogue of critical messages.

Self-defeating thoughts are irrational (unhelpful) ideas about one's own weaknesses. Albert Ellis (1962, 1984,1993a,1993b, and 2004) has written a great deal about what he defined as irrational thinking and its impact on emotions and behaviour. Ellis argues that people's belief systems influence how they respond to and understand problems and events. When their beliefs are irrational and characterized by an unrealistic *should*, they are likely to experience emotional anxiety or disturbance. This thinking is often accompanied by self-deprecating internal dialogue: "I'm no good," "Everyone must think I'm an idiot," and "No one likes me." Ellis believed that irrational beliefs come from self-imposed rigid demands or *shoulds*, such as "I have to be perfect" and "Everyone has to love me."

MOANS: An acronym for the words *must, ought, always, never,* and *should*, which signal irrational or self-defeating thought.

Golden and Lesh (1997) use the acronym **MOANS** for five words that often signal negative self-talk: *must, ought, always, never,* and *should*.

- I *must* succeed or I am worthless.
- I *ought* to be able to do it.
- I *always* screw up.
- I will *never* be able to get a job.
- I *should* feel differently.
- Everything *must* be perfect.

SUCCESS TIP

Clients will profit from considering what triggers self-defeating thoughts. For those with addiction problems, triggers are a prelude to substance abuse. By successfully countering cognitive triggers such as "the only way I can relax is to use drugs," substance abuse and relapse can be prevented.

Helping Clients Increase Helpful Thinking

When people learn to pay attention to their thoughts, they can begin to identify those thoughts and patterns that are unhelpful and then take action to change their thinking. Thinking patterns are often well established and firmly anchored by core beliefs, so considerable practice may be necessary to effect change.

An important first step is to help clients become aware of their automatic thoughts. Counsellors can ask questions such as:

- What were (are) you thinking?
- How strong was this thought?
- How much (1–10) do you believe it to be true?
- How does this thought/image link to feelings and behaviour?
- Helpful? Not Helpful?

If clients have trouble identifying thoughts, counsellors can ask them to visualize and "replay" the problem situation. Or clients can do homework to monitor their thoughts and reactions. (There are numerous online sites that offer thought monitoring forms—example: https://www.psychologytools.com and search for the heading "CBT tools.")

Thought-Stopping/Diversion Negative self-talk can easily become an automatic response. **Thought-stopping** is a technique for interrupting repetitive unhelpful thinking that impedes action and confidence with positive, empowering substitutions. After identifying negative self-talk, clients need to develop positive statements to replace intrusive negative thoughts. Here are some examples:

> **Unhelpful Thought:** "I'm so stressed about going for the job interview, I'm going to panic and make a complete fool of myself."
>
> **Thought Substitution:** "I'm qualified for the job. I can control my anxiety through deep breathing."
>
> **Unhelpful Thought:** "If I don't do everything well, then I am a failure."
>
> **Thought Substitution:** "I don't have to be perfect. I'm human and sometimes I'll miss the mark."

(see Beck & Beck, 2011, p. 213 for more examples)

Clients might find it useful to think the word STOP to interrupt unhelpful thinking, then immediately use thought substitution to introduce helpful thinking. Alternatively, other cues can be used as a thought-stopper. One client carried a picture of her son as a baby. This helped her interrupt negative thinking about him that was triggered by his current drug abuse. Another imagined an axe as a cue to substitute a new helpful thought. Figure 7.5 illustrates the sequence.

Thought-stopping works, but it requires practice. Negative self-talk patterns may represent years of learning that must be "unlearned," and the best way to do this is to learn new ways of thinking. Intrusive thoughts can also be countered by diverting attention with activity, music, physical activity, or meditation.

Mindfulness In recent years, many cognitive behavioural counsellors have integrated mindfulness techniques in their work. **Mindfulness** is simply defined as "awareness of present experience with acceptance" (Siegel, 2010, p. 27). With mindfulness,

thought-stopping: A technique for breaking the pattern of repetitive self-defeating thought patterns. Techniques include thought replacement, yelling "stop" in your mind until the undesired thought disappears, snapping an elastic band on the wrist to shift thinking, and activity diversion.

mindfulness: Focusing on moment-to-moment experiences without judgment

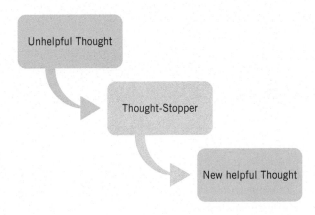

Figure 7.5 Thought-Stopping Sequence

"the intention is for participants not only to bring their awareness to present-moment experience but also to become aware of the tendency of the mind to wander away from the moment and to learn to gently guide it back without judgment" (Bowen, Chawla, & Marlatt, 2011, p. 34). It helps people to disengage from worry about past, current, and future problems that may not occur.

Mindfulness is not difficult, but practice is essential. Mindfulness has shown to be an effective adjunct to cognitive behavioural therapy in the treatment of a range of disorders, including depression, obsessive-compulsive disorder, post-traumatic stress disorder, and others (Firouzabadi & Shareh, 2009; Godfrin & van Heeringen, 2010; and Vujanovic, Niles, Pietrefesa, Schmertz, & Potter, 2011).

SUCCESS TIP

"Mind the Gap"—The time gap between thinking and action provides an opportunity to make new choices. In the absence of effort and attention, the same unhelpful patterns of thinking and behaviour will be repeated and strengthened. Mindfulness slows down experiences and giving people an opportunity to identify thinking patterns. Subsequently, they can practise helpful ways of thinking and responding. Practice then creates and strengthens new neural pathways.

Evidence Finding   Beliefs may arise from faulty assumptions and other errors in thinking, or they may be based on emotions, not fact. Unchallenged beliefs can limit new learning, and they may keep clients locked in old, ineffective ways of acting or thinking. Evidence finding is a CBT technique that teaches clients to be their own "devil's advocate" through the use of disputing questions to test the validity of their beliefs. As well, counsellors can also encourage clients to seek out information and data by suggesting they talk to others to expand their perspective. Counsellors can also directly challenge beliefs with facts, examples, or they can use brainstorming techniques to generate alternate ideas. Guided discovery (Neenan & Dryden, 2006) involves asking questions to help clients consider perspectives that are currently outside their awareness.

Here are some counsellor responses that will stimulate evidence finding:

- How much of what you believe is based on how you feel and how much is based on fact?
- How do you know this to be true? Do you have facts or are you assuming?
- Let's try to explore evidence that this may not be true. Play devil's advocate.
- What are some other ways of thinking about your situation?
- If a friend thought this way about his situation, what would you say to him?

SUCCESS TIP

Don't believe everything you think (Thomas Kida, 2006).

Reframing

reframing: A technique for helping clients look at things differently by suggesting alternative interpretations, perspectives, or new meanings. Reframes should present logical and positive alternative ways of thinking.

Reframing is a counselling skill that helps clients shift or modify their thinking by suggesting alternative interpretations or new meanings. It empowers clients by focusing on solutions and redefining negatives as opportunities or challenges. Client stubbornness might be reframed as independence or greediness as ambition.

Neuroplasticity refers to the brain's ability to grow and rearrange neural pathways based on new experiences or learning. Conversely, neural pathways that are not used will be pruned. Neural growth can be positive or negative, but in the absence of awareness, effort, or new experience the brain tends to act on autopilot, repeating and reinforcing established patterns. Mindfulness creates awareness of thoughts and feelings as well as the ability to change mental focus with the goal of influencing brain growth in a positive way.

Although mindfulness can stimulate relaxation, that is not its goal. Mindfulness involves a wide range of strategies that might involve all five senses. It helps people develop self-awareness and acceptance of their moment-to-moment thoughts and feelings by paying attention to one experience at a time. Mindfulness can focus on sounds, thoughts, smells, taste, visual images, and bodily sensation using techniques such as the following:

- Mindfully attending to a sensory experience, such as eating a banana.
- Focusing on breathing; paying attention to the flow of thoughts.
- Simply paying attention to any daily activity such as washing the dishes.
- Performing the "body scan," which helps people become aware of physical sensations that often precede or accompany habitual responses. The process involves systematically focusing attention on each part of the body, including breathing. (See Bowen, Chawla, & Marlatt, 2011, p. 42, or Siegel, 2010, p. 72 for detailed instructions).

Example: Carl, age 11, is playing baseball by himself. He throws the ball into the air and exclaims, "I'm the greatest batter in the world." He swings and misses. Once again, he tosses the ball into the air and says, "I'm the greatest batter in the world." He swings and misses. A third time he throws the ball into the air proclaiming emphatically, "I'm the greatest pitcher in the world."

(See Table 7.5 for additional examples.)

Before presenting reframed ideas, counsellors should use active listening skills to fully understand the client's current perspective. As well, empathy is crucial—otherwise, clients may conclude that their feelings are being discounted or trivialized.

SUCCESS TIP

Five ways to reframe:
- Turn problem statements into goals.
- Help clients accept their emotions and reactions as "normal."
- Look at perceived weaknesses as strengths.
- See "triggers" as an opportunity to act differently.
- Explore the positive outcomes of adversity.

Reframing should not be confused with platitudes, such as "It's always darkest just before dawn," which are typically not very supportive or helpful. An example of a well-meaning but misguided reframe that people give in times of grief over the loss of a child is "You're young—you can have more children." A response such as this ignores

Exploring the past may help clients develop some insight into their behaviour and emotions. However, it may reinforce neural pathways that have sustained unhelpful thinking and actions. Consequently, it is important to use techniques such as thought-stopping, behavioural rehearsal, and the "miracle question," because these actions will create new neural connections that will support goals and changes that clients target.

TABLE 7.5 Reframing

Client's Perspective or Statement	Reframing Lead
This counselling is a waste of time.	Sounds as if you've done some thinking about how our work could be more relevant to you.
I don't fit in. I come from a different culture and my ideas and values must seem strange.	Of course. Some people have not had experience with your culture, and they may be frightened. Perhaps you could look at this in a different way. Your experiences might also be fascinating for people who have not lived outside the country. They might welcome your fresh ideas.
I'm very shy. When I first join a group, I usually don't say anything.	You like to be patient until you have a sense of what's happening. People who are impulsive are working to develop this skill. You also seem to want to develop alternatives, such as being more expressive in the beginning.
For the first time in 20 years, I'm without a job.	Obviously, this is devastating. At the same time, I wonder if this might also be an opportunity for you to try something different.
Whenever I am late for curfew, my mother waits up for me and immediately starts screaming at me.	I'm curious about why she might do this. Perhaps she has trouble telling you how scared she is that something may have happened to you. It might seem strange, but her anger could be her way of saying how much she loves you.
My life is a mess. I've lived on the street for the last six months.	Sounds like you've had to survive under conditions that might have defeated most people. How did you do that?

the person's grief by offering well-meaning but simplistic and ineffective advice. Reframing should not trivialize complex problems with pat answers; rather, it should offer a reasonable and usable alternative frame of reference that challenges clients to break out of unhelpful ways of thinking about their problems.

Timing is important. Even though it may be obvious that a client's thinking is distorted, it may be wise to hold back on reframing until the client's problem is fully explored. Moreover, as previously suggested, it is important that the client's feelings be acknowledged through empathy. Exploration and empathy ensure that the counsellor understands the client's feelings and situation, and they provide a basis for the client to consider reframed ideas as reasonable or worthy of consideration. If counsellors push clients too quickly, clients may feel devalued and misunderstood, and in response they may resist new ideas. Empathy helps counsellors to establish and maintain credibility with their clients.

In addition, counsellors can use reframing to invite clients to take control over feelings and behaviour:

- Client might say, "I can't get organized." Here, a counsellor can challenge the client by proposing that the client reframe this statement with "I won't let myself get organized."

- Client might say, "She makes me feel hopeless." In response, the counsellor can propose that the client rephrase the statement by saying, "I have decided to feel hopeless." The latter response underscores the client's control over personal feelings. As part of this work, counsellors can empower their clients by explaining that clients have ownership over their feelings and that no one can make them feel a certain way.

Reframing can energize clients. When clients are locked into one way of thinking about their problems, their solutions are limited. But when they consider new perspectives, problems that seemed insurmountable can yield new solutions. Moreover, reframing can serve to redirect client anxiety away from self-blame and onto other rational explanations that are less self-punishing. In these ways, effective reframing empowers clients to action, problem resolution, and management of debilitating feelings.

Cognitive Behavioural Counselling

Canadian neuropsychologist Donald Hebb (public domain; 1949) made the now famous statement, "neurons that fire together wire together." The meaning is that repetitive actions or thoughts strengthen neural pathways and links. For example, if one experiences anxiety in a social situation, repeated experiences may cause the person to become stuck in a pattern of social anxiety fueled by unhelpful self-talk. With CBT clients learn to break this pattern and, in the process, new neural pathways are created and strengthened.

There is experimental evidence that CBT alters the brain. For example, a study by Kumari et al. (2011) found that there are measureable changes in the brain as an outcome of CBT. In particular, the positive symptoms of psychosis, especially delusions reduced in severity. As well, after treatment, clients had decreased fear and anger responses. A report by Mayor (2004) noted that while antidepressant medication attacks depression by altering the neurotransmitters, cognitive behavioural therapy also changes the brain, but in a different way by changing activity in the prefrontal cortex, hippocampal and dorsal cingulate areas of the brain. Another study by de Lange et al. (2008) using patients with chronic fatigue syndrome (CFS) demonstrated that brain shrinkage (cerebral atrophy) associated with CFS might be partially reversed by CBT.

>>> INTERVIEW 7.1 Cognitive Behavioural Techniques

The following interview excerpt illustrates some of the essential strategies of cognitive behavioural counselling. The client, a 40-year-old first-year university psychology student, has sought help to deal with the fact that she has been "overwhelmed and depressed" since returning to school.

Counsellor: Feelings, thinking, and behaviour are all connected. Change one and the other two also change. In particular, it's critical to explore how your thinking affects your feelings and your behaviour.

Client: I'm at the point where, if I don't do something fast, I'm going to lose the whole term. I might as well drop out.

Analysis: Cognitive behavioural counselling requires a collaborative relationship. An important component of this is educating the client on how the process works. This will also help the client to make her own interventions when she recognizes problematic thinking.

Counsellor: You're feeling desperate.

Analysis: With all counselling approaches, empathy is an important response. More than any other skill, it tells clients that they have been heard and that their feelings have been understood.

Counsellor: Can you remember a time in the last few days when these feelings were particularly strong? What was going through your mind at the time just before class?

Client: Yesterday, I was scheduled to make my first-class presentation. I was thinking that I was going to make a fool of myself in front of the whole class. Everyone else seems so confident when they talk, but I haven't been in school for 20 years.

Counsellor: And that made you feel . . .

Client: Stupid and terrified. I finally phoned in sick.

Analysis: Eliciting and exploring examples such as this provides a database for helping this client understand how her thoughts contribute to her feelings. Significantly, probes to discover thinking patterns may reveal "inner dialogue" (self-defeating thought patterns) or images.

Counsellor: So, here we have an example of how what you were thinking—"I'm going to make a fool of myself"—influenced how you were feeling and what you did. Does this make sense to you? Let's use the ABC model to illustrate it. *(The counsellor uses a flip chart: A [activating situation]—thinking of making the presentation; B [belief]—"I'm going to look like a fool"; and C [consequent emotion]—fear, feeling overwhelmed.)*

Analysis: Earlier the counsellor and the client discussed the essential elements of cognitive behavioural counselling. Now the client's example can be used to reinforce the principles. Using a flip chart or drawing is very helpful for many clients, particularly for those who are less comfortable in the verbal modality.

Counsellor: If you agree, I'd like to ask you to make notes during the next week when you find yourself feeling worse. When this happens, I want you to pay attention to what's going through your mind.

Analysis: Homework is essential to effective cognitive behavioural counselling. Here, the homework creates an opportunity for the client to become more familiar with how her feelings and behaviour are intimately connected to her thinking.

In the next session (excerpted later), the counsellor uses reframing and thought-stopping as tools to help the client change her thinking.

Counsellor: Your journal is great. You've identified lots of great examples. Let's try something different for a minute. What if it were possible to look at your fears differently? (Client nods approval.)	**Analysis:** The counsellor introduces the possibility of reframing.
Counsellor: I think it's natural when we have a problem to dwell on all its unpleasant aspects. I know that I tend to do that unless I discipline myself not to. For example, when you think of how nervous you are, you think of all the negatives, such as you might make a fool of yourself, or your mind might go blank while you're talking. **Client:** (Laughs.) Or that I might throw up in front of everyone.	**Analysis:** The counsellor's short self-disclosure communicates understanding and a nonjudgmental attitude.
Counsellor: Okay, those are real fears. But by considering only your fears, you become fixated on the negatives, and you may be overlooking some important positives. If you can look at it differently, you might discover a whole new way of dealing with your class presentation.	**Analysis:** One tenet of cognitive behavioural counselling is that people tend to pay too much attention to the negative aspects of their situations while ignoring positives or other explanations.
Counsellor: Want to try it? (The client nods.) Okay, try to identify some positive aspects of your fear.	**Analysis:** As a rule, it's more empowering for clients to generate their own suggestions before counsellors introduce their ideas and suggestions. In this way, clients become self-confronting and are more likely to come up with ideas that they will accept as credible.
Client: Well, I guess I'm not the only one who is scared of public speaking. **Counsellor:** So, you know that there will be other people in the class who understand and will be cheering for you to succeed. **Client:** I never thought of that before. Here's another idea: Because I'm so nervous, I'm going to make sure that I'm really prepared.	**Analysis:** In this example, the client is able to generate a reframe, which the counsellor embellishes. In other situations, counsellors might introduce reframes of their own.
Counsellor: Great! Do you think it might be possible to look at your fears differently? Consider that it's normal to be nervous. Or go a step further and look at it positively. Maybe there's a part of it that's exciting—kind of like going to a scary movie.	**Analysis:** The counsellor offers the client a reframed way of looking at nervousness.
Client: I did come back to school because I hated my boring job. One thing is for sure, I'm not bored.	**Analysis:** The client's response suggests that this notion is possible.
Counsellor: So, the more you scare yourself, the more you get your money's worth. (The counsellor and the client laugh.)	**Analysis:** Spontaneous humour helps the client see her problems in a lighter way (yet another reframe).
Counsellor: Here's an idea that works. If you agree, I'd like you to try it over the next week. Every time you notice yourself starting to get overwhelmed or feeling distressed, imagine a stop sign in your mind and immediately substitute a healthier thought.	**Analysis:** Another example of counselling homework. The counsellor introduces thought-stopping—a technique to help clients control self-defeating thinking (Dattilio & Freeman, 2010). The basic assumption is that if self-defeating thoughts are interrupted, they will eventually be replaced by more empowering, positive perspectives.

Reflections:

■ How might you introduce cognitive behavioural counselling to a 10-year-old child?

■ Suppose the client returns for the next session and reports that "thought-stopping did not work." Suggest counsellor choices for dealing with this outcome.

■ Identify this client's neural pathways.

At this point, the counsellor could also help the client develop different choice strategies for dealing with dysfunctional thinking, such as an activity diversion to shift attention, use of a prepared cue card with a positive thought recorded, imagining success, or substituting a different image.

CONVERSATION 7.2   When Buttons are Pushed

STUDENT: Can we use CBT to deal with our own reactions?

CBT Counsellor: Absolutely! Clients can "push our buttons," test our patience, and leave us doubting our ability to work effectively. Sometimes, negative feelings such as anger, frustration, or fear can cloud our objectivity and impair our ability. Feelings of attraction or protectiveness can be just as problematic. When we begin to take client behaviour personally, when we become disconnected from essential skills and attitudes such as being nonjudgmental and empathic, it's time to do some work on self. That's where CBT strategies can be very helpful.

STUDENT: How?

CBT Counsellor: The CBT approach involves paying attention to the connection among how we think, feel, and behave. Self-awareness regarding client behaviours, which trigger unhelpful thinking gives us an opportunity to critically examine their validity, then challenge unhelpful thoughts by using strategies such as thought-stopping. I always find it helpful to consider that my client's behaviour may be their usual way, so if, for example, they are rude to me, I can understand that this is part of their personality, and I am much less likely to take it personally.

Student: People in recovery from substance misuse learn to recognize triggers that could lead to relapse. Counsellors can do the same thing by identifying client situations or behaviours, which trigger problematic feelings.

HELPING CLIENTS MAKE BEHAVIOURAL CHANGES

Goal Setting

> *Obstacles are those frightful things you see when you take your eyes off your goals.*
>
> —Henry Ford, public domain

Goal setting is a counselling process that helps clients define in precise, measurable terms what they hope to achieve from the work of counselling. Goals can be classified as process or outcome goals (Shebib, 1997; Nystul, 2011). An **outcome goal** relates to what the client hopes to achieve from counselling. These goals have to do with changes in the client's life, such as getting a job, improving communication with a spouse, dealing with painful feelings, or managing self-defeating thoughts. A **process goal** concerns the procedures of counselling, including such variables as the frequency of meetings and the nature of the counselling relationship. Process goals are strategies for reaching outcome goals.

There is wide support in the counselling literature for the importance of setting goals (Nystul, 2011; Martin & Pear, 2011) Goal setting serves many important purposes, including giving direction, defining roles, motivating, and measuring progress.

goal setting: A counselling process that helps clients define in precise, measurable terms what they hope to achieve from the work of counselling.

outcome goal: A goal related to what the client hopes to achieve from counselling.

process goal: The methods and procedures that will be used in counselling to assist clients in reaching their goals.

Giving Direction   Goals help to give direction, purpose, and structure to the work of counselling, thus, helping counsellors and clients decide which topics and activities are relevant. When clients and counsellors are clear about their goals, they can begin to structure their thinking and action toward their attainment. Setting goals helps clients make reasoned choices about what they want to do with their lives. Goal setting helps clients prioritize these choices.

Defining Roles   Goals provide a basis for defining roles. When goals are clear, counsellors know which skills and techniques are appropriate, and clients know what is expected of them. Moreover, when counsellors know the goal of the work they can make intelligent decisions regarding whether they have the skills, capacity, and time to work with the client. If not, they may make a referral.

Motivating   Goals motivate clients. Setting and reaching goals is also therapeutic. It energizes clients and helps them develop optimism and self-confidence about change. Goal achievement confirms personal capacity and further promotes action. Writing down goals may add an extra measure of motivation.

Measuring Progress   Goals help provide benchmarks of progress, including defining when the counselling relationship should end—that is, when the goals have been reached or their pursuit is no longer viable.

Developing Effective Goal Statements

Sometimes clients are able to clearly articulate what they hope to achieve as a result of counselling. At other times, they have difficulty identifying their goals; however, through systematic interviewing counsellors can help these clients define and target their goals. The widely used acronym S.M.A.R.T. (Bovend'Eerdt, Botell, & Wade, 2009; Harms & Pierce, 2011) defines the characteristics of effective goals: Specific, Measureable, Achievable, Realistic, and Timely.

Effective Goals Are Specific   One defining feature of a counselling relationship is its goal-directed nature. But some clients begin counselling with vague and undefined goals:

- "I want to feel better."
- "My husband and I need to get along better."
- "I need to make something of my life."

These goals are starting points, but they are useless until they are described as clear and concrete targets. Beginning phase work that explores problems and feelings should lead to the development of goals that define and structure subsequent work. Then in the action phase, clients can develop these goals as specific and measurable targets. This step is a prerequisite for action planning—the development of strategies and programs to achieve goals. Vague goals result in vague and ill-defined action plans, whereas explicit goals lead to precise action plans.

In Chapter 5, concreteness was introduced as the remedy for vagueness. Concreteness can add precision to unclear and ambiguous goals. For example, when clients are describing their goals, counsellors can use simple encouragers, such as "Tell me more" and "Yes, go on" to get a general overview of what clients hope to achieve. This is the first step in shaping workable goals.

The next step is to use questions to define terms, probe for detail, and develop examples. This step helps to cast the emerging goals in precise language and move from good intentions and broad aims to specific goals (Egan & Schroeder, 2009). Here are some sample probes:

- What is your goal?
- When you say you'd like to feel better, what exactly do you mean?
- Describe how your life would be different if you were able to reach your goal. Try to be as detailed as possible.
- If your problem were to be solved, what would need to be different in your life?
- What do you think would be the best resolution to your problem?
- What are some examples of what you would like to achieve?
- As a result of counselling, what feelings do you want to increase or decrease?
- What do you want to be able to do that you can't do now?
- If I could watch you being successful, what would I see?

Some clients are reluctant or unable to identify goals, and they may respond with a dead-end statement like "I don't know" when they are asked for their goals. To break this impasse, counsellors can use some of these responses:

- "Guess."
- "What might your best friend (mother, father, teacher, etc.) suggest as your goal?"
- "What would you like to achieve but don't think is possible?"

A good general technique is to encourage clients to visualize themselves reaching their goals.

When clients say, "I don't know," their responses may indicate friction in the counselling relationship, and this answer is a way of sabotaging the work. In such cases, goal setting might be premature, and the focus of the interview may need to shift to relationship problem solving (immediacy). Moreover, when clients say, "I don't know" they might also be saying, "I can't do it" or "I'm afraid." Here, counsellors can suggest setting a very small goal as a starting point (e.g., "If you could make just one tiny change in your life, what would it be?").

SUCCESS TIP

When clients say, "I don't know," don't rush in too quickly with another question or comment. Often, after a short silence, clients will generate new ideas, feelings, or thoughts.

Effective Goals Can Be Measured   When goals are measurable, clients are able to evaluate progress, and they know precisely when they have reached their goals. Moreover, clear goals sustain client enthusiasm and motivation. Vague and unmeasurable goals, on the other hand, can result in apathy and vague action plans.

Baseline   A baseline is a measure of what is happening now. It becomes the reference point for measuring future change. For example, a baseline might be how often during any 15-minute interval a child is off task in a classroom. Baselines might be taken over one or many selected time frames to obtain an average. Measureable goals identify how much change in the baseline is targeted. In this example, suppose the baseline shows that the child is off task an average of 8 minutes during any 15-minute interval. The goal might be to increase the frequency of on-task behaviour to 12 minutes during any 15-minute interval in the next three weeks (i.e., reduce off-task behaviour to maximum 3 minutes).

Thus, goals need to be defined in terms of changes (increases or decreases) in baseline behaviours, thoughts, or feelings. Goals should also have a realistic schedule (a target date to start working on them and a target date to reach them). Counsellors can help clients frame goals in quantifiable language with questions such as, "how often?" "how many times?" and "how much?" The question "When will you start?" is a simple but powerful way to ensure client commitment to the change.

> **Example (skill):** "My goal is to express my opinion or ask a question once per class."

> **Example (thoughts):** "My goal is to manage self-deprecating thought patterns by substituting positive affirmations each time I say to myself that I can't do it."

> **Example (feelings):** "My goal is to reduce anxiety when I speak in public from a subjective level of 8/10 to 3/10 within the next six months."

Other measurable goals would include, "Target weight reduction of 9 kilograms in 10 weeks" or "Make five calls per day to potential employers."

Effective Goals Are Achievable and Realistic   A goal has to be something that clients can reasonably expect to achieve, even though it may require effort and commitment. So counsellors need to consider variables such as interest in achieving the goals, skills and abilities, and resources (including the counsellor) available to help in reaching the goals. In addition, the goals need to be significant enough to contribute to managing or changing the core problem situation.

But some clients may be reluctant to set challenging goals or even to set goals at all. This situation can occur for a number of reasons:

- Poor self-esteem
- Fear of failure
- Lack of awareness of capacity for change
- Fear of change and reluctance to give up established patterns
- Lack of resources to support pursuit of the goal (Shebib, 1997, p. 210)

Addressing these reluctance issues is a prerequisite for goal setting. When problems are complex and the client's capacity or self-esteem is low, setting short-term goals or subgoals is particularly useful. Short-term goals represent small, attainable steps toward long-term goals, and they help clients build confidence that long-term goal achievement is possible.

Clients need to see goals as relevant to their needs and consistent with their values. Thus, when clients are involved in the process of deciding what their goals are, they are more likely to be motivated to work toward achieving them. Counsellors can suggest goals, as in the following:

> Example: Evelyn was referred to the counsellor for help in coping with Trevor, her 18-year-old stepson, who was involved in petty crime. Evelyn's immediate goal was to encourage Trevor to move out of the house, and she hoped that the counsellor might help her do this. During the interview, it became apparent to the counsellor that Evelyn needed help developing parenting skills for dealing with Trevor and her two other teenage stepsons. Without dismissing Evelyn's objective, the counsellor suggested that this be part of their agenda.

When clients are forced to come to counselling by a third party, they may not feel committed to any of the goals of counselling. Thus, the chances of success are diminished greatly unless some mutually acceptable working agreement can be reached.

Understanding a client's values is an important part of goal setting. Some clients are motivated by spiritual values, some by material gain, and others by family values. Other clients focus on immediate gratification, while still others have objectives that are long term.

Ming left his family in China to come to North America. He has seen his wife only once in the last five years, when he returned to China for a short visit. He maintains regular contact with her and their six-year-old son. He sends much of his monthly pay home to support his wife and extended family. Although he hopes that one day his family will be able to join him, he has accepted that his purpose is to position future generations of his family for a better life.

Sometimes clients set goals that require others to change, such as "I want my husband to stop treating me so badly." Counsellors need to encourage clients to form goals based on what is under their control, namely their own feelings, behaviour, and thoughts.

Client complaints and problem statements can usually be reframed as positively worded goal statements. Here are some examples:

Example 1

Client: Everyone always takes advantage of me.

Counsellor: Sounds as though you'd like to learn to stand up for yourself.

Example 2

Client: I'm tired of not working.

Counsellor: Put simply, your goal is to get a job.

Example 3

Client: My life is a mess.

Counsellor: You would like to find a way to get your life in order.

The above responses change the focus of the interview from problems to goals. Of course, the counsellor and client will have to work together to shape these vague goals into more explicit terms.

Effective Goals Are Timely   Setting goals in a time frame, that is, identifying a target for goal achievement, is important for planning the work. The time frame should also be realistic—not too quick and not too slow. Whenever possible, goal statements should include "by when" the goal will be achieved. For example:

- To improve my grade-point average from C to B by the end of the semester.
- To make prayer a daily part of my life.
- To develop skills at organizing my time and setting priorities. I need to set up a schedule so I can plan at least a month in advance.

▶▶▶ INTERVIEW 7.2 | Goal Setting

The following interview excerpt illustrates goal-setting techniques. Prior to this dialogue, exploration and active listening enabled the counsellor to develop a solid base of understanding. With this work apparently finished, it seems timely to move on to goal setting.

Counsellor: I'd like your opinion. Are you ready to move on to making a change? If so, the next steps would be set a goal, then explore how you can achieve it. **Client:** Yeah, I'm not getting any younger. It's now or never. **Counsellor:** Help me understand what you'd like to change.	*Analysis:* The counsellor uses a phase transition to suggest moving from problem exploration to making a change. This will also change the contract. The client's response signals that he is ready to move from the contemplative stage to the preparation for change phase.
Client: I need to refocus my life on the things that are important. **Counsellor:** What do you mean? **Client:** I've been so busy with work that I really haven't had too much time for family. That has to change.	*Analysis:* At this point, the counsellor will have the criteria for effective goals (i.e., specific, measureable, achievable, realistic, and timely) as a reference point. Subsequent questions will be designed to help frame the goal around these criteria.

Counsellor: Just so we can be clear, can you try to be more specific? Suppose you're successful. What will be different from the way things are now?

Client: Less work, more family time. Now, work takes so much of my time and energy I don't have anything left for family.

Counsellor: Okay, you'd like to be able to give more time and commitment to family. To do that you'd have to cut back on work. What's the situation now?

Client: I'm lucky if I can have dinner with my family once a week, and I can't remember the last time my wife and I had a night out.

Counsellor: So, in a typical week, what do you see as the balance between work and family?

Client: If possible, weekends—strictly family. One night a week reserved as "date night" with my wife.

Analysis: The counsellor establishes the baseline and encourages goal setting in behavioural terms that are clear and measureable. Goals should specify what clients will be doing, not in terms of what they want to stop doing. A clear measurable target for change emerges.

Counsellor: You smile and seem excited as you talk about this.

Client: I think it's what I need to do to be happy.

Analysis: Empathy is still an important component of the work even though the conversation has become more focused on the behavioural domain. The client's response confirms that the empathic statement is accurate. It gives this client an opportunity to be more definitive about his emotional needs.

Counsellor: You said "if possible" when you talked about cutting back on work. What problems do you anticipate?

Client: I'd like to try for a management position at the company, but everyone's so competitive. I've got to put in the hours if I'm going to keep my sales above the others. And high sales is the first thing they look for when it's time for promotion.

Analysis: Counsellors have a responsibility to help clients consider the implications (positive and negative) of their goals and action plans.

Counsellor: You're torn. To compete, you've got to put in the hours. But if you do that, it takes away from your time and energy with the family. That's a lot of stress.

Client: Now that you point it out, it seems obvious. I've been under stress for so long, I don't even think about it anymore. It's clear to me now that the price of success is just too much.

Counsellor: Meaning that if you have to sacrifice time with your family to get ahead, you're not interested.

(Client nods.)

Analysis: The counsellor acknowledges the client's ambivalence—a factor that often impedes decision making and action. Identification of ambivalence helps the client get clarity on the choices.

Counsellor: Sounds as if you've made a decision, but let me play devil's advocate. Suppose you cut back on your job and lost a promotion. How would you feel about that?

Client: It would be hard on me, but I think not nearly so hard as what's happening now. At heart, I'm really a family man. I'm certain of it. Family has to be number one. My career is important to me, but it's my second priority.

Analysis: By exploring the implications of the client's goal, the counsellor helps to prevent the client from acting impulsively. Goals and action plans are much more likely to be pursued if the costs and benefits are clearly understood and anticipated.

Counsellor: Let's go back to your goal. What other problems do you anticipate?

(20 seconds of silence.)

Client: Here's one. My family is so used to getting along without me, they've developed lives of their own. I guess I can't expect them to drop everything for me.

Counsellor: So how can you deal with that reality?

Client: That's easy. I guess I'll just have to negotiate with the family on how much time we'll spend together.

Counsellor: One thought occurs to me. How will your boss react if you suddenly start spending less time on the job? Do you think that's something to consider?

Analysis: The counsellor continues the process of exploring risks and problems. By doing so, problems may be anticipated and strategies to overcome them developed. Often goals and action plans fail or are abandoned because of unanticipated obstacles. The counsellor is free to be an active participant in identifying risks, but, as a rule, clients should have the first opportunity.

Reflections

■ What indicators suggest it is appropriate to move on from problem exploration to goal setting and action planning?

THE PROBLEM-SOLVING PROCESS

Counselling is a developmental process. In the beginning phase, the process goal is the development of a strong client-counsellor working relationship and contract that describes the work to be done and the respective roles of both the counsellor and the client. If clients are motivated to make changes, then problems can be identified and explored, which provides the foundation for goal setting and action planning. Clear goals and a systematic action plan help to prevent failure that often comes from impulsive or premature action.

Problem Exploration ⟶ Goals ⟶ Problem Solving

Problem solving has four steps: (1) identify alternatives for action, (2) choose an action strategy, (3) develop and implement plans, and (4) evaluate outcomes.

Step 1: Identify Alternatives

The first task in selecting a plan is to list alternative ideas for achieving the goals. This step holds clients back from impulsive action based on the first alternative available, which may simply be a repeat of previous unsuccessful attempts at change. When there is choice, clients can make more rational decisions. Brainstorming is one way to quickly generate a list of possibilities. To encourage clients to generate ideas, counsellors can use leads such as these: "Let your imagination run wild and see how many different ideas you can come up with that will help you achieve your goals," "Don't worry for now about whether it's a good idea or a bad one." Sometimes counsellors can prompt clients to be creative by generating a few "wild" ideas of their own.

Step 2: Choose an Action Strategy

Once a creative list of alternative action strategies is identified, the next task is to assist clients in evaluating alternatives and making choices. This involves helping clients intelligently consider each alternative by exploring questions such as:

- Is it sufficient to make a difference to the problem?
- Is it within the capacity (resources and ability) of the client?
- Is it consistent with the client's values?
- What are the costs?

Cost might be measured by time, money, and energy expended in finding resources to execute the alternative. As well, alternatives might result in other losses for the client. For example, suppose a client wishes to end a pattern of alcohol abuse, but the person's friends are drinking buddies. If quitting drinking involves developing new activities, the potential loss of friends and social structure must be considered as a negative consequence that will have an impact on the client. Understanding and exploring this loss is important, for unless clients are aware of and prepared for these contingencies, they may be unable to sustain any efforts at changing.

> ### SUCCESS TIP
>
> Help clients conduct autopsies (also known as post-mortems) on past experiences as a tool to help them identify errors in thinking, triggers, problematic responses, and successes. Help them answer the questions "What went wrong?" "What could I have done differently?" and "What worked well?"

Step 3: Develop and Implement Plans

Developing and implementing plans involves four substeps: (1) sequencing plans, (2) developing **contingency plans**, (3) putting plans into action, and (4) evaluating plans.

contingency plans: Preventive plans that anticipate possible barriers that clients might encounter as they carry out action plans.

Effective plans are maps that detail the sequence of events leading to the final goal. Counsellors should avoid tailor-made plans in favour of customized strategies that are designed in collaboration with individual clients. Some of the important questions that need to be answered include the following:

- What specific strategies will be used?
- In what order will the strategies be used?
- What resources or support will be needed at each step?
- What are the risks and potential obstacles?

Contingency Planning Effective plans anticipate the potential obstacles that clients might encounter along the way. Once clients know and accept the possible barriers that could interfere with their plans, they can develop contingency plans to deal with these barriers. This preventive work helps keep clients from giving up when things don't go smoothly. A variety of different strategy choices can be used to support contingency planning:

- Anticipatory questions such as "What will you do if . . . (detail possible obstacles)?"
- Role playing (including counsellor modelling) to explore and practise strategies.
- Use of contracting—before problems occur, counsellors can ask clients for advice on how they can respond when the time comes. For example (to a client who has just begun a job search): "What would you want me to do if a few weeks from now I notice that you're becoming frustrated with your job search?"

With flight simulators, airline pilots learn to fly aircraft in emergencies. Should a real-life emergency happen, they are able to respond with confidence knowing that their training has prepared them. Similarly, contingency planning helps clients prepare for personal challenges and sustain their goals. It helps to prevent relapse to previous but ineffective ways of thinking and reacting.

Other Selected CBT Techniques   A wide range of behavioural change techniques can be used and customized to address the needs of clients (Maclaren & Freeman, 2007; Neenan & Dryden, 2006; Vonk & Early, 2009). These include the following:

- *"Autopsies"* help clients evaluate and learn from past experiences. As we have discussed, clients often repeat and reinforce the same thoughts and actions, sometimes with full knowledge that they are not working. A counselling autopsy involves systematic review of past actions to identify "triggers," unhelpful thinking and their link to behaviour and feelings. Of course, there is also considerable value in reviewing what worked. This enables clients to identify and build on proven strategies.

- *Relaxation training* helps clients manage anxiety and tension.

- *Assertion training*, where clients learn to express feelings or thoughts and achieve their rights while respecting the rights of others.

- *Relationship problem solving*, where clients can learn communication skills and conflict management strategies.

- *Homework* enables clients to implement and practise change strategies discussed during CBT, such as activities that provide pleasure. Homework may also include charting and monitoring emotions or behaviour through the use of diaries and checklists to measure baselines and progress to goals. Homework enables clients to see tangible and positive results from counselling, which builds confidence for further change. If clients encounter implementation barriers, these can be addressed quickly.

- *Exposure* provides gradual desensitization to anxiety-provoking events. Real or imagined exposure may be combined with relaxation training to inhibit anxiety.

SUCCESS TIP

HALT (hungry, angry, lonely, and tired) is an acronym for common feelings that can trigger relapses. Help clients explore what they tend to do, and what they might do differently, when they are hungry, angry, lonely, or tired.

HALT: An acronym for hungry, angry, lonely, and tired. HALT is a quick way to help clients assess triggers and plan alternative responses.

Counsellors need to support and encourage clients as they deal with the stress of change. One way they can help is to remind clients that anxiety, awkwardness, and periodic slumps are normal when change is occurring. Meanwhile, counsellors can look for ways to reframe failure or setbacks as learning opportunities. Empathy should be used to support clients dealing with feelings that accompany change or setbacks. During implementation, counsellors should also encourage clients to use family, friends, and support groups to assist them.

Step 4: Evaluate Outcomes

Effective plans include continual evaluation during the implementation phase. Evaluation recognizes and confirms success and is a powerful motivator; however, evaluation may also uncover problems that need to be addressed. For example, it may become apparent that the goals are too unrealistic. If they are too challenging and unreachable, counsellors can help clients define smaller goals. Similarly, if goals prove to be too easy, they can be modified to provide more challenge. Thus, regular review of progress ensures that goals and action strategies remain relevant and realistic.

When evaluation reveals that the plan is unlikely to be successful, efforts can be redirected toward redesigning the plan or selecting a different strategy for action. In some cases, the client may need help that is beyond the capacity of the counsellor; in this case, referral to another counsellor or service is appropriate.

STUDENT: I get stuck when a client says, "I've tried everything and nothing seems to work."

TEACHER: You feel stuck, which is precisely how the client feels. Clients often bring out in counsellors the same feelings that they are experiencing. This reality can be a useful tool for empathy. When clients say they've tried everything, it's important not to get into a "yes, but" game, whereby counsellors generate ideas and clients dismiss them with a "yes, but" response.

STUDENT: So what are my choices?

TEACHER: I'd be interested in exploring what the client did. Did he or she try long enough? At the right time? In the right way? Sometimes problems get worse before they get better, and clients may give up too soon. A mother might try ignoring her child when he has a tantrum and then tell you ignoring doesn't work, but she may have abandoned this tactic after a few minutes when it appeared that the intensity of her child's tantrum was increasing. In this situation, you could help her anticipate this obstacle so that she would not be demoralized if it recurred. Or maybe she has been giving her child lots of nonverbal attention, not realizing how this has been reinforcing the tantrum.

STUDENT: I can think of another example. One of the members of my work group was having trouble with her supervisor. She told us that there was no point in talking to him because he didn't listen anyway. But from the way she described how she talked to him, I wouldn't listen either. She was vicious and cruel.

TEACHER: So, if she were your client, she would need some help developing awareness about how she affects others.

BRIEF COUNSELLING

brief counselling: An approach to counselling characterized by a focus on resources and solutions rather than problems.

Since the 1980s, the assumption that counselling needed to be lengthy to be effective has been successfully challenged. In many settings, counselling relationships are brief, sometimes limited to a few sessions, a single session, or even a brief encounter. **Brief counselling** approaches, with their emphasis on strengths, resources, problem solving, solutions, and collaboration with clients, are now accepted as effective for many clients (Battino, 2007; Cameron, 2006; Carpetto, 2008; Hoyt, 2009; and Presbury, Echterling, & McKee, 2008).

Steve de Shazer (1985), one of the early pioneers of brief counselling, argues that it is not necessary to spend time searching for the root causes of a problem, nor is it necessary to have elaborate knowledge about the problem. In brief counselling, the goal is to help clients do something different to improve their situation rather than repeat the same ineffectual solutions. Small changes (e.g., insight, reduction of painful feelings, and new skills) can have a dramatic long-term impact by moving clients from a point of despair to one of optimism and motivation to work on changes in other areas of their lives. Because of its emphasis on action and change, brief counselling helps clients become "unstuck" from ineffectual ways of thinking, feeling, and acting. Clients can be encouraged to reframe by focusing their attention on what's working, thus, interrupting their preoccupation with problems and failure. This focus may generate or renew the clients' optimism that change is possible. In addition, brief counselling, even a single session, can be therapeutic for clients if they are able to unload pent-up feelings. A caring and empathic counsellor can encourage such ventilation and reassure clients that their reactions and feelings are normal. This can significantly reduce feelings of isolation by disputing the belief that many clients hold: "I'm the only one who feels this way."

Selected Brief Counselling Techniques

Precounselling Change   Momentum for change is often established at the moment clients seek counselling. Carpetto (2008) notes that studies have shown that changes frequently occur in the interval between the time clients make an appointment to see a counsellor and the first meeting. Thus, counsellors can make use of the fact that some clients realize progress while waiting for their first scheduled appointment.

The Miracle Question A typical **miracle question** might be formulated as follows: "Suppose that tonight while you're sleeping a miracle happens and your problem is solved. When you wake up, what will be different about your life?" Variations of this question may need to be developed to accommodate different clients. For example, some clients may object to the religious overtones in the question and a more neutral term, such as something *remarkable*, could be used. The following example illustrates the process:

> **Counsellor:** Suppose when you woke up tomorrow something remarkable has happened and your problem is gone. How would you know that your problem is solved?
>
> **Client:** Well, for one thing, I'd be worrying less.
>
> **Counsellor:** What might your family see as different?
>
> **Client:** I'd be more willing to get involved in family activities.
>
> **Counsellor:** Activities?
>
> **Client:** Things like sports, family outings—movies and so forth.
>
> **Counsellor:** What else would they find different? [Note: It is important for the counsellor to use probes such as this to elicit detail. If a change can be imagined, the more possible it will seem and the more the behavioural changes to make it possible will become apparent.]
>
> **Client:** I think that we'd be happier. Not just because we're doing fun things together, but we'd be arguing less about money and our other problems.
>
> **Counsellor:** How much of this is already happening?

The above excerpt shows how quickly the counsellor can move the interview to focus on change and solution possibilities, which helps clients become more hopeful about their situation. As Carpetto (2008) concludes, "they are already on their way to finding solutions to their problems" (p. 181). Since the client has imagined and described some of what needs to happen to solve the problem, the counsellor's next task is to get the client moving in the direction of the "miracle" with questions such as "What would you need to do now to begin to move toward the miracle?" or "What would it take to make the first step?"

miracle question: Used in brief or single-session counselling as a way to help clients who have difficulty coming up with defined goals. The miracle question challenges clients to imagine how their lives would be different if a miracle solved their problems.

Helping Clients Get on Track Counsellors don't need to stay with clients until all their problems are solved and their lives are in order. With brief counselling, the relationship may end when the client has a plan in mind, and they are headed in the right direction. Once clients start the process, counsellors should consider getting out of their way.

Looking for Exceptions Clients often stay fixated on their problems and on what doesn't work, and they continue to repeat or exaggerate "solutions" that have already proved unworkable. By doing so, they fail to notice times when they are successfully managing their problems. Looking for exceptions challenges clients to focus on those moments, however rare, when they are coping successfully. The assumption is that there are times when clients are successfully managing their problem, and they do many positive things that they are not aware of (Wehr, 2010). There are moments when anxious persons feel calm, acting-out children listen to their parents, and angry people are peaceful. By drawing clients' attention to these moments, they can remember and discover potentially successful answers to chronic problems. Challenging clients in this way stimulates them to think about more exceptions in their lives, thus, increasing self-confidence and their awareness of proven success experiences.

When clients are asked, "What is different about those occasions when your child obeys you or at least responds more receptively to your requests?" or "What is different about those times that you're not angry or only minimally upset?" the counsellor is requesting that clients report on experiences to which they have paid almost no attention.

Working with exceptions provides a quick and powerful way to motivate and energize clients to think about solutions rather than problems. The process is as follows:

1. Identify exceptions to those times when the client is having difficulty.
2. Help the client explore what was different about those times; including what (specifically) the client was doing differently.
3. Identify elements (e.g., behaviour, setting, and timing) that contributed to a successful solution.
4. Help the client plan to do more of what was successful.

In the following brief excerpt, the counsellor uses the technique to assist a client who is having trouble dealing with her teenage son:

Counsellor: From what you've been saying, it's a rare moment when you and your son can sit together and talk calmly.

Client: Maybe once or twice in the last year.

Counsellor: Let's look at those two times. I'm really curious about what was different about them that enabled you to talk without fighting. Pick one time that worked best.

Client: That's easy. My son was excited because he was going to a rock concert, and he was in a really good mood. I felt more relaxed too. He just seemed more approachable that day.

Counsellor: Have you considered that part of your success might have to do with your mood? Perhaps your son was more approachable because you were more relaxed.

Client: Interesting point.

Counsellor: Let's explore that a bit further. Because you were more relaxed, what else was different about the way you handled this encounter?

Client: I didn't feel stressed, so I think I was more open to listening to him.

Counsellor: What were you doing differently?

Client: I let him talk without jumping into argue.

Finding Strengths in Adversity Hardships and difficulties often have positive spin-offs in that people develop skills to deal with their misfortunes or discover capacities that they did not know they had. Following are some sample probes:

- How have you managed to keep going in conditions that would have defeated a lot of people?

- You have dealt with this problem for a long time. Many people would not have survived. How did you manage to keep going? What strengths were you able to draw on?

- What have you learned from life's trials and tests?

- Have hardships helped to shape your values and character in positive ways?

- People often develop talents or discover strengths from facing challenges. How has this been true for you?

Using Solution Talk   To get clients to notice their skills and capacities, counsellors can use statements and questions such as, "When you've successfully coped, how did you do it?"

In addition, counsellors need to be alert for opportunities to reinforce clients' strengths. Personal qualities, actions that underscore their determination, attitudes, positive decisions, accomplishments, effort toward change, and courage in the face of adversity can all be used to bolster clients' sense of capacity and self-esteem.

Clients may already have a rich understanding of their problems and the ways in which they might be solved. Counsellors need to tap their clients' expertise about possible answers to their problems:

- What solutions have you already tried?

- What would your best friend advise you to do?

- To solve your problem, what will you have to do?

- Let's try to identify something different for you to do to solve your problem.

- Let's brainstorm solution ideas. The wilder the idea, the better.

SUCCESS TIP

Use a question such as "What do you want to change about yourself today?" as a quick way to set a goal-directed sessional contract.

The Change Continuum   Often clients are overwhelmed with the number and depth of their problems. Their despair can easily infect counsellors. The continuum is a tool to assist clients to become motivated in the direction of positive change (see Figure 7.5). When clients can gain some control over their situation through small successes, this promotes further optimism and change. Counsellors do not have to be involved for the whole change process. Sometimes helping clients head in the right direction is the extent of their involvement. Here's an example of the use of the continuum with Figure 7.6a to e illustrating how it might be presented to the client: Kim, a young woman of 19 who is heavily involved in drugs, seeks counselling for help "to get her life in order."

> **Counsellor: (Uses a flip chart to draw the continuum depicted later.)** Kim, think about an area of your life where you would like to make a change. The continuum represents things as bad as they could be if things got worse at one end, and your ultimate goal at the other end.
>
> **Kim:** I need to change my whole life.

As Bad as It Could Be
(Negative)

My Ultimate Goal
(Positive)

Figure 7.6a

Counsellor: Okay, let's work on the big picture. Let's add descriptors that represent each end of the continuum.

Kim: *(Response depicted later.)*

As Bad as It Could Be
(Negative)

– Using hard narcotics
– Prostitution
– HIV-positive
– Criminal activity

My Ultimate Goal
(Positive)

– Job
– Drug-free
– Money in the bank
– Friends who are "clean"

Figure 7.6b

Counsellor: Where are you on the continuum?

Kim: (Draws a circle.) I'm about here, pretty near the bottom.

Figure 7.6c

Counsellor: What direction are you heading?

Kim: (Draws an arrow.) "My life is a mess, and it's getting worse."

Figure 7.6d

Counsellor: Maybe you'd agree that the direction you're heading in is ultimately more important that where you are on the continuum.

Kim: Absolutely, I can see that.

Counsellor: So what's one thing that would need to happen for you to change directions?

Kim: That's easy. I need a place of my own, and I need to get out of this area.

Counsellor: Let's start there and make that the focus of our work.

Figure 7.6e

Comments: The continuum has a number of useful features. It is visual, which makes it easier for some clients to understand. It is a quick way to prioritize complex problems and goals. This helps clients generate a sense of control and direction. Once completed, it provides shorthand communication for counsellors and clients. The two basic questions of the continuum can be used at the beginning of subsequent interviews to assess progress and to identify emergent issues: "Where are you on the continuum?" and "What direction are you headed?"

SUMMARY

- Empowerment counselling rests on the foundational belief that clients are capable and that they have the right to manage their own lives.

- Canada's senior population, now almost 6 million, represents a growing diverse group with a wide range of differing needs and expectations.

- Crisis intervention aims to empower clients by helping them regain physical and psychological safety, control, and balance.

- Motivational interviewing is a practice approach that uses the stages of change model to help clients overcome ambivalence to changes. Its central features include active listening, especially empathy, developing discrepancies, and rolling with resistance.

- The stages of change model (precontemplative, contemplative, preparation, action, and maintenance) provide a useful framework for understanding where clients are in the process of change and for making intelligent decisions regarding the usefulness of particular counselling skills.

- Cognitive behavioural counselling helps clients understand how unhelpful thinking can lead to problematic behavioural and emotional responses. Cognitive behavioural counselling helps clients break out of established (but ineffective) patterns of thinking and behaviour.

- Brief counselling recognizes that short encounters have the potential to be helpful for clients. Brief counselling techniques include the use of skills such as the miracle question, looking for exceptions, finding strengths in adversity, using solution talk, and the change continuum.

EXERCISES

Self-Awareness

1. Reflect on areas in your life where change is possible, is necessary, or has already occurred. Classify your stage of change with each issue based on the stages of change model: precontemplative, contemplative, preparation, action, and maintenance. What could potentially "move" you from one stage to another?

2. Start a log that chronicles your automatic thinking, for example, when you meet someone new, before asking a question in class, when you want to ask for help, etc.

3. Think of a crisis that you have faced. Try to recall your reactions in each of the three major domains: feelings, thinking, and behaviour. What helped you cope with and recover balance following the crisis? What factors acted against recovery?

4. Use the concepts from this chapter to practise goal setting and action planning for yourself. Pick one or more target areas (behaviour, feelings, thoughts, skills, or relationship). Develop a baseline.

5. Practise mindfulness:

    a. Go for a walk. Focus on coordinating your breath with your steps.

    b. Eat a banana or other fruit. Pay careful attention (sequentially) to the structure, colour, and feel of the fruit. Next, slowly chew it while focusing on the taste and feel of the fruit in your mouth.

    c. Breath meditation. Find a quiet place where you can be comfortable. Observe your breathing by attending to the flow of air through your nose and into your lungs. Watch your thoughts, and when a judgment arises, silently label it "judging." (Adapted from Siegel, 2010, p. 83)

6. Interview seniors. Discuss their current needs and expectations. Meet with colleagues to share your findings and to explore implications for counselling this group.

Skill Practice

1. Working with a colleague, take turns exploring a time in your life when you were unmotivated. What feelings were associated with this period? What helped you get unstuck?

2. Working with a partner, use selected brief counselling techniques from this chapter to help him or her deal with a problem area.

3. Conduct a practice interview with a colleague that focuses on goal setting.

4. Conduct an interview with a colleague (as client) using the principles of cognitive behavioural counselling. Explore a

problem area that the client identifies as real and current where they wish to make a change. Try to help your client:

   a. identify automatic thoughts.

   b. evaluate automatic thoughts.

   c. develop strategies for controlling and modifying automatic thoughts that are not helpful.

   d. set a goal for action (homework).

5. Record an interview with a colleague (as client) where you explore a problem or situation where they are ambivalent. Review the recording and identify statements that "sustain talk" and "change talk."

Concepts

1. Suggest questions you might ask clients to assess their stage of change.

2. Identify which stage of change best describes each of the following clients:

   a. "I hardly know anyone who smokes anymore. I'll get there too one day."

   b. "What's the point of looking for work? Since the big stock market crash there aren't any jobs out there anyway."

   c. "It's been almost six months since my last drink. I don't even crave it like I used to."

   d. "I wish I could find a way to get off drugs."

3. Explore how each of the client statements might impact their behaviour and emotions. What errors in thinking are apparent?

   a. "I'll never get a job."

   b. "She didn't even say hello when she saw me at the store. I guess she doesn't like me."

   c. "I have to be number one."

4. Suggest reframed responses for each of the following client statements:

   a. I can't do it.

   b. *(A student counsellor.)* I feel so unnatural and phony expressing empathy all the time.

   c. I really want my kids to avoid making the same mistakes I did. I don't know why they don't listen to me.

   d. If he really loved me, he'd send me flowers.

   e. My life is a mess.

   f. I'm tired of being depressed all the time.

5. Name at least 10 different ways to motivate clients.

6. Evaluate how the following statements meet the criteria for effective goals:

   a. To be a better person.

   b. To get my boss to stop hassling me.

   c. To drink less.

   d. To be able to disagree with someone without dismissing them or their ideas.

   e. To improve my fitness by next year to the point where I can run 1 kilometre in eight minutes.

7. Practise brainstorming techniques. Identify 5–7 different action strategies for a client who wishes to quit drinking.

WEBLINKS

Links and resources on the topic of motivational interviewing

www.motivationalinterviewing.org

Links to articles and resources on goal setting

www.selfgrowth.com/goal.html

Beck Institute for Cognitive Behavior Therapy

www.beckinstitute.org

Online tools for CBT

https://www.psychologytools.com and search for the heading "CBT tools"

Substance Abuse Mental Health Service Administration (SAMHSA) publication: "Brief Interventions and Brief Therapies for Substance Abuse"

www.ncbi.nlm.nih.gov/books/NBK64947

Short article on anti-oppressive practice from a child and youth care perspective

http://cyc-net.org/cyc-online/cycol-1203-moore.html

Mindfulness Exercises

www.stillmind.com.au/mindfulnessandrelaxation.htm

A practical guide to elder abuse and the law

http://www.bcli.org/sites/default/files/Practical_Guide_English_Rev_JULY_2011_0.pdf

Chapter 8
Difficult Situations: Engaging with Hard-to-Reach Clients

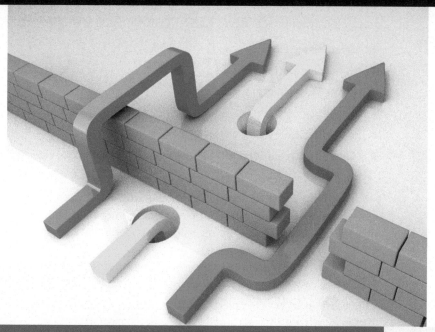

Inozemtsev Konstantin/
Shutterstock

LEARNING OBJECTIVES

- Understand the nature of client resistance.

- Describe techniques for dealing with resistance.

- Explain the use of confrontation.

- Identify key variables for violence risk assessment.

- Identify and describe strategies for preventing violence.

- Describe strategies for intervening at each phase of violence.

- Understand the importance of debriefing critical incidents.

- Describe counselling interventions for dealing with angry and potentially violent situations.

RESISTANCE

Resistance, a term first introduced by Freud, refers to a normal defensive reaction that comes from the natural drive to preserve the status quo. Changing one's patterns of thinking and behaving, even when desired, creates anxiety. It requires people to alter existing and familiar patterns of communicating or coping which, however painful or

resistance: A defensive reaction by clients that interferes with or delays the process of counselling.

unhelpful, are at least familiar, and so the prospect of change represents some risk as well as potential gain. Thus, resistance protects clients from the stress and threat of change.

Thus, resistance may be the client's reaction to being pushed (by the counsellor) to do or accept something the client does not want. In fact, the psychological need to stay connected to the familiar may cause clients to resist the very changes they are seeking. For example, a client may verbalize a strong desire to curb drinking, but fail to engage with agreed-upon goals or action plans to work toward that goal. Clients may be ambivalent about change and the risks and fears of change may cancel any momentum toward action.

Active listening, particularly empathy, reduces or prevents resistance. Other counsellor responses may increase it. These include the following:

- Arguing for change
- Assuming the expert role
- Criticizing, shaming, or blaming
- Labelling
- Being in a hurry
- Claiming pre-eminence ("I know what is best for you") (Miller & Rollnick, 2002, p. 50)

By paying attention to client resistance, counsellors can examine how their own responses might contaminate the interview, and what they might do differently to prevent, neutralize, or reduce resistance.

SUCCESS TIP

Newton's third law of motion states that for every action there is an equal and opposite reaction. Resistance is the equal and opposite reaction that happens when clients feel pressured or coerced. Counsellors need to monitor and reduce their responses that are accelerating resistance while increasing responses that reduce it.

Signs of Resistance

Resistance may reveal itself in a variety of ways, ranging from overt hostility to passivity that impedes the work. Here are some client behaviours and signs that may suggest resistance (Cormier & Hackney, 2008; Gladding & Alderson, 2012; Miller & Rollnick, 2002, 2013; and Shulman, 2009).

1. Failure to comply with the basic procedures of counselling, including keeping appointments, being on time, and paying fees.
2. Hostile or argumentative statements (e.g., "This is a waste of time," "You can't make me cooperate," "That's none of your business," and "I don't want to be here").
3. Passivity (e.g., silence, withholding information, persistent short responses such as "I don't know," extreme self-censorship of ideas and feelings)—such passivity may indicate that the client does not want to be there, or it may mean that the feelings, content, and challenges of the interview are more than the client is willing or able to face.
4. Diversion as a way of avoiding difficult, threatening, or incriminating content (e.g., changing the subject, using excessive humour, making small talk, introducing irrelevant material, being overly talkative, intellectualizing, and restricting the conversation to particular topics).

5. Uncooperative behaviour (e.g., failure to follow through with plans or homework, false promises).

6. Subtle undermining (e.g., acting seductively, attempting to redefine the counselling relationship as a friendship, excessive praising, being sarcastic).

7. Creating the illusion of work, described by Shulman (2009) as engaging in conversations that appear important but that in reality are empty and have no real meaning because they do not empower clients to change.

8. Nonverbal cues suggesting a passive–aggressive response, such as not making eye contact, folding arms, sitting on the edge of the seat, using an angry tone of voice, clenching fists, raising eyebrows, frowning, and sighing.

9. Blaming, making excuses, and expressing unwillingness to change.

Understanding and Responding to Resistance

Some Resistance Is Normal and Desirable Counsellors do not have to view all resistance as problematic. Skilled counsellors recognize resistance, but they are not threatened by it. They see resistance as a signal that clients' defences are engaged, and this insight opens a pathway to greater understanding of their clients. For example, in the beginning phase of counselling, before trust and a working contract are negotiated, many clients tend to hold back. At this stage, their counsellors are strangers, and it would be unwise for clients to open up too quickly without knowing how precious personal information might be treated.

Sheafor and Horejsi (2008) note that it is common for clients to be somewhat defensive, particularly in the beginning phase when a person's natural resistance to change can be triggered by fear of what lies ahead: "Even a small amount of change can create a discomfort or fear for clients, especially if they hold rigid beliefs, are inflexible in their thought processes and behaviors, or are fearful about risking change in their relationships with others" (p. 205). Some clients resist because they do not understand the expectations or the process of counselling, so they wisely remain cautious and guarded. Until relationship contracting establishes the goals and purpose of the work, clients may hold back from fully participating. Counsellors also need to be explicit regarding their expectations. They should not assume that what is obvious to them will also be obvious to their clients.

> **SUCCESS TIP**
>
> Help clients understand how anxiety and ambivalence about change may create more anxiety which sabotages action plans, then use anticipatory contracting to strategize how this can be addressed.

Resistance and the Stages of Change The stage of change model (Prochaska & Norcross, 2001) was introduced in Chapter 7 as a model for understanding the developmental nature of change. Different skills and strategies are used to engage clients during different stages. For example, clients who are at the precontemplative stage of change do not accept that they have a problem and are not thinking about making changes, even though their behaviour is problematic for them and others. At this stage, strategies such as confrontation to push a client toward change are likely to be met with resistance, but other strategies (e.g., open questions and empathy) will help to neutralize the resistance. Some clients who are precontemplative hold to their current mode of thinking, feeling, and acting because they lack the energy necessary for change, or because they are pessimistic about the possibility of change. Whatever the reason, these clients resist counselling because it is easier and safer than embracing change. Counsellors might deal with this resistance by communicating optimism and by helping clients set small but achievable goals. By supporting and reinforcing small successes, counsellors contribute to the empowerment of their clients. However, during this process, counsellors should express empathy regarding the challenges and fears associated with any change. Clients need to understand that they will not be humiliated or overwhelmed by the demands of counselling. Counselling can be presented as a way for them to find the resources, support, and motivation for change.

At the contemplative stage, clients are ambivalent about the change process and may simultaneously desire and resist efforts and opportunities for change, "even when such action is counterproductive and dysfunctional" (Gladding & Alderson, 2012, p. 141). The messages from clients seem to say, "I want to change, but I don't want to change." This ambivalence can freeze clients in a state of indecision; and the resolution of ambivalence is the key to change (Miller & Rollnick, 2013). Even for those clients who are highly motivated to change, the prospect of changing involves risk; risk creates anxiety, and the simplest way to reduce anxiety is avoidance. From this perspective, resistance is viewed as self-protective. To resolve ambivalence in favour of change, the benefits of change must outweigh the risks and anxiety associated with change, or anxiety regarding change must be reduced.

SUCCESS TIP

Openly expressed resistance from a client can be a great opportunity for relationship building and goal setting if it leads to frank discussion of roles, expectations, barriers, and fears.

Relationship Issues   Sometimes clients become increasingly resistant as counselling progresses. This may signal that the process is moving too quickly or that there is unresolved conflict in the counsellor–client relationship. Clients may be resistant because of transference reactions or simply because they do not feel a good connection with their counsellors.

psychological reactance: The tendency for people to increase problem behaviour if they believe their freedom is threatened. This theory can help us understand why nagging by concerned friends and family may have a paradoxical effect.

Resistance may emerge when counsellors challenge long-established behaviours or attempt to encourage discussion or goal setting in areas that clients would like to avoid. Miller and Rollnick (2002) developed the theory of **psychological reactance** to describe how painful consequences (e.g., personal suffering from drug addiction, nagging from concerned family members) may actually increase the undesired behaviour. This theory predicts "an increase in the rate and attractiveness of a 'problem' behaviour if a person perceives that his or her personal freedom is being infringed or changed" (p. 18).

Some clients have dealt with the social service system for many years and sometimes their whole lives. They have had many experiences with social workers, psychiatrists, foster homes, counsellors, and the criminal justice system, which have shaped their expectations. Frequently, they have had bad experiences with helping professionals or other persons in authority, and they fear the same outcome again. For example, if they experienced other counsellors as rude or untrustworthy, they may be guarded with new workers. This defense protects them from further rudeness, inconsistency, or breach of trust. Armed against the counsellor before they even meet, these clients may view caring as manipulative and empathy as intrusive. Asking about prior experiences helps to bring feelings and issues into the open, including any preconceptions or fears about the current relationship. When counsellors do this, they should provide a brief explanation to let their clients know they are not prying for gossip:

> **Counsellor:** Have you had any other experiences with counselling in the past?
>
> **Client:** Yes, my husband and I went for marital counselling about two years ago.
>
> **Counsellor:** What did you like and dislike about that experience? I'm asking because I think it will help me to understand a bit about your expectations. I'd like to learn what worked for you and what didn't.

Resistance may also develop because of conflict in the current relationship. Counselling relationships, like all relationships, are subject to periodic stress and conflict. Counsellors can make mistakes and say the wrong thing, and they can offend their clients. Vulnerable clients may be overly sensitive, or they might misinterpret messages and feel angered. This is an inevitable reality of the chemistry of human encounters.

It's also true that resistance may have origins that began long before the current relationship. Many clients have had negative experiences that leave them suspicious and doubtful about the value of yet another encounter with someone representing the system.

What sets effective counsellors apart is their ability to be sensitive to clues such as verbal and nonverbal shifts in the tone of the interview that signal that there is friction in the relationship. Effective counsellors are further distinguished by their willingness and capacity to address these issues with nondefensive caring. By doing so, they not only prevent further resistance but they also build trust and understanding with their clients.

Immediacy was introduced in Chapter 3 of this book as a process for exploring, deepening, and evaluating counselling relationships. When resistance blocks the work of counselling, immediacy provides a way to deal directly with client concerns regarding the counselling process or the relationship itself. As a rule, if resistance is increasing, it is wise to deal directly with it; otherwise, the client may never return. The following questions and statements illustrate the potential variety of responses that can be used to move the interview toward a discussion of resistance:

- How do you feel about being here?
- I'm wondering what's happening between us. Are you feeling angry toward me?
- Let's see if we can agree on what we want to accomplish.
- If I'm not mistaken, every time I mention your father you change the subject. Would you rather avoid that topic?
- How committed are you to making changes?
- Do you believe it is possible for you to change?
- What does it mean to you to be seeing a counsellor?
- Are you worried that I will try to force you to do something you don't want to do?

When nonverbal cues suggest resistance (e.g., lack of eye contact, single word answers, crossed arms, and abrupt tone), counsellors might try "breaking the ice" with statements such as, "If I felt forced to come to counselling, I think I'd feel quite resentful."

Shulman (2009) comments on the fact that communication is frequently indirect in that feelings and concerns are expressed in ways that might not be immediately clear. Such indirect communication challenges counsellors to understand what clients might be trying to say behind the words expressed. For example, a client who asks whether a worker has children may be communicating her fear that a childless worker might not understand her struggles. By picking up on the question behind the question, workers create an opportunity to explore these fears. Similar indirect communication might be embedded in clients' questions such as these:

- Have you ever been in jail?
- Do you know what it is like to be on welfare?
- Have you used street drugs?

Table 8.1 presents alternative ways of responding to personal questions such as those mentioned earlier.

Resistance and Fear of Change For most people, it is difficult to change from established routines and ways of coping. They communicate fears regarding the imagined consequences of change through resistance. Some clients have trouble with intimacy, and

TABLE 8.1 Five Choices for Responding to Personal Questions

Client: Do you have children?

1. Answer the question: "I do not have any children."
2. Explore the meaning of the question: "I'm curious about your reasons for asking."
3. Explore the implication of different answers: "What would it mean to you if you heard that I don't have any children?" or " . . . if you heard that I have children?"
4. Empathy: "Are you perhaps worried that I might not understand what it's like for you, a single mom with two kids?"
5. Silence: Provides an opportunity for the client to elaborate and perhaps share concerns and feelings associated with the question.

counselling may be seen as an unwanted intrusion that threatens their need to maintain personal distance and privacy. A variety of counsellor responses might be considered:

- Candid discussion with clients about their fears and the real risks of change.
- Target small but achievable goals.
- Empathize with the clients' fears.
- Reassure clients that they will not be pushed beyond their capacity and that they are in control of the pace of change.
- Limited counsellor self-disclosure to normalize fears about change.

Resistance and Personal Beliefs Some clients are resistant because they believe that taking help is a sign of weakness. They may believe that counselling will undermine their personal autonomy. For others, cultural or familial values promote privacy about one's personal struggles and the belief that they should not be shared with strangers. One way for counsellors to address this resistance is to look for appropriate opportunities to reframe counselling as a sign of strength rather than feebleness. Counsellors can also deal with fears about loss of independence by making sure that clients are active and informed partners in the work of counselling.

Involuntary Clients and Resistance Sometimes resistance stems from clients' resentment at being forced to come for counselling and an inability to see a need for change. These clients may see themselves as fighting "the system," and the counsellor who represents it. Involuntary clients typically receive services from large bureaucratic organizations, but the structure and procedures of these agencies can make it difficult for counsellors to support their clients. Systems designed to help clients may overwhelm them with rules and regulations, and counsellors often have to make troubling decisions on how to use their scarce resources and time. It is important that counsellors understand how clients may perceive them.

Johnson and Yanka (2004) remind us that clients may overestimate the extent of a worker's power. When clients assume counsellors have more power than they actually have, they might withhold information, avoid meetings, or otherwise resist counselling; therefore, frank discussion of roles, responsibilities, and the limits of power may assist in clients' fears.

With involuntary clients, it is important to restore their sense of control and right to self-determination. These clients need to be able to answer the question "What can counselling do for me?" They need to see goals and outcomes that they desire as opposed to those imposed on them. Counsellors need to be patient with unwilling clients by remaining nonjudgmental and caring. Moreover, they can decrease resistance by demonstrating their ability to talk calmly with their clients about their reasons for not wanting to be there. Counsellors should be especially diligent about informing unwilling clients about their rights, including the limits of confidentiality. Clear, succinct statements about these issues will help to reduce their suspicions.

The brain is wired to keep us safe. Neural pathways over time result in "hard wired" ways of thinking or doing. Emotional reactions to risk taking, changing behaviour, or feeling pressured by others may be experienced as threats to the comfort of the status quo. This creates anxiety about change, even when the changes are seen by clients as good and desirable. The brain reduces this anxiety by avoiding the change or creating pressure to revert to familiar patterns, thus, sabotaging the change. Significantly, some of this anxiety may be displaced as resistance or anger toward counsellors, even when clients are willing partners in the objective to change. Counsellors can help by assisting clients to anticipate and plan for the natural anxiety associated with modifying established patterns.

Sometimes counsellors can modify expectations through reframing. The following interview excerpt provides a brief illustration:

Counsellor: What do you hope to achieve?

Client: Nothing.

Counsellor: What's behind that answer?

Client: I just think that counselling is a waste of time. What good does it do to talk about problems anyway?

Counsellor: You also seem to be saying that if counselling could in some way help you with your problems, you would be more satisfied.

Client: I guess so.

In Chapter 7, "rolling with resistance" was introduced as a way to avoid any direct challenges that might precipitate a power struggle. This strategy identifies but accepts the resistance. This approach is illustrated as follows:

Client: I just think that counselling is a waste of time. What good does it do to talk about problems anyway?

Counsellor: Given your pessimism, it seems to me that you're wise to be cautious about what we might accomplish here.

The following story provides another example:

A holy man and an atheist met one day. The atheist challenged the holy man to debate, exclaiming, "I don't believe in God!" The holy man replied, "Tell me about the God you don't believe in." The atheist talked at length about the absurd wars that had been fought in the name of God. He attacked the "hypocrites" who espoused their religious values and beliefs but behaved in quite the opposite fashion. The holy man listened patiently until the atheist had said his piece. Only then did he respond: "You and I have a lot in common. I don't believe in that God either."

Figure 8.1 outlines some counsellor responses that both increase resistance and decrease resistance.

Resistance and Counsellor Self-Awareness

Counsellors should monitor and manage their own emotional reactions to resistance. Client resistance can be unsettling and demoralizing, and it can test almost any counsellor's ability to be nonjudgmental. Common counsellor reactions include fear, anxiety, avoidance, defensiveness, anger, pessimism, and a sense of rejection. Counsellors may turn against their clients, blame them for their problems, and look for ways to refer them to another counsellor.

In response, clients may view their counsellors' defensive reactions as proof that the situation is hopeless. Thus, it is important that counsellors find ways to depersonalize

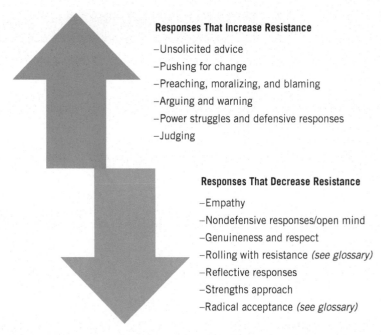

Responses That Increase Resistance

–Unsolicited advice
–Pushing for change
–Preaching, moralizing, and blaming
–Arguing and warning
–Power struggles and defensive responses
–Judging

Responses That Decrease Resistance

–Empathy
–Nondefensive responses/open mind
–Genuineness and respect
–Rolling with resistance *(see glossary)*
–Reflective responses
–Strengths approach
–Radical acceptance *(see glossary)*

Figure 8.1   Resistance

⟫⟫ CONVERSATION 8.1 | Working with "Involuntary" Clients

COUNSELLOR: You work with street-involved youth. What have you learned about working with involuntary clients?

YOUTH COUNSELLOR: I learned the hard way doesn't work. There's no point in lecturing, moralizing, or preaching about the dangers of drugs. What seems to work best is to focus on the relationship.

COUNSELLOR: How do you do that?

YOUTH COUNSELLOR: Sometimes it's just little things, like bringing a cup of coffee to a sex-trade worker, or checking to see if they are all right or need anything. I try to be ready for the "teachable moment." That can happen anytime, such as after a "bad date" or when they're feeling down. Then, empathy and listening skills are best, especially empathy. Spending time with clients without having an "agenda" goes a long way toward establishing trust. When the time is right, you'll be the "go to" person.

COUNSELLOR: That's right. As you know, involuntary clients can be rebellious, and being forced into counselling arouses their defences. For example, I recently met with one who was referred by his employer because he could not get along with his co-workers. He claimed that others in his work team simply had difficulty dealing with his assertive manner and his

high standards. He came in to see me, but it was evident that his main motivation was to preserve his job. With him I found that it worked best to encourage him to express his anger about being told what to do. This diffused his resistance to the point where he no longer saw me as the enemy.

YOUTH COUNSELLOR: It's like that with our clients as well. With youth on probation, I like to look for ways to give them power and involve them in decision making. Here again, empathic listening can help them arrive at a plan that suits them, one that doesn't feel imposed.

COUNSELLOR: So involuntary clients are not necessarily pre-contemplative. Many are well aware of their problems and the need to change. They just don't like being told what to do, and that's the key to working successfully with them. When I worked in corrections, I found that many of my clients were initially resistant and overtly hostile to authority. Clients with such anti-authoritarian values are not going to respond to directive, rigid attempts to control them. Such strategies will only serve to increase resistance. As always, paying attention to the relationship is crucial. For example, with clients coming out of prison, relationship credibility can be developed by helping them with basic needs, such as housing, clothes, food, and a job.

---

the situation. Otherwise, they run the risk of further worsening the situation by rejecting the client or retaliating in subtle ways.

Counsellors need to be able to objectively evaluate their own conduct and take their fair share of responsibility for resistance. When counsellors have high self-awareness of their actions, they are able to monitor themselves and change their behaviour to be

The following interview excerpt shows some ways avoid and reduce resistance when dealing with an angry client. The client is a young male, age 19, who has been referred to an addiction counsellor as a condition of his probation. It is clear from the client's nonverbal behaviour that he doesn't want to be there (e.g., he has not removed his coat, he gives single-word or short answers to questions, and his voice tone is hostile).

Client (*with angry tone*): Are we going to be here long. I got things to do.	***Analysis:*** *The client's opening comment clearly communicates his resistance in a way that should not be ignored.*
Counsellor: I know that you were forced to come here by your probation officer. I'm wondering how you feel about that. **Client:** I'm really not in the mood to be cross-examined. **Counsellor:** Of course, you are free to leave at any point. But before you do, why don't we take a moment to talk straight.	***Analysis:*** *At this point, the counsellor needs to control her own emotional response to ensure that she does not become defensive, a response that would almost certainly increase resistance. Instead, the counsellor encourages the client to say more about his feelings. The counsellor reminds the client that he does have a choice about whether to stay or go, which is designed to give him back some of the power he feels he has lost.*
Client (*sarcastically*): I think this is all crap. It makes no sense. What's the point? **Counsellor:** I appreciate your honesty. **Client:** I'm here, so let's get this done.	***Analysis:*** *Use of "radical acceptance" (see Chapter 7). The counsellor tries to find a point of agreement, but her response is greeted by more anger. At this point, it is important that the counsellor not give up. Even though the client's response is less than ideal, he has heard what the counsellor said. The counsellor needs to remain calm, patient, and empathic. This will give the client an opportunity to spill out some of his anger, which often helps to soften it.*
Counsellor: It sounds like you've been through this before, and it didn't work out. **Client:** Yep! More than once. **Counsellor:** If you want, I'd be happy to listen to what went wrong. **Client:** I'm tired of people trying to control my life.	***Analysis:*** *The client's earlier statement that he "doesn't want to be cross-examined" is a good indication that it might be wise, at least at this point, to avoid directly questioning the client. Questions would be inappropriate in this interview.* *The counsellor proceeds, while trying to honour the client's need for autonomy and control.*
Counsellor: Fair enough. We agree. You don't want to be cross-examined, and I don't intend to try. You don't have to tell me about anything you don't want to talk about. **Client:** Let's get one thing clear. I do not need your permission to do anything.	***Analysis:*** *The counsellor continues to honour the client's right to self-determination and autonomy.*
Counsellor: Agreed. But since you have decided to stay, let's talk. If you're feeling angry because your probation officer thinks you need counselling, I can understand. I sure do not like it when I'm forced to do something against my will.	***Analysis:*** *The counsellor continues to "roll with resistance." The counsellor tries to ally herself with the client by using self-disclosure to encourage him to talk about his resistance. She emphasizes that the client has made choices.*
Client: It's not you. I just don't see the point. There's nothing wrong with me. I don't understand why I have to come here.	***Analysis:*** *The counsellor's persistence works, as the client begins to open up. At this point, it is important for the counsellor to avoid becoming defensive. If she starts to "sell" her client on the merits of counselling, she may lose him.*
Counsellor: Sounds as if you really want to stand up and say, "This is my life. Butt out."	***Analysis:*** *An inferred empathic response acknowledges the client's feelings.*
Client: Yeah. What gives them the right to say I'm crazy?	***Analysis:*** *Cautiously, the client begins to share his feelings, including his reservations about what will happen in the relationship.*
Counsellor: And now that you're here, you might be worried that I'll do the same thing. That I will try to get into your head, tell you what to do.	***Analysis:*** *The counsellor uses immediacy to verbalize the client's central concern, which the client has expressed implicitly.*

Client: Of course. Isn't that how it works? I have been to counselling before. (Laughs.) You guys aren't happy unless you're mucking someone up.	**Analysis:** Despite his initial resolve to keep his distance from the counsellor, the client is beginning to connect. He is seeing the counsellor as less of a threat.
Counsellor: (Laughs.) Well, we have to shrink our quota of heads. **Client:** (Laughs.) My head is staying just where it is.	**Analysis:** A little humour from the counsellor helps build rapport while showing empathy with the client's feelings. The counsellor's humour affirms her ability to talk about the issues without becoming defensive. However, when using humour timing is critical. What works very well in one situation might result in disaster in another.
Counsellor: I am impressed that you're able to say what you want. **Client:** I do not believe in playing games.	**Analysis:** The counsellor does not attempt to break down her client's defences, which are helping this client cope with a threatening situation. Instead, she reframes his stance as a strength.
Counsellor: Me neither. So, let's talk about what you'd like to see happen here. I will need some help from you. And if it's okay with you, I'll share some of my ideas. **Client:** I guess so. It is not like I have a choice. I've seen dozens of social workers in my life. They all talked a good game, but it didn't help me one bit! How is this going to be any different?	**Analysis:** There is much work to be done to establish a solid working relationship with this client. The counsellor's responses allow the process to move forward, but her manner gives the client some much-needed control and power. Asking for the client's help about process and direction is very empowering. An important beginning has been established.

Reflections:

■ How might this interview have evolved differently if the counsellor had used questioning as her main tool for inquiry?

■ What are some of the personal feelings you might need to control if you were the counsellor in this scenario?

■ How can you approach clients who have had multiple "bad" experiences with counsellors or others in the social service system?

■ How would you respond to the client's last question, "How is this going to be any different?

more effective. Hill (2004) echoes sentiments from many sources with the simple yet profound advice to counsellors to "respond to client anger as they would to any other emotion" (p. 417).

Counsellors can use colleagues and supervisors for support when dealing with highly resistant clients, who can tax the patience of even the most dedicated counsellor. Collegial support can help counsellors unwind from tough sessions. They can help counsellors to be more objective, or they can be a source of fresh ideas for reaching difficult clients.

CONFRONTATION: PROCEED WITH CAUTION

Many people associate confrontation with conflict and hostility, an association arising from the fact that confrontation often comes from frustration or anger. For counsellors, effective confrontation is not a hostile act. Confrontation is simply a way of directing clients' attention to aspects of their personality or behaviour that they might otherwise overlook. It is a tool to move clients to a higher level of understanding of themselves and others. Moreover, caring confrontation can deepen the level of trust in the counselling relationship. It is also a major skill for helping clients develop fresh perspectives on

STUDENT: What are some ways to say "no" to clients? I really hate it when I have to deny them what they want or need.

TEACHER: That is my reaction too. None of us in the helping professions wants to be seen as harsh or uncaring. Saying "no" may evoke feelings of guilt in us, as well as strong negative reactions from our clients. We really need to be able to address our own emotions as well as those of the client.

STUDENT: I suppose it's a reality of the business. Sometimes we have to make tough decisions, such as who gets the training money and who qualifies for assistance. In the residential part of the program where I work, we often have to say no when the kids want exceptions to the rules. No problem when you're able to give them what they want. But what about when you have to turn down requests?

TEACHER: Even when you're saying "no," it's important that clients know you care. You need to listen and be available to respond with empathy and compassion. Find a way to show you understand, even if you are not able to give your clients what they want. Or see if there is a way to compromise to help your client save face. What do you think?

STUDENT: I have learned a couple of things. Be direct, clear, and brief. Don't waffle, hint, or avoid the "bottom line." With kids, I've found that, even when they test the limits, they may need limits and even welcome them when imposed. It increases their sense of safety and control when they learn the boundaries of acceptable behaviour.

TEACHER: I agree. I think it is important that you don't make a hasty retreat. Expect that anger, defensiveness, and counter-attack are the ways that some clients respond to frustration. In extreme situations, you need to protect yourself. Anticipate potentially violent situations and take defensive action. Also, be sure to debrief with a colleague or supervisor after difficult encounters. And if necessary, take a break to ensure that your reactions do not contaminate your ability to deal with your next client objectively. Finally, remind yourself that no matter how your client reacts, you must stay in a professional role.

STUDENT: When someone says "no" to me, I find it a lot easier to accept it if I know why. So, I try to explain my rationale or the policy. Then I invite questions while remaining clear when the policy is nonnegotiable.

TEACHER: If you can, help your clients identify other ways to meet their needs.

---

themselves and their behaviour. Nevertheless, it is a skill that should be used sparingly and with caution. As a general rule, confrontation has the greatest chance of success when clients accept it as part of the counselling contract.

Types of Confrontation

The two main types of confrontation are feedback confrontation and confrontation of incongruities. **Feedback confrontation** provides new information to clients about who they are, including how they are perceived by others and the effects of their behaviour on others. Feedback confrontation can be used to help clients become aware of the consequences of their decisions and actions. It is not reserved for negative or critical feedback; it can also be used to identify strengths.

> **feedback confrontation:** Used to provide new information to clients about who they are, including how they are perceived by others and the effects of their behaviour on others.

In some cases, clients do not recognize the harmful effects of their behaviour on themselves and others. They continue to behave in ways that are hurtful, yet they lack insight into how they are affecting others. Because they are unaware and fail to see their behaviour as problematic, they have no motivation to change. Feedback confrontation can help these clients examine the consequences of their actions. The following are examples of client blind spots:

- Jerry thinks of himself as humorous, but he is unaware that his jokes are offensive and sexist.
- Nathan has bad breath and body odour.
- Parvinder is unaware of how his aggressive behaviour pushes others away.
- Estelle has been in a series of relationships in which she has been battered. She does not understand how this has affected her children.

Despite its potential power as a helping tool, feedback confrontation is often misused. Some counsellors avoid it, perhaps because they fear that they might alienate their clients or arouse their anger. Other counsellors feel the need to keep the helping relationship pleasant, so they distort or lie to clients to sustain their approval; however, effective counsellors need to be willing and able to confront clients when necessary. Thus, counsellors must remain aware of their beliefs, fears, and expectations regarding confrontation to use this skill appropriately.

Sometimes beginning counsellors (and some experienced ones too) are reluctant to confront. They may hold beliefs such as the following, which potentially limit their effectiveness:

- "I was brought up to believe that if you don't have something good to say, then don't say anything at all."
- "If I confront, I might damage the relationship. I don't want to upset my clients."
- "I don't want to hurt my clients."
- "My clients might retaliate."

Yet most of the preceding beliefs arise from an erroneous understanding of confrontation as a "no holds barred" assault on clients. Assault-type confrontation strategies should, of course, be avoided. At the other extreme, refraining from confronting clients under any circumstance is an evasion of responsibility that cuts clients off from the potential benefits of new information and feedback. Competent counsellors should not withhold potentially useful feedback.

confrontation of incongruities: Used to point out inconsistencies in a client's verbal and nonverbal messages, values or beliefs, and behaviour.

The second type of confrontation, **confrontation of incongruities** (Ivey, Ivey, & Zalaquett, 2010), is directed at inconsistencies and mixed messages:

- Discrepancy between a client's verbal and nonverbal messages.
  Client: (*Crying.*) It's really nothing. I'm not bothered.
- Discrepancy between a client's values or beliefs and behaviour.
  Client: There's nothing more important to me than my kids. I know I haven't spent much time with them. It's just so hard to say no to my buddies when they ask me to help.
- Discrepancy between what a client says and what he or she does.
  Client: I'm committed to looking for work. Yesterday something came up before I could get to the employment office.

In confronting discrepancies, counsellors need to remain calm and nonjudgmental while presenting clients with facts. Ivey, Ivey, and Zalaquett (2010) look at confrontation as a way to support clients in a gentle and respectful manner rather than a harsh challenge. Its purpose is to aid clients to have a more complete understanding by offering additional information or perspective. It opens up new possibilities for changes in thinking and behaving.

The Misuse of Confrontation

Although confrontation has potential for motivating clients to change and can assist clients in developing insight, misuse of confrontation can be destructive. As a rule, counsellors should use it sparingly and should be prepared to offer support and caring to ensure that confrontation does not overwhelm or devastate their clients.

There are risks to confrontation, and some clients do react poorly. They may respond with hostility and attempt to question the integrity or credibility of the counsellor. Such a hostile reaction may be a type of denial, indicating that the client is simply not ready to acknowledge the validity of the confrontation. Hostile reactions are more likely to occur when feedback or confrontation is unsolicited, but they may occur even when clients appear to be seeking information or feedback. Counsellors also need to consider that harsh client reactions may arise for legitimate reasons. Sometimes feedback is confusing or the manner and tone of the counsellor are abrupt. Secure counsellors have to be open to the possibility that they may have erred.

Confrontation is not an outlet for a counsellor's anger or frustration. When counsellors are not in control of their own feelings, clients are more likely to view them as aggressive and to feel their confrontation is unsupportive. The counselling relationship is formed to meet the needs of clients, and responsible counsellors forgo their own needs to this end. In addition, counsellors should be self-aware enough to know their reasons for wanting to confront.

Overly confrontational styles have been found to result in a high client dropout rate and poor outcomes. "Counsel in a directive, confrontational manner and client resistance goes up. Counsel in a reflective, supportive manner, and resistance goes down while change talk increases" (Miller & Rollnick, 2002, p. 9). Ultimately, "the manner in which we present confrontations affects the way they are heard and accepted or rejected by the client" (Sperry, Carlson, & Kjos, 2003, p. 120).

SUCCESS TIP

"Do not confront another person if you do not wish to increase your involvement with that individual" (Hamachek, 1982, p. 230).

Principles for Effective Confrontation

Principle Number 1   Unsolicited confrontation tends to result in resistance, hostility, and defensiveness, but solicited (invited) feedback is more likely to be accepted.

The skill of anticipatory contracting can be used to engage clients in accepting feedback:

> **Counsellor:** One of the ways I might be able to help is by sharing some of my impressions about what you are doing, or even about our relationship. What do you think?
>
> **Client:** Sure. I would appreciate that.
>
> **Counsellor:** Well, let's look ahead. Suppose I wanted to give you some feedback about something I thought you were doing wrong that you were not aware of. What would be the best way for me to approach you?
>
> **Client:** I do not like to be overwhelmed. And I like the good mixed with the bad.

This example shows how contracting can be used to help the counsellor "customize" feedback to meet the needs and expectations of the client. Some clients like blunt feedback; others prefer it "sandwiched" between positive statements. Anticipatory contracting empowers clients and communicates respect for their rights to make choices. When confrontation is invited, it is much less likely to meet with resistance.

Principle Number 2   Confrontation should be used sparingly and in combination with other skills, particularly sensitivity and empathic listening.

Confrontation may involve feedback that is unsettling for clients, and empathy reminds counsellors to remain sensitive to the impact of confrontation. In addition, counsellors should not confront clients without assisting them to develop new alternatives. Confrontation should also be measured to avoid overwhelming clients with more information than they can handle. Ideally, confrontation should not undermine the self-esteem of clients. At first, clients may respond defensively to feedback, but after reflection, they may be more accepting. Alternatively, they may appear to be accepting but later become resentful. Thus, it is important to check with clients how they feel about the feedback or confrontation. Counsellors should monitor immediate reactions. As well, checking back with the client during the next session is a useful tool for identifying delayed reactions and for noticing any feelings that might impair the relationship. The following example illustrates the process:

> **Counsellor:** I'm wondering how you felt about our last meeting. Remember, I shared with you some of my opinions about the things you are doing that seem to distance you from your family.
>
> **Client:** I almost did not come today. (*Silence.*)
>
> **Counsellor:** Because?
>
> **Client:** I was embarrassed by what you thought of me.
>
> **Counsellor:** You thought that I might think less of you?
>
> **Client:** Yes.
>
> **Counsellor:** Would you like to find out for sure what I think?
>
> **Client:** Okay.

This counsellor's strategy sets the stage to help the client correct any distortions, and it is crucial for dealing with the aftermath of confrontation. It also reinforces the understanding that any feelings about what happens in the counselling relationship can be dealt with openly.

Principle Number 3 Confrontation should serve the goals of counselling by leading the client to improved ways of behaving, thinking, and feeling.

Relevant confrontation always meets the needs of the client. Thus, it is inappropriate for a counsellor to use confrontation as a means to vent frustration, anger, or to punish clients.

Counsellors can best deal with feelings related to the relationship or the work by using I-statements rather than trying to mask their feelings as helpful feedback. I-statements are assertions about personal feelings or reactions that do not blame or judge others. Instead of saying "You don't care," an I-message would be "I feel confused when you don't answer my questions." I-statements are much less likely to cause resistance.

Principle Number 4 Confrontation must be timed appropriately at a point when clients are ready and willing to take advantage of feedback and when there is a reasonable possibility that feedback can motivate them to change.

Counsellors need to pay attention to timing and ensure that there is a well-developed counselling relationship to support confrontation. As a rule, it is preferable to avoid strong confrontation in the beginning phase of counselling. Clients are more receptive and likely to accept feedback as credible when there is a relationship and climate of trust, when they do not feel insulted and misunderstood. Otherwise, they may never return.

Confrontation should be done as close as possible to the relevant behaviour, events, or circumstances that are being addressed. In some cases, such as when strong emotions are clouding communication, it may be best to wait. A client's ability to handle confrontation is a crucial variable. If clients are already overwhelmed with feelings, confrontation may add to their stress but contribute little to their ability to cope. Moreover, clients who are highly defensive and guarded may respond poorly to confrontation. In such situations, counsellors may find it wise to delay or avoid confrontation entirely.

Effective confrontation is an investment in the relationship. After confronting, counsellors need to be able and willing to invest time to help their clients understand any feedback. As well, counsellors must be available to help clients deal with any feelings that may result from the confrontation. Consequently, the end of a counselling interview is generally a poor time to confront.

Principle Number 5 Effective confrontation needs to be specific without attacking the personality of the client.

> **Counsellor (Choice 1—ineffective confrontation):** You don't seem at all interested in what's happening here. If you're too lazy to care about our work, why don't you just quit? (*Counsellor is attacking and judging the client without offering any concrete feedback.*)

> **Counsellor (Choice 2—more effective confrontation):** When you don't show up for appointments, I wonder whether you're as committed to your goals as you say you are. (*Counsellor's comments are linked to specific client behaviour.*)

> **Counsellor (Choice 3—most effective confrontation):** I think your best work has happened on those days when you came on time and when you took the effort to focus. My sense is that if you could make every appointment, you'd get a lot more out of our time together. (*Counsellor focuses on strengths and what the client can do that will be more effective—people are motivated more by positive feedback than negative feedback.*)

AGGRESSION AND VIOLENCE

Counsellors, social workers, child care counsellors, and other social service professionals, especially those who work in residential care, are increasingly vulnerable to violence (Macdonald & Sirotich, 2005, 2001; Newhill, 1995, 2003). For example, a counsellor's denial of a client's request for financial assistance may evoke retaliation. Hospitals, especially emergency rooms, can be a particularly dangerous place. A survey of over 9000 registered nurses in Canada revealed that almost 40 percent had experienced some form of workplace violence and about 20 percent had been physically assaulted (spit on, bitten, hit, or pushed) (Canadian Institute for Health Information, 2012). A study at one private psychiatric hospital found that the frequency of violence by male patients was 50 percent higher than a decade before, and that violence by female patients was 150 percent higher than a decade before (Tardiff, Marzuk, Leon, Portera, & Weiner, 1997). One study (Alink, Lenneke, Euser, Bakermans-Kranenbury, & Van IJzendoorn. 2014) of workers in residential care revealed that 81 percent experienced some type of victimization (verbal, physical, and sexual harassment) and 37 percent were subject to physical violence.

Situations that may increase counsellors' risk for violence include:

- Dealing with people who are using street drugs.
- Dealing with mentally ill people who are not taking their medication or mixing prescribed medication with street drugs.
- Investigating situations of child abuse and neglect.
- Institutional work in prisons, group homes, and hospitals.
- Work that includes some elements of social control (e.g., probation, involuntary clients, and establishing eligibility for income assistance).
- Assisting police intervention in domestic abuse.
- Hospital emergency work.

Canadian studies by MacDonald & Sirotich (2001, 2005), de Léséleuc (2004), and Ryan (2016) found the following:

- Almost 90 percent of social workers have experienced verbal harassment.
- 90 percent of Canadian front-line residential care workers experienced physical violence from residents (or their relatives).
- About 65 percent have been threatened with physical harm.
- About 30 percent have been sexually harassed.

- Close to 8 percent have been physically assaulted and injured.
- One-third of all workplace violence incidents took place in social service or health care settings, with about 71 percent involving physical assault.
- About 50 percent of incidents were linked to substance abuse.
- Males were accused in 93 percent of the assaults, and 54 percent of them were under 35 years of age.

Sometimes clients cause fear because their behaviour is threatening, or they have a history of violent behaviour. At other times, counsellors' fears are based on intuition or hunches, the internal response to subtle signals that not all is well. In fact, some clients provide abundant reasons for fear, because of either intimidating behaviour or overtly violent acts.

Intimidating behaviour includes name calling, obscene or sexually harassing language and gestures, shouting, threatening displays of power such as fist shaking, invasion of personal space, stalking, and verbal threats. Clients also behave in an intimidating manner when they will not take no for an answer or when they refuse to leave the office. As well, clients may attack workers with personal insults, or they may intimidate them with threats to call the newspaper or civil rights groups. In general, intimidating behaviour should be controlled or managed to prevent escalation to violence. The following case examples of threatening behaviour are all based on real incidents:

- New client in a welfare office says, "If I don't get some help, you'll be sorry."
- Man, in his late twenties stares obstinately at an intake worker.
- Angry parent tells child protection workers that if his child is not returned, the worker will know what it's like to lose someone you love.
- Teenager in a group home refuses to comply with house rules. He tells his child care counsellor, "I've had enough. Things are going to change around here."
- Parole officer meets a new parolee for the first time. He is pleasant and cooperative, but the parole officer knows the man has a short fuse and a long history of assault charges.
- Mental health counsellor deals with her client, a young male with a history of self-destructive behaviour. It is obvious that he is not taking his medication, and he seems unusually agitated.
- Ten-year-old child who witnessed abuse at home grabs a pair of scissors and lunges toward the counsellor.

Violent behaviour means hitting, pushing, biting, slapping, kicking, throwing objects, and using weapons such as guns, knives, or syringes. It also refers to kidnapping and stalking.

- Social worker in a hospital emergency ward is threatened with a syringe by an angry HIV-positive patient.
- Angry client picks up a chair and hurls it at the counsellor.
- Client, disgruntled with the counsellor's refusal to provide him with money, spits in the counsellor's face.

Nonetheless, it is important that counsellors do not become hypervigilant and conduct their work in constant fear. Such a stance makes it difficult for them to separate actual hazards from situations that present no real risk. Moreover, unwarranted fear of clients leads to uninformed responses. Though very real dangers exist in the workplace,

intimidating behaviour: Behaviours such as name calling; using obscene or sexually harassing language and gestures; shouting; and threatening through displays of power such as fist shaking, invading personal space, stalking, and issuing verbal threats. These behaviours should be restrained to prevent escalation to violence.

violent behaviour: Hitting, pushing, biting, slapping, kicking, throwing objects, and using weapons such as guns, knives, or syringes.

by and large it is a place of safety. The challenge is to be able to answer some basic questions:

- Which clients are likely to become violent? What are the indicators of potential violence?

- Under what conditions should a client's anger be cause for concern?

- What are the skills and behaviours that can be used to de-escalate dangerous situations?

> **SUCCESS TIP**
>
> Anger, when expressed assertively, is a normal and potentially useful part of relationship communication. Assertive anger respects the rights, obligations, and feelings of self and others. Aggressive anger involves intimidation, misuse of power, and disrespect for others.

Risk Assessment for Violence

Violence arises from a complex array of psychological, social, biological, and physiological factors. Although certain variables are more likely risk factors, risk assessment is difficult and violence cannot be predicted with precision (Miller, 2000). There is simply no foolproof way to predict with certainty who is likely to become violent.

Violence may be perceived as a desperate act by an angry client to regain control and power. Multiple stressors, such as poverty, the loss or absence of supportive relationships, and substance abuse, may magnify a client's vulnerability and stress to the breaking point. Moreover, counsellors may be in positions of authority with the right to deny clients access to goods or services. Clients may perceive such denials as further threats to their fragile power and self-esteem, and the risk of violence may escalate. Attacking others works as a psychological defense against feelings of shame and humiliation.

Based on his review of the academic literature, Ross (1995) identifies five primary causes of violent crime in Canada: "interpersonal conflict situation (over status, resources, power, control, and reputation), presence of weapons, influence of drugs and/or alcohol, media facilitation, and cultural or subcultural reinforcement" (p. 348). The key variables that have been found to have some validity for predicting violence include: (1) past and current behaviour, (2) substance abuse, (3) age and gender, and (4) personality (see Figure 8.2). The more risk factors present, the greater the risk, but the presence of a risk factor does not mean that a given person will become violent in a given situation.

Past and Current Behaviour   The best predictor of future violence is a history of violence (Miller, 2000), and the more recent and severe the violent behaviour, the greater the risk. Kelleher's (1997) conclusion that a history of violent behaviour should always be given serious consideration is echoed consistently in the research on violence: "Although the argument can be made that historical evidence of violence is not a guarantor future violent behavior, an understanding of any form of violent criminal activity clearly supports the contention that a history of violence is often a predictor of future violence" (p. 13).

Counsellors should be particularly interested in noting how a client has handled difficulties and frustrations in the past. Some clients who were victims of abuse as children have grown up without a capacity for warmth and empathy for others, which can make them oblivious to the suffering of others (Miller, 2000). In extreme cases, violence may even bring these clients pleasure or sexual gratification. Counsellors should also be interested in the level of remorse that clients show for past acts of violence, particularly

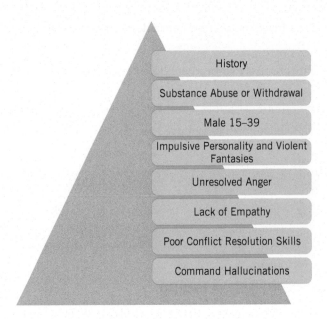

Figure 8.2 Risk Factors for Violence

for those who show no regret. On the other hand, clients who have learned other ways of managing their anger now have more choices and are less likely to act out physically. In this respect, it might be revealing for counsellors to explore how their clients are managing stress outside the counselling relationship. For example, do they show evidence of a lack of concern for the safety of others? Are there indicators of inappropriate or uncontrolled anger? Are they typically extremely defensive, irritable, or self-centred? To what extent are they prone to impulsive behaviour? Impulsive clients might assure counsellors that they have no intent to harm anyone and then attack another client in the waiting room 10 minutes later.

Furthermore, clients who have a specific plan of violent action and the means to carry it out represent an immediate risk of violent behaviour. Counsellors need to consider their professional obligations and legal requirements to warn any intended victim by examining their codes of ethics as well as relevant legislation or legal precedent.

Substance Abuse   Violence from substance abuse is associated with

- the effect of drugs,
- violence to get drugs, and
- violence in the drug culture.

Common sense and empirical research suggest that intoxicated and agitated clients should be approached cautiously. Substance abuse, particularly in combination with other risk factors, compounds the risk of violence (Miller, 2000). Reviewing the role of drugs in violence, Roth (1987, pp. 13–14) concludes the following:

- Hallucinogens such as LSD and PCP, glue sniffing, amphetamines, and barbiturates have been associated with aggressive and homicidal behaviour.
- Narcotics tend to suppress violence, but individuals might become violent in order to get these drugs.
- Alcohol reduces inhibitions, and it is implicated as the most frequent drug linked to violence.

Furthermore, many studies link substance misuse to violent behaviour (Swanson et al., 1997; Tardiff et al., 1997). Newhill (1992) reviewed the available research and recorded that certain drugs subdue aggression, whereas others escalate it:

"Anticholinergics, antipsychotics, antidepressants, sedative hypnotics, and analgesics tend to suppress aggression. Amphetamines and withdrawal from drugs such as morphine or alcohol induce aggression" (p. 70). Moreover, people who abuse drugs are at an increased risk of victimization. The link between drug abuse and violent behaviour may arise, at least in part, from the fact that alcohol and other drugs are more likely to be abused in a dangerous place.

Age and Gender   The vast majority of people who are violent and who have been arrested for violent behaviour are male. The highest risk for violence is found in people from 15 to 39 years of age. The rate of violent acts for this age group is three times that of the general population (Newhill, 2003). Violence declines with age, but dementia and other cognitive problems can result in an increase in violence by those over 65.

Personality   Some clients deal with their sense of personal fragility by lashing out at others, and they are hypervigilant about protecting themselves from perceived threats from others. Miller (2000) notes:

> Tendencies toward low frustration tolerance, impulsive behavior, vulnerability to criticism, feeling humiliated and powerless, superficial relationships, lack of empathy, a pattern of externalizing problems, and failing to accept responsibility for one's own actions are all associated with more-violent behavior. (p. 300)

De Becker (1997) cautions that some people assume the worst possible motives and character and that they write their own scripts: "The Scriptwriter is the type of person who asks you a question, answers it himself, then walks away angry at what you said . . . The things that go wrong are the work of others who will try to blame him. People are out to get him, period" (pp. 148–149). These clients believe that you are uncaring and bent on harming them. Whatever counsellors do and however caring their actions, these clients will react based on their expectations. They may try to control the relationship through manipulation and intimidation; however, this behaviour should be interpreted as a warning signal only. These clients may not escalate to violence.

Violence and Mental Illness

The question whether people with mental illnesses are more dangerous than the general public continues to be the subject of research, debate, and controversy. Not surprisingly, many people believe that there is a strong link between mental illness and violence. But advocacy groups argue that the media, through selective and exaggerated reporting, have stimulated the development of false assumptions about the dangers posed by people with mental illnesses. Sensationalized headlines such as "Schizophrenic Man Kills Wife, Then Turns Gun on Himself" and "Voices Told Me to Kill My Child" create the impression that mental illness is associated with violence; however, objective research evidence supports different conclusions.

SUCCESS TIP

Violence that originates from psychoses and other neurological problems can for the most part be prevented through medication and support services. This underscores the importance of working with clients to enhance medication compliance, as well as providing ready access counselling for crisis management, peer support, and basic needs such as housing.

One comprehensive Canadian study of the literature on the link between mental illness and violence concluded that there is no scientific evidence that mental illness causes violence (Arboleda-Florez, Holley, & Crisanti, 1996). Echoing many other research findings, they also implicated substance abuse as the most significant risk

Organic brain disease and head trauma may reduce clients' impulse control and lead to an increase in aggression and violence, as well as changes in memory and ability to reason.

A study of prisoners links a history of brain trauma with an increased likelihood for violence (McCook, 2011).

factor, noting that studies suggest that "individuals are at greater risk of being assaulted by someone who abuses substances rather than someone who is suffering from major mental illness such as affective disorder, anxiety disorder, or schizophrenia." Another study (Swanson et al., 1997) confirms the link between violent behaviour and substance abuse, particularly when there has been absence of recent contact with mental health service providers. A different study concluded that predictions of violence based on a history of violence were more accurate than clinical predictions based on diagnosis (Gardner, Lidz, Mulvey, & Shaw, 1996). Overall, persons with mental illness are over 2.5 times more likely to be victims rather than perpetrators of violence, particularly when other factors such as poverty and substance abuse are present (Canadian Mental Health Association, 2005). The vast majority of violence comes from people who are not mentally ill, yet the widespread belief that persons with mental illness pose a threat contributes to the stigmatization of this group (University of Washington, School of Social Work, 2015).

Although "major mental disorder and psychiatric disturbance are poor predictors of violence" (Harris & Rice, 1997), Miller (2000) found that certain mental disorders, such as schizophrenia with paranoia and command hallucinations, mania, substance use disorders, antisocial personality disorders, and borderline personality disorders, are more likely to be associated with violence. Moreover, in recent decades, deinstitutionalization of psychiatric patients has resulted in unprecedented numbers of people with mental illnesses in the community. Clients with a history of severe mental illness and violence who stop taking their medications can be very dangerous, particularly if they have command hallucinations (voices and images directing them to be violent).

A comprehensive follow-up study of patients discharged from psychiatric hospitals concluded that former patients who do not abuse drugs are no more violent than a random population sample (Bower, 1998). Pastor (1995) concluded that unrealistic and delusional thinking tends to increase the likelihood that violence will result. He also noted, "Manic symptoms, such as irritability, increased energy or activity, psychomotor agitation and grandiosity, also increase the risk of violent behavior. A belief that 'others' are responsible for the person's misfortune increases the likelihood of striking out against those persons" (p. 1173).

Violence Risk Assessment: Key Questions

Although long-term prediction of violence is difficult, counsellors should be able to make reasonable short-term forecasts based on consideration and assessment of the following questions and issues:

1. Does the client have a history of violent behaviour or an arrest record for violent crime? The counsellor should review agency file records and other anecdotal evidence for information.

2. To what extent does the client appear dangerous, as evidenced by marked or escalating agitation or threatening behaviour? The counsellor should consider verbal threats as well as nonverbal expressions of aggression.

3. If the client is threatening violence, are the threats concrete and specific? Does the client have a plan? Does the client have the means to carry out the stated plan? Does the client have a weapon or access to one, especially a gun?

4. Is the client under stress (e.g., recent death, poverty, unemployment, or loss of social support)? Has there been a recent event that represents the last straw for the client? Noticeable changes in baseline behaviour (the client's usual personality and manner) should be noted, such as the following examples:

   ▪ Haydon, usually quite demanding and argumentative, becomes quiet.
   ▪ Jeff, a 16-year-old group home resident, who is typically very social, withdraws to his room.

5. What systemic factors might be exacerbating the situation (e.g., missed or delayed appointments and denial of benefits)?

6. What counsellor variables might be heightening the client's anger? Is the counsellor acting in ways that the client might see as provocative? For example, is the counsellor defensive or judgmental toward the client?

7. What high-risk symptoms are present? For example, is the client experiencing command hallucinations? Is the client impulsive? Is the client near panic? Is the client narcissistic or self-centred and prone to blaming others for his or her misfortune? Is the client hypersensitive to any criticism or hint of rejection?

8. Is there evidence of substance abuse?

9. Has the client failed to take psychiatric medications? Has the client cut off or failed to keep scheduled contact with a psychiatric caregiver?

10. Does the client believe that he or she is able to control his or her behaviour? Is the client socially isolated?

11. Is there a history of brain injury or organic brain disease?

These questions are references for the purpose of assessment only. The presence of any of the factors does not mean that the client will necessarily become violent. However, when there are numerous strong clues that suggest violence, counsellors should proceed cautiously and look for ways to reduce risk factors to establish safety.

Managing Angry and Potentially Violent Behaviour

Preventing Violence Effective intervention begins with prevention. Organizations need to be open to the fact that there may be elements of their service system that act as triggers for clients who are stressed or have short fuses. Additionally, workers need high self-awareness to recognize their own triggers, as well as how their responses and behaviour might escalate frustrated and angry clients to violent responses.

Systemic Factors Many clients come to counselling in a state of crisis, with low tolerance for added stress. Consequently, it is important that agency policies and routines

---

⟫⟫ BRAIN BYTE | Aggression

Society for Neuroscience (2007) reported findings on the neurobiology of aggression. It found evidence of brain damage in neural circuits related to moral decision making in violent individuals. Damage to the prefrontal cortex, and the angular gyrus can also increase violent behaviour.

Hyperactive responses in the amygdala (responsible for managing threats and fear) and decreased activity in the frontal lobe are also implicated. As well, low levels of the neurotransmitter serotonin may help predict violence.

---

do not compound the risk by exacerbating client frustration. Parada, Barnoff, Morratt, and Homan (2011) comment on this Canadian reality:

> Community members who use social services often have to wait too long for an appointment, wait too long to be seen on the day of their appointment, and have too little time with you or other professionals when they are finally seen. The forms they must complete are often lengthy and confusing. Some agency staff can be insensitive, unhelpful, or downright rude. Then together, these practices reinforce the idea that community members who have to use these services are unworthy and lack dignity (p. 6)

Organizations need to understand that for many clients, systemic change is what is needed. Part of this ought to include review of the structure and service delivery systems of the agencies whose mandate is to help.

Agency Safety Precautions   In settings where there is significant risk for violence, procedures should be developed for dealing with potentially violent clients. In fact, employers usually have a legal responsibility to provide a safe working environment. Minimum safety precautions might include the following:

Policy   Agencies should develop and regularly review policies and procedures for dealing with potentially violent situations. Policies should address issues such as the procedures for visiting homes, giving clients home phone numbers, using last names, and interviewing after hours. Generally, counsellors should not make home visits alone if there is a possibility for violence. Many counsellors who work with potentially dangerous clients use unlisted phone numbers as a way to ensure privacy and safety. In extreme situations, such as dangerous child abuse investigations, counsellors may need to be protected by police. Generally, counsellors should avoid making unescorted visits to high-crime areas. And only those counsellors with legal authority should investigate allegations of child abuse or neglect.

Staff Training   Training should address tactics for dealing with difficult clients, including those who are involuntary, angry, or acting out. Front office and reception staff should also be trained so that they can relate to clients in ways that do not escalate the clients' frustration or anger. Periodic team simulations will ensure that everyone is familiar with their roles and responsibilities. This prevents members of the team from becoming confused during a critical incident. Simulations also help staff build confidence in themselves and trust in their colleagues as backups.

Interviewing Procedures and Office Design   Counsellors who are interviewing difficult or dangerous clients should work in offices where access to immediate help can be provided. A silent system for alerting others that a dangerous situation is developing should be implemented (e.g., panic button and encrypted phone message). Leaving the

>>> BRAIN BYTE   Flight or Fight

When counsellors or clients feel fear or threat from the other, the classic "flight or fight" response may result for either or both. Stored memories of similar threatening events have an enormous influence on how individuals respond. Five major areas of the brain, amygdala, hippocampus, hypothalamus, thalamus, and sensory cortex all play a part in the decision to run (flight) or fight, (although some may respond by freezing). When the threat is perceived as real, hormones such as epinephrine (adrenaline) and norepinephrine (noradrenaline) are released which cause an increase in heart rate and blood pressure. Muscles tense, breathing rate increases, digestion slow or stops and blood glucose levels increase. Because attention is fully directed at the threatening situation, individuals may be unaware of other things such as how their responses are affecting others (Layton, 2015; Sherrard, 2015). Thus, some angry and aggressive clients may be quite unaware how frightening their behaviour is to other people.

door open during the interview can allow other staff to monitor any increasing danger, but this practice may violate the client's confidentiality.

Files on clients with a history of violence should clearly document details of any past violent behaviour or threats. For clients with a high propensity toward violence, a team approach may be desirable, with two or more persons being present during the interview. In such cases, it is usually preferable if only one person does the interviewing. This can lessen any feelings the client might have of being ganged up on. Too many people may heighten the client's anxiety. Backup help can be stationed out of sight, but on quick standby for dangerous situations.

Office furnishings should be carefully chosen to minimize risk. For example, shatterproof glass can be used, and items that are potential weapons, such as scissors, should be removed. Also, soft lighting and calming colours may have some modest effect on mood. In addition, the agency itself should have good external lighting. Finally, during high-risk hours, such as late at night or early in the morning, access doors should be locked, and workers should not have to walk alone into dark parking lots.

Table 8.2 on the next page provides some tips on how to prevent and manage anger and violent behaviour. The table is organized according to the phases of violence, which are discussed in the next section.

The Phases of Violence

The National Crisis Prevention Institute (2012) has developed a model for nonviolent crisis intervention that is widely used in Canada. It is based on four **phases of violence**: (1) anxiety, (2) defensiveness, (3) acting out, and (4) tension reduction (see Figure 8.3). Each phase is characterized by particular indicators and demands specific responses.

phases of violence: The four-phase model (anxiety, defensiveness, acting out, and tension reduction) that describes how crises escalate to violence.

Phase 1: Anxiety In the anxiety phase, there are often early warnings that are marked changes in the client's behaviour. The client's agitation and anxiety may include verbal challenges, such as the refusal to follow directions or questioning of authority. Statements such as "You can't tell me what to do" accompanied by finger pointing may suggest escalating anger. Signs of escalation, such as pacing, intense staring, and refusing to sit down, should be noted (Shea, 1998). Other indicators may include excessive euphoria, angry facial expressions, increased voice volume, and prolonged staring. Counsellors should watch for changes in client baseline behaviour or personality patterns.

During the anxiety phase, the client may respond to gentle directives and invitations, such as "Let's talk and see if we can work things out" and "I'm willing to listen." This phase offers counsellors the best opportunity to intervene early to prevent anger from intensifying into acting-out behaviour.

TABLE 8.2 Preventing and Managing Anger and Violent Behaviour

Preventive Phase

- Recognize risk factors.
- Identify and minimize systemic factors that might be triggers for clients.
- Structure the agency to reduce client stress and danger to personnel.
- Set up emergency response protocols.
- Practise crisis responses with simulations.
- Take steps to protect identified intended victims.
- Self-awareness.

Early Warning Phase (Anxiety)

- Pay attention to changes in client behaviour such as increased anxiety.
- Attempt to identify and rectify client "triggers."
- Promote client involvement in decision making to give them a sense of empowerment and control.
- Take "gut instincts" and threats seriously.
- Use empathy and reassurance to acknowledge and attend to client needs.

Late Warning Phase (Defensive)

- Pay attention to changes in client behaviour such as increased defensiveness, challenges, and verbal threats.
- Set clear, reasonable, and enforceable limits.
- Respect client need for increased space.
- Remain calm and avoid sudden movements.
- Avoid using an authoritarian tone; respond assertively.
- Use basic counselling skills.
- Search for compromises and "win–win" solutions.

Uncontrolled Anger and Violence (Acting Out)

- Call the police (do not try to disarm clients who have weapons and do not risk personal safety unless unavoidable).
- Try to ensure the safety of everyone, including bystanders, other staff, and the client.
- Use a team approach, including, if necessary and appropriate, physical restraint, but extreme caution is required as untrained persons can inflict injury or death.
- Refer or arrange to transport clients to hospital for assessment or medication.
- Try to re-establish verbal communication.

Tension Reduction

- Support the client's return to a state of calm.
- Re-establish communication.
- Elicit available family support.

Post-Event Follow Up

- Involve clients in long-term counselling.
- Help clients learn nonviolent solutions to problems.
- Implement consequences, if any.
- Conduct individual and team debriefing.
- When clients have plans to harm a specific victim, warn the victim and notify the police.
- Review procedures for handling disruptive clients.

Usually, clients enter the anxiety phase because of stress, which can come from multiple sources, including jobs, relationships, health, and finances. Clients define stressful events; thus, counsellors cannot measure stress just by knowing the facts about a situation. What one client might see as an opportunity, another might experience as a threat. Kelleher (1997) describes the triggering event as an incident that pushes the potentially

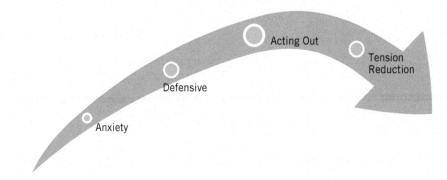

Figure 8.3 The Phases of Violence

violent person toward violence: "It is the proverbial 'straw that broke the camel's back,' and, like the straw, may often be perceived by others with far less significance than it's perceived by the perpetrator" (p. 11). Before clients see counsellors, they may already be feeling helpless and abandoned. Any counsellor or agency behaviour that the client views as provocative or rejecting may further propel the client toward violence. Counsellors may have to deny assistance, and clients may believe that they are denying them access to goods or services. These clients may perceive themselves as "losers" and look for ways to save face, including resistance, with statements such as "I don't have to put up with this treatment."

Individuals who are predisposed to violence respond to stress with increasing anger and anxiety. A person's emotional reaction can also influence whether he or she might become violent. Labig (1995) suggests that people who are prone to anger, hatred, and those who tend to blame others are at higher risk of becoming violent, while those who are more empathic are less likely.

Dealing with Threats   Counsellors need to take action when clients exhibit changes in their normal behaviour. This action could include referral for psychiatric assessment and re-evaluation of medication. Immediate crisis intervention might result in moving the client out of the environment where others might be injured, for example, a crowded waiting room. As well, long-term counselling might focus on anger management or relaxation training. The immediate goal is crisis management, but the long-term goal is crisis prevention. This interesting conclusion reached by Quinsey, Harris, Rick, and Cormier (1998) challenges one common misbelief: "encouraging angry individuals to relieve anger through catharsis (e.g., boxing, using a punching bag) is contraindicated because it may lead to increased hostility and aggression" (p. 204).

> ### SUCCESS TIP
>
> "When any type of threat [from a client] includes indirect or veiled references to things they might do, such as 'You'll be sorry' or 'Don't mess with me,' it is best to ask directly, 'What do you mean by that?' Ask exactly what the person is threatening to do. His elaboration will almost always be weaker than his implied threat. If, on the other hand, his explanation of the comment is actually an explicit threat, better to learn it now than to be uncertain later" (de Becker, 1997, p. 117).

Counsellors need to be attuned to their own fears and anxieties. Appropriate anxiety is a clue that the situation is escalating and that remedial action is necessary. De Becker (1997) argues that people have a basic intuition that tells them when all is not well, but that they often disregard the red flags of danger. It is only in the aftermath that they reflect and realize that they had sufficient information to make better choices but that they ignored it.

Phase 2: Defensive   This is a late warning phase with clear indicators that the person is about to lose control. The client may become more challenging and belligerent by making direct threats and provocations. The client has become irrational and clear warning indicators may be present, including clenching or raising of fists, rapid breathing, grasping objects to use as weapons, and showing signs of movement toward attack (e.g., grasping the arms of the chair and denoting that the client is about to rise and advance) (Shea, 1998; Sheafor & Horejsi, 2008).

At this point, it is crucial that counsellors refrain from reciprocating with the same aggressive behaviour that the client is using. This requires some self-discipline, as the counsellor's natural reaction might be to respond in kind, which only serves to escalate or precipitate violence. Decreased eye contact might be appropriate with some clients. As well, counsellors are wise to increase the physical distance between themselves and their clients since potentially violent persons may have an increased need for space. Note that physical contact, however well intentioned, should be avoided. Sometimes counsellors try to calm clients by touching their shoulders, but this is ill-advised as clients may interpret it as aggression.

During this phase, counsellors need to be self-disciplined and to model calmness. When counsellors stay calm, clients are more likely to emulate their composure. This calmness should be reflected in their voice and manner with slow, non-jargonistic language. Counsellors who speak calmly and avoid any loud or authoritarian tone have a greater chance of calming their anxious clients. On the other hand, counsellors who match their clients' defensiveness and anger exacerbate the situation and increase the possibility of violent retaliation. Rigid and authoritarian counsellor reactions may leave clients feeling pressured or trapped.

It is essential that counsellors maintain their own equilibrium and remain in control. They need to develop their capacity to monitor their own feelings and behaviour, including their ability to ask for help or to withdraw when they are not in control. Counsellors also need to resist any tendency to be baited by clients into angry confrontation or retaliation, which only escalates the crisis. If clients perceive that their counsellors are anxious and not in control, they may become more irrational.

Labig (1995) reminds us of the importance of emotional tone. He notes that a loud or aggressive voice can quickly precipitate retaliation, while a voice tone that is calm and supportive inhibits violence. Simply put, a threatening environment increases the risk of violence.

Basic communication and counselling skills are excellent tools both for preventing violence and for dealing with clients who are on the verge of losing control. In particular, active listening skills communicate that counsellors are willing to listen to and learn about clients' wants and needs. Counsellors should try to speak calmly and avoid any mannerisms that clients might interpret as threatening (e.g., touching a client, making a sudden movement, or invading a client's personal space). Encourage the client to sit and to be comfortable. Listen, empathize, paraphrase, and summarize while avoiding defensiveness. As a rule, respond to clients in the anxiety and defensive phases with supportive and empathic statements.

However, some clients may misinterpret empathy as an unwanted intrusion on personal privacy and react defensively. Counsellors should be alert to clients' reactions to certain topics or questions. This will help counsellors make intelligent decisions about when it is appropriate to challenge or confront, and when they should back off because the subject is agitating the client to a dangerous level.

The Power of Compromise   Violent clients often feel disempowered and disadvantaged. When counsellors promote compromise, they restore some balance of power in the relationship and show their willingness to reach a solution. Conversely, when counsellors argue with, threaten, or ignore the needs of their clients, the clients may become increasingly belligerent.

Compromise helps clients find a way to save face and retain their dignity. While counsellors have the responsibility to set appropriate limits, they must not argue with, ridicule, challenge, threaten, or unfairly criticize clients. The language used by the counsellor can help establish an atmosphere of compromise and mutual problem solving—for example, "Let's work together to find a solution we can both live with" and "I really do want to find a solution."

Client: (*Yelling loudly.*) I am sick and tired of getting the runaround.

Counsellor: (*Calmly.*) Your anger makes it clear to me how strongly you feel about this. I can see that this is an important issue for you, but I will be able to work better with you if you stay calm and don't threaten me. Let's see if there's another way to approach it.

Client: (*Pacing and yelling.*) Are you going to help me or not?

Counsellor: (*Calmly.*) I'm willing to work with you on the problem.

Client: (*Sits and stares intently.*)

Counsellor: I understand that you think that this is the best solution. I also appreciate your reasoning, but there are two of us here. We need to find a solution that both of us can live with.

Client: (*Loudly, but not yelling.*) I am trying to be reasonable!

Counsellor: Okay, I'm listening. I'd like to hear your ideas.

Hocker and Wilmot (1995) identify five principles for establishing effective collaboration: (1) join with the other, (2) control the process, not the people, (3) use productive communication, (4) be firm in your goals, flexible in your means, and (5) remain optimistic about finding solutions to your conflict (p. 212). They suggest a variety of means for operationalizing the principles, such as using "we" language to affirm common interests, actively listening even when you disagree, and persuading rather than coercing. As well, they emphasize the importance of separating the issues from the relationship and dealing with the important items one at a time. Such a collaborative approach requires that counsellors remain positive, creative, and constructive. The general goal must be "We, working together, can solve this problem that is confronting us" (Hocker & Wilmot, 1995, p. 205). Dubovsky and Weissberg (1986) underscore the importance of promoting collaboration. They contend that the client "protects himself from feeling powerless, inadequate and frightened by attempting to demonstrate how powerful and frightening he can be. His threatening behavior increases if he feels he is not being taken seriously" (p. 262).

SUCCESS TIP

If aggressive behaviour is escalating, the safety of others must be a priority. This might include evacuating the waiting room, removing objects that might be used as weapons, and seeking backup from other available staff.

Setting Limits Setting and enforcing reasonable limits makes it possible for counsellors and clients to continue working together. Failure to set limits reinforces acting-out behaviour, which if unchecked could lead to more violent and destructive consequences. In the defensive phase, clients may still respond to appropriate limits. Limits let clients know what will and will not be tolerated, but counsellors need to apply certain principles in setting limits. Counsellors should be specific and tell clients which behaviour is inappropriate since they may not be aware what is acceptable.

Moreover, they may not know how their behaviour is affecting others. Limits should include enforceable consequences, and counsellors should state the consequences of noncompliance.

Phase 3: Acting Out   At this stage, the client has lost control and has become assaultive. Protection of self and others is the primary goal. Ideally, agency procedures are operative, and counsellors who are dealing with such situations will receive immediate assistance from the staff team. Police intervention and restraint of the acting-out client may also be required. When dealing with acting-out clients, a team approach with a well-organized and trained staff is the preferred way to address the crisis. A team approach provides increased safety for everyone, including the client. A well-trained team may subdue violent clients before they injure themselves or others, but staff should be trained in techniques for physical restraint and control. The team members provide support and can act as witnesses if litigation should arise because of the incident.

Police Intervention   Counsellors should not hesitate to call the police if a client becomes too threatening or aggressive. No counsellor is expected to risk his or her life or endure physical assault as part of the job. Moreover, sometimes clients are unwilling or unable to constrain their hostility, and police or psychiatric restraint is essential for managing the crisis. Police intervention is particularly crucial when dealing with clients who have weapons. In addition, counsellors should not try to prevent a client who is determined to leave by blocking the exit. In general, counsellors who are assaulted by clients should consider laying criminal charges. This establishes the importance of clients' taking responsibility for their actions.

Never interview when you are alone in the office. Never enter a client's home when you know the client is talking about hurting someone.

Phase 4: Tension Reduction   The tension reduction phase is characterized by a gradual reduction in aggressive behaviour and a return to more rational behaviour. The client may still be driven by adrenalin, so it is important that counsellors proceed cautiously to avoid reactivating aggressive acting out.

Follow-up Counselling Interventions   Clients can be counselled to become alert to their own warning signs, such as "tenseness, sweating palms, a tightening of the stomach, pressure in the chest and a surge to the head" (Morrissey, 1998, p. 6). Once clients are aware of their own triggers, they can be counselled on appropriate diversionary tactics, such as employing relaxation techniques, taking time out, and using **assertiveness** and other behavioural response alternatives. Morrissey (1998) describes a technique that a counsellor used with a client who was on the verge of violence. The counsellor reassured the client "that he was there to help him and commended the client for coming to see him rather than acting on his feelings of rage. He also asked the client what was keeping him in control thus far and used that as proof to reinforce the fact that he could indeed control himself" (p. 6).

At the end of the tension reduction phase and after the client has returned to normal, the client may be mentally and physically exhausted and show signs of remorse and shame. Consequently, counselling can be directed toward helping the client use the experience as a learning opportunity—for example, to develop alternative responses for future similar stresses. Interview 8.2 provides an example.

Counsellors are well prepared to teach their clients techniques for resolving conflict and crises nonviolently. The skills of counselling are also, to some extent, the skills of effective everyday communication. Communication skill training equips clients with more choices for asserting their rights and respecting others. Assertiveness training can help clients express feelings in a nonaggressive manner. When clients are able to respond assertively, they establish an atmosphere of cooperation and conflict can be peacefully resolved. Often conflict is difficult for clients to settle because they are unable to see the perspectives or feelings of others in the conflict. Clients who learn empathy and other active listening skills are better able to compromise because they are less likely to judge their own behaviour as absolutely right and that of others as absolutely wrong.

Sometimes, long before violence erupts, counsellors intuitively feel that the situation is worsening. This feeling may be based on unconscious reactions to subtle cues and indicators. Counsellors and clients might find it useful to try to concretely identify these clues. Doing so will assist clients in becoming sensitive to those initial psychological responses that signal the imminent onset of the anxiety phase. Clients who become adept at recognizing early warning indicators are in a much better position to take early warning action, such as withdrawing from an explosive situation or switching to healthier problem-solving strategies.

Critical Incident Debriefing

An organization needs to have a mechanism in place for debriefing after a violent or hostile act. This enables the counsellor to restore a sense of equilibrium. It is important to remember that a critical or violent incident may also affect and traumatize staff who were not directly involved, including clerical, janitorial, and kitchen personnel; therefore, they should be involved in the debriefing.

Counsellors who have been assaulted or threatened with assault may be traumatized. They may experience symptoms such as recurrent images or thoughts of the event, distressing dreams, flashbacks, and intense stress when returning to the scene of the incident. There may be a marked decline in their ability to handle routine work tasks, and they may feel detached and isolated from colleagues. They may develop sleep difficulties and have difficulty concentrating. Frequently, they return to work in a state of hypervigilance, constantly expecting further trauma. Often, they describe themselves as "numb" and unable to enjoy activities that usually give them pleasure. Macdonald and Sirotich (2005) reviewed studies and reported that victims of client violence might experience the following:

- Troubled relationships (with colleagues and family)
- Reduced ability to function in the workplace
- More absenteeism
- Higher levels of burnout, depression, anxiety, and general irritability stemming from threats or abuse

When symptoms such as these are present, counsellors should consider obtaining medical assessment or professional counselling.

In the following example, the counsellor, a group home worker, is reviewing an incident with her client. The incident occurred two hours ago and was precipitated when the counsellor denied the client, a 16-year-old male, permission to meet with some of his friends later that night. The client threw his chair across the room and stormed out of the office while screaming obscenities.

Counsellor: I'm wondering if this is a good time to talk about what happened earlier today.

Client: It won't happen again. Can we just forget it ever happened?

Counsellor: You're right. We need to move on. However, I think it's important we both take a look at it to make some plans so it doesn't occur again. Okay?

Analysis: Whenever possible, it's important that clients be invited to review prior incidents.

Client: I guess I got a bit carried away.

Counsellor: I was scared.

Client: I'm sorry. I won't let it happen again.

Counsellor: I accept your apology.

Analysis: Often, violent or acting-out clients are so preoccupied with their own needs and fears that they don't realize the impact they have on others. By telling the client how she felt, the counsellor hopes to increase his capacity for empathy. Acceptance of her client's apology does not condone his behaviour, as would a statement such as "It's okay. Don't worry about it. No real harm was done."

Counsellor: It might be helpful for both of us to go over what happened to see how it might have been prevented.

Client: I was still upset from seeing my mother. When you said no, it was just too much.

Analysis: One goal of counselling is to help clients recognize their own early warning indicators that they are in danger of losing control.

Counsellor: It's never been easy for you to talk to your mom. You always seem to come back really wound up.

Analysis: Empathy confirms that feelings have been heard and understood.

Client: Yeah, those are the days that people should stay out of my face.

Counsellor: Good point. Sounds like you know that you need some time alone when you're stressed.

Client: You got it.

Analysis: The client rationalizes his behaviour, putting the responsibility on others. Without directly challenging the rationalization, the counsellor shifts the focus back to a client strength.

Counsellor: As we talk, I'm wondering what prevented you from taking that time. If you'd taken the time to cool off before approaching me, things would have been a lot different.

Client: Sure, I know I have to learn to control my temper, but once I get going I just can't seem to stop myself.

Counsellor: Put another way, your hope is to find a way to deal with your feelings so that you don't get angry and hurt someone.

Client: I don't know if that's possible.

Analysis: Feedback confrontation challenges the client to consider some new alternatives. The counsellor takes advantage of an opportunity to reframe the client's problem statement into a goal.

Counsellor: You've already shown me that you have some skill at doing this. You threw the chair and you said some awful things, but afterward you left the room without doing any more damage. This tells me that you have the ability to bring things under control.

Analysis: Acknowledgment of the client's restraint, however late, provides a base for further development. This recognizes the client's strengths by acknowledging and reinforcing nonaggressive behavioural alternatives.

Reflections:

■ How would you assess that the time is right to initiate a follow-up interview?
■ Suggest how anticipatory contracting might be used as a next step.

Youth Worker: What should a counsellor do if assaulted by a client?

Counsellor: There are many types of assaults ranging from verbal threats to physical attacks causing injury. All of them are frightening and potentially traumatic.

Youth Worker: We should not forget that any assault on a counsellor also impacts other workers in the agency, even those who were not present during the altercation. Their psychological needs should not be ignored or minimized. An assault on one worker is a reminder to others that they are also vulnerable. In some cases, the assaulted worker (or their colleagues) are traumatized. This can have serious repercussions for their personal and professional work.

Counsellor: Individuals may experience a myriad of emotions, including fear, anger, shame, denial, contempt for clients, or even guilt. All of them are normal; all of them need to be processed. People who work in the counselling field already know the benefit of the counselling process, and they should not hesitate to use counselling to deal with their own emotions. To do so is a sign of strength, not weakness. Debriefing with a trusted colleague or supervisor or using employee assistance services are possible options.

Youth Worker: A team debrief where individuals are encouraged to share their feelings about the incident is an important way to regroup. The team debrief should include all personnel in the setting, not just the professional counselling staff. It may be helpful to have an outside facilitator conduct the team debrief.

STUDENT: What should happen during the debrief?

Youth Worker: The basic goal of any counselling or team debrief is to re-establish a sense of control and safety. The debrief is an opportunity to share feelings and concerns. By doing so, individuals typically discover that others are affected in similar ways and the power of group support is mobilized.

Counsellor: In addition, re-examining the circumstances of the assault is important. A number of key questions should be addressed, including: Were there indicators of an escalating risk of violence that were missed? Were there aspects of the setting's structure or policy that contributed to the assault? Was there adequate sharing of information within the agency (e.g., history of violence, substance misuse, and non-compliance with psychiatric medications)? What changes are necessary to prevent further incidents? Exploring these questions can help the team to develop better procedures and confidence for handling future incidents.

Youth Worker: Since an assault increases peoples' feeling of vulnerability, it is important to monitor how it might affect relationships with other clients. For example, individuals, or even the entire setting, may overestimate the risks posed by the entire client population. This might result in excessive procedural rules or structural changes that impair the agency's overall effectiveness. Counsellors must also be wary of transferring unresolved feelings to other clients.

Counsellor: Good point. I know one worker who, after an assault at the agency, decided to leave his office door half-opened during interviews which compromised confidentiality. He also became very reluctant to address potentially sensitive issues fearing that it might arouse client anger or defensiveness. As a result, many of his counselling interviews remained superficial with opportunities for meaningful work passed over. Fortunately, an alert supervisor intervened with supportive supervision and referred the worker to an employee assistance counselling service.

Even when counsellors are not injured, the threat of violence can be just as traumatic. Typical responses may include helplessness and thoughts of leaving the profession. These feelings may develop immediately or emerge after a delay of months or even years. Consequently, it is important to debrief critical incidents to lessen shock, reduce isolation, and restore personal control. Team debriefing should take place as soon as possible after the incident. Debriefing should be conducted by an objective third party in a safe setting. It should be held as soon as possible after the critical incident, usually within 24 to 72 hours, to minimize the effects of any trauma that victims or witnesses may be experiencing. This is important in promoting a return to the normal routine of the agency. A typical debriefing session is like a counselling interview. The debriefing should reinforce team interdependence. Sometimes counsellors are reluctant to ask colleagues for assistance, believing that asking for help is a sign of incompetence. One goal of a debriefing is to develop a staff culture in which asking for help is understood

critical incident debriefing: A team meeting held to defuse the impact of a violent or traumatic event such as an assault on a staff member. Debriefing assists workers to normalize and deal with the feelings that may be aroused because of the event. As well, debriefing is used to review and revise preventive and crisis intervention procedures.

as a sign of strength rather than a weakness. A **critical incident debriefing** generally has the following elements:

1. All team members are invited to share feelings and reactions about the current or prior incidents. Active listening can be used to promote this process. This helps individuals who were threatened or assaulted to "normalize" their own reactions. Counsellors should require little persuasion about the benefits of talking about their feelings. They might be reminded that sharing feelings is something they routinely ask of their clients. Helping team members manage feelings is the major objective of the debriefing. At this time, it is important to identify the potential physical and emotional reactions that staff may experience. As well, information regarding services, such as employee assistance programs (EAPs) that are available to staff who need additional help to manage their emotions, should be detailed.

2. The team conducts a post-mortem on the violent event. A thorough analysis of what transpired is used to review and reinforce procedures for dealing with violent clients. An important question for the team to consider is "What, if anything, could we have done to prevent this incident?" For example, the team can explore whether any early warning indicators of pending violence were overlooked. They can investigate whether there were things that individuals or the agency did or did not do that contributed to the client's behaviour.

3. The team debriefing is an important "teachable moment" when staff are highly motivated to develop their skills. It is a chance to explore alternative responses that might have been used at all stages of the critical incident. Role-play and simulations can be used to practise alternative responses. This step helps empower individuals, and the team by moving them away from any tendency to feel helpless.

COUNSELLING ANGRY AND VIOLENT CLIENTS

The obvious counselling goal is to assist these clients to develop skills and responses that do not harm others. Safety is the top priority. While there is no single best strategy, the following intervention choices can be tailored to meet the needs of individual clients.

Prevention

Sometimes, long before violence erupts, counsellors intuitively feel that the situation is worsening. This feeling may be based on unconscious reactions to subtle cues and indicators. Counsellors and clients might find it useful to try to concretely identify these clues. Doing so will assist clients in becoming sensitive to those initial psychological responses that signal the imminent onset of the anxiety phase. Clients who become adept at recognizing early warning indicators are in a much better position to take early warning action, such as withdrawing from an explosive situation or switching to healthier problem-solving strategies.

Assertiveness Training

Assertiveness: Assertiveness involves exercising personal rights, including the ability to express feelings and ideas without guilt or undue anxiety, without denying the rights of others

Assertiveness involves exercising personal rights, including the ability to express feelings and ideas without guilt or undue anxiety, without denying the rights of others (Shebib, 1997). It requires respect and empathy for other people. Assertiveness training helps clients express feelings in a nonaggressive manner. When clients are able to respond assertively, they establish an atmosphere of cooperation where conflict can be peacefully resolved. It is clearly distinguished from aggression, which involves the use of power, domination, and intimidation to achieve one's goals, and passivity, which foregoes personal rights and needs. Counsellors can help clients develop assertive communication skills such as active listening, especially empathy. Some clients know how to respond assertively, but low self-esteem or fear inhibits them from making appropriate assertive choices. Cognitive behavioural counselling can be used to address these issues. Strategies such as relaxation training, deep breathing, and mindfulness can be used to assist clients to deal with anxiety.

The skills of counselling are also, to some extent, the skills of effective everyday communication. This puts counsellors in a good position to teach their clients techniques for resolving conflict and crises nonviolently. Communication skill training equips clients with more choices for asserting their rights and respecting others. Often conflict is difficult for clients to settle because they are unable to see the perspectives or feelings of others in the conflict. Clients who learn empathy and other active listening skills are better able to compromise because they are less likely to judge their own behaviour as absolutely right and that of others as absolutely wrong.

Cognitive Behavioural Counselling (Therapy)

As discussed in Chapter 7, Cognitive Behavioural Therapy (CBT) helps clients to identify and manage unhelpful thinking patterns such as catastrophizing or blaming others. CBT can also focus on helping clients learn alternate behavioural choices which, when practised, will lessen any tendency to default to the anger mode.

Anger Management

Anger is a normal emotion and the appropriate expression of anger can deepen relationships. Out of control anger can destroy relationships. Anger management skills include recognizing and managing triggers (e.g., avoiding problematic situations). Counsellors can use role playing and modeling as a way to help clients develop alternate responses. They can also teach breathing and relaxation techniques.

Substance Misuse Interventions

The use of illicit substances is strongly linked to increased violence, so intervention targeting this important area is crucial. A wide range of choices include 12-step programs, residential treatment, CBT, harm reduction, treatment of co-occurring mental disorders, traditional healing practices, exercise, nutrition, spirituality, and many other strategies have proven effective.

Psychiatric Intervention

Psychiatric assessment can determine whether medication is warranted. Antidepressant or antianxiety medication may be useful as an adjunct to counselling. Medication alone is not recommended.

Reduction of Stressors

Resolution of issues related to unemployment, poverty, relationship dysfunction, and housing are important targets for intervention.

Counselling Victims

Counsellors may be called upon to deal with domestic violence where the majority of victims are women. A 2015 survey by the Canadian Women's Foundation provides startling statistics that underscore the extent of the problem for women in Canada:

- Fifty percent of women over 16 report having experienced at least one incident of physical or sexual violence since the age of 16.

- Every six days a woman in Canada is killed by her intimate partner.

- On any given day in Canada, more than 3,300 women (along with their 3,000 children) are forced to sleep in an emergency shelter to escape domestic violence.

- Each year, over 40,000 arrests result from domestic violence—that's about 12 percent of all violent crime in Canada. Since only 22 percent of all incidents are reported to the police, the real number is much higher.

- As of 2010, there were 582 known cases of missing or murdered Aboriginal women in Canada.

- In a 2009 Canadian national survey, women reported 460,000 incidents of sexual assault in just one year, but only about 10 percent of all sexual assaults are reported to police.

- More than one in ten Canadian women say they have been stalked.

When counsellors are working with victims of violence, the number one concern is to help them take steps to ensure their safety. Clients should be made aware of their rights and options, including use of police (phone 911), restraining orders, and transition homes. When dealing with perpetrators of victims of spousal violence, counsellors may face the challenge of dealing with cultural or religious ideologies that favour patriarchal dominance and control. Further, cultural norms may preclude disclosure and the victim, fearful of judgment and shame, may suffer the abuse in private. Counsellors might explore whether there are culture-specific resources such as support groups or community leaders that might be of assistance.

For many and varied reasons, women may choose to stay in abusive relationships. Counsellors need to remain empathic and suspend any tendency to impose judgment or to push women to leave. While counsellors can help women understand the inherent risks of remaining in the home, they need to support the decision to stay or leave as belonging to the woman, even where this choice seems to defy logic.

SUCCESS TIP

A common, repeating pattern (cycle), often emerges in abusive relationships. This cycle of abuse or violence develops through four stages: (1) build-up of tension, (2) abusive incident (verbal, emotional, physical, and sexual), (3) abuser remorse, and (4) honeymoon period (when all is calm).

≫ BRAIN BYTE | Children and Abuse

The brains of children who are abused (or witness abuse) can be profoundly affected and lead to a wide range of problems, including emotional regulation (damage to the amygdala, and changes in brain chemistry affecting neurotransmitters such as epinephrine, dopamine, serotonin, and the stress hormone cortisol), learning deficits such as difficulty concentrating/focusing, language acquisition, organizing, loss of interest (damage to the cortex and hippocampus), sleep disturbances, relationship issues, and low self-esteem (American Psychological Association, 2015; Kendall, 2002).

SUMMARY

- Resistance is a common defensive reaction that interferes with or delays the process of counselling. It may be evident in a variety of ways, such as failure to cooperate with the basic routine of counselling, subtle or direct attacks, passivity, and non-verbal cues.

- It is important for counsellors to evaluate their own feelings and behaviour as well as aspects of the agency that might be triggering resistance.

- Effective confrontation helps clients come to a different level of understanding, behaving, or feeling.

- Clients may become violent or threatening for a number of reasons. Although it is difficult to predict with certainty which clients will become violent, some risk factors can be isolated. The best predictor of violent behaviour is a history of violence; substance abuse is also a common variable. Other factors that counsellors should consider when assessing risk are age, gender, and personality characteristics.

- Effective management of potentially violent situations includes prevention and appropriate responses to the four phases of violence: anxiety, defensiveness, acting out, and tension reduction. It is important to debrief critical incidents to lessen shock, reduce isolation, and restore personal control. Team debriefing should take place as soon after the incident as possible. It should provide an opportunity for people to talk about their feelings and to review what went wrong.

- Counselling interventions include a focus on safety, assertiveness training, anger management, cognitive behavioural counselling, harm reduction, psychiatric assessment and treatment, and support for victims of spousal abuse.

EXERCISES

Self-Awareness

1. Self-evaluate your personal comfort when confronting others.
   a. What people would you have difficulty confronting?
   b. Do you avoid confronting?
   c. Think of times when it was reasonable to confront but you didn't. What prevented you from confronting?
   d. Finish the following sentence: When I confront, I feel . . .

2. Review your experiences dealing with individuals who are angry, resistant, or potentially violent. What is your natural reaction when someone's anger starts to escalate? Do you tend to fight back? Or do you withdraw? What aspects of your experience will help you deal effectively with difficult situations? What aspects will impede your ability?

3. Reflect on your thoughts, feelings, and behaviour when you were forced or pressured to do something against your will. How might your reactions help you to understand and work with clients who are "involuntary"?

Skill Practice

1. Work with a colleague to role-play an appropriate counsellor confrontation in each of the following situations:

   a. Youth who has hygiene problems
   b. Colleague who has, in your opinion, behaved in an unprofessional manner
   c. Client who consistently arrives late for appointments

2. Evaluate the effectiveness of each of the confrontations that follow; suggest improvements:
   a. Try to do better next time.
   b. You're an idiot.
   c. You're saying that you're okay, yet you're crying.
   d. Grow up and act your age.
   e. As long as you continue to act like a doormat, you're going to get abused. If you're serious about protecting yourself, leave him.

3. Interview counsellors from different settings regarding their experiences with violent or potentially violent clients. Discuss strategies that they have found effective.

4. Work in a small group. Assume that you are members of an inner-city needle exchange centre. Develop detailed policies and procedures for dealing with violent and potentially violent clients.

5. Suppose you review the file on your next client, a 16-year-old male, and discover that he was loud and abusive with his previous counsellor. What are some possible explanations for this client's behaviour? Suggest some strategies for working with this client.

6. Work in a small group to explore the potential benefits and risks of each of the following:

   a. Having an unlisted phone number

   b. Making home visits alone

   c. Making home visits only when accompanied by a colleague

   d. Conducting joint interviews for potentially hostile clients

   e. Using only your first name with clients

   f. Knowing that a client has a history of violence

   g. Interviewing a client with a police officer present

   h. Refusing to see a client with a history of violence

   i. Striking a client to defend yourself

   j. Calling the police

   k. Warning an intended victim

   l. Seeing a client who has been drinking

7. The setting is a residential centre for youth. Your last interview with Peter was particularly distressing. It ended with his throwing the chair against the wall, swearing loudly at you, and then storming out of your office, slamming the door in the process and breaking one of the hinges. This incident seems to have been precipitated by his frustration at not being allowed to smoke in the centre. Develop a plan for dealing with Peter during the next interview and in the coming months. Suggest specific leads you can use in the next interview. Consider three possible scenarios:

   a. He displays remorse over what happened.

   b. He downplays the serious nature of the incident.

   c. He's still angry.

8. Work with one or two colleagues to practise assertiveness:

   a. Expressing anger

   b. Saying "no" to a request

   c. Sharing positive feelings such as love or affection

   d. Accepting a compliment

   e. Expressing disagreement

   (Suggestion: Role play aggressive and passive responses for each of the preceding scenarios, then discuss how assertiveness differs).

9. Conduct an extended role play based on the following situation: You have just begun a new job as a youth worker in a residential group home. Your client is a 14-year-old boy who has been in care since he was six years old. During that time, he has lived in over 17 foster homes. After meeting you, he says, "Why should I trust you? You guys are all alike. You make all sorts of promises, but nothing ever happens. This is just a job for you, but it's my life. Next month, there will probably be another new worker."

Concepts

1. Research legal and ethical codes to explore your responsibility to notify intended victims of violence. Talk to counsellors and agencies for their opinions.

2. Write a short concept paper that describes what you believe are the elements of effective confrontation.

3. Hamachek (1982) says, "Do not confront another person if you do not wish to increase your involvement with that individual" (p. 230). Develop a rationale that supports this statement.

4. How can assertively expressed anger deepen relationships?

WEBLINKS

The Crisis Prevention Institute provides information about training programs and resources for nonviolent crisis information

https://www.crisisprevention.com/Specialties/Nonviolent-Crisis-Intervention

Canadian Centre for Occupational Health and Safety provides information about violence and violence prevention

www.ccohs.ca/oshanswers/psychosocial/violence.html

This website provides access and links to a wide range of health and emotional issues (use the search feature to find material on violence).

www.mayoclinic.com

A comprehensive Canadian study on mental illness and violence

www.phac-aspc.gc.ca/mh-sm/pubs/mental_illness/index-eng.php

Canadian Centre for Threat Assessment and Trauma Response offers information and training for responding to threats and potentially violent situations

http://www.cctatr.com

Chapter 9
Mental Disorders and Substance Misuse

LEARNING OBJECTIVES

- Understand the nature and breadth of mental illness in Canada.

- Explain the structure, use, and limitations of the *Diagnostic and Statistical Manual of Mental Disorders* (DSM).

- Describe the characteristics of and treatment for major mental disorders, including schizophrenia, mood disorders, anxiety disorders, eating disorders, and personality disorders.

- Explore the mental health issues of children and youth.

- Describe the nature and impact of substance abuse.

- Identify best-practice approaches for working with clients with substance use problems, including those with co-occurring disorders.

- Identify suicide warning signs and strategies for dealing with clients who are suicidal.

MENTAL HEALTH IN CANADA

Attempts to treat mental illness date back thousands of years, but they were typically inhumane and cruel when judged by today's standards. Historically, treatment of people with mental disorders was barbaric and ineffective with practices such as exorcising, burning "witches," bloodletting, whipping, starving, imprisoning, or housing in over-crowded "snake pits" or insane asylums. During the twentieth and twenty-first centuries, especially in the last 50 years, mental disorders have gradually been recognized as health problems, and more humanitarian practices have been developed to replace procedures based on superstition, fear, and ignorance.

Over the past 70 years in Canada, there has been a major and continuous shift in the delivery of mental health services from long-term treatment in hospitals to treatment of patients in the community, a process known as deinstitutionalization. Today, the population of mental hospitals in Canada is only a small fraction of what it was 40 years ago (Sealy & Whitehead, 2004) and some, such as Riverview Hospital in Coquitlam, British Columbia, which once housed thousands of patients, are virtually closed. However, there are some proposals to reopen abandoned facilities based on models of treatment different from the traditional "warehousing" methods of the past. The development and refinement of a range of psychotropic drugs has been the driving force behind deinstitutionalization because these drugs enable patients to control hallucinations and behaviour that might otherwise preclude their living in the community. However, this move toward community treatment has often been poorly funded, and new problems for those with mental disorders have resulted, particularly homelessness (Davis, 2006). Deinstitutionalization in Canada left many people with mental illness in communities with inadequate treatment, support, and outreach. While no one would argue for a return to the "warehouses" of the nineteenth and early twentieth centuries, it is clear that many people discharged from the mental hospitals are now living in dire conditions, often in poverty-stricken inner cities such as the Downtown Eastside in Vancouver. Table 9.1 outlines some facts about mental health in Canada. The Mental Health Commission of Canada (2012) proposed an overhaul of the mental health system that called for broad changes, including the promotion of mental health throughout life, suicide prevention, support of recovery through use of optimum integrated services, removal of systemic barriers to work and education, and the strengthening of services to Northerners, First Nations, and Inuit peoples.

Mental Health Assessment

The purpose of psychiatric diagnosis is not to label clients but to match diagnosis to treatment decisions based on the best scientific evidence regarding which treatments are likely to be most effective with each disorder (Corcoran & Walsh, 2009). Psychiatric assessment and diagnosis involves (ideally) an in-depth interview, including a thorough history of the person's situation. Physical examinations, including brain scans, electro-encephalograms (EEGs), and lab tests, may be used to rule out organic illness, which can cause psychiatric symptoms. Psychological tests may be used to assess thinking, personality, and other variables. In addition, families and friends are an important source of information, particularly when clients are denying the presence of psychiatric symptoms.

Psychiatric diagnosis is influenced by cultural and societal values. For example, at various times in history, homosexuality has been considered both an aberration and a gift. It is no longer considered a mental disorder.

There may be vast differences among individuals with the same mental disorder. Psychological, social, and biological variables influence how illness manifests in each

TABLE 9.1 Mental Health: Canadian Facts

- One in five Canadians of all educational backgrounds, income levels, and cultures will experience a mental illness or substance misuse problem during their lifetime.
- Most mental illnesses begin in adolescence and young adulthood.
- Mental illness arises from a complex interaction of biological, genetic, personality, and environmental factors.
- Social and workplace pressures, poverty, substance abuse, and learned behavioural and thinking patterns can influence the onset and outcome of mental illness.
- Studies have shown that at least 23 percent and as many as 67 percent of homeless people have a mental illness.
- During any one-year period:
  - Over 8 percent of the Canadian population experience a mood disorder
  - 0.3 percent experience schizophrenia
  - 12 percent experience an anxiety disorder
  - Almost 2.5 percent experience an eating disorder
  - One in ten people experience some disability from a diagnosable mental disorder.
- In Canada during 2001–2002, there were almost 200, 000 psychiatric hospital admissions with an average stay of 43 days—over 8 million patient days.
- More hospital beds in Canada (8 percent) are filled with persons with schizophrenia than with any other condition.
- Mental illness costs the healthcare system as much as $7 billion, while the annual total impact of mental health (healthcare, lost productivity) exceeds $51 billion.
- As many as one-third of the homeless have a mental disorder.
- Approximately 1 percent of Canadians will experience bipolar disorder.
- At least 2 percent of all deaths are from suicide.
- Personality disorders affect between 6 percent and 9 percent (estimated) of the Canadian population.
- Suicide accounts for 24 percent of all deaths among those 15 to 24 years of age and 16 percent among those aged 25 to 44 years.
- Psychiatric problems are the second leading cause of hospital admissions among those 20 to 44 years old.
- Most mental illness can be treated.
- Best-practice intervention favours treatment in the community using a variety of counselling interventions, occupational therapy, and medication.

Sources: British Columbia Schizophrenia Society, 2008; Centre for Addiction and Mental Health, 2017; Corcoran & Walsh, 2009; Davis, 2006; Government of Canada, 2017a; Health Canada, 2002a; NIMH, 2012; Public Health Agency of Canada, 2002; Regehr & Glancy, 2010; and Statistics Canada, 2005.

person. In addition, people with mental disorders may have concurrent problems, such as poverty, substance abuse, and social or relationship difficulties. A co-occurring disorder is present when a person has both a substance abuse problem or addiction and a psychiatric disorder.

Psychiatric diagnosis is made by a physician, preferably a psychiatrist, or a psychologist who is trained in clinical assessment. Some jurisdictions allow social workers who have completed considerable training and supervised experience to make a diagnosis. Everyone who works in the field should be alert to signs and symptoms that warrant a referral for medical and psychiatric assessment. Significant warning signs include: hallucinations, delusions, identity confusion, memory loss, paranoia, inappropriate anxiety, euphoria or sadness, mood swings, eating and body image problems, obsessions and compulsions, self-harm (e.g., cutting), and substance misuse.

The Diagnostic and Statistical Manual of Mental Disorders (DSM)

Diagnostic and Statistical Manual of Mental Disorders: Published by the American Psychiatric Association, it is used by psychologists, psychiatrists, and other psychotherapists to classify and diagnose mental disorders.

The *Diagnostic and Statistical Manual of Mental Disorders* (DSM), published by the American Psychiatric Association, is used by psychologists, psychiatrists, and other psychotherapists throughout the United States, Canada, and many other countries to classify and diagnose mental disorders. **DSM** does not include guidance or information on treatment. In Europe and some other countries, the International Classification of Diseases–10 (ICD–10) is used. The first edition, known as DSM-I, was published in 1952, and it was largely based on psychoanalytic principles. DSM-I listed 106 diagnoses and with each subsequent revision, the number increased to the current number of almost 300.

With the publication of the third edition in 1980, psychoanalytic theory was abandoned in favour of a system based on diagnostic criteria. The criteria were researched and developed to help increase reliability—the probability that different clinicians would assess a client with the same diagnostic result or conclusion regarding a person's mental disorder.

DSM-III and DSM-IV used a multiaxial system (five axes) to facilitate a more comprehensive assessment.

- *Axis I and II:* to classify clinical disorders, with Axis II reserved for personality disorders and mental retardation
- *Axis III:* to report relevant medical conditions such as hypothyroidism (which can cause depression) that affect a mental disorder
- *Axis IV:* to report significant stressors such as job and housing problems that might be contributing to the mental disorder
- *Axis V: Global Assessment of Functioning Scale (GAF):* used to score on a scale of 0–100 an individual's highest level of functioning in three major areas: social functioning, occupational functioning, and psychological functioning. Predictably, people who have a higher level of functioning before their illness generally do better than those with a lower level (Saddock & Saddock, 2004).

DSM-5 DSM-5, the latest edition, was published in late spring, 2014. It contains a number of significant changes including the following:

1. The traditional Roman numeral has been dropped and subsequent revisions will be identified as DSM-5.1, DSM-5.2, and so on.

2. The multiaxial system introduced in DSM-III has been eliminated, and all disorders are now classified in a single section with 22 chapters.

3. Chapters are organized with a lifespan approach, beginning with disorders that are most likely diagnosed in childhood.

4. Asperger's syndrome has been eliminated.

5. Revised model for classifying substance use disorders, which also includes the addition of gambling disorder

6. New disorders: hoarding and disruptive mood dysregulation

7. The archaic term "mental retardation" has been replaced by intellectual disability and intellectual developmental disorder

Appropriate Uses of the DSM   The overview in this chapter is a brief introduction to the basic structure of the manual. Counsellors should use the DSM classification system as a diagnostic tool only if they have appropriate specialized clinical training. Typically, individuals who use the DSM in their counselling practice are licensed psychiatrists or those with graduate degrees in counselling or psychology. Untrained practitioners should not attempt to make psychiatric diagnoses.

However, all counsellors should have a thorough knowledge of mental disorders and their effect on individuals and families. At the very least, they should be able to recognize behavioural, emotional, and cognitive difficulties that suggest the need for further assessment (see Figure 9.1). The DSM contains valuable information regarding variations in culture, age, and gender with respect to particular mental disorders. The manual also provides counsellors with reference material on the prevalence of mental disorders, including lifetime risk, the typical patterns of disorders, and data on the frequency of specified disorders among biological family members.

Figure 9.1   Signs of a Potential Mental Disorder

CAUTION: The presence of one or more of these warning signs does not mean the individual has a mental disorder; however, they may signal the need for a professional assessment to assess medical or psychiatric illness.

Definition of a Mental Disorder DSM-5 defines a mental disorder as follows:

> A mental disorder is a syndrome characterized by clinically significant disturbance in an individual's cognition, emotion regulation, or behavior that reflects a dysfunction in the psychological, biological, or developmental processes underlying mental functioning. Mental disorders are usually associated with significant distress in social, occupational, or other important activities. An expectable or culturally approved response to a common stressor or loss, such as the death of a loved one, is not a mental disorder. Socially deviant behavior (e.g., political, religious, or sexual) and conflicts that are primarily between the individual and society are not mental disorders unless the deviance or conflict results from a dysfunction in the individual, as described above (American Psychiatric Association, 2013, p.20).

> Unlike medical disorders such as diabetes, there are no clear lab tests that help clinicians to diagnose mental disorders. Consequently, mental health clinicians must rely on DSM-5 criteria and their judgement to determine if the DSM threshold for a mental disorder has been reached—"significant distress in social, occupational, or other important activities" (American Psychiatric Association, 2013, p.20).

There can be significant differences among individuals with the same diagnosis. One person with schizophrenia may suffer debilitating effects and his or her behaviour may present as bizarre, but another may respond to medication to the point where he or she functions "normally," with no one suspecting that this person has a mental disorder. In addition to the severity of the disorder, other factors, such as age of onset, presence of social supports, availability of treatment, and willingness to follow treatment regimes, affect how well people cope.

SUCCESS TIP

Everyone can have intense emotions and thoughts when dealing with stress. These reactions should not be confused with a mental disorder. A diagnosis of a mental disorder can only be justified when these reactions happen over an extended period, and there is significant impairment of a person's ability to function in daily life.

Critique of the DSM-5 Even before it was published, DSM-5 attracted a high level of criticism. Among the most vocal was Dr. Allen Frances, author of *Saving Normal: An Insider's Revolt Against Out-of-Control Psychiatric Diagnosis, DSM-5, Big Pharma, and the Medicalization of Ordinary Life*. Frances, chair of the task force that compiled DSM IV argued that the new DSM-5 will "lead to massive overdiagnosis and harmful over-medication" with new or sharply revised mental disorders such as disruptive mood dysregulation disorder, medicalizing normal grief, minor neurocognitive disorder, and many others.

The DSM, however, useful as a tool for intellectually understanding mental disorders, is based on the medical model of diagnosis with an emphasis on symptoms and pathology. Counselling is primarily concerned with individuals in a social context, with an emphasis on helping them to deal with relationship problems, crisis events, difficulties related to inadequate resources, and problems dealing with organizations such as schools or government welfare offices. Effective counsellors adopt a strengths approach to problem solving that assumes the power of individuals to overcome adversity. With a strengths perspective, they emphasize "human resilience—the skills, abilities, knowledge, and insight that people accumulate over time as they struggle to surmount adversity and meet life challenges" (Corcoran & Walsh, 2009, p. 10). They endeavour to find and respect the successes, assets, and resources of people, including those resources available within their culture such as sweat lodges and other healing rituals. While Compton and Galaway (2004) recognize the advantages of the DSM in terms of its wide use and common language for professionals, they also urge caution, reminding us that:

- Many phenomena included as mental disorders are more usefully explained in social, economic, or environmental terms.
- Psychiatric labels often lead to lifetime stigmatization.
- Diagnostic reliability remains suspect (p. 196).

Lloyd Sederer, medical director of the New York State Office of Mental Health offers this succinct comment on the value of the controversial DSM:

> A diagnostic manual of mental disorders cannot be eluded. Clinicians need specific ways of declaring what they observe to be one condition or another so they can speak to each other and to patients and families. Researchers need reliable diagnoses to study whether treatments work, and the course and prognosis of diseases (Sederer, 2012.)

SUCCESS TIP

Most practitioners as well as people with mental disorders and their families will find much more useful and user-friendly information on psychiatric illness through organizations such as the Canadian Mental Health Association (chma.ca) or the Canadian Centre for Addiction and Mental Health (camh.ca) than they will from the DSM. Both sites provide comprehensive information and advice on specific illness, medications, treatment, and support for recovery, not just treatment of symptoms.

Structure of the DSM   DSM-5 organizes mental disorders under 20 major chapters with each diagnostic class further subdivided into specific disorders (APA, 2013). The chapters are organized based on a developmental lifespan, starting with disorders first diagnosed in childhood, then progressing to adult disorders. Table 9.2 provides an overview of the structure.

Major Mental Disorders

This section provides only a very brief synopsis of some of the most common mental disorders that counsellors are likely to encounter, including schizophrenia, mood disorders, anxiety disorders, eating disorders, and personality disorders.

Schizophrenia   According to the Schizophrenia Society of Canada (2009), **schizophrenia** is a chronic (continuing) mental disorder affecting about 1 percent of the population. In rare cases, children can develop schizophrenia, but it usually starts in the late teens or early twenties for men, and in the twenties and early thirties for women. Although the exact cause remains unknown, it is believed that the disease is a biochemical brain disorder involving suspect neurotransmitters such as dopamine and serotonin. The children of a parent who has schizophrenia are 10 times more likely to develop the disorder compared to children of a parent who does not have it (National Institute of Mental Health [NIMH], 2012). Schizophrenia is a chronic, lifelong illness with no cure; however, it can be treated, and most people are able to recover and continue with their lives. Nevertheless, an estimated one of every ten people with the illness dies by suicide (NIMH, 2012).

> schizophrenia: A chronic mental disorder involving symptoms such as hallucinations, delusions, disordered thinking, and social isolation.

Contrary to popular opinion, people with schizophrenia do not have split personalities, like Dr. Jekyll and Mr. Hyde. Furthermore, although some once accepted it as truth, parents do not cause schizophrenia. The current perspective on the disorder is that it is caused by an imbalance of the complex, interrelated chemical systems of the brain (NIMH, 2012), but there may be no single cause. The symptoms of schizophrenia vary among individuals, sometimes dramatically. The symptoms are commonly classified as

TABLE 9.2 DSM-5 Structure

Major Category	Specific Disorders Under This Category
Neurodevelopmental disorders	• Intellectual; communication; autism spectrum; attention deficit/hyperactivity; learning; motor
Schizophrenia spectrum and other psychotic disorders	• Schizotypal personality, delusional; brief psychotic; substance-induced psychotic; catatonic; schizophreniform; schizoaffective
Bipolar and related disorders	• Bipolar I; bipolar II; cyclothymic; substance induced bipolar
Depressive disorders	• Disruptive mood dysregulation disorder; major depressive disorder; persistent depressive disorder (dysthymic) premenstrual dysphoric disorder; substance/medication-induced depressive disorder
Anxiety disorders	• Separation anxiety; selective mutism; specific phobia; social anxiety; panic; agoraphobia; generalized anxiety; substance induced
Obsessive-compulsive and related disorders	• Obsessive-compulsive; body dysmorphic; hoarding; hair pulling (trichotillomania); excoriation/skin picking; substance induced
Trauma and stressor-related disorders	• Reactive attachment; disinhibited social engagement; post-traumatic stress; acute stress disorder; adjustment
Dissociative disorders	• Dissociative identity; dissociative amnesia depersonalization/derealization
Somatic symptom disorders	• Somatic symptom; illness anxiety; conversion; psychological factors affecting medical conditions; factitious
Feeding and eating disorders	• Pica; rumination; avoidant restrictive food intake; anorexia nervosa; bulimia nervosa; binge eating
Elimination disorders	• Enuresis, encopresis
Sleep–wake disorders	• Insomnia; hypersomnolence; narcolepsy; sleep apnea; central sleep apnea; sleep-related hypoventilation; circadian rhythm sleep wake; disorder of arousal; nightmare; rapid eye movement sleep behaviour; restless leg; substance induced
Sexual dysfunctions	• Delayed ejaculation; erectile; female orgasmic; female sexual interest/arousal disorder; genito-pelvic pain penetration disorder; male hypoactive sexual desire; premature ejaculation; substance induced
Gender dysphoria	• Gender dysphoria in children; gender dysphoria in adolescents or adults
Disruptive, impulse control, and conduct disorders	• Oppositional defiant; intermittent explosive; conduct; antisocial personality disorder: pyromania; kleptomania
Substance use and addictive disorders	• Alcohol; caffeine; cannabis; hallucinogen; inhalant; opioid; sedative hypnotic; stimulant; tobacco; unknown substance; gambling
Neurocognitive disorders	• Delirium; mild & major neurocognitive (e.g., Alzheimer's, vascular neurocognitive, traumatic brain injury, due to HIV infection)
Personality disorders	• Paranoid; schizoid; schizotypal; antisocial; borderline; histrionic; narcissistic; avoidant; dependent; obsessive-compulsive
Paraphilic disorders	• Voyeuristic; exhibitionistic; frotteuristic; sexual masochism; sexual sadism; pedophillic; fetishistic
Conditions for further study (further research encouraged with possibility of inclusion in future editions of DSM)	• Attenuated psychosis syndrome; depressive episodes with short-duration hypomania; persistent complex bereavement; caffeine use disorder; Internet gambling disorder; neurobehavioural disorder associated with prenatal alcohol exposure; non-suicidal self-injury; suicidal behaviour

Source: Based on Diagnostic and Statistical Manual of Mental Disorders (DSM-5®), American Psychiatric Association

positive symptoms: Symptoms of psychosis that include hallucinations, delusions, bizarre behaviour, agitation, thought disorder, disorganized speech and behaviour, and catatonic behaviour. (See also *negative symptoms*.)

positive or negative. **Positive symptoms** may include hallucinations, delusions, bizarre behaviour, agitation, thought disorder, disorganized speech and behaviour, and catatonic behaviour. **Negative symptoms** include blunted or flattened affect, poverty of speech, emotional and social withdrawal, lack of pleasure (anhedonia), passivity, difficulty in abstract thinking, and lack of goal-directed behaviour (Ralph, 2003). Antipsychotic medications (neuroleptics) are the most effective way of treating the positive symptoms of schizophrenia.

There are a wide variety of early warning signs of schizophrenia, including noticeable social withdrawal, deteriorating personal hygiene, irrational behaviour, sleep disturbances, extreme reactions, inappropriate laughter, cutting or strange use of words, and many others (for a more complete list, see British Columbia Schizophrenia Society, 2008, p. 6).

negative symptoms: Symptoms of psychosis that include blunted or flattened affect, poverty of speech, emotional and social withdrawal, lack of pleasure (anhedonia), passivity, difficulty in abstract thinking, and lack of goal-directed behaviour. (See also *positive symptoms*.)

SUCCESS TIP

Psychotropic medication, where warranted, is only the first step in treatment. After medication, counsellors play a key role in assisting clients to manage the negative symptoms of schizophrenia and other mental disorders. This is crucial since negative symptoms can be far more disruptive for people with mental disorders and their families than positive symptoms. Counsellors can also educate families about negative symptoms, which will help them to realize that these are symptoms of the disorder, not the result of lack of willpower. (Velligan & Alps, 2008).

Hallucinations   There are wide variations in the symptoms of persons with schizophrenia. Most sufferers, however, experience **hallucinations**, usually auditory but sometimes visual or olfactory (related to smell). These hallucinations may be voices that tell clients what to do (**command hallucinations**), or they may be visions of things that do not exist. Persons with command hallucinations telling them to harm themselves or others are dangerous risks for suicide, homicide, or other violent behaviour (Saddock & Saddock, 2004).

hallucination: A false or distorted sensory perception such as hearing, seeing, tasting, touching, or smelling what others do not.

command hallucination: A distorted perception of voices and images directing one to perform some action (e.g., attack or kill someone).

Hallucinations can affect any of a person's senses, causing them to hear, see, taste, touch, or smell what others do not. Auditory hallucinations are the most frequent type of hallucination and are most common for people with schizophrenia (60–90%) (Clark, 2015; Fauman, 2002). Visual hallucinations are much less common, and they are more likely to occur as a result of acute infectious disease. Olfactory hallucinations may occur because of schizophrenia and organic lesions in the brain. Tactile hallucinations (touch) may occur as a reaction to drugs. Kinesthetic hallucinations may occur after the loss of a limb ("phantom limb") and owing to schizophrenia. Withdrawal from drugs may cause vivid hallucinations, such as the sensation that insects are crawling under the skin (delirium tremens, common with alcohol withdrawal; Saddock & Saddock, 2004). In fact, the symptoms of alcohol withdrawal may be clinically indistinguishable from schizophrenia (NIMH, 2012). With disorders such as schizophrenia, people may have auditory hallucinations with voices that are complimentary, but more often the voices are hostile (Shea, 1998). These voices may be so real that clients believe that they have had broadcasting devices planted in their bodies. For example, one client was convinced that her dentist had secretly implanted "radio receivers" in her dental fillings. It was so real to her that she could not dismiss it as imagination.

It is important to know that many things can cause hallucinations, including psychosis, high fever, mind-altering drugs (marijuana, psilocybin, LSD, and opium), medications, withdrawal from depressant drugs such as alcohol, brain disease and injury, epilepsy, sensory deprivation or sensory overload, oxygen deprivation, hyperventilation, hypoglycemia, extreme pain, extended fasting, dehydration, and social isolation (Beyerstein, 1998; Regehr & Glancy, 2010; Saddock & Saddock, 2004). Hallucinations can also occur in persons who have impaired vision but no mental disorder.

Delusions   **Delusions** are false beliefs that "cannot be influenced or corrected by reason or contradictory evidence (Fauman, 2002, p. 149). Persons with schizophrenia may experience delusions or distorted beliefs involving bizarre thought patterns. Delusions of persecution, typical in paranoid schizophrenia, may lead people to believe they are

delusion: Distorted beliefs or thought patterns that cannot be challenged by others using reason or evidence.

thought broadcasting: The delusional belief that one's thinking can be heard by others.

thought insertion: The delusional belief that thoughts are being inserted into one's brain by others.

being cheated, controlled, or poisoned. Other common delusions include religious delusions (belief that one is a manifestation of God), delusions of grandeur (bizarre beliefs about one's abilities), delusions of being controlled (e.g., belief that one is being directed by radio messages), **thought broadcasting** (belief that one's thinking can be heard by others), and **thought insertion** (belief that thoughts are being inserted into one's brain by others). Not all delusions are bizarre. Examples of non-bizarre delusions are the client's belief that he or she is being watched or that a famous person loves the client (erotomania) (Fauman, 2002; Saddock & Saddock, 2004).

Disordered Thinking   Another common feature of schizophrenia is disordered thinking. Individuals may be unable to think logically, or they may jump from one idea to another without any apparent logical connection. Thinking may be so disorganized and fragmented that it is totally confusing to others.

Social Isolation   Persons with schizophrenia are often socially isolated and withdrawn. They may be emotionally numb, have poor communication skills, and show decreased motivation and ability for self-care.

Treatment of Schizophrenia   Hospitalization may be a necessary first step in the effective treatment of acute psychotic symptoms, particularly if there is a risk of violence (Ralph, 2003). Antipsychotic medications such as clozapine and risperidone are used to decrease the positive symptoms of the disorder—hallucinations, agitation, confusion, distortions, and delusions. There is no cure for schizophrenia, but long-term drug maintenance now enables most people with the disease to live outside a psychiatric institution.

Counselling is an important adjunct to antipsychotic medication. Counsellors typically target their activities at helping clients deal with the social aspects of the disease. As well, counsellors can be instrumental in encouraging clients to seek psychiatric attention when necessary, and they can support psychiatric initiatives by encouraging clients to continue with any prescribed medication. This is crucial since about 50 percent of people with schizophrenia are noncompliant in taking their medication and for those with co-occurring disorders, medication noncompliance is more common than not (Substance Abuse and Mental Health Services Administration, 2008). Long-acting (one to six weeks) antipsychotic medication is an option for those who have difficulty (Ralph, 2003).

One client, a young university student, gives us a sense of what the world of a person with schizophrenia is like:

> I want to sue my dentist. Over the past year, he has been installing radio transmitters in my fillings. Now he uses them to control me. At first, he was nice, and then he raped me while he worked on my teeth. Sometimes he makes me sleep with complete strangers. If I don't get them removed soon, I might be forced to do something awful. There are others. I talked to a woman on the phone the other day. Her dentist did the same thing. We need to go underground where we can be safe from the enemy.

depression: Pervasive deflation in mood characterized by symptoms such as sadness, hopelessness, decreased energy, and difficulty concentrating, remembering, and making decisions.

bipolar disorder: A mood disorder characterized by alternating periods of depression and abnormally heightened mood, sometimes to the point of grandiosity. People with bipolar disorder may behave irrationally (e.g., going on uncontrolled buying sprees, committing sexual indiscretions, and taking part in foolish business investments).

Mood Disorders   The two most severe mood disorders (also known as affective disorders) are major **depression** and **bipolar disorder**, or manic-depressive illness.

Depression   About 8 percent of Canadians will deal with depression at some point in their lives; however, it is diagnosed twice as often among women, who may be more vulnerable to it or they may be more likely to seek treatment (Davis, 2006). Although everyone has bad days, the depressed feelings usually pass quickly. A clinical diagnosis of depression is made when a person's depressed mood becomes pervasive over time and interferes with the person's ability to cope with or enjoy life. In this way, depression is differentiated from the normal mood swings that everyone experiences. Depression is almost certainly more widespread than statistics suggest since it often goes

CONVERSATION 9.1 Paranoia

STUDENT: What is paranoia?

MENTAL HEALTH WORKER: Paranoia is a very common type of delusion that involves false or irrational beliefs that others are intent on causing one harm. A certain level of suspicion is normal and desirable as it protects us from venturing into dangerous situations and from others taking advantage of us. However, individuals with paranoia persist in their mistrust of others, even when evidence to the contrary is presented. They are hypervigilant, and they are obsessed about the hidden motives of others. Typically, their interactions with people, including counsellors and other professionals, are filtered through their paranoid lens.

STUDENT: How can you tell if it's a delusion or not?

MENTAL HEALTH WORKER: Sometimes, delusions are bizarre and easily identified such as the patient who believes that someone has put transmitters in her teeth in order to send her messages and control her behaviour. Other times, it may be difficult to determine if it is a delusion or if the client's fears are justified. It's important to keep an open mind. One woman, who had schizophrenia and a number of bizarre delusions, had trouble convincing people she had been sexually abused by her doctor. They assumed that because of her illness, her accusation was yet another delusion. In fact, it later proved to be true.

STUDENT: My grandmother, who had dementia, thought that her kids were stealing from her. She also believed that they planned to kill her in order to get her money. In fact, it was her failing memory. She was misplacing her possessions, then she would conclude she was a victim of theft.

MENTAL HEALTH WORKER: Your grandmother's situation is not uncommon with dementia. However, we need to be open to the possibility of elder abuse. Seniors with dementia are a vulnerable group, and there are certainly situations where family members take advantage of them by controlling and using their money for personal gain.

STUDENT: So, what's the root cause of paranoid delusions?

MENTAL HEALTH WORKER: The cause is still unknown, but the consensus is that there is no single cause. Environment,

genetics, stress, lack of sleep, high fever, side effects of medication, street drugs, and medical conditions such as strokes can all contribute to paranoia. Paranoia is also a common symptom in many mental disorders including dementia, schizophrenia, paranoid personality disorder, and mood disorders such as depression and bipolar disorder.

STUDENT: How do you treat it?

MENTAL HEALTH WORKER: Medications and counselling can be effective, but often people are unwilling to seek treatment because they do not believe they have a problem. Moreover, they are highly suspicious of their doctors and counsellors. Antidepressant, antianxiety, and antipsychotic medications are often used. Counsellors can help by working with their clients to ensure medication compliance. When symptoms get noticeably worse, it is often a sign that they are off their medication.

STUDENT: What are some counselling strategies?

MENTAL HEALTH WORKER: Counsellors and others should avoid being drawn into arguments regarding the delusion. Most often, such an approach will be met with resistance and the client will only further question the motives of the helper.

As always, relationship is the key to working effectively with someone who is paranoid, but this will require patience, as it is common that the client with paranoid delusions will be highly distrustful of counsellors, particularly if they challenge the validity of strongly held beliefs. Generally, you'll want to empathize with the client's feelings without supporting the delusion. However, with some clients, empathy may be experienced negatively as an "attempt to get inside their heads," so the counsellor may need to shift to a less threatening topic.

Sometimes, the best course of action is to distract the client by changing the subject or activity. Clients who are motivated to overcome paranoia can use anxiety management techniques and cognitive behavioural strategies to address unhelpful thinking. Innovative approaches are also available. One uses customized avatars to represent a person's paranoia, then the person learns to confront and control the paranoia (avatar) through role plays and simulations.

untreated. In fact, it is sometimes referred to as the "common cold of mental illness." The signs of depression, sometimes described as clinical depression or major depression to separate it from ordinary sadness, can be organized into four major categories with specific symptoms:

1. Mood disturbances
   - constant sad, anxious, or empty mood
   - feelings of hopelessness or pessimism
   - feelings of guilt, worthlessness, or helplessness

Over 80 billion neurons in the brain and body communicate with each other by sending tiny chemicals called neurotransmitters from one neuron to another. A neuron may have active neural pathway connections to 10,000 or more neurons. Dysfunction in the neurotransmitter may be one contributing factor in a number of mental and physical disorders. A complex array of factors including heredity, social factors, environment, life stress, and other unknown factors make it unlikely that a single cause for mental illness is present.

GABA: anxiety and fear (deficit)

Serotonin: depression, mood, sleep, appetite, impulse control, and aggression

Dopamine: Parkinson's disease, schizophrenia, attention deficit hyperactivity disorder, motivation, and depression, movement

Glutamate: obsessive-compulsive disorder (OCD), schizophrenia, depression, and autism

Acetylcholine: depression (excess) and deficit (dementia)

Norepinephrine: depression (deficit) and schizophrenia (excess)

Sources: NIMH, 2015; Hefner, 2015; Möhler, 2013; and Belsham, 2001.

2. Changes in behaviour
   - diminished interest or pleasure in daily activities, including sex
   - decreased energy and fatigue
   - withdrawal from others

3. Alterations in thinking
   - difficulty thinking, concentrating, and remembering
   - inability to make decisions
   - recurrent thoughts of death or suicide

4. Physical complaints
   - restlessness or irritability
   - fatigue or loss of energy
   - sleep disturbances, including insomnia
   - loss or gain of appetite and weight
   - chronic pain or other persistent bodily symptoms that are not caused by physical disease
   - suicide attempts (American Medical Association, 1998; American Psychiatric Association, 2013; NIMH, 2012).

Scott Simmie, a Canadian journalist, describes how his depression included obsession with thoughts of suicide:

> I spent weeks in bed, unable to find a reason to get up. Sleep was my drug—the only, albeit temporary, way to escape what had befallen me. When awake I brooded, almost obsessively, on death. Pictured myself rigging pulleys so I could hang myself in the condo. . . . Most mornings, the first thought that entered my head was to put a gun to it. Bang. Problem solved. (Simmie & Nunes, 2001, p. 27)

In a report on diagnosis trends by Intercontinental Medical Statistics Inc. (IMS, 2001), which compiles statistical information for the Canadian healthcare community, researchers noted that visits to a doctor for depression have shown the largest increase among Canada's leading diagnoses. During the period of 1995 to 2000, IMS statistics revealed that visits to doctors in Canada for depression increased 36 percent, with 7.8 million consultations with doctors for depressive disorders. Put another way, almost 3 percent of all physician visits were for depression. Women represented 66 percent of those diagnosed with depression. About 47 percent of individuals (male and female) diagnosed with depression were in the age group 40 to 59, and 31 percent were from the next largest group, made up of individuals aged 20 to 39. Significantly, depression

STUDENT: What should I do when clients begin hallucinating?

TEACHER: The first concern should be the safety of the client and others, including yourself. Pay particular attention to clients who describe voices ordering them to hurt themselves or others (command hallucinations). This might be a psychiatric emergency, particularly if there is evidence that the client has little ability to resist the commands. Police intervention may be necessary to bring the person to the hospital.

Let's talk about what not to do. Counsellors need to resist the temptation to argue with clients about the reality of their hallucinations. Although some clients are aware of when they are hallucinating and have learned to live with it, others are convinced of their hallucination's authenticity and dismiss arguments to the contrary. Their experience is very real and has to be accepted as such. This is also true when clients are delusional; however, improbable or bizarre the delusion, it is real to them.

Remember that many things can cause hallucinations. When someone is hallucinating because they have taken a street drug such as LSD, the best approach is to ensure safety and wait until the effects of the drug clear. In some circumstances, such as when the client has schizophrenia, hallucinations are generally treated with antipsychotic medications. Consequently, referral to a physician or psychiatrist is essential to make sure that clients have been assessed for an appropriate medication to control their hallucinations. Subsequently, it is important to ensure that clients are taking their medication and that their dosage is appropriate.

Hallucinations can be frightening, so it is important that counsellors remain calm and offer reassurance to clients that they are safe. The Canadian Mental Health Association (2015 online) emphasizes the importance of respecting a client's personal space and not touching them without invitation. They suggest minimizing distractions and noise, remaining calm, and allowing clients more time to process and respond are important when dealing with clients who are hallucinating.

Counsellors should avoid patronizing or humouring clients about their hallucinations, as this behaviour may promote further hallucinating. One way that counsellors can respond without arguing is to simply state that they do not sense what their clients are sensing. They can express empathy that acknowledges the feelings that clients may be experiencing because of their hallucinations. Counsellors also can help clients deal with any stressors that may be increasing the frequency of hallucinations. For example, if being in large crowds or missing sleep brings on hallucinations, clients can take steps to minimize these precursors. It may be helpful to work with clients to help them learn skills for controlling their hallucinations. For example, they can discipline themselves to direct their thoughts and activities elsewhere. One researcher found that silence, isolation, and attention to oneself tend to promote hallucinations, but distraction, exploratory activity, movement, and external stimulation tend to impede hallucinations (Silva & Lopez de Silva, 1976). So simply diverting client attention can be a useful strategy.

STUDENT: I learned something from one of my clients that I found helpful and profound. I remember him saying to me, "I have a mental disorder, but don't forget I have the same needs and fears as everyone else." I was reminded that he and I were more alike than unlike each other.

TEACHER: Moreover, hallucinations and delusions, which often define illnesses such as schizophrenia, are common in normal life. Clark (2015) reported that "hallucinations, despite common misconceptions, are a part of normal healthy life."

For example, we might hear a noise and think someone has called our name. Or, in the period between waking and sleeping, we might temporarily lose contact with reality.

now ranks second behind essential hypertension as the leading reason for visiting a physician. Moreover, the report suggested that almost 3 million Canadians have serious depression, but less than a third of them seek help.

SUCCESS TIP

Premorbid functioning is a measure of how well an individual coped before the onset of mental disorder or the misuse of substances. As a rule, those who have a history of success in broad areas of life such as career, relationships, and management of emotions will have a more positive prognosis for success. Asking clients to describe times in their lives when they did not have a problem (e.g., when they were not misusing drugs) is an effective way of identifying strengths as well as reasonable success goals (i.e., return to premorbid functioning).

Depression is believed to be caused by a complex combination of three primary variables—biological, genetic (inherited), and emotional or environmental (American Medical Association, 1998). Biological origins are associated with brain chemistry and hormonal activity. Research has demonstrated that some families are more likely to have members who suffer from depression. Although no specific gene has been linked to depression, there appears to be ample evidence that heredity leads to an increased vulnerability to depression. Emotional and environmental causes might include stressors such as the death of a loved one, a job loss, or the breakup of a relationship. As well, depression might be the result of sleep disturbances, illness, or drug reaction. Depression that originates from physical illness usually abates once the physical illness is treated. Depression is symptomatic of a medical condition in about 10 percent to 15 percent of all cases. Known physical causes of depression include thyroid disease, adrenal gland disorders, hyperparathyroidism, diabetes, stroke, infectious diseases such as viral hepatitis, autoimmune disorders, vitamin and mineral deficiencies, and cancer (American Medical Association, 1998). Thus, clients who are dealing with depression should be referred for a medical check-up as an adjunct to counselling.

Counsellors can assist people who are depressed in a number of ways:

- Help them recognize and identify the symptoms of depression.
- Refer them for appropriate medical examination and treatment, which might include medication or hospitalization.
- Help them to develop coping strategies for dealing with stress.
- Counsel them for loss or grief.
- Assess and manage suicide risk.
- Help them develop cognitive/behavioural strategies for overcoming low self-esteem and other self-defeating thought patterns that often accompany depression.
- Support and understand emotions.
- Provide family counselling to interrupt communication patterns that contribute to or escalate depression.

Bipolar Disorder   With bipolar disorder, depression alternates with manic episodes. During manic periods, people typically experience heightened energy, a euphoric mood, and a greatly increased sense of confidence, sometimes to the point of grandiosity. They may have sharpened and unusually creative thinking, along with a much-decreased need for sleep. Or they may experience a flight of ideas (thoughts without logical connection). Although they may engage in increased goal-directed activities at work or school, they often engage in them without regard to the consequences, thus, leading to irrational behaviour such as uncontrolled buying sprees, sexual indiscretion, and foolish business investments (American Psychiatric Association, 2013; NIMH, 2012). Scott Simmie's recollection of his mindset when he was in the midst of the manic phase illustrates the irrationality of this state:

> Despite everything I'd been through, I was still convinced that I was in perfect health, that the real problem was the failure of others to recognize that something extraordinary and wonderful had happened to me. That I had been spiritually reborn. That my limitless potential had finally been freed. (Simmie & Nunes, 2001, p. 25)

>>> **BRAIN BYTE**   Depression

Current thinking suggests that it is a combination of factors that results in depression. For example, if people with a predisposition to depression experience stressful life crises, they may develop depression. Subsequently, their first depressive episode may stimulate changes in brain chemistry that leave them more vulnerable to further episodes, when even small stressful events can trigger depression (American Medical Association, 1998). Thyroid problems (overactive or underactive) and hormonal imbalances (e.g., after childbirth) can also play a role in depression (Tartakovsky, 2015).

Thus, it is very difficult, though not impossible, to persuade people to accept treatment, including hospitalization, during the manic phase of the illness. Supportive counsellors, family, and friends may convince them to seek treatment, but in some cases, particularly where behaviour has become self-destructive or dangerous, involuntary hospitalization may be necessary.

Bipolar disorder usually begins in adolescence or early adulthood and continues throughout life. It is often not recognized as an illness, and people who have it may suffer needlessly for years or even decades. There is evidence that bipolar disorder is inherited (NIMH, 2012). Persons with untreated bipolar disorder may experience devastating complications, including marital breakup, job loss, financial ruin, substance abuse, and suicide. However, almost everyone with bipolar disorder can be helped through the use of medications such as lithium, which has demonstrated effectiveness in controlling both depression and mania. Bipolar disorder cannot be cured, but for most people, treatment can keep the disease under control.

Anxiety Disorders

Anxiety disorders are characterized by higher than normal levels of fear, worry, tension, or anxiety about daily events. High anxiety may be present without apparent reason. Four serious anxiety disorders are obsessive-compulsive disorder (OCD), phobias, panic disorder, and post-traumatic stress disorder (PTSD).

Obsessive-Compulsive Disorder (OCD)

An **obsessive-compulsive disorder (OCD)** involves recurrent, unwanted thoughts and conscious, ritualized, seemingly purposeless acts, such as counting the number of tiles on the ceiling or needing to wash one's hands repetitively. Behavioural techniques and medication have proved effective in treating this disorder.

Phobia

A **phobia** is an irrational fear about particular events or objects. Phobias result in overwhelming anxiety in response to situations of little or no danger. Most people have phobias of one sort or another, such as fear of flying, heights, public speaking, or snakes. For the most part, people deal with their phobias through avoidance, which decreases the anxiety associated with the fear. Unfortunately, avoidance increases the fear of the particular object or situation. Treatment of phobias is necessary when they interfere with a person's capacity to lead a normal life. For example, agoraphobia (fear of open or public spaces) prevents people from leaving the safety of their homes. Treatment in such cases is essential to help clients escape what would otherwise be severely restricted lives.

With systematic desensitization, individuals with a phobia are first taught how to manage anxiety through relaxation. With the help of the counsellor, they construct a hierarchy of anxiety-provoking events associated with the phobia. Finally, they learn how to control their anxiety with progressively more difficult exposures to the anxiety-producing object or event. In addition, other specialized behavioural techniques, such as flooding (immersing a person in the situation causing fear or anxiety), relaxation training, and pharmacologic (drug) treatment, may be necessary to relieve anxiety disorders.

Panic Disorder

A **panic disorder** involves sudden attacks of terror and irrational fear accompanied by an overwhelming sense of impending doom. During a panic attack, a person may experience symptoms such as an accelerated heart rate, sweating, shaking, shortness of breath, chest pain, and nausea, as well as a fear of dying or losing control (American Psychiatric Association, 2000). Medication and psychotherapy have proven effective in treating this disorder.

Post-Traumatic Stress Disorder (PTSD)

Post-traumatic stress disorder (PTSD) symptoms develop following traumatic events such as rape, assault, natural disasters (earthquakes, floods, etc.), war, torture, or an automobile accident. Symptoms may

anxiety disorders: More than normal levels of fear, worry, tension, or anxiety about daily events.

obsessive-compulsive disorder (OCD): Recurrent, unwanted thoughts and conscious, ritualized, seemingly purposeless acts, such as counting the number of tiles on the ceiling or needing to wash one's hands repetitively.

phobia: An irrational fear about particular events or objects that results in overwhelming anxiety in response to situations where there is little or no danger.

panic disorder: Sudden attacks of terror and irrational fear accompanied by an overwhelming sense of impending doom. During a panic attack, a person may experience symptoms such as an accelerated heart rate, sweating, shaking, shortness of breath, chest pain, nausea, and fear of dying or losing control.

post-traumatic stress disorder (PTSD): Disabling symptoms such as emotional numbness, sleep disturbance (nightmares, difficulty sleeping), or reliving the event following a traumatic event such as rape, assault, natural disaster (earthquakes, floods, etc.), war, torture, or an automobile accident.

occur immediately after the event or may be delayed by months or years. Recollections of the event result in disabling symptoms, such as emotional numbness; sleep disturbance (nightmares, difficulty sleeping); reliving the event; intense anxiety at exposure to cues that remind the person of the trauma; avoidance of activities, people, or conversations that arouse recall of the trauma; hypervigilance; and outbursts of anger (American Psychiatric Association, 2013). PTSD symptoms often dissipate within six months, but for some people the symptoms may last years. Relaxation training and counselling are effective tools for treating this disorder.

Eating Disorders   The two most common eating disorders, anorexia nervosa and bulimia, are most likely to affect adolescent and young adult women, with about 90 percent of all those afflicted coming from this group (NIMH, 2012). Approximately 1 percent of adolescent girls develop anorexia nervosa and as many as 10 percent develop bulimic disorder (NIMH, 2012). Eventually, half of those with anorexia will develop bulimia (NIMH, 2012). Eating disorders are difficult to treat because many people refuse to admit that they have a problem and resist treatment. Counsellors and family need to persuade those affected to seek treatment, but this can be hard because people with these disorders may argue that their only problem is the "nagging" people in their lives. Because of the life-threatening nature of eating disorders, involuntary treatment or forced hospitalization may be necessary, particularly when there has been excessive and rapid weight loss, serious metabolic disturbances, and serious depression with a risk of suicide.

The National Eating Disorder Information Centre (NEDIC), a Toronto-based nonprofit organization, offers this explanation of the cause of eating disorders:

> Eating disorders are caused by a combination of societal, individual, and family factors. They are a manifestation of complex underlying struggles with identity and self-concept, and of problems that often stem from traumatic experiences and patterns of socialization. Eating disorders are coping behaviours that provide the individual with an outlet for displacement of feelings or with a (false) sense of being in control. Common to all eating disorders is a pervasive underlying sense of powerlessness. (2005)

Social and Cultural Variables   For most of recorded history, plumpness in women was deemed desirable and fashionable. But during the last 60 years, particularly in Western cultures, women have been bombarded with media messages that promote slimness as the route to a successful and happy life. Societal emphasis on body image, combined with the unrealistically thin ideal of the supermodel, has contributed to an obsessive preoccupation with weight control and dieting (Davis, 2006). One study found that the top wish of a group of girls aged 11 to 17 was "to be thinner," while another survey discovered that girls were more afraid of becoming fat than they were of cancer, nuclear war, or losing their parents (Berg, 1997, p. 13). Mothers and fathers who are overly concerned or critical about their daughters' weight and physical attractiveness may put the daughters at increased risk of developing an eating disorder. People pursuing professions or activities that emphasize thinness, such as modelling, dancing, or gymnastics, are more susceptible to the problem (NIMH, 2012).

anorexia nervosa: An eating disorder that occurs when people reject maintaining a minimally healthy body weight. Driven by low self-esteem and an intense fear of gaining weight, people with anorexia use techniques such as purging (e.g., fasting, vomiting, and taking laxatives) and excessive exercise to reduce body weight.

Anorexia Nervosa   **Anorexia nervosa** occurs when people reject maintaining minimally healthy body weight. Driven by low self-esteem and an intense fear of gaining weight, people with anorexia use techniques such as purging (e.g., fasting, vomiting, and taking laxatives) and excessive exercise to reduce body weight. Even though they may diet to the point of starvation and they look emaciated, they will still insist that they are too fat. Anorexia nervosa can be life threatening, and as many as 10 to 15 percent of sufferers die of the effects of prolonged starvation (NIMH, 2012).

The symptoms of anorexia include excessive weight loss, belief that the body is fat, continuation of dieting despite a lower than normal body weight, cessation of menstruation, obsession with food, eating in secret, obsessive exercise, and depression. People with anorexia are often perfectionists with superior athletic ability. There is some evidence to suggest that people with anorexia starve themselves to gain a sense of control in some area of their lives (NIMH, 2012).

Treating eating disorders requires a team approach consisting of physicians, counsellors, nutritionists, and family therapists. Group therapy may be a helpful adjunct to individual counselling to reduce isolation. Reframing and other methods for helping clients change their distorted and rigid thinking patterns may be extremely helpful (see Chapter 7). As well, antidepressant medications such as fluoxetine (Prozac) and imipramine may be used.

Bulimia   Bulimia occurs when people adopt a pattern of excessive overeating followed by vomiting or other purging behaviours to control their weight. Individuals with bulimia usually binge and purge in secret. Typically, people with bulimia feel isolated, and they deal with their problems through overeating; then, feeling guilty and disgusted, they purge. Because they may have normal or even above normal body weight, they often hide their problem from others for years. By the time, they finally seek treatment (sometimes not until they are in their thirties or forties), their eating disorder is firmly entrenched and difficult to treat.

> **Bulimia:** An eating disorder that occurs when people adopt a pattern of excessive overeating followed by vomiting or other purging behaviours to control their weight.

The symptoms of bulimia may include cessation of menstruation; obsession with food; eating in secret; obsessive exercise; serious depression; binging, vomiting, and other purging activities (often with the use of drugs); and disappearances in the bathroom for long periods of time. In addition, as a result of excessive vomiting, the outer layer of the teeth can be worn down, scarring may be present on the backs of hands (from teeth when pushing fingers down the throat to induce vomiting), the esophagus may become inflamed, and glands near the cheeks can become swollen (NIMH, 2012). Individuals with bulimia are at increased risk for substance abuse and suicidal behaviour.

Personality Disorders: "Stable Instability"   A personality disorder is characterized by significant impairments in such areas as empathy, capacity for intimacy, ability to regulate emotions, self-esteem, disregard for the rights of others, and impulse control. The diagnosis requires that the impairments have an onset in adolescence or early adulthood and that they are enduring over time.

Personality disorders involve extensions (excesses or deficits) of personality traits that we all possess, but to warrant the diagnosis the criteria for the particular disorder must be met and must result in significant distress or disability for the individual or others. Diagnosis requires considerable time and expertise, and counsellors should avoid a common tendency to quickly conclude that someone has a personality disorder because of his or her behaviour. Personality disorders are diagnosed based on history, observation, and collateral information, not solely on current behaviour. Psychometric tests might also be used. Proposed changes to DSM-5 classification of personality disorders met with considerable resistance from the mental health community, and they were not approved. Instead, an alternate model has been introduced for further study and at the same time, the DSM-IV classification has been retained. The new model attempts to address the limitations of the DSM-IV classification, for example, the fact that most people do not fit into one of the subtypes. Often, they meet the criteria for two or more personality disorders (comorbidity).

In DSM-5, the 10 personality disorders (retained from DSM-IV) are:

- Paranoid: distrust and suspicion
- Schizoid: detachment and restricted emotional range

- Schizotypal: acute discomfort in relationships, cognitive distortions—odd beliefs and superstitions
- Antisocial: disregard for the rights of others
- Borderline: unstable relationships and self-image; impulsivity; emotional swings
- Histrionic: excessive emotionality and attention seeking
- Narcissistic: grandiosity; lack of empathy
- Avoidant: socially inhibited and feelings of inadequacy
- Dependent: submissive and needy; lack of confidence
- Obsessive-compulsive disorder: preoccupation with orderliness, perfection and control
- Personality disorder trait specified

Table 9.3 outlines challenges to the counselling relationship that clients with personality disorders might present, along with appropriate counselling responses.

TABLE 9.3 Personality Disorders: Common Challenges and Responses

Nature of Challenge	What to Expect in the Client–Counsellor Relationship	Counselling Choices
Distrust and suspicion	Accusations; suspicion; misinterpretation of counsellor's intentions and behaviour	Be cautious with humour, warmth, and empathy; be concrete and straightforward; probe with caution; client may be uncomfortable with eye contact; sit beside client if convenient
Detachment and social inhibition	Discomfort with intimacy; avoidance; client may be awkward and uneasy during interview, especially when dealing with the emotional domain	Assist client to develop social and interactive skills (if willing); accept that the relationship may be emotionally superficial; anxiety management
Disregard for the rights of others (antisocial personality)	Deception; manipulation; attacking; bullying; breaking rules; bragging; may be charming with great ability to convince even experienced workers of their sincerity	Avoid challenging; establish a clear contract and limits, explain rules; accept that it is unlikely that the client will change ways of thinking, so help clients find good reasons for changing
Unstable relationships and self-image; impulsivity; emotional swings (borderline personality disorder)	Emotional volatility; anger and threats; self-destructive acting out; self-injury; complaints to management; expectation to be taken care of; flirting; acting helpless; constant crisis	Set relationship boundaries; remain calm; manage your own negative reactions; help clients manage emotions, self-injury, and suicide attempts
Sense of entitlement; grandiosity; lack of empathy; self-centred (narcissistic personality disorder)	Manipulation; breaking rules; competing for attention; expectation of service and admiration; wanting special rules	Focus on helping client develop self-esteem and more realistic expectations of others
Excessive emotionality and attention seeking (histrionic)	Temper tantrums; suicide gestures; charm; dramatic affect; approval seeking	Help client modulate emotions, impulsive actions, and sensitivity
Preoccupation with orderliness, perfection, and control	Criticism; problems with ambiguity or lack of structure; vulnerability	Help client learn to recognize and modify unhelpful thinking; anxiety management; help client-set realistic goals; help client develop flexibility and comfort with ambiguity
Excessive dependency; submissiveness and neediness; and lack of confidence	Dependency; advice seeking and compliance; acting helpless	Train client in assertiveness; foster independence; recognize strengths; set short-term goals to reinforce capacity and success

ADHD is characterized by problems with staying on task, but a number of medical conditions can also present with the same symptoms including seizure disorders, HIV infection, anxiety disorders, reactions to chemotherapy, drugs (e.g., marijuana, cocaine, and caffeine), hypothyroidism, PTSD, abuse or trauma, sleep disturbance, and learning disorders.

Child and Youth Mental Health

Many mental disorders, such as schizophrenia and bipolar disorder, typically emerge in late adolescence or early adulthood (Davis, 2006), but indicators (premorbid symptoms) may show up in children. Other disorders, including mood and anxiety disorders, may start in childhood or later in life. Common childhood disorders include the following:

- Anxiety disorder, the most common disorder seen in children
- Attention-deficit/hyperactivity disorder
- Attachment disorder
- Oppositional defiance
- Conduct disorder
- Obsessive-compulsive disorder

The following are some case examples illustrating some of the complex behavioural problems that youth workers and other professionals might encounter in their work with children:

- Neema, age 7, goes from being completely calm to blindly running, screaming, and hitting anyone in his path. He's triggered by changes in his environment, even seemingly small and insignificant stressors.
- Rebecca, age 10, throws herself on the ground as soon as she enters the schoolyard. She clings to her mother, begging to be taken home.
- Emilio, age 12, loves wrapping plastic bags around his penis and masturbating during class. His behaviour was so disruptive that he needed to be placed in a special class away from other students.
- Nasim, age 9, poured gasoline on the family cat, and then tried to burn the house down.
- Pierre, age 15, was introduced by the teacher to the rest of the class. She jumped on the desk, pretending that she had a gun, screaming obscenities, and threatening to kill everyone.

Early marijuana use among Canadians aged 15 to 24 years has harmful impact on their brains in the areas of memory, attention, information processing, learning, coordination, appetite, mood, motivation, response to pain and pleasure, as well as risks to mental health (association with psychosis and schizophrenia). Structural damage to the brain and reduced frontal lobe brain mass damages executive functioning related to planning, decision making, motivation, self-awareness, and goal setting. Cannabis dependency and impairment of the brain's reward system can occur for as many as one out of six adolescent users. (Canadian Centre on Substance Abuse, 2015). Cannabis use at an earlier age alters the brain's dopamine system and is associated with a higher risk of psychosis and increased negative emotionality—depression, anxiety, and poor ability to deal with stress. (Manza, Tomasi, & Volkow, 2017) This reality has important implications for counsellors who work with youth.

- Pierre, age 9, is preoccupied with arranging the books and materials at his work desk to the point that he cannot engage with class activities.

- Pari, age 18, is prone to intense emotional reactions. When stressed, she threatens suicide or cuts herself. She is sexually promiscuous and uses any street drug available. When asked about her cutting, she says, "I don't know why I do it. It just feels good. It makes the pain go away."

Each of the preceding examples must be understood in the context of the environmental factors that have contributed to the child's extreme behaviour. For example, Nick was abandoned by his mother at birth, and even though he is only 7, he has been in over 30 foster homes. Although any child of any background can develop a mental disorder, a number of factors can increase vulnerability, including poverty, violence, abuse, illness, school difficulties, family breakdown, death of a family member or friend, and others (Gladding & Newsome, 2010). Mental disorders in children compound developmental challenges. The complications of mental illness, particularly when left untreated, can lead to an increase in suicidal behaviour and addictions.

Simon Davis (2006) from the University of British Columbia School of Social Work, reviewed a number of Canadian studies and reported the following:

- As many as 14 percent of children have a mental disorder at any given time.

- Eight to 14 percent of children in Ontario have visited a mental health professional in the last year.

- Children are a high-risk suicide group with the rate of suicide ideation ranging from 12 to 20 percent (one-year prevalence), and suicide representing 24 percent of all deaths among those aged 15 to 24.

- For children, an anxiety disorder is the most common mental disorder, with a one-year prevalence rate of about 10 percent.

In 2002, the British Columbia Ministry of Children and Family Development (MCFD) commissioned a study that summarized existing research on child and youth mental health. Their analysis concluded that the prevalence of mental disorders in children and youth that cause significant symptoms and problems was about 15 percent, with anxiety, conduct, attention, and depressive disorders the most common.

General Considerations   Here are some issues counsellors should consider when working with children and adolescents who have mental disorders:

- Assessment and intervention need to consider the context of family, culture, and social milieu. Attempt to modify environmental factors that are contributing to the child's behaviour.

- Modify interview strategies to meet developmental and individual needs. For example, with younger children games, art, and play can be used to facilitate expression as well as to develop rapport.

- Support or advocate for a thorough assessment that will determine the child's needs for medication and academic supports.

- Use best-practice approaches that are adapted for children. For example, Dr. Jane Garland at BC Children's Hospital developed a program called "Taming the Worry Dragons" that uses cognitive behavioural therapy to help children who have been diagnosed with anxiety disorder. This program is now used in many parts of Canada with adaptations for various age groups. The "Friends for Life" program (2012) was

Adolescent brains are particularly vulnerable to drug misuse. Early use increases the risk of developing a substance disorder, interferes with brain maturation, which is normally accelerated during adolescence, and damages the brain in areas associated with learning, language, and memory such as the hippocampus, which shows a decrease in volume (Winters & Arria, 2011). The authors stress the importance of teaching teenager's assertive decision making to enable them to say "no" to drug use, providing education to help them understand how their developing brains are impacted by drug use, and safe risk taking that supports personal growth without the need to use drugs. One strategy suggested by Winters and Arria is to teach teens how to use a "red light (stop), yellow light (caution), and green light (proceed)" model for decision making.

developed in Australia and is now used throughout the world, including Canada, as a structured approach to helping children cope with anxiety and depression. It focuses on building resilience and self-esteem.

■ Family intervention is essential. Families need education to understand the nature of any mental disorder that their child is dealing with as well as information regarding medications that are being used. As well, family counselling can assist the family to make changes to environmental factors that are contributing to the illness.

Counselling and Working with People Who Have Mental Disorders

Ideally, people with mental disorders should be dealt with through a team approach that includes psychiatrists, psychiatric social workers, social service workers, counsellors, occupational counsellors, nurses, and volunteers. As a team, they share common objectives:

1. Motivating clients to seek and remain in treatment and, in severe cases, arranging for involuntary treatment.

2. Supporting clients to return to or remain in the community (helping with housing, life skills training, employment and career counselling, and assistance with the negative symptoms of the illness).

3. Assisting clients in dealing with the challenges of medication (e.g., compliance and side effects).

4. Educating clients and their families about the nature of the disorder.

5. Assisting clients in dealing with the consequences of mental disorders, including stigma.

6. Helping clients and their families develop and use support systems, including self-help groups and professionals.

Clubhouses Social support is offered to clients with chronic mental illness through clubhouses. These organizations emerged in 1940s with the first clubhouse, Fountain House, opening in New York, which became the visionary model for all subsequent clubhouses. They operate in the community as a means to promote recovery for their clients, who are referred to as "members." A typical clubhouse will provide food, social interaction, employment assistance, recreation, and support to find housing in a safe environment. Members, who work along with staff, fully participate in all aspects of programming and management of the centres. Staff view themselves as colleagues of the members, and they often develop real and lasting friendships with members in much the same way as they would in a typical work environment (International Centre for Clubhouse Development, 2012).

Mental Health and Employment   Davis (2006) reported that unemployment and underemployment rates in North America for persons with serious mental disorders range from 70 to 90 percent. The devastating impact of unemployment and job loss is well documented in the literature (Bolles, 2011; Borgen, Amundson, & McVicar, 2002; and Soper & Von Bergen, 2001). Aside from the obvious loss of income from not having a job, there may be significant consequences to job loss, such as increased stress, loss of self-esteem and identity, and negative effects on health and well-being (Bolles, 2011; Davis, 2006). Davis observes that "unemployment may significantly impact the mental health of someone who is already struggling with the stigma associated with a psychiatric illness" (2006, p. 260).

For most people, a job or career is a pivotal part of their identity. A protracted period of unemployment can result in a loss of self-esteem and personality. Moreover, persons who are unemployed lose the routine of their daily lives, the structure of the workday, their sense of purpose, and the social contact with friends and colleagues at the workplace.

In addition, the financial impact of job loss can be devastating. Day-to-day survival can be tenuous at best as individuals and families struggle to survive on savings or meagre social assistance benefits. Financial problems become a crisis when unanticipated expenses such as car repairs, school fees, or medical bills appear. Job loss can easily result in the loss of one's savings, one's home, and the ability to sustain a social and recreational life.

Assisting people who have mental disorders often requires medication, but this is insufficient to achieve full recovery. A British Columbia Ministry of Health report on best practices concluded:

> The literature and experts provided strong evidence that work has many benefits for people with serious mental illness, including improvements in their psychiatric symptoms, reduced hospitalization, greater social interaction, decreased levels of anxiety, enhanced self-esteem and self-confidence and overall improvement in their quality of life. (2002, pp. 5–6)

Although a full discussion of employment counselling with individuals who have mental disorders is beyond the scope of this text, the following broad initiatives can form the basis of support:

- Marketing to employers, dispelling myths about clients and promoting the positive contributions that they can make to an organization.
- Offering pre-employment services, including career counselling, skills training, work experience, job search skills (e.g., networking, résumé preparation, and interview rehearsal).
- Assisting clients to identify and access educational resources.
- Life skills counselling for clients who lack basic abilities in such areas as managing finances, maintaining proper hygiene, getting to work on time, and getting along with supervisors and co-workers.
- Using volunteer work as a way to improve self-esteem and develop job skills.
- Using a variety of employment paths such as supported employment, where sustained assistance for skill development and adaptive strategies for dealing with the challenges of the workplace are provided.

- Personal counselling that assists clients to develop positive self-esteem and optimism by recognizing strengths that they have acquired through hobbies, personal life experience, volunteer work, and other employment.

- Using group and peer support to help reduce isolation.

- Using the **job club method** (Azrin & Besalel, 1980), a structured group approach that provides support, job search skills training, and materials and supplies for completing a successful job hunt.

- Assisting clients in dealing with work-related stress issues (Azrin & Besalel, 1980; British Columbia Ministry of Health, 2002; Cattan & Tilford, 2006; Davis, 2006; Niles, Amundson, & Neault, 2011; and Sears & Gordon, 2011).

job club method: An intensive and structured approach to job finding based on group support and structured learning activities. The sole purpose of a job club is to help participants find work.

Psychiatric Medications The 1950s witnessed the introduction of powerful chemicals that have resulted in dramatic advances in the treatment of mental disorders. Medications have enabled the vast majority of people with mental disorders to be treated and managed in the community and not locked up in psychiatric facilities. Medications may be able to control the symptoms of mental disorders, such as hallucinations, but they do not cure the illness. They can increase the effectiveness of counselling by increasing the capacity of the clients to hear and respond. Many people need to take medication to control their illness for the rest of their lives. Counsellors do not prescribe medications, but they provide support to clients in a number of important ways: making referrals to physicians, helping clients assess the pros and cons of taking medication, discussing adverse side effects, helping clients and families access information about medication (purpose, side effects, and risks), and advocating on behalf of clients to health providers.

There may be wide variations in people's reactions to medication (e.g., some respond better to one than another; some need larger doses; some experience side effects; and others do not). Medications may result in unwanted side effects, such as tardive dyskinesia (characterized by uncontrollable movement), drowsiness, weakness, tremors, slurred speech, sleep disturbances, sexual dysfunction, increased heart rate, dry mouth, and headaches (Walsh & Bentley, 2002). Some clients may stop taking medication to avoid these side effects.

Psychotropic medications alter the neurotransmission processes, the chemical and electrical system of the brain. There are five main categories of psychotropic medication (Walsh & Bentley, 2002), as outlined as follows:

- **Antipsychotic (or neuroleptic) medications** such as loxapine, haloperidol, clozapine, and risperidone are used to treat psychotic illnesses such as schizophrenia. Antipsychotic medications may be taken daily, but some medications are available through injection (once or twice a month). Injections are particularly useful for ensuring that clients take the medication. Newer antipsychotic medications (e.g., clozapine, risperidone, olanzapine, and quetiapine), also known as novel or atypical antipsychotics, do not have the same level of adverse side effects as some of the older (conventional) drugs such as chlorpromazine (Thorazine) and haloperidol

antipsychotic (or neuroleptic) medication: Medications such as chlorpromazine, haloperidol, clozapine, and risperidone that are used to treat illnesses such as schizophrenia.

⟫⟫⟫ BRAIN BYTE   Psychotropic Medication

A psychotropic drug is any medication used to treat a mental health condition such as depression or schizophrenia. These medications help to manage symptoms by changing brain neurotransmitters, but they are not designed to cure the illness. They can also have harmful side effects, and they may structurally alter the brain for better or worse.

antidepressant medication: Medications such as Prozac, Paxil, and Zoloft that are used to help people deal with serious depression.

mood-stabilizing medications: Medications such as lithium carbonate that are used to control the manic symptoms and mood swings of bipolar disorder.

anti-anxiety medication: Medications such as Valium and Librium that are used to control serious and persistent anxiety, phobia, and panic attacks.

psychostimulants: Medications such as Ritalin that are used to treat attention deficit/hyperactivity disorder (ADHD).

addiction medications: Medications such as naltrexone, buprenorphine, and methadone that are used to support addiction recovery and treatment.

(Haldol). Antipsychotic medications have enabled most people with schizophrenia to be treated in the community rather than in institutions, the primary method used for the first half of the twentieth century.

- **Antidepressant medications** such as Prozac, Paxil, Wellbutrin, and Zoloft are used to help people deal with serious depression and anxiety disorders (NIMH, 2012; Walsh & Bentley, 2002).

- **Mood-stabilizing medications** such as lithium carbonate, valproic acid, and carbamazepine are used to control the manic symptoms of bipolar disorder.

- **Anti-anxiety medications** such as Valium, Librium, beta-blockers, and benzodiazepines, are used to control serious and persistent anxiety, phobias, and panic attacks.

- **Psychostimulants** such as Adderall, Ritalin, and Cylert are used to treat attention deficit/hyperactivity disorder (ADHD).

- **Addiction medications** such as naltrexone, Antabuse, and methadone are used to support addiction recovery and treatment. There are also a variety of medical aids such as the drug Bupropion, patches, sprays, gums, and lozenges for dealing with nicotine addiction. Medication may also be used to assist people through the withdrawal process from drugs such as alcohol and heroin.

⟫⟫ CONVERSATION 9.3 When Clients Don't Take Their Medication

STUDENT: My practicum is at an inner-city drop-in centre for people with mental disorders. One of the biggest challenges we face is working with clients who don't take their drugs. They end up relapsing or going to the emergency room on a regular basis.

TEACHER: I know when you say drugs you're referring to their prescribed medications. Since many clients use street drugs, it's better to use the term "medication" to maintain the distinction. As you suggest, failure to take prescribed medication is an enormous problem. I read recently that approximately 50 percent of individuals with schizophrenia are noncompliant, and there is a high correlation between medication noncompliance, violence, and suicide, particularly when there is a co-occurring substance abuse problem (Leo, Jassal, & Bakhai, 2005). Noncompliance can mean not taking medication at all, not using it correctly, or mixing it with street drugs.

STUDENT: So what can we do about it?

TEACHER: First, I think it's important to understand factors that contribute to clients not taking their medications, such as adverse side effects, medication costs, or the complex nature of their medication regimen. Their illness may also cause a lack of will or motivation to take their medication. Some may simply be unable to understand or follow the routines. Moreover, clients who are paranoid might fear they are being poisoned or controlled by medication and thus be unwilling to comply. Clients who are manic may prefer to stay that way.

STUDENT: I think a big problem is homelessness and isolation.

TEACHER: Yes, clients will tend to do better if they live in a supportive environment. And for some this means a structured and supervised setting, such as a mental health boarding home, where professional help and encouragement are available. When clients resist medication because of adverse side effects, it is crucial that this be discussed with their doctors since side effects can often be addressed with alternative medications, particularly if the client is taking some of the older medications. Long-acting injections are another useful alternative.

STUDENT: What can counsellors do?

TEACHER: They can make sure that clients have access to adequate information about their illness and its treatment. They can also assist clients in developing and using routines to manage their medication. Moreover, counselling can help clients resolve ambivalence about using medication (e.g., by providing information about the potential consequences of prolonged noncompliance and the benefits of compliance). As well, counsellors may be able to help family members with information and ideas on how they can support medication compliance. And, as you said, it's important to assist clients in finding supportive housing.

Medications are approved after research studies demonstrate their effectiveness in treating a particular disorder. However, once they are approved, physicians may legally prescribe them "off-label" for other disorders. For example, an anti-psychotic medication could be prescribed to treat depression or to manage excessive anger. Although off-label prescription is common and accepted medical practice, there are risks. There may be adverse reactions that have not been documented, or the usefulness of the drug for the targeted disorder may not have been proven.

SUBSTANCE USE DISORDERS

Substance abuse is estimated to cost Canadians about $40 billion per year for healthcare, law enforcement, and lost productivity (Herie & Skinner, 2010). The Canadian Centre on Substance Abuse (2012) estimates that alcohol and tobacco represent about $31 billion of this cost. Beyond the financial costs are the devastating impacts that substance abuse can have on individuals and families:

- Disruption or breakdown of family, job, and social life
- Loss of control and the ability to exercise good judgment
- Increased rates of violence and abuse
- Mental and physical health deterioration, including premature death from the continued use drugs or accidental death from overdose
- Fetal alcohol spectrum disorder caused by alcohol use during pregnancy
- Legal problems arising from the pursuit of illicit drugs or the consequences of behaviour such as impaired driving or disorderly conduct
- Death from overdose. In 2016, there were almost 3000 opioid deaths in Canada with the majority (about 75%) occurring in males (Government of Canada, 2017b).

Herie and Skinner (2010) highlight alcohol and tobacco as the substances causing the most harm in Canada: "tobacco is by far the most harmful drug; tobacco accounted for 16.6 percent of all deaths and $17 billion in lost productivity and healthcare costs in 2002" (p. 37). "Alcohol accounted for 1.9 percent of all deaths, with $14.6 billion in costs" (p. 37). A Canadian Centre on Substance Abuse (CCSA) survey (2004) on addiction reported the following:

- Nearly 80 percent of Canadians aged 15 years and older drink.
- Seventeen percent of past-year drinkers are considered high-risk drinkers.
- High-risk drinkers are predominantly males and are under the age of 25.
- Fourteen percent of Canadians reported using cannabis in the past year, but 30 percent of 15–17-year-old youth and just over 47 percent of 18–19-year-old youth reported having used cannabis in the past year.

A Health Canada (2007) study on substance abuse by youth produced the following statistics:

- About 61 percent of youth have used cannabis in their lifetime.
- About 16 percent have used hallucinogens.
- About 12 percent have used cocaine or ecstasy.
- Almost 10 percent have used speed, and almost 2 percent have used inhalants.

The medications prescribed by a physician are manufactured under strict conditions to ensure purity. They are approved for distribution based on scientific evidence of their effectiveness. Physicians consider factors such as a person's age, weight, and other

substance abuse: Continued use of substances despite significant difficulties in areas such as health (physical, emotional, and cognitive), family and other relationships, legal problems, and use in hazardous situations. Individuals may also experience increased tolerance, which leads to increases in the amount used, and withdrawal symptoms and cravings, which often precipitate relapse.

medications that an individual may be taking. Notwithstanding these controls, there are risks. Medications can have significant and dangerous side effects for some individuals, so physicians monitor the effectiveness of the medication, and they intervene when necessary to mediate any adverse reactions.

Street drugs, on the other hand, have no such controls and the risks are compounded. The drug may be different than users expect, or it may be mixed with other unknown or toxic substances. Moreover, the street drug may interact poorly with any prescribed medication, causing a risk of significant health problems or death. As well, there are other well-known problems associated with illicit drug use, including HIV and hepatitis infections from contaminated needles, violence and crime in the pursuit of drugs, and family breakdown. Table 9.4 outlines some commonly abused substances.

The Opioid Crisis   The misuse of opioids is now a national crisis in Canada. In 2016, there were almost 3000 opioid deaths in Canada and in 2017, the number exceeded 4000 (Government of Canada, 2017c). About 75 percent of the deaths were male. In Canada's major cities, emergency intervention with naltrexone (Narcan) has saved thousands of lives, but escalating opioid use still results in over 10 deaths a day prompting governments in Canada and the United States to declare it a national emergency. Recently, Narcan emergency kits have been made available to users and others who are likely to encounter overdose situations. Prescription drugs such as suboxone, methadone, and buprenorphine HCI can assist with short- and long-term withdrawal from opioids.

Many people became addicted to opioids when they used medications or illicit drugs such as oxycodone, Vicodin, fentanyl, heroin, and morphine. Fentanyl is a deadly opioid 50 times more potent than heroin that continues to take many lives every day in Canada. Sometimes, people migrate to street drugs when they are unable to get prescription oxycodone.

Opioids cause a burst of the neurotransmitter dopamine, which precipitates a surge of pleasure known as a "high." Drug dependence, addiction, and tolerance can happen very quickly. Opioid drugs can be snorted, injected intravenously, or smoked.

Withdrawal from Drugs: Detoxification

There is no set timeline on how long it takes to detox from addictive drugs. It depends on factors such as type of drug, how long it was used, how much, method of injection, general health, history, and genetics.

Withdrawal (detox) from drugs, including opioids, can range from mild to severe. Prolonged use of opioids can alter the functioning of the brain, including the limbic system, the brain stem, as well as the spinal cord. Dependency occurs when the person requires the drug to deal with pain or to avoid withdrawal.

Detox is often undertaken in a hospital or specialized centre that is equipped to deal with the medical symptoms and risks of withdrawal. For those who are not at high risk of severe physical withdrawal symptoms, there are outpatient detox programs.

With opioids, acute withdrawal symptoms (first 72 hours) usually start after about 12 hours and may include muscle aches, anxiety, sleep disturbance, diarrhea, cramping, nausea, rapid heartbeat, and high blood pressure (Healthline, 2018). Symptoms are at their worst during the first few days and weeks and they will gradually decrease, but protracted effects from withdrawal can last up to six months or longer. Since opioids offer immediate release from the pain of withdrawal, relapse during this period

TABLE 9.4 Commonly Abused Substances

Substance	Reasons for Using	Potential Risks
Tobacco (cigarettes, cigars, snuff, and chewing tobacco)	• Habit, prevent discomfort of withdrawal, relieve boredom, and peer group pressure	• Heart disease, stroke, cancer and many other significant health risks, and addiction
Alcohol (liquor, beer, and wine)	• Elevated mood and relaxation (low dose) • Lowered inhibitions	• Nausea, emotional volatility, loss of coordination, violence, fetal alcohol spectrum disorder, liver and heart disease as well as hundreds of other significant health risks, addiction, and death from overdose
Cannabinoids (marijuana and hashish)	• Euphoria, increased heart rate • Medicinal uses (pain or nausea relief, appetite stimulant) • Slowed reaction time	• May trigger psychosis, anxiety, or depression; respiratory infection; worsens outcomes for people with psychotic disorders
Opioids (heroin, opium, codeine, fentanyl, and co-fentanyl)	• Sedation, euphoria, and pain management	• Dizziness, confusion, nausea, addiction, HIV and hepatitis infection from sharing needles, and death from overdose
Stimulants (cocaine, amphetamines, and meth)	• Increased energy and exhilaration	• Anxiety, panic, violence, heart and cardiovascular problems, weight loss, severe dental problems (meth), stroke, seizures, and addiction
Club Drugs (MDMA-ecstasy and GHB)	• Lowered anxiety, hallucinations, and muscle relaxation	• Anxiety, sleep disturbances, depression, seizures, coma, death
Dissociative (ketamine, PCP, salvia, dextromethorphan [cough suppressant])	• Feelings of detachment from body and perceptual distortions	• Tremors, memory loss, nausea, delirium, dangerous physiological changes (respiration, heart rate, and blood pressure), increase in violence, loss of coordination, and death
Hallucinogens (LCD, mescaline, peyote, and psilocybin)	• Hallucinations and euphoria	• Flashbacks, increases in body temperature, heart rate and blood pressure, rapid emotional shifts, nervousness, anxiety, and paranoia
Inhalants (paint, glue, and gasoline)	• Stimulation and loss of inhibition	• Headache, nausea, loss of motor coordination, depression, memory impairment, serious damage to cardiovascular and nervous systems, unconsciousness, and sudden death
Prescription meds (opioid pain relievers such as oxycodone, central nervous system depressants used to treat anxiety and sleep disorders, and stimulants)	• Pain relief, stimulation, reduction of anxiety, and assistance with sleep disorders	• Addiction (increased tolerance and need for higher doses), hostility, psychosis, elevated body temperatures, irregular heartbeat, cardiovascular failure, and seizures
Synthetic drugs (a.k.a. bath salts sold under a variety of names such as Bliss and Ivory Wave)	• Similar to methamphetamine, but much more intense	• Intense hallucinations and psychotic breaks, paranoia, self-mutilation, rapid heart rates, suicidal thoughts, and death

Sources: Harvard Medical School, 2012; Herie & Skinner, 2010; National Institute of Drug Abuse, 2012; and National Institute of Health, 2012.

is a high risk, hence the need for significant medical and counselling support during this period. Physicians can provide medications to deal with many of the withdrawal symptoms.

Withdrawal from alcohol may result in significant symptoms and health risks including anxiety, insomnia, vomiting, fatigue, tremors, heart arrhythmia, mental confusion, problems with mood and temper. The most severe symptom is delirium tremens (but not everyone will experience them) characterized by hallucinations, high fever, confusion, agitation, and seizures (American Addictions Centers, 2018)

Counsellors can support clients during withdrawal (detox) in a number of ways:

- Preparatory discussion that helps them anticipate and strategize ways to manage symptoms of withdrawal.
- Provide encouragement, empathy, and optimism while directing clients' attention to long-term goals and payoffs of successful detox.
- Use of cognitive behavioural strategies to help clients address "unhelpful thinking" that might otherwise sabotage detox and recovery. Reframe symptoms as evidence of the body healing itself.
- Relapse prevention counselling during and after detox.
- Referral and advocacy for long-term treatment and support following the detox process. Ideally, this should begin immediately.
- Using detox as a "teachable moment" to support clients to undertake long-term treatment.
- Encouraging peer and family understanding and support.
- Making sure clients understand that after detox, tolerance decreases. If they relapse, the same amount of the drug that they once used may now result in an overdose or even death.

> ### SUCCESS TIP
>
> Since many clients have co-occurring disorders that involve addictions and one or more mental disorders, detox from substance misuse, while important, is insufficient on its own. Other disorders need to be assessed and treated at the same time.

Substance Use Disorders and the DSM

DSM-5 classifies substance use disorders under the category "Substance Use and Addictive Disorders." It offers diagnostic criteria for disorders related to the following substances: alcohol, caffeine, cannabis, hallucinogens, inhalants, opioids, sedative/hypnotics, stimulants, tobacco, and unknown substances. The Substance Use and Addictive Disorders section also features the non-substance addiction of gambling disorder, which was previously classified as an impulse control disorder. This section of DSM lists a broad range of mental disorders that can be caused by substances (e.g., substance-induced psychotic disorder, substance-induced bipolar disorder, substance-induced depressive disorder, and many others). In fact, physicians and other professionals who assess psychiatric symptoms will first assess whether substance use is causing the symptoms.

Brain Plasticity and Addiction

brain plasticity: The brain's ability to modify itself through experience and learning.

tolerance: A need for more of a drug to obtain the desired effect or less effect with the same amount of the substance.

withdrawal: The presence of physical symptoms when a drug is no longer taken.

Brain plasticity refers to the brain's ability to modify itself through experience and learning. **Tolerance** is a need for more of the substance to obtain the desired effect, or experiencing less of an effect with the same amount of the substance. **Withdrawal** is the presence of physical symptoms when the drug is no longer taken; withdrawal symptoms stop when more of the drug is taken.

Many drugs affect the natural reward pathways of the brain and cause addiction by altering the brain's ability to produce dopamine (Gibb, 2007). Euphoria from using addictive drugs comes from the massive increase in dopamine that results. In response, "the brain attempts to re-establish some form of equilibrium by decreasing the brain's responsiveness to the dopamine. . . . It does so by reducing the number of dopamine receptors. . . . As a consequence, the person becomes tolerant to the drug, requiring more to achieve the same effect" (Gibb, 2007, p. 178). Simply put, the brain is using its ability to be plastic to "protect" itself from the excess dopamine made available by using the drug. Significantly, if individuals stop using the drug, the brain's plasticity in adjusting (reducing) the dopamine receptors leave the user more depressed than they were before they began taking the drug. In turn, this leads to withdrawal symptoms such as anxiety, anger, and irritability. Given time, the brain *may* be able to reset the dopamine system back to a normal level; however, changes to the brain "may even be lifelong, depending on the duration and intensity of drug use" (Mate, 2008, p. 142). Moreover, "the worse the addiction is, the greater the brain abnormality and the greater the biological obstacles to opting for health" (Mate, 2008, p. 146). Such changes to the brain are one reason for the high rates of relapse among addicted opioid users.

Supporting Recovery from Addiction

Addiction is associated with a wide range of associated problems which may affect individuals to a greater or lesser extent including: criminal behaviour, birth defects, hepatitis, HIV, heart/lung diseases, sexually transmitted diseases, financial ruin, psychiatric comorbidities, increased incidence of suicide, homicide, violence, child abuse, job loss, and family/relationship stress. The impact of these problems often remains even after individuals recover from addition. A comprehensive counselling intervention should include assessment and action plans to address these complex challenges.

SUCCESS TIP

A study by Fraser Health in British Columbia found that most overdose deaths do no occur on the streets as commonly believed. Their study revealed that 90 percent happen indoors with 70 percent occurring in homes (Chan, 2018). This underscores the importance of counselling discussions with clients that focus on safe drug use habits.

There is no single best path to recovery. The uniqueness of each client's needs, preferences, and readiness for change means that strategies that work well for one client may not be appropriate for another. Consequently, it makes sense that counsellors avail themselves of all possible avenues for change, including the following:

■ *Detoxification (Detox) programs* provide medical supervision and support for people who are withdrawing from drugs. Withdrawal from drugs often results in uncomfortable

---

>>> **BRAIN BYTE** | Pleasure Pathway

The neurotransmitter dopamine acts as a natural reinforcer producing pleasure, which motivates us to continue behaviours that support our needs. Any of the five senses—smell, touch, hearing, seeing, or tasting—can trigger a pleasing dopamine burst. The pleasure pathway includes a part of the brain called the ventral tegmental area, which releases dopamine to other parts of the brain, including the nucleus accumbens, the septum, the amygdala, and the prefrontal cortex. Drugs such as cocaine interfere with the normal functioning of the pleasure pathway. They produce a flood of dopamine, which causes euphoria. In the process they may damage the pleasure pathway limiting its ability to experience pleasure from the routines of daily living. As a result, withdrawal from many drugs results in depression as the brain is unable to produce or utilize sufficient dopamine to sustain a sense of well-being. (Erickson, & Wilcox, 2001; Ashwell, 2012; Lees & Lingford-Hughes, 2012; Capuzzi & Stauffer, 2016).

and sometimes dangerous physical reactions (e.g., anxiety, agitation, tremors, pain, and sometimes nausea, vomiting, and diarrhea), which need to be monitored and treated. Alcohol withdrawal can be extremely dangerous, with symptoms such as hallucinations, heart attack, and stroke. Detoxification programs are from three days to two weeks in duration, and they can be offered on an in-patient or out-patient (Daytox) format.

- *Psychoeducation* provides education to individuals who have a substance abuse or mental health problem and their families. The goal is to help them better understand the physical, psychological, economic, and social implications of their substance use, including the reality that relapses are often part of the recovery process.
- *Cognitive behavioural counselling* was introduced in Chapter 7 as an approach to assist clients to develop new ways of thinking and responding. An important part of this approach is relapse prevention, which involves helping people to recognize social, psychological, or physical triggers that precede substance abuse, and then plan alternate response strategies.
- *Motivational interviewing* was introduced in Chapter 7 as a way of engaging and working with clients who are at different stages of change.

harm reduction: Methods such as needle exchange programs and methadone maintenance that reduce the damaging effects of drugs without requiring users to stop using substances.

- **Harm reduction** involves methods of reducing the damaging effects of drugs without requiring users to stop using substances. The Centre for Addiction and Mental Health (CAMH) has strongly endorsed the value of harm reduction programs: "There is evidence that programs that reduce the short- and long-term harm to substance users benefit the entire community through reduced crime and public disorder, in addition to the benefits that accrue from the inclusion into mainstream life of previously marginalized members of society. The improved health and functioning of individuals and the net impact on harm in the community are notable indicators of the early success of harm reduction" (CAMH, Position on Harm Reduction: Its Meaning and Applications for Substance Use Issues). Examples of harm reduction programs that have proved effective include needle exchange programs and safe injection sites as well as others as per Figure 9.2
- *Addiction medications* are now available and give physicians a wide range of pharmaceutical supports for addictions treatment. Here are some of the most common addiction medications:
  - Methadone maintenance replaces illicit opioids (e.g., heroin) with medically prescribed and regulated methadone, a synthetic opioid. It has proven to be effective in substantially decreasing illicit drug use and reducing crime and violence (Health Canada 2002b; Razzaghi, 2005). Methadone maintenance is viewed as a viable alternative for those who are unable to obtain the more desirable drug-free condition. Buprenorphine (Suboxone) is an alternative to methadone.

Harm Reduction Strategies (examples)		
➢ Safe Injection Sites	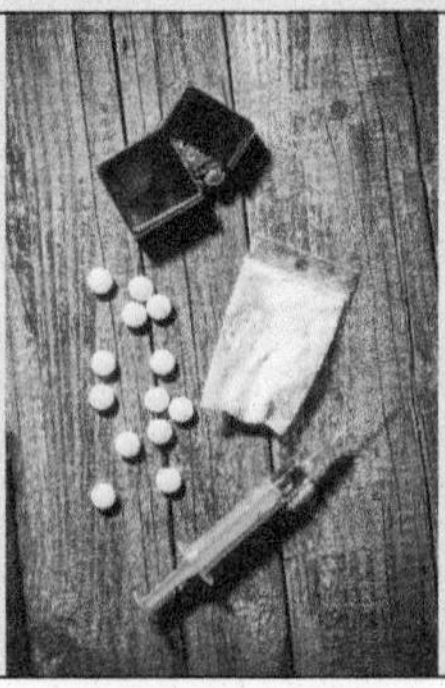	➢ Needle Exchange
➢ Reduction of drug use		➢ Drug substitution (e.g. methadone)
➢ Safer sex		➢ Heroin maintenance
➢ Naloxone		➢ Vapor alternative to cigarettes
➢ Decriminalization		➢ Buddy System

Figure 9.2 Harm Reduction Strategies

SOURCE: Leszek Czerwonka/Shutterstock

- Naltrexone used to block the effects of opioids and alcohol.
- Disulfiram (Antabuse) has been used for over 50 years to treat alcohol addiction. It works by making users sick if they have a drink.
- Campral is used to reduce alcohol cravings, and it is now available in Canada.
- Narcan is an emergency medicine used to treat heroin overdoses.
- Smokers now have many different medications and nicotine replacements available to help them quit, including patches, gum, varenicline (Champix), and bupropion (Zyban).
- Anti-anxiety and antidepressants can be used to treat co-occurring mood and anxiety disorders. As well, many of these medications have demonstrated effectiveness in reducing cravings for some users.

- *Self-help programs* include well-established groups such as Alcoholics Anonymous (AA) and Narcotics Anonymous (NA). These groups provide support and fellowship for those who are working to become drug free (abstinence). Although these groups, which are based on a twelve-step program, are not appropriate for everyone, they have proven effective for many people who are struggling with addiction.

- *Residential treatment programs* provide intensive counselling, including housing to individuals and their families. Residential programs can be short term (three to six weeks) or long term (up to two years or more).

- *Assertive Community Treatment (ACT)* is a method of working with people who have significant mental health or addictions problems. The model involves a multidisciplinary team with 24/7 availability that is able to deliver services in the community. The team provides service where the client lives rather than waiting for or expecting the client to come to the agency office. The National Alliance on Mental Health (2012) concludes that "ACT clients spend significantly less time in hospitals and more time in independent living situations, have less time unemployed, earn more income from competitive employment, experience more positive social relationships, express greater satisfaction with life, and are less symptomatic."

SUCCESS TIP

Supporting clients to stop or reduce smoking has been shown to result in higher rates of recovery from other addictions. Smoking during recovery may increase cravings for other substances that were used together. (McClure et al., 2015). This finding contradict a widely held belief that quitting smoking threatens recovery. Clients who stop smoking have overall better general health and improved financial status, which contribute to stress reduction thus increasing strength for the challenges of recovery. Therefore, there is no reason to delay cessation until other addictions are addressed.

Co-occurring Disorders

A **co-occurring disorder** exists when an individual has one or more substance use problems and one or more mental disorders. For example, a person with schizophrenia might also be addicted to alcohol, or an individual with bipolar disorder might abuse sedatives. In fact, the individual might have more than two disorders; for example, he might be addicted to amphetamines but also have major depression and a personality disorder. *Co-occurring disorders* is the emerging term of choice, but the terms *concurrent*

co-occurring disorder: A term used to describe a situation in which a person has both a substance use disorder and a psychiatric disorder.

disorders and *dual diagnosis* are also commonly used. The most challenging situation is where there is both a severe substance misuse disorder and a severe mental disorder. In these cases, high-level coordination of service providers (physicians, social workers, mental health professionals, and residential coordinators) is essential in order to provide integrated intervention.

The Centre for Addiction and Mental Health (CAMH) reports that "studies show that about half of the people with either a mental health or substance use disorder have had problems in the other domain at some point in their life" (2009). Meuser, Noordsy, Drake, and Fox (2003) reviewed the literature and found the lifetime probability of someone in the general population having a substance abuse or dependence disorder is about 17 percent, but for people with schizophrenia the rate jumps to 47 percent, for those with depression the probability is 32 percent, and for those with bipolar disorder the probability is 56 percent.

Despite the very high incidence of co-occurring disorders, historically it has been very difficult for individuals with co-occurring disorders to get proper treatment. CAMH (2009) offers this overview:

> When people with co-occurring substance use and mental health problems seek help, the treatment they receive is too often directed at only one of these problems. Helping clients to address one key problem can sometimes start a process of change that goes on to have far-reaching positive effects; other times this approach does little to improve clients' overall situation, and may even make both problems worse. To understand how we can best help a client, we need to look at that person as a whole, and see how that person's problems overlap, disguise, or exaggerate one another. Only then we can begin to offer help that is effective (Treating Concurrent Disorders: Preface).

SUCCESS TIP

Best-practice service for people with co-occurring disorders requires that treatment for their mental illness and their substance abuse be offered at the same time by the same counsellor. Assertive community treatment (ACT) is a proven way to engage people in treatment or harm reduction.

SUICIDE COUNSELLING

The American Association of Suicidology (2009) describes suicide as a permanent solution to a temporary, treatable problem. Suicide intervention is crisis counselling that requires counsellors to assess the immediate risk (see Figure 9.3) and intervene to prevent their clients from completing the suicide. This challenges counsellors to rapidly establish a supportive relationship. Active listening skills are crucial, for unless suicidal clients can be convinced that the counsellor is genuinely interested in their welfare, they may cut off communication. In Canada, it is not illegal to attempt suicide, but aiding or abetting suicide is an illegal act. Table 9.5 provides some facts about suicide in Canada.

Warning Signs and Risk Assessment

While there is no assured way of predicting that a person will attempt suicide, there are some important warning signs: threats of suicide, history of attempts, methodology, stressors, personality factors, alcoholism, social supports, and gender and demographic variables (American Association of Suicidology, 2009; Centre for Suicide

Figure 9.3   Suicide Risk Factors

TABLE 9.5   Suicide: Canadian Facts

- In Canada, the known annual suicidal death rate (all ages) is about 17 per 100, 000 for males and 5.5 per 100, 000 for females. Overall, almost 4,000 people a year die by suicide, but the real figure may be much higher due to underreporting.
- In 1999, suicide was the leading cause of death for Indigenous people up to age 44.
- Suicide accounts for 38 percent of deaths among Indigenous youth.
- Men complete suicide at a rate of four times that of women, whereas women attempt suicide at a rate of four times that of men.
- Men are more likely than women to use lethal methods (e.g., guns and hanging).
- Physical illness is estimated to be a contributing factor in up to 50 percent of suicides.
- Approximately 40 percent of people who have completed a suicide have made a previous attempt.
- Some drugs can produce depression that leads to suicide.
- The death rate from suicide is higher than the death rate from motor vehicle accidents.
- The suicide rate for persons married with children is about half that of never-married, single people.
- The suicide rate for persons under psychiatric care is 3 to 12 times that of non-patients (over 90 percent of people who die by suicide have a mental disorder, usually a mood disorder). Key risk factors are substance abuse, depression, personality disorders, and schizophrenia.
- The suicide rate is higher among people who are unemployed, and it increases with economic recessions and depressions.
- High-risk groups are male physicians (whose rate is two to three times that of the general male population), dentists, musicians, law enforcement officers, lawyers, and insurance agents.

Sources: American Association of Suicidology, 2009; Centre for Suicide Prevention, 2009; Health Canada, 2002a; Saddock and Saddock, 2004; and Statistics Canada, 2012a.

Prevention, 2009; Harvard Medical School, 1996; Saddock & Saddock, 2004; and San Francisco Suicide Prevention Institute, 2009).

Threats of Suicide   Clients who talk about suicide, or who appear preoccupied with death and dying, should be considered at risk. Research has shown that eight out of ten suicidal persons give some sign of their intentions. Sometimes the clues are clear, such as when clients directly threaten to take their lives. At other times, there are only hints of suicidal objectives, such as giving away possessions, making final arrangements (e.g., expressing wishes for their funeral, writing a will), or involving themselves in increased risk-taking behaviour. Threats of suicide and other warning signs are a cry for help, and counsellors should take them seriously.

History of Suicide Attempts   About 30 to 40 percent of people who commit suicide have made a previous attempt, and about 10 percent of those who attempt suicide succeed within 10 years. But eight to ten times as many people make a suicide attempt as those who complete it (Cleghorn & Lee, 1991; Harvard Medical School, 1996); however, it is likely that the number of completed suicides is underreported, since in some cases what appear to be accidental deaths are, in fact, suicides.

SUCCESS TIP

Look at suicide warning signs as an invitation to communicate.

Methodology   As a rule, clients who have a specific plan and a lethal method for taking their lives are at greater risk than those who do not have such a plan and method. Moreover, the more developed the plan and the greater the potential lethality of the proposed method, the greater the risk.

Certain drugs, such as antipsychotic medications, sleeping pills, antidepressants, and analgesics (such as ASA), are all potential overdose drugs, especially when taken in combination with other drugs.

Stress   Clients who are currently coping with significant stress, such as a death, divorce, spiritual crisis, or loss of job, money, status, self-confidence, or self-esteem, are at greater risk. As well, a recent medical illness may be a factor. About two-thirds of the clients who commit suicide have seen a doctor shortly before their death (Hirschfeld & Russell, 1997).

Personality Changes   Counsellors should explore whether there have been recent and drastic changes in their clients' usual manner. Changes such as social withdrawal, sudden changes in mood, loss of interest in activities that previously gave them pleasure (sex, work, friends, family, job, and hobbies), increased substance abuse, changes in sleep patterns, and loss of interest in personal appearance ought to be closely assessed. As well, counsellors should look for signs of depression, apathy, anxiety, and general pessimism about the future. Not all suicidal people are depressed, nor are all depressed people suicidal. Some people contemplating suicide may seem at peace, even euphoric; however, depression is a signal to counsellors to assess suicide risk.

Alcohol Addiction   Research has shown that people who are addicted to alcohol have an increased risk of suicide compared with the general population. As many as 15 percent of people addicted to alcohol commit suicide, and the suicide rate for people who are heroin dependent is 20 times that of the general population (Saddock & Saddock, 2004, pp. 391–392).

Gender and Demographic Differences Women attempt suicide three or four times as often as men, but men tend to use more lethal methods and account for 75 percent of all completed suicides (Statistics Canada, 2012a). High-risk groups include those with a mental disorder, young people, seniors, Indigenous people, homosexuals, and those in prison (Health Canada, 2002a). The highest suicide rates for men are in the 40–54-year-old group, with about 25 completed suicides per 100, 000 of population, but the rate rises after age 65 and peaks for those over 90 at about 33 per 100, 000. For women, those at most risk are in the 40–54-year-old age group, with an average of 9 completed suicides per 100, 000 of population (Statistics Canada, 2012a). Suicide is also a serious problem among youth. In a survey of 15, 000, Grade 7 to 12 students in British Columbia, 34 percent knew of someone who had attempted or died by suicide; 16 percent had seriously considered suicide; 14 percent had made a suicide plan; 7 percent had made an attempt; and 2 percent had required medical attention due to an attempt (Canadian Children's Rights Council, 2012).

Suicide Intervention The counselling principles discussed in this text form the basis for working with clients who are suicidal. Suicide intervention can start with the assumption that the person is ambivalent. The fact that the person is still alive and reaching out for help is a positive indicator that part of him or her wants to live. The strategies described subsequently provide a basis for intervention that may help to tip the scale in favour of living. Table 9.6 dispels some common myths about suicide.

Active Listening This skill cluster, particularly empathy, creates safety for the client to express and explore feelings. Counsellors must resist any impulse to moralize, give advice, or judge, which might create a dangerous power struggle. Active listening communicates to clients that they are not alone.

Risk Assessment Although no counsellor can determine with certainty whether a client will try to commit suicide, knowing about and exploring risk factors is essential for intelligent intervention. As described earlier in this section, some of the key risk factors that counsellors should consider include past attempts, current mental and physical status, the presence of a viable plan, the means to kill oneself, talk about suicide, personal losses, efforts to put one's affairs in order, and substance abuse. Counsellors need to explore these variables in a calm, nonjudgmental manner, without moralizing, and offer support and empathy throughout the process. To assess the potential lethality of a plan, counsellors should investigate factors such as the lethal potential of the suicide method (e.g., time between attempt and likely death), the extent to which the person has access to the means (e.g., presence of a gun or sleeping pills), and the possibility of discovery and access to rescue. Protective factors should also be considered. Strong spiritual beliefs and a social support system, including a positive relationship with the counsellor, are strengths that should be mobilized.

TABLE 9.6 Suicide Myths

Myth	Fact
Suicide occurs without warning.	There are warning signs about 80 percent of the time.
People who talk about suicide are not serious about killing themselves; they are just trying to get attention.	This is a cry for help that, if ignored, may result in a suicide attempt. The attention they need is to be listened to.
Asking about suicide may put the idea in someone's mind.	Talking about suicide in a calm, supportive way reduces isolation and gives people a chance to talk about their despair. Not talking about it may increase the risk.

Sources: Canadian Association for Suicide Prevention, 2009; Oakville Distress Centre, 2012.

Ask the Intent Question   Counsellors need to overcome any reluctance to ask clients if they have considered suicide as a solution to their problems. Asking about suicide will not plant the idea in the client's mind. In fact, bringing the issue into the open can relieve clients of the stress of trying to hide their intent, whereas avoiding the topic increases feelings of isolation and hopelessness in the suicidal person. A counsellor should always take seriously any veiled or vague comment about suicide. When clients make statements such as "Sometimes life doesn't seem worth it," a follow-up question such as "Have you thought about killing yourself?" should be used to put the issue on the discussion table.

Crisis Intervention   Counsellors have a responsibility to prevent suicide once the client makes this intent known. Crisis intervention strategies may include the following:

- Removing the means of suicide from the client (e.g., flushing pills down the toilet and confiscating guns). This prevents clients from acting impulsively.

- Negotiating plans for the next step: This plan should be very concrete and detailed, outlining exactly what the client will be doing, hour by hour, until the next contact with the counsellor. Some counsellors use a "no suicide" contract, which involves an agreement that the client will not hurt himself or herself until the next contact with the counsellor, when a new contract may be negotiated.

- Decreasing isolation and withdrawal: For many clients, talking about their problems with a counsellor is sufficient to reverse the drive to suicide. In addition, counsellors should make every effort to recruit capable family members or friends to be with the client through the crisis phase. For their support to be helpful, the client must perceive these people as credible and supportive. They may need to be available on a 24/7 basis during the crisis period.

- Emergency hospitalization: All jurisdictions have mental health legislation that defines when clients can be hospitalized. Typically, imminent risk for suicide is a compelling reason for involuntary hospitalization.

- Address environmental stressors such as harassment and bullying: In late 2012, Amanda Todd, a 15-year-old British Columbia girl killed herself and left a strong video message on the Internet detailing her continued harassment and cyber-bullying by her peers. Subsequently, her case received unprecedented international attention. The bullying was not the only factor leading to her death, but it clearly contributed to her final decision to take her own life. Amanda's death underscores the responsibility of counsellors, particularly those who work with youth, to explore and attempt to remedy problems such as bullying. Clearly, youth counsellors need to be willing to talk to youth about depression, suicide, and bullying.

Suicide Relapse Prevention   The long-term goal is to address the circumstances that led to the need to make a suicide attempt. This might involve counselling or medication to treat serious problems such as depression and other mental disorders, addictions, or uncontrollable pain. Advocacy and support can help alleviate the stress of unemployment, homelessness, and bullying. Cognitive behavioural counselling can be useful as a way to help clients deal with issues such as low self-esteem, as well as controlling and managing emotions and self-defeating thinking patterns.

SUMMARY

- The *Diagnostic and Statistical Manual of Mental Disorders* (DSM) is published by the American Psychiatric Association to guide psychologists, psychiatrists, and other psychotherapists who use it to classify and diagnose mental disorders. It uses a multiaxial system—a comprehensive evaluation system that includes not only mental disorders but also medical conditions, psychosocial and environmental problems, and an assessment of a client's overall level of functioning.

- Major mental disorders include schizophrenia, a serious mental illness that results in a range of symptoms, including hallucinations, delusions, disordered thinking, and social isolation; mood disorders such as depression and bipolar disorder; anxiety disorders such as obsessive-compulsive disorder (OCD), phobias, panic disorder, and post-traumatic stress disorder (PTSD), which are characterized by greater than normal levels of fear, worry, tension, or anxiety about daily events, or anxiety without apparent reason; eating disorders such as anorexia and bulimia; and personality disorders.

- At any given time, as many as 14 percent of children may be dealing with a significant mental health problem, which can compound developmental challenges. Untreated mental illness in children can lead to an increase in suicidal behaviour and addictions.

- Substance use disorders may result in dependence, withdrawal, and serious disruptions to work, social, and family life as well as legal problems.

- A co-occurring disorder is present when the individual has one or more substance use problems and one or more mental disorders.

- There is no certain way to predict that a person may attempt or complete suicide, but certain warning signs and risk factors can be considered. The principal risk factors include past attempts, current mental and physical status, the presence of a viable plan and the means to kill oneself, talk about suicide, personal losses, efforts to put one's affairs in order, and substance abuse.

EXERCISES

Self-Awareness

1. If you were responsible for defining mental illness, how would you define it?

2. Explore how you and your family or friends might react to the following events and situations:

   a. You or someone else has a mental illness.

   b. You or a member of your family is HIV-positive or has AIDS.

   c. Someone has lost a job.

   d. You or someone in your family has an eating disorder.

   e. Someone you know carries out suicide.

3. Examine your own attitudes and beliefs about mental illness. How have your values been shaped by personal experience? By the media?

4. Should counsellors be required to prevent clients in advanced stages of fatal illnesses from killing themselves?

5. How can you manage your own negative feelings that might be triggered when you are working with clients who have personality disorders?

6. Under what conditions do you think a person with a mental disorder should be forced to treatment?

Skill Practice

1. A client asks you to explain his or her diagnosed mental disorder. What might you say? Assume that the doctor has told the client very little about the nature of the disorder. Role-play your response with a colleague. Practise your response using different mental disorders (e.g., schizophrenia, depression, and borderline personality disorder).

2. Clients with personality disorders might challenge you with provocative behaviour such as:

   a. Missing sessions

   b. Jumping from crisis to crisis

   c. Open displays of anger or paranoia

   d. Anti-authoritarian attitudes

   e. Dependency

   Suggest strategy choices for dealing with each of these behaviours:

3. Practise a suicide intervention interview with a colleague who plays the role of someone who is contemplating suicide. Try to complete an assessment of risk and protective factors. At an appropriate point in the interview, ask the intent question.

4. Imagine that you are a youth worker (community based) who is working as part of a multidisciplinary team with the following clients:

   • Neema, age 7, goes from being completely calm to blindly running, screaming, and hitting anyone in his path. He's triggered by changes in his environment, even seemingly small and insignificant stressors.

   • Rebecca, age 10, throws herself on the ground as soon as she enters the schoolyard. She clings to her mother, begging to be taken home.

   • Emilio, age 12, loves wrapping plastic bags around his penis and masturbating during class. His behaviour was so disruptive that he needed to be placed in a special class away from other students.

   • Nasim, age 9, poured gasoline on the family cat, and then tried to burn the house down.

   • Pierre, age 15, was introduced by the teacher to the rest of the class. She jumped on the desk, pretending that she had a gun, screaming obscenities and threatening to kill everyone.

   • Pierre, age 9, is preoccupied with arranging the books and materials at his work desk to the point that he cannot engage with class activities.

   • Pari, age 18, is prone to intense emotional reactions. When stressed, she threatens suicide or cuts herself. She

is sexually promiscuous and uses any street drug available. When asked about her cutting, she says, "I don't know why I do it. It just feels good. It makes the pain go away."

What might be an appropriate role for a community-based child and youth care counsellor on the multidisciplinary team in each case? What additional information would you need to develop a case plan from a child and youth counselling perspective?

5. Imagine that a client is showing some of the signs of a serious mental illness. Brainstorm different ways to address this. Assume your goal is to motivate your client to seek assessment and treatment. What are some of the different responses you might expect to hear from the client?

6. A person reveals that he is thinking of suicide. He asks that you promise not to tell anyone. How might you respond?

7. Practice asking the intent question with student colleagues.

8. You are a youth care counsellor working in a high school. Recently, one of the grade 11 students killed herself. In an Internet posting, she detailed her depression and a long history of being subject to cyberbullying. You have been asked to participate as part of a team to develop a bullying and suicide prevention program for the school. Describe the potential role for youth care workers in such a program.

9. Suggest counselling options for working with clients who have "negative symptoms" associated with psychosis.

10. Discuss the counselling implications of the use of cannabis among young teens.

Concepts

1. Why do people stop taking their psychotropic medication? Describe what a counsellor might say to a client who refuses to take or appears to be off his medication.

2. Scan magazines to identify feature stories highlighting dieting. Discuss how these might have an impact on readers' self-image and behaviour.

3. Imagine that you are a counsellor working with a 21-year-old woman who asks you to explain what borderline personality disorder means. What might you say? Assume she has been diagnosed with it, but her doctor has told her little about the nature of the disorder.

4. Rudy has a history of serious depression. During a recent visit, he seemed unusually "upbeat." He took the opportunity to thank you for all your help. What might be happening for Rudy?

5. This chapter describes personality disorders as "stable instability." What does this mean?

6. In what specific ways might street drugs "self-medicate" mental disorders?

7. Suggest how answers to the question "What has kept you from killing yourself so far?" might be used to assist clients.

8. Discuss why there is societal (and often self-imposed) stigma attached to having a mental disorder, while no stigma is attached to having a physical disease such as diabetes.

WEBLINKS

The Centre for Addiction and Mental Health (formerly, the Clarke Institute of Psychiatry and Addictions Research Foundation) has resources on addiction and mental health issues

www.camh.ca

The Centre for Suicide Prevention is a Canadian-based organization providing information, training, and research on suicide

http://suicideinfo.ca

The Public Health Agency of Canada has comprehensive reports and information on mental illness in Canada

www.phac-aspc.gc.ca/publicat/miic-mmac/index-eng.php

The Canadian Mental Health Association has fact and information sheets on a wide range of mental health issues

www.cmha.ca

The American Association of Suicidology is a leading source of information on suicide

www.suicidology.org

Canadian Association for Suicide Prevention

http://suicideprevention.ca

Mental Health First Aid Canada

http://www.mentalhealthfirstaid.ca/en

Mental Health Commission of Canada—strategy for overhauling Canada's mental health system

http://strategy.mentalhealthcommission.ca (then search for Changing Directions, Changing Lives)

The National Institute of Mental Health provides information on mental health medications, including known side effects

www.nimh.nih.gov/health/publications/mental-health-medications/complete-index.shtml

The pros and cons of marijuana

https://medicalmarijuana.procon.org/view.resource.php?resourceID=000141

Chapter 10
Cultural Intelligence

LEARNING OBJECTIVES

■ Define cultural intelligence.

■ Understand the Canadian multicultural mosaic including the diversity of its' citizens and the challenges faced by immigrants, including the impact of oppression and racism.

■ Describe the key elements of cultural understanding.

■ Explain the basics of multicultural counselling.

■ Demonstrate knowledge of skills and attitudes necessary for working with Indigenous people.

■ Describe the importance of spirituality in counselling.

CULTURAL INTELLIGENCE AND DIVERSITY: WORKING WITH COMPETENCE

Competent counsellors don't just tolerate or accept diversity; they welcome and value differences. By working to achieve empathic connections with their culturally different clients, counsellors are best able to position themselves to respond effectively to clients with a different worldview. According to Arthur and Stewart (2001), to achieve knowledge about the factors that shape their client's worldviews,

> [c]ounsellors need to possess knowledge about the history, values, and socialization practices of cultural groups within Canadian society, and how their heritages, including the socio-political issues facing these groups, may have influenced their personal and social development . . . . Cultural knowledge includes information about the client's cultural roots, values, perceived problems and preferred interventions, as well as any significant within group diversity, including differing levels of socioeconomic status, acculturation and racial-identity commitment. (p. 7)

Table 10.1 outlines **cultural intelligence** competencies for Canadian counsellors. These competencies encompass the core beliefs, knowledge, and skills that are essential for working with Canada's multicultural community. Under ideal conditions, clients can receive service from agencies and workers from their own communities in their own language. In large urban areas, this may be possible for some groups, but more often minority group clients must engage with mainstream agencies, but often these settings are structured to meet the needs of the dominant culture. The reality of Canada's diversity and increased sensitivity to the needs of diverse groups has resulted in movement, albeit slow, to reorganize agency structure, policy, and staffing to become more inclusive. As part of this transformation, all counsellors need to pursue developing their cultural intelligence.

Cultural Intelligence: The ability to adapt and integrate skill, knowledge, and attitudes consistent with the culture of clients.

TABLE 10.1	Profile of a Culturally Intelligent Canadian Counsellor
Skills	✓ Adapts counselling skills and procedures to be consistent with the needs, values, and healing practices of different groups ✓ Utilizes resources, people, and counselling supports from the client's own community ✓ Integrates culturally appropriate spirituality into counselling practice ✓ Works from an anti-oppressive, strengths-based philosophy ✓ Prevents stereotyping by learning about the individuality of each client
Knowledge	✓ Explores the cultural values, beliefs, customs, and worldviews of clients ✓ Understands the dynamics of power and privilege enjoyed by dominant culture ✓ Recognizes that minority groups are often the targets of oppression ✓ Aware of the oppression that Indigenous people, minority groups and immigrants have faced while valuing their inherent strength and resilience (e.g., Residential Schools, Japanese internment, and job discrimination) ✓ Appreciates the sacrifices immigrants and refugees have made in their journey to Canada in order to escape personal, religious, or political oppression
Values/Self-awareness	✓ Alert to monitor how one's own culture, values, and beliefs might lead to bias and difficulty making empathic connections with others who are different ✓ Honours diversity as a powerful force for unity ✓ Values the importance of French language and culture to Canadian identity
Behaviour	✓ Makes multicultural competence a priority for personal and professional development ✓ Open to hearing the individual stories of culturally different clients ✓ Develops friendships and involvement with individuals and groups from diverse communities ✓ Advocates on behalf of minority group clients

The Importance of Multicultural Involvement

Books, films, courses, and seminars can be invaluable sources of information for counsellors in their quest for cultural sensitivity and understanding. These tools can greatly deepen intellectual knowledge and awareness about cultural customs and variations. They are also important for stimulating thought and broadening knowledge about diversity; however, counsellors also need to embrace experiential learning. Multicultural events, travel, and visits to various churches, synagogues, and other places of worship will expose counsellors to the subtleties of culture, including the wide variations in style and practice that exist within various groups. Multifaith calendars can be used as a starting point to learn about the religious holidays and festivals that different people celebrate. Cultivating multicultural friendships and involvement in multicultural organizations help counsellors broaden their worldview, increase their tolerance, and learn about the many different ways to make sense of the world.

Cross-cultural experiential learning exposes counsellors to the reality that there are many different ways to view and solve the same problem. But achieving cross-cultural competence is difficult, perhaps impossible, if counsellors remain personally isolated within their own cultural community of friends and family.

In addition, contact with different cultures provides opportunities to rehearse adaptive functioning skills that help us survive in the diversified global village of the future. By learning to work with those different from ourselves, we learn that we can develop the facility for working with future cultures that we do not yet know (Pedersen, 2001, p. 20).

THE CANADIAN CONTEXT: CULTURE AND DIVERSITY

Despite being the second largest country in the world geographically, with an area of almost 10,000,000 square kilometres, Canada is one of the most sparsely populated, with the bulk of the population of about 37 million (2018 estimate) residing within 300 kilometres of the United States border, and more than 50 percent living in four major metropolitan centres. Canada is larger than China, yet has less than 3 percent of China's population. Canada has six different time zones and shares an 8891 kilometre east–west border with the United States. Canada has two official languages (French and English), and all official government documents must be published in both languages.

Canada's multicultural mosaic is defined by the presence of dozens of different cultural and language groups, each of which brings their own traditions and beliefs to the Canada's collective identity. Below is a quick snapshot of Canada's ethnic and religious diversity:

- Canada has a higher proportion of immigrants than any other G7 country.

- In 1971, Canada adopted an official policy of multiculturalism. This was followed by the 1982 *Charter of Rights and Freedoms* that protected multiculturalism.

- Over 20 percent of Canada's population are immigrants (80% of whom live in Canada's six largest cities) with over 200 languages spoken as their mother tongue.

- Among Canadians, approximately 66% identify as Christian; 3.2% as Muslim; 12.5% as Hindus; 1.4% as Sikhs; 1.1% as Buddhists; and 1.0% as Jewish (Statistics Canada, 2018; Canadian Population, 2018).

The diversity of Canada's population goes beyond culture, language, and religion to include a wide range of variables that define our differences, including age, gender, economic status, sexual orientation, and marital status. Figure 10.1 presents some of the

The emergent field of cultural neuroscience has found different brain activity among cultural groups. For example, there are significant differences in neural activity in areas such as pain perception, visual perception, face recognition, and resting state activity (Han, 2015). Put simply, two people from divergent cultures may behave, think, and feel in very dissimilar ways, with unique neural pathways firing for each. The simple truth is that culture shapes how one views and interacts with the world.

Figure 10.1   Selected Elements of Diversity

many elements of diversity. Table 10.2 defines some of the key terms that counsellors should understand when working within Canada's multicultural environment.

Diversity defines and unifies the country. Throughout its history, the people of Canada have maintained a commitment to diversity. Among nations, Canada has acquired a leadership role as a model for diversity. The country's receptivity to diversity is reflected in a broad range of federal and provincial legislation. Concurrently, the Canadian workplace itself has come to realize and recognize the value of diversity as a desirable goal for organizations. This perspective was underscored by Prime Minister Trudeau celebrating Canada's Multiculturalism day:

> Today, Canadians from coast to coast join together to celebrate the multiculturalism and openness that make us who we are as a country. Canadians come from every corner of the world, speak two official languages and hundreds more, practice many faiths, and represent many cultures. Multiculturalism is at the heart of Canada's heritage and identity—and as Canadians, we recognize that our differences make us strong (2017).

SUCCESS TIP

The importance of avoiding stereotypes needs to be emphasized. Individuals of any group or culture may or may not hold to the values and customs of their group. Some adhere completely, while others may be assimilated into the mainstream society. Never assume from physical appearance that the person was born outside Canada, speaks a foreign language, or adheres to the culture that he or she appears to represent.

TABLE 10.2 Selected Definitions

- **Aboriginal:** First Nations, Metis, or Inuit people. (Note: Indigenous is now the preferred term.)
- **Acculturation:** The process by which people adapt and blend in with a different culture.
- **Cultural appropriation:** Borrowing, adopting, or distorting elements of another culture inappropriately or in a way that is disrespectful.
- **Culture:** How people define themselves; may include shared behavioural patterns with respect to food, the arts, customs, ritual, identity, and traditions.
- **Culture shock:** Disorienting and stressful physical and psychological reactions to a new culture that may include depression, homesickness, and feelings of helplessness.
- **Diversity:** The vast range of differences among us, including such variables as age, gender, race, economic status, sexual orientation, religious/spiritual beliefs, ethnicity, marital status, abilities, and language.
- **Ethnicity:** Shared components of race, language, customs, and religion.
- **Ethnocentrism:** The belief that one's values, beliefs, and traditions are inherently superior to those of others.
- **First Nations:** Status and nonstatus Indian people.
- **Immigrant:** A person from another country who has been accepted by the Canadian government as a permanent resident.
- **Indigenous people:** Original residents of North America including their decendants.
- **Indian Status:** The status enjoyed by person recognized and registered under the Canadian *Indian Act* for a range of government programs and services as well as certain land, hunting, fishing, and monetary rights. Precise treaty rights differ among the various First Nations.
- **Indigenous or Aboriginal self-government:** Governance designed, established, and administered by Indigenous people.
- **LGBTQ:** Lesbian, gay, bisexual, transgender, and queer community.
- **Marginalization:** Formal or informal exclusion of groups or individuals from full participation in society.
- **Nonstatus Indians:** Persons who have Indian ancestry and retain their Indian identity but have lost their legal status under the *Indian Act*.
- **Norms:** Shared expectations regarding what is acceptable such as clothing, greeting routines, manners, and eye contact.
- **Prejudice:** Disempowerment and denial of rights of others based on membership in a group.
- **Race:** Group of people with similar skin tone and facial characteristics (Note: the concept of race is a social construct, not a biological reality based on discreet genetic differences among people).
- **Racism:** Oppression and discrimination based on race.
- **Refugee:** A person offered protection by the Government of Canada because of a justified fear of persecution in his or her country.
- **Worldview:** Beliefs that are the foundation for the meaning people attribute to the world, themselves, and life.
- **Xenophobia:** Fear, suspicion, or distrust of people who are different or foreign.

Although we share common human values and needs, we are uniquely different. Some differences such as skin colour, gender, age, race, height, weight, and other body characteristics are clearly visible. Other differences such as sexual orientation, religious affiliation, and economic status are less obvious.

SUCCESS TIP

Counsellors have a responsibility to advocate for systemic change to reduce oppression and the misuse of power, and improve clients' access to services and resources.

Canadian Immigration

Canadian art and community celebrations mirror the rich diversity of its citizens. Throughout the year, festivals, religious ceremonies, and various cultural events provide people with opportunities to honour their own heritage and take part in the ceremonies of others. But this has not always been the case. Until 1968, immigrants to Canada were largely of European ancestry. The *Immigration Act* of 1968 replaced criteria for entry that were perceived as racist. As a result, the ratio of visible minorities among immigrants changed from less than 1 percent (pre-1960) to more than 75 percent today. These changing demographics have challenged all institutions, including social service providers, to re-examine their structures, philosophies, and service delivery methodologies. Even the theoretical basis of counselling practice is under pressure to become more culturally sensitive to the diverse worldviews of the client population.

Immigration policies in the latter part of the twentieth century increased the need for counsellors to develop skills to relate to increasingly heterogeneous caseloads. In fact, typical counselling caseloads in Canada are characterized by diversity in terms of culture, age, race, gender, and sexual orientation. It is a certainty that counsellors will work with clients who have different cultural backgrounds from their own. Canadian census data reveals that over 20 percent of Canada's people were born in another country and immigrated to Canada. In Vancouver and Toronto, over 40 percent of the population has a mother tongue other than English or French. Statistics Canada (2012b) estimates that by 2031, between 25 and 28 percent of the population will be foreign born, and almost 50 percent of those age 15 and over will be foreign born.

When working with immigrants, it is important to understand the circumstances under which they came to Canada. Some come as investors and are independent, while others arrive destitute from refugee camps, where they may have waited years under harsh conditions for permission to immigrate. Some refugees and their families have experienced unimaginable violence and trauma, and they may have undiagnosed mental health problems such as post-traumatic stress disorder.

The Canadian *Immigration and Refugee Protection Act* establishes many different categories of immigrants, including the following:

- Skilled workers who qualify based on education, skills, and work experience
- Entrepreneurs and investors who can create jobs or stimulate the economy
- Provincially-nominated immigrants who fill regional labour shortages
- Live-in caregivers who can apply for permanent resident status after completing two years of employment in Canada
- Family class immigrants—those sponsored by close relatives
- Foreign children adopted by Canadians
- Refugee claimants—people who are seeking protection as defined by the United Nations' Geneva Convention relating to the Status of Refugees

Comparisons of Canadian internal approaches to ethnic relations with those of the United States often suggest that the American "melting pot" contrasts with the Canadian "cultural mosaic." The assumption is that the United States promotes integration of cultures whereas Canadians encourage preservation of ethnic culture; however, studies have shown that the differences between the two countries are not as distinct as the two models suggest (Isajiw, 1999). In fact, the United States more closely resembles the Canadian mosaic metaphor than the melting pot. In both countries, the tendency is for ethnic groups to retain their distinct individual identity. Of course, each culture contributes to the national identity and is in turn subject to its influence. One clear example is the extent to which the non-Asian population in North America celebrates the Chinese New Year.

Nevertheless, Isajiw (1999) highlights one important difference in race relations between Canada and the United States: "In the United States, the largest groups setting priorities for ethnic relations are Blacks, now called Afro-Americans, and the Hispanics, mainly immigrants from Latin America, particularly Mexico. In Canada, the two main groups that set priorities are, above all, the French of Quebec, and the Native Peoples" (p. 58).

In Canada, Indigenous peoples claims for self-government and territorial rights have reached a much higher profile than in the United States. In addition, French Canadian struggles for cultural equality and preservation of their language parallel those of Hispanics in the United States. For French Canadians, language has become the principal battleground for preserving their cultural heritage; however, the issue of Quebec separation from Canada continues to remain important. Increases in Asian immigration to Canada have also greatly affected the cultural mix of many areas, particularly large urban centres such as Vancouver, Toronto, and Montreal. Isajiw (1999) suggests that substantial increases in immigration have resulted in tension and "an uneasy balance between an understanding and acceptance of the immigrants and feelings of suspicion and even moderate hostility towards them and towards minority ethnic groups in general. A factor in this mood is a degree of racist feeling against the predominately non-white immigrants" (p. 93).

SUCCESS TIP

Counsellors actively work to understand the diverse cultural background of the clients with whom they work, and do not condone or engage in discrimination based on age, colour, culture, ethnicity, disability, gender, religion, sexual orientation, marital, or socio-economic status (Canadian Counselling and Psychotherapy Association, 2007, p. B9).

Problems Faced by Immigrants and Refugees

Immigrants to Canada face a wide range of practical problems that may result in their coming for or being referred for counselling. Here are some examples of the issues that counsellors might expect to emerge when working with immigrants:

1. **Language:** Clearly, one of the most challenging problems for any immigrant is to acquire sufficient knowledge of the country's language so that he or she can fully participate in the community. For children, language acquisition comes quickly, but for many adults, it may be many years before they are proficient. For others, the challenges are formidable, and they may withdraw to the safety of their own ethnic group, never fully assimilating to their new country.

2. **Employment:** For many immigrants, coming to Canada results in loss of status, as credentials acquired in their home country may not be accepted in Canada. In conjunction with other problems including language barriers, prejudice, and lack of familiarity job finding techniques, some never return to their former occupations.

3. **Poverty:** Immigrants who have escaped oppressive conditions may have been forced to leave their possessions and wealth behind. Others may be required to take entry-level or minimum wage jobs in Canada and, as a result, subsist on marginal income.

4. **Discrimination:** Discrimination can frustrate an immigrant's ability to find employment and housing, and it can evoke feelings of bitterness or hostility and affect their psychological well-being. Economic stressors, including company downsizing and consequent unemployment, can result in the scapegoating of immigrants and minorities for societal problems.

5. **Culture shock:** This phenomenon, which may be experienced in varying degrees, can include bewilderment, increased self-consciousness, embarrassment, shame, longing for their home country, and loss of self-esteem.

6. **Parent–child relationship friction:** As a rule, children learn the host language more quickly than their parents do, and they adapt more quickly to Canadian life. Thus, parents may adapt by over-reliance on their children for translation or interacting with their new country. Fears for their children may lead them to become overprotective, which can lead to parent–child conflicts or acting-out behaviour.

7. **Male–female role adjustment issues:** Clients may come from cultures where male dominance is accepted and embedded in the routines and beliefs of their society.

8. **Seniors:** Some seniors, particularly those who immigrated to Canada in their later years may have limited ability to communicate in French or English. During the time, they lived with extended family this would have been manageable, as others in the family could assist them with daily tasks and translation. However, if they now find themselves in institutional care, they could find themselves in a facility where no one speaks their language or understands their cultural customs.

Immigrant Stories

- Noushein, a plastic surgeon from Pakistan, not able to practice in Canada, was forced to take a minimum wage job at a pizza restaurant where she works with two other foreign-trained physicians, a teacher, and an accountant, all of them destined to remain underemployed.
- Fareema, a specialized oral surgeon, retrained as a dental assistant. Her new employer never knew that she had more training than him.
- Issam came to Canada in 2016 as a Syrian refugee. Determined to adopt his new country, he immersed himself in learning the language. He works seven days a week at three low-paying jobs to provide for his family of 9. To avoid prejudice, he changes his first name to Tom.
- Tofig, age 55, a refugee from Iran, has not been successful in learning English. He relies on his teenage children to help him navigate the challenges of living in Canada. He struggles to understand his teenage children who have little memory of the values and customs of his native country.
- Monifa, age 23, immigrated with her family twelve years ago. She works as a settlement worker at a local immigrant services society. Fully integrated to Canadian life, she's in continual conflict with her parents who are committed to traditional values including arranged marriages.
- Thirty years after being expelled from Uganda, Kiaan is a prosperous businessman and active as a philanthropist promoting healthcare in his country of origin.
- Jessa, determined to pioneer a new life in Canada for her family, is employed on a temporary work visa as a live-in nanny. She sends a large portion of her meagre earning to her mother in the Philippines who is caring for her two children, age 4 and 5.
- Mike, after 15 years in Canada, still longs to return to his birthplace in England where most of his extend family still live.
- Maryam, age 86, from Afghanistan, is a resident in a long-term care home. She receives only occasional visits from her family. She speaks only a few words of English, and there is no one who speaks her first language, Pashto. She is depressed and expressed a desire to die.

Recent Canadian Immigrants and Refugees   There are unique challenges for counsellors who work with recent immigrants, particularly those who do not speak English or French. These challenges are magnified when clients are refugees, who may be poorly prepared for life in Canada:

> Not only is their arrival usually preceded by an arduous, often dangerous journey, their flight was usually precipitated by social, ethno-racial, religious, or political strife—even war. Many refugees have been the victims of, or witnessed, torture and other atrocities. (Turner & Turner, 2001, p. 171)

Counsellors who cannot draw on their own experiences for understanding need to be willing to learn from their clients about the enormous trauma and suffering they have experienced. A trauma-informed approach with empathic interest will help them avoid duplicating the experience of many survivors of concentration camps, who were prevented from getting treatment and assistance "because the examining psychiatrists were unable to comprehend the enormity of their suffering" (Ruskin & Beiser, 1998, p. 428).

> Example: Parivash fled from her home in the Middle East after a long period of religious persecution. Her father and her brother were both executed for refusing to deny their Baha'i Faith, although she claims the official explanation cited various fictitious crimes against the state. As a teenager, she was imprisoned and was subjected to torture, but then without explanation she was released from jail. Her eldest brother remains imprisoned with his fate unknown. Newly arrived in Canada, Parivash has only marginal English but strong determination to make a new life. Her spiritual commitment remains central to her worldview.

Westwood and Ishiyama (1991) offer this caution counsellors working with immigrants:

> Client resistance and distrust in the counselling process may be set in motion by cross-cultural insensitivities, such as the counsellor's disregarding the client's age and social status and calling him or her by the first name, using excessive informality and friendliness, probing into private feelings, demanding high levels of self-disclosure and expressiveness, and advice giving. (p. 137)

Sociopolitical Realities

With ethnic minority clients and Indigenous people, there are typically historical and sociopolitical realities of oppressive racism that cannot be ignored. In Canada, this is particularly relevant when working with Indigenous clients, whose cultures, including their languages, spirituality, customs, leadership, and social structure, have been eroded through colonization and systematic undermining by Canadian government policies and legislation (Poonwasie & Charter, 2001; Backhouse, 1999). Residential schools were established to force children to assimilate and accept Christian values. These schools, which shockingly operated until 1996, left behind a well-documented legacy of physical and sexual abuse (Truth and Reconciliation Commission of Canada, 2015).

Counsellors should not be surprised to find that their culturally different clients present with suspicion and caution, expecting that counselling will be yet another experience where overt or subtle evidence of bias will come to the foreground. Sue and Sue (2008) argue that counsellors need to consider the problems that minority clients face that are not under clients' control, such as bias, discrimination, prejudice, and so on, and clients should not be blamed for these obstacles. To do so is victim blaming. They suggest that in counselling sessions with culturally different clients, "suspicion, apprehension, verbal constriction, unnatural reactions, open resentment and hostility, and passive or cool behavior may all be expressed" (p. 93). They conclude that culturally effective counselling requires professionals to understand these behaviours nonjudgmentally, to avoid personalizing them, and to resolve questions about their credibility.

Counsellors should consider acknowledging diversity differences early in the relationship. Davis and Proctor (1989) argue that "acknowledgment by the worker of a worker–client dissimilarity will convey to the client the worker's sensitivity and awareness of the potential significance of race to the helping relationship. It will also convey to the client that the worker probably has the ability to handle the client's feelings regarding race" (p. 120).

When counsellors and clients are from different cultures, frank discussion of their differences is an opportunity to "put on the table" variables related to dissimilar values and perspectives that might otherwise adversely affect the work. Although this is an important process with all clients, it should be a priority whenever there are sharp differences between counsellors and clients. This will assist counsellors in understanding their clients' worldviews, including their priorities for decision making.

> **Counsellor:** Clearly, you and I are very different. I wonder if it might help me to spend a bit of time talking to you about your culture and your take on things.
>
> **Client:** Many people here in Canada think it's rather odd that my wife's mother and father live with us. But they just don't understand.
>
> **Counsellor:** What don't they understand?
>
> **Client:** In Canada, kids grow up and, once they reach 19 or 20, they can't wait to get away from home to establish their independence. In our culture, we want to be with our families as much as possible. Living with our parents is natural and expected. We don't see it as a burden. It's a great blessing that we can be together.

Counsellors also need to consider the notion that not all groups in Canada have the same status or power, despite the fact that all groups have the same legal rights. Power differentials that lead to oppression and discrimination can exist by virtue of race ("white privilege"), sexism, heterosexism, and classism (Miley, O'Melia, & Dubois, 2004).

Power and Privilege   Despite the fact that the majority of Canadians value diversity, some individuals or groups remain vulnerable to oppression, marginalization, prejudice, and violence based on their membership in a group, and this fact has significant implications for the counselling relationship. Discrimination and oppression continue to be realities for visible minorities and Indigenous peoples and "racism is widely perceived to be a major problem in Canada" (Fleras, 2012, XX).

Rothman (2008) reminds us of the power differential that surrounds our relationships with clients including the reality that counsellors are typically educated and middle class and the fact that they may have considerable power in many settings (e.g., the ability to deny service and remove children from homes). When counsellors are also members of the dominant culture, the imbalance of power and privilege is even more pronounced. Consequently, counsellors need to be especially sensitive to the fact that their actions, even when well meaning, may be experienced and interpreted very differently by their clients.

SUCCESS TIP

The onus is on counsellors to adjust their style to meet the needs and expectations of the clients they serve.

KEY ELEMENTS OF CULTURAL UNDERSTANDING

Worldview

Worldview is the looking glass through which clients see the world. Dodd (1995) describes worldview as:

> . . . a belief system about the nature of the universe, its perceived effect on human behavior, and one's place in the universe. Worldview is a fundamental core set of assumptions explaining cultural forces, the nature of humankind, the nature of good and evil, luck, fate, spirits, the power of significant others, the role of time, and the nature of our physical and natural resources. (p. 105)

Because the worldviews of counsellors and their clients may involve different belief systems based on different assumptions and explanations, communication misunderstandings can easily occur and, as Sue and Sue (2008) note, cultural oppression may

worldview: A person's "belief system about the nature of the universe, its perceived effect on human behaviour, and one's place in the universe. Worldview is a fundamental core set of assumptions explaining cultural forces, the nature of humankind, the nature of good and evil, luck, fate, spirits, the power of significant others, the role of time, and the nature of our physical and natural resources" (Dodd, 1995, p. 105).

result. Counsellors may, for example, encounter clients whose essential worldview is fatalistic (i.e., they believe that they have little control over what happens to them and that luck is the primary factor governing their fate). This fatalism has profound implications for counselling and may serve to explain (at least partially) why some clients persist with passivity and pessimism. If we look only at the individual (and possibly yield to the temptation to blame the victim), then we are ignoring the systemic problems and discrimination that must be redressed for minority groups to have equal return for their efforts.

Culture is not an adjunct to counselling. It is not "something to be gotten over or gotten around in order to get on with the real business" (Ruskin & Beiser, 1998, p. 438). Instead, it provides the essential context for understanding and responding to clients. Counsellors need to understand how cultural origin influences client behaviour and worldview. Similarly, they need to be aware of how their own cultural past influences their assumptions and responses. Moreover, counsellors need to remember that they are members of a professional community that adheres to a specific social or political ideology and that they hold to a belief system that may be at odds with those of their clients. This awareness is a prerequisite for developing the consciousness to ensure that counsellors don't impose their worldview on their clients. Subsequently, they will be less likely to make erroneous assessments or judgments based on their own perspectives regarding behaviours such as lack of eye contact—considered inappropriate by some cultural groups, but valued by others as important to relationship intimacy.

SUCCESS TIP

"Whenever we find ourselves beginning to draw negative conclusions from what the other has said or done, we must take the time to step back and ask whether those words and acts might be open to different interpretations, whether that other person's actions may have a different meaning from within his cultural conventions." (Ross, 1995, p. 5)

Table 10.3 suggests sample questions for exploring worldview. They will help counsellors to understand differences and control the tendency to be ethnocentric—to believe that one's beliefs, values, culture, and behaviour are "normal" while those that are different are abnormal. Culturally intelligent counsellors know that people can see or do things in markedly different and acceptable ways.

TABLE 10.3 Sample Questions for Exploring Worldview

- What are your views and feelings about counselling?
- What do you value in life?
- What relative importance do you place on family? (Work, leisure, making money, being successful, etc.)
- What makes you laugh? (Cry, become sad, etc.)
- How, when, and with whom do you express emotions?
- To what extent are gift giving and other gestures of hospitality important to you and your family?
- Who has power in your family?
- What is the importance of spirituality or religion in your life?
- What are your views on bringing up children?
- What do you think is the purpose in life?
- What do you think should be the roles of men and women?
- What happens when you die?

Personal Priorities, Values, and Beliefs

Everyone is differently motivated. Some people are career oriented and others are driven by spiritual beliefs. Counsellors may find themselves working with clients whose views and attitudes on such major issues as gender equality, spirituality, and sexuality differ sharply from their own. But when counsellors understand their clients' priorities, they are in a much better position to support decision making and problem solving that is consistent with their clients' beliefs. Counsellors need to be self-aware and to have self-discipline in keeping their personal views and values from becoming a burden to their clients. If counsellors cannot work with reasonable objectivity, referral may be necessary.

For some clients, ideas and values that define personal and familial responsibilities and priorities are deeply rooted and defined in the traditions of their culture. There may be little room for individual initiative and independent decision making that is separate from considerations of family and one's position in the hierarchy of the family. For these clients, family and community are their sources of help, and this reality has enormous implications for counsellors. To proceed without understanding, involving, or considering central family figures predestines counselling initiatives to failure.

European and North American notions of healthy adaptation include a focus on "self-reliance, autonomy, self-actualization, self-assertion, insight, and resistance to stress" (Diller, 1999, p. 61). In contrast, Asians have different value priorities that include "interdependence, inner enlightenment, negation of self, transcendence of conflict, and passive acceptance of reality" (Diller, 1999, p. 61). Thus, individualism and personal assertion may not be as important for Asians as they tend to be for the dominant cultures of Canada. To process information correctly and make accurate assessments, "counsellors need to determine what is relevant behaviour within the client's current cultural context that may be quite different from that of the dominant group" (Arthur & Stewart, 2001, p. 8). For example, they need to know when the value of family or tribal responsibility supersedes personal need. Moreover, with some Asian groups, humility and modesty are preferred over confrontation, and conflict or disagreement may be expressed through silence or withdrawal. Thus, all behaviour must be interpreted based on its learned and cultural origins.

Pedersen (2001) offers an amusing but profound comment on the natural tendency to assume that others see the world the same as ourselves: "We have been taught to 'do unto others as you would have them do unto you' whether they want it done unto them or not" (p. 21).

A client's personal values can be identified through interviewing or simple tests and questionnaires. Lock (1996), for example, uses an inventory that assists people to rank-order 21 different values (e.g., need for achievement, creativity, power, and wealth) based on their relative priority.

Identity: Individualism versus Collectivism

When working with clients of different cultures, it is important to determine where the client's identity emphasis lies within the individual or within the family or community

---

⟫⟫ BRAIN BYTE — Culture and the Pleasure Centre

Brain imaging has revealed how the brain's response varied among people from cultures viewed as individualistic (Western) and those that valued collectivism (East Asian). When Westerners were exposed to stimuli that featured dominance (being in control) and independence, their brains limbic system responded showing pleasure, while the brain pleasure centres of East Asians fired in response to more submissive imagery (Azar, 2010).

Figure 10.2 Individualism versus Collectivism

(Hackney & Cormier, 2005). North Americans place high value on individuals becoming independent from their families, but in many cultures, separation from family is neither sought nor desired. In North America, rugged individualism tends to be prized, but among many Asian and Hispanic groups, greater priority is given to family and community (Sue & Sue, 1999). In general, counsellors should remember that for many African, Asian, Middle Eastern, and Indigenous clients, "individual identity is always subsumed under the mantle of family" (Ruskin & Beiser, 1998, p. 427). Consequently, counsellors can expect that extended family or even members of their community should be included in counselling.

The bipolar axis of individualism–collectivism (see Figure 10.2) is frequently used to compare cultures. Individualism pertains to societies in which ties between individuals are loose; everyone is expected to look after himself or herself and his or her immediate family. Collectivism refers to societies in which people from birth onward are integrated into strong, cohesive in-groups, which throughout the people's lifetimes continue to protect them in exchange for unquestioning loyalty (Hofstede, cited in Pedersen, Draguns, Lonner, & Trimble, 2008, p. 28).

Generally, Canada and the United States have high ratings in individualism, whereas East Asian and Middle Eastern countries are more collectivistic. Failure to understand cultural differences in this area can easily lead to erroneous conclusions. For example, in Western society, it is expected that emotionally healthy individuals will, as they become adults, achieve independence and physical separation from their families. Conversely, in a collectivist culture emotionally healthy individuals continue to be emotionally and socially enmeshed with their families. From a Western perspective, a 30-year-old adult living with his parents might be judged as overly dependent. This bias is evident in all Western theories of development, which "agree that normal development starts in full dependency and ends in full independency" (Pedersen et al., 2008, p. 150).

Culturally sensitive counsellors need to be aware of the influence of extended family in decision making. Consider, for example, the potential dilemmas regarding confidentiality with the client who comes from a family where the family leader, not the client, is responsible for decisions regarding counselling. There may be sharply different role and relationship expectations among cultures. In addition, culture-bound counsellors who define a healthy male–female relationship as one based on equal division of household responsibilities will find themselves in difficulty if they try to impose their assumptions on a family who holds a more traditional gender division of roles and power. See Figure 10.3 for some other common elements counsellors need to be aware of to achieve cross-cultural understanding.

Although all cultures tend to have at least some respect for their elders, some cultures place very high value on the elders of the community. Many Africans, especially younger ones, defer decision making until they consult with older family members (Dodd, 1995). The North American tendency to stress individuality and personal decision making might be regarded as disrespectful to parents in many African, Middle

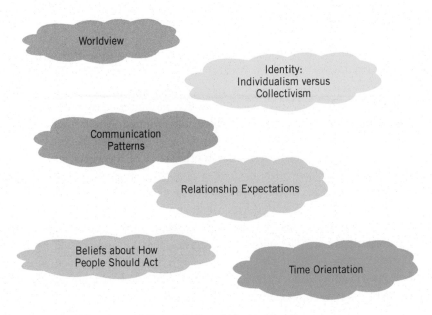

Figure 10.3 Key Elements of Cross-Cultural Understanding

Eastern, and Asian cultures. In these cultures "to honour one's parents throughout life is considered one of the highest virtues" (Dodd, 1995, p. 117). Obligation to one's family or even to the community may take precedence over self, and failure to fulfill one's obligations may bring shame and embarrassment to the family.

Counsellors should consider family and community as helping networks that exist within their clients' cultural communities. Such natural helping opportunities should be used as adjuncts or alternatives to professional counselling. However, involving others should be with the permission of the client, except under unusual circumstances such as when the client is incapacitated or incapable of making an informed choice. Some cultural groups include deceased persons as part of their natural helping network. For example, many Iranians believe that deceased relatives can appear in their dreams to offer guidance and support. Morrisseau (1998), from the Ontario Couchiching First Nation, eloquently describes his belief:

> Since all life is based on a circle, and a circle has no beginning and no end, life cannot end in death but rather takes on a different form and meaning. When we understand "all our relations," we will know our ancestors are just as much a part of us today as when they were physically walking Mother Earth. In this sense, we are never alone. Our relations are still present to help us. (p. 90)

The 1978 Iranian revolution resulted in large numbers of Iranians, mostly Muslims and Baha'is, coming to Canada. Shahmirzadi (1983) noted that Iranians are highly family oriented, and counsellors can expect that elder relatives may accompany clients to counselling. As well, Iranians will tend to be formal, particularly when dealing with people in authority, so last names should be used until familiarity is established.

> ⟩⟩⟩ **BRAIN BYTE** Individualism and Collectivism
>
> Cultural neuroscience investigates how culture shapes the brain. One recent finding using brain imaging techniques discovered differences in brain activation when Westerners and Easterners were asked to think about "self" (one's identity and traits). With both groups, the medial prefrontal cortex became active. With the Eastern group, the same area activated when they thought about a mother, but no such activity was evident with the Westerners. This research suggests how individualism and collectivism are hardwired in the brain. (Azar, 2010)

Verbal and Emotional Expressiveness

An important consideration is the client's beliefs regarding emotional expression and disclosure of personal information. The Western approach to counselling "involves heavy dependence on verbal expressiveness, emotional disclosure, and examination of behaviour patterns" (Hackney & Cormier, 2005, p. 125). This may be in stark contrast to other cultures, notably Asian and Hispanic, where emotional control is favoured. Also, what is acceptable in one culture may be offensive in another. For example, what is considered assertive behaviour in North America might be seen as arrogance in other parts of the world, and what North Americans interpret as shyness might be defined as respectful behaviour elsewhere.

Many counsellors place heavy emphasis on the exploration of problems and feelings as a means to assist clients to develop insight and understanding. But this course of action may conflict with the approach favoured by some cultures, namely to ignore feelings by concentrating on activity with an expectation that counsellors will be directive. Many Western counsellors favour a Rogerian approach, which encourages clients to express feelings and counsellors to respond with empathy. Sue and Sue (2008) highlight the danger of this approach with some cultural groups:

> Emotional expressiveness in counselling and psychotherapy is frequently a highly desired goal. Yet many cultural groups value restraint of strong feelings. For example, many Hispanic and Asian cultures emphasize that maturity and wisdom are associated with one's ability to control emotions and feelings. This applies not only to public expressions of anger and frustration, but also to public expressions of love and affection. Unfortunately, therapists unfamiliar with these cultural ramifications may perceive their clients in a very negative psychiatric light. Indeed, these clients are often described as inhibited, lacking in spontaneity, or repressed. (p. 143)

Similarly, Sue and Sue (1999) observe that since many Asians have difficulty expressing their feelings openly to strangers, counsellor attempts to empathize and interpret feelings may result in shaming the client. Consequently, they propose more indirect or subtle responses: "In many traditional Asian groups, subtlety is a highly prized art, and the traditional Asian client may feel much more comfortable when dealing with feelings in an indirect manner" (p. 45). Whereas Western counselling methods tend to emphasize open expression and exploration of feelings as a method to develop insight and manage pain, many cultural groups do not favour this approach. Indigenous people, for example, may feel threatened by demands for personal disclosure from counsellors (Diller, 1999). Sue and Sue (1999) observe that many Asians believe that "the reason why one experiences anger or depression is precisely that one is thinking about it too much! 'Think about the family and not about yourself' is advice given to many Asians as a way of dealing with negative affective elements" (p. 65). Consequently, counsellors should consider that keeping one's emotions private is for some cultures an indicator of maturity. This will assist counsellors to avoid negatively labelling such clients as resistant, uncooperative, or depressed; however, this does not rule out open discussion between counsellors and clients about the merits of dealing with repressed or painful feelings.

Versatile counsellors are able to shift away from introspective approaches that emphasize insight and exploration of feelings when this shift meets the needs of culturally different clients. For example, action-based strategies that focus on developing skills or accessing resources are sometimes more culturally appropriate. This shift has equal validity when working with clients with limited economic means whose primary need may relate to getting a job, finding housing, or feeding their families.

Alexander and Sussman (1995) suggest creative approaches to multicultural counselling that draw on the minority client's everyday life experiences. Culturally relevant music, for example, might be used in waiting rooms as a way of welcoming clients. Similarly, agency and office architecture and art should be culturally inviting.

Communication Style

Some clients are expressive and keen to talk about their experiences and feelings, whereas others are more reserved and carefully guard their privacy. Some clients like to get to the point and task quickly, but others prefer to informally build up to it. Clients may also differ sharply in their nonverbal communication style, including how comfortable they are with eye contact, their need for physical space and distance, their comfort with touch, their concept of time, and the way they use silence. Some clients find that a conversational distance of 1 to 1.5 metres (arm's length) is comfortable, whereas others find the same distance intrusive. For example, many people from the Middle East stand close enough to breathe on others. "In fact, the breath is like one's spirit and life itself, so sharing your breath in close conversation is like sharing your spirit" (Dodd, 1995, p. 166).

Generally, Indigenous people tend to speak more softly, use less eye contact (indirect gaze), and delay their responses (using silence) (Sue & Sue, 2008). A similar style is evident among Asians, who also maintain a low-key approach and are more likely to defer to persons in authority. McDonald (1993) offers this simple but impressive suggestion: "Interviewers must also be careful to remember that a response is not necessarily over when the speaker pauses. There may be more. Give time for full expression" (p. 19).

Eye contact is another area of difference. In the dominant white Canadian community, eye contact is experienced as a sign of listening and showing respect, and lack of eye contact is perceived as evasive and inattentive. But in other cultures, casting one's eyes downward is a sign of respect. For the Navajo and many other Indigenous people, direct eye contact communicates harsh disapproval (Dodd, 1995). Ross (1995) relates some important principles he learned from an Indigenous mentor and elder from Northern Ontario, Charlie Fisher, who commented on communication errors Ross made in speaking to an elder in the local community:

> Verbal expressions of praise and gratitude are embarrassing and impolite, especially in the presence of others. The proper course is to quietly ask the person to continue making his contribution next time around. Looking someone in the eye, at least among older people in the community, was a rude thing to do. It sends a signal that you consider that person in some fashion inferior. The proper way to send a signal of respect was to look down or to the side, with only occasional glances up to indicate attention. (p. 3)

Ross also notes that Fisher reassured him that his errors probably did not offend the elder who "knew, after all, that a great many white men simply hadn't learned how to behave in a civilized manner" (p. 4).

Sue and Sue (2003), emphasizing how communication styles are strongly linked to culture, make this observation:

> Whether our conversation proceeds with fits or starts, whether we interrupt one another continually or proceed smoothly, the topics we prefer to discuss or avoid, the depth of our involvement, the forms of interaction (ritual, repartee, argumentative, persuasive, etc.) and the channel we use to communicate (verbal-nonverbal versus nonverbal-verbal) are all aspects of communication style. (p. 126)

Language

Counsellors need to listen carefully to the vocabulary and idioms that their clients use to express ideas and feelings, while keeping in mind that those minority clients who are not fluent in the counsellor's language will have trouble expressing their thoughts. The more that counsellors can match their clients' style, the greater their rapport with them will be. When counsellors use jargon or unfamiliar words, clients may feign understanding, or the experience may leave them feeling vulnerable and disempowered. Of course, counsellors also need to avoid talking down to clients. Sometimes interpreters will be necessary, but family and friends of the client should not be used because of the risk of breaking confidentiality and the fact that their inclusion may introduce bias.

In addition, words may have different meanings or connotations for different cultures. For example, the word *school* may evoke terror from some people who associate the term with the abuses of residential schools. Counsellors should also consider the degree of formality that may be expected by clients. Addressing clients as Mr. or Mrs. may be much more appropriate than using first names. Some clients may see indiscriminate use of first names as overly familiar and insulting.

Culturally different clients are often particularly attuned to nonverbal communication (Sue & Sue, 2008), and they will respond very quickly to subtle indicators of counsellor bias. In counselling, they may test counsellors with questions about their racial views and attitudes to measure how much they can be trusted. Counsellors' nonverbal responses to such inquiries will often reveal more about their real views than their words.

Relationship Expectations

Clients from some cultural groups may have expectations that test the North American guidelines for counsellors. Ruskin and Beiser (1998) provide examples related to the field of psychiatry that parallel the challenges faced by counsellors:

> In many cultures, people expect to express positive feelings by giving a gift. Should a therapist accept patients' gifts? Is this an aspect of transference that must always be interpreted? Is a gift a bribe? Giving a gift to a therapist may be a culturally appropriate expression of gratitude and respect. Depriving the patient of this culturally sanctioned process may invoke feelings of hurt pride, shame, or anger that interfere with the therapy. Inviting the psychiatrist to family ceremonies and special occasions may at first seem inappropriate, but is not at all unusual. In such instances, the therapist may be well advised to consult with other therapists or culturally literate colleagues before making a decision. (p. 437)

> Example: Joyce, a young social worker, recalled how she became anxious when her client, a Jamaican single parent, told her that she wished to give her a gift to thank her for her help. Joyce did not want to insult the woman by refusing the gift, but she was acutely aware that her client was poor and could barely afford to feed her family. Moreover, she was concerned with not violating professional ethics. Fortunately, her client resolved the dilemma when she presented Joyce with a grapefruit tied with a red ribbon. For Joyce's client, the grapefruit had great symbolic value.

Another domain that counsellors need to navigate carefully is the area of physical contact and culture. Cultural groups differ on the extent that touch is expected or tolerated, and further issues related to gender are a complicating factor. The codes of ethics of both the Canadian Counselling and Psychotherapy Association and the Canadian Association of Social Workers are silent on the issue except to prohibit contact of a sexual nature. The code of the National Association of Social Workers (1996) outlines the responsibility of social workers to set "culturally sensitive boundaries" (Standard 1.10) regarding physical contact, but no specific guidance beyond this directive is offered.

Moreover, there are cross-cultural variations on how people greet each other and the spatial distance that is maintained during conversation or greeting. Whereas a handshake is common in North America, people from other cultures bow, hug, nod, or kiss on introduction, and this may vary depending on setting, degree of intimacy, or nature of the relationship. Some Vietnamese men do not shake hands with women or their elders; nor do some Vietnamese women shake hands (Dodd, 1995). Another variation concerns how people greet each other. Some clients are comfortable with first names only, but others are more formal and prefer to use titles. Some cultures expect one to greet the head of a family or elders first (Dodd, 1995). Iranians, who favour formality, may stand up when counsellors enter or leave the room (Shahmirzadi, 1983). Iranian same-sex members stand closer than in North America, but opposite-sex members are likely to be farther apart (Shahmirzadi, 1983). Middle Easterners may expect that offers of refreshments be given several times with encouragement to accept.

Relationships among various cultures may have historic roots of friction and oppression. Counsellors may expect that the feelings minority group clients have toward the dominant culture will influence the counselling relationship, particularly when counsellors are perceived to be representatives of the controlling culture. In some cases, feelings such as anger and suspicion will be overtly expressed, but they may also be unexpressed and revealed only through subtle or indirect ways. Clients who are overly compliant or ingratiating may, in fact, be masking their anger or hiding the fact that they feel inadequate in a relationship of unequal power. In any case, clients will carefully observe how counsellors process and deal with their feelings, with the future of the relationship or decisions about returning for a second session hinging on their counsellors' capacity to address such feelings nondefensively.

Many cultural groups may have limited experience with counselling (Shahmirzadi, 1983). Consequently, it is important that roles and procedures be defined clearly, a step that is, of course, important for all counselling relationships regardless of experience with the process.

Beliefs about How People Should Act

This includes clients' beliefs about receiving help from counsellors. Do they believe that taking help is a sign of weakness? Do they think that families should be able to solve their own problems without outside intervention? Who do they believe should initiate conversations? What are their expectations of the role of the counsellor? What expectations do they have of people in authority? How do they feel men and women should relate to each other?

Clients from some cultures will tend to defer to authority and wait for their counsellors to take the lead in the interview, rarely volunteering information or taking the initiative. They may be reluctant to challenge the authority of their counsellors or even to admit that they do not understand.

Time Orientation

There are interesting and important differences among cultures regarding how they view time. The dominant Canadian society tends toward preoccupation with time, with people's lives divided and regulated by appointments and time constraints. The common saying "Time is money" describes the drive toward getting ahead and making progress. But other societies may be less future oriented and more focused on the present or past. Consider, for example, the importance that Asians and Indigenous people place on one's ancestors and elders in defining one's life. Indigenous people may be more grounded in the present and "artificial division of time (schedules) is disruptive to the natural pattern" (Sue & Sue, 2008, p. 199). Some clients will make considerable sacrifices by coming to Canada and working for years separated from their children and families in order to provide future opportunities for their families (including those who are not yet born), to improve their lives. Their time orientation may extend well beyond their own lifetime.

COUNSELLING IMMIGRANTS AND MULTICULTURAL CLIENTS

Multiculturalism has been identified as a key force that has influenced the philosophy and practice of counselling (Pedersen & Locke, 1996). It takes its place along with five other influential forces: psychoanalysis, behaviourism, humanism, social justice, and, most recently, neuroscience (see Chapter 11 for a complete discussion of the six forces). Diversification of society has made it imperative that counsellors develop new attitudes and skills to deliver effective service to their multicultural clientele, particularly since research has shown that "many traditional counselling approaches are not effective (and in some cases are even harmful) when used among culturally and racially diverse client populations" (D'Andrea, 1996, p. 56).

Counsellors need to be familiar with the cultural milieu that has defined their clients' identities. This will help guard counsellors from judging client behaviour as abnormal or symptomatic of mental illness when, in fact, it is perfectly acceptable within their clients' cultural frame of reference. Trust issues in the client–counsellor relationship need to be understood and addressed with due consideration of any history of oppression and abuse by the dominant culture. This will decrease the likelihood of assessing the client as unmotivated, resistant, and hostile.

Barriers to Culturally Intelligent Practice

A review of the literature (Turner & Turner, 2001; Sue & Sue, 2008) suggests a number of barriers and recurrent themes that prevent culturally sensitive practice from being the norm:

1. Ignorance regarding the underlying philosophical, structural, and technological alterations that are necessary.

2. Inability or reluctance to develop agency services from a "one-size-fits-all" approach to one founded on respect for multicultural diversity.

3. Failure of professionals to recognize, accept, and honour cultural diversity.

4. Lack of counsellor self-awareness regarding how their cultural values and socialization affect their practice.

5. Evidence that counsellors do not invest equal time and energy in their work with minority group clients.

6. Failure of training programs to address ethnic issues adequately.

Capuzzi and Gross (2009) report that research has demonstrated that ethnic minority clients tend to avoid seeking help from mainstream counselling agencies except in emergency situations. In addition, they are typically not satisfied with the outcomes of counselling and "may distrust the counselling experience which may be viewed as intrusive, objectifying, and dehumanizing" (p. 417). Sheafor and Horejsi (2008) suggest that "overlooking client strengths, misreading nonverbal communication, and misunderstanding family dynamics are among the most common errors made in cross-cultural helping. Behaviours motivated by religion and spirituality, family obligation, and sex roles are often misunderstood" (p. 177).

Ruskin and Beiser (1998) conclude that Asians are more likely to avoid seeking mental health services because of the fear of stigma. They may also be less likely to accept referrals for assistance and may terminate service more prematurely than white clients. This is not surprising, given Ivey's (1995) observation that "traditional counselling and therapy theory are White, male, Eurocentric, and middle-class in origin and practice" (p. 55).

One Canadian study documented the barriers that inhibit ethnic groups from accessing the mental health system. The study reported that many find the barriers insurmountable and avoid it, while others who utilize it find the services inappropriate and ineffective (Canadian Task Force on Mental Health Issues Affecting Immigrants and Refugees, 1988).

In addition, ethnic groups may differ in their expectations of counselling. While Western-trained counsellors may favour more passive approaches that empower clients to develop solutions to problems, other cultures may expect that the helper will be more active and give them direct answers. Hays and Erford (2010) highlight that the importance that counselling places on promoting values such as self-awareness and emotional disclosure are not congruent with many cultural groups who favour limited self-disclosure of emotions.

Controlling the Tendency to Stereotype

Counsellors are expected by their codes of ethics to appreciate and respect the uniqueness and individuality of each client and to avoid being blinded by stereotyping groups and cultures. Stereotyping may be defined as holding firm judgments about people based on preconceptions. This is illustrated by ideas like believing one ethnic or racial group is miserly or another "can't hold their liquor." Abundant evidence of stereotypes can be found in ethnic jokes that typecast and smear various groups.

It is critical that counsellors realize and accept that people from different cultures have different standards of behaviour and that they often respond to or interpret actions in widely divergent ways. Counsellors can study particular cultures and may reach conclusions that support certain broad generalizations about that culture, but this is no guarantee that any one member of that culture will adhere to the defining norms of their subgroup. Consequently, counsellors should make no assumptions. In fact, clients are often simultaneously under the influence of many cultural groups that may exert powerful but contradictory leverage.

> Example: Baljit, a 20-year-old Asian, is a first-generation Canadian. Her parents emigrated from India shortly before her birth. They retain many of the values of their traditional culture, including the expectation that Baljit will have an arranged marriage. Baljit respects her parents, but this conflicts with her growing desire to choose her own marriage partner. She also wants to honour her spiritual traditions. Baljit is active in her community, but she also has many friends from difficult cultures and religions.

Thus, a client like Baljit belongs "to multiple groups, all of which influence the client's perceptions, beliefs, feelings, thoughts, and behavior. The counselor must be aware of these influences and of their unique blending or fusion in the client if counseling is to be successful" (Patterson, 1996, p. 230). In general, one's personal culture is influenced by many factors, including family of origin, social circle, community, and education. As well, it may change over time and be influenced by catastrophic events such as illness and war or by economic realities such as poverty.

Although individuals within cultural or other groups tend to share certain values and customs, individual differences may prevail, and any one person within the group may or may not conform to the cultural norms. There may also be wide diversity within the same group. In Canada, for example, there are many Indigenous peoples, including (to name only a few) Algonquin, Blackfoot, Cree, Haida, and Ojibway. Two key questions need to be considered:

1. To what extent does the client hold cultural values and traditions consistent with his or her own culture of origin?
2. What cultural values and traditions are unique to this individual (i.e., differing from those of their culture of origin)?

Exploring and understanding the culture, language, and history of the populations counsellors work with is an important step in preventing stereotyping. To some extent, books and films can provide this knowledge base, but direct contact and experience with different cultures is a better way to learn. Counsellors can gain this experience in a number of ways, such as by visiting ethnic districts, attending cultural festivals, and cultivating friendships with a diversity of people. However, it is important to remember that a member of a particular culture does not necessarily hold the cultural values that characterize that culture. Within any culture, there can be a wide range of individual differences. Even members of an individual family may exhibit wide variations in their cultural identity.

SUCCESS TIP

Expect that you will not be able to fully understand the cultural values and customs of every individual or diversity group. An attitude of curiosity and a willingness to learn will help you to avoid cultural mistakes. If you do make a mistake, admit it, apologize, learn from it, and modify your responses.

Respecting Diversity and Individual Differences

As noted earlier in this chapter, there have been dramatic shifts in the demographics of Canada, with a significant increase in non-white populations. In some cities and provincial areas, non-white populations have become or soon will become the majority. The implications of these changes have meant that counsellors are increasingly called on to serve clients from diverse cultures. But Speight, Myers, Cox, and Highlen (1991) caution counsellors against seeing multicultural counselling as something different from "regular" counselling. They warn against using a "multicultural 'cookbook' with each group receiving a 'recipe' that includes a checklist of the group's characteristics and some instructions regarding how the counseling should proceed" (p. 30). Such an approach may result in stereotypes and in a failure to recognize individual differences. Since within-group cultural differences may actually exceed between-group differences, "all counselling, and, in fact, all communications are inherently and unavoidably multicultural" (Pedersen, 2001, p. 18).

Respect for diversity challenges counsellors to modify their approaches to fit the needs and expectations of their clients. Counsellors need to become alert to any conflicts between how they see and do things and the different worldviews that drive their clients' perceptions and actions. To achieve this, counsellors need to develop self-awareness of their own cultural worldview, including their values, assumptions, biases, and assumptions about others. They need to remember that everyone is somewhat culture-bound and that counsellors' heritage and socialization limits their capacity to be fully objective about the worldviews of others.

Learning from Clients

Given the diverse range of clients that counsellors work with, it is not realistic to expect that they can know about the cultural values and customs of all groups. Fortunately, counsellors can use clients as sources of information by asking clients to teach them about their beliefs. Smith and Smith & Morrisette (2001) stress that counsellors should avoid the "expert role" by becoming students of their client's culture. Simple questions such as "What do you think I need to know about your culture and values to understand your situation?" can start the process. Additionally, the process of inquiry serves to deepen the development of the basic foundation of counselling—namely, the counsellor–client relationship. In fact, this approach empowers clients, and it should be followed with all clients, not just those who are culturally different from the counsellor.

Every client represents diversity with his or her own cultural mix. In this respect, Kadushin's (1990) comments on cultural attitudes are particularly relevant:

> What may ultimately be more important than knowledge is an attitude. The interviewer needs to feel with conviction that her culture, way of life, values, etc., are only one way of doing things; that there are equally valid ways, not better or worse, but different. Cultural differences are easily transmuted into cultural deficiencies. There needs to be an openness and receptivity toward such differences and a willingness to be taught by the client about such differences . . . . Because the interviewer is less likely to have had the experience, which permits empathic understanding of the racially different interviewee, she needs to be more ready to listen, less ready to come to conclusions, more open to guidance and corrections of her presuppositions by the interviewee . . . . (p. 304)

Table 10.4 summarizes major guidelines for working with multicultural clients.

TABLE 10.4 Guidelines for Multicultural Work

1. Openly acknowledge and discuss differences in race, gender, sexual orientation, and so forth.
2. Avoid stereotyping by expecting individual differences. Encourage clients to teach you about their values, beliefs, and customs. Physical appearance does not necessarily mean that a person speaks the language or adheres to the values or customs of the culture he or she appears to represent.
3. Increase multicultural self-awareness through personal study, professional development, and personal involvement (e.g., cultivate multicultural friendships and attend multicultural events). Understand and appreciate how your culture, attitude, beliefs, customs, experience, and religion influence what you say and do in counselling.
4. Seek to understand how historical events, such as residential schools and the internment of Japanese Canadians during World War II, influence current beliefs and behaviour.
5. Explore how problems like poverty, unemployment, agency policies and procedures, and systemic prejudice affect your client. Whenever possible, advocate for appropriate systemic change. For example, examine how agency structure, policy, staffing, and even architecture serve dominant groups while excluding minorities.
6. Remain nondefensive when dealing with clients who have experienced discrimination. Expect that they may be distrustful, sometimes hostile, toward professionals who represent what they perceive as the oppressive power of the dominant group.
7. Stay alert to how language, including nonverbal variables, has different meanings for different people.
8. Adapt counselling strategies and goals to meet the needs of individual clients instead of expecting clients to fit into your style and expectations. Consider cultural context when working with all clients, especially ethnic minority clients.
9. Pay particular attention to family, community, or tribal expectations and roles. (Who makes important decisions? Who should be invited to counselling meetings?)
10. Seek and use natural helping networks and traditional healing practices, including family and community resources. Remember that spiritual and religious values are important components of multicultural understanding. Spiritual leaders from the client's community may in some cases be used in the counselling process.
11. Basic needs (food, shelter, and employment) may need to be discussed first.
12. When dealing with clients for whom English is a second or subsequent language, speak more slowly (not more loudly). Sometimes single words or phrases are easier for them to understand than complete sentences.
13. If you are using a translator, look at your client, not the translator. When using translators, avoid using family and friends of the client. The client's permission to use a translator should be secured. Ideally, the counsellor should be fully fluent in both languages and familiar with the client's cultural background.

Counselling Seniors

Counsellors may find themselves working with seniors in residential care facilities where their client is isolated because they are unable to speak the language. In such settings, counsellors will need to look for creative ways to address this problem. For example, they can work with staff to find ways to acknowledge and honour their client's religious holidays. Or, they can encourage the inclusion of culture specific food on the menu. They can facilitate links to individuals or organizations from their client's culture. They could encourage and assist the client to display artifacts, pictures, or mementos. The use of translators or volunteers who speak the client's language can be used to help establish rapport and increase the client's ability to express themselves in their own language. In larger urban settings, there may be opportunities for the client to be housed in a facility that has a higher proportion of residents who speak their language.

It is especially important that counsellors, particularly those who are culturally different from their clients, take some time to learn about the customs and values of their senior clients. This knowledge will inform them as they try to adapt their work to respectfully include their client's worldview. As always, cultural stereotypes need to be avoided and individual differences acknowledged.

The Importance of Counsellor Self-Awareness

Counsellors who presume that they are free of racism seriously underestimate the impact of their own socialization.

—P.B. Pedersen (1994, p. 58)

Culturally competent counsellors are committed to understanding their own ethnic and value base. They consider how factors such as their own race, culture, sexual orientation, and religion shape their worldview and affect their work with clients who are different from them. They strive to develop and demonstrate understanding and comfort with diversity.

ethnocentrism: The inclination to judge other cultures negatively in relation to one's own cultural values and norms.

Counsellors must constantly question the relevance of their behaviour, values, and assumptions for particular clients and cultures. **Ethnocentrism** is the inclination to judge other cultures negatively in relation to one's own cultural values and norms. Counsellors who work from an ethnocentric perspective may be predisposed to discount the importance of cultural traditions and beliefs. Worse still, they may see cultural traits as something to be treated or changed because they use their traditions, standards, and majority norms as a measure of normal behaviour. But respect for individual and cultural diversity implies more than just tolerance. It requires counsellors to accept that other cultures and lifestyles are equally valid, albeit different. This is an ethical responsibility for professional counsellors. For example, Standard A.9 of the Canadian Counselling and Psychotherapy Association's *Code of Ethics* directs counsellors to pursue knowledge and experiences that help them understand diversity:

> Counsellors strive to understand and respect the diversity of their clients, including differences related to age, ethnicity, culture, gender, disability, religion, sexual orientation, and socio-economic status. (CCPA, 2007)

Typically, counsellors are well-meaning individuals who see themselves as moral and accepting. Thus, as Sue and Sue (1999) suggest, it may be very difficult for them to understand how their actions may be hurtful to their minority clients through the following:

- Stereotyping. It may be tempting to accept a commonly held but erroneous belief about a particular ethnic group.

- Adhering to counselling strategies that are culture-bound. For example, many people of colour prefer that "the helper [be] more active, self-disclosing and not averse to giving advice and suggestions where appropriate" (Sue & Sue, 1999, p. 29).

- Believing that one's own cultural heritage and way of doing things is superior. Unchecked, this can lead to oppression.

INDIGENOUS CLIENTS

It is important to acknowledge the diversity of the more than 600 Indigenous groups in Canada. Although there are great similarities among them, and they share many common values and characteristics, each of them has a unique identity. Moreover, the individuals within each community may share all, some, or only a few of their Nation's values and traditions.

The term *Aboriginal* refers to the descendants of the original inhabitants of North America. In Canada, the Constitution defines three groups of Aboriginal people—Indians, Metis, and Inuit—each of which has a unique culture, language, custom, religious practices, and so forth. Metis have mixed First Nation and European ancestry. They may have cultures influenced by their ancestral roots, such as French, Scottish, Ojibway, and Cree.

Currently, the term Indigenous Peoples is preferred over the terms *First Nations* or *Aboriginal*, but some Indigenous people prefer to acknowledge their nation, for example, the Oweekeno or the Klahoose. Each Indigenous community is diverse and has its own governing system, but the members of different groups are bonded by common values, traditions, and practices from their ancestral heritage.

Statistics Canada (2015) presented the following data based on a 2011 survey:

- About 1.4 million people or 4.3 percent of the total Canadian population had an Indigenous identity and increase of over 20 percent since 2006.

- There are more than 600 reserves (land reserved for the exclusive use of the Indigenous peoples) in Canada, most with populations of less than 1000.

SUCCESS TIP

One way for counsellors to deepen their knowledge about Indigenous issues is through film. Since 1996 the National Film Board of Canada (NFB) has supported the Aboriginal (Indigenous) Film-making Program. The NFB has a rich variety of culturally informative and sensitive films that explore Indigenous issues such as (to name a few) cultural heritage, healing practices, arts, family, and sweat lodges. Online resource catalogues are available at www.nfb.ca.

Indigenous Values and Worldviews

France, McCormick, and Rodriguez ((2013) identified Indigenous values and worldviews that shape how they view themselves and their relationship with the majority culture, including the central role of spirituality, harmony with nature, kindness, honest, integrity, bravery, balance, and humility. In order to work effectively with Indigenous peoples, counsellors need to understand and incorporate these values. Balance, for example, modeled in the medicine wheel, looks at the interconnectedness of one's emotional, spiritual, mental, and emotional being. France et al (2013) underscore the spiritual aspect of healing noting that, "it is to the Great Spirit or Creator, perceived everywhere, that Indigenous people turn to in times of need" (p. 296).

Indigenous people view mental and physical health in a unique way. "Illnesses, both mental and physical, are thought to result from disharmony of the individual, family, or tribe from the ways of nature and the natural order. Healing can only occur when harmony is restored" (Diller, 1999, p. 61). Traditional healing practices are directed at restoring this harmony. Jack Lawson, an Indigenous addictions counsellor, describes how balance can be restored:

> We sit in a talking circle, but it is the issues we talk about that are important. The issues have to do with Native culture, identity, how they see themselves as Native People, the effects of stereotyping, justified anger, positive identity development, and ceremony. And we use ritual objects and ceremonies as part of the process: eagle feathers and pipes, smudging, sweat lodges, and so on, introducing our culture into the treatment process and acknowledging what they are going through ritually and with ceremonies. Such a process fits naturally with our cultural understanding of health and sickness. We also discuss the effects of oppression, while at the same time addressing the issues around denial, relapse prevention planning, and recovery maintenance. (Quoted in Diller, 1999, p. 171)

Poonwassie and Charter (2001) describe the clash of worldviews that occurred when European Christians first encountered Indigenous people:

> European Christian Canadians believed that they were meant to dominate the Earth and its creatures. The Aboriginal peoples believed that they were the least important creatures of the universe and that they were dependent upon the four elements (fire, water, earth and air) and all of creation for survival. (p. 65)

Oppression of Indigenous people in Canada has created much pain as they were robbed of their land and their children were removed to abusive residential schools, where they were forbidden to practise their own cultures or speak their languages. In the boarding schools, the goal was to make the children forget their traditional culture and adopt white and Christian values. Government policies were based on the assumption that Indigenous people were primitive and that they needed to adopt the culture of the European settlers. Canadian governments systematically attacked the tribal systems, and this resulted in marginalization and a loss of Indigenous identity.

In recent years, the Canadian government has drafted and ratified legislation to redress some of the historical wrongs against Indigenous populations. Land rights were first recognized in 1973; the *Canadian Charter of Rights and Freedoms* in 1982 identified the rights of Indigenous people to protection of their cultures and languages; and a federal government report, *Gathering Strength: Canada's Aboriginal Action Plan*, tried to establish collaboration with Indigenous people in health, social, political, and economic arenas (Arthur & Collins, 2005). The Truth and Reconciliation Commission was established in 2008 with a mandate to explore and acknowledge the abuses of the Residential School System. Acknowledgement of the severe harm that the residential schools caused for Indigenous people was seen as a first step in a long-term healing process to deal with the aftermath of policies and programs that promoted cultural genocide of the Indigenous communities.

The final report of the Commission in 2015 identified 94 "Calls to Action." Many of these have significant implications for social workers and other counsellors who work with Indigenous communities including:

- Emphasis on keeping Indigenous children in care in culturally appropriate settings.
- Social service professionals, child welfare agencies, and courts to receive training that sensitizes them to the history and impact of the residential schools and that all decisions regarding Indigenous children take this into account. (Truth and Reconciliation Commission, 2015).

Working with Indigenous People

Given the wide diversity among Indigenous peoples, it is impossible to offer precise counselling guidelines that apply to everyone in the group. McDonald (1993) offers a number of general pointers for working with Indigenous people, but these must be used with great respect for individual differences:

1. In contrast to mainstream Canadians, whose responses are quick, Indigenous people may pause before offering a response.

2. Indigenous people tend not to engage in "small talk." As a result, they may be misjudged as "shy, reticent, or uncooperative by an interviewer when, in fact, the behaviour may actually indicate they feel that there is nothing worthwhile to say, so there is no reason to comment" (p. 19).

3. Indigenous people may appear stoic or unconcerned because of a belief that it is improper to share personal feelings or information with a stranger.

4. Expect short and direct answers to questions. As well, there may be a cultural tendency not to "volunteer" information.

5. Lack of eye contact from Indigenous people may mean respect for the person.

SUCCESS TIP

"In order to facilitate community empowerment, all those who collaborate with Aboriginal communities in healing initiatives must understand and accept that Aboriginal peoples have practiced viable healing methods based on their worldview throughout their history, and these methods must be recognized and accepted as equal to Euroamerican therapeutic approaches." (Poonwassie & Charter, 2001, p. 70)

Smith and Morrissette, 2001 conducted a study of the experiences of white counsellors who work with Indigenous clients. Some of their key observations and conclusions are summarized as follows:

- Honouring difference, maintaining flexibility, and using creative approaches is critical to effective counselling. A central part of this is the willingness of counsellors to understand Indigenous experiences and culture in terms of their traumatic historical context.

- Counselling relationships may need to include extended families, elders, and traditional healers. Counsellors need to believe in the community's capacity to solve its own problems.

- Willingness to learn from clients, elders, and Indigenous co-workers is important to relationship development and success in counselling. Counsellors must be willing to relinquish the expert role and adopt "a willingness to have one's knowledge challenged, to work with uncertainty, and seek guidance from the Native community" (p. 80).

- Counsellors need to respect and be open to the power of Indigenous spirituality. They need to be willing to become involved in community events, which may test and redefine contemporary professional boundaries.

These conclusions are echoed by Choney, Berryhill-Paapke, and Robbins (1995), who also remind counsellors to consider such variables as "differences in communication styles, gender role definitions, medicine, and social support networks, including family relationships" (p. 87).

Traditional Healing Practices

For Indigenous people, various practices and ceremonies are used in which the "underlying goal . . . is almost always to offer thanks for, create, and maintain a strong sense of connection through harmony and balance of mind, body, and spirit with the natural environment" (Garrett, Garrett, & Brotherton, 2001, p. 18). Some examples of the various ceremonies include the sweat lodge, vision quest, and powwow. They are used in a number of ways such as "honouring or healing a connection with oneself, between oneself and others (relationships; i.e., family, friends, and community), between oneself and the natural environment, or between oneself and the spirit world" (p. 19). In Indigenous traditions, life is embraced through the senses, which includes the awareness of medicine, which might include physical remedies (herbs and spices) but also extends beyond:

> Medicine is in every tree, plant, rock, animal, and person. It is in the light, the soil, the water, and the wind. Medicine is something that happened 10 years ago that still makes you smile when you think about it. Medicine is that old friend who calls you up out of the blue because he or she was thinking about you. There is medicine in watching a small child play. Medicine is the reassuring smile of an elder. There is medicine in every event, memory, place, person and movement. There is even medicine in empty space if you know how to use it. And there can be powerful medicine in painful or hurtful experiences as well. (Garrett et al., 2001, p. 22)

Elders are being reaffirmed as central figures, and many Indigenous people are once again adopting traditional holistic healing approaches. Poonwassie and Charter (2001) include the following examples:

- medicine wheels (used to represent the balance of mental, physical, emotional, and spiritual dimensions of the person)
- storytelling
- teaching and sharing circles
- ceremonies (e.g., sun dances, medicine lodges, fasts, sweats, pipe ceremonies, moon ceremonies, giveaways, and potlatches)
- traditional role models, such as elders, healers, medicine people, traditional teachers, or healthy community members

SPIRITUALITY AND COUNSELLING

"In the matter of religion, people eagerly fasten their eyes on the difference between their own creed and yours; whilst the charm of the study is in finding the agreements and identities in all the religions of humanity."

—Ralph Waldo Emerson

The Statistics Canada National Household Survey (2011) highlighted the continued shift in the religious affiliation of Canadians. The majority of Canadians (67%) are still Christian, but this is a significant drop from a rate of over 80 percent in 1991 (Statistics Canada, 2005). The changing nature of the nation's religious makeup is a result of the shifts in immigration described earlier in this chapter.

Cunningham (2012) defines spirituality and religion as follows:

Religion: the institutionalized, formal beliefs, dogmas, and practices to which followers of a particular spiritual path adhere.

Spirituality: the inner, more personal experiences of clients, especially the search for meaning and purpose . . . which may be expressed within or without the structure of religion. (p. 23)

Some counsellors are uncomfortable addressing spirituality in counselling. Fear of imposing one's values and beliefs, general discomfort with discussing religious issues, and lack of knowledge or skill in addressing religious issues may lead counsellors to unnecessarily avoid making spiritual beliefs a target for counselling discussion. Cunningham (2012) questions whether "we can truly understand our clients, their difficulties, or their strengths if we do not understand their spiritual worldview, including the fact that they do not embrace spirituality in any form" (p. xv).

Historically, many counselling texts failed to address or even mention spirituality. One major counselling textbook with more than 600 pages is completely silent on the issue. When spirituality was addressed, typically the discussion was confined to ethical issues and discussion of the professional requirement that practitioners respect and accept diversity. However, spiritual or religious dimensions, often intimately entwined with culture, are beginning to receive increased attention in the literature and professional organizations. For example, the Association for Spiritual, Ethical, and Religious Values in Counseling has been formed under the auspices of the American Counseling Association.

Most people are likely to report some religious affiliation or conviction. Moreover, for some individuals and many cultural subgroups, religious practice plays a central role in their social lives and may be seen as a major source of support. Indeed, all cultures have important religious perspectives that must be understood as part of the process of understanding clients and their worldviews. Consequently, counsellors should not refrain from working in this important area, particularly when it meets the needs and expectations of their clients.

Counsellors may work in a religious setting where their work is clearly framed and guided by the values of their particular faith. Others may work in secular settings without any religious connection. In such settings, spiritual counselling is geared to the client's spiritual values and beliefs, not the counsellor's. This requires that counsellors become comfortable with religious diversity. They do not impose their religious or personal views on their clients. Examples of spiritual issues that might be discussed in counselling include the following:

- Emotional struggles to reconcile emerging personal beliefs that are in conflict with one's religious background (e.g., a client "losing faith").

- Feelings such as guilt that emerge from lifestyle choices that are in conflict with one's religious values (e.g., a client contemplating an abortion).

- Client feelings such as anger toward God (e.g., a client whose child has died).

- Familial conflict (e.g., common-law unions in violation of religious laws).

- Family discord related to one's level of involvement (e.g., children who lose interest in attending religious services).

- The meaning of life (e.g., exploring experiences that clients describe as spiritual or religious to discern the meaning of these experiences for them).

- Death and dying (e.g., position regarding an afterlife and the meaning of life's difficulties).

- Establishing a life plan or problem solving that is consistent with spiritual values (e.g., dealing with a divorce).

Frequently, cultural identity is meshed with religious identity. To understand culture, counsellors must understand religion and spirituality. Religion influences the way people think; it shapes their values and sways their behaviour. Ethnic customs, calendar observances, music, and art may all be rooted in religious beliefs and practices. For people in many cultural minorities (and some from the dominant culture), their lives are centred on their religious institution.

Moreover, ethnic minority clients may be more inclined to seek help from elders and religious leaders from within their own community. Clients with a strong religious connection respond best to counselling initiatives that take into account their spiritual community, values, and practices. This might include helping them to access and consider relevant sacred writings as well as helping them to use the resources and practices of their faith, including prayer and meditation. But counsellors who are not informed or do not consider spiritual issues when they are important for their clients have difficulty establishing credibility in this kind of counselling relationship. Not surprisingly, research has demonstrated that highly religious clients do better in counselling and are less likely to drop out prematurely when they are matched with counsellors who have similar religious values (Kelly, 1995). For example, members of the Baha'i faith, who tend to come from a variety of ethnic origins, generally strive to obtain counselling services from professionals who are versed in their faith. Cultural understanding requires appreciation of spiritual values.

SUCCESS TIP

Failure to introduce spirituality as a topic for discussion and a target for initial assessment may discourage clients from talking about their spiritual connections. The implicit message to clients may be that their counsellors are not comfortable with the topic or that they do not see it as important.

Counsellors who are versed in the spiritual teachings of their clients' belief system should discuss with them the extent that they wish counselling to be framed within tenets of their faith. Counsellors who are not versed in the spiritual teachings of their clients can establish credibility by demonstrating that they are open to spiritual elements as their clients experience them. Subsequently, they can best assist clients by helping them to articulate or sort out spiritual and religious issues. As well, counsellors can refer clients to religious leaders from their faith or enlist their assistance. Kelly (1995) offers this perspective:

> A counsellor who understands and respects the client's religious dimension is prepared to enter that part of the client's world. At this point, the counsellor does not need an expert knowledge of the client's particular spiritual or religious belief but rather an alert sensitivity to this dimension of the client's life. By responding with respectful understanding to the spiritual/religious aspect of the client's problem, the counsellor in effect is journeying with the client, ready to learn from the client and to help the client clarify how his or her spirituality or religiousness may be understood and folded into fresh perspectives and new decisions for positive growth and change. (p. 117)

Empathic responses are powerful ways to respect clients and communicate understanding of clients' feelings. An illustrative counsellor response to a client struggling with spiritual issues might be "Seems like you're feeling a bit lost or disconnected. This frightens you, and you're looking for a way to find spiritual peace."

But in the same way that there are wide variations within cultures, it is important to remember that there may be variations within religions. For some, religion and spirituality are central to their lives, and all of their decisions and choices in life are considered in the context of their spiritual commitment. Others may identify with a particular religious belief, but their involvement and the extent that religion influences their actions may be marginal. Moreover, complexity is increased because individuals may give a different interpretation to religious teachings. Clients may self-identify as spiritually oriented without being affiliated with any organized religion, or they may be members of a particular faith but report that spirituality is not central to their lives.

STUDENT: What should you do if a client asks you to pray with him or her?

COUNSELLOR: It's unlikely that you'd ever get such a request in a secular or nonreligious setting. However, in religious settings, or when clients seek help from counsellors affiliated with an organized religion, prayer might be used at the beginning and the end of a session. For clients, this helps to establish the spiritual nature of this particular counselling work. Certainly, clients who come for religious counselling expect that prayer may be part of the work. But in a secular setting, most counsellors and agencies would agree that it is usually inappropriate to pray with clients. They might witness a client who wishes to pray but not participate actively.

STUDENT: In fact, it did happen to me. I have a field placement at a hospital where I assisted a Catholic woman. Her husband was terminally ill, and she asked if I would join the family as they celebrated last rites with their priest. I accepted, but I wonder if perhaps I've broken any ethical or professional rules.

COUNSELLOR: From the circumstances you describe, I don't believe that anyone could reasonably accuse you of unprofessional conduct. In a situation such as this, I think you need to ask two important questions. First, did you interfere with your client's right to self-determination? The request was initiated by your client, and given the context, your response seems supportive and appropriate. What's important is that you did not impose your religious views on her. Second, did you violate the legitimate boundaries of your role? It doesn't appear that you compromised your role with her by entering into a dual relationship. This would occur if you started to meet her outside your professional mandate, for instance, if

you agreed to accompany her to church on a regular basis or invited her to attend one of your religious ceremonies. In fact, you may have enhanced your capacity to work with her in that you gained further insight into her spiritual values and beliefs. Kelly (1995) argues that when a counsellor and a client have the same religious values, the counsellor may accept an invitation to participate in a prayer, but he advises extreme caution.

STUDENT: Suppose clients ask me about my religion. What should I do?

COUNSELLOR: Our role is to help clients make informed choices based on independent investigations. You might answer the question about your religion directly and then ask what prompted the question. You could assist the client to explore spiritual questions, but this must be done from a position of neutrality without any attempt to convert the client to your religion, which would clearly interfere with his or her right to self-determination. As for teaching the client your religion, I wouldn't go there. Instead, refer clients to religious specialists to help them meet their spiritual needs.

STUDENT: When prayer and spirituality are important for clients, I think it's okay to assist in setting goals and action plans that will help them fulfill this need.

COUNSELLOR: Sure, and this might include encouraging them to use prayer—if they believe that this is an important part of their life.

STUDENT: I also think that it's okay to pray for your clients. A significant part of the population believes that others will benefit from our prayers. So why should we deny our clients this benefit?

Counsellors need to acquire a broad knowledge of the world's major religions. This is a formidable task considering the wide array of beliefs and traditions that exist. In Canada, counsellors will certainly encounter clients from the following groups: Christianity, Judaism, Islam, Hinduism, Sikhism, Buddhism, and Baha'i. Although basic knowledge can be obtained from books, this should be supplemented with appropriate field exploration. Many faiths permit visitors at religious ceremonies and sponsor public information events.

SUMMARY

- Counsellor cultural intelligence is the ability to adapt and integrate skill, knowledge, and attitudes consistent with the culture of clients.

- Canada's multicultural mosaic is defined by the presence of dozens of different cultural and language groups, each of which brings their own traditions and beliefs to the Canada's collective identity. It is further defined by individual differences such as sexual orientation, education, economic status, and many others. Immigrants to Canada may face many challenges, including language barriers, unemployment or underemployment, poverty, discrimination, and culture shock.

- The key elements of cultural understanding include: worldview, personal priorities, identity orientation (individualism versus collectivism), verbal and emotional expressiveness, communication style, language, relationship expectations, beliefs about how people should act, and time orientation.

- Research has shown that many ethnic minority clients avoid seeking counselling, and when they do, they are typically not satisfied with the outcome. Successful counselling includes controlling any tendency to stereotype by acknowledging individual differences, learning from clients, and making self-awareness a priority.

- Successful work with Indigenous people is more likely to occur when counsellors honour differences, include extended families and elders in the process, and demonstrate their openness to learn from Indigenous peoples' spirituality.

- For many people and most cultural groups, spirituality and religion are an important part of their worldviews. Consequently, counsellors should develop comfort working in this important area.

- Culturally competent counsellors try to understand their own ethnic and value base, including how factors such as their own race, culture, sexual orientation, and religion shape their worldview. They need to deepen their understanding of different cultures. Although books, films, courses, and seminars can be rich sources of information about other cultures, counsellors also need to embrace experiential learning.

EXERCISES

Self-Awareness

1. Develop a personal plan for increasing your multicultural sensitivity. Include strategies for experiential learning (e.g., increasing your circle of multicultural friends and involvement in multicultural events).

2. What is your emotional reaction when you meet or counsel someone from a different culture?

3. To what extent does your cultural membership give you privilege?

4. In what ways is your worldview the same as or different from that of your parents? Your colleagues? Your teacher?

5. Take a cultural inventory of your friends. To what extent do they come from different cultures?

6. What does being Canadian mean to you? What values are linked to being a Canadian?

7. Explore your spiritual values through the following questions:

   a. Are religions good or bad?

   b. Is my religion the only correct one?

   c. Should cults be illegal?

   d. What does spirituality mean to you?

   e. Should spiritual issues be introduced by counsellors?

   f. When is it appropriate to discuss religion with clients?

   g. What are the implications of your religious views when working with someone with a similar perspective and when working with someone with radically different views?

8. Pedersen (1994) says, "Counsellors who presume that they are free of racism seriously underestimate the impact of their own socialization" (p. 58). Explore the validity of this quote with respect to your own life.

9. Spend an hour with someone who speaks another language that you do not understand. Communicate <u>only</u> in their language. What did you learn this experience that will add to your understanding of working with new immigrants?

Skill Practice

1. Interview several people who are culturally different to learn about their worldviews.

2. Spend an hour or so with a person from a different culture. Use the sample questions from this chapter to begin an exploration of his or her worldview.

3. Practise different choices for responding to a client who asks, "Do you believe in God?"

4. Suggest how you might work with a client, Ruth, who is dealing with the following problem: Ruth is a devout Christian who is very close to her family. She has become romantically involved with Jacob, a Jewish man, but her father insists that she marry within her own faith.

5. Invite an Indigenous person to share with you some of his or her experiences in a residential school. Remember that this is a very sensitive topic, so be prepared to be empathic in response to powerful feelings that might be revealed.

Concepts

1. In what ways do diversity issues such as ethnicity, gender, and sexual orientation affect counsellor effectiveness?

2. Research how mental illness may be interpreted by different cultures.

3. Describe how counsellors can be sensitive to cultural norms while honouring individual differences.

4. What are some of the barriers that clients from ethnic minorities face when seeking counselling services?

5. Explore the religions of the world (e.g., attend services and festivities and acquire a multifaith calendar).

6. How can counsellors assist clients to explore spiritual and religious issues without imposing their own religious values?

7. Do you think it's appropriate for counsellors to privately pray for their clients?

8. Use library databases or the online database of Statistics Canada (www.statcan.gc.ca) to research the demographic characteristics of your community. Identify the places of birth and mother tongues of the local immigrant community. Explore statistics related to Indigenous groups in your area. What are the implications of your data for counsellors who hope to work in your area?

9. Invite an Indigenous person to share with you some of his or her experiences as a student in a residential school. Caution: This is a very sensitive topic, so be prepared to be empathic in response to powerful feelings that might be shared.

10. What unique problems might arise when counsellors and clients are from the same culture?

11. Think about specific customs and beliefs that you might encounter when you work with clients from different cultures. In what areas do you have difficulty working with objectivity? (Possible examples: arranged marriages, male dominance in the family, and female genital mutilation) Are there circumstances where counsellors should express their opinion and challenge the views or behaviour of their clients?

12. Identify different choices for how a counsellor might respond to this client question, "What are your religious/spiritual beliefs?"

WEBLINKS

Canadian Heritage promotes Canadian content and cultural understanding

www.canadianheritage.gc.ca/index_e.cfm

Indigenous Services Canada and Crown-Indigenous Relations and Northern Affairs Canada (formerly Indigenous and Northern Affairs Canada) provide extensive information on federal programs and services as well as readings on the culture and history of Indigenous peoples.

https://www.canada.ca/en/indigenous-services-canada.html

https://www.canada.ca/en/crown-indigenous-relations-northern-affairs.html

Statistics Canada

www.statcan.gc.ca

An online magazine about Canadian immigrants

www.canadianimmigrant.ca

Links to the Truth and Reconciliation Commission's websites

http://www.trc.ca/websites/trcinstitution/index.php?p=890

Chapter 11
Neuroscience and Counselling

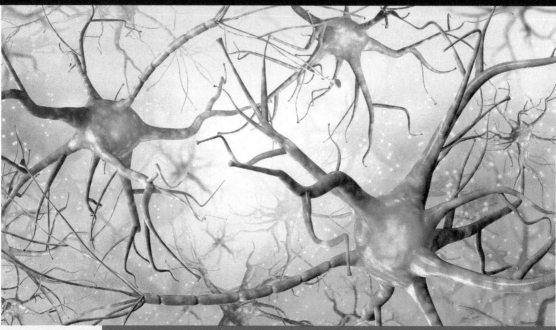

Romanova Natali/Shutterstock

LEARNING OBJECTIVES

- Acquire a basic understanding of the brain and mind.
- Describe how neuroscience is emerging as a new force in counselling.
- Identify methods for studying the brain, including neuroimaging.
- Explore how the concept of neuroplasticity can be used in counselling.
- Explain the basic structure of the brain.
- Understand the function of neurons and neurotransmitters.
- Describe the range of acquired brain injuries.

THE REMARKABLE AND MYSTERIOUS BRAIN

On a cold and wet winter morning, Bob overcomes his "excuses" and begins his daily run. As expected, the first few kilometres are gruelling and painful but, midway through the run, something magical is about to happen.

Astonishing electrical and chemical events are unfolding. Aroused by electricity, small molecules awaken and move across tiny gaps in his brain, exciting billions of others that send signals down familiar pathways creating a euphoric feeling that Bob experiences as a "runner's high," his reward for persevering.

A vicious dog interrupts the serenity of Bob's run and begins the chase. Instantly, Bob's brain assembles its stress and danger response team under the command of the hypothalamus. It signals other parts of the brain and body to release neurotransmitters and hormones such as adrenaline, glutamate, and cortisol to deal with the threatening dog. Responding to energizing signals from the brain, Bob's heartbeat increases to pump more blood to the limbs, his lungs dilate to allow extra oxygen intake, he runs faster, and he escapes to run another day.

Returning to the solitude of the run, in a way that remains a mystery, the greatest miracle of all occurs. Bob's mind energizes with self-awareness; freeing him to contemplate his existence, his place in the universe, his future, and his connection with God.

Throughout the run, outside of his conscious awareness, Bob's brain functions as an active coach and trainer. It organizes and commands a vast team of neurons to make his run possible. It moves his legs, regulates his breathing, monitors his heartbeat, and processes visual signals to produce ultra-high definition 3D pictures with stereophonic sound in order to coordinate his movement, avoid hazards, maintain equilibrium, and return him safely home.

It's clear that Bob's brain, not his legs, deserves the credit for the run.

The brain is a complex, perpetual motion machine that controls everything we see, do, hear, and think twenty-four hours a day, non-stop for our entire lives. Usually, we associate the brain with thinking and making decisions. In reality, its role is far more reaching. It powers amazing electrical and chemical interactions involving hundreds of different organs and structures within the body and the brain itself. The human brain, with its vast network of alive constantly changing neural connections is the ultimate multitasker, simultaneously managing everything from our heartbeat to our dreams, from our immune system to our imagination. Although we associate the heart with our feelings, it is in fact the brain that controls our emotions.

The brain is a ceaseless director, observer, participant, choreographer, and scriptwriter of our existence. It also relentlessly reinvents itself, literally altering its structure and chemistry in response to our experiences.

Most of the work of our brain is done without requiring our conscious attention. It works silently to make our hearts beat, forge memories, and orchestrate complex chemical and behavioural reactions to protect us from danger, even before we are consciously aware of any threat. Without our brain, survival is impossible.

A New Era   We've only just begun. With breathtaking speed, over the last 20 years, neuroscientists have uncovered vast knowledge about the brain and its mechanics, but they are still at the early stages of unravelling the mysteries of the most complex and capable object in the universe. Until recent years, the brain remained mysterious, and little was known or understood about how the brain actually works. Now, in a new era, with amazing brain imaging techniques and extraordinary emphasis on research, the brain is slowly divulging its secrets.

Worldwide, brain research has become a priority, with work proceeding at an unprecedented rate. For example, the government and The Brain Canada Foundation, a nonprofit public-private partnership formed to support brain research, by the end of March 2018 invested almost 210 million dollars to over 900 researchers. Such research is generating a constant stream of discoveries that inform innovative and effective interventions for brain disorders.

Serious interest in the brain is no longer confined to professionals. Books, television specials, and popular magazines like *National Geographic*, *Scientific American*, *Time*, and *Discover* are publishing content on the brain for all to read. Libraries and bookstores now regularly feature displays on the brain, including a growing body of material on the topic of brain health and vitality. Terms like "frontal lobe," "serotonin," "dopamine," "neurotransmitter," and "brain plasticity," once the jargon of researchers, academics

At birth, a single brain cell has become 80 billion neural cells eager to define our existence. The brain is an instant supercentre of learning. Two decades later, the brain is still maturing (hopefully) to create a mind with good judgment and impulse control. In every instant, the brain is changing, adapting, and, if necessary, repairing damage. New neurons are created (neurogenesis), and the massive neural highways that control everything are formed, strengthened, or pruned. Over a lifetime, experience and reflection give rise to wisdom, a fair trade for the memory, and cognitive declines of aging.

>>> BRAIN BYTE | The Amazing Brain

The brain is 75 percent water and weighs only 1400 grams, but it uses 20 percent of the body's energy and blood to fuel 80 billion neurons, each of which is connected electrochemically to as many as 40,000 others at a speed of over 400 km per hour. Contrary to popular myth, we use all of our brain, all of the time. Unlike the pictures in the books, the parts of the brain are not colour coded. The brain is mostly grey with the same consistency as tofu.

and doctors, are now part of everyday language. Empowerment comes with this knowledge. People have access to the knowledge that can make them informed consumers of mental health and counselling services. They can take charge of their brain health by learning strategies for dealing with disorders such as Alzheimer's.

This chapter can only provide brief information about a selected range of topics that are important for counsellors. Given the growing importance of neuroscience for counsellors, readers should take advantage of opportunities for further study available on the web, in research reports, journals, and books.

NEUROSCIENCE: AN EMERGING FORCE IN COUNSELLING

Over the past 100 years, five key forces (Figure 11.1) or approaches have influenced the direction and philosophy of counselling. Neuroscience is on track to become the sixth force. Each force offers counsellors important perspective, knowledge and guidance.

>>> CONVERSATION 11.1 | Mind and Brain

Counsellor: What's the difference between the mind and the brain?

Teacher: It depends on who you ask. Philosophers, theologians, biologists, and neuroscientists will each have their own definition and, even within their discipline, they will not find consensus.

I'll give you my opinion. The brain is the physical organ at top of our heads. The mind is what we are able to do with our brain, our capacity for problem solving and creativity, our consciousness, and our capacity to experience love and joy as well as deep sadness. It also distinguishes us from others by defining our individuality and personality.

The greatest marvel of the mind is it allows us to reflect on our own existence and find spiritual significance and purpose to life. In the last 35 years, neuroscientists have made remarkable progress in understanding the brain. New research findings are coming at such a rapid rate that even neuroscientists have trouble keeping up. In the future, we will probably achieve an almost complete description of the structure, chemistry, and electrical circuitry of the brain. What about the mind? It's still a mystery. We know very little.

Counsellor: I wonder if traditional scientific research and analysis are inadequate tools for studying the mind. The mind is concerned with the nature of reality, consciousness, curiosity, and spirituality. These matters aren't part of the physical world that can be studied in the same way. They don't adhere to the laws of physics. Maybe, because of this, we'll never be able to fully understand the nature of the mind. In fact, I hope this is true.

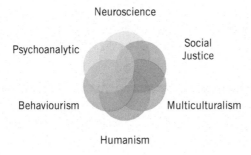

Figure 11.1 Key Forces in Counselling

While some counsellors may strongly align themselves with a particular approach, most recognize the value of drawing on the insights offered by different theories and models. This has been the essential theme of this book based on the premise that wise counsellors make informed choices based on individual situations and client needs.

Six Key Forces in Counselling

1. **Psychoanalysis** focuses on helping clients develop understanding and insight regarding the origins of their thoughts, feelings, and behaviour. Heavy emphasis is placed on exploring the unconscious.

2. **Behaviourism** looks at human behaviour as a product of learning and the environment. In this approach, behaviour is shaped by reinforcement.

3. **Humanism** with Carl Rogers at the forefront, is based on the philosophy that people are innately driven toward growth and fulfillment. Core conditions (empathy, genuineness, and unconditional positive regard) are seen as "necessary and sufficient" qualities needed by counsellors to help clients manage problems and emotions.

4. **Multiculturalism** involves framing counselling interventions in the context of our clients' cultural worldviews. In a multicultural society such as Canada, it a necessary perspective, regardless of the counselling approach adopted.

5. **Social justice** recognizes the importance of counselling professionals working to help establish more equity regarding the distribution of wealth, resources, and opportunity. Social justice accepts that client problems may be the unfortunate outcome of oppression, poverty, and marginalization.

6. **Neuroscience** is the study of the nervous system (see Figure 11.2), which includes the central nervous system (brain and spinal cord) and the peripheral nervous system (nerves outside of the brain and spinal cord). Neuroscience explores the electrical and chemical activity of the brain using a variety of experimental and brain imaging techniques.

Neuroscience explores how the brain controls thinking, behaviour, and emotions, and how the brain reacts to such things as physical or mental illness, trauma, and substance misuse. **Neurocounselling**, a term not yet in widespread use, is the integration of neuroscience into the practice of counselling. A neuropsychiatrist is a medical doctor who specializes in the treatment of neurological injury or disease. A neuropsychologist is a psychologist (usually with a Ph.D.) who deals with the psychological problems associated with brain injury or disease. In Canada, only those with a medical degree can prescribe medication, but in the United States (in some jurisdictions), specially trained psychologists can prescribe a limited number of medications.

neurocounselling: The integration of neuroscience into the practice of counselling.

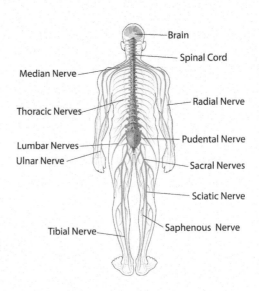

Figure 11.2 The Nervous System
SOURCE: Snapgalleria/Shutterstock

Competent counsellors try to understand their clients by considering many variables, including genetics, developmental level, prior learning, relationship and family dynamics, impact of substance misuse, presence of mental disorders, overall health, the influence of cultural and spiritual beliefs, as well as systemic issues such as poverty, unemployment, and oppression. Neuroscience, as an emergent force, will add yet another dimension for counsellors to consider. It represents no threat. It won't negate the long-established and important cornerstones of effective counselling such as relationship and the core conditions, especially empathy. In fact, as will be explored later in this chapter, neuroscience has endorsed the validity of these cornerstones.

WHY NEUROSCIENCE IS IMPORTANT FOR COUNSELLORS

Neuroscience Endorses Counselling

A growing body of neuroscience research is providing counsellors with scientific proof of the value of their work as well as guidance on which counselling strategies are effective in given situations. McHenry, Sikorski, & McHenry (2014) call on counsellors to embrace neuroscience as an important additional tool regardless of their theoretical approach, noting that "all of the main theories of counselling can be supported through the use of brain imaging that provides evidence of brain changes in clients" (p. 12)

Neuroscience will add credibility to the field, empowering counsellors with the confidence that comes knowing that their interventions are based on solid science. As Hill and Dahlitz (2014) note:

> Confirmation by neuroscience of what were largely intuitive practices opens an unprecedented way forward for us as therapists to refine our technique, and ourselves, for even greater success, while leaving behind those practices revealed to be ineffectual or even detrimental (p. 11)

In the future, neuroscience will no doubt continue to offer significant insight and precise guidance on what works and what doesn't. Here are some examples of notable and relevant neuroscience research findings for counsellors:

- Neuroscience has confirmed the effectiveness of the mainstays of counselling, listening, empathy, and a focus on wellness (Ivey, Ivey, & Zalaquett, 2010).

- Counselling aids in the generation of new neurons, a process known as **neurogenesis** (Ivey et al., 2010). This is important because neurogenesis aids damaged brains to recover, and it can slow brain degeneration caused by dementia.

    neurogenesis: The production of new neurons.

- Neuroscience is providing specific guidance on how to promote neurogenesis. It supports the efficacy (effectiveness) of counselling strategies that include exercise and diet (Arden, 2015), an argument in favour of counsellors encouraging clients to add these lifestyle changes to their action and recovery plans. Similarly, stress management, having positive relationships (including the client/counsellor relationship), spirituality, and mental stimulation increase neurogenesis.

- Social interaction stimulates the brain's reward circuitry and the release of dopamine and oxytocin, neurotransmitters that increase motivation, feelings of well-being (dopamine) and levels of attachment and trust (oxytocin) (Stanford, 2017). This finding reinforces the importance of the counsellor/client relationship, which is strongly linked to counsellor empathy.

- The counselling relationship, long recognized as the most important catalyst for client change, creates the fertile conditions for healing the damages created by stress and supporting the growth of new neural pathways fundamental to wellness and mental health.

- Mindfulness helps the brain to refocus, decrease worry, increase working memory, and decrease stress.

- Exercise helps to slow cognitive decline.

- Specific interventions such as exposure therapy can help to repair the damage caused by trauma damages to two important parts of the brain, the amygdala and the hippocampus (Trouche, Sasaki, Tu, & Reijmers, 2013).

- Problem-solving work and selected computer games enhance cognitive functioning.

- Most counsellors are aware that confrontation is generally a poor strategy for effecting change (Miller & Rollnick, 2013). Neuroscience tells us why. Confrontation arouses the brain's fight or flight response as it mobilizes for what is experienced as an attack. As a result, valuable energy that might otherwise be harnessed for change is diverted to defence of the status quo. Empathy, on the other hand, offers no such threat and, in fact, acts to calm the brain and add to the development of the counsellor/client relationship, a major variable associated with favourable outcomes in counselling.

- Counsellors who use a strengths approach stimulate their clients' prefrontal cortex to shift to positive thinking and emotions, which in turn helps to overcome unhelpful and negative thinking patterns (Ivey, Ivey, Zalaquett & Quirk, 2009).

- Dahlitz (2017) cited research showing that when clients are involved in decision making and have choices, there is increased activity in the caudate nucleus and other areas of the brain that are involved in motivation. The research suggests that clients with choices have a greater sense of control, increased motivation, and an overall more positive mood.

Neuroscience Adds a Biological Perspective Emergent research that reveals the biological basis of many mental disorders is helping to guide the development of preventive and interventive strategies. The research is also informing counsellors about

Evidence-Based Practice and Neuroscience

Evidence-based best practice (EVP) means that we counsel clients using the best available evidence that what we are doing has a reasonable chance of successfully meeting client needs and goals. Typically, EVP was based on research (outcome and controlled studies), cultural considerations, codes of ethics, and individual client variables, as well as practitioner and colleague experience. Now, neuroscience is providing counsellors with EVP in growing a scientific body of knowledge about how specific strategies can positively impact the brain and facilitate change or repair of damaged brains. This EVP research makes a strong case in support of an eclectic and customized approach to counselling that allows for change and adaptation based on the individual needs of clients and situations. A "one-size-fits-all" model of counselling may work well in one situation, but fail miserably in another.

how the brain is impacted by crisis, trauma, substance misuse, and social determinants such as poverty.

Since many counsellors have had little or no training in neuroscience, they will need to include this topic in their reading and professional development agenda. Counsellors do not need to become experts in neuroscience, but it is imperative that they have at least a basic understanding of the brain and the terminology. This will enable them to be active consumer of neuroscience information.

Neuroscience Provides Counsellors with Another Rationale for Systemic Change   Research endorsing the value of counselling interventions is providing compelling arguments for increased funding for counselling preventive and treatment programs. The Centre for Addiction and Mental Health (2017) estimated that the total cost of untreated mental illness in Canada is more than 51 billion dollars. Data such as this provide an empirical base for counsellors who are active in lobbying for political and systemic change to grossly underfunded mental health and addictions system.

Neuroscience Offers Guidance on the Use of Technology for Treatment
Counsellors who are well versed in neuroscience can inform and refer clients to take advantage of rapidly emerging technology. For example, Li, Montaño, Chen, & Gold (2011) described how virtual reality can be used to rewire the brain to deal with pain management. Techniques such as biofeedback can be utilized to supplement more traditional counselling approaches. Another promising technological advance is Transcranial Magnetic Stimulation (TMS), which involves the use of magnetic pulses to stimulate the brain. An effective alternative to medication, this technique has proved very useful in treating depression, including for those who have not responded to medication.

Neuroscience Reduces Stigma   Moral and cultural judgments can inflict shame on those dealing with mental disorders, a reality that often leads people to forgo treatment and suffer in silence. Neuroscience research has made great strides proving that there are genetic and biological causes of mental disorders. These findings support the argument that mental disorders ought to be understood and treated in the same way that biological disease or injury is addressed. Stigma will be reduced when people learn and accept that mental illness is not a choice caused by moral weakness. Neuroscience knowledge will help to change thinking so that brain based disorders are viewed no differently than any biological disease or injury. Counsellors can play a major role in communicating this notion to clients, their families, and the community.

Neuroscience Provides Explanations Useful for Psychoeducation   Psychoeducation, long a mainstay of counselling, involves helping clients and their families learn about the nature of their problems, including practical information on how they might address social, psychological, economic, and other concerns. Neuroscience explanations can be used by counsellors to help clients understand how their brains are impacted by their life experiences, trauma, illness, and substance misuse. Most counsellors are not experts in neuroscience, so they must be careful that they do not exceed the limits of their competence in this area. They need to refrain from giving medical advice or offering opinions on neurological issues in which they are not qualified.

Neuroscience is Available on the Internet As a result of widespread access to information online, clients have opportunities to become better informed regarding their conditions. There is, however, a real risk that clients, or even professionals, will be misled by false or misleading information. Sometimes, people will post to the Internet based on their beliefs or personal experience, but their statements may be malicious, fabricated, or simply wrong. An informed client is empowered, but a misinformed client may delay or suspend treatment based on an unverified opinion expressed on the Internet. Counsellors can best support clients by encouraging them to consult with reputable sources such as government or national user sites. When counsellors have a basic working knowledge of neuroscience and the brain, they are in a much better position to help clients access and utilize factual and reliable information.

What counsellors can do is help clients acquire a basic understanding of how their problems might be influenced by the brain. To do so, counsellors need at least a rudimentary appreciation of how the brain works. For example, research has demonstrated that excessive anxiety might be due (in part) to an overactive amygdala (Arden, 2015). This knowledge can form the basis of a simple explanation that can help a client understand and deal with their anxiety. Here's an example:

> **Counsellor:** One of the interesting things they've discovered is that when people feel overly anxious, there's a part of the brain that's overactive. However, the good news is, it can be managed.

> **Client:** How?

> **Counsellor:** Some people are helped with medication, but that's something for you and your doctor to discuss. You've told me that it helps to avoid situations where you get overwhelmed, and that's one good coping strategy. It's the everyday situations and moments that you can't avoid where you need a solution. Right? (Client nods) Generally, avoidance decreases anxiety, but increases fear, so the next time you face the situation, you will be even *more* anxious. If you want, we can work to develop a strategy that will help you take small steps to overcome both fear and anxiety. You'll be in charge, and I won't try to force you to do anything.

In the example above, the next step might involve the use of a best-practice counselling strategy such as systematic desensitization, a technique that combines relaxation with incremental exposure to an anxiety-provoking situation. (Caution: the use of systematic desensitization should be within the counsellor's area of competence.) Clients such as the one in the example often report feeling relieved when they finally understand the reasons for their problems and empowered as they learn that their problems can be managed.

SUCCESS TIP

Neuroeducation

Counsellors can use neuroscience information to help others to understand behaviour. For example, children in a classroom who might otherwise be labelled as "bad," "difficult," or "spoiled" are, in fact, responding to faulty brain chemistry or behavioural patterns long shaped by repetition.

Neuroscience Provides Guidance on Medication   Knowledge of how medications enhance, inhibit, or augment brain and bodily functioning is essential for assessment and goal setting with clients. For example, many psychotropic medications lead to weight gain, so counsellors can support clients with wellness initiatives (e.g., diet and exercise). As a result, medication compliance may be improved since clients will be less likely to abandon their medication because of the discouragement associated with weight gain.

Neuroscience Offers Hope   Because our brains are wired based on past experiences, there is strong pressure to act and think in a manner consistent with this wiring. Put simply, we are creatures of habit, even when our habits of thinking and behaving are problematic, the usual position that brings clients to counselling. However, the good news is that we can change our brains and change our futures.

Neuroplasticity   One of the most exciting and relevant discoveries in neuroscience, **neuroplasticity** refers to the brain's ability to change itself by forming new neural connections in response to learning, changes in the environment, or as compensation for injury or disease. Neuroscientists have found that not only can the brain change, it is constantly changing. (Neuroplasticity will be explored in more detail later in this chapter.)

neuroplasticity: The brain's ability to change itself by forming new neural connections in response to learning.

Neuroplasticity concepts can be used by counsellors to convey hope to our clients. They can help clients understand that they are not permanently doomed to their current thinking, behaviour, or emotions. They can provide guidance regarding how clients can change or "rewire their brains" in ways that reduce or eliminate their current problems. Neuroplasticity can show clients how tools such as cognitive behavioural counselling, mindfulness, risk taking, meditation, exercise, and diet can be the roots of positive change in their lives. For both counsellors and clients, neuroscience provides the factual basis for the use of techniques, such as cognitive behavioural therapy, that harness the brain's amazing neuroplasticity to form new neural pathways to replace and extinguish unhelpful and harmful thinking and behavioural patterns. Peckham (2017) offers this perspective:

> The very definition of neuroplasticity shows us that acceptance of circumstance does not have to be the end of the story. If experiences have shaped us in ways that currently cause distress (both to ourselves and to others in our lives), what experiences could change us to have better lives? What experiences might we need? (p. 15)

Neuroplasticity research confirms that new learning is not only possible throughout the lifespan, it is also inevitable. Old dogs can, in fact, learn new tricks.

Here's how a counsellor might explain it to a client:

Counsellor: In the last 30 years, brain researchers have discovered that our brains are constantly changing.

Client: So, what's the big deal. It's not something I can control.

Counsellor: That's what everyone believed until recently. Now, they've learned that there is actually a lot we can do to help our brains grow and heal. Since your brain is going to change anyway, you might as well be helping it change for the better. And the good news is that we now know how to do it.

Neuroimaging   Modern advances in neuroimaging have provided facts and information with enormous implications for counsellors. Research is increasingly guiding and informing counsellors how their clients' brain structure and chemistry might respond to different intervention strategies. We are well on our way to understanding how specific counselling strategies change the brain to promote positive growth, including neurogenesis, the growth of new neurons, something that a short time ago was considered impossible. Clients can change their brains. Counselling can support, enhance, and accelerate this outcome.

A Look Ahead   In the coming decades, neuroscience will continue to have a major impact on our understanding of mental and physical disorders. Counsellors, social workers, psychologists, child care workers, and other social service providers will need to have at least a basic understanding of the brain and the implications of neuroscience research for their fields of practice.

Academics and researchers in the counselling field will no doubt begin to generate their own research and commentary from a neuroscience perspective. Educators will be challenged to integrate neuroscience into professional training programs. Research reports in any discipline are often difficult for the average person to understand and absorb. Frequently, this result in a disconnect between the empirical results of science and their application to field practice. Counselling specific literature utilizing neuroscience has the potential to bridge this gap.

In the same way that multiculturalism has become a continuing theme in virtually all counsellor education programs, neuroscience will confirm its' place as a new force. There is still much to learn, but there is abundant room for optimism that neuroscience discoveries will continue to provide hope for clients, and guidance to counsellors on how to help people repair damaged brains and slow age-related decline. Neuroscientific research will develop greater precision regarding how chemical, electrical, and structural abnormalities in the brain lead to brain disorders like Alzheimer's and mental disorders such as depression and schizophrenia. Along with this will come new psychotropic medications, custom designed to restore equilibrium and function to wounded brains. The future holds fantastic possibilities!

STUDYING THE BRAIN

Neuroscientists and psychologists can learn about the brain in many ways, including through dissection, neuroimaging, the study of electrical activity in the brain, animal studies, and behavioural research. They can also learn a great deal by exploring how injury or disease affects normal functioning and behaviour, or by monitoring the brain as it struggles to heal and recover. For example, if doctors needed to remove a tumour from your brain and this affected your vision, they could assume that this part of your brain was involved in vision. Double-blind experiments are used to study the effects of medication on the brain. In a double-blind experiment, one group is given a placebo, another the medication, and the results are compared. Neither the subjects nor the researcher know which group is receiving placebo or medication.

Frontal lobotomies, which involved destroying a piece of the brain, were often used in the mid-twentieth century before the advent of antipsychotic medication. The results were unpredictable and often horrendously debilitating. The damage from lobotomies showed the important role that the frontal lobe of the brain plays with respect to personality and other higher-order operations.

Brain Imaging

Neuroimaging or brain imaging involves the use of various tools to explore the structure and function of the brain. It has evolved considerably since the discovery of X-rays by Wilhelm Röntgen at the end of the nineteenth century. Since the 1970s, technological innovation has produced machines that now provide unprecedented maps and images of the structure and activity of the brain.

Although brain imaging techniques cannot be used for psychiatric diagnosis, they are useful for ruling out physical causes that may lead to psychiatric symptoms. In addition, they can show how the brains of people with psychiatric conditions function differently. For example, "[s]tudies showed that during tasks involving emotions, people with depression, compared to those without depression, had activity in a region in the middle of the front of the brain. Another study helped us understand why people with attention deficit

neuroimaging: The use of various tools to explore the structure and function of the brain.

hyperactivity disorder have trouble paying attention because a part of the frontal lobe that helps us focus is less active (Sitek, 2016). Findings such as this supported the development of counselling strategies that help people with (Attention Deficit Hyperactivity Disorder) ADHD stay on task, such as establishing routines and selecting quiet spaces to work where there is not too much stimulation.

MRI (Magnetic Resonance Imaging)

A procedure that utilizes magnetic fields and radio waves to take three-dimensional structural pictures of the brain and body organs, **Magnetic Resonance Imaging (MRI)** aids in the detection of brain abnormalities such as tumours, multiple sclerosis (MS), damage from strokes, infections, and accidents. A **Functional MRI (fMRI)** also utilizes magnetic fields, but it measures activity in the brain while the individual is involved in different activities or thoughts. Although fMRI can identify areas of abnormal activity in the brain, this technology has not reached the point where it can be confidently used to diagnose mental illness. Future innovations may make this more feasible and reliable.

CAT (Computerized Axial Tomography)

A **CAT (Computerized Axial Tomography)** scan uses X-rays to detect abnormalities in organs. CAT scans of the brain can be used to diagnose a wide range of problems, including strokes, tumours, damage from head trauma, bleeding, skull malformations, and other conditions.

PET (Positron Emission Tomography)

A **PET (Positron Emission Tomography)** scan uses a radioactive dye that is injected into the body to measure blood flow and to detect problems with the heart, brain, and central nervous system (brain and spinal cord).

EEG (Electroencephalography)

EEG (Electroencephalography) painlessly and without risk measures electrical activity in the brain. This is used to assess or rule out conditions such as tumours, stroke, head injury, and epilepsy. Neuroscientists have identified five distinct types of electrical brain waves, delta, theta, alpha, beta, and gamma (Figure 11.3), which increase or decrease depending on what we are doing or feeling.

Magnetic Resonance Imaging (MRI): A procedure that utilizes magnetic fields and radio waves to take three-dimensional structural pictures of the brain and body organs.

Functional MRI (fMRI): Use of magnetic fields to measure activity in the brain while an individual is involved in different activities or thought.

CAT (Computerized Axial Tomography): Use of X-rays to detect abnormalities in organs.

PET (Positron Emission Tomography): Radioactive dye injected into the body to measure blood flow, and detect problems with the heart, brain, and central nervous system (brain and spinal cord).

EEG (Electroencephalography): A tool used to measure electrical activity in the brain.

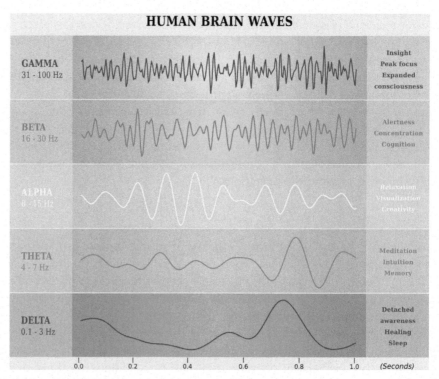

Figure 11.3 Brain Waves
SOURCE: Artellia/Shutterstock

Techniques such as neurofeedback or biofeedback, which use EEG to show clients their brain's electrical activity, teach them through trial and error to control brain wave activity as a way to reduce anxiety and stress (Myers & Young, 2012). Research also suggests this strategy may be useful for conditions such as migraines, post-traumatic stress disorder (PTSD), and ADHD (Nordqvist, 2017).

Emergent Technologies Diagnostic methods for studying the brain are advancing rapidly. **Emergent technologies**, include new techniques such as: Magnetoencephalogram (MEG), used to record magnetic fields; functional near-infrared spectroscopy, (FNIRS) which uses light to record changes in brain oxygen levels; diffusion MRI (DMRI), used to measure water diffusion in the brain, event-related optical signal (EROS), used to assess changes in optical properties in the brain; voxel-based morphometry (VBM), used to measure anatomical difference in the brain; and many others (Mental Health Daily, 2017).

Emergent Technologies: New diagnostic tools for studying the brain, including Magnetoencephalogram (MEG), functional near-infrared spectroscopy (FNIRS), diffusion MRI (DMRI), event-related optical signal (EROS), and voxel-based morphometry (VBM).

>>> **BRAIN BYTE** Types of Depression

Weill Cornell Medicine (2017) reported research utilizing fMRI analysis of over 1000 people with depression. It revealed four distinct subtypes of depression, each with unique patterns of abnormal brain activity. The results helped doctors to determine which patients were more likely to respond to different therapies such as deep brain stimulation, a procedure where electrodes planted in the brain are used to stimulate it.

NEUROPLASTICITY: AN EMPOWERING DISCOVERY

An exciting and relevant neuroscience finding with enormous implications for counsellors and clients was the discovery in the 1990s of brain neuroplasticity. As noted earlier in this chapter, neuroplasticity refers to the brain's *constant* changing of neural pathways as a result of new learning, experiences, disease, and injury. Prior to this discovery, it was believed that the brain remained relatively unchanged after early childhood. It was assumed that we are born with all the neural capacity that we will ever have, and that brain damage, stress, depression, and other life events will result in permanent loss of this neural capacity.

Peckham (2017) makes this interesting observation, "nature assumes that the experiences of our future will be similar to the experiences of our past (p. 14)." So, our brain's neural pathways form and strengthen based on our experiences and are programmed to expect more of the same. Unfortunately, neural pathways may form that strengthen unhelpful thoughts or behaviour such as self-criticism, violence, or the belief that one cannot cope without using alcohol or street drugs. This reality has profound implications for a person's overall ability to deal with life challenges as the following examples illustrate:

Example 1: Andrea grew up in an environment where she learned that "children should be seen and not heard." On the rare occasions when she expressed feelings or ideas, she was berated or punished. As an adult, she has difficult speaking in groups or forming intimate relationships because of her constant fear of rejection. She copes by keeping to herself, essentially leading a solitary life.

Example 2: Mildred was encouraged from an early age to pursue her dreams. Her parents provided her with a rich childhood full of challenging experiences that gave her a chance to develop a wide range of interests and hobbies. As an adult, she is an independent risk taker.

Clearly, Mildred's brain is "wired" for success while Andrea has many neural pathways that, if unchallenged, program her for failure. Although Andrea's past has left her ill-equipped for life as an adult, with time, patience, effort, and practice, her neuroplastic brain can be changed. She does not have to be destined to a future defined by the realities of her past. Counselling can help her to reprogram her brain. Using cognitive behavioural techniques such as those introduced in Chapter 7, she can be helped to recognize problematic thinking, and how this negatively impacts her behaviour and emotions. Then, with the help of a counsellor, she can take steps to reprogram unhelpful thinking and automatic responses.

How to Stimulate Neuroplasticity

Neuroscience has demonstrated that brain change is continuous. Every day of our lives, our brains change in response to every interaction, thought, feeling, and experience. For better or worse, the structure and chemistry of the brain is in a constant state of flux. The counselling challenge is to help clients increase the probability that neuroplastic change will be productive and positive. Here are some things counsellors can do and/or be familiar with that promote neuroplasticity:

- Encourage creativity and new experiences, such as learning to play a musical instrument or a new language. Pathways in the brain that are not used are pruned, so the old adage "use it or lose it" applies to the brain.

- Promote client participation in exercise. Exercise has been shown to stimulate the growth of neural connections, slow brain decline in people with dementia, and even stimulate the growth of new neurons (Budde, Wegner, Soya, Voelcker-Rehage & McMorris, 2016).

- Help clients visualize solutions and success. Neuroscience research has found that visualizing solutions and success "prewires" the brain with neural pathways to those desired ends. One counselling strategy is the "miracle question" (see text Chapter 7), which helps clients fantasize how their lives might change if their problems disappeared. Conversely, dwelling on past failures or imagining future failure reinforces neural pathways supporting failure. Consequently, counsellors should teach their clients how to build and strengthen (through practice) neural pathways by visualizing success.

- Encourage goal setting, which stimulates the brain with challenges. This is particularly important for Canada's aging seniors as a way to slow age-related cognitive decline. As they retire from the challenges of their jobs, it is important that seniors retain a sense of purpose, so working with them to set goals that meet the SMART criteria discussed in Chapter 7 (specific, measurable, achievable, realistic, and in a time frame) (see Chapter 7) helps to nurture positive brain plasticity.

- Help clients deal with the anxiety and stress that happens with change or risk taking. Excessive stress diverts energy that could otherwise be used for learning and action plans. Counsellors can assist by helping clients recognize that change stress is normal and predictable. They can help clients predict and manage potential stress points.

- Remember that the counselling relationship itself is a powerful ally to change. It can provide clients support, empathy, and a milieu for emergent problem solving. As such, its importance as a motivator and sustainer of the change process should never be underestimated.

- Encourage clients to access physical rehabilitation services for brain injuries. For example, using repetitive movements helps the brain form new neural connections for a movement such as walking that may have been damaged by injury or illness (Liou, 2015).

- Use cognitive behavioural counselling to extinguish unhelpful thinking (negative thought patterns) by replacing them with helpful thinking (see Chapter 7). Learned unhelpful thinking is also a product of neuroplasticity.

- Help clients recognize the importance of sleep and the need to deal with problems such as sleep apnea. Research has shown that sleep boosts neural plasticity and lack of sleep is damaging (Gorgoni et al., 2013).

- Be aware that that early life experiences can play an important part in the recovery of individuals who are later impacted by such things as trauma or substance misuse. A key consideration is whether a client's neuroplastic brain is wired for problem solving, resilience, and healthy living, or not. An example will illustrate:

  > Devin and his friend Marco became heavily involved with drugs in their late teens. Both had a five-year-long history of arrests and incarcerations when they finally entered a Montreal drug rehab treatment centre in their early twenties. Devin was raised in a loving environment where he had access to enriching experiences and sports. Marco was physically and sexually abused as a child, then spent over ten years in a long series of foster homes.

In rehab, Devin has some advantages. Although long dormant, his brain already has neural pathways supporting good values and sound judgment, whereas Marco learned that the world is an unsafe place where his physical and emotional needs will be unmet. With Devin, a counsellor might strategize ways to re-energize dormant neural pathways that support mental and social coping such as by encouraging him to recall early memories where he felt safe and loved. With Marco, a counsellor needs to prioritize the development of a trusting relationship with him. The strengths approach philosophy suggests that Marco, as a result of his experiences, may have developed resilience and capacity, the counsellor should look for ways to recognize and build on these strengths. This approach will help counterbalance neural networks programmed with expectations that he will be abused and rejected.

STRUCTURE OF THE BRAIN

The brain is composed of three parts: the cerebrum, cerebellum, and the brain stem.

- *Cerebrum:* The largest part, the **cerebrum** controls higher-order functions, including emotions, learning, and sensory processing. The cerebrum has two hemispheres (right and left) and four lobes: frontal, parietal, temporal, and occipital. Within the lobes, there are a large number of parts, each of which has at least one and more often, multiple functions. One of the major parts of the cerebrum is the limbic system, which, because of its critical role with respect to emotions, is of major interest to counsellors. The limbic system includes the thalamus, hypothalamus, amygdala, and the hippocampus. For any function controlled by the cerebrum, such as emotion, memory, or decision making, there may be a major centre which regulates it, but often as not, many other brain parts play a role.

  cerebrum: Part of the brain that controls higher-order functions, including emotions, learning, and sensory processing.

- *Cerebellum:* The **cerebellum**, sometimes referred to as the "little brain" comprises about 10 percent of brain volume. It can be found behind the top part of the brain stem (Figure 11.4). The cerebellum is associated with movement, sensory perception, and motor coordination, so it is not surprising that damage to the cerebellum could result in paralysis, tremors, and problems with motor coordination (body movements) and ataxia (loss of control of bodily movements). As well, this part of the brain is one of the areas that is adversely affected by schizophrenia (Moberget et al., 2017). It is also believed that the cerebellum is involved in a wide range of

  cerebellum: The part of the brain associated with movement, sensory perception, and motor coordination.

This brief interview excerpt illustrates a number of important counselling strategies. It introduces the idea that the client's unhelpful thinking is an outcome of learning, not personal failure or inadequacy. The client has been talking about his fear of taking risks, which has held him back in his career and personal life.

Counsellor: The brain is like a muscle. Exercise it and it gets stronger. Sometimes, and it can happen to anyone, we train our minds to do things that aren't helpful.	**Analysis:** *A brief introduction is given, which helps to normalize the client's situation with the notion that the client is not the only one with this problem.*
Client: That makes sense. I think I'm programmed for failure. Whenever I face a challenge or new situation, I keep thinking, "What's the point? I can't do it." So, I don't even try.	**Analysis:** *The client engages with the concept and relates it to his thinking patterns.*
Counsellor: I'm guessing you've been doing this for a long time **Client:** All my life. **Counsellor:** Well, not yet. (Client laughs.)	**Analysis:** *"Not yet," lightens the mood–appropriate and timely humour is an important part of counselling. However, "not yet" also conveys the implicit message that what's been true in the past does not have to be true in the future. This communicates hope for change.*
Counsellor: How strong is this belief? Scale of 1–10? **Client:** About an 11! (Client chuckles, then tears up.) (Pause of 10 seconds.)	**Analysis:** *The counsellor wants to get a sense of the degree that the client is committed to his belief. It's no surprise that he also shares (nonverbally) his pain.*
Counsellor: It hurts to think about it. **Client:** A lot.	**Analysis:** *Counsellor empathy is important when feelings are expressed.*
Counsellor: It's not easy but what your brain has learned can be unlearned. The brain can be rewired. **Client:** My first reaction is, "It won't work for me." (Pause of 10 seconds.) See, I've done it again. **Counsellor:** Good for you. You've already started by recognizing the pattern. That's an important first step.	**Analysis:** *The counsellor conveys hope. The interview continues with an example of the strengths approach in practice. The counsellor's patience during the 10-second pause gave the client a chance to challenge his own reaction. This provided the counsellor with an opening to recognize this as an empowering strength. The counsellor might have picked up on his pessimism with empathy, but there was some value in ignoring the pessimism and suggesting a reframe instead. The client has already declared his "normal" thinking pattern, so there is merit in not getting drawn into this too heavily.*
Counsellor: In the last 20 years, a lot of work has been done exploring how the brain works. This has given us lots of guidance on how to change thinking patterns. The principles are quite simple and they work, but they require a lot of persistence and patience to rewire your brain. **Client:** Can you give me an example?	**Analysis:** *The relationship is now well-positioned to further discuss the process, then contract to explore change strategies and action plans.*
Counsellor: There are many ways, but here's one. Research has shown that visualizing success can be just as effective in changing the brain as actually doing it. Here's how it works. You'll choose a situation you want to change, one where you've been saying to yourself, "I can't do it." Then, I'll help you imagine or play out the situation where you are successful. With practice, you'll actually change your brain by changing the way you think. Repetition is the key to this wiring. It won't be easy– like you said, it's an "11/10." So, we'll fight the old pattern with a "12."	**Analysis:** *The counsellor provides a simple, non-jargonized example of an action plan that can be used to help the client change unhelpful thinking patterns.* *Letting the client know there will be challenges ahead allows the client to anticipate and strategize how to handle them. This makes it less likely that he will lose motivation when he faces obstacles.* *Implicit in the action plan is the neuroscience concept that new learning is enhanced with practice and repetition.*

Reflections:

■ Suggest what the counsellor's next steps might be.

■ What cognitive behavioural counselling principles are illustrated in the interview.

■ What are some of the obstacles that the client might encounter. Suggest strategies to handle them.

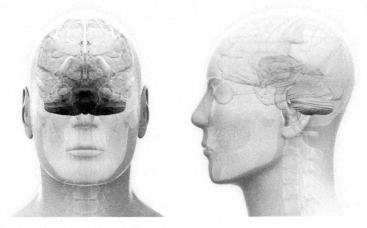

Figure 11.4 The Cerebellum
SOURCE: Decade3d - anatomy online/Shutterstock

disorders, including ADHD and autism spectrum disorders, as well as mood and anxiety disorders (Phillips, Hewedi, Eissa, & Moustafa, 2015). Counsellors can support clients in seeking treatment from psychotherapists for exercises that will help them to deal with movement and balance problems in order to reduce the risk of injury from falling.

■ *Brain Stem:* The **brain stem** connects the brain to the spinal cord and provides nerve pathways for passing sensory information from various sources (e.g., spinal cord and inner ear). The brain stem is essential for essential body functions such as breathing, heart control, and sleep cycles. It is responsible for controlling central nervous system functioning, including breathing, consciousness, and blood pressure. Because of the vital role regulating bodily functions, damage to it can be life threatening. It has three main parts: midbrain, pons, and medulla (Figure 11.5).

brain stem: Part of the brain above the spinal cord that controls breathing, heart, and blood pressure.

■ The **midbrain (mesencephalon)** plays a role in sleep, hearing, vision, and the regulation of body temperature. It is also associated with vision, hearing, motor control, sleep/wake, and arousal (alertness).

Midbrain (mesencephalon): Brain structure associated with sleep, hearing, vision, body temperature, vision, hearing, motor control, sleep/wake, and arousal (alertness).

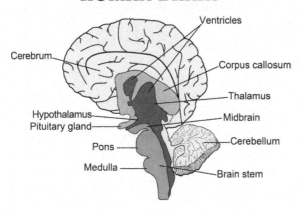

Figure 11.5 The Brain Stem
SOURCE: Ducu59us/Shutterstock

Pons: Part of the brain that aids in the transmission of messages between the cortex and the cerebellum, as well as playing a role in breathing, sleep, biting, chewing, and swallowing.

Medulla: Brain structure responsible for breathing and regulating blood pressure.

- The **pons** aids in the transmission of messages between the cortex and the cerebellum. As well, it is also involved in breathing and sleep. Nerves from the pons play a role in biting, chewing, and swallowing.
- The **medulla**, responsible for breathing and regulating blood pressure, is essential for survival.

The thalamus, at the top of the brain stem, acts as the brain's switchboard and relaying sensory information to the appropriate part of the brain. It also has a part in how we perceive pain and in some aspects of motivation, learning, memory, and emotions. The hypothalamus, located between the thalamus and the brain stem, is involved with body functions such as thirst, hunger, temperature, sleep, and blood pressure.

Hemispheres

The cerebrum, protected by the eight fused bones of the skull, is divided into two hemispheres, right and left, each of which has different functions. Generally, the right hemisphere controls the left side of the body and the left hemisphere controls the right side. The right side of the brain is more involved in artistic and creative tasks while the left side of the brain is better at tasks that involve critical thinking, logic, and language (see Figure 11.6). A stroke on the left side of the brain will affect the right side of the body, while a stroke on the right side of the brain will affect the left side of the body. The two hemispheres are connected by the nerve fibres of the **corpus callosum**, which facilitates communication between the two hemispheres.

corpus callosum: Nerve fibres that connect the two hemispheres of the brain.

white matter: Brain tissue that supports connections in the brain by helping the transmission and speed of information sharing between parts of the brain.

grey matter: Brain tissue composed of cells that help us think.

White and Grey Matter   The terms "**white matter**" and "**grey matter**" are often used to describe brain tissue. Grey matter is composed of cells that help us think.

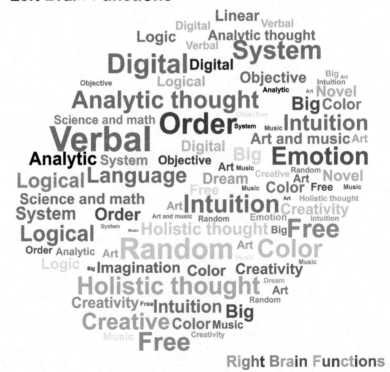

Figure 11.6   Right and Left-Brain Functions
SOURCE: Kitsana Baitoey/123RF

A common belief is that people can be classified as "right-brained" or "left-brained," suggesting that one part of the brain is used more than the other. However, recent research (University of Utah, 2013) has found no support for this belief. The reality seems to be that both sides of the brain are involved in most functions.

White matter supports connections in the brain and help the transmission and speed of information sharing between parts of the brain. Most white matter functions somewhat like the insulation on an electric wire. In the central nervous system (brain and spinal cord), the white matter insulation, known as myelin or myelin sheath, protects nerve cells (Figure 11.5). Many things can damage the myelin sheath, including MS, stroke, infection, and excessive use of alcohol. Damage to the myelin sheath is called demyelination, which can cause wide-ranging damage, including problems with emotions, movement, sight, hearing, and thinking. Damaged myelin (Figure 11.7) is a central feature of MS. Medication and counselling should be utilized to help clients deal with the emotional and psychological effects of demyelination.

Brain Lobes

Each of the two hemispheres has four lobes (Figure 11.8). Although it is common to identify certain responsibilities for each lobe, the reality is that all parts of the brain are involved and activated during any function through intricate connections that are not fully understood. Neuroscientists are only at the beginning stages of unravelling this complexity.

A University of California, Irvine study (2005) found that men had 6.5 times more grey matter than women while women had 10 times the amount of white matter. While general intelligence between the sexes was found to be equal, the results help explain why men tend to be better with precise sciences like mathematics while women more often excel with language.

Figure 11.7 Healthy Myelin (bottom neuron) and Damaged Myelin (top neuron)
SOURCE: BlueRingMedia/Shutterstock

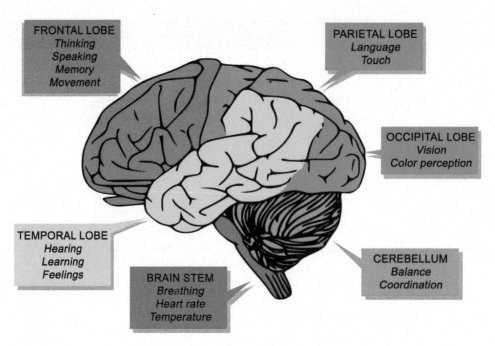

Figure 11.8 Lobes of the Brain
SOURCE: Noiel/Shutterstock

frontal lobes: Part of the brain responsible for higher-order functions such as decision making, problem solving, judgment, and impulse control.

The **frontal lobes** are often referred to as the executive portion of the brain because of their involvement in higher-level thinking. These lobes are enormously important for managing complex behaviour, including decision making, prediction, appropriate behaviour, problem solving, working memory, impulse control, judgment, sexual and social behaviour, and various aspects of personality. Misuse of substances, stroke, or injury to this part of the brain can cause significant problems or impairment in all of these areas. Alcohol, for example, may lead to permanent frontal lobe damage that limits an individual's ability to make rational decisions, including the decision to limit or cease drinking. In addition, alcohol and other substance may lower inhibitions and cause an individual to act irrationally in ways that would be otherwise controlled by the frontal lobes (e.g., impulsive behaviour, violence, and suicide).

Adolescents, particularly males, are more likely to engage in risky or impulsive behaviour such as substance misuse, reckless driving, casual sex, and violent behaviour. This is partly explained by the fact that the prefrontal cortex, the front of the frontal lobe, does not fully develop until late adolescence. In addition, peer relationships and strong needs for approval may lead adolescents to increased risk behaviour. Steinberg (2008) uses neuroscience research to argue that this risk taking is inevitable. He also cites research suggesting that preventive educational programs have been largely ineffective. He argues that attention should shift to tactics such as raising the driving age, greater policing of alcohol sales, and increasing access to mental health and contraceptive services.

Although schizophrenia and other psychotic disorders are most often associated with the positive symptoms of hallucinations and delusions, cognitive impairment (e.g., memory, thinking, and judgment), involving significant problems with frontal lobe executive functioning, is often far more debilitating. Early recognition and treatment of psychosis is essential in order to prevent and minimize brain deterioration that results from untreated psychosis.

occipital lobes: The parts of the brain responsible for visual processing.

The **occipital lobes** at the back of the head are responsible for visual processing. When the occipital lobe is damaged, a person will have trouble correctly processing

Broca's area is located in the left hemisphere of the frontal lobe. It plays a vital role with respect to language and speech. Damage to this part of the brain can result in a speech disorder known as Broca's Aphasia. Wernicke's area in the parietal and temporal lobe is essential for understanding speech and finding the right words to express thoughts. People with Wernicke's Aphasia can speak, but not understand others.

what they see. For example, **prosopagnosia**, or face blindness, is a disorder in which people cannot recognize faces, even with people with whom they are familiar. Counsellors can assist by helping people with prosopagnosia to develop recognition strategies such as using voice, mannerisms, or clothing for identity clues.

prosopagnosia: A disorder where people cannot recognize faces, even with people with whom they are familiar (aka as face blindness).

Vision problems such as macular degeneration can cause disorders such as **Charles Bonnet Syndrome (CBS)**, a condition that often causes visual hallucinations among people who have lost their sight or have severely impaired vision. Given Canada's aging population, this reality has important implications for counsellors who work with seniors. Consequently, counsellors who work with this population will want to acquire specialized skills to assist them in dealing with age-related visual problems. Psychoeducation is vital in order to help the client and family to understand the condition, and to offer reassurance that the person with CBS is not losing his or her mind (Bier, 2017). Referral for specialized assessment and treatment will introduce clients to strategies for managing the condition. These might include eye exercises (Bier, 2017), alterations in lighting that might precipitate or exacerbate the problem (Murphy, 2012, cited in Bier, 2017), and counselling to deal with any social or psychological condition resulting from CBS.

Charles Bonnet Syndrome (CBS): a condition that often causes visual hallucinations among people who have lost their sight or have severely impaired vision.

The **temporal lobes** process auditory information, as well as some responsibility for visual memory and speech. Damage to the temporal lobes (e.g., trauma and epilepsy) can impact functioning in any or all of these areas and also result in problems with emotional response and personality changes. Both Alzheimer's and Parkinson's can cause temporal lobe damage involving memory, especially in the hippocampus (Goodtherapy, 2017).

temporal lobes: portion of the brain that controls visual memory and speech.

The **parietal lobes** process body sensations such as touch, pain, and temperature, as well as playing a role in vision, reading, and in solving mathematical problems. Left parietal lobe damage can result in a number of problems, including "Gerstmann's Syndrome," characterized by difficulty with writing (agraphia), mathematics (acalculia), language, and left-right confusion. Right parietal lobe damage may lead to problems with self-care. A stroke in the parietal lobe can cause a number of spatial, visual, and sensory problems.

parietal lobes: part of the brain responsible for processing body sensations such as touch, pain, and temperature as well as playing a role in vision, reading, and solving mathematical problems.

Brain Lobes and Counselling

Effective counsellors utilize a range of different counselling approaches that honour individual and situational needs. Different strategies stimulate different parts of the brain. For example, a client may have great difficulty tracking and understanding language, but remain quite adept at processing visual cues that draw on the occipital lobe. Activities such as mindfulness and relaxation training activate the parietal lobe. All educators know that people learn better by doing, which enhances skill as well as memory. Hence the importance of helping clients set and implement action plans for change. As a rule, the more that counsellors use a variety of strategies, the greater the extent that they will be able to engage different parts of the brain for understanding and problem-solving process.

McHenry and colleagues (2014) propose that counsellors tailor their approach depending on which lobe is dominant for a given client. For example, suppose a client overly intellectualizes her problem with little emotionality. Here, the frontal lobe may be dominant so she may respond better to approaches such as CBT that focus on logic and thinking. At the same time, invitational empathy (see Chapter 6) might be used to stimulate and encourage new thinking in the emotional areas of the brain. However, delving into the emotional area may evoke more resistance from this client since it is not her usual mode of processing. Nevertheless, it may ultimately be more useful for the client because it opens up new (emotional) perspectives that previously have not been part of her thinking. The challenge for counsellors is to balance respect for this client's natural disposition and strength (i.e., logic) with appropriate and well-timed encouragement to consider emotions (invitational empathy). Contracting and counsellor transparency regarding the process and rationale for doing this will be helpful, as illustrated in the example below.

> *Counsellor:* One of your great strengths is your ability to logically analyze your issues, and this is important. Not everyone is good at this and you are. I'm also aware that we haven't talked much about your feelings. In my experience, I've found emotions play a very important role in problem resolution. Research also confirms this. So, I'm wondering if it might be useful for us to spend a bit of time talking about your feelings. What do you think? [Note: In this example, the counsellor attempts to contract with the client to move the interview to the affective (feeling) domain by appealing to the client's strength, logic, and reasoning ability].

The Limbic System

limbic system: The brain's control centre for emotions.

Although other parts of the brain are involved, the **limbic system** (Figure 11.9) is often referred to as the control centre for our emotions. It's also involved in motivation and memory (Dahlitz & Hall, 2016). Because of its central role regarding emotions, it is important for counsellors to have at least a basic understanding of this part of the brain, particularly the amygdala and hippocampus.

The Limbic System

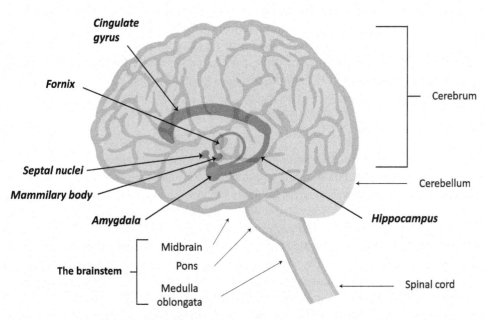

Figure 11.9 The Limbic System
SOURCE: Joshua Abbas/123RF

Counsellor: Are there inherent differences between the brains of men and women?

Neuroscientist: The short answer is yes. In an article, psychologist Gregory Jantz, PhD (2014) summarized a number of variances. He noted that differences in the relative proportion of gray and white matter in male versus female brains leave women (in general) more adept at multitasking, while men do better with highly task-focused work. Although males and females have the same brain parts and neurotransmitters, the evidence is that they utilize them differently leading to a tendency for men to be more impulsive. Women utilize more oxytocin, the bonding chemical. Research supports the conclusion that men are more interested in technical details and are better at the exact sciences such as mathematics. Women are better with social sciences. But let's never forget that these are generalizations. There are plenty of female scientists who outshine their male counterparts. Canadian neurologist, Dr. Roberta Bondar, the first Canadian female astronaut, is one great example.

Counsellor: Culture and socialization are also at play here.

Neuroscientist: Yes indeed. And the number of women in science is growing. One study (Ontario Network of Women in Engineering, 2017) found that the number of women in engineering programs in Canada, once a male bastion, has grown 68 percent since 2007.

Counsellor: We often hear that women are more feeling oriented than men. Is this supported by neuroscience research?

Neuroscientist: With respect to feelings, Jantz (2014) offered that women have a larger hippocampus and are inclined to be more sensitive to stimulation from our five major senses. Additionally, before boys or girls are born, their brains have developed with different hemispheric divisions of labour. Female brains are able to draw on verbal centres in both sides of the brain and women are often better communicators and more expressive, particularly with respect to feelings. In this sense, women are likely to process feelings longer than men, whereas men are more likely to move quickly on to the next task. As Baron-Cohen (2005) put it, "women are hard-wired for empathy." Here again, remember this is a generalization. No one would argue that the famous Dr. Carl Rogers, the founder of person-centred counselling, was not adept at empathy.

Counsellor: Why are females more likely to be diagnosed with depression?

Neuroscientist: Females have a larger, more developed limbic system, which gives them more ability to recognize and process emotions, but this may make them more susceptible to depression. We should also consider that they are more likely to seek treatment for depressive disorders. While we are on the topic, research has shown that women are more likely to experience generalized anxiety disorder, panic disorder, and social and other phobias (Eaton et al., 2012).

Counsellor: Are there areas where men are more likely to experience problems?

Neuroscientist: Yes, men are more likely to have substance abuse problems, antisocial personality disorders, ADHD, syndrome, and they have a higher incidence of dyslexia. It is often said that women are more likely to internalize problems whereas men externalize them and have more of a tendency to act out (Eaton et al., 2012). In this sense, anger and aggression in men may actually be symptoms of depression.

Neuroscientist: I want to stress that we cannot ignore environmental forces (nurture) when we consider difference between the brains of men and women. Our brains are shaped by experience, so the socialization of men and women must be considered when we compare.

Counsellor: I'm wondering about the counselling implications of what you've been saying. It seems more likely that women would more readily respond to counsellors who featured empathic responses and a greater opportunity to discuss and understand their emotions. Action plans could feature cognitive behavioural strategies to avoid internalizing and self-blame, which would help combat depression. Men might be more responsive to action approaches strategizing specific activities and actions to overcome depression in order to reduce any behaviour that is harmful to themselves of others.

Neuroscientist: I agree. As always, exploring individual needs and differences through the contracting process is essential for defining which counselling approach is best. In any case, empathy is still an effective and necessary skill for working with men.

Counsellor: You've alerted me to one very important point. Next time, I'm dealing with an angry male client, I'm going to explore whether I'm actually dealing with someone who is depressed.

amygdala: An important part of the brain associated with emotions such as fear and anger.

hippocampus: The part of the brain in control of storing memories.

The Amygdala and Hippocampus   The **amygdala**, an often-studied almond-shaped brain part (limbic system and temporal lobe), is involved in emotions such as fear and anger. As with most brain structures, there is duplication with two amygdalae, one in each hemisphere of the brain.

The **hippocampus** is another critical part of the limbic system. It is responsible for storing memories. The hippocampus and the amygdala are connected, and this partnership is responsible for the strong emotions that are connected to memories.

Trauma and depression can damage the amygdala and the hippocampus, but counselling can repair or lessen the damage. After trauma, the amygdala often becomes hypersensitive, and it may quickly react to even minor stress by activating high intensity stress responses, panic, or even PTSD. From both trauma and depression, the hippocampus shows a reduction in volume, which results in greater difficulty distinguishing between current and past experiences (Bremner, 2006, Wlassoff, 2017). As a result, flashbacks may occur where an individual re-experiences a past event. Neuroscience research confirms that both medication and counselling contribute to repairing the hippocampus and calming the amygdala to make it less reactive (Sapolsky, 2001). There are a number of strategies trained counsellors can teach clients who are dealing with traumatic flashbacks, including:

- Breathing and relaxation training to calm emotions
- Diversion
- Stopping techniques to remind oneself that what is occurring is not current
- PTSD treatment such **as Eye Movement Desensitization and Reprocessing (EMDR)**, an evidence-based approach to dealing with trauma based on the theory that emotional problems are caused by memories that have not been stored properly (Shapiro & Solomon, 2010).

Eye Movement Desensitization and Reprocessing (EMDR): A treatment approach for dealing with trauma based on the theory that emotional problems are caused by memories that have not been stored properly.

Consider a client who is afraid of public speaking to the point where even the thought of it sparks his anxiety. In response, he may use avoidance to cope with his fear. Avoidance may temporarily reduce his anxiety, but ultimately it increases both his fear and his anxiety about speaking in public. Exposure counselling, a best-practice technique, provides a systematic way to reduce both fear and anxiety (Trouche, et al., 2013). Counsellor management and support during the process increases the likelihood of success. Counsellors can also help clients become empowered by utilizing progressive relaxation, mindfulness, meditation, exercise, and breathing as tools to reduce anxiety, thereby retraining the amygdala. Damage to the hippocampus can be addressed by medication and cognitive behavioural counselling (Gradin & Pomi, 2008).

cingulate: Part of the limbic system that plays an important part in the regulation of emotions.

The **cingulate** in the limbic system plays an important part in the regulation of emotions. Problems such as PTSD, schizophrenia, and anxiety disorders have been found to be (in part) related to over or underactivation of the cingulate (Stevens, Hurley, & Taber, 2011). Counselling strategies such as the use of cognitive behavioural therapy are recommended for clients who have difficulty with emotional regulation. The goal here is to help clients learn how to manage anxiety (relax) and to develop more choices for dealing with emotional challenges in their lives.

》》》 BRAIN BYTE | Psychopathic Brains

There is evidence that the amygdalae of people diagnosed as psychopaths are smaller than those of other people, which results in the often-noted lack of fear among this group. They may also have damage to the frontal lobe, which impairs their ability to exercise self-control and good judgment (Scientific American, 2017).

Cranial Nerves

The brain has twelve pairs of nerves known as cranial nerves. They perform various functions, including connecting sense organs such as the nose or eyes to the brain. Other cranial nerves form connections from glands and organs. Here is a list of the cranial nerves (by convention assigned a Roman numeral) with their primary function:

I. Olfactory – smell

II. Optic – vision

III. Oculomotor – eye muscle and pupil

IV. Trochlear – eye movement

V. Trigeminal – facial touch pain and chewing

VI. Abducens – eye movement

VII. Facial – taste and facial expression

VIII. Vestibulocochlear – hearing and balance

IX. Glossopharyngeal – taste and swallowing

X. Vagus – heart rate and glands

XI. Spinal accessory – head movement

XII. Hypoglossal – tongue

Damage to cranial nerves can be caused by disease or injury. Some cranial nerve damages can be very serious causing loss of senses such as vision and hearing. Neuropathic nerve damage adversely affects a person's ability to feel or move. Sometimes, over an extended period of time, people can recover from cranial nerve damage. Counsellors can support this recovery by helping clients to make lifestyle changes to reduce high blood pressure, increase physical activity, cease smoking, and manage excessive use of alcohol. (John Hopkins Medicine, 2017).

The Endocrine System

The body's **endocrine system** consists of a network of glands in the body and brain, which secrete hormones into the blood stream. These glands produce hormones such as insulin, oxytocin, estrogen, cortisol, somatostatin, and dozens of others that control a wide range of body functions. The pea-sized pituitary gland is often referred to as the body's "master gland" because of its control over many other glands such as the thyroid, ovaries, and adrenal glands. Figure 11.10 presents some of the other major glands that counsellors need to understand.

endocrine system: Network of glands in the body and brain, which secrete hormones into the blood stream.

Problems such as diabetes occur when the glands over or underproduce hormones. For example, adrenalin is a hormone produced by the renal glands that mobilize the body to deal with fear and threat. When the adrenalin level goes out-of-balance

---

▶▶▶ BRAIN BYTE Endocrine System versus Nervous System

The body's endocrine and nervous systems control the operation of the body and mind. The central nervous system (CNS) is composed of the brain and spinal cord, while the peripheral nervous system consists of nerves and ganglia outside the CNS. The nervous system uses rapid firing electrical impulses to release neurotransmitters and activate neural pathways. The endocrine system involves glands that secrete hormones into the blood stream. Its' actions are slow, but long lasting.

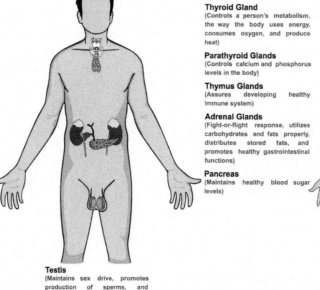

Endocrine Glands of Human Body

Hypothalamus
(Controls pituitary gland hormones)

Pituitary Gland
(Influences other organs, and its function is vital to the overall well-being of a person)

Pineal Gland
(Helps maintain circadian rhythm, regulate reproductive hormones, and recognize sleeping time)

Thyroid Gland
(Controls a person's metabolism, the way the body uses energy, consumes oxygen, and produce heat)

Parathyroid Glands
(Controls calcium and phosphorus levels in the body)

Thymus Glands
(Assures developing healthy immune system)

Adrenal Glands
(Fight-or-flight response, utilizes carbohydrates and fats properly, distributes stored fats, and promotes healthy gastrointestinal functions)

Pancreas
(Maintains healthy blood sugar levels)

Testis
(Maintains sex drive, promotes production of sperms, and maintains healthy levels of muscles and bones mass)

Ovary
(Promotes development of breasts, and maintain healthy menstrual periods)

Figure 11.10 Major Glands

SOURCE: udaix/Shutterstock

problems ensue (Figure 11.11). When the delicate balance of other hormones is disrupted, depression, sleep, sexual, anxiety, and weight problems may result. Counsellors who are alert to this possibility will want to consider referring their clients for medical assessment.

In addition to medical intervention, clients with endocrine problems may benefit from lifestyle counselling that focuses on nutrition, exercise, and anxiety management. Counsellors can help clients set goals, develop action plans, and strategize to deal with obstacles that might otherwise sabotage goal attainment. Family and social support system involvement is also an important component of success. Counsellors can play an important role by helping clients find support groups to assist them with chronic (long-term) management of endocrine conditions. Support groups are especially useful for clients who are dealing with conditions such as diabetes, which, as it require continuous daily attention and motivation, can be emotionally taxing.

NEURONS: THE BRAIN'S INFORMATION SYSTEM

The nervous system is dominated by two types of cells, neurons and glia. Generally, neurons transmit information and glia cells support neurons, although recent research has revealed that glia cells are also capable of transmitting information (Dahlitz, 2017).

There are over 80+ billion nerve cells or neurons in the brain that produce chemicals called neurotransmitters which are the key to brain functioning. Neurons are responsible

Adrenalin

HORMONE FEAR

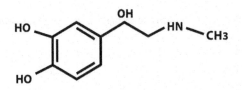

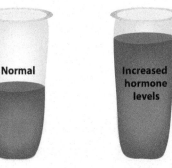

Reduced hormone levels

Normal

Increased hormone levels

WEIGHT GAIN, FATIGUE, POOR CONCENTRATION, AND LOW SEXUAL AROUSAL

ANXIETY, IRRITABILITY, HYPERACTIVITY, ANXIETY, ACUTE STRESS, INSOMNIA, AND HIGH BLOOD PRESSURE

Figure 11.11 Adrenalin
SOURCE: Timonina/Shutterstock

for transmission of information in the brain and spinal cord. There are three main parts of the neuron (Figure 11.12):

1. The *soma* (cell body) controls the neuron.
2. The *dendrites* receive information from other neurons that are then sent to the cell body.
3. The *axon* is covered by myelin (myelin sheath), which protects it and aids in the transmission of electrical signals that are critical for activating neurotransmitters, chemicals which enable one neuron to communicate with another. Dendrites on neurons receive and transmit electric signals.

Neural Transmission **Neural transmission** is the process by which neurons are activated or fired thus enabling neurons to communicate with each other. Neurons could not communicate and the brain could not do its job without neurotransmitters. The neurotransmitters are released by one neuron, and they then travel across a small gap called a synapse or synaptic cleft (Figure 11.13) to another neuron (receptor neuron or postsynaptic cell). Their release is triggered by chemicals in the body (e.g., sodium and potassium) which create an electrical charge that causes the neuron to fire (i.e., release the neurotransmitters). Neural pathways, once activated, allow us to complete all of the functions of daily living—for example, thinking, moving, and breathing.

If the neurotransmitter causes the receptor neuron to fire, it is now activated to signal other neurons to fire. This creates a neural pathway that may involve hundreds of thousands of neurons in the brain. Neural transmission ends when the neurotransmitter returns to the neuron that released it, a process called **reuptake**. Reuptake is an

neural transmission: Connections between neurons in the brain for transmitting information.

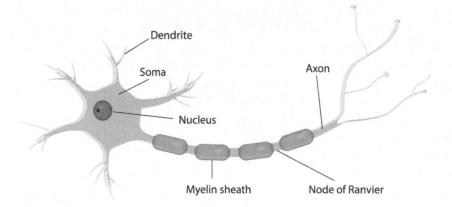

Figure 11.12   The Parts of the Neuron
SOURCE: joshya/Shutterstock

Signal transmission at a chemical synapse

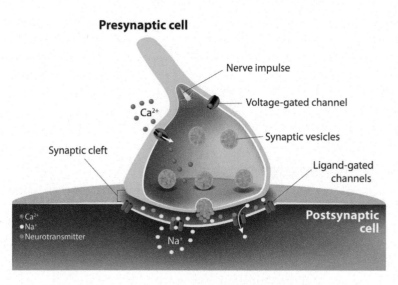

Figure 11.13   Synapse
SOURCE: Designua/Shutterstock

efficient process that allows for "recycling" of the neurotransmitter. Some medications temporarily prevent reuptake allowing the neurotransmitter to remain active longer. For example, Prozac© prevents the reuptake of serotonin which relieves the symptoms of depression.

Different neurons have different shapes and functions. Sensory neurons transmit information from the sensory organs (skin, eyes, and ears). Motor neurons carry information from the brain to the limbs. When a neuron receives a neurotransmitter, it is called a receptor neuron or postsynaptic cell. Receptor neurons are programmed to accept one specific neurotransmitter for which it is programmed. Its' shape is like a lock that can only be opened by a key, its assigned neurotransmitter. Figure 11.14 illustrates types of neuron receptors.

RECEPTORS

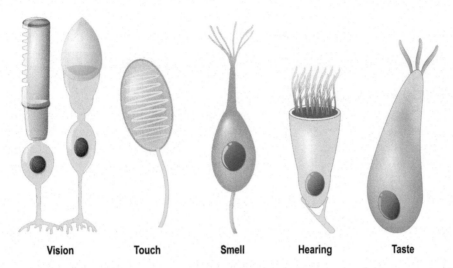

Figure 11.14 Types of Neuron Receptors
SOURCE: Designua/Shutterstock

"Neurons that fire together wire together"   This famous phrase was coined by the Canadian neuropsychologist Donald Hebb who observed that learning and repetition creates strong and enduring neural pathways. Neural pathways strengthen with repetitive behaviour, thoughts, or emotions. Subsequently these "wired" neural pathways become entrenched and automatic.

Ideally, children grow in a consistent and nurturing environment where neural pathways develop that support healthy self-esteem, empathy for others, and a capacity for appropriate risk taking. Unfortunately, problematic neural pathways such as those that sustain unhelpful thinking (e.g., unrealistic anxiety and self-defeating thought), can form. With every replay of an unhelpful thought, the neural pathway becomes stronger and more resistant to change. Practice makes the thought automatic.

Newton's famous first law of motion states that objects at rest tend to stay at rest, and objects in motion tend to stay in motion unless acted on by some force. This law also seems like an apt description of how the will brain continues to repeat established patterns unless something is done to interrupt it.

There Is Hope!   Problematic neural pathways can be replaced and neuroscience teaches us how to do it. Counsellors, using techniques such as cognitive behavioural therapy, help clients to curb unhelpful thinking by replacing unhealthy neural pathways with new pathways that support mental wellness. Since the problematic neural pathways are "wired together," considerable repetition with the replacement thoughts or behaviour will be necessary in order to effect change. Counselling can be the force that changes the fixed momentum of the brain. Counsellors can support clients by helping them to understand, anticipate, and manage the challenges that changes to wired neural pathways entails.

> **Counsellor:** If we continue to do, think, or feel something, it becomes automatic. Even when we know it's not helpful, we may keep doing it because our brains are programmed

reuptake: Process whereby neurotransmitters are reabsorbed by the neuron that released them.

to keep us on the same path. When we try to change, our brains, out of habit, may sabotage the change, and we end up going back to the same old pattern.

Client: So, am I stuck?

Counsellor: No! The good news is that change is possible, but it takes a plan, patience, and practice. As part of this, it will be important to expect to feel some anxiety, maybe fear. But, anxiety can be a positive sign that you are moving forward and making changes. If you agree, we can work together to make this happen.

SUCCESS TIP

Neuroplasticity and Change

This simple truth, long a mainstay of cognitive behavioural counselling, and now confirmed by neuroscience research on brain plasticity, is that the key to change and managing problematic behaviour is practice and repetition of new behaviour to build new or replacement neural pathways.

Major Neurotransmitters

Neuroscientists have identified over 100 different neurotransmitters. Some neurotransmitters such as dopamine, serotonin, and norepinephrine also act as hormones, released by the endocrine system into the blood stream, whereas neurotransmitters are released from one neuron of the brain to another (firing). Among the more significant neurotransmitters are serotonin, dopamine, glutamate, acetylcholine, and GABA. Neurotransmitters are further classified according to function as excitatory or inhibitory.

Abnormally low or high levels of a particular neurotransmitter or breakdowns in the electrical signalling that fires neurons are often major causes of physical and psychiatric disorders. For example, faulty electrical signals can lead to epilepsy or cause the tremors associated with Parkinson's disease.

excitatory neurons: Neurons that send neurotransmitters that stimulate the brain and increase the likelihood that a receptive neuron will fire.

Excitatory Neurons   **Excitatory neurons** send neurotransmitters such as epinephrine and norepinephrine that stimulate the brain and increase the likelihood that a receptive neuron will fire.

glutamate: Excitatory neuron associated with learning and memory.

Glutamate—an excitatory neuron associated with learning and memory. **Glutamate** abnormalities have been linked to a number of mental disorders, including Alzheimer's, autism, obsessive compulsive disorder (OCD), schizophrenia, and depression. (National Institute of Mental Health, 2015) Glutamate is the main excitatory and most plentiful neurotransmitter in the brain.

norepinephrine: An excitatory neurotransmitter that activates and the body's stress response.

Norepinephrine (also called noradrenaline)—excitatory neurotransmitter activates and mobilizes the body's stress response. Abnormal levels of **norepinephrine** can lead to physical and psychological problems (see Figure 11.15).

dopamine: Neurotransmitter involved in movement, attention, and problem solving.

Dopamine—involved in many functions, including movement, attention, and problem solving. **Dopamine** is most often associated with mood, and it is released when we are involved in activities that we find pleasurable. Subsequently, this motivates us

---

⟫⟫ BRAIN BYTE   Endorphins

Endorphins (endogenous morphine) pituitary gland and the hypothalamus interact with opioid receptors (neurons) in the brain to produce pleasure and reduce pain. Exercise, chocolate, and sex are known to release endorphins.

Norepinephrine
RAGE HORMONE

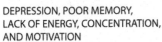

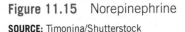

DEPRESSION, POOR MEMORY, LACK OF ENERGY, CONCENTRATION, AND MOTIVATION

INCREASES BLOOD PRESSURE, HEART RATE, CAUSES HYPERACTIVITY, ANXIETY AND STRESS, ANXIETY, IRRITABILITY, AND INSOMNIA

Figure 11.15 Norepinephrine
SOURCE: Timonina/Shutterstock

to repeat actions which release dopamine. A deficit in dopamine can result in Parkinson's disease. As well, there is evidence that dopamine abnormalities may be a factor in schizophrenia or attention deficit hyperactivity disorder (National Institute of Mental Health, 2015). However, it is likely that other neurotransmitters and causative factors are also involved when a person has schizophrenia (Brisch et al., 2014). Figure 11.16 illustrates the impact of excess and deficient dopamine.

Inhibitory Neurons   **Inhibitory neurons** send neurotransmitters (such as serotonin and gamma-aminobutyric acid (GABA)) to calm the brain and decrease or inhibit other neurons from firing.

> **inhibitory neurons:** Neurons that produce neurotransmitters that calm the brain and decrease or inhibit other neurons from firing.

Serotonin—a major inhibitory neurotransmitter found mostly in the gastrointestinal tract and the brain stem. **Serotonin** helps regulate mood, body temperature, pain, appetite, and sleep. Lower levels of serotonin are believed to be associated with depression, impulsiveness, and aggression. (It should be noted that there is some controversy about whether depression is in fact a result of low serotonin levels and some neuroscientists such as Arden (2015) argue that the actual causation is much more complicated.) Excessive serotonin can lead to a potentially fatal and very dangerous condition known as serotonin syndrome (Mayo Clinic, 2017a) with symptoms of high fever, irregular

> **serotonin:** An inhibitory neurotransmitter found in the gastrointestinal tract and the brain stem that helps regulate mood, body temperature, pain, appetite, and sleep.

>>> BRAIN BYTE   Dopamine

Addictive drugs create an enormous surge of dopamine in the brain creating an elevated level of pleasure (drug high or rush). In turn, this increases the drive (motivation) to continue to use drugs in order to recapture the rush from the drug.

Dopamine

HORMONE PLEASURE

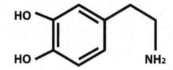

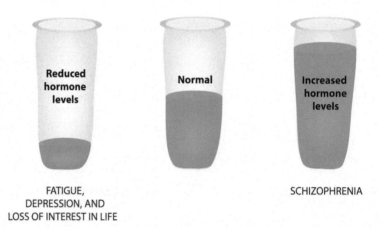

Reduced hormone levels

Normal

Increased hormone levels

FATIGUE, DEPRESSION, AND LOSS OF INTEREST IN LIFE

SCHIZOPHRENIA

Figure 11.16 Dopamine
SOURCE: Timonina/Shutterstock

heartbeat, and seizures. This may occur if clients take too much medication or if they take their medication with other medicines or illegal drugs. Figure 11.17 depicts the impact of excess or deficient serotonin.

Antidepressant medications such as Prozac can rapidly increase serotonin levels; however, counsellors should be aware that it may take weeks for medications to impact depression (Andrews, Bharwani, Lee, Fox, & Thomson Jr, (2015). Counsellors can remind clients of this fact and encourage them not to abandon treatment prematurely before the medication has had a chance to take effect. In the following example, the counsellor, while careful not to give medical advice, supports the client's relationship with the doctor, provides general guidance regarding medication compliance, and acknowledges the strengths of the client.

> **Client:** The doctor put me on an antidepressant a few weeks ago, but it's not working. I haven't given up, but I'm wondering if it's worth the effort.
>
> **Counsellor:** What did the doctor tell you about the meds.
>
> **Client:** Lots! But, I don't remember any of it.
>
> **Counsellor:** Did she say anything about how long it might take for the medication to work?
>
> **Client:** Now that you mention it, she did say it might take a while.
>
> **Counsellor:** Sure. Sometimes these meds can take a month or longer to kick in. And sometimes, you might need a higher dose, or even a different drug. So, you need to be . . . .
>
> **Client:** Patient?
>
> **Counsellor:** Also, street drugs may interfere, so it's important to let your doctor know if you are using. By the way, I'm impressed that you've been able to hang in there. That's a real strength.

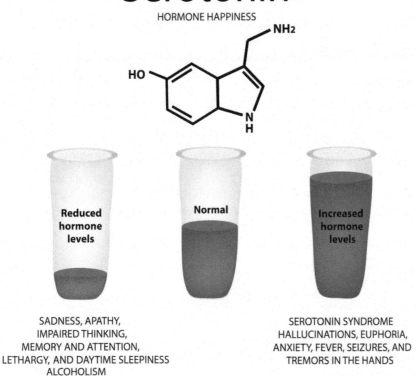

Serotonin

HORMONE HAPPINESS

Reduced hormone levels

Normal

Increased hormone levels

SADNESS, APATHY,
IMPAIRED THINKING,
MEMORY AND ATTENTION,
LETHARGY, AND DAYTIME SLEEPINESS
ALCOHOLISM

SEROTONIN SYNDROME
HALLUCINATIONS, EUPHORIA,
ANXIETY, FEVER, SEIZURES, AND
TREMORS IN THE HANDS

Figure 11.17 Serotonin

SOURCE: Timonina/Shutterstock

Acetylcholine—linked to central nervous system functions, including wakefulness, attentiveness, anger, aggression, sexuality, and thirst. **Acetylcholine** also plays a role in Alzheimer's. (Francis, 2005) (McGill University, 2015 (Note: Sometimes acetylcholine acts as an excitatory neurotransmitter while at other times, it functions as an inhibitory neurotransmitter. This depends on the type of receptor neuron that absorbs it.)

> **acetylcholine:** neurotransmitter linked to central nervous system functions, including wakefulness, attentiveness, anger, aggression, sexuality, and thirst

GABA (gamma-aminobutyric acid)—plays a role in controlling fear and anxiety, motor control, and vision. Adequate levels of **GABA** are critical for relaxation. Abnormalities can cause anxiety, disturbances in mood, sleep, epilepsy, and pain (WebMD, 2015). It is the main inhibitory neurotransmitter in the brain.

> **GABA:** Inhibitory neurotransmitter that helps to control fear and anxiety, motor control, and vision.

Mirror Neurons

Mirror neurons are neurons that fire when we observe another person doing or saying something. Significantly, our brains mirror those of the other person by firing in the same way as if we were doing or saying it. Mirror neurons are active when we watch a hockey game, attend a movie, and especially when we witness or hear the emotions of others. When a client expresses emotions, mirror neurons in the counsellor may react with the same emotions. This phenomenon has powerful implications. For one thing, it may leave counsellors vulnerable to vicarious trauma from the cumulative impact of working with clients who have been traumatized. It also presents counsellors with opportunities for empathy if they pay close attention to their own emotional responses. For example, if a counsellor is feeling lost and confused as he listens to his client, he could use this observation to inquire whether his client is feeling the same.

> **mirror neurons:** Neurons that fire when we observe another person doing or saying in the same way as if we were doing or saying it.

Counsellor: I'd like to know how you might be feeling right now. I'm feeling a bit lost, and I wonder if that's also happening for you.

Client: Oh good! It's not just me. I'm totally muddled.

Counsellor: Okay, what do we need to do to get back on track?

Although our own mirror neurons might be one cue that aids in the experience and expression of empathy, they are only one part of a very complex system of empathic perception. Counsellors need to remember that their own prior learning, experience, culture, and their present mood impact the receptivity and accuracy of their mirror neuron reactions. Siegel (2012) presents an example that underscores the importance of tentativeness when interpreting client behaviour or inferring emotions:

> If you are from New York City and I raise my hand in front of you, you may imagine that I am hailing a cab. If you are currently a student, you may imagine that I am intending to ask a question. If you have been abused, you may feel that I am going to hit you. (p. 166)

Glial Cells

glial cells: Cells which provide support to neurons.

In the brain, **glial cells** or glia, which are far more plentiful than neurons, provide essential support to neurons. Without them, neurons would be unable to do their work. There are five main types of glial cells with the exotic names, Astrocyte, Microglia, Oligodendroglia, Ependymal, Satellite, and Schwann. Each of them have specialized functions such as carrying nutrients, disposing of dead neurons, or protecting the neuron (myelination).

Reward Pathway

reward pathway: Neural circuit that rewards pleasurable activities with dopamine.

The **reward pathway** (or pleasure pathway) is a pathway in the brain that reinforces or rewards activities with dopamine that it finds pleasurable. The reward pathway involves ventral tegmental area, the nucleus accumbens, the prefrontal cortex, the hippocampus, and the amygdala.

Pleasurable sensory experiences (e.g., food, sex, and positive relationships) cause the reward pathway in the brain to release dopamine, which creates feeling of well-being. Dopamine also acts as a reinforcer, which increases the probability (motivation) that the individual will repeat the experience that generated the reward. Many prescribed medications, such as opiate-based pain killers, and most street drugs, such as heroin, cocaine, and methamphetamine, also activate the pleasure pathway. They do so in dramatic ways that flood the brain with massive amounts of dopamine, which causes disruption and damage to the normally balanced reward pathway. This damage reduces the person's capacity to experience pleasure for normal activities and thus the drug becomes the only way to feel okay. As a result, the drive to use the drugs increases, and it may become the dominant force in the person's life. Continued use of the drug leads to tolerance and ever increasing levels of it are required to achieve the desired effect, or even to feel "normal."

Epigenetics   Genes, which we inherit from our parents, contain the code or instructions that define us, including the colour of our eyes, how we look, and our susceptibility to certain diseases. **Epigenetics** is the study of how certain genes can be activated or deactivated by life experiences such as nutrition, environment, poverty, and especially trauma. Studies have shown that epigenetic gene changes from life experience may trigger depression, schizophrenia, alcohol abuse, anxiety, and many other conditions in those already predisposed genetically to them (Albert, 2010, Ptak, & Petronis, 2010). For example, a review by Radhakrishnan, Wilkinson, & D'Souza (2014) revealed

epigenetics: The study of how certain genes can be activated or deactivated by life experiences, such as nutrition, environment, poverty, and especially trauma.

how marijuana can trigger psychosis in some individuals who are predisposed to it. Of significance to counsellors is the fact that epigenetic gene changes caused by experience can be passed down to future generations.

Further research will no doubt reveal more specific information regarding how and when intergenerational genetic change occurs, and this will offer guidance regarding customized counselling interventions to prevent (ideally) or address problems. What we already know is that a range of counselling interventions, including the counselling relationship itself, diet, exercise, sleep, and the provision of safe environments for those affected by trauma, can lessen the effects of adverse epigenetic experiences (Dahlitz, 2016). Epigenetics offers the empowering idea that our clients' genetic codes do not fully define the outcome of their lives. Change is possible. Using techniques, they learn in counselling, clients have the ability to influence whether genes activate.

BRAIN PROBLEMS

The brain has undeniable remarkable ability and capacity, yet it is very fragile. Although protected somewhat by the skull, it is vulnerable to injury as well as disease. Sometimes, recovery is possible, and the brain has the capacity to reprogram itself to compensate for damage. Sometimes damage is irreversible and degenerative, as with Alzheimer's a condition for which there is not yet a cure. There are over 400 different neurological diseases and disorders (Brainfacts.org, 2017). The following subsections will explore common and significant disorders of the brain.

Mental Disorders

The Diagnostic and Statistical Manual of Mental Disorders (DSM-5) describes and classifies hundreds of different disorders arranged in developmental sequence. See Chapter 9 for a full discussion of this important topic.

Meningitis

Meningitis is a viral inflammation of the lining of the spinal cord or brain. Spread by close contact with others, and it is an extremely serious condition that requires immediate medical attention.

Encephalitis

Encephalitis is an inflammation of the brain. It is usually caused by a viral infection. Symptoms might include fever or headache and sometimes the inflammation can cause confusion or seizures. Some people experience personality changes, memory loss, and hallucinations (HealthLinkBC, 2017). It is treated with antiviral medication and recovery can take months.

Brain Tumours

Brain tumours can be benign (non-cancerous) or malignant (cancerous). They are treated in a variety of ways, including surgery, chemotherapy, and radiation.

Amyotrophic lateral sclerosis (ALS or Lou Gehrig's disease)

Amyotrophic lateral sclerosis (ALS) is a progressive, fatal disorder in which the brain's motor neurons, which carry signals from the brain to the body, break down and lose their ability to communicate with muscles. There are about 3000 Canadians living with ALS (ALS Society of Canada, 2017).

Cerebral palsy

Cerebral palsy (CP) is a disorder resulting from brain damage before or during birth that affects body and muscle movement. CP affects 1 of every 500 people in Canada (Cerebral Palsy Association of British Columbia, 2017). Symptoms vary widely from person to person with some only mildly affected while others require constant care.

Epilepsy

Epilepsy is a non-contagious brain disorder in which nerve cells in the brain cause a person to have seizures, although not all seizures involve convulsions. In Canada, about 0.6 percent of people have epilepsy (Epilepsy Canada, 2017). It may be caused by such things as tumours, infection, or injury to the brain. It is usually treated with anticonvulsant medication. One additional challenge for people with epilepsy is dealing with the stigma and discrimination that often accompanies the disease.

Huntington's disease

Huntington's disease (HD) is an inherited brain disorder which causes the brain cells to die, leading to a gradual, eventually fatal inability to control movement, as well cognitive and emotional decline. Approximately 1 in every 1000 Canadians has HD, and children who have a parent with the disorder have a 50 percent chance of developing the disease (Huntington Society of Canada, 2017). There is now a test to determine if an individual will develop HD disease. Counsellors may have a role supporting people who are trying to decide whether to take the test.

Multiple sclerosis (MS)

MS is an autoimmune disease, in which myelin, a cover protecting nerves, is damaged, resulting in the disruption of nerve impulses. Symptoms are unpredictable, vary widely, and may include fatigue, muscle weakness, vision, or mood problems. Significantly, for reasons not yet known, Canada has one the world's highest rate of MS with 1 in 340 Canadians living with the disease (Multiple Sclerosis Society of Canada, 2017).

SUCCESS TIP

What to do if Someone is Having a Seizure

Stay calm. Don't try to restrain the person or put anything in their mouth—they will not swallow his tongue. Make sure the area around them is safe by moving hazards such sharp objects or items that could injure. Cushion the person's head. After the seizure stops, position the person on their side.

Counsellors can assist clients with MS deal with the social, emotional, and financial effects of the disease. Family counselling can provide a safe venue for people to deal with the often difficult emotional and relationship issues associated with the disease.

Parkinson's disease

Parkinson's is a progressive brain disorder caused by the brain's deteriorating inability to produce dopamine, a neurotransmitter critical to movement and the regulation of emotions. Most people are familiar with the tremors caused by Parkinson's, but symptoms can also include fatigue, movement problems, sleep disturbance, cognitive decline, and mood problems, especially depression. L-dopa, which the brain converts to dopamine, is the most common medication. Parkinson's, affecting over 100,000 Canadians (mostly seniors), is the second most common neurodegenerative disorder after Alzheimer's (Parkinson Canada, 2017).

Tourette syndrome

Tourette syndrome (TS) is a neurological disorder characterized by repetitive vocalizations and involuntary tics. It was named for Dr. Georges Gilles de la Tourette, a French neurologist who diagnosed the condition in 1885. Tics can include eye blinking, lip-licking, shoulder shrugging, and head jerking. It might involve involuntary hopping, jumping, or spinning, as well as meaningless vocalizations (Tourette Canada, 2017). The Canadian Psychological Association (2017) suggests that the prevalence of TS is about 0.005 percent of the population and is more likely to affect males.

Medication and specially designed behavioural and cognitive counselling techniques are used to treat TS. Deep stimulation and transcranial magnetic stimulation are also being explored as potential treatment options (Tourette Canada, 2017).

Dementia

Most people have heard of the terms dementia and Alzheimer's and often they are used interchangeably, but there are differences. **Dementia**, now known as neurocognitive disorder in DSM-5 is a general term that includes a large number of disorders such as Alzheimer's, HD, Parkinson's disease, and Creutzfeldt-Jakob disease, and is characterized by problems associated with memory and thinking (alzheimers.net, 2017). Of particular significance is the fact that up to 50 percent of persons with dementia, including Alzheimer's, are clinically depressed, but, adult depression does not increase the likelihood of dementia (Singh-Manoux et al., 2017).

dementia (neurocognitive disorder): A general term that includes a number of disorders where there are problems with memory and thinking.

Alzheimer's disease, the most common form of dementia, was first described by Dr. Alois Alzheimer in 1906. It is an irreversible, fatal disorder that results in behavioural and emotional decline as well as brain shrinkage (especially in the hippocampus), deterioration, and cell death. Post-mortem microscopic analysis of the brain tissue of people with Alzheimer's show abnormal protein clusters (plaques) and twisted strands of other proteins called tangles. Plaques and tangles will be very prevalent in areas of the brain related to learning and memory (see Figure 11.18). This helps explain the reasons for some of the common symptoms of dementias such as Alzheimer's (see Figure 11.19).

Alzheimer's mostly affects people over 65 years old with the risk increasing with age, but early onset can occur in people as young as 40 (Graff-Radford, 2017). Canada's rapidly aging population means that there will be a dramatic increase in the number of Canadians who are dealing with this disease. The Alzheimer's Society of Canada (2017) estimates that there are currently about 565,000 Canadians with Alzheimer's, but this number will grow to 937,000 in the next 15 years. In addition to the enormous costs (currently estimated by the Alzheimer's Society at 10.1 billion dollars a year),

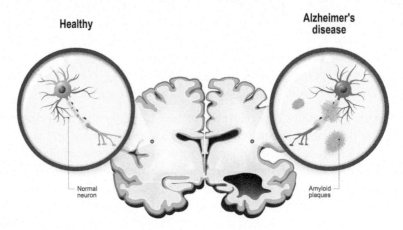

Figure 11.18 Cell Deterioration with Alzheimer's
SOURCE: Designua/Shutterstock

this disease will increasingly require professional counsellors who are well versed in its presentation to provide support services to patients and caregivers.

The Alzheimer's Society of Canada (2017) identifies four stages to the disease:

- *Early*: **M**ild symptoms and problems with memory, communication, mood, and behaviour. At this stage, people are generally able to cope, perhaps with some assistance.

- *Middle*: **W**orsening of symptoms. People may require assistance with daily living tasks. Clearly, this puts steadily increasing demands on caregivers, so they may also need considerable support.

- *Late*: **S**evere impairment with profound inability to communicate, recognize family and friends, or care for themselves. Continuous care is required.

- *End of Life*: **S**ymptoms progress further, and 24-hour-per-day care is necessary.

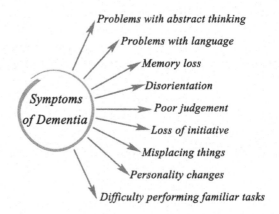

Figure 11.19 Symptoms of Dementia
SOURCE: arka38/Shutterstock

BRAIN BYTE | Sundowning

As many as 20 to 45 percent of people with dementia experience "sundowning" or late day confusion characterized by a deterioration in their condition in late afternoon and evening. Counsellors and caregivers can watch for and manage triggers such as low or fading light, fatigue, depression, and sleep disturbance (WebMD, 2017). Sticking to routines, minimizing stress, dietary management, and exercise can help reduce frequency and symptoms (Roth, 2017).

Counselling People with Dementia and Alzheimer's

■ *Empathy*: Counsellors should be aware that an Alzheimer's diagnosis is a terrifying experience, not only for the patient, but also for everyone in their lives. Patients and caregivers may be reluctant to share their feelings with each other, but be quite willing to open up to a nonjudgmental counsellor who is willing to listen as they share powerful emotions. In this regard, counsellor empathy is an important part of helping people deal with the emotional impact of the disease.

SUCCESS TIP

Dementia

Put emphasis on what clients *can do* and what they can be supported to do rather than on what they can't do or are incapable of doing. Be creative!

■ *Hope*: Alzheimer's is a progressive disease, meaning that the symptoms worsen with time. The Alzheimer's Society of Canada (2017) notes that although some dementias are reversible, Alzheimer's is not. Counsellors need to avoid conveying false hope that "everything is going to be all right." On the other hand, hope and optimism can be built on the knowledge that some of the symptoms can be managed with medication and counselling. People diagnosed with it can lead meaningful lives for many years. Enormous brain research is now under way to find ways to diagnose, prevent, and cure this complex disease. Although a cure has still evaded researchers, new medications and insights about the disease give reasons to be hopeful that a cure and treatment will be found.

■ *Structure*: Establishing routines and familiarity can help to calm people with dementia who are anxious and dealing with an increasingly forgetful mind. Counsellors can review their client's pre-dementia routines with their families, with the goal of retaining as much of this as possible, even if the client is now in institutional care.

■ *Empowerment*: Based on individual capacities, counsellors can look for ways to help clients regain or retain control and power over their lives. Many of the counselling strategies discussed in earlier chapters might be adapted including: involvement in decision making, respect for choices such as where and how clients wish to live their lives, and the identification of activities and tasks that give clients a sense of purpose.

■ *Support for Caregivers*: Taking care of someone with dementia requires relentless dedication and personal sacrifice. Counsellors can contract to offer caregivers assistance such as: information and guidance about dementia and its' stages, education on strategies for communicating and dealing with the challenges presented by the person with dementia, links to support groups, assistance to access respite care, and personal counselling to deal with their emotions and the difficult decisions caregivers must make such as moving their loved one to a care facility.

⟩⟩⟩ BRAIN BYTE ▎ Is it Normal or Dementia?

About 40 percent of people over 65 will have some memory loss—this "age associated memory loss" is normal and not a sign of dementia. Dementia is characterized by more severe memory loss, such as not being able to recall the names of family members or recent conversations and events (Alzheimer's Society of Canada, 2017).

Student: I've just found out that my training placement will be in a centre that deals with clients who have dementia. What are the important things for counsellors to remember when working with people who have dementia?

Counsellor: For one thing, it is important to remember that symptoms can range from very mild to severe. Consequently, no single recipe for counselling is possible, and interventions must be customized to individual needs and capacities, just as they are for clients without dementia. Even those with significant impairment may retain some cognitive capacity and strengths. For example, clients with advanced dementia may still be able to express themselves with music or art. Accordingly, counsellors might place a priority on finding and using strengths, including areas of the brain that have not been damaged.

Student: What else?

Counsellor: Although many dementia's, especially Alzheimer's, have no cure, some of the commonly coexisting conditions such as anxiety and depression can be addressed medically and with counselling. As much as possible, keep clients involved in decision making and planning. This helps them retain a sense of control and purpose. Since boredom is a major cause of depression among seniors, including those with dementia, help them find meaningful and stimulating recreational activity that can help combat depression. For example, counsellors can help those with vision problems to access audio books. Anxiety can be reduced by promoting such things as consistent routines and reminders for those with short-term memory loss. Putting out familiar objects (e.g., pictures and memorabilia) can serve as comforting reminders. Counsellors can help caregivers understand the importance of keeping living quarters organized and, if useful, putting signs on doors such as the bathroom to reduce confusion.

Student: What about specific interviewing and counselling skills?

Counsellor: Here again, there is no one-size-fits-all answer. But generally, counsellors should speak in a slow, calm, reassuring manner. Because of cognitive decline, counsellors need to allow time for their clients to answer. Counsellors need to be comfortable with silence and the onus is on them to adjust pace to meet their clients' needs. When short-term memory loss is an issue, frequent simple repetitions and summaries may help. Targeted short answer or questions are preferable to those that require extended or complex responses. It's also important for counsellors to remember the tremendous strain that caregivers often face. Discuss with them the importance of self-care. And that also applies to you too! There's lots more information out there. I'd suggest the local Alzheimer's Society as a good place to start.

Stroke

stroke: A clot blockage which causes rupture of arteries in the brain.

A **stroke** occurs when blood flow to the brain is blocked. Some of the major warning signs of stroke are depicted in Figure 11.20. Although a stroke can occur at any age, nearly three-quarters happen to people over age 65 years of age (The Internet Stroke Center, 2017).

There are three major types of strokes:

Ischemic stroke: A blockage or clot in the brain caused by a buildup of plaque.

1. **Ischemic stroke** occurs when plaque causes a blockage or clot in the brain.

Hemorrhagic stroke: A stroke that that occurs when conditions such as high blood pressure causes arteries to burst.

2. **Hemorrhagic stroke** occurs when conditions such as high blood pressure cause arteries in the brain to burst.

Transient ischemic attack (T.I.A.): A mini stroke that strikes when a clot blocks an artery.

3. **Transient ischemic attack (T.I.A.)** or mini stroke occurs when a clot blocks an artery. Although they may not cause damage, their occurrence is a warning sign that should be taken seriously.

Broca's Aphasia: Difficulty with speech, understanding, and language.

Wernicke's Aphasia: Difficulty finding words and/or using nonsensical words.

The effects of a stroke can vary greatly from mild to catastrophic. The Cleveland Clinic (2017) reports that a stroke in the right side of the brain can lead to symptoms such as attention and perception difficulties, trouble processing information, poor judgment and communication problems, as well as attention and memory problems. Left-brain strokes may result in paralysis on the right side, and communication problems such as slurred speech, **Broca's Aphasia** (difficulty with speech, understanding, and language), and **Wernicke's Aphasia** (difficulty finding words and/or using nonsensical

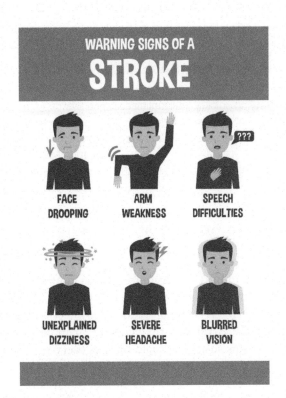

Figure 11.20 Stroke Warning Signs
SOURCE: Irina Strelnikova/Shutterstock

words). People with aphasia have difficulty with language and communication, but their difficulty is **not** a measure of their intelligence.

A variety of medications are used to treat and/or prevent stroke, including blood thinners, cholesterol lowering medications, clot busters, blood pressure, and cholesterol-lowering medications (Heart and Stroke Foundation of Canada, 2017). As well, medications to treat anxiety and depression, which Hackett & Pickles (2014) found occur in 33 percent or more of stroke patients, may be used.

SUCCESS TIP

FAST Stroke Signs

Face, is it drooping
Arms, can you raise both arms
Speech, is it slurred
Time to call 911 (Heart and Stroke Foundation of Canada, 2017)

Counsellors may be involved in a variety of ways, including lifestyle stroke prevention, cognitive behavioural and problem-solving counselling to deal with the aftermath of a stroke, and family counselling. There are a number of risk factors for stroke which counselling can appropriately address, including smoking, weight control, sedentary lifestyle, and heavy drinking.

Counsellors can refer or encourage clients to use services such as physiotherapy, occupational therapy, and neurotherapy. Neurotherapy centres, available in most major cities in Canada, can customize brain treatment to specific areas of the brain that have been damaged by stroke.

Traumatic Brain Injury (TBI) and Acquired Brain Injuries (ABI)

Traumatic Brain Injury (TBI): Brain injuries from blow to the head, sports injuries, disease, poisoning, or drug abuse.

Acquired Brain Injuries (ABIs): ABIs are brain injuries that happen after birth rather than as a result of genetic factors.

Traumatic Brain Injuries (TBIs) and **Acquired Brain Injuries (ABIs)** include head trauma (from whiplash, falling, or blows to the head), as well as damage caused by sports injuries, disease (e.g., heart attack, seizure, tumours, and infections), poisoning, and drug abuse (Brain Injury Canada, 2017). The frequency of brain injury in Canada is rising with over 160,000 Canadians sustaining brain injuries every year, about 50 percent of which are the result of motor vehicle accidents and falls (Brain Injury Canada, 2017).

One common type of brain injury is a concussion, which can cause symptoms such as loss of consciousness, headache, dizziness and confusion, and mood changes. Usually, with rest, a concussion will heal, but sometimes medical intervention is required to deal with more serious symptoms such as internal bleeding.

Canada's aging seniors are one group at risk of abuse by a family member or caregiver, usually an adult child. Counsellors should consider the possibility that TBI could be the result of abuse. Sensitive and nonjudgmental interviewing can be used to provide an opportunity for the person to disclose abuse. Although there is no legal "duty to report" abuse of adults, counsellors have a professional responsibility to look for ways to ensure that their client has a safety plan, with options, including police intervention, transition homes, family counselling, and anger management for the abuser. Where abuse of a child is suspected, Canadian laws require that this be reported to the appropriate child welfare authorities. Further in-depth interviewing should be suspended and deferred to the responsible child welfare specialist.

Oakview Studios/ Shutterstock

After injury or stroke, the brain does not regenerate damaged tissue. However, the brain's remarkable plasticity may enable it to reorganize (reprogram) neural pathways to allow partial or full recovery over a period of time. It is analogous to a road detour. When a part of the brain is unable to continue its work because of injury, it is capable of rewiring itself to move the work to a different, healthy area. Recovery outcome is impacted by many factors, including age and the nature of the injury, but recovery can be maximized through repetition of rehabilitation exercises to enhance brain plasticity. Counsellors can help by assisting clients to access local rehabilitation professionals, and by providing supportive counselling to sustain client motivation during what might be a long period of recovery requiring patience and continued effort.

Brain and spinal cord injury are potentially catastrophic events with the potential to cause paralysis as well as impact consciousness. The Mayo Clinic (2017b) describes five different states of consciousness:

- **Coma**—a state of unconsciousness that may be temporary or permanent.
- **Vegetative state**—person is unaware of what is happening, but they may retain some responses (open eyes, sounds, and respond to reflexes).

- **Minimally conscious state**—severed altered consciousness, but some awareness of surroundings.
- **Locked-in syndrome**—person is aware, unable to respond, but may be able to communicate with eye movement.
- **Brain death**—no activity in the brain and brainstem.

TBI can precipitate a wide range of social and psychological problems. Since affected individuals may not be able to work in their chosen profession, employment counselling professionals can work with them to secure retraining or income replacement. They can also help clients deal with the emotional loss (grief) associated with an unplanned interruption in their work, which may result in "depression, anxiety, relationship strain, failed attempts at returning to work, substance use, loss of self-esteem, and PTSD related to a TBI" (Maucieri, 2012). Since family members are directly impacted by a loved one's TBI, they may need to be considered or included in any counselling intervention.

SUCCESS TIP

Brain Health

The positive impact on brain health of factors such as exercise, diet, social relationships, reduction of substance use, including smoking, housing, sleep, reduction of stress, positive thinking, employment, engaging in stimulating brain activity (reading, education, and games), and spirituality have been well documented in the literature. All of them are valid targets for contracting in a comprehensive counselling plan.

SUMMARY

- The brain is a complex organ that controls all the functions of the body, including what we do, see, hear, and think.
- Neuroscience as a new force in counselling joins psychoanalysis, behaviourism, humanism, multiculturalism, and social justice.
- There are diverse ways to study the brain, including dissection, animal studies, the impact of injury or disease, and neuroimaging.
- Neuroplasticity refers to the brain's continuous changing of neural pathways as a result of experience and learning.
- A range of counselling strategies can be used to enhance neuroplasticity.
- The brain is composed of three parts: the cerebrum, cerebellum, and brainstem.
- Eighty billion nerve cells or neurons produce neurons, which are the key to brain functioning and communication.
- Neurons communicate with neurotransmitters such as dopamine and serotonin.
- Learning and experience create neural pathways, which may involve hundreds of thousands of neurons.
- There are over 400 named neurological disorders and diseases, including dementias, such as Alzheimer's disease.

EXERCISES

Self-Awareness

1. How might your genetics be affected by your life experiences?

2. Think about how you might react if you or a member of your family was diagnosed with Alzheimer's. Reflect on the overall impact for you, your friends, and your community.

3. Make a list of things you could do to "exercise" your mind.

4. Imagine that you are an individual whose parent has HD. Share your thoughts on the pros and cons of taking the genetic test to determine if you will develop the disease.

5. What are your strongest neural pathways? What events or experiences made them strong? Which are helpful to you in leading your life? Which are problematic?

6. Do you think biology and neuroscience will be able to explain the "mind?"

Skill Practice

1. Change your neural patterns by visualizing (imagining) change. Identify a situation in your life where you would like to change how you think, behave, or act. Set a specific goal. Now close your eyes and visualize the ideal result. Use thought stopping to manage unhelpful thinking.

2. Option: Work with a partner who can assist you with prompts that help you visualize—For example, Where are you? Who else is present? Imagine that you are to . . . (situational details). Now, imagine yourself saying . . . . You are feeling (add positive emotion consistent with success).

3. Suggest how a counsellor might deal with a client recently diagnosed with Alzheimer's at the early stages who remarks, "My life is over."

4. What unique issues might arise for a client age 40 who develops early onset Alzheimer's?

5. Your client is a 75-year-old man living with his wife, age 68. They have been happily married for over 40 years. Three years ago, she was diagnosed with Alzheimer's, and the disease has progressed rapidly. She has reached a point where she can no longer be left alone. Often, she has trouble recognizing family and friends and, on occasion, even

her husband. He is in good health and determined to keep his wife at home. However, he admits that the burden of her care is becoming overwhelming. Develop a plan for supporting him in the coming months.

6. Talk to your circle of family and friends. Ask them, "What words and phrases do you think of when you hear the word Alzheimer's." Now ask them, "What would you say, feel, and think if someone close to you said they had Alzheimer's." Share your answers in a group discussion with classmates.

7. Your client has recently experienced a stroke. He says, "My life is over." Suggest counselling priorities for working with this client.

8. Your client is a woman, age 28, who has been diagnosed with MS. In recent months, her symptoms have become more pronounced where she is having difficulty caring for her twin boys, age 6. She also reports that this is putting a severe strain on her 10-year marriage to her high school sweetheart. As her counsellor, how might you assist her to deal with her challenges.

9. Your client is a 20-year-old man who has recently been diagnosed with epilepsy. He reports that he feels ashamed and embarrassed by his condition. Suggest a simple, non-jargonized response to help him deal with his feelings. Use neuroscience concepts.

10. A third-grade teacher is adamant that her nine-year-old student diagnosed with ADHD is just "being bad." Suggest a neuroscience response to the teacher.

Concepts

1. Scientists are a very early stage using technology to "read the mind." Suggest ethical issues that might arise if this technology is perfected.

2. Describe how neuroplasticity can be used to explain cognitive behavioural counselling concepts.

3. Dispute the common myth that we only use part of our brain.

4. How can we best help our clients utilize information on the Internet?

5. If the brains of psychopaths are damaged, to what extent should they be held accountable for their behavior?

WEBLINKS

Note: There are many national, international, and local agencies that have been formed to provide information and support to people who are dealing with brain related problems. They are excellent resources for clients, families, and professionals. Here are some examples

http://www.alzheimer.ca

http://www.heartandstroke.ca

https://braininjurycanada.ca

www.epilepsy.ca

http://braincanada.ca/

Link to initiatives and research from Brain Canada, a national nonprofit agency that supports innovative brain research projects.

http://www.alz.org/research/overview.asp

A site with up-to-date current research, information, data, and links to resources on Alzheimer's.

Glossary

absolute confidentiality: An assurance that client disclosures are not shared with anyone.

acetylcholine: Neurotransmitter linked to central nervous system functions, including wakefulness, attentiveness, anger, aggression, sexuality, and thirst.

action planning: Helping clients make changes in their lives; involves setting goals, identifying strategies for change, and developing plans for reaching goals.

active listening: A term describing a cluster of skills that are used to increase the accuracy of understanding. Attending, using silence, paraphrasing, summarizing, questioning, and showing empathy are the basic skills of active listening.

addiction medications: Medications such as naltrexone and methadone that are used to support addiction recovery and treatment.

affect: A term that counsellors use to describe how people express emotions.

- blunted: Emotional expression is less than one might expect.
- flat: There is an absence or near absence of any signs of emotional expression.
- inappropriate: The person's manner and mood contradict what one might expect. For example, a client might laugh while describing the death of his mother.
- labile: There is abnormal variability in affect, with repeated, rapid, and abrupt shifts in affective expression.
- restricted or constricted: There is a mild reduction in the range and intensity of emotional expression.

affective disorders: Disturbances in mood, including depression and mania.

affective domain: How clients feel.

amplified reflection: A technique that exaggerates what a client has said with the hope that the client will present the other side of ambivalence.

amygdala: Important part of the brain associated with emotions such as fear and anger.

anorexia nervosa: An eating disorder that occurs when people reject maintaining a minimally healthy body weight. Driven by low self-esteem and an intense fear of gaining weight, people with anorexia use techniques such as purging (e.g., fasting, vomiting, and taking laxatives) and excessive exercise to reduce body weight.

anti-anxiety medications: Medications such as Valium and Librium that are used to control serious and persistent anxiety, phobia, and panic attacks.

anticipatory contract: An agreement between counsellors and clients that plans for predictable events. Anticipatory contracts provide guidance for counsellors and answer the question, "What should I do if . . .?"

antidepressant medications: Medications such as Prozac, Paxil, and Zoloft that are used to help people deal with serious depression.

anti-oppressive practice: When counsellors work for structural changes in organizations, policy, and in promoting equity in the distribution of resources, opportunities, and power.

antipsychotic (or neuroleptic) medications: Medications such as chlorpromazine, haloperidol, clozapine, and risperidone that are used to treat illnesses such as schizophrenia.

anxiety disorders: More than normal levels of fear, worry, tension, or anxiety about daily events.

assertiveness: Behaving and expressing thoughts and feelings in an open and honest manner that respects the rights of others.

assumptions: Distortions or false conclusions based on simplistic reasoning, incomplete information, or bias.

attended silence: Counsellor silence characterized by making eye contact, physically and psychologically focusing on the client, and being self-disciplined to minimize internal and external distraction.

attending: A term used to describe the way that counsellors communicate to their clients that they are ready, willing, and able to listen. Verbal, nonverbal, and attitudinal cues are the essence of effective attending.

Link resources for social work terms: https://www.carthage.edu/social-work/student-resources/vocabulary/; http://cwrp.ca/sites/default/files/publications/en/Glossary_of_Social_Work_Terms_February_2013_EN.pdf automatic thoughts: Thoughts that occur spontaneously and are often outside of one's awareness.

basic empathy: A counsellor's acknowledgment of a client's clearly communicated feelings.

behavioural domain: What clients are doing.

bipolar disorder: A mood disorder characterized by alternating periods of depression and abnormally heightened mood, sometimes to the point of grandiosity. People with bipolar disorder may behave irrationally (e.g., going on uncontrolled buying sprees, committing sexual indiscretions, and taking part in foolish business investments).

brain plasticity: The brain's ability to modify itself through experience and learning.

brain stem: Part of the brain above the spinal chord that controls breathing, heart, and blood pressure.

brief counselling: An approach to counselling characterized by a focus on resources and solutions rather than problems.

Broca's Aphasia: Difficulty with speech, understanding, and language.

bulimia: An eating disorder that occurs when people adopt a pattern of excessive overeating followed by vomiting or other purging behaviours to control their weight.

burnout: A state of emotional, mental, and physical exhaustion that reduces or prevents people from performing their job.

CAT (Computerized Axial Tomography): Use of X-rays to detect abnormalities in organs.

catharsis: Verbalization of ideas, fears, past significant events, and associations, which results in a release of anxiety or tension.

cerebellum: Part of the brain associated with movement, sensory perception, and motor coordination.

cerebrum: Part of the brain that controls higher-order functions including emotions, learning, and sensory processing.

cingulate: Part of the limbic system that plays an important part in the regulation of emotions.

corpus callosum: Nerve fibres that connect the two hemispheres of the brain.

challenging skills: Skills used to encourage clients to critically evaluate their behaviour and ideas.

change talk: Client statements favouring change.

Charles Bonnet Syndrome (CBS): Condition that often causes visual hallucinations among people who have lost their sight or have severely impaired vision.

closed questions: Questions that can easily be answered with a simple yes or no (e.g., "Did you go by yourself?").

cultural intelligence: The ability to adapt and integrate skill, knowledge, attitudes consistent with the culture of clients.

cognitive behavioural counselling (therapy): A counselling approach that assists clients to identify and modify unhelpful thinking and problematic behaviour.

cognitive domain: How clients think about their situations.

command hallucination: A distorted perception of voices and images directing one to perform some action (e.g., attack or kill someone).

concreteness: A term used to measure the clarity and specificity of communication.

confrontation: Counselling initiatives that challenge clients to critically examine their actions and/or consider other viewpoints.

confrontation of incongruities: Used to point out inconsistencies in a client's verbal and non-verbal messages, values or beliefs, and behaviour.

congruence: The capacity to be real and consistent with clients; matching behaviour, feelings, and actions.

content summary: A summary that focuses on content and is an unedited condensing of the client's words.

contingency plans: Preventive plans that anticipate possible barriers that clients might encounter as they carry out action plans.

contract: A negotiated agreement between counsellors and clients regarding the purpose of the work, their respective roles, and the methods and routines that will be used to reach their agreed-on objectives. (See also *sessional contract* and *work contract*.)

co-occurring disorder: A term used to describe a situation in which a person has both a substance use disorder and a psychiatric disorder.

core conditions: Warmth, empathy, and genuineness.

counselling: An empowerment process of helping clients to learn skills, deal with feelings, and manage problems.

counselling relationship: A time-limited period of consultation between a counsellor and a client dedicated to achieving a defined goal.

counsellor self-disclosure: When counsellors disclose personal opinions, feelings, or anecdotes, it can be a useful tool that models appropriate sharing, and it might normalize the clients' feelings or experiences. Counsellor self-disclosure should be used sparingly, solely to meet the needs of clients in a way that does not shift the focus to the counsellor.

countertransference: "The positive or negative wishes, fantasies, and feelings that a counsellor unconsciously directs or transfers to a client, stemming from his or her own unresolved conflicts" (Gladding, 2011, p. 42).

critical incident debriefing: A team meeting held to defuse the impact of a violent or traumatic event such as an assault on a staff member. Debriefing assists workers to normalize and deal with the feelings that may be aroused because of the event. As well, debriefing is used to review and revise preventive and crisis intervention procedures.

defence mechanisms: Mental process or reaction that shields a person from undesirable or unacceptable thoughts, feelings, or conclusions that, if accepted, would create anxiety or challenges to one's sense of self. Common defence mechanisms include denial, displacement, rationalization, suppression, and regression.

delusion: Distorted belief involving bizarre thought patterns that cannot be challenged by others using reason or evidence.

dementia (neurocognitive disorder): A general term that includes a number of disorders where there are problems with memory and thinking.

dependent relationship: A counselling relationship in which clients become overly reliant on their counsellors for decision making. Symptoms include excessive permission seeking, frequent phone calls or office visits for information, and an inability to make simple decisions or take action without consulting with the counsellor first.

depression: Pervasive deflation in mood characterized by symptoms such as sadness, hopelessness, decreased energy, and difficulty concentrating, remembering, and making decisions.

directives: Short statements that provide direction to clients on topics, information, and pace (e.g., "Tell me more").

diversity: Variations in terms of lifestyle, culture, behaviour, sexual orientation, age, ability, religion, and other factors.

Diagnostic and Statistical Manual of Mental Disorders: Published by the American Psychiatric Association, it is used by psychologists, psychiatrists, and other psychotherapists to classify and diagnose mental disorders.

doorknob communication: A phenomenon described by Shulman (2009) wherein clients bring up important issues at the end of the interview/relationship when there is little or no time to address them.

dopamine: Neurotransmitter involved in movement, attention, and problem solving.

dual relationship: A relationship in which there is both a counselling relationship and another type of relationship, such as friendship or sexual intimacy.

duty to warn: The professional responsibility that counsellors have to inform people whom they believe a client may harm.

dysthymia: A chronic condition with symptoms similar to depression but that are less severe.

EEG (Electroencephalography): A tool used to measure electrical activity in the brain.

Emergent Technologies: New diagnostic tools for studying the brain, including Magnetoencephalograms (MEG), functional near-infrared spectroscopy (fNIRS), diffusion MRI (DMRI), event-related optical signal (EROS), and voxel-based morphometry (VBM).

empathy: The process of accurately understanding the emotional perspective of another person and the communication of this understanding without imposing one's own feelings or reactions.

empowering skills: Skills used to help clients develop confidence, self-esteem, and control over their lives.

empowerment: The process of helping clients discover personal strengths and capacities so that they are able to take control over their lives; the expected outcome of successful counselling.

endocrine system: Network of glands in the body and brain that secrete hormones into the blood stream.

epigenetics: The study of how certain genes can be activated or deactivated by life experiences such as nutrition, environment, poverty, and especially trauma.

ethical dilemma: A situation involving competing or conflicting values or principles.

ethics: Guidelines that define the limits of permissible behaviour.

ethnocentrism: The inclination to judge other cultures negatively in relation to one's own cultural values and norms.

excitatory neurons: Neurons that send neurotransmitters that stimulate the brain and increase the likelihood that a receptive neuron will fire.

exploring and probing skills: Skills counsellors use to gather information, clarify definition, seek examples, and obtain necessary detail.

Eye Movement Sensitization and Reprocessing (EMDR): A treatment approach for dealing with trauma based on the theory that emotional problems are caused by memories that have not been stored properly.

feedback confrontation: Used to provide new information to clients about who they are, including how they are perceived by others and the effects of their behaviour on others.

frontal lobes: Part of the brain responsible for higher-order functions such as decision making, problem solving, judgment, and impulse control.

Functional MRI (fMRI): Use of magnetic fields to measure activity in the brain while an individual is involved in different activities or thought.

GABA (gamma-aminobutyric acid): Inhibitory neurotransmitter that helps to control fear and anxiety, motor control, and vision.

glial cells: Cells that provide support to neurons.

glutamate: Excitatory neuron associated with learning and memory.

goal setting: A counselling process that helps clients define in precise, measurable terms what they hope to achieve from the work of counselling.

grey matter: Brain tissue composed of cells that help us think.

hallucination: A false or distorted sensory perception such as hearing, seeing, tasting, touching, or smelling what others do not.

HALT: An acronym for hungry, angry, lonely, and tired. HALT is a quick way to help clients assess triggers and plan alternative responses.

harm reduction: Methods such as needle exchange programs and methadone maintenance that reduce the damaging effects of drugs without requiring users to stop using substances.

Hemorrhagic stroke: A stroke that occurs when conditions such as high blood pressure causes arteries to burst.

hippocampus: Part of the brain in control of storing memories.

humour: A counselling tool that—when appropriate and well timed—may support the development of the relationship, reduce tension, encourage the client to take a lighter view of his or her problems, or provide an alternate perspective on their situation.

immediacy: A tool for exploring, evaluating, and deepening counselling relationships.

indirect questions: Statements that imply questions (e.g., "I'm curious how you responded.").

inferred empathy: Identification of a client's feelings based on nonverbal cues and indirect communication.

Inhibitory neurons: Neurons that send neurotransmitters (such as serotonin and GABA) to calm the brain and decrease or inhibit other neurons from firing.

interviewing: Acquiring and organizing relevant information using active listening skills, including attending, silence, paraphrasing, summarizing, questioning, and empathy.

interview transition: A shift in the topic of the interview.

intimidating behaviour: Behaviours such as name calling; using obscene or sexually harassing language and gestures; shouting; and threatening through displays of power such as fist shaking, invading personal space, stalking, and issuing verbal threats. These behaviours should be restrained to prevent escalation to violence.

invitational empathy: A tool a counsellor uses to encourage clients to explore emotions.

Ischemic stroke: A blockage or clot in the brain caused by a buildup of plaque.

I-statements: Clear assertions about personal feelings or reactions that do not blame or judge others.

job club method: An intensive and structured approach to job finding based on group support and structured learning activities. The sole purpose of a job club is to help participants find work.

kinesics: The study of body language, including such variables as posture, facial expressions, gestures, and eye motion.

leading question: A question that suggests a preferred answer (e.g., "Don't you think our session went really well today?").

learned helplessness: A state of mind that occurs when individuals have learned through failure that their efforts will not result in change.

limbic system: The brain's control centre for emotions.

LIVE: An acronym that describes the four essential steps in summarizing: listen, identify, verbalize, and evaluate.

Magnetic Resonance Imaging (MRI): A procedure that utilizes magnetic fields and radio waves to take three-dimensional structural pictures of the brain and body organs.

medulla: Brain structure responsible for breathing and regulating blood pressure.

metacommunication: The message that is heard (interpreted), which may differ from the words spoken or the intended message of the speaker.

midbrain (mesencephalon): Brain structure associated with sleep, hearing, vision, body temperature, vision, hearing, motor control, sleep/wake, and arousal (alertness).

mindfulness: Focusing on moment-to-moment experiences without judgment.

miracle question: Used in brief or single-session counselling as a way to help clients who have difficulty coming up with defined goals. The miracle question challenges clients to imagine how their lives would be different if a miracle solved their problems.

mirror neurons: Neurons that fire when we observe another person doing or saying in the same way as if we were doing or saying it.

MOANS: An acronym for the words *must, ought, always, never,* and *should,* which signal irrational or self-defeating thought.

mood disorders: See *affective disorders.*

mood-stabilizing medications: Medications such as lithium carbonate that are used to control the manic symptoms and mood swings of bipolar disorder.

motivational interviewing (MI): A nonconfrontational counselling approach that promotes behavioural change by assisting clients to resolve and overcome ambivalence.

negative symptoms: Symptoms of psychosis that include blunted or flattened affect, poverty of speech, emotional and social withdrawal, lack of pleasure (anhedonia), passivity, difficulty in abstract thinking, and lack of goal-directed behaviour. (See also *positive symptoms.*)

neural transmission: Connections between neurons in the brain for transmitting information.

neurocognitive disorder: (See also *dementia.*)

neurocounselling: The integration of neuroscience into the practice of counselling.

neurogenesis: Production of new neurons.

neuroimaging: The use of various tools to explore the structure and function of the brain.

neuroplasticity: The brain's ability to change itself by forming new neural connections in response to learning.

norepinephrine: An excitatory neurotransmitter that activates and the body's stress response.

objectivity: The ability to understand feelings, thoughts, and behaviour without allowing personal values, beliefs, and biases to interfere.

obsessive-compulsive disorder (OCD): Recurrent, unwanted thoughts and conscious, ritualized, seemingly purposeless acts, such as counting the number of tiles on the ceiling or needing to wash one's hands repetitively.

occipital lobes: Part of the brain responsible for visual processing.

open questions: Questions that promote expansive answers. These types of questions cannot be answered with a simple yes or no (e.g., "How do you feel about her?").

outcome goal: A goal related to what the client hopes to achieve from counselling.

panic disorder: Sudden attacks of terror and irrational fear accompanied by an overwhelming sense of impending doom. During a panic attack, a person may experience symptoms such as an accelerated heart rate, sweating, shaking, shortness of breath, chest pain, nausea, and fear of dying or losing control.

paraphrasing: A nonjudgmental restatement of the client's words and ideas in the counsellor's own words.

parietal lobes: Part of the brain responsible for processing body sensations such as touch, pain, and temperature as well as playing a role in vision, reading, and solving mathematical problems.

PET (Positron Emission Tomography): Radioactive dye injected into the body to measure blood flow, and detect problems with the heart, brain, and central nervous system (brain and spinal cord).

phases of counselling: Sequential steps through which counselling tends to evolve. The four phases are preliminary, beginning, action, and ending.

phases of violence: The four-phase model (anxiety, defensiveness, acting out, and tension reduction) that describes how crises escalate to violence.

phobia: An irrational fear about particular events or objects that results in overwhelming anxiety in response to situations where there is little or no danger.

Pons: Part of the brain that aids in the transmission of messages between the cortex and the cerebellum, as well as playing a role in breathing, sleep, biting, chewing, and swallowing.

positive regard: The ability of counsellors to recognize the inherent worth of people.

positive symptoms: Symptoms of psychosis that include hallucinations, delusions, bizarre behaviour, agitation, thought disorder, disorganized speech and behaviour, and catatonic behaviour. (See also *negative symptoms*.)

post-traumatic stress disorder (PTSD): Disabling symptoms such as emotional numbness, sleep disturbance (nightmares, difficulty sleeping), or reliving the event following a traumatic event such as rape, assault, natural disaster (earthquakes, floods, etc.), war, torture, or an automobile accident.

preparatory empathy: A counsellor's attempt to consider (in advance of the interview) the feelings and concerns that the client may communicate indirectly.

process goal: The methods and procedures that will be used in counselling to assist clients in reaching their goals.

prosopagnosia: A disorder where people cannot recognize faces, even with people with whom they are familiar (aka as face blindness).

proxemics: A term used to describe how people use space and distance in social behaviour.

pseudo-counselling (illusion of work): A process in which the worker and the client engage in a conversation that is empty and that has no real meaning. Counselling involves irrelevant exploration of issues, use of clichés and patronizing platitudes, intellectual exploration of issues, and avoidance of subjects or feelings that involve pain in favour of "safe" topics.

psychological reactance: The tendency for people to increase problem behaviour if they believe their freedom is threatened. This theory can help us understand why nagging by concerned friends and family may have a paradoxical effect.

psychostimulants: Medications like Ritalin that are used to treat attention-deficit/hyperactivity disorder (ADHD).

psychotherapy: Advanced counselling targeting severe emotional or behavioural difficulties or disorders.

questioning: An active listening skill that involves probing for information to confirm understanding and seek clarification.

radical acceptance: A strategy that involves encouraging expression of statements that you tend to disagree with or philosophically oppose.

reframing: A technique for helping clients look at things differently by suggesting alternative interpretations, perspectives, or new meanings. Reframes should present logical and positive alternative ways of thinking.

relationship-building skills and strategies: Tools for engaging clients and developing trust.

relationship contract: A negotiation of the intended purpose of the counselling relationship, including an agreement on the expected roles of both counsellor and client.

relative confidentiality: The assumption that client disclosures may be shared within the agency with supervisors or colleagues, outside the agency with client permission, or with others because of legal requirements, such as those contained within child-abuse legislation.

rescuing: Also called band-aiding, this involves a counsellor's actions that prevent or protect clients from dealing with issues or feelings. Rescuing arises from the counsellor's need to avoid tension and keep the session cheerful.

resistance: A defensive reaction by clients that interferes with or delays the process of counselling.

reuptake: Process whereby neurotransmitters are reabsorbed by the neuron that released them.

reward pathway: Neural circuit that rewards pleasurable activities with dopamine.

schizophrenia: A chronic mental disorder involving symptoms such as hallucinations, delusions, disordered thinking, and social isolation.

selective attention: See *selective perception*.

selective perception: A term used to describe the natural tendency to avoid being overwhelmed by information by screening out material that is irrelevant.

self-awareness: The process of becoming alert and knowledgeable about one's own way of thinking, acting, and feeling.

self-defeating thoughts: Inner dialogue of critical messages.

self-determination: The principle that promotes the rights of clients to have autonomy and freedom of choice.

self-talk: Mental messages people give to themselves (e.g., "I'm no good").

serotonin: An inhibitory neurotransmitter found in the gastrointestinal tract and the brain stem that helps regulate mood, body temperature, pain, appetite, and sleep.

sessional contract: An agreement between counsellor and client regarding the topic and expected outcome of an interview or session. (See also *contracting*.)

silence: A tool used in counselling when the client is thinking, the client is confused and unsure of what to say or do, or the client has encountered painful feelings. Because it is culturally defined, silence can also signal trust issues or closure.

simple encouragers: Short phrases and gestures such as "Tell me more," "Go on," "Uh-huh," and head nods that encourage clients to continue with their stories.

skill and strategy clusters: Categories of skills based on their intended purpose or helping activity.

stages of change model: A theory of motivation that recognizes five changes of stage: precontemplation, contemplation, preparation, action, and maintenance.

strengths approach: A counselling perspective that assumes the inherent capacity of people. Individuals and communities are seen to have assets and resources that can be mobilized for problem solving.

stroke: Clot blockage that causes rupture of arteries in the brain.

structured interview: An interview that follows a predetermined sequence of questions.

substance abuse: Continued use of substances despite significant difficulties in areas such as health (physical, emotional, and cognitive), family and other relationships, legal problems, and use in hazardous situations. Individuals may also experience increased tolerance, which leads to increases in the amount used, and withdrawal symptoms and cravings which often precipitate relapse.

summarizing: A way of condensing content. (See also *content summary* and *theme summary*.)

sustain talk: Client statements favouring the status quo.

temporal lobes: Portion of the brain that controls visual memory and speech.

theme summary: A summary that edits unnecessary detail and attempts to identify key patterns and areas of urgency.

thought broadcasting: The delusional belief that one's thinking can be heard by others.

thought insertion: The delusional belief that thoughts are being inserted into one's brain by others.

thought-stopping: A technique for breaking the pattern of repetitive self-defeating thought patterns. Techniques include thought replacement, yelling "stop" in your mind until the undesired thought disappears, snapping an elastic band on the wrist to shift thinking, and activity diversion.

tolerance: A need for more of a drug to obtain the desired effect or less effect with the same amount of the substance.

transference: The tendency of clients to communicate with their counsellors in the same way that they communicated to significant people in the past.

Transient ischemic attack (T.I.A.): A mini stroke that strikes when a clot blocks an artery.

Transtheoretical Model of change: A model that identifies five stages of change—precontemplation, contemplation, preparation, action, and maintenance. Counsellor response choices are different depending on the client's stage of change.

Traumatic Brain Injury (TBI): Brain injuries from blow to the head, sports injuries, disease, poisoning, or drug abuse.

unhelpful thinking patterns: Faulty reasoning caused by distortion, incomplete analysis, egocentricity, rigidity, and self-defeating thought.

unstructured interview: An interview that does not have a preset plan that restricts direction, pace, or content.

values: What individuals and groups consider important or worthwhile.

versatility: The need for counsellors to develop a broad range of skills so they can adapt their approach to fit the distinctive complexities of each individual and context.

vicarious trauma: An occupational hazard for people in the helping professions, where they develop the same symptoms as their clients who have been traumatized.

violent behaviour: Hitting, pushing, biting, slapping, kicking, throwing objects, and using weapons such as guns, knives, or syringes.

warmth: An expression of nonpossessive caring that requires genuineness and involvement, the acceptance of the equal worth of others, a nonjudgmental attitude, and avoidance of blaming.

Wernicke's Aphasia: Difficulty finding words and/or using nonsensical words.

white matter: Brain tissue that supports connections in the brain by helping the transmission and speed of information sharing between parts of the brain.

withdrawal: The presence of physical symptoms when a drug is no longer taken.

work contract: An agreement that specifies the intended goals or outcome of counselling.

worldview: The way one perceives, explains, and makes sense of the world including beliefs about topics such as God, politics, family, justice, respect for others, and the environment.

References

Adler, R., Towne, N., & Rolls, J. (2001). *Looking out/looking in* (1st Cdn ed.). Orlando, FL: Harcourt.

Albert, P. R. (2010). Epigenetics in mental illness: Hope or hype? *Journal of Psychiatry & Neuroscience: JPN, 35*(6), 366–368. http://doi.org/10.1503/jpn.100148

Alexander, C.M., & Sussman, L. (1995). Creative approaches to multicultural counseling. In J.G. Ponterotto, J.M. Casas, L.A. Suzuki, & C.M. Alexander (Eds.), *Handbook of multicultural counseling* (pp. 375–384). Thousand Oaks, CA: Sage Publications.

Alink, L. A., Euser, S., Bakermans-Kranenburg, M. J., & van IJzendoorn, M. H. (2014). A challenging job: Physical and sexual violence towards group workers in youth residential care. *Child & Youth Care Forum, 43*(2), 243–250.

ALS Society of Canada. (2017). Accessed September 26, 2017, from https://www.als.ca

Alzheimer's Foundation of America. (2015). *Education and care: Music.* Retrieved July 11, 2015, from http://www.alzfdn.org/EducationandCare/musictherapy.html

Alzheimers.net. (2017) http://www.alzheimers.net/difference-between-alzheimers-and-dementia/

Alzheimer's Society of Canada. (2017). Retrieved September 20, 2017, from http://www.alzheimer.ca

American Association of Suicidology. (2009). Website. Retrieved March 24, 2009, from www.suicidology.org/web/guest/home

American Addictions Centers. (2018). *Alcohol withdrawal treatment, symptoms, and timeline.* Retrieved January 10, 2018, from https://americanaddictioncenters.org/withdrawal-timelines-treatments/alcohol/

American Medical Association. (1998). *Essential guide to depression.* New York, NY: Pocket Books.

American Psychiatric Association. (2000). *Diagnostic and statistical manual of mental disorders* (4th ed., text revision). Washington, DC: American Psychiatric Association.

American Psychiatric Association. (2013). *Diagnostic and statistical manual of mental disorders* (5th ed.). Washington, DC: American Psychiatric Association.

American Psychological Association. (2015). *Children and trauma.* Retrieved July 3, 2015, from http://www.apa.org/pi/families/resources/children-trauma-update.aspx

American Speech Language Hearing Association. (2015). *Right hemisphere brain damage.* Retrieved May 290, 2015, from http://www.asha.org/public/speech/disorders/RightBrainDamage.htm

Amyotrophic Lateral Sclerosis Society of Canada. (2017). Accessed September 26, 2017, from https://www.als.ca

Andrews, P. W., Bharwani, A., Lee, L. R., Fox, M., & Thomson Jr., J. A. (2015). Is serotonin an upper or a downer? The evolution of the serotonergic system and its role in depression and the antidepressant response. *Neuroscience & Biobehavioral Reviews, 51*: 164 DOI: 10.1016/j.neubiorev.2015.01.018.

Angus, L.E., & Greenberg, L.S. (2011). *Working with narrative in emotion-focused therapy: Changing stories, healing lives.* Washington, DC: American Psychological Association.

Arboleda-Florez, J., Holley, H.L., & Cristianti, A. (1996). *Mental illness and violence: Proof or stereotype.* Ottawa, ON: Health Canada. Retrieved June 12, 2005, from www.phac-aspc.gc.ca/mh-sm/pubs/mental_illness/summary-eng.php

Arden, John B. (2015). *Brain2Brain.* Wiley. Retrieved July 20, 2017, from <http://0-www.myilibrary.com.orca.douglascollege.ca?ID=692351>

Arthur, N., & Collins, S. (Eds.). (2005). *Culture-infused counselling: Celebrating the Canadian mosaic.* Calgary, AB.

Arthur, N., & Stewart, J. (2001). Multicultural counselling in the new millennium: Introduction to the special theme issue. *Canadian Journal of Counselling, 35* (1), 3–14.

Ashwell, K. (2012). *The Brain book.* Richmond Hill, Ont: Firefly.

Azar, B. (2010). *Your brain on culture.* Retrieved July 4, 2015, from http://www.apa.org/monitor/2010/11/neuroscience.aspx

Azrin, N.H., & Besalel, V.A. (1980). *Job club counselor's manual: A behavioral approach to vocational counseling.* Austin, TX: Pro-Ed.

Backhouse, C. (1999). *Colour-coded: A legal history of racism in Canada, 1900–1950.* Toronto, ON: University of Toronto Press.

Baron-Cohen, S. (2003). *The essential difference: The truth about the male and female brain.* New York, NY: Basic Books.

Baron-Cohen, S. (2005). The Essential Difference: The Male and Female Brain. *Phi Kappa Phi Forum, 85*(1), 23–26.

Barth, A. (2011). Good listeners get inside your head. *Discover, 32* (1), 71.

Battino, R. (2007). Expectation: Principles and practice of very brief therapy. *Contemporary Hypnosis, 24* (1), 19–29. doi:10.1002/ch.325

BC Provincial Mental Health and Substance Use Planning Council. (2013). *Trauma informed practice guide.* Retrieved May 9, 2015, from http://bccewh.bc.ca/wp-content/uploads/2012/05/2013_TIP-Guide.pdf

Beck, A.T. (1976). *Cognitive therapy and the emotional disorders,* New York International Universities Press Beck, J.S., & Beck, A.T. (2011). *Cognitive behavior therapy: Basics and beyond* (2nd ed.). New York, NY: Guilford Press.

Beckman, C.S., Turner, S.G., Cooper, M., Polnerow, D., & Swartz, M. (2000). Sexual contact with clients: Assessment of social workers' attitudes and educational preparation. *Social Work, 45* (3), 223–235.

Belsham B. (2001). Glutamate and its role in psychiatric illness. *Human Psychopharmacology: Clinical & Experimental* [serial online]. *16* (2):139–146. Available from: Academic Search Complete, Ipswich, MA. Accessed June 3, 2015.

Berg, F.M. (1997). *Afraid to eat: Children and teens in weight crisis.* Hettinger, ND: Healthy Weight Publishing Network.

Beyerstein, B.L. (1998). Believing is seeing: Organic and psychological reasons for hallucinations and other anomalous psychiatric symptoms. *Medscape.* Retrieved August 7, 1998, from www.medscape.com/Medscape/MentalHealth

Bier, D. (2017). *Learning to live with Charles Bonnet-syndrome.* Retrieved September 25, 2017, from https://psychcentral.com

Bolles, R.N. (2011). *What color is your parachute? A practical manual for job-hunters and career changers.* Berkeley, CA: Ten Speed Press.

Bombay, A., Matheson, K., & Anisman, H. (2014). The intergenerational effects of Indian Residential Schools: Implications for the concept of historical trauma. *Transcultural Psychiatry, 51*(3), 320–338. doi:10.1177/1363461513503380

Borgen, W.A., Amundson, N.E., & McVicar, J. (2002). The experience of unemployment for fishery workers in Newfoundland: What helps and hinders. *Journal of Employment Counseling, 39* (3), 117–126.

Bovend'Eerdt, T.H., Botell, R.E., & Wade, D.T. (2009). Writing SMART rehabilitation goals and achieving goal attainment scaling: A practical guide. *Clinical Rehabilitation, 23* (4), 352–361.

Bowen, S., Chawla, N., & Marlatt, G.A. (2011). *Mindfulness-based relapse prevention for addictive behaviors: A clinician's guide.* New York, NY: Guilford Press.

Bower, B. (1998). Study tracks violence among mentally ill. *Science News (5),* 309.

Boyle, S., Hull, G., Mather, J., Smith, L., & Farley, O. (2006). *Direct practice in social work.* Boston, MA: Pearson.

BrainFacts.org. (2017). *Neurological diseases and disorders.* Retrieved August 29, 2017, from BrainFacts.org

Brain Canada Foundation. (2018) accesses June 13, 2018, from https://braincanada.ca/canada-brain-research-fund

Brain Injury Canada. (2017). Retrieved September 10, 2017, from https://braininjurycanada.ca/acquired-brain-injury/

Brammer, L.M., & MacDonald, G. (1999). *The helping relationship: Process and skills* (7th ed.). Needham Heights, MA: Allyn & Bacon.

Bremner, J. D. (2006). Traumatic stress: effects on the brain. *Dialogues in Clinical Neuroscience, 8* (4), 445–461.

Brill, N.I., & Levine, J. (2005). *Working with people: The helping process* (8th ed.). Boston, MA: Pearson Education.

Brisch, R., Saniotis, A., Wolf, R., Bielau, H., Bernstein, H.-G., Steiner, J., . . . , & Gos, T. (2014). The role of dopamine in schizophrenia from a neurobiological and evolutionary perspective: Old fashioned, but still in vogue. *Frontiers in Psychiatry, 5,* 47. http://doi.org/10.3389/fpsyt.2014.00047

British Columbia Ministry of Children and Family Development. (2002). *Prevalence of mental disorders in children and youth.* Vancouver, BC: UBC.

British Columbia Ministry of Health. (2002). *Best practices: Psychosocial rehabilitation and recovery.* Victoria, BC: Ministry of Health Services.

British Columbia Provincial Mental Health and Substance Use Planning Council. (2013). *Trauma informed practice guide.* Retrieved May 9, 2015, from http://bccewh.bc.ca/wp-content/uploads/2012/05/2013_TIP-Guide.pdf

British Columbia Schizophrenia Society. (2008). *Basic facts about schizophrenia* (14th ed.). Richmond, BC: BC Schizophrenia Society.

Butler, A.C., Chapman, J.E., Forman, E.M., & Beck, A.T. (2006). The empirical status of cognitive-behavioral therapy: A review of meta-analyses. *Clinical Psychology Review, 26* (1), 17–31.

Budde, H., Wegner, M., Soya, H., Voelcker-Rehage, C., & McMorris, T. (2016). Neuroscience of exercise: Neuroplasticity and its behavioral consequences. *Neural Plasticity,* vol. 2016, Article ID 3643879, 3 pages, 2016. doi:10.1155/2016/3643879

Cameron, C.L. (2006). Brief psychotherapy: A brief review. *American Journal of Psychotherapy, 60* (2), 147–152. Retrieved October 24, 2018, from EBSCOhost.

Canadian Association for Suicide Prevention. (2009). Website. Retrieved May 20, 2012, from www.suicideprevention.ca

Canadian Association of Social Workers. (2005). *Guidelines for ethical practice.* Ottawa, On: Author

Canadian Centre for Elder Law. (2017), Retrieved December 31, 2017, from http://www.bcli.org

Canadian Centre on Substance Abuse. (2004). *Canadian addiction survey.* Retrieved April 30, 2012, from www.ccsa.ca/Eng/Priorities/Research/CanadianAddiction/Pages/default.aspx

Canadian Centre on Substance Abuse. (2012). Website. Retrieved May 15, 2012, from www.ccsa.ca/eng/priorities/research/CostStudy/Pages/default.aspx

Canadian Centre on Substance Abuse. (2015). *The effects of cannabis use during adolescence.* Retrieved June 15, 2015, from http://www.ccsa.ca/Resource%20Library/CCSA-Effects-of-Cannabis-Use-during-Adolescence-Report-2015-en.pdf

Canadian Children's Rights Council. (2012). *Child and teen suicides in Canada.* Retrieved September 30, 2018, from www.canadiancrc.com/Youth_Suicide_in_Canada.aspx

Canadian Counselling and Psychotherapy Association. (2007). *Code of ethics.* Ottawa, On: Author

Canadian Counselling and Psychotherapy Association. (2012). *Who are counsellors?* Retrieved March 16, 2012, from www.ccpa-accp.ca/en/theprofession/whoarecounsellors

Canadian Immigrant. (2018). *Diversity in Canada: An overview.* Retrieved January 22, 2018, from http://canadianimmigrant.ca/guides/moving-to-canada/diversity-in-canada-an-overview

Canadian Institute for Health Information. (2012). *Canada's health care providers.* Retrieved May 17, 2012, from https://secure.cihi.ca/free_products/hctenglish.pdf

Canadian Mental Health Association. (2005). *Violence and mental illness.* Retrieved June 12, 2005, from www.cmha.pe.ca/bins/content_page.asp?cid&equals

Canadian Mental Health Association. (2015). *Hallucinations and delusions: How to respond.* Retrieved June 8, 2015, from http://www.cmha.bc.ca/files/6-hallucinations_delusions.pdf

Canadian Population. (2018). Retrieved March 2, 2018, from http://worldpopulationreview.com/countries/canada-population/

Canadian Psychological Association. (2017). *"Psychology works" fact sheet: Tourette syndrome.* Retrieved October 1, 2017, from http://www.cpa.ca

Canadian Task Force on Mental Health Issues Affecting Immigrants and Refugees. (1988). *After the door has been opened: Mental health issues affecting refugees and immigrants in Canada.* Ottawa, ON: Multiculturalism and Citizenship Canada.

Canadian Women's Foundation. (2015). *The facts about violence against women.* Retrieved June 28, 2015, from http://canadianwomen.org/facts-about-violence

Capuzzi, D., & Gross, D.R. (2009). *Introduction to the counseling profession* (5th ed.). Needham Heights, MA: Allyn & Bacon.

Capuzzi, D., & Stauffer, M. (2016). *Foundations of addictions counseling* (3rd ed.). Boston, MA: Pearson Education.

Carniol, B. (2010). *Case critical: Social service and social justice in Canada* (6th ed.). Toronto, ON: Between the Lines.

Carpetto, G. (2008). *Interviewing and brief therapy strategies: An integrative approach.* Boston, MA: Pearson.

Cattan, M., & Tilford, S. (2006). *Mental health promotion: A lifespan approach.* Berkshire, UK: McGraw-Hill.

Centre for Addiction and Mental Health. (2009). *Treating concurrent disorders: Preface.* Retrieved March 31, 2009, from www.camh.net/Publications/Resources_for_Professionals/ Treating_Concurrent_Disorders_Preface/index.html

Centre for Addiction and Mental Health. (2012). *Harm reduction: Its meaning and application for substance use issues position statement.* Retrieved May 3, 2012, from www.camh.net/Public_ policy/Public_policy_papers/harmreductionposition.html

Centre for Addiction and Mental Health. (2017). Mental illness and addiction: Facts and statistics. Accessed August 1, 2017, from http://www.camh.ca/en/hospital/about_camh/ newsroom/for_reporters/Pages/addictionmentalhealthstatistics.aspx

Centre for Suicide Prevention. (2009). Website. Retrieved July 29, 2009, from www.suicideinfo. ca

Cerebral Palsy Association of British Columbia. (2017). Accessed July 31, from http:// bccerebralpalsy.com/

Chambless, D.L., & Ollendick, T.H. (2001). Empirically supported psychological interventions: Controversies and evidence. *Annual Review of Psychology, 52*, 685–716.

Chan, C. (2018). Majority of overdose deaths happen behind closed doors. *The Vancouver Sun,* p. A6

Choney, S.K., Berryhill-Paapke, E., & Robbins, R. (1995). The acculturation of American Indians: Developing frameworks for research and practice. In P.B. Pedersen & D.C. Locke (Eds.), *Cultural and diversity issues in counseling* (pp. 73–92). Greensboro, NC: ERIC Counseling and Student Services Clearinghouse.

Clark, A.J. (2007). *Empathy in counseling and psychotherapy: Perspectives and practices.* Mahwah: Lawrence Erlbaum Associates.

Clark, A.J. (2010). Empathy: An integral model in the counseling process. *Journal of Counseling & Development, 88* (3), 348–356.

Clark, C. (2015). *Are we all schizophrenic? Part II – Hallucinations.* Retrieved June 8, 2015, from http://www.brainblogger.com/2015/05/22/are-we-all-schizophrenic-part-ii-hallucinations/

Cleghorn, J.M., & Lee, B.L. (1991). *Understanding and treating mental illness: The strengths and limits of modern psychiatry.* Toronto, ON: Hogrefe & Huber.

Cohen, L. (1968). *Selected poems, 1956–1968.* New York: Viking Press, [1968].

Compton, B., & Galaway, B. (2004). *Social work processes* (7th ed.). Pacific Grove, CA: Brooks/ Cole.

Cochran, J. L., & Cochran, N. H. (2015). *The heart of counseling: Counseling skills through therapeutic relationships.* New York: Routledge.

Corcoran, J., & Walsh, J. (2009). *Mental health in social work: A casebook on diagnosis and strengths based assessment.* Boston, MA: Pearson.

Cormier, S., & Hackney, H. (2008). *Counseling strategies and interventions.* Boston, MA: Pearson.

Cormier, W.H., & Cormier, L.S. (1985). *Interviewing strategies for helpers.* Monterey, CA: Brooks/ Cole.

Cozolino, L. J. (2010). *The neuroscience of psychotherapy: Building and rebuilding the human brain.* New York: Norton.

Cozolino, L.J., & Santos, E. (2014). Why we need therapy – and why it works: A neuroscience perspective. *Smith College Studies in Social Work, 84*:2–3, 157–177.

Cunningham, M. (2012). *Integrating spirituality in clinical social work practice: Walking the labyrinth.* Boston, MA: Pearson.

Dale, O., Smith, R., Norlin, J., & Chess, W. (2009). *Human behaviour and the social environment: Social systems theory.* Boston, MA: Pearson.

D'Andrea, M.J. (1996). White racism. In P.B. Pedersen & D.C. Locke (Eds.), *Cultural and diversity issues in counseling.* Greensboro, NC: ERIC Counseling and Student Services Clearinghouse.

Dahlitz, M. (2017). *The psychotherapist's essential guide to the brain* Part 9, Epigenetics. Neuroscience.

Dahlitz, M. (2016). The limbic system, Neuroscience. Retrieved July 25, 2018, from https://www.neuropsychotherapist.com/the-limbic-system/

Dattilio, F.M., & Freeman, A. (2010). *Cognitive-behavioral strategies in crisis intervention* (3rd ed.). New York, NY: Guilford.

Davis, L.E., & Proctor, E.K. (1989). *Race, gender, and class: Guidelines for practice with individuals, families, and groups.* Englewood Cliffs, NJ: Prentice-Hall.

Davis, S. (2006). *Community mental health in Canada: Theory, policy, and practice.* Vancouver, BC: UBC Press.

De Becker, G. (1997). *The gift of fear: Survival signals that protect us from violence.* Boston, MA: Little, Brown and Co.

de Lange, F.P., Koers, A., Kalkman, J.S., Bleijenberg, G., Peter Hagoort, P., van der Meer & J.W., Toni, I. (2008). Increase in prefrontal cortical volume following cognitive behavioural therapy in patients with chronic fatigue syndrome. *Brain: A Journal of Neurology, 131* (8) 2172–2180. http://dx.doi.org/10.1093/brain/awn140 2172-2180 First published online: June 28, 2008.

de Léséleuc S. (2004). *Criminal victimization in the workplace.* Ottawa, ON: Canadian Centre for Justice Statistics.

de Shazer, S. (1985). *Keys to solution in brief therapy.* New York, NY: Norton.

Dewar, G. (2015). *Empathy and the brain.* Website. Retrieved March 27, 2015, from http://www.parentingscience.com/empathy-and-the-brain.html

DiClemente, C.C., & Velasquez, M. (2002). Motivational interviewing and the stages of change. In W.R. Miller & S. Rollnick (Eds.), *Motivational interviewing: Preparing people for change* (2nd ed.). New York, NY: The Guilford Press.

Diller, J.V. (1999). *Cultural diversity: A primer for the human services.* Toronto, ON: Brooks/Cole.

Dodd, C.H. (1995). *Dynamics of intercultural communication* (4th ed.). Dubuque, IA: Brown & Benchmark.

Drolet, J., Clark, N., & Allen, H. (2012). *Shifting sites of practice: Field education in Canada,* Toronto, ON: Pearson.

Dubovsky, S.L., & Weissberg, M.P. (1986). *Clinical psychiatry in primary care* (3rd ed.). Baltimore, MD: Williams & Wilkins.

Eaton, N. R., Keyes, K. M., Krueger, R. F., Balsis, S., Skodol, A. E., Markon, K. E., . . . , & Hasin, D. S. (2012). An invariant dimensional liability model of gender differences in mental disorder prevalence: Evidence from a national sample. *Journal of Abnormal Psychology, 121*(1), 282–288. http://doi.org/10.1037/a0024780

Egan, G., & Shroeder, W. (2009). *The skilled helper: A problem management and opportunity development approach to helping* (1st Cdn ed.). Toronto, ON: Nelson.

Ellis, A. (1962). *Reason and emotion in psychotherapy.* New York, NY: Stuart.

Ellis, A. (1984). *Rational-emotive therapy and cognitive behavior therapy.* New York, NY: Springer.

Ellis, A. (1993a). Fundamentals of rational-emotive therapy for the 1990s. In W. Dryden and I. Hill (Eds.), *Innovations in rational-emotive therapy* (pp. 1–32). Newbury Park, CA: Sage.

Ellis, A. (1993b). Reflections on rational-emotive therapy. *Journal of Counseling and Clinical Psychology, 62* (2), 199–201.

Ellis, A. (2004). *The road to tolerance: The philosophy of rational emotive behavior therapy.* Amherst, NY: Prometheus.

Epilepsy Canada. (2017). Accessed June 27, 2017, from http://www.epilepsy.ca

Erford, B.T. (2010). *Orientation to the counselling profession: Advocacy, ethics, and essential professional foundations.* Boston, MA: Pearson.

Erickson, C.K., & Wilcox, R.E. (2001). Neurobiological causes of addiction. *Journal of Social Work Practice in the Addictions, 1* (3), 7–22.

Fauman, M.A. (2002). *Study guide to DSM-IV–TR.* Washington, DC: American Psychiatric Publishing.

Firouzabadi, A., & Shareh, H. (2009). Effectiveness of detached mindfulness techniques in treating a case of obsessive compulsive disorder. *Advances in Cognitive Science, 11* (2), 1–7. Retrieved Nov. 1, 2015, from EBSCOhost.

Fleras, A. (2012). *Unequal relations: An introduction to race, ethnic, and aboriginal dynamics in Canada* (7th ed.). Don Mills: Pearson.

Fortune, A.E. (2002). Terminating with clients. In A.R. Roberts & G.J. Greene (Eds.), *Social workers' desk reference* (pp. 458–463). New York, NY: Oxford University Press.

France, M., McCormick, R, Rodriguez. (2013). The red road: Spirituality, the medicine wheel and the sacred hoop. In M. France, C. Rodriguez, G. Hett (Eds.), *Diversity, culture and counselling: A Canadian perspective*. Edmonton, Alberta: Brush Education Inc.

Frances, A. (2013a). *Saving normal: An insider's revolt against out-of- control psychiatric diagnosis, DSM-5, big pharma, and the medicalization of ordinary life*. New York: William Morrow.

Friends for Life. (2012). Website. Retrieved May 11, 2012, from www.friendsforlife.org.nz

Gabbard, G.O. (2006). A neuroscience perspective on transference. *International Congress Series*, 1286 (Beyond the Mind-Body Dualism: Psychoanalysis and the Human Body. Proceedings of the 6th Delphi International Psychoanalytic Symposium held in Delphi, Greece between 27 and 31 October 2004), 189–196. doi:10.1016/j.ics.2005.09.049

Gardner, W., Lidz, C., Mulvey, E., & Shaw. E. (1996). Clinical versus actuarial predictions of violence in patients with mental illness. *Journal of Consulting and Clinical Psychology, 64* (3), 602–610.

Garfat, T. (2008). On the fear of contact, the need for touch, and creating youth care contexts where touching is okay. *Journal of Child and Youth Care, 12* (3), iii–x.

Garrett, M.T., Garrett, J.T., & Brotherton, D. (2001). Inner circle/outer circle: A group technique based on Native American healing circles. *Journal for Specialists in Group Work, 26* (1), 17–30.

Gibb, B.J. (2007). *The rough guide to the brain*. New York, NY: Rough Guides.

Gilliland, B.E., & James, R.K. (1998). *Theories and strategies in counseling and psychotherapy* (4th ed.). Needham Heights, MA: Allyn & Bacon.

Gladding, S.T. (2011). *The counseling dictionary: Concise definitions of frequently used terms*. Upper Saddle River, NJ: Pearson.

Gladding, S.T., & Alderson, K.G. (2012). *Counselling: A comprehensive profession* (Cdn ed.). Toronto, ON: Pearson.

Gladding, S.T. & Newsome, D. (2010). *Clinical mental health counseling in community and agency settings* (3rd ed.). Boston, MA: Merrill.

Glicken, M.T. (2004). *Using the strengths perspective in social work practice: A positive approach for the helping professions*. New York, NY: Allyn & Bacon.

Godfrin, K.A., & van Heeringen, C.C. (2010). The effects of mindfulness-based cognitive therapy on recurrence of depressive episodes, mental health and quality of life: A randomized controlled study. *Behaviour Research and Therapy, 48* (8), 738–746. doi:10.1016

Golden, B.J., & Lesh, K. (1997). *Building self-esteem: Strategies for success in school and beyond* (2nd ed.). Scottsdale, AZ: Gorsuch Scarisbick.

Goleman, D. (2005). *Emotional intelligence: 10th anniversary edition*. New York, NY: Bantam Books.

Goodtherapy. (2017). *Temporal lobe*. Accessed October 1, 2017, from https://www.goodtherapy.org

Gorgoni, M., D'Atri, A., Lauri, G., Rossini, P. M., Ferlazzo, F., & De Gennaro, L. (2013). Is sleep essential for neural plasticity in humans, and how does It affect motor and cognitive recovery? *Neural Plasticity, 2013*, 103949. http://doi.org/10.1155/2013/103949

Government of Canada. (2017a). *About mental illness*. Retrieved December 1, 2017, from https://www.canada.ca/en/public-health/services/about-mental-illness.html

Government of Canada. (2017b). *National report: Apparent opioid-related deaths in Canada (January 2016 to March2017)*. Ottawa, Ont.: Author.

Government of Canada. (2017c). *National report: Apparent opioid-related deaths in Canada* (January 2016 to March 2017). Ottawa, Ont.: Author.

Gradin, V. B., & Pomi, A. (2008). The role of hippocampal atrophy in depression: A neurocomputational approach. *Journal of Biological Physics, 34*(1-2), 107–120. http://doi.org/10.1007/s10867-008-9099-7

Graff-Radford, J. (2017). Early onset Alzheimer's: When symptoms begin before age 65. Retrieved August 29, 2018, from http://www.mayoclinic.org

Granello, D.H., & Young, M.E. (2012). *Counseling today: Foundations of professional identity.* Boston, MA: Pearson.

Gravotta, L. (2013). *Be mine forever: Oxytocin may build long lasting love.* Retrieved June 19, 2015, from http://www.scientificamerican.com/article/be-mine-forever-oxytocin

Greenberg, M. (2011). *The neuroscience of relationship breakups: Is the pain all in the brain?* Retrieved July 13, 2015, from https://www.psychologytoday.com/blog/the-mindful-self-express/201104/the-neuroscience-relationship-breakups

Grohol, J. (2015). *15 Common defence mechanisms.* Retrieved July 10, 2015, from http://psychcentral.com/lib/15-common-defense-mechanisms/

Hackett, M. L., & Pickles, K. (2014). Part I: frequency of depression after stroke: an updated systematic review and meta-analysis of observational studies. *International Journal of Stroke,* 9(8), 1017–1025. doi:10.1111/ijs.12357

Hackney, H.L., & Cormier, L. S. (2005). *The professional counselor: A process guide to helping* (5th ed.). Needham Heights, MA: Pearson Education.

Hall, E.T. (1959). *The silent language.* Greenwich, CT: Fawcett Publications.

Hamachek, D.E. (1982). *Encounters with others: Interpersonal relationships and you.* New York, NY: Hold, Rinehart and Winston.

Hammond, W. (2015). *Principles of strength-based practice.* Retrieved May 3, 2015, from http://www.ayscbc.org/Principles%20of%20Strength-2.pdf

Han, S. (2015). Understanding cultural differences in human behavior: A cultural neuroscience approach. *Current Opinion in Behavioral Sciences,* 3 (1), 68–72.

Harms, L., & Pierce, J. (2011). *Working with people: Communication skills for reflective practice* (Cdn ed.). Toronto, ON: Oxford University Press.

Harris, G.T., & Rice, M.E. (1997). Risk appraisal and management of violent behavior. *Psychiatric Services,* 48 (9), 1168–1176.

Harvard Medical School. (1996). *Harvard Mental Health Letter,* 13 (6).

Harvard Medical School. (2012). *Understanding marijuana's risk to the brain.* Retrieved April 2, 2012, from www.health.harvard.edu/press_releases/understanding-marijuanas-risks-to-the-brain

Hays, D.G., & Erford, B.T. (2010). *Developing multicultural counseling competence: A systems approach.* Boston, MA: Pearson.

Health Canada. (2002a). *A report on mental illness in Canada.* Ottawa, ON: Health Editorial Board.

Health Canada. (2002b). *Literature review: Methadone maintenance treatment.* Retrieved May 15, 2012, from www.hc-sc.gc.ca/hc-ps/pubs/adp-apd/methadone/effectiveness-efficacite-eng.php#evi

Health Canada. (2007). *Substance use by Canadian youth: A national survey of Canadians' use of alcohol and other drugs.* Retrieved May 29, 2012, from www.hc-sc.gc.ca/hc-ps/pubs/adp-apd/cas_youth-etc_jeunes/index-eng.php

Healthline. (2018). *Withdrawing from Opiates and Opioids.* Retrieved January 8, 2018, from https://www.healthline.com/health/opiate-withdrawal

HealthLink BC. (2017). *Encephalitis.* Retrieved September 10, 2017, from https://www.healthlinkbc.ca/health-topics/hw145207

Heart and Stroke Foundation of Canada. (2017). Accessed September 3, 2017, from http://www.heartandstroke.ca.

Hebb, D.O. (1949). *The Organization of behavior: A Neuropsychological theory.* New York: Wiley and Sons.

Hefner, C.L. (2015). *Neurotransmitters.* Retrieved May 31, 2015, from http://allpsych.com/psychology101/neurotransmitters/#.VW3g5EaXd8E

Heinonen, T., & Spearman, L. (2010). *Social work practice: Problem solving and beyond* (3rd ed.). Toronto, ON: Nelson.

Herie, M., & Skinner, W. (2010). *Substance abuse in Canada.* Toronto, ON: Oxford.

Hick, S. (2010). *Social work in Canada: An introduction* (3rd ed.). Toronto, ON: Thompson.

Hill, C.E. (2004). *Helping skills: Facilitating exploration, insight, and action* (2nd ed.). Washington, DC: American Psychological Association.

Hill, R. & Dahlitz, M. (2014). What's hot in neuroscience for psychotherapy. Retrieved November 24, 2017, from http://www.neuropsychotherapist.com/whats-hot-in-neuroscience-for-psychotherapy/

Hill, C.E., Thompson, B., & Ladany, N. (2003). Therapist use of silence in therapy: A survey. *Journal of Clinical Psychology, 59* (4), 513–525.

Hirschfeld, R.M., & Russell, J.M. (1997). Assessment and treatment of suicidal patients. *New England Journal of Medicine, 337* (13), 910–916.

Hocker, J.L., & Wilmot, W.W. (1995). *Interpersonal conflict* (4th ed.). Dubuque, IA: Wm. C. Brown Communication.

Horowitz, S. (2012). *The science and art of listening.* Retrieved August 1, 2015, from http://www.nytimes.com/2012/11/11/opinion/sunday/why-listening-is-so-much-more-than-hearing.html?smid=pl-share&_r

Huntington Society of Canada (2017). Accessed September 30, 2017, from https://www.huntingtonsociety.ca

Hoyt, M.R. (2009). *Brief psychotherapies: Principles and practices.* Phoenix, AZ: Zeig, Tucker & Theisen.

Intercontinental Medical Statistics Inc. (2001). Retrieved March 31, 2001, from www.imshealth-canada.com/htmen/4_2_1_35.htm

International Center for Clubhouse Development. (2012). *International standards for clubhouse development.* Retrieved April 4, 2012, from www.iccd.org/quality.html

Isajiw, W.W. (1999). *Understanding diversity, ethnicity and race in the Canadian context.* Toronto, ON: Thompson Educational Publishing.

Ivey, A.E. (1995). Psychotherapy as liberation: Toward specific skills and strategies in multicultural counseling and therapy. In J.G. Ponterotto, J.M. Casas, L.A. Suzuki, & C.M. Alexander (Eds.), *Handbook of multicultural counseling* (pp. 53–72). Thousand Oaks, CA: Sage.

Ivey, A.E., Ivey, M., Zalaquett, C., & Quirk, K. (2009). *Counseling and neuroscience: The cutting edge of the coming decade.* Retrieved October 7, 2017 from https://ct.counseling.org

Ivey, A.E., Ivey, M., & Zalaquett, C. (2010). *Intentional interviewing & counseling: Facilitating client development in a multicultural society.* Belmont, CA: Brooks/Cole.

James, R.K., & Gilliland, B. (2013). *Crisis intervention Strategies,* 7th ed., Belmont, CA: Brooks/Cole.

Jantz, G. (2014). *Brain differences between genders.* Retrieved August 31, 2017, from https://www.psychologytoday.com

Jantz, G. (2015). *The role of the brain in love and relationship dependency.* Retrieved January 3, 2018, from https://www.psychologytoday.com/blog/hope-relationships/201510/the-role-the-brain-in-love-and-relationship-dependency

John Hopkins Medicine. (2017). *Cranial neuropathies.* Retrieved September 1, 2017, from http://www.hopkinsmedicine.org/healthlibrary/conditions/nervous_system_disorders/multiple_cranial_neuropathies_134,4

Johnson, L.C., McClelland, R.W., & Austin, C.D. (2000). *Social work practice: A generalist approach* (Cdn ed.). Scarborough, ON: Prentice Hall/Allyn & Bacon Canada.

Johnson, L.C., & Yanka, S.J. (2004). *Social work practice: A generalist approach* (8th ed.). Needham Heights, MA: Allyn & Bacon.

Jones, K. (2006). Quick and smart? Modularity and the pro-emotion consensus. In L. Faucher & C. Tappolet (Eds.), *The modularity of emotions.* Calgary, AB: University of Alberta Press.

Justice Education Society, n.d., Retrieved April 2, 2015, from http://www.justiceeducation.ca

Kadushin, A. (1990). *The social work interview: A guide for human service professionals* (3rd ed.). New York, NY: Columbia University Press.

Kadushin, A. (1997). *The social work interview: A guide for human service professionals* (4th ed.). New York, NY: Columbia University Press.

Kelleher, M.D. (1997). *Profiling the lethal employee: Case studies of violence in the workplace.* Westport, CT: Praeger.

Kelly, E.W. (1995). *Spirituality and religion in counseling and psychotherapy: Diversity in theory and practice.* Alexandria, VA: American Counseling Association.

Kendall, J. (2002). *How child abuse and neglect damage the brain.* Retrieved July 15, 2015, from http://www.snapnetwork.org/psych_effects/how_abuse_andneglect.htm

Kida T.E. (2006). *Don't believe everything you think: The 6 basic mistakes we make in thinking.* Amherst, NY: Prometheus Books.

Kivlighan, D. J., Gelso, C. J., Ain, S., Hummel, A. M., & Markin, R. D. (2015). The therapist, the client, and the real relationship: An actor–partner interdependence analysis of treatment outcome. *Journal of Counseling Psychology, 62* (2), 314–320. doi:10.1037/cou0000012

Knapp, M. & Hall, J. (2006). *Nonverbal communication in human interaction.* Toronto, ON: Thompson/Wadsworth.

Korb, A. (2014). *The problems with the love hormone:* How oxytocin is shaped by your parents and wrecks your relationships. Retrieved June 18, 2018, from https://www.psychologytoday.com/blog/prefrontal-nudity/201401/the-problems-the-love-hormone

Korb, A. (2015). *The problems with the love hormone:* How oxytocin is shaped by your parents and wrecks your relationships. Retrieved July 15, 2015, from https://www.psychologytoday.com/blog/prefrontal-nudity/201401/the-problems-the-love-hormone

Kumari, V., Fannon, D., Peters, E., Ffytche, D., Sumich, A., Premkumar, P., . . . & Kuipers, E. (2011). Neural changes following cognitive behaviour therapy for psychosis: a longitudinal study. *Brain: A Journal of Neurology, 134* (8), 2396–2407 12p. doi:brain/awr154

Labig, C.E. (1995). *Preventing violence in the workplace.* New York, NY: AMACOM.

Layton, J. (2015). *How fear works.* Retrieved June 11, 2015, from http://science.howstuffworks.com/life/inside-the-mind/emotions/fear2.htm

Lees, R., & Lingford-Hughes, A. (2012). Neurobiology and principles of addiction and tolerance. *Medicine, 40* (12), 633.

Leo, R.J., Jassal, K., & Bakhai, Y. (2005). Nonadherence with psychopharmacologic treatment among psychiatric patients. *Primary Psychiatry* (June), 33–39.

Li, A., Montaño, Z., Chen, V. J., & Gold, J. I. (2011). Virtual reality and pain management: current trends and future directions. *Pain Management, 1*(2), 147–157. http://doi.org/10.2217/pmt.10.15

Liou, S. (2010). *Neuroplasticity.* Accessed October 7, 2017, from https://web.stanford.edu/group/hopes/cgi-bin/hopes_test/neuroplasticity/

Lock, R.D. (1996). *Taking charge of your career direction* (3rd ed.). Pacific Grove, CA: Brooks/Cole.

Locke, S. (2014). *Four ethical dilemmas raised by the brain science of the future.* Retrieved May 2015, from http://www.vox.com/2014/5/14/5714724/four-ethical-problems-that-brain-science-will-raise-in-the-future

Macdonald, G., & Sirotich, F. (2001). Reporting client violence. *Social Work, 46,* 107–114.

Macdonald, G., & Sirotich, F. (2005). Violence in the social work workplace: The Canadian experience. *International Social Work, 48* (6), 772–781.

MacLaren, C., & Freeman, A. (2007). Cognitive behavior therapy model and techniques. In T. Ronen & A. Freeman (Eds.), *Cognitive behaviour therapy in clinical social work practice.* New York, NY: Springer.

Manza, P., Tomasi, D., Volkow, N. (2017). Subcortical local functional hyperconnectivity in cannabis dependence. *Biological psychiatry: Cognitive neuroscience and neuroimaging.* Published online November 21 2017. doi:10.1016/j.bpsc.2017.11.004

Martin, G., & Pear, J. (2011). *Behavior modification: What it is and how to do it* (9th ed.). Upper Saddle River, NJ: Pearson.

Maslow, A.H. (1954). *Motivation and personality.* New York, NY: Harper & Row.

Mate, G. (2008). *In the realm of hungry ghosts: Close encounters with addiction.* Toronto, ON: Knopf.

Maucieri, L. (2012). *Traumatic brain injury: What counselors need to know.* Retrieved September 30, 2017, from https://www.psychologytoday.com

Mayo Clinic. (2017a) Serotonin syndrome. Retrieved August 22, 2017, from http://www.mayoclinic.org/diseases-conditions/serotonin-syndrome/home/ovc-20305669

Mayo Clinic. (2017b). Traumatic brain injury. Retrieved September 12, 2017, from http://www.mayoclinic.org/diseases-conditions/traumatic-brain-injury/basics/complications/con-20029302

Mayor, S. (2004). Cognitive behaviour therapy affects brain activity differently from antidepressants. *British Medical Journal, 328* (7431), 69.

McClure, E. A., Campbell, A. N. C., Pavlicova, M., Hu, M., Winhusen, T., Vandrey, R. G., . . . , & Nunes, E. V. (2015). Cigarette smoking during substance use disorder treatment: Secondary outcomes from a National Drug Abuse Treatment Clinical Trials Network study. *Journal of Substance Abuse Treatment, 53*, 39–46. http://doi.org/10.1016/j.jsat.2014.12.007

McCook, A. (2011). *Head injuries linked to later violence.* Retrieved May 30, 2015, from http://www.reuters.com/article/2011/06/02/us-head-injuries-idUSTRE7 5101D20110602

McDonald, N. (1993). *Interviewing Aboriginal peoples: A guide to effective cross-cultural interviews* Winnipeg, MB: Cross-Cultural Communications International.

McHenry, B., Sikorski, A. M., & McHenry, J. (2014). *A counselor's introduction to neuroscience.* New York, NY: Routledge.

McLeod, S. (2008). *Defence mechanisms.* Retrieved July 2, 2015, from http://www.simplypsychology.org/defense-mechanisms.html

Medina, J. (2008). *Brain rules: 12 principles for surviving and thriving at work, home, and school.* Seattle, WA: Pear.

Mental Health Commission of Canada. (2012). *Changing directions, changing lives: The mental health strategy for Canada.* Calgary, AB: Author.

Mental Health Daily. (2017). *Brain imaging techniques.* Retrieved October 6, 2017, from http://mentalhealthdaily.com/2015/08/05/brain-imaging-techniques-neuroimaging/

Meuser, K., Noordsy, D., Drake, R., & Fox, L. (2003). *Integrated treatment for dual disorders: A guide to effective practice.* New York, NY: Guilford Press.

Miley, K.K., O'Melia, M., & DuBois, B. (2004). *Generalist social work practice: An empowering approach.* Boston, MA: Allyn & Bacon.

Miller, M.C. (2000). A model for the assessment of violence. *Harvard Review of Psychiatry, 7,* 299–304.

Miller, P. (2007). *Ethical decision making in social work and counselling.* Toronto, ON: Thomson/Nelson.

Miller, W.R., Forcehimes, A., & Zweben. (2011). *Treating addiction: A guide for professionals.* New York, NY: Guilford.

Miller, W.R., & Rollnick, S. (2002). *Motivational interviewing: Preparing people for change* (2nd ed.). New York, NY: The Guilford Press.

Miller, W.R., & Rollnick, S. (2013). *Motivational interviewing: Preparing people for change* (3rd ed.). New York, NY: The Guilford Press.

Moberget, T., Doan, N., Alnæs, D., Kaufmann, T., Córdova-Palomera, A., Lagerberg, T., Diedrichsen, J., Schwarz, E., Zink, M., Eisenacher, S., Kirsch, P., Jönsson, E, Fatouros-Bergman, H., Flyckt, L., Pergola, G., Quarto, T, Bertolino, A., Barch, D., Meyer-Lindenberg, A., Agartz, I., Andreassen, O., Westlye, L. (2017). Cerebellar volume and cerebellocerebral structural covariance in schizophrenia: a multisite mega-analysis of 983 patients and 1349 healthy controls. *Molecular Psychiatry,* 2017; DOI: 10.1038/mp.2017.106

Möhler, H., & Ressler, K. (2013). Differential roles of GABA receptors in anxiety. In D. S. Charney, J. D. Buxbaum, P. Sklar, E. J. Nesler, (Eds.), *Neurobiology of mental illness* (4th ed.) (pp. 567–579). New York, NY, US: Oxford University.

Moore, P. (2001). Critical components of an anti-oppressive framework. *Journal of Child and Youth Care.* 14 (3) pp. 25–32.

Morrisseau, C. (1998). *Into the daylight: A wholistic approach to healing.* Toronto, ON: University of Toronto Press.

Morrissey, M. (1998). Safety issues for counselors who work with violent clients. *Counseling Today* (February), 6.

Mount Sinai Medical Center. (2012). *Area of the brain that processes empathy identified. Science-Daily.* Retrieved October 31, 2015, from www.sciencedaily.com/releases/2012/10/121024175240.htm

Murdock, N.L. (2009). *Theories of counseling and psychotherapy: A case approach* (2nd ed.). Upper Saddle River, NJ: Pearson.

Multiple Sclerosis Society of Canada. (2017). Accessed September 1, 2017 from https://mssociety.ca.

Myers, J. E., & Young, J. S. (2012). Brain wave biofeedback: benefits of integrating neurofeedback in counseling. *Journal of Counseling & Development, 90*(1), 20–28.

Naqvi N., Shiv B., & Bechara, A. (2006). The role of emotion in decision making: A cognitive neuroscience perspective. *Current Directions in Psychological Science, 15* (5), 260–264.

National Alliance on Mental Health. (2012). *Assertive community treatment.* Retrieved May 25, 2012, from www.nami.org/Template.cfm?Section=About_Treatments_and_Supports&template=/ContentManagement/ContentDisplay.cfm&ContentID=8075

National Association of Social Workers. (1996). *Revised code of ethics.* Washington, DC: NASW Press.

National Child Traumatic Stress Network (2015). *Effects of complex trauma.* Retrieved July 15, 2015, from http://www.nctsn.org/trauma-types/complex-trauma/effects-of-complex-trauma

National Crisis Prevention Institute. (2012). Website. www.crisisprevention.com

National Eating Disorder Information Centre. (2005). *Questions and answers.* Retrieved June 21, 2005, from www.nedic.ca/qa.html#3

National Institute of Drug Abuse. (2012). *Prescription drugs: Abuse and addiction.* Retrieved April 10, 2012, from www.drugabuse.gov/publications/research-reports/prescription-drugs/what-are-some-commonly-abused-prescription-drugs

National Institute of Health. (2012). *Hallucinogens and dissociative drugs.* Retrieved April 5, 2012, from www.drugabuse.gov/publications/research-reports/hallucinogens-dissociative-drugs

National Institute of Mental Health (NIMH). (2012). Website. Retrieved April 1, 2012, from www.nimh.nih.gov/index.shtml

National Institute of Mental Health. (2015). *Brain basics.* Retrieved August 5, 2015, from http://www.nimh.nih.gov/health/educational-resources/brain-basics/brain-basics.shtml

Neenan, M., & Dryden, W. (2006). *Cognitive therapy in a nutshell.* Thousand Oaks, CA: Sage.

Nesbitt, Nancy A. (2017). *Tarasoff v. Regents of the University of California*: Psychotherapist's obligation of confidentiality versus the duty to warn. *Tulsa L. J., 12,* 747.

Newhill, C.E. (1992). Assessing danger to others in clinical social work practice. *Social Service Review* (March), 65–79.

Newhill, C.E. (1995). Client violence toward social workers: A practice and policy concern for the 1990s. *Social Work, 40* (5), 631–639.

Newhill, C.E. (2003). *Client violence in social work practice: Prevention, intervention, and research.* New York, NY: Guilford.

Niles, S.G., Amundson, N., & Neault, R. (2011). *Career flow: A hope centered approach to career development.* Boston, MA: Pearson.

Noesner, G.W., & Webster, M. (1997). Crisis intervention: Using active listening skills in negotiations. *FBI Law Enforcement Bulletin, 66* (8), 13–20.

Nordqvist, J. (2017). *What is biofeedback therapy and who can benefit.* Accessed June 21, 2017, from http://www.medicalnewstoday.com/articles/265802.php

Nystul, M.S. (2011). *Introduction to counseling: An art and science approach* (4th ed). Boston, MA: Pearson.

Oakville Distress Centre. (2012). *Suicide myths and facts.* Retrieved May 15, 2012, from www.distresscentreoakville.com/suicide-myths-facts.php

Ontario Network of Women in Engineering (ONWiE). (2017). *Percentage of female undergraduates in engineering.* Retrieved September 20, 2017, from http://www.onwie.ca/resources

Parada, H., Barnoff, L., Morratt, K., & Homan, M. (2011). *Promoting community change: Making it happen in the real world* (1st Cdn ed.). Toronto, ON: Nelson.

Parkinson Canada. (2017). Accessed September 10, 2017, from http://www.parkinson.ca/

Pastor, L.H. (1995). Initial assessment and intervention strategies to reduce workplace violence. *American Family Physician, 52* (4), 1169–1175.

Patterson, C.H. (1996). Multicultural counseling: From diversity to universality. *Journal of Counseling and Development, 74* (3), 227–231.

Peckham, H. (2017). Neuroplasticity: A new paradigm for understanding and treating mental health issues. Retrieved September 25, 2017, from http://www.neuropsychotherapist.com neuroplasticity-a-new-paradigm-for-understanding-and-treating-mental-health-issues/.

Pedersen, P.B. (1994). *A handbook for developing multicultural awareness* (2nd ed.). Alexandria, VA: American Counseling Association.

Pedersen, P.B. (2001). Multiculturalism and the paradigm shift in counselling: Controversies and alternative futures. *Canadian Journal of Counselling, 35* (1), 15–25.

Pedersen, P.B., Draguns, J., Lonner, W., & Trimble, J. (Eds.). (2008). *Counseling across cultures* (6th ed.). Los Angeles, CA: Sage.

Pedersen, P.B., & Locke, D.C. (Eds.). (1996). *Cultural and diversity issues in counseling.* Greensboro, NC: ERIC Counseling and Student Services Clearinghouse.

Phillips, J. R., Hewedi, D. H., Eissa, A. M., & Moustafa, A. A. (2015). The cerebellum and psychiatric disorders. *Frontiers in Public Health, 3*, 66. http://doi.org/10.3389/fpubh.2015.00066

Pierce, J., & Schmidt, G., (2012). Rural and remote education: Practice dynamics in smaller communities. In J. Drolet, N. Clark, & H. Allen (Eds.), *Shifting sites of practice: Field education in Canada.* Toronto, ON: Pearson.

Poonwassie, A., & Charter, A. (2001). An Aboriginal worldview of helping: Empowering approaches. *Canadian Journal of Counselling, 35* (1), 63–73.

Presbury, J.H., Echterling, L.G., & McKee, J. (2008). *Beyond brief counseling and therapy: An integrative approach* (2nd ed.). Upper Saddle River, NJ: Pearson.

Prochaska, J.O., & Norcross, J. (2001). Stages of change. *Psychotherapy: Theory, Research, Practice, Training 38* (4), 443–448.

Ptak, C., & Petronis, A. (2010). Epigenetic approaches to psychiatric disorders. *Dialogues in Clinical Neuroscience, 12*(1), 25–35.

Public Health Agency of Canada. (2002). *A report on mental illness in Canada, 2002.* Retrieved June 25, 2005, from www.phac-aspc.gc.ca/publicat/miic-mmac/index.html

Quinsey, V.L., Harris, G.T., Rice, M. E., & Cormier. C. (1998). *Violent offenders: Appraising and managing risk.* Washington, DC: American Psychological Association.

Radhakrishnan, R., Wilkinson, S. T., & D'Souza, D. C. (2014). Gone to pot – A review of the association between cannabis and [Psychosis. *Frontiers in Psychiatry, 5*(54). http://doi.org/10.3389/fpsyt.2014.00054

Ralph, I. (2003). *Psychotropic agents* (13th ed.). Grand Forks, BC: IGR Publications.

Razzaghi, E.M. (2005). *Effectiveness of methadone maintenance program in reducing illicit drug use and HIV related high-risk behavior: A multi-center study.* Retrieved May 3, 2012, from www.unodc.org/pdf/iran/publications/MMT%20Pilot%20report%20for%20UNODC%20final%20%28March%202005%29.pdf

Reamer, F.G. (1998). *Ethical standards in social work: A critical review of the NASW code of ethics.* Washington, DC: NASW Press.

Reamer, F.G. (2002). Ethical issues in social work. In A. Roberts & G. Greene (Eds.), *Social workers' desk reference.* New York, NY: Oxford University Press.

Regehr, C., & Glancy, G. (2010). *Mental health social work practice in Canada.* Toronto, ON: Oxford.

Reiter, M. (2008). *Therapeutic interviewing: Essential skills and contexts of counseling.* New York, NY: Pearson.

Riddle, T. (2013). *How your moral decisions are shaped by a bad mood: Weighty choices can be shifted by surprising factors.* Retrieved May 19, 2015, from http://www.scientificamerican.com/article/how-your-moral-decisions-shaped-by-mood/

Rogers, C.R. (1951). *Client-centered therapy: Its current practice, implications, and theory.* Boston, MA: Houghton Mifflin.

Rogers, C.R. (1961). *On becoming a person.* Boston, MA: Houghton Mifflin.

Rogers, C.R. (1980). *A way of being.* Boston, MA: Houghton Mifflin.

Rogers, C.R. (1987). *A way of being.* Boston, MA: Houghton Mifflin.

Ross, J.I. (Ed.). (1995). *Violence in Canada: Sociopolitical perspectives.* Toronto, ON: Oxford.

Roth, L.H. (1987). *Clinical treatment of the violent person.* New York, NY: Guilford Press.

Roth, E. (2017). 7 tips for reducing sundowning. Retrieved September 10, 2017, from http://www.webmd.com/alzheimers/guide/manage-sundowning#1

Rothman, J.C. (2008). *Cultural competence in process and practice: Building bridges.* Boston, MA: Pearson.

Royce, T. (2005). The negotiator and the bomber: Analyzing the critical role of active listening in crisis negotiations. *Negotiation Journal, 21* (1), 5–27.

Ruskin, R., & Beiser, M. (1998). Cultural issues in psychotherapy. In P. Cameron, J. Ennis, & J. Deadman (Eds.), *Standards and guidelines for the psychotherapies* (pp. 422–445). Toronto, ON: University of Toronto Press.

Ryan, S. (2016). Violence and harassment in health and social services. Retrieved January 15, 2018, from https://cupe.ca/violence-and-harassment-health-and-social-services

Saddock, B.J., & Saddock, V. (2004). *Concise textbook of clinical psychiatry*. Philadelphia, PA: Lippincott Williams & Wilkins.

Saleeby, D. (2009). *The strengths perspective in social work practice* (5th ed.). New York, NY: Allyn & Bacon.

San Francisco Suicide Prevention Institute. (2009). *Suicide facts and statistics*. Retrieved March 23, 2009, from www.sfsuicide.org/html/facts.html

Sapolsky, R. M. (2001). Depression, antidepressants, and the shrinking hippocampus. *Proceedings of the National Academy of Sciences of the United States of America, 98*(22), 12320–12322. http://doi.org/10.1073/pnas.231475998

Schizophrenia Society of Canada. (2009). Retrieved July 29, 2009, from www.schizophrenia.ca/home.htm

Science Daily. (2001). *Brain imaging study sheds light on moral decision-making*. Retrieved May 19, 2015, from http://www.sciencedaily.com/releases/2001/09/010914074303.htm

Scientific American. (2017). *Can you make sociopath through brain injury or other types of trauma?* Retrieved October 13, 2017, from www.scientificamerican.com/article/can-you-make-sociopath-through-brain-injury-trauma

Scoffield, H. (2008). *UN criticizes Canada on child rights*. Retrieved April 2, 2015, from http://www.huffingtonpost.ca/2012/09/26/un-canada-child-rights_n_1916876.htm

Sealy, P., & Whitehead, P. (2004). Forty years of deinstitutionalization of psychiatric services in Canada: An empirical assessment. *Canadian Journal of Psychiatry, 49*, 249–257.

Sears, S.J., & Gordon, V. (2011). *Building your career: A guide to your future* (4th ed.). Boston, MA: Pearson.

Sederer, L. (2012). *The DSM-5: Will it work in clinical practice?* Retrieved May 10, 2012, from www.huffingtonpost.com/lloyd-i-sederer-md/dsm-5_b_1256123.html

Seligman, L. & Reichenberg, L.W. (2010). *Theories of counseling and psychotherapy: Systems, strategies, and skills* (3rd ed.). Toronto, ON: Pearson.

Seligman, M.E. (1975). *Helplessness: On depression, development and death*. San Francisco, CA: W.H. Freeman.

Shahmirzadi, A. (1983). Counseling Iranians. *Personnel and Guidance Journal*, 487–489.

Shapiro, F (2001). Eye movement desensitization and reprocessing: Basic principles, protocols and procedures (2nd ed.). New York: Guilford Press.

Shapiro, F. and Solomon, R. M. (2010). Eye movement desensitization and reprocessing. *Corsini Encyclopedia of Psychology*. 1–3.

Shea, S.C. (1998). *Psychiatric interviewing: The art of understanding* (2nd ed.). Philadelphia, PA: W.B. Sanders.

Sheafor, B.W., & Horejsi, C.R. (2008). *Techniques and guidelines for social work practice* (7th ed.). Boston, MA: Allyn & Bacon.

Shebib, B. (1997). *Counselling skills*. Victoria, BC: Province of British Columbia, Ministry of Education, Skills and Training.

Sherrard, M. (2015). *Parts of the brain involved in flight or fight*. Retrieved June 20, 2015, from http://www.ehow.com/list_6907783_parts-brain-involved-fight-flight.html

Shulman, L. (2009). *The skills of helping individuals, families, groups, and communities* (6th ed.). Belmont, CA: Brooks/Cole.

Shulz, W.E. (2000). *Counselling ethics casebook 2000*. Ottawa, ON: Canadian Counselling and Psychotherapy Association.

Siegel, R.D. (2010). *The mindfulness solution: Everyday practices for everyday problems*. New York, NY: Guilford Press.

Siegel, D.J. (2012). *The developing mind: How relationships and the brain interact to shape who we are* (2nd ed.). New York, NY: Guilford Press.

Silva, F., & Lopez de Silva, M. (1976). Hallucinations and behavior modification. *Analisis y Modificacion de Conducta, 2* (2).

Simmie, S., & Nunes, J. (2001). *The last taboo: A survival guide to mental health care in Canada.* Toronto, ON: McClelland & Stewart.

Simon-Dack, S.L. & Marmarosh, C.L. (2014). Neurosciences and adult health behaviors: Recent findings and implications for counseling psychology. *Journal of Counseling Psychology, 61,* 4, 528–533.

Singh-Manoux, A., Dugravot, A., Fournier, A., Abell, J., Ebmeier, K., Kivimäki, M., & Sabia, S. (2017). trajectories of depressive symptoms before diagnosis of dementia: A 28-Year Follow-up Study. *JAMA Psychiatry, 74*(7), 712–718. doi:10.1001/jamapsychiatry.2017.0660

Sitek, K. (2016) Can computers use brain scans to diagnose psychiatric disorders? Retrieved July 1, 2017, from http://sitn.hms.harvard.edu/flash/2016/can-computers-use-brain-scans-to-diagnose-psychiatric-disorders

Smith, D.B., & Morrissette, P.J. (2001). The experiences of white male counsellors who work with First Nations clients. *Canadian Journal of Counselling, 35* (1), 74–88.

Smith, Kerri. (2013). Brain decoding: Reading minds. *Nature: International Weekly Journal of Science.* http://www.nature.com/news/brain-decoding-reading-minds-1.13989

Society for Neuroscience. (2007). Brain chemicals involved in aggression identified: May lead to new treatments. *ScienceDaily.* Retrieved June 5, 2015, from www.sciencedaily.com/releases

Soper, B., & Von Bergen, C.W. (2001). Employment counseling and life stressors: Coping through expressive writing. *Journal of Employment Counseling, 38* (3), 150–160.

Speight, S.L., Myers, L.J., Cox, C.I., & Highlen, P.S. (1991). A redefinition of multicultural counseling. *Journal of Counseling and Development, 70* (1), 29–36.

Sperry. L. (2006). *Cognitive behavior therapy of DSM-IV-TR personality disorders* (2nd ed.). New York, NY: Taylor & Francis Group.

Sperry, L., Carlson, J., & Kjos, D. (2003). *Becoming an effective therapist.* Boston, MA: Allyn & Bacon.

Stanford (2017). How 'Love Hormone' Oxytocin Spurs Sociability. *NeuroscienceNews.* August 23, 2018, from http://neurosciencenews.com/oxytocin-sociability-7623/

Starr, M. (2017). *When your brain is overloaded, you listen better with your right ear.* Retrieved January 12, 2018, from https://www.sciencealert.com/when-your-brain-is-overloaded-you-listen-better-with-your-right-ear

Statistics Canada. (2005). *Overview: Canada still predominantly Roman Catholic and Protestant.* Retrieved February 28, 2005, from www12.statcan.ca/english/census01/Products/Analytic/companion/rel/canada.cfm#noreligion

Statistics Canada. (2011). *2011 National household survey.* Retrieved July 16, 2015, from http://www12.statcan.gc.ca (search for 2011 National Household Survey)

Statistics Canada. (2012a). *Suicides, and suicide rate, by sex and by age group.* Retrieved May 15, 2012, from www.statcan.gc.ca

Statistics Canada. (2012b). *Projections of the diversity of the Canadian population.* Retrieved June 14, 2012, from www.statcan.gc.ca/daily-quotidien/100309/dq100309a-eng.htm

Statistics Canada. (2015). *Aboriginal peoples in Canada: First Nations people, Métis and Inuit.* Retrieved July 17, 2015, from http://www12.statcan.gc.ca/nhs-enm/2011/as-sa/99-011-x/99-011-x2011001-eng.

Statistics Canada. (2017). *Seniors.* Retrieved November 5, 2017, from http://www.statcan.gc.ca/pub/11-402-x/2010000/chap/seniors-aines/seniors-aines-eng.htm

Statistics Canada. (2018). *Immigration and ethnocultural diversity in Canada.* Retrieved January 22, 2018 from http://www12.statcan.gc.ca/nhs-enm/2011/as-sa/99-010-x/99-010-x2011001-eng.cfm Statistics Canada. (2018). Retrieved March 2, 2018, from https://www.statcan.gc.ca/eng/start

Steinberg, L. (2008). A Social Neuroscience Perspective on Adolescent Risk-Taking. *Developmental Review: DR, 28*(1), 78–106. http://doi.org/10.1016/j.dr.2007.08.002

Stevens, F. L., Hurley, R. A., & Taber, K. H. (2011). Anterior cingulate cortex: unique role in cognition and emotion. *The Journal of Neuropsychiatry and Clinical Neurosciences, 23*(2), 121-125. doi: 10.1176/appi.neuropsych.23.2.121

Substance Abuse and Mental Health Services Administration. (2008). *Substance abuse treatment for persons with co-occurring disorders: Treatment improvement protocol tip 42.* Rockville, MD: Division of Service Improvement.

Substance Abuse and Mental Health Services Administration. (2014). *SAMHSA's concept of trauma and guidance for a trauma-informed approach.* HHS Publication No. (SMA) 14-4884. Rockville, MD: Substance Abuse and Mental Health Services Administration.

Sudman, S., & Bradburn, N.M. (1983). *Asking questions: A practical guide to questionnaire design.* San Francisco, CA: Jossey-Bass.

Sue, D.W., & Sue, D. (1999). *Counseling the culturally diverse: Theory and practice* (3rd ed.). New York, NY: John Wiley and Sons.

Sue, D.W., & Sue, D. (2003). *Counseling the culturally diverse: Theory and practice* (4th ed.). New York, NY: John Wiley and Sons.

Sue, D.W., & Sue, D. (2008). *Counseling the culturally diverse: Theory and practice* (5th ed.). New York, NY: John Wiley and Sons.

Swanson, J., Estroff, S., Swartz, M., Borum, R., Lachicotte, W., Zimmer, C., & Wagner, R. (1997). Violence and severe mental disorder in clinical and community populations: The effects of psychotic symptoms, comorbidity, and lack of treatment. *Psychiatry: Interpersonal and Biological Processes, 60* (1), 1–22.

Tarasoff v. Regents of the University of California [1976] Retrieved July 25, 2018, from https://scocal.stanford.edu/opinion/tarasoff-v-regents-university-california-30278

Tardiff, K., Marzuk, P., Leon, A., Portera, L., & Weiner, C. (1997). Violence by patients admitted to a private psychiatric hospital. *American Journal of Psychiatry, 154* (1), 88–94.

Tartakovsky, M.S. (2015). *Is thyroid dysfunction driving your depression?* Retrieved June 2, 2015, from http://psychcentral.com/blog/archives/2012/04/26/is-thyroid-dysfunction-driving-your-depression

Taylor, J., (2011). *Technology: myth of multitasking. Is multitasking really more efficient.* Retrieved June 30, 2015, from https://www.psychologytoday.com/blog/the-power-prime/201103/technology-myth-multitasking

The Cleveland Clinic. (2017). Stroke and the brain. Accessed September 5, 2017, from https://my.clevelandclinic.org/health/articles/stroke-and-the-brain

The Franklin Institute. (2015). *The human brain.* Retrieved August 13, 2015, from http://learn.fi.edu/learn/brain/stress.html

The Internet Stroke Center. (2017) *Stroke statistics.* Retrieved September 12, 2017, from http://www.strokecenter.org/patients/about-stroke/stroke-statistics/

Thoreson, R.W., Shaughnessy, P., Heppner, P.P., & Cook, S.W. (1993). Sexual contact during and after the professional relationship: Attitudes and practices of male counselors. *Journal of Counseling and Development, 71* (4), 429–434.

Tourette Canada. (2017). Deep brain stimulation, Part One: How does it work? Retrieved November 13, 2017, from https://tourette.ca/deep-brain-stimulation-part-one-how-does-it-work.

Trouche, S., Sasaki, J.M., Tu, T., & Reijmers, L.G. (2013). Fear extinction causes target-specific remodeling of perisomatic inhibitory synapses. *Neuron, 80*(4) 1054–1065.

Trouche, S., Sasaki, J. M., Tu, T., & Reijmers, L. G. (2013). Fear extinction causes target-specific remodeling of perisomatic inhibitory synapses. *Neuron, 80*(4), 10.1016/j.neuron.2013.07.047. http://doi.org/10.1016/j.neuron.2013.07.047

Trudeau, J., (2017). Statement by the Prime Minister on Multiculturalism Day. Retrieved April 6, 2018, from https://pm.gc.ca/eng/news/2017/06/27/statement-prime-minister-canadian-multiculturalism-day

Truth and Reconciliation Commission of Canada. (2015). *Calls to action.* Retrieved July 1, from https://waynekspear.files.wordpress.com/2015/06/calls_to_action_english2.pdf

Turner, J.C., & Turner, F.J. (Eds.). (2001). *Canadian social welfare* (4th ed.). Toronto, ON: Pearson Education Canada.

University of California, Irvine. (2005, January 22). Intelligence in Men and Women Is a Gray and White Matter. *ScienceDaily.* Retrieved September 21, 2017, from www.sciencedaily.com/releases/2005/01/050121100142.htm

University of Maryland. (2015). Stress. Retrieved August 13, 2015, from http://umm.edu/health/medical/reports/articles/stress

University of Utah Health 2013. *Researchers debunk myth of 'right-brained' and 'left-brained' personality traits.* Retrieved 14 August 2013, from www.sciencedaily.com/releases/2013/08/130814190513.htm

University of Washington, School of Social Work. (2015). *Facts about mental illness and violence.* Retrieved July 1, 2015, from http://depts.washington.edu/mhreport/facts_violence.php

Van Hasselt, V., Baker, M.T., Romano, S.J., Schlessinger, K.M., Zucker, M., Dragone, R., & Perera, A.L. (2006). Crisis (hostage) negotiation training: A preliminary evaluation of program efficacy. *Criminal Justice and Behavior, 33* (1), 56–69.

Velligan, D.I., & Alphs, L. (2008). *Negative symptoms in schizophrenia: The importance of identification and treatment.* Retrieved June 12, 2015, from http://www.psychiatrictimes.com/schizophrenia/negative-symptoms-schizophrenia-importance-identification-and-treatment

Vonk, E., & Early, T. (2009). Cognitive-behavioral therapy. In A. Roberts (Ed.), *Social workers' desk reference* (2nd ed.). New York, NY: Oxford University Press.

Vujanovic, A.A., Niles, B., Pietrefesa, A., Schmertz, S.K., & Potter, C.M. (2011). Mindfulness in the treatment of posttraumatic stress disorder among military veterans. *Professional Psychology: Research and Practice, 42* (1), 24–31. doi:10.1037

Walsh, J., & Bentley, K. (2002). Psychopharmacology basics. In A. Roberts & G. Greene (Eds.), *Social workers' desk reference.* New York, NY: Oxford University Press.

WebMD. (2017). How to manage sundowning. Retrieved September 30, 2017, from http://www.webmd.com/alzheimers/guide/manage-sundowning#1

WebMD. (2015). *Vitamins and supplements.* Retrieved August 2, 2015, from http://www.webmd.com/vitamins-and-supplements/gaba-uses-and-risks

Wehr, T. (2010). The phenomenology of exception times: Qualitative differences between problem-focused and solution-focused interventions. *Applied Cognitive Psychology, 24* (4), 467–480. Retrieved from EBSCOhost.

Weill Cornell Medicine. "Neuroimaging categorizes four depression subtypes." *ScienceDaily. ScienceDaily*, December 8, 2016. <www.sciencedaily.com/releases/2016/12/161208143451.htm>

Westwood, M.J., & Ishiyama, F.I. (1991). Challenges in counseling immigrant clients: Understanding intercultural barriers to career adjustment. *Journal of Employment Counseling, 28* (4), 130–143.

Wicks, R.J., & Parsons, R.D. (1984). *Counseling strategies and intervention techniques for the human services.* New York, NY: Longman.

Wills, F. (2008). *Skills in cognitive behaviour counselling and psychotherapy.* Los Angeles, CA: Sage.

Winters, K.C., & Arria, A. (2011). Adolescent brain development and drugs. *The Prevention Researcher, 18* (2), 21–24.

Wlassoff, V. (2017). How does post-traumatic stress disorder change the brain. Retrieved July 31, 2017, from http://brainblogger.com/2015/01/24/how-does-post-traumatic-stress-disorder-change-the-brain/

Young, M.E. (1998). *Learning the art of helping.* Upper Saddle River, NJ: Merrill.

Tables, Figures, Conversations, Interviews, and Brain Bytes Index

Index of Interviews

Index of Tables

Author Index

A

Adler, R., 110
Albert, P. R., 374
Alexander, C. M., 324
Alink, L. A., 249
Alzheimer's Society of Canada. (2017), 376, 377, 378, 379
Alzheimers.net., 377
American Addictions Centers, 297
American Association of Suicidology, 302, 303, 304
American Medical Association, 282, 283
American Psychiatric Association, 39, 64, 168, 276, 282, 284, 285, 286
American Psychological Association, 268
Amyotrophic Lateral Sclerosis Society of Canada, 376
Andrews, P. W., 372
Angus, L., 172
Arboleda-Florez, J., 253
Arden, J. B., 347, 349, 371
Arthur, N., 311, 321, 334
Ashwell, K., 196, 299
Azar, B., 321, 323
Azrin, N. H., 293

B

Backhouse, C., 318
Baron-Cohen, S., 169, 363
Barth, A., 97
Battino, R., 228
Beck, A.T., 210
Beck, J. S., 207, 213
Beckman, C. S., 18
Belsham, B., 282
Berg, F. M., 286
Beyerstein, B. L., 279
Bier, D., 361
Bolles, R. N. 291, 292
Bombay, A., 375
Borgen, W. A., 291
Bovend'Eerdt, T. H., 220
Bowen, S. 214, 215
Bower, B., 254
Boyle, S., 14
Brain Injury Canada, 382
BrainFacts.org., 375
Brammer, L. M., 25
Bremner, J., 364
Brill, N. I., 36, 47, 72, 89, 90
Brisch, R., 371
British Columbia Mental Health and Substance Use Planning Council, 38
British Columbia Ministry of Children and Family Development, 290
British Columbia Ministry of Health, 292

British Columbia Schizophrenia Society, 273, 279
Budde, H., 354
Butler, A. C., 207

C

Cameron C. L., 228
Canadian Association of Social Workers, 1, 3, 4, 5, 7, 9, 13, 18
Canadian Association for Suicide Prevention, 305
Canadian Centre for Elder Law, 145
Canadian Centre on Substance Abuse, 289, 295
Canadian Children's Rights Council, 305
Canadian Counselling and Psychotherapy Association, 1, 4, 5, 7, 9, 10, 13, 18, 34, 88, 316, 332
Canadian Institute for Health Information, 249
Canadian Mental Health Association, 254
Canadian Psychological Association, 377
Canadian Women's Foundation, 267
Capuzzi, D., 20, 67, 167, 199, 299, 328
Carniol, B., 194
Carpetto, G., 38, 228, 229
Cattan, M., 293
Centre for Addiction and Mental Health, 273, 300, 302, 348
Centre for Suicide Prevention, 302, 303
Cerebral Palsy Association of British Columbia, 376
Chambless, D. L., 207
Choney, S. K., 335
Clark, A. J., 169, 170, 184, 279, 283
Cleghorn, J.M., 304
Compton, B., 47, 60
Corcoran, J., 66, 272, 273, 276
Cormier, S., 147, 166, 236
Cozolino, L., 66, 87, 112
Cunningham, M., 336, 337

D

D'Andrea, M. J., 328
Dahlitz, M., 347, 362
Dale, O., 3
Dattilio, F. M.
Davis, L. E., 272, 273, 280, 286, 289, 290, 293
Davis, S., 168, 318
de Becker, G., 253, 259
de Lange, F., 217
de Léséleuc, 249
de Shazer, S., 228
DiClemente, C., 205, 206
Diller, J.V., 321, 322, 323, 325, 327
Dodd, C. H.
Drolet, J., 194
Dubovsky, S. L., 261

Mental Health Commission of Canada, 272
Mental Health Daily, 353
Meuser, K., 302
Miley, K. K., 67, 319
Miller, M. C., 251, 252, 253, 254
Miller, P., 6, 47, 236, 238, 247, 347
Miller, W.R., 106, 167, 170, 171, 199, 200, 201, 202
Moberget, T., 355
Möhler, H., 282
Moore, P., 194
Morrisseau, C., 323
Morrissey, M., 262
Multiple Sclerosis Society of Canada, 376
Murdock, N. L., 162
Myers, J. E., 353

N

Naqvi, N., 210
National Alliance on Mental Health, 301
National Association of Social Workers, 326
National Child Traumatic Stress Network, 39
National Crisis Prevention Institute, 257
National Eating Disorder Information Centre, 286
National Institute of Drug Abuse, 296
National Institute of Health, 296
National Institute of Mental Health (NIMH), 273, 277, 279, 282, 285, 286, 287, 293, 370, 371
Neenan, M., 214, 227
Nesbitt, N., 7
Newhill, C.E., 249, 252, 253
Niles, S.G., 293
Noesner, G., 103
Nordqvist, J., 353
Nystul, M.S., 66, 219

O

Oakville Distress Centre, 305
Ontario Network of Women in
    Engineering (ONWiE), 363

P

Parada, H., 256
Parkinson Canada, 377
Pastor, L. H., 254
Patterson, C. H., 329
Peckham, H., 350, 353
Pedersen, P.B., 312, 321, 322, 330, 332, 340
Phillips, J. R., 357
Pierce, J., 6
Poonwassie, A., 318, 334, 335
Presbury, J. H., 38, 163, 198, 228
Prochaska, J. O., 199, 204, 237
Ptak, C., 374
Public Health Agency of Canada, 273

Q

Quinsey, V. L., 259

R

Radhakrishnan, R., 374
Ralph, I., 278, 280
Razzaghi, E., 300
Reamer, F. G., 6
Regehr, C., 273, 279
Reiter, M., 169
Riddle, T., 11
Rogers, C. R., 43, 44, 66, 67, 69, 70, 72, 87, 169, 170, 171, 200
Ross, J. I., 251, 320, 325
Roth, L., 252
Roth, E., 378
Rothman, J.C., 319
Royce, T., 102
Ruskin, R., 318, 322, 326, 328
Ryan, S., 249

S

Saddock, B., 274, 279, 303, 304
Saleeby, D., 46, 162, 196
San Francisco Suicide Prevention Institute, 304
Sapolsky R. M., 364
Schizophrenia Society of Canada, 277
Science Daily, 11
Scientific American, 364
Scoffield, H., 11
Sealy P., 272
Sears, S.J., 293
Sederer, L.I., 277
Seligman, L., 162, 163
Seligman, M. E., 205
Shahmizadi, A., 323, 327
Shapiro, F., 41, 364
Sharrard, M., 256
Shea, S. C., 178, 257, 260
Sheafor, B. W., 3, 27, 46, 49, 77, 82, 87, 90, 107, 193, 194, 237, 260, 328
Shebib, B., 44, 49, 61, 68, 89, 132, 163, 169, 219, 222, 266
Shulman, L., 48, 49, 59, 66, 74, 89, 90, 149, 150, 170, 177, 178, 236, 238
Shulz, W. E., 4
Siegel, R. D., 213, 215, 233
Siegel, D.J., 374
Silva, F., 283
Simmie, S., 282, 284
Simon-Dack, S., 68
Singh-Manoux, A., 377
Sitek, K., 352
Smith, D. B., 320, 335
Society for Neuroscience, 255
Soper, B., 291
Speight, S. L., 330
Sperry, L., 209, 247
Stanford, 347
Starr, M., 100
Statistics Canada, 197, 273, 303, 305, 312, 315, 336

Steinberg, L., 360
Stevens, F. L., 364
Substance Abuse and Mental Health Services
    Administration, 39, 280
Substance Use Planning Council
Sudman S., 136
Sue, D. W., 107, 165, 318, 319, 322, 324,
    325, 326, 327, 328, 332, 333
Swanson, J., 252, 254

T

Tardiff, K., 249, 252
Tartakovsky, M., 284
Tatera, K.
Taylor J., 105
The Centre for Addiction and Mental Health, 273, 300, 302
The Cleveland Clinic, 380
The Franklin Institute, 196
The Internet Stroke Center, 380
Thoreson, R. W., 5
Tourette Canada, 377
Trouche, S., 347
Trudeau, J., 313
Truth and Reconciliation Commission of
    Canada, 318, 334
Turner, J. C., 317, 328

U

University of California Irvine, 359
University of Maryland, 196
University of Utah, 254
University of Washington, 254

V

Van Hasselt, V., 102
Vonk, E., 227
Vujanovic, A., 214

W

Walsh, J., 293
WebMD, 373, 378
Weill Cornell Medicine, 353
Wehr, T., 230
Westwood, M. J.
Wicks, R. J., 75, 76, 201
Wills, F., 208
Winters, K.
Wlassoff, V.

Y

Young, M., 48, 85, 86, 89

Subject Index

CBT (see cognitive behavioural therapy)
cerebellum, 355, 357
cerebrum, 355
change continuum, 231–232
change talk, 200–201
Charles Bonnet syndrome, 361
children
    abuse, 268bb
    mental health, 289–291
    rights, 11
chronic fatigue syndrome, 217
cingulate, 364
clients
    involuntary, 242c
    personal involvement with, 18c
    physical contact with, 5
    praying with, 339c
    saying no, 243c
    sexual relationship with, 5–6
    tried everything, 228c
    working with "lazy", 203c
    working with involuntary, 242c
closed question, 127–128
Clubhouse, 291–292
cognitive behavioural counselling/therapy (CBT), 41, 207–219,
    267, 355
    interdependence of feelings thinking and behaviour, 209f
    techniques, 217–219i
cognitive domain, 132–133
cognitive triad, 210
collectivism, 321
coma, 382
command hallucination, 254
communication stoppers, 62
communication style, 325
competence, 18–19
compromise, 260
computerized axial tomography, 352
concreteness, 147–152
    strategies for achieving, 148f, 150–153
concurrent disorders (see co-occurring disorders)
confidentiality, 6–8
    absolute, 6
    guidelines, 8t
    relative, 8
confrontation, 47, 244–249
    misuse of, 246–247
    principles, 247–249
    types, 245–246
congruence, 43
connect (interview) transition, 156
contemplative stage of change, 205–206
content summary, 120
contingency planning, 226
contract, 44, 73–80
    anticipatory, 76
    leads, 78t
    questions for establishing, 131
    relationship, 74–76
    sessional, 77–78
    work, 77

control (interview) transition, 154–155
control (need for), 25
co-occurring disorder, 301–302
core beliefs (schema)
    helpful and unhelpful, 209t
core conditions, 43, 69–72
corpus collosum, 358
counselling, 33–35
    barriers to success, 54–60
    definition, 33
    ending phase, 57
    pitfalls, 57–64
    psychotherapy, 55t
    skill levels, 34t
    skills and strategies, 41–47
    top ten errors, 59t
    victims of violence, 267
counselling contract (see contract)
counselling relationship (see relationship)
counsellor self-disclosure (see self-disclosure)
counsellor
    competent, 16–19
    managing feelings, 40
    personal reactions/problems, 58–59, 100
    values beliefs and attitudes that help and hinder, 26t
countertransference, 84–86
cranial nerves, 365
crisis intervention, 197–199, 199t
critical incident debriefing, 263–266
cultural appropriation, 314
cultural intelligence
    barriers, 328–329
    defined, 311
    profile of a Canadian counsellor, 311f
cultural neuroscience, 313bb
culture, 166
    definitions, 314t
    eating disorders, 286
    individual differences, 166
    key elements of understanding, 323f
    nonverbal communication, 110
    personal values, 25
    pleasure centre and, 321bb
culture shock, 314, 316
cut-offs, 18

D

decisional balance sheet, 201
defence mechanisms, 23, 63–64
defensive phase (of violence), 260–262
deinstitutionalization, 272
delusions, 279–280
dementia, 370–380
    is it normal or, 379
dendrites, 357
denial, 63
dependent relationship, 83
depression, 280–284, 284bb
    types of, 353bb
detoxification, 296–298
developing discrepancy, 201–202

music, 36*bb*
myelin sheath, 359
   healthy and damaged, 359*f*

N

narcan, 301
Narcotics Anonymous, 2
natural transition, 153–154
Navajo, 325
negative symptom, 278–279
nervous system, 345*f*
neural development, 147*bb*
neural alarms, 162
neural pathways, 353, 369
   creating new, 215*bb*
neural transmission, 367–369
neurocounselling, 345
neuroeducation, 349
neurogenesis, 347
neuroimaging, 350–353
neuron, 366
   parts, 368*f*
"neurons that fire together", 217, 369
neuroplasticity, 135, 350, 370
   helping clients harness, 356*i*
neuroscience, 344–345
   technology and, 348
   why important for counsellors, 346–351
neurotransmitters, 343, 347, 363, 365–368, 370–373
   mental illness, 282*bb*
nonmaleficience, 4, 12
norepinephrine, 370, 371*f*
nonverbal communication, 106–111
   emotions, 165
   meaning of, 107–108
   resistance, 239
   what to observe, 107*t*
norm (defined), 314
note taking, 156*c*

O

objectivity, 15–18, 59
   maintaining, 17*t*
obsessive compulsive disorder
   (OCD), 285
occipital lobes, 360–361
office design, 256–257
"one-size-fits-all" approach, 36
open ended question, 128–129
opioid crisis, 296
opioids, 296
outcome goal, 219
overidentification, 17
overinvolvement, 17
oxytocin, 68

P

pacing, 55, 155–156
Parkinson's disease, 377
panic disorder, 285
paranoia, 281*c*

paraphrasing, 44, 117–119
   effective, 119*c*
   empathy, 119
   language of, 118*t*
parietal lobes, 361
passive aggression, 63
perfectionism, 25, 211–212
personal distance, 108–109
personal feelings, 16*c*
personal needs, 23–25
   managing, 24*t*
personal questions, 240*t*
personality disorders, 287–288
   common challenges and responses, 288*t*
phase (interview) transition, 155
phases of counselling, 47–57
   relationship, 68–70
phobias, 285
physical contact, 5
pitfalls (of counselling), 57–64
placating (*also see* rescuing), 62
"playing psychologist", 62
pleasure pathway, 299*bb*, 321*bb*
police intervention, 262
pons, 358
positive regard, 43
positive reinforcer, 179
positive symptom, 278
post-traumatic stress disorder (ptsd), 4, 285–286
positron emission tomography (PET), 352
poverty, 316
power and privilege, 47, 319
praying with clients, 339*c*
precontemplative stage of change, 204–205
precounselling change, 228
prejudice, 314
preliminary phase (of counselling),
   50–53, 68
premorbid functioning, 283
preparation stage of change, 206
preparatory empathy, 177–178
privileged communication, 6
problem solving, 225–227
   questions for, 133–134
process goal, 130, 219
professional associations, 2*t*
professional survival, 26
projection, 63
promoting change skills, 42t, 46–47
prosopanosia, 361
proxemics, 109
pseudocounselling, 59
psychiatric diagnosis, 273
psychiatric medications, 293–295, 293*bb*,
   when clients don't take, 294*c*
psychoanalysis, 345
psychoeducation, 300, 348–349
psychological reactance theory, 238
psychostimulant, 294
psychotherapy, 35
   counselling, 35*c*

ptsd (see Posttraumatic stress disorder)
public distance, 109

Q